THE INTERNATIONAL RESPONSIBILITY
OF INTERNATIONAL ORGANISATIONS

The International Responsibility of International Organisations addresses the joint responsibility of organisations for violations of international law committed during the deployment of peacekeeping operations. More specifically, it inquires if and under which circumstances – in terms of the notion of control – international organisations can be jointly responsible. The author analyses the practice of international organisations (the United Nations, the North Atlantic Treaty Organisation, the European Union, the African Union and the Economic Community of West African States) on an inter-institutional level, as well as in the field in the form of five case studies. The likelihood and distribution of responsibility between international organisations engaged in peacekeeping operations is affected by the different layers of applicable primary norms (Security Council mandates, internal law of the organisations, international humanitarian and human rights law). Although external pressure may contribute to enhancing the effectiveness of holding international organisations jointly responsible, any substantial measures and mechanisms can only be implemented with the participation of states and international organisations.

MORITZ P. MOELLE is working as a legal adviser in the Federal Foreign Office in Berlin, Germany. He gained previous work experience in the peacekeeping training programme of UNITAR, the International Law Commission of the UN, at the International Tribunal for the Law of the Sea and at the *Leiden Journal of International Law*.

THE INTERNATIONAL RESPONSIBILITY OF INTERNATIONAL ORGANISATIONS

Cooperation in Peacekeeping Operations

MORITZ P. MOELLE

CAMBRIDGE
UNIVERSITY PRESS

University Printing House, Cambridge CB2 8BS, United Kingdom

One Liberty Plaza, 20th Floor, New York, NY 10006, USA

477 Williamstown Road, Port Melbourne, VIC 3207, Australia

314-321, 3rd Floor, Plot 3, Splendor Forum, Jasola District Centre, New Delhi - 110025, India

79 Anson Road, #06-04/06, Singapore 079906

Cambridge University Press is part of the University of Cambridge.

It furthers the University's mission by disseminating knowledge in the pursuit of education, learning and research at the highest international levels of excellence.

www.cambridge.org
Information on this title: www.cambridge.org/9781107556553
10.1017/9781316415757

© Moritz P. Moelle 2017

This publication is in copyright. Subject to statutory exception and to the provisions of relevant collective licensing agreements, no reproduction of any part may take place without the written permission of Cambridge University Press.

First published 2017
First paperback edition 2018

A catalogue record for this publication is available from the British Library

Library of Congress Cataloging in Publication data
Names: Moelle, Moritz P., author.
Title: The international responsibility of international organisations : cooperation in peacekeeping operations / Moritz P. Moelle, Université de Genève.
Description: Cambridge, United Kingdom ; New York, NY : Cambridge University Press, 2017. | Based on author's thesis (doctoral - Université de Genève and Universiteit Leiden, 2014), issued under title: Cooperation of International Organisations in Peacekeeping Operations and Issues of International Responsibility. | Includes bibliographical references and index.
Identifiers: LCCN 2016041131 | ISBN 9781107124158 (hard back)
Subjects: LCSH: Peacekeeping forces.
Classification: LCC KZ6374 .M64 2017 | DDC 351.5/84–dc23
LC record available at https://lccn.loc.gov/2016041131

ISBN 978-1-107-12415-8 Hardback
ISBN 978-1-107-55655-3 Paperback

Cambridge University Press has no responsibility for the persistence or accuracy of URLs for external or third-party internet websites referred to in this publication, and does not guarantee that any content on such websites is, or will remain, accurate or appropriate.

CONTENTS

Preface *page* vii
List of Abbreviations xi

Introduction 1

1 Cooperation in Peacekeeping and Peace Enforcement Activities under the UN Charter 16

2 The (Emerging) System of Collective Security Consisting of the UN and Regional Organisations 67

3 From the Broader Legal Framework to International Responsibility 160

4 The Case Studies 203

5 The Law Applying in Peacekeeping Operations 272

6 Conclusions and Recommendations 321

Select Bibliography 331
Index 361

PREFACE

> We often hear it said that the United Nations has succeeded here, or has failed there. What do we mean? Do we refer to the purposes of the Charter? They are expressions of universally shared ideals, which cannot fail us, though we, alas, often fail them. Or do we think of the institutions of the United Nations? They are our tools. We fashioned them. We use them. It is our responsibility to remedy any flaws there may be in them. It is our responsibility to correct any failures in our use of them.
>
> – Dag Hammarskjöld, New York, May 1956

Seventy years after the onset of the Cold War, the scourge of war is still as present as it was in 1945 or even more so. A peaceful world has not yet been achieved. In fact, the number of armed conflicts has tripled since 2008. Violent crises around the globe are drawing unprecedented levels of international engagement by the UN, as well as regional organisations. The UN is currently deploying more than 128,000 people in thirty-nine missions, more than at any previous time. Peacekeeping operations are also deployed by African and Euro(-Atlantic) regional organisations and on occasion beyond their own continents.

The UN and regional organisations are not able to address these challenges on their own; cooperation between international organisations in peacekeeping operations has become the most essential tool to address these new and often unprecedented challenges. As was expressed by Secretary-General Ban Ki-moon on 31 March 2015, 'We have thus entered an era of "partnership peacekeeping", where close cooperation among multiple multilateral actors throughout every phase of a crisis is becoming the norm – and an essential component of each organization.'

The greater the powers of international organisations and states, the more essential it is to guarantee an effective administration of justice. The UN and other international organisations have also failed if there are no effective mechanisms guaranteeing that they are responsible for violations of international law arising from their activities. This book will inquire into this very aspect – holding international organisations effectively responsible for cooperation during peacekeeping operations.

The present book is based on a revised and updated version of my PhD thesis which was submitted to Leiden University and the University of Geneva in autumn 2014 and publicly defended on 18 December 2014. Documents published until 31 January 2016 have been included.

Working on a PhD thesis is a very lonesome undertaking, and I would not have been able to finish it successfully without the help and moral support of the following people and institutions.

First and foremost, I am particularly indebted to Laurence Boisson de Chazournes (University of Geneva) and Niels Blokker (Leiden University) who agreed to jointly supervise my PhD dissertation. Their profound expertise in international law, along with their support, encouragement, wisdom, excellent feedback and friendship, has guided me along this long journey. There could not have been a better pair of *Doktoreltern* for the supervision of my thesis. Moreover, their joint supervision illustrated that cooperation between two institutions and joint responsibility of one "mission" – my PhD thesis – can be successfully implemented in practice; hopefully this should be possible in the near future for the UN and regional organisations!

A huge thank you is due to the other members of the reading and the opposition committee, in particular Johann Lammers, Nicolas Michel, Nico Schrijver and Ramses Wessel. I particularly need to thank my dearest friends Max Kanzow and Shabnam Mirsaeedi-Farahani for their support throughout the course of my PhD and in particular on the day of my viva in their capacity as my paranymphs.

I am also grateful to my fellow academic 'comrades-in-arms' and the larger academic community in Geneva, *ma deuxième patrie*, in particular Edouard Fromageau and Andrzej Gadkowski.

I was fortunate to have spent a major period of time of writing my PhD at the Lauterpacht Centre for International Law, University of Cambridge, and it has become a place where I feel at home. This is foremost due to those great people working there. I am particularly thankful to James Crawford, to Marc Weller for granting me the opportunity to visit the centre, and also to Anita Rutherford and Karen Fachechi, who provided all the logistical and administrative support. I am equally grateful to the other Visiting Fellows and the academic staff of the centre. Your friendship, support and feedback, which you provided over countless lunches and dinners, were priceless. I also need to thank Sir Elihu Lauterpacht for a great discussion on the topic of my thesis.

Another four months of this long endeavour were spent at Columbia Law School in New York, and I was lucky enough to follow the course of Roy S. Lee on 'Peacekeeping and the United Nations'. I also benefitted from discussions with Jean-Marie Guéhenno, Michael Doyle and Elisabeth A. Lindenmayer and, of course, all the discussions and inputs from my fellow Visiting Scholars.

Katarina Grenfell at the Office of Legal Affairs at the UN also provided me with the practitioner's view on the issue of peacekeeping operations, as did Jaap de Hoop Scheffer in The Hague. Further practical inputs were provided by colleagues at the Federal Foreign Office, the Federal Ministry of Defence and the General Staff College of the German Armed Forces.

My research would have been more tedious without the excellent support provided by the staff at Squire Law Library and University Library, University of Cambridge; Arthur W. Diamond Law Library, Columbia Law School, and last but not least the Library of the United Nations in Geneva.

Georg Nolte provided me with the opportunity to work one summer at the International Law Commission of the United Nations in Geneva, while the commission was discussing the Articles on Responsibility of International Organisations.

I am also very grateful to Elizabeth Spicer at Cambridge University Press for all the help, support and guidance along the process of publishing my thesis and to the three anonymous reviewers of my book proposal.

Finally, I am infinitely indebted to my family – my parents, Claudia and Peter Moelle; my twin sister, Michaela Frosz; my brother-in-law Michael Frosz, and my grandmother, Doris Meese. Completing this lengthy endeavour would not at all have been possible without you. I dedicate this book to you.

ABBREVIATIONS

ADB	African Development Bank
AFISMA	African-Led International Support Mission to Mali
AICRC	African Immediate Crisis Response Capacity
AJOC	Abyei Joint Oversight Committee
AMIS	AU Mission in Sudan
AMISOM	AU Mission in Somalia
AMU	Arab Maghreb Union
APF	African Peace Facility
APSA	African Peace and Security Architecture
ARIO	Articles on the Responsibility of International Organizations
ARSIWA	Articles on the Responsibility of States for Internationally Wrongful Acts
ASF	African Standby Force
AU	African Union
AUHIP	AU High-Level Implementation Panel on Sudan
AU PSC	AU Peace and Security Council
BINUCA	UN Integrated Peacebuilding Office in the Central African Republic
CAR	Central African Republic
CDI	Commission du droit international; see ILC
CENSAD	Community of Sahelo-Saharan States
CINCSOUTH	Commander-in-Chief, Allied Forces Southern Europe
CFSP	Common Foreign and Security Policy
CONOPS	Concept of Operations
CPLP	Community of Portuguese-Speaking Countries
CSDP	Common Security and Defence Policy
DPKO	Department for Peacekeeping Operations
DRC	Democratic Republic of Congo
ECCAS	Economic Community of Central African States
ECHR	European Convention on Human Rights
ECOMIL	ECOWAS Mission in Liberia
ECOWAS	Economic Community of West African States

EDC	European Defence Community
EDF	European Development Fund
EGOMOG	ECOWAS Ceasefire Monitoring Group
ESDP	European Security and Defence Policy
ESF	ECOWAS Standby Force
EU	European Union
EUFOR Chad/CAR	EU Force Chad/CAR
EUFOR Tchad/RCA	See EUFOR Chad/CAR
EUMC	EU Military Committee
EUMS	EU Military Staff
EU PSC	EU Political and Security Committee
EUPT	EU Permanent Planning Team
EUTM Mali	EU Training Mission Mali
EUTM Somalia	EU Training Mission for Somalia
FARDC	Forces Armées de la République Démocratique du Congo
GA	General Assembly
ICC	International Criminal Court
ICCPR	international Covenant on Civil and Political Rights
ICJ	International Court of Justice
ICTR	International Criminal Tribunal for Rwanda
ICTY	International Criminal Tribunal for the Former Yugoslavia
IDB	Islamic Development Bank
IFOR	Implementation Force
IGAD	Intergovernmental Authority on Development
IHL	International Humanitarian Law
ILA	International Law Association
ILC	International Law Commission
ISAF	International Security Assistance Force
JEM	Justice Equality Movement
JSCM	Joint Support and Coordination Mechanism
KFOR	Kosovo Force
KLA	Kosovo Liberation Army
LoN	League of Nations
LRA	Lord's Resistance Army
MCPMRPS	Protocol Relating to the Mechanism for Conflict Prevention, Management, Resolution, Peacekeeping and Security
MICIVIH	International Civilian Mission in Haiti
MINUSCA	UN Multidimensional Integrated Stabilisation Mission in the Central African Republic
MINUSMA	UN Multidimensional Integrated Stabilisation Mission in Mali
MISAHEL	AU Mission for Mali and the Sahel

MISCA	African-Led International Support Mission in the Central African Republic
MITF	Mali Integrated Task Force
MONUC	UN Mission in the Democratic Republic of Congo
MONUSCO	UN Organisation Stabilisation Mission in the Democratic Republic of Congo
MTA	Military-Technical Agreement
NAC	North Atlantic Council
NATO	North Atlantic Treaty Organisation
NMLA	National Movement for the Liberation of Azawad
NPFL	National Patriotic Front of Liberia
OAS	Organisation of American States
OAU	Organisation of African Unity
OCHA	UN Office for the Coordination of Humanitarian Affairs
OIC	Organisation of Islamic Cooperation
OIF	International Organisation of *La Francophonie*
ONUC	UN Operation in the Congo
OSCE	Organisation for Security and Cooperation in Europe
PCIJ	Permanent Court of International Justice
PSOs	Peace Support Operations
RECs	Regional Economic Communities
SACEUR	Supreme Allied Commander Europe
SC	Security Council
SDN	Société des Nations; see League of Nations
SFOR	Stabilisation Force
SHAPE	Supreme Headquarters Allied Powers Europe
SLM/A	Sudanese Liberation Movement/Army
SOFA	Status of Forces Agreement
SOMA	Status of Mission Agreement
TCC	Troop-Contributing Country
TEU	Treaty on European Union
TFEU	Treaty on the Functioning of the EU
UNAMID	AU/UN Hybrid Operation in Darfur
UNAMIR	UN Assistance Mission for Rwanda
UNAMSIL	UN Mission in Sierra Leone
UNEF	UN Emergency Force
UNHCR	UN High Commissioner for Refugees
UNISFA	UN Interim Security Force for Abyei
UNMIK	UN Interim Administration in Kosovo
UNMIL	UN Mission in Liberia
UNMIS	UN Mission in Sudan
UNMISS	UN Mission in the Republic of South Sudan

UNOCI	UN Operation in Côte d'Ivoire
UNOM	UN Office in Mali
UNOMIL	UN Observer Mission in Liberia
UNOMSIL	UN Observer Mission in Sierra Leone
UNOWA	UN Office for West Africa
UNPROFOR	UN Protection Force
UNSOA	UN Support Office for AMISOM
VCLT	Vienna Convention on the Law of Treaties
WEU	Western European Union
WTO	World Trade Organisation
WWII	World War II

Introduction

Es gibt keine Handlung, für die niemand verantwortlich wäre.

– Otto von Bismarck[1]

The purpose of this book is to contribute to the understanding of the regime of international responsibility as it applies to international organisations cooperating in matters of international peace and security and, in particular, peacekeeping operations. This covers cooperation under Chapter VIII of the UN Charter which regulates the relationship of the UN with regional organisations in the field of maintaining international peace and security, as well as peacekeeping operations under Chapter VII of the UN Charter.[2]

Peacekeeping operations have been essential for maintaining international peace and security, and they have evolved tremendously over the years. On 20 December 2012, the Security Council (SC) adopted Resolution 2085 on the situation in Mali. In this Resolution, the SC requested 'that the Secretary-General, in close coordination with Mali, ECOWAS, the AU, the neighbouring countries of Mali, … and all other interested bilateral partners and international organizations, continue to support the planning and the preparations for the deployment of AFISMA'.[3] The SC also expressed its gratitude to the Organisation of Islamic Cooperation (OIC) for the efforts in mediation and to the EU which started to plan for the deployment of a military training mission in Mali (EUTM Mali).[4]

Although Mali is only one example of a crisis in a country that calls for international action to guarantee the maintenance of international peace and security, it reflects the current reality of cooperation between

---

[1] 'There is no deed for which not anybody would be responsible.'
[2] In the practice of the Security Council concerning peacekeeping operations, Chapter VI of the Charter has lost its relevance and is – particularly in the recent practice – not invoked anymore.
[3] UN Doc. S/RES/2085 (2012), para. 11.
[4] Ibid., Preamble and para. 8.

international organisations.[5] Cooperation among international organisations is not only at the core of the maintenance of international peace and security; it also applies across all areas, starting with the planning of the mission and training of forces and extending to the deployment of troops and putting boots on the ground. This increased cooperation is not a feature unique to the maintenance of international peace and security, but it is generally a consequence of and a catalyst for globalisation;[6] international organisations are *fora* to deal and cope with the increased interdependence among states while simultaneously accelerating the process.[7] It is therefore surprising that the term 'cooperation' has never been defined by either an international treaty or in a resolution of an international organisation.[8]

As was stated by Mexico:

> Cooperation among states has become one of the most important factors – if not the key factor – in international relations. In that regard, the role of international organisations has assumed increasing significance.
>
> The most ordinary matters of daily life have an international dimension ... States have come to realise that only through the joint and coordinated action made possible by international organisations we can confront these threats ...
>
> In keeping with this development, the legal and actual capacities of international organisations to take action have been strengthened. As a logical consequence, the likelihood that their conduct (whether actions or omissions) may generate international responsibility has also increased.[9]

These observations were made with regard to the Articles on the Responsibility of International Organizations (ARIOs) as developed and adopted in second reading by the International Law Commission of the

---

[5] Cf. D. M. Tull, 'UN Peacekeeping Mission during the Past Two Decades. How Effective Have They Been?', in J. Krause, N. Ronzitti (eds.), *The EU, the UN and Collective Security. Making Multilateralism Effective* (London, Routledge 2012), 117, 136.
[6] See, e.g., M. Hirsch, 'Compliance with International Norms in the Age of Globalization: Two Theoretical Perspectives', in E. Benvenisti, M. Hirsch (eds.), *The Impact of International Law on International Cooperation. Theoretical Perspectives* (Cambridge University Press, 2004), 166, 168–170. Hirsch concludes that states, in particular developed states, are actually more likely to comply with international norms in the course of globalisation, ibid., 193.
[7] B. Dold, *Vertragliche und ausservertragliche Verantwortlichkeit im Recht der internationalen Organisationen* (Zürich, Schulthess, 2006), 1. Generally, on theories of international cooperation, cf. J. Klabbers, *An Introduction to International Institutional Law* (2009), 25–37.
[8] R. Wolfrum, 'Cooperation, International Law of', in R. Wolfrum (ed.), *The Max Planck Encyclopedia of Public International Law (2008–)*, online edition, (www.mpepil.com), para. 2. The Friendly Relations Declaration also starts from a 'preconceived terminology', ibid.
[9] General Remarks of Mexico, UN Doc. A/CN.4/547 (2004), 3–4.

United Nations in 2011.¹⁰ They capture the developments which have taken place in the past decades. On the one hand, an increased number of international organisations exist, but on the other, the powers and competences entrusted to these entities by their members have grown. Their increased activity has raised questions concerning the lack of clear and established rules of accountability or responsibility, in particular under international law.

Codification Projects on the Responsibility of International Organisations and the Changing System of International Law

Various codification projects relating to the responsibility of international organisations have been carried out by international bodies to engage intellectually and from a legal point of view with the increased activity in a variety of areas by international organisations. In addition to the International Law Commission, the *Institut de droit international*¹¹ and the International Law Association (ILA)¹² actively started addressing the topic in the mid-1990s, while the *Instituto Hispano-Luso-Americano de Derecho Internacional* engaged with the topic of responsibility of international organisations in the mid-1980s.

The approach taken by these three latter bodies varied and the dates of adoption mirrored the changing debate on the topic. The *Instituto Hispano-Luso-Americano* focused on international organisations as bearers of rights and obligations.¹³ The *Institut de droit international* added a new layer, realising that acts of international organisations can entail the

---

[10] The articles and commentaries are contained in UN Doc. Suppl. No. 10 (A/66/10) (2011).
[11] *Institut de Droit Transnational*, Resolution (Session of Lisbon 1995), The Legal Consequences for Member States of the Non-fulfilment by International Organizations of their Obligations toward Third Parties, Articles 4–6.
[12] ILA, Berlin Conference (2004); Accountability of International Organisations, ILA, New Delhi Conference (2002); Committee on Accountability of International Organisations, third report consolidated and enlarged version of recommended rules and practices ("RRP-S"). Generally, on the project, cf. I. F. Dekker, 'Making Sense of Accountability in International Institutional Law. An Analysis of the Final Report of the ILA Committee on Accountability of International Organizations from a Conceptual Legal Perspective', *Netherlands Yearbook of International Law*, 36 (2005), 83–118. See also the follow-up project of the ILA, Sofia Conference (2012), Study Group on the Responsibility of International Organizations.
[13] Instituto Hispano-Luso-Americano de Derecho Internacional, Las organizaciones internacionales y el Derecho de la responsabilidad, El XIV Congreso del Instituto Hispano-Luso-Americano de Derecho Internacional, San José 1985, 2–3, Preamble. The work of the Instituto is limited in its approach, focusing on international organisations as bearers of rights and obligations and thus falling under the law of responsibility. It does, however,

responsibility of the member states of that organisation. Finally, the ILA chose a socio-political-legal approach, analysing the topic under the criterion of 'accountability', which covers both legal and quasi-judicial as well as other forms of holding international organisations responsible for their actions.

It is often said of the relationship between International Humanitarian Law (IHL) and armed conflicts that the law always plays catch-up with the respective new forms of conflicts.[14] This statement holds true equally for the regulation of acts of international organisations. The common feature of these studies is the state-centric approach by which they are characterised. Their modus operandi is state-centric in the sense that the studies focus on the responsibility of international organisations per se and the responsibility of international organisations in connection with their respective members. They therefore ignore the question of inter-organisational cooperation and consequently also the possibility of joint responsibility of international organisations or the responsibility of an international organisation for acts or another organisation.[15] In academic writing, most attention has been paid to the topic of the distribution of responsibility between international organisations and their member states excluding, therefore, '*den Dritten im Bunde*' (the third in the alliance),[16] which, in the conduct of peacekeeping or peace enforcement operations, is often another international organisation.

A major change emerged through the Articles of the International Law Commission on the Responsibility of International Organisations, which contain dispositions regulating the responsibility of an international organisation in connection with the acts of another international organisation.[17] The key question is whether these articles reflect sufficiently the complexities of inter-organisational cooperation and whether they include

---

discuss the possibility that an internationally wrongful act may be attributed to an international organisation or to the state on whose territory it operates, 3, para. 5.

[14] Be it new means and methods of warfare or new types of conflicts such as 'internationalised' internal armed conflicts.

[15] The same critique was formulated by L. Boisson de Chazournes, 'Les relations entre organisations régionales et organisations universelles', *Recueil des cours de l'Académie de La Haye*, 347 (2010), 79, 401–402.

[16] One has to emphasise that one of the reasons for the disregard of this particular angle is possibly the immunity of international organisations which has so far prevented the consideration of international and other courts and tribunals of that particular question, besides doing so incidentally in connection with acts of states. Another potential reason relates to the issue of judicial review of resolutions issued by the Security Council.

[17] Articles 7, 14–18, 48.

the necessary flexibility and *marge de manoeuvre* in their interpretation which allows regulating adequately the highly complex field of peacekeeping operations.

Whereas the Articles on State Responsibility[18] were the work of roughly fifty years, the Articles on the Responsibility of International Organisations were finished within eight years. As was observed by one member of the International Law Commission,

> [t]he topic currently under consideration was much more complex, for while relations between States and international organizations were, in the last analysis, fairly limited, those between international organizations themselves continued to evolve, particularly in the area of peacekeeping, where their functions and *modus operandi* were increasingly often called into question.[19]

Furthermore, the forces of globalisation, interconnectivity and interdependence have also moved the system of international law further away from being self-contained and applicable exclusively to states towards 'an intricate network of laws governing a myriad of rights and duties that stretch across and beyond national borders'.[20] While, in the 1940s, Kelsen's view of the *Reine Rechtslehre* might have been suitable, which argued that the nature of the law can only be truly understood if one examines the relations between particular rules of a legal order and not a single isolated rule on its own,[21] the current understanding of international law can only be that one cannot grasp the nature of international law if one limits one's attention to this specific field. Non-legal arguments and considerations are equally important.

It is particularly true for the context of the present book that insofar as cooperation among international organisations in maintaining international peace and security touches not only upon international law but also upon essential geopolitical, strategic, economic and other interests of states and international organisations, this necessitates a broadening of the perspective – and while applying the law – to take duly into account policy-induced arguments and considerations.[22] In addition, '[t]he more essential

---

[18] For the articles and commentaries, see UN Doc. A/CN.4/SER.A/2001/Add.1 (Part 2) (2001), 20–143.
[19] Mr Al-Marri, UN Doc. A/CN.4/SR.2963 (2008), 16–17.
[20] T. M. Franck, *Fairness in International Law and Institutions* (Oxford University Press, 1995), 5–6.
[21] H. Kelsen, *General Theory of Law and State* (Cambridge, Harvard University Press, 1945), 3.
[22] The understanding of the notions of 'peace and security' has also evolved: 'The absence of war and military conflicts amongst States does not in itself ensure international peace and

interests are for politics, the more politics are opposed to the penetration of the legal system with its principles of legality and equality'.[23] Following two disastrous world wars, states and the wider international community consider the maintenance of international peace and security to be one of their main concerns. Accordingly, the contentions between international law and politics can be particularly harsh; one may only think of the Iraq War in 2003 or the current crisis in Syria. One can therefore duly speak of an 'increasingly politicized legal landscape', and this trend is also reflected in jurisprudence which relies heavily on policy documents.[24] Thus, there is a certain dichotomy with which the law of international responsibility applicable to international organisations is confronted. Interconnectivity and interdependence of issues and actors and globalisation are transforming international law from a state-centred, self-contained system to a multipolar system with various entities, but simultaneously the system for maintaining international peace and security as codified in the UN Charter is constructed around one principal actor, the SC, and the influence of politics over international law remains particularly dominant in this specific field.

The Proliferation of International Organisations and the Multiplication of Tasks (in Peacekeeping Operations)

The bar to establish suitable rules pertaining to the law of international responsibility for international organisations is further raised by the very nature of international organisations and their organs of which the SC of the UN is the most apposite example. Their respective constituent instruments, such as the UN Charter,[25] form the legal basis of their existence and their activities. However, the organisations and their organs act through various forms of diplomacy and policy; they are political 'animals' with a legal skeleton. The SC is the beacon of the system of global collective security, and although a political body per se, its actions nonetheless often have

---

security. The non-military sources of instability in the economic, social, humanitarian and eco-logical fields have become threats to peace and security.' UN Doc. S/23500 (1992), 3.

[23] R. Kolb, G. Porretto, S. Vité, *L'application du droit international humanitaire et des droits de l'homme aux organisations internationales. Forces de paix et administrations civiles transitoires* (Brussels, Bruylant, 2005), 8.

[24] P. Koutrakos, *The EU Common Security and Defence Policy* (Oxford University Press, 2013), 80; C-91/05, *Commission of the European Communities v. Council of the European Union* [2005], Judgment (Grand Chamber) of 20 May 2008.

[25] UN Charter (1945).

legal consequences.²⁶ Generally speaking, the field of international peace and security could be defined as being situated between international politics and international law.

In the past few decades, a plethora of regional and sub-regional, non-universal international organisations have been created and evolved with mandates for maintaining international peace and security, of which many have taken over tasks previously carried out by universal organisations or they act conjointly with such. This rise of regionalism is a global phenomenon and not limited to the area of peace and security,²⁷ but is especially true for the field of peacekeeping operations. Notwithstanding the prohibition of the use of force which is enshrined in Article 2(4) of the UN Charter, armed conflicts still occur regularly in various regions around the globe. Of the seventy-one peace operations conducted under the auspices of the UN in the period from 1945 to 2015, forty-eight have taken place in the period of 1991–2015.²⁸

The increased number of peacekeeping operations in recent decades has been accompanied by a multiplication of tasks and functions exercised by those forces, which range from classic peacekeeping operations such as neutral troops between two opposing states to multifaceted operations including military and civil components, amounting even to operations which administer complete territories as was seen in Cambodia, East Timor and Kosovo.²⁹ The UN operation in the

---

²⁶ As Gowlland-Debbas also points out, '[o]ne is highly aware of the political nature of the Security Council which may make a legal analysis of its activities sound derisory. It is unquestionable that the mechanisms instituted under Chapter VII of the UN Charter grant extensive, discretionary powers to an elitist, political organ whose primary responsibility is the maintenance of a political conception of international ordering, i.e., the maintenance of international peace and security': V. Gowlland-Debbas, 'The Security Council and Issues of Responsibility under International Law', *Recueil des cours de l'Académie de La Haye*, 535 (2012), 185, 206. Boutros-Ghali once remarked that the SC is a place where international law and international policy 'happily mix', as cited in D. Türk, 'Impact of International Humanitarian Provisions on the Decision-Making Process in Crisis Management: The Practice of the Security Council', in S. Kolanowski, Y. Salmon (eds.), *Proceedings of the Bruges Colloquium. The Impact of International Humanitarian Law on Current Security Policy Trends* (2001), 97, 100.

²⁷ As will be discussed in Chapter 1, the rise of regionalism has been problematic in the field of maintenance of international peace and security as the legal framework under the UN Charter is an area of conflict between universalism and regionalism.

²⁸ All figures are drawn from the UN homepage (Fact Sheet as on 31 August 2015).

²⁹ According to Berdal, this development is explained by 'these changes in operational (focus on intra-state conflict) and normative context (emphasis on "humanitarian" issues broadly conceived)': M. Berdal, 'The Security Council and Peacekeeping', in V. Lowe, A. Roberts, J. Welsh (eds.), *The United Nations Security Council and War* (Oxford University

DRC lists no less than forty-five different tasks to be carried out by the operation.[30]

An Increasing Network of Cooperation

In recent years a number of other important developments have taken place in the organisation and the conduct of peace operations. The opening paragraphs of the introduction illustrated that cooperation has become increasingly common in the planning and implementation of peacekeeping operations. The UN relies regularly on regional organisations to carry out peacekeeping operations under a mandate by the SC, although the legal framework is not always very clear.[31]

Indeed, it was held by the AU–UN panel:

> The *complexity of modern peacekeeping means that no single organization is capable of tackling the challenge on its own*. More than ever, security threats require a collective approach premised on a range of partnerships which should seek to establish coordination both at the strategic and programmatic levels. They should also take maximum advantage of the strengths that respective organizations, especially regional organizations, can contribute.[32] [Emphasis added]

Other reports go further still, and suggest that 'hybrid peace operations and other innovative approaches to peacekeeping ... are the way of the future as the strength of such joint ventures draws from the universal character of the UN and the advantages embedded in regionalism'.[33]

International organisations are generally complex structures, which act through their member states, and in turn these act through individuals, thereby creating three layers of responsibility. In addition, and adding to the complexity, international organisations rarely act on their own,

---

Press, 2008), 175, 190. For a summary of this evolution, see General Assembly/Security Council, Supplement to an Agenda for Peace: Position Paper of the Secretary-General on the Occasion of the Fiftieth Anniversary of the United Nations, UN Doc. A/50/60-S/1995/1 (1995), 3–5.

[30] Department of Peacekeeping Operations and Department of Field Support, a New Partnership Agenda. Charting a New Horizon for UN Peacekeeping (2009), 10.

[31] Peacekeeping was created by the UN and has developed through practice alone.

[32] Report of the African Union–United Nations Panel on Modalities for Support to African Union Peacekeeping Operations, UN Doc. A/63/666-S/2008/813 (2008), 7, para. 10. Cf. AU Doc. PSC/PR/2.(CCCVII) (2012), 3, para. 8; Statement of the SG in the Security Council, UN Doc. S/PV.7112 (2014), 2.

[33] AU Doc. PSC/PR/2.(CCCVII) (2012), 33, para. 105; UN Doc. S/2002/979 (2002), 3, para. 2(g).

but often in cooperation with other organisations and increasingly also with private actors, impeding upon the application of the law of responsibility: '[E]ven, in those rare cases where most would agree that some wrongful act has taken place, it is by no means self-evident to whom the wrongfulness can be attributed.'[34]

The SC is responsible for the maintenance of international peace and security under Chapters VI and VII of the Charter. Chapter VIII of the Charter of the UN, entitled 'Regional Arrangements', regulates the relationship between regional arrangements or agencies[35] and the UN for the settlement of local disputes. Cooperation in the area of maintenance of international peace and security may take various forms, for example, the 'dual-key' arrangements between the UN and NATO in Yugoslavia[36] for the authorisation of air-strikes or the establishment of the hybrid peace-keeping operation between the UN and the AU, UNAMID in Darfur. In the past few years the UN has started to enhance inter-mission cooperation by redeploying troops from one peacekeeping operation to another if an urgent need arises or by authorising cross-border inter-mission activities.[37] These activities are also a reaction to the current economic climate and tight financial budgets.[38] Private military and security contractors have also become more influential in the context of peacekeeping operations,

---

[34] J. Klabbers, 'Self-Control: International Organisations and the Quest for Accountability', in M. Evans, P. Koutrakos (eds.), *The International Responsibility of the European Union* (Oxford, Hart Publishing, 2013), 75, 97–98. In similar fashion, F. Naert, *International Law Aspects of the EU's Security and Defence Policy, with a Particular Focus on the Law of Armed Conflict and Human Rights* (2010), 353; A. Tzanakopoulos, *Disobeying the Security Council. Countermeasure against Wrongful Sanctions* (2011), 18–19.
[35] In this book, the generic term of 'regional organisation' will be used when possible.
[36] UN Doc. A/49/681 (1994), 7, para. 25.
[37] See, e.g., UN Doc. S/2005/135 (2005), especially, 2, paras. 5–7; S/RES/1609 (2005), 5, para. 6; S/RES/1657 (2006), 1, para. 1. Inter-mission cooperation can be quite extensive; a budget performance report for UNAMID lists the following activities as being closely coordinated or being accomplished with UNMIS: 'joint situational analysis and brainstorming meetings on the referendum on the status of South Sudan ..., bimonthly joint UNAMID/UNMIS video-telephone conferencing with the headquarters Integrated Mission Task Force ..., the areas of security management, assessment of public information activities on subjects of mutual interest or endeavour, ... capacity-building and other activities involving the police, ... human rights, child protection and gender activities. Common services, including space/office utilization, security management, air and ground transport services and fleet management, joint movement control operations, property management and medical services continued to be shared with UNMIS. Particularly on air transportation, while no aircraft were shared with UNMIS, air asset support to UNMIS was provided when requested and when UNAMID commitments allowed for such support', UN Doc. A/66/596 (2011), 9, para. 34.
[38] Statement by Major General Iqbal Asi, UN Doc. S/PV.6987 (2013), 5.

being charged with important tasks as well as being involved even in the training and planning of UN peacekeeping operations.[39]

It is against this background that this book will set out to examine the scope and content of the international responsibility of international organisations cooperating in peacekeeping operations. The approach taken and the method of analysis are multipolar, focusing not on one particular organisation, but examining several and their interplay.

Research and Methodology

At the heart of the inquiry presented in this book is the question of whether international organisations cooperating in peacekeeping operations can be jointly responsible for internationally wrongful acts committed by peacekeeping forces. This can be divided into three main questions. The first is: Are there internationally wrongful acts which can be attributed to more than one international organisation? This involves an examination of the forms and methods of cooperation between the involved organisations, first, *in abstracto*, under the framework of the UN Charter – in particular, Chapters VII and VIII – as well as on an inter-organisational level. The legal framework of the UN Charter determines the "playing field" on which regional organisations and the UN interact in order to maintain international peace and security. In other words, the UN Charter assigns the general roles of the UN and regional organisations in this field of international law. The mechanisms and arrangements of cooperation as developed on an inter-institutional level further define and develop the role of each organisation and the framework of cooperation between the UN and regional organisations. They serve simultaneously as the foundation and as the interface for cooperation, *in concreto*, within a specific operation. The analysis of the attribution of conduct operates on the basis of an examination of the command and control arrangements in a given scenario.

---

[39] ECOWAS, for example, relies on private military and security companies (PMSCs) s to rectify the lack of capabilities of its members in certain given areas, UNAMSIL and MONUC used PMSCs for logistical support and demining is nearly completely sourced out by the UN, see R. Buchan, H. Jones, N. D. White, 'The Externalization of Peacekeeping: Policy, Responsibility and Accountability', *Journal of International Peacekeeping*, 15 (2011), 15 281, 286. Although the treaties concluded by the UN specify that the employees of these companies will not in any form be considered as agents of the UN and it also appears highly unlikely that the UN will exercise 'effective control' over them, the issue per se is problematic (ibid., 293–296). For an excellent overview, see, A. G. Østensen, 'In the Business of Peace: The Political Influence of Private Military and Security Companies on UN Peacekeeping', *International Peacekeeping*, 20 (2013), 33–47.

Therefore, any analysis of the attribution of conduct of acts arising in the context of international organisations cooperating in peacekeeping operations needs to address and examine the inter-institutional and in-mission cooperation mechanisms existing between the UN and regional organisations.

Secondly, one has to ask whether the ARIOs by the International Law Commission, by which the current book will be principally guided, are appropriate for the specific context of regulating conduct of international organisations cooperating in peacekeeping operations or whether a *sui generis* regime would be more appropriate. As the law of responsibility has developed in the context of bilateral relations of states and the predominant view still adheres to the idea that cases of joint responsibility are rare, it might, indeed, be necessary to rely upon a *lex specialis* rule of attribution for the specific context of peacekeeping operations.

Indeed, the Articles on State Responsibility and on International Responsibility of International Organisations provide a similar legal framework containing references to the other set of articles, but they both deal with cases of mutual responsibility in specific cases only. Depending on the cooperation arrangements and agreements between the involved international organisations, it is not unlikely that there are peacekeeping operations in which a high level of cooperation between international organisations is evident, but which are not adequately covered by the ARIOs.

Although currently, it is not foreseeable that the European Union (EU) will accede to the European Convention on Human Rights (ECHR), such an analysis is also particularly relevant because the EU's accession to the ECHR would have implications on many levels.[40] It would make it possible to hold the EU legally responsible and it would therefore not only prompt a change in analysis in cases, but equally contribute to the elucidation and clarification of the applicable legal framework to international organisations. It could further encourage the implicit judicial review of acts of other international organisations than the EU and it would simultaneously put pressure on those organisations to submit themselves to judicial review. Finally, it could possibly spark a new debate on the legal framework applicable to determining the responsibility of international organisations in the context of peacekeeping operations.[41]

---

[40] ECtHR, Opinion 2/13 of the Court (Full Court), 18 December 2014.
[41] The first and highly criticised case concerning conduct arising in the context of a peacekeeping operation of an international organisation by the European Court was *Agim Behrami and Bekir Behrami against France, Ruzdhi Saramati against France, Germany and Norway*, Decision on Admissibility, 2 May 2007.

If any conduct can be attributed to one or more international organisations, the question arises if it is in violation of an international legal norm, so the third question concerns the applicable legal framework for peacekeeping operations. The present book does not analyse the application of IHL or human rights law to specific circumstances during the deployment of a peacekeeping operation because these aspects are beyond the scope of this book. This being said, the analysis of the applicable legal framework is important for two principal reasons. First of all, it underlines the complexity of the application of IHL and human rights to international organisations and it also allows shedding some light on many specific issues whose legal regulation has not yet been sufficiently explored. Secondly, the applicable legal framework has to be seen as part of the wider picture of a breach of an international obligation and it may have repercussions for the attribution of conduct. As the present book will also explore further legal bases for a breach of an international obligation, it may be possible that the UN and one or several organisations might be bound by different legal obligations which entail their responsibility under international law.

The analysis of the applicable legal framework in this book is limited to the conduct of international organisations, which – in contrast to states – are not bound by international human rights and IHL treaties and conventions. Customary international law is less developed than treaty law and its application to the conduct of international organisations is particularly difficult for various reasons, including that most of the customary rules were developed on the basis of state practice alone so that they can only be applied *mutatis mutandis* to international organisations. Similar issues are raised by the application of IHL, particularly in the exact nature of the relationship between these two bodies of law.

Objectives and Scope of the Book

The book will examine the applicable legal framework for peacekeeping operations. But reaching beyond the legal debate, it seeks to provide practical guidance to relevant practitioners in the field. As peace operations operate in difficult areas, and even under conditions of armed conflict in which law and order break down, the violation of fundamental rights of individuals by peacekeepers is not imaginary, but a simple fact.[42] All

---

[42] C. Ryngaert, 'Apportioning Responsibility between the UN and Member States in UN Peace-Support Operations: An Inquiry into the Application of the "Effective Control" Standard after Behrami', *Israel Law Review*, 45 (2012), 151, 152.

evidence suggests that the cooperation between international organisations will increase in the future, thus also increasing the potential for the occurrence of cases of internationally wrongful acts which could be attributed to multiple international organisations.[43] The overall objective is to arrive at conclusions which take into account in particular the primary sources and the practice of international organisations, the specific features of individual organisations, and which allow for the proposition of a reasonable responsibility regime for cases of cooperation of international organisations in peacekeeping operations – including a point of view of *de lege ferenda*.

The book focuses on the following international organisations: the EU, the NATO, the AU, the ECOWAS and the UN.

The discussion is limited to these five organisations for the following reasons. Firstly, it is necessary to find a balance between a comprehensive approach to the issue and an in-depth analysis of the topic. An analysis of all international organisations which are involved in peacekeeping activities risks a superficial analysis of the subject. Secondly, some organisations are less active than others and thereby also less relevant for the present book. The Organisation of Southeast Asian Nations (ASEAN), for example, has only been involved in one peacekeeping operation.[44] A third factor is the geographic distribution of conflicts and peacekeeping operations. Africa unfortunately remains the continent with the highest number of conflicts and is consequently particularly interesting for the purposes of this book. Finally, the legal make-up of the different organisations is yet another feature relevant to this book as it has a direct bearing on the existing cooperating mechanisms, and thereby incidentally on the law of international responsibility.

The EU is a supranational organisation, an organisation *sui generis*, and has been involved in thirty-three military and civil operations since the implementation of the European Defence and Security Policy in 2003.[45] The EU not only sends its own troops and people, but it also holds a prominent role in cooperation with other organisations, particularly, for peace operations on the African continent.

---

[43] UN Doc. A/70/95 and S/2015/446 (2015).
[44] This was the surveillance mission in Aceh, Réseau francophone de recherché sur les opérations de paix, www.operationspaix.net/ANASE. See the Memorandum of Understanding between the Government of the Republic of Indonesia and the Free Aceh Movement, available at: www.consilium.europa.eu/uedocs/cmsUpload/MoU_Aceh.pdf.
[45] Numbers (as of June 2015) are drawn from www.eeas.europa.eu/csdp/missions-and-operations/.

The AU is, next to the EU, a major regional organisation engaged in activities concerning peace and security. This is also due to the high number of conflicts on the African continent and it is therefore significant for the content of this book.[46] The same assumption applies to the ECOWAS.

NATO was founded as a military alliance among certain Western states and is by its mandate a 'military' international organisation and therefore one of the major players in all matters concerning peace and security and peacekeeping operations.

The comparative methodology used throughout the book has several advantages. Firstly, it allows the identification of similarities and differences among the legal frameworks of these organisations, in their relations with another, and in the cooperation arrangements during peacekeeping operations. Regarding the framework of the UN Charter, the analysis is conducted both on the basis of Chapters VII and VIII.[47] Secondly, on the basis of these findings, it is possible to determine and to pinpoint the applicable legal rules of international responsibility to peacekeeping operations in the context of cooperation therein by international organisations. Thirdly, general conclusions can be drawn, providing an outlook for the future and recommendations.

Structure of the Book

This book is divided into six chapters and follows a top-down approach. Chapter 1 introduces the legal framework applicable under the UN Charter for the maintenance of international peace and security and for cooperation with international organisations. The argument made is that the compromise solution under the UN Charter between universalism and regionalism is inspiring cooperation between the UN and regional organisations.

---

[46] For example, between 1963 and 1998, twenty-eight armed conflicts erupted in Africa affecting 61 per cent of the continent's population; seventy-five to eighty conflicts were recorded since 1945, Africa, our common destiny, Guideline Document (2004), 11.

[47] It is moreover necessary because enforcement action under Chapter VII and enforcement activities under Chapter VIII may also be intertwined, cf., for example, Security Council Resolution 787, UN Doc. S/RES/787 (1992), 4, para. 12, in which it is written as follows: 'Acting under Chapter VII and Chapter VIII of the Charter of the United Nations, [the Security Council] calls upon States, acting nationally or through regional arrangements or agencies, to use such measures commensurate with the specific circumstances as may be necessary under the authority of the Security Council to halt all inward and outward maritime shipping in order to inspect and verify their cargoes and destinations and to ensure strict implementation of resolutions 713 (1991) and 757 (1992).'

In Chapter 2, the relations between the UN and NATO, the EU, the AU and ECOWAS are traced in peacekeeping and peace enforcement activities of the UN and between these organisations. This analysis allows for the formulation of general conclusions regarding the potential distribution of roles among international organisations as well as the consequences for responsibility arising from wrongful conduct.

Chapter 3 deals specifically with the law of international responsibility as applied to international organisations. It specifically analyses the compatibility of the ARIO with the scenario of international organisations cooperating in peacekeeping operations. It further refines and clarifies the methodology used in Chapter 4 which consists of various case studies.

Chapter 4 contains a comparative analysis of case studies to ascertain and verify the findings of Chapters 1–3 and it seeks to further develop and define the proposed special criterion of attribution (*lex ferenda*).

Chapter 5 analyses the material law applicable to military contingents deployed in peacekeeping operations.

Finally, Chapter 6 provides the conclusions reached by the analysis in this book, as well as recommendations for the future, addressed in particular to practitioners and legal scholars.

1

Cooperation in Peacekeeping and Peace Enforcement Activities under the UN Charter

> The architects of the United Nations Charter were visionary in foreseeing a world where the United Nations and regional organizations worked together to prevent, manage and resolve crises. However, it is hard to imagine that they could have anticipated the interconnected nature of the threats we face today or the range of cooperation between the United Nations [sic] regional and subregional organizations.
>
> Secretary-General Ban Ki-moon[1]

The central research question of this book is whether international organisations cooperating in peacekeeping operations can be jointly responsible under international law. The primary foundation for cooperation between the UN and regional organisations is Chapter VIII of the UN Charter. In practice, however, the Security Council (SC) increasingly resorts solely to Chapter VII to mandate peacekeeping operations by regional organisations. This first introductory chapter, therefore, traces several developments within the field of collective security as established under the UN Charter. First of all and to put it into perspective, this chapter analyses the general evolution of the system of collective security from the Dumbarton Oaks conference to the developments after the end of the Cold War.

The second part of this chapter introduces the concept of peacekeeping. It attempts to circumscribe peacekeeping and peace enforcement activities. In practice the distinction between both concepts has become increasingly blurred, although a distinction is essential as the following third part will illustrate. Depending on the qualification of an international military operation as a peacekeeping or peace enforcement operation, an authorisation of the SC for the deployment of such an operation may or may not be necessary. Consequently, the qualification of an international military

---

[1] During the debate on cooperation between the UN and regional and sub-regional organisations in maintaining international peace and security, Security Council, 7015th meeting, UN Doc. S/PV.7015 (2013), 3.

operation as either a peacekeeping or peace enforcement operation may also have a direct bearing upon the question of international responsibility.

An analysis of practice shows that a certain division of labour between the UN and regional organisations with regard to the deployment of military forces is emerging as will be highlighted in the second part of this chapter.

Cooperation under the UN Charter: Between Universalism and Regionalism

The Creation of the UN: Regionalism vs Universalism

The Dumbarton Oaks proposals for the UN Charter had already envisioned the framework of the Charter as it exists today.[2] The proposal contained already explicit dispositions concerning the distribution of competences and responsibility between the SC and regional organisations with regard to maintaining international peace and security. Due to the history of the Society of Nations, on whose model the proposals were based, they were concerned with the legitimacy of regional organisations to deal with issues of international peace and security on an appropriate regional level, provided that they conformed to the legal obligations under the Charter.[3] The proposed principles further included the authorisation for the SC to use regional arrangements and organisations for coercive measures, and the obligation for the latter to inform the SC of enforcement measures taken.[4]

One of the most significant aspects of these propositions, which were only altered slightly before they became part of the UN Charter in Chapter VIII, is that cooperation with regional organisations, as well as the integration of these organisations into universal organisations, became

---

[2] For a comprehensive review of the drafting history of the UN, see, D.-E. Khan, 'Drafting History', in B. Simma, D.-E. Khan, G. Nolte et al. (eds.), *The Charter of the United Nations. A Commentary. Volume I* (Oxford University Press, 2012), 1–23.

[3] As a lesson learned from the history of the Society of Nations, one can record that 'une conception trop rigide de l'universalisme, couplée avec une attitude de mépris à l'égard du phénomène régional, n'a pas renforcé l'autorité de l'organisation universelle', L. Boisson de Chazournes, *Les relations entre organisations régionales et organisations universelles*, Recueil des cours de l'Académie de La Haye, Volume 347 (2010), 79, 163. Consequently, 'les rédacteurs de la Charte n'ont jamais eu pour ambition d'anéantir le phénomène des ententes particulières/régionales', ibid.

[4] United Nations, Documents de la Conférence des Nations Unies sur l'Organisation Internationale, San Francisco, 1945, Tome IV, Propositions de Dumbarton Oaks, Commentaires et Projets d'Amendements (1945), pp. 17–18.

legitimate[5] – and the norm rather than the exception.[6] Nevertheless, regionalism was placed at a disadvantage by the imposed supremacy of the SC and its primary responsibility for maintaining international peace and security. The Charter also established that the SC should act in the name of all members of the organisation while exercising its duties, so that it consequently confirms and reasserts the universalist approach favoured by the great powers while negotiating the UN Charter.[7] Regionalist efforts include the conclusion of the Australian–New Zealand Agreement 1944, which stipulated the following:

> Pending the re-establishment of law and order and the inauguration of a system of general security, the two Governments hereby declare ... that it would be proper for Australia and New Zealand to assume full responsibility for policing or sharing in policing such areas in the South West and South Pacific as may from time to time be agreed upon.[8]

Reacting to and rebutting of the proposals of Dumbarton Oaks, Australia furthermore proposed an amendment to the proposals, anticipating the propositions made approximately five years later in the *Uniting for Peace* Resolution. It said the following:

> Si le Conseil de sécurité ne prend pas de mesures lui-même et ne permet pas que des mesures soient prises en vertu d'un arrangement ou d'un mécanisme régional en vue de maintenir ou rétablir la paix internationale, aucune disposition de la présente Charte ne sera considérée comme abrogeant le droit des parties à contacter tout arrangement compatible avec la présente Charte ou d'adopter toutes mesures paraissant justes et nécessaires pour maintenir au rétablir la paix et la sécurité internationales en vertu de cet arrangement.[9]

---

[5] U. Villani, *Les Rapports entre l'ONU et les organisations régionales dans le domaine du maintien de la paix*, Recueil des cours de l'Académie de La Haye, Volume 290 (2001), 225, 244. Churchill and some other realists remained unsuccessful with their idea of independent regional agencies for the preservation of peace, Khan, 'Drafting History', supra note 2, 1, 15, marginal number (mn), 40.

[6] UN Doc. S/2015/229 (2015), 2, para. 4.

[7] Villani, supra note 5, 225, 244, 246; cf. also P.-M. Dupuy, 'Les grands secteurs d'intérêt des organisations internationales', in R.-J. Dupuy (ed.), *Manuel sur les organisations internationals/A Handbook on International Organizations* (Leiden, Martinus Nijhoff, 1998), 563, 598–599.

[8] Australian–New Zealand Agreement of 21 January 1944, para. 15.

[9] The documents of the conference are published in either French or English; the latter version of this particular volume is not available online. United Nations, Tome IV, supra note 4, Amendements aux Propositions de Dumbarton Oaks présentés par l'Australie, 773, 783.

The Latin American countries, relying heavily on their tradition of Pan-Americanism, went a step further and adopted a Resolution containing the Act on Reciprocal Assistance and American Solidarity.[10] The Act provided not only for the authorisation of the use of coercive measures and military measures in order to defend an American state, but also allowed the prevention of an attack, contravening consequently Article 51 of the UN Charter.[11] The supporters of the universalist approach, inter alia, the Netherlands, argued that nothing would be more dangerous for world peace than regional organisations if, notwithstanding the good intentions leading to their creation, they could at any moment turn against each other or any given state due to a lack of appropriate coordination.[12]

The results of the San Francisco conference can be therefore seen either as a compromise between the universalist, centralist approach favoured by the great powers and the regionalist, decentralised approach,[13] or as a clash between two opposing doctrines, the wartime Churchillian view calling for regional councils and the centralist Wilsonian view.[14] The concessions made to the regionalist proponents concern primarily the peaceful settlement of disputes,[15] but whereas the Dumbarton Oaks proposals did not contain any disposition regarding a right of (collective) self-defence, the conference of San Francisco led to the adoption of Article 51.[16] The

---

[10] Further opposition came, inter alia, from France and the Arab States, Villani, supra note 5, 225, 252. In a similar fashion, the Arab States created the Arab League, ibid. For further details, C. Walter, 'Chapter VIII Regional Arrangements. Introduction to Chapter VIII', in B. Simma, D.-E. Khan, G. Nolte et al. (eds.), *The Charter of the United Nations. A Commentary. Volume II* (Oxford University Press, 2012), 1429, 1437 mn. 10–1438 mn. 14.

[11] Inter-American Reciprocal Assistance and Solidarity (Act of Chapultepec), 6 March 1945, available at http://avalon.law.yale.edu/20th_century/chapul.asp.

[12] United Nations, Tome IV, Suggestions du Gouvernement des Pays-Bas sur les Propositions de Dumbarton Oaks, supra note 4, 448, 461.

[13] Walter, 'Chapter VIII Regional Arrangements', supra note 10, 1429, 1434; E. Griep, *Regionale Organisationen und die Weiterentwicklung der VN-Friedenssicherung seit dem Ende des Kalten Krieges* (Baden-Baden, Nomos, 2012), 60.

[14] I. Claude, *Swords into Plowshares: The Problems and Progress of International Organizations* (Random House, 1965), 113.

[15] Either by the parties under Article 33 or by regional organisations under Article 52(2).

[16] The insertion of Article 51 was due to the insistence of the Latin American and the Arab states, C. Schreuer, 'Regionalism v. Universalism', *European Journal of International Law*, 6 (1995), 477, 478. These states also pushed heavily for the distinction in the Charter between regional arrangements and organisations of collective defence leading to the inclusion of Chapter VIII, D. L. Tehindrazanarivelo, 'The African Union's Relationship with the United Nations in the Maintenance of Peace and Security', in A. A. Yusuf, F. Ouguergouz (eds.), *The African Union: Legal and Institutional Framework* (2012), 375; C. Walter, 'Hybrid Peacekeeping: Is UNAMID a New Model for Cooperation between the United Nations and Regional Organizations?', in H. Hestermeyer, D. König, N. Matz-Lück et al. (eds.),

procedure under the Charter for the adoption of decisions by certain organs is another element that prompted an effort towards regionalism. In order for states to achieve the necessary majority vote to adopt a decision in a UN organ, a certain number of votes have to be mobilised by states, which is easier within a group containing common ties.[17]

The Cold War and the opposition of the two blocs in the SC and on the international stage were partly beneficial and partly detrimental for regional organisations and cooperation. Whereas the block construction led to the establishment of new regional organisations with the objective of securing the respective spheres of interest, as well as the creation of possible defence mechanisms such as NATO, the opposing veto powers in the SC also prevented all efforts for cooperation, including on a regional basis. Consequently, the end of the Cold War also constituted a veritable break for international cooperation between international organisations,[18] but the Cold War itself – somewhat ironically – allowed regional organisations to emancipate themselves 'from any unwelcome assertion of controlling authority by the Security Council'.[19] Notwithstanding the identification of a need for greater regional cooperation in the maintenance of peace and security, its usefulness persisted throughout the Cold War, and particularly in the last few years of this conflict. In 1988, the General Assembly adopted a declaration in which it recommended that states that were members of regional organisations use these mechanisms to settle local disputes. Furthermore, significant recommendations were introduced which suggested that the SC, the General Assembly and the Secretary-General should encourage and endorse efforts at the regional level to prevent or remove a conflict or situation.[20]

Coexistence, Cooperation and Solidarity. Liber Amicorum Rüdiger Wolfrum (Leiden, Brill, 2012), 1327, 1328.

[17] M. Virally, *L'Organisation Mondiale* (Paris, A. Colin, 1972), 281.
[18] It is also suggested by a member of the ILC that the 'failure of imperfect implementation of the security system set up by the United Nations was prompting some regional organizations to fill the vacuum' by changing their original aims, Mr. Kateka, UN Doc. A/CN.4/SR.2755 (2003), para. 59. See also Griep, *Regionale Organisationen*, supra note 13, 30.
[19] Claude, *Swords into Plowshares*, supra note 14, 116. However, this was often due to one of the two great powers, thus the US has consistently resisted the submission of the OAS under the UN Charter within the SC, ibid.
[20] UN Doc. A/RES/43/51 (1988), Annex, paras. 4, 13, 17 and 24. See also T. Rensmann, 'Reform', in B. Simma, D.-E. Khan, G. Nolte et al. (eds.), *The Charter of the United Nations. A Commentary. Volume I* (Oxford University Press, 2012), 25, 34 mn. 30–31; 50 mn. 87; 51 mn. 90.

The End of the Cold War and the Rebirth of the SC: What Role for Regional Organisations?

After the end of the Cold War and the apparent rejuvenation the SC,[21] concerns arose on the hand that the SC was becoming too active, and on the other hand that it was being sidelined by its inability to take enforcement action on its own and, therefore having to rely on the so-called 'coalition of the willing'.[22] The form of a coalition serves two main purposes: the sharing of costs and the provision of some form of legitimisation.[23] The early 1990s was a period in which the UN struggled to find its identity, being as it was inhibited by the compromise between universalism and regionalism as codified in its Charter.

Thus, in his *Agenda for Peace*, Secretary-General Boutros-Ghali declared that '[t]he adversarial decades of the cold war made the original promise of the Organization impossible to fulfill', continuing that

> [i]n these past months a conviction has grown among nations large and small, that an opportunity has been regained to achieve the great objectives of the Charter – a United Nations capable of maintaining international peace and security ... This opportunity must not be squandered. The Organization must never again be crippled as it was in the era that has now passed.[24]

But his agenda had a broader aim than simply to boost the capacities of the UN. Part of his vision for the maintenance of international peace and

---

[21] Of the 477 Chapter VII Resolutions adopted by 2009, 456 have been adopted since the end of the Cold War, according to P. Johansson, 'The Humdrum Use of Ultimate Authority: Defining and Analysing Chapter VII Resolutions', *Nordic Journal of International Law*, 78 (2009), 309, 327. As noted by the Secretary-General in 2008, '[u]ntil 1990, there were no references in Security Council resolutions to regional organizations', UN Doc. S/2008/186 (2008), 6, para. 4. A study of resolutions of the SC of 1988 stated that references to regional organisations were, indeed, rare and it only cites two examples since 1945, according to R. Sonnenfeld, *Resolutions of the United Nations Security Council* (Leiden, Martinus Nijhoff, 1988), 103–104. See also Rensmann, 'Reform', supra note 20, 25, 52 mn. 92.

[22] C. Gray, 'The Charter Limitations on the Use of Force: Theory and Practice', in V. Lowe, A. Roberts, J. Welsh (eds.), *The United Nations Security Council and War* (Oxford University Press, 2008), 86, 90. In this context, the concepts of peacekeeping and authorisations given to coalitions of the able and willing were not always fully distinguishable. N. Blokker, 'The Security Council and the Use of Force: On Recent Practice', in N. Blokker, N. Schrijver (eds.), *The Security Council and the Use of Force: Theory and Reality. A Need for Change?* (Leiden, Brill, 2005), 1, 15.

[23] A. J. Bellamy, P. D. Williams, 'Who's Keeping the Peace? Regionalization and Contemporary Peace Operations', *International Security*, 29 (2005), 157, 162.

[24] UN Doc. S/25996 (1993), paras. 2–3; cf. also UN Doc. A/65/762 (2011), 6–7, para. 15; A/RES/47/120 (1993), Preamble, I. para. 4, II. para. 1, IV. Preamble.

security in this new era was the promotion of the role of regional organisations. He wrote in the Agenda that 'regional action as a matter of decentralization, delegation and cooperation with United Nations efforts could not only lighten the burden of the Council but also contribute to a deeper sense of participation, consensus and democratization in international affairs'.[25] The Secretary-General consequently took a middle course between a universal approach – a strong UN with its own troops at its disposal – and a regional approach – cooperation with regional organisations – for maintaining international peace and security. This approach can be seen as holistic and comprehensive, as it is addressing the issue through various actors, but it also reflects the limitations of the charter by which the UN is bound.

His successor in office, Kofi Annan, took a more accentuated approach. He argued for an increased involvement of regional organisations, saying that

> [a] considerable number of regional and subregional organizations are now active around the world, making important contributions to the stability and prosperity of their members, as well as of the broader international system. The United Nations and regional organizations should play complementary roles in facing the challenges to international peace and security.[26]

However, Kofi Annan went even further in his report, titled *In Larger Freedom*, in which he expressed the view that 'the time is now ripe for a decisive move forward: the establishment of an interlocking system of peacekeeping activities that will enable the United Nations to work with relevant regional organizations in predictable and reliable partnerships'.[27] Consequently, an argument was made for synergy between peacekeeping activities, which are based on ad hoc agreements, and cooperation with regional organisations.[28] This approach conflates the previously proposed standing UN forces, under Article 43 of the UN Charter, with the practice

---

[25] UN Doc. S/25996 (1993), 18, para. 64. The SC itself issued a presidential statement in early 1993 acknowledging the role regional organisations can play. See UN Doc. S/25184 (1993).

[26] UN Doc. A/59/2005 (2005), 52, para. 213. The very same idea is also put forward in SC Resolution 1809, UN Doc. S/RES/1809 (2008), para. 9; cf. UN Doc. A/RES/49/57 (1994), Annex. See also UN Doc. S/2008/186 (2008), 7, para. 9 and UN Doc. A/61/204 and S/2006/590 (2006), 18, paras. 87–88.

[27] UN Doc. A/59/2005 (2005), 31, para. 112.

[28] Another argument submitted is that it became difficult for UN forces to carry out the complexity of attributed tasks with the insufficient means they had at their disposal, leading the SC to authorise member states or regional organisations to support these UN forces, R. Kolb, G. Porretto, S. Vité, *L'application du droit international humanitaire et des droits de l'homme aux organisations internationales. Forces de paix et administrations civiles transitoires* (Brussels, Bruylant, 2005), 39.

and structure of UN peacekeeping, and the cooperation with regional organisations. A clear expression of this policy is also found in the Report of Secretary-General Ban Ki-moon on the relationship between the UN and regional organisations in the maintenance of international peace and security. He points out that

> [t]he past decade has witnessed a strengthened relationship, at different levels, between the United Nations and regional organizations ... This has yielded interesting perspectives and fruitful cooperation between the United Nations and regional organizations. It is, therefore, critical that regional organizations be encouraged and empowered to take actions to restore peace and security in conflicts and areas under their respective purview. These actions, however, cannot be viewed in isolation as many actors have a part to play in attaining overall global security.[29]

The proposition of the conclusion of agreements under Article 43 and the vision of standing UN forces with enforcement capacity failed to receive the necessary support by the member states.[30] States had started to rely on regional organisations with their more advanced military capabilities for peacekeeping and peace enforcement purposes. Arguably, one can speak of the establishment of standing UN forces through 'outsourcing' to regional organisations which might have united proponents of regional organisations and supporters of standing UN forces. The 2004 High-Level Panel recognised that 'in recent years, decisions to authorize military force for the purpose of enforcing the peace have primarily fallen to multinational forces' and that

> there has been a trend towards a variety of regional- and sub-regional based peacekeeping missions ... [which] poses a challenge for the Security Council to work closely with each other and mutually support each other's efforts to keep the peace and ensure that regional operations are accountable to universally accepted human rights standards.[31]

Boutros-Ghali's proposal of standing UN forces was thus abandoned in favour of more modest ideas and cumulative ameliorations, including

---

[29] UN Doc. S/2008/186 (2008), 5, para. 3.
[30] Cf. R. Higgins, 'Peace and Security Achievements and Failures', *European Journal of International Law,* 6 (1995), 445, 451; with further reasons for the opposition, UN Doc. A/55/305 and S/2000/809 (2000), 15, para. 85. The SC also reacted to Boutros-Ghali's Proposal for UN Rapid Reaction Force for Peacekeeping Operations. See UN Doc. A/50/60-S/1995/1 (1995), 11, para. 44; Statement by the President of the Security Council, and UN Doc. S/PRST/1995/9 (1995), 2, final paragraph.
[31] UN Doc. A/59/565 (2004), 58, para. 210; 60, para. 220.

regional initiatives.³² Consequently, throughout the 1990s the UN remained unable to deploy forces quickly and effectively on the ground. The Brahimi Report stated clearly that 'few of the basic building blocks are in place for the United Nations to rapidly acquire and deploy the human and material resources required to mount any complex peace operation in the future'.³³

The increased support for regional organisations by member states was interconnected with traditional troop contributors decreasing their support to UN peacekeeping operations.³⁴ This development was primarily due to the end of the Cold War and the omission of the conflict between the West and the East.

Whereas the Charter preserves a compromise between a universalist and regionalist approach regarding the maintenance of international peace and security, the practice of the 1990s demonstrates that this task could not be fulfilled differently than through a multilateral, decentralised construction in which the SC acted primarily as the authorising entity. Nevertheless, also in the current era of cooperation with regional organisations there are new problems and challenges to face which necessitate a professional, concerted approach to peacekeeping. The Secretary-General declared frankly in 2008 that 'the real challenge for the Security Council is to replace the improvised, at times selected, resource-skewed approach with more planned, consistent and reliable arrangements'.³⁵

This part focused on the wider framework as well as on the development of the broader area of maintenance of international peace and security by the UN and regional organisations. The effect of these developments on the applicable legal framework for peacekeeping and peace enforcement

---

[32] A. Roberts, 'Proposals for UN Standing Forces: A Critical History', in V. Lowe, A. Roberts, J. Welsh (eds.), *The United Nations Security Council and War* (Oxford University Press, 2008), 99, 120.

[33] Panel on UN Peace Operations, supra note 30, 15, paras. 85, 90.

[34] Berdal lists a few of these non-UN peacekeeping operations during the 1990s: 'various NATO-led missions to the Balkans since 1995; the Italian-led operation in Albania in 1997 (Operation Alba); the 1997 Mission Interafricaine de Surveillance des Accords de Bangui (MISAB) in the Central Africa Republic; the ECOWAS Monitoring Group (ECOMOG) in Sierra Leone from 1998 to 2000; the International Force in East Timor (INTERFET) between 1999 and 2000; ... the European Union Mission in the FYROM (Operation Concordia) in 2003; the EU Mission in the Democratic Republic of Congo (Operation Artemis) in 2003; the African Mission in Burundi (AMIB) in 2003; and the (US-, South African- and Moroccan-led) ECOWAS mission to Liberia in 2003', M. Berdal, 'The Security Council and Peacekeeping', in V. Lowe, A. Roberts, J. Welsh et al. (eds.), *The United Nations Security Council and War* (Oxford University Press, 2008), 175, 198 fn. 75. See also D. B. Bobrow, M. A. Boyer, 'Maintaining System Stability: Contributions to Peacekeeping Operations', *The Journal of Conflict Resolution*, 41 (1997), 723, 735–741.

[35] UN Doc. S/2008/186 (2008), 7, para. 12. See also Chapter 2.

operations as well as in practice and in the legal framework applicable in the domain of cooperation between the UN and regional organisations are analysed in the following parts. Chapter 2 will then focus exclusively on the cooperation between the UN and regional organisations and will, in particular, trace the developments since the beginning of this millennium.

The Legal Framework of Peacekeeping and Peace Enforcement Operations: Chapters VI and VII of the UN Charter

Chapters VI and VII of the UN Charter set out the legal framework applicable to the peaceful settlement of disputes as well as to action with respect to threats to the peace, breaches of the peace and acts of aggression. The blockade within the SC during the Cold War led to the failure of the implementation of the agreements under Article 43.[36] Nevertheless, 'the UN system proved sufficiently flexible to allow the Security Council to take force measures not expressly provided for in the Charter'.[37] As the SC could not order the use of force using its own standing army, it resorted to either 'authorising' or 'calling upon' member states to use force.[38] The establishment of the concept of peacekeeping was therefore a reaction to both the blockade in the SC and the lack of agreements under Article 43, although there was no explicit legal basis for peacekeeping operations in the Charter.[39]

---

[36] Virally, supra note 17, 469–470; C. Gray, *International Law and the Use of Force* (Oxford University Press, 2008), 254; N. Krisch, 'Chapter VII Action with Respect to Threats to the Peace, Breaches of the Peace, and Acts of Aggression. Introduction to Chapter VII: The General Framework', in B. Simma, D.-E. Khan, G. Nolte et al. (eds.), *The Charter of the United Nations. A Commentary. Volume II* (Oxford University Press, 2012), 1237, 1241 mn. 7. Another reason was more generally the lack of unanimity of all the permanent members within the Council, M. Bothe, 'Peacekeeping', in B. Simma, D.-E. Khan, G. Nolte et al. (eds.), *The Charter of the United Nations. A Commentary. Volume I* (Oxford University Press, 2012), 1171, 1175 mn. 2.

[37] Gray, 'The Charter Limitations', supra note 22, 86, 88; T. Lie, *In the Cause of Peace: Seven Years with the United Nations* (New York, Macmillan, 1954), 98. Generally regarding UN standing forces, see Roberts, 'Proposals', supra note 32, 99–130.

[38] Gray, 'The Charter Limitations', supra note 22, 86, 88.

[39] Ibid. 86, 88. The Legality of Peacekeeping Operations was confirmed in the Certain Expenses Case by the ICJ and is now not disputed. The very same reasoning should apply for authorisations of peace enforcement operations and it is now widely accepted. Furthermore, it is supported by UN practice, see, for instance, N. Krisch, 'Article 42', in B. Simma, D.-E. Khan, G. Nolte et al. (eds.), *The Charter of the United Nations. A Commentary. Volume II* (Oxford University Press, 2012), 1330, 1337 mn. 11–1338 mn. 13; N. Blokker, 'Is the Authorization Authorized? Powers and Practice of the UN Security Council to Authorize the Use of Force by "Coalitions of the Able and Willing"', *European Journal of International Law*, 11 (2000), 541, 547–549; E. de Wet, *The Chapter VII Powers of the United Nations Security*

Throughout its existence, the SC has relied only on the determination of a situation as a 'threat to international peace and security' or sometimes a 'breach of the peace' as the trigger for the application of Chapter VII of the Charter.[40] The term 'threat to the peace' in particular involves wide powers of discretion as

> il s'agit en effet d'une hypothèse très vague et élastique qui, contrairement à l'agression et à la rupture de la paix, n'est pas nécessairement caractérisée par des opérations militaires ou en tout cas impliquant l'utilisation de la force, et qui par conséquent peut correspondre aux comportements les plus variés des Etats.[41]

A determination of an act of aggression would also entail the responsibility of the aggressor state under international law, and possibly even individual criminal responsibility[42] and both reasons explain the political preference

---

Council (2004), 260–263; T. M. Franck, *Recourse to Force. State Action against Threats and Armed Attack* (Cambridge University Press, 2002), 24–31; A. Orakhelashvili, *Collective Security* (Oxford University Press, 2011), 223–226. A contrary view is taken, e.g., by B. H. Weston, 'Security Council Resolution 678 and Persian Gulf Decision-Making: Precarious Legitimacy', *American Journal of International Law*, 85 (1991), 516, 518–522; M. Bothe, 'Les limites des pouvoirs du Conseil de Sécurité', in R.-J. Dupuy (ed.), *The Development of the Role of the Security Council* (Leiden, Brill, 1993), 67, 73–74; J. Quigley, 'The "Privatization" of Security Council Enforcement Action: A Threat to Multilateralism', *Michigan Journal of International Law*, 17 (1995–1996), 249, especially 261–283. Other authors give a more cautious, policy-oriented view such as Chesterman who considers the delegation of enforcement powers at least partially to be based on national interests by states, S. Chesterman, *Just War or Just Peace? Humanitarian Intervention and International Law* (Oxford University Press, 2001), 163–218. Dinstein considers that the authorisation to use force amounts to a mere recommendation under Article 39, Y. Dinstein, *War, Aggression and Self-Defence* (Cambridge University Press, 2005), 310. For a critique of Dinstein's view, see Orakhelashvili, ibid., 225–226; see also UN Doc. A/59/565 (2004), 57, para. 203; 58, para. 210.

[40] J. Allain, 'The True Challenges to the United Nations System of the Use of Force: The Failures of Kosovo and Iraq and the Emergence of the African Union', *Max Planck Yearbook of United Nations Law*, 8 (2004), 237, 245.

[41] B. Conforti, 'Le pouvoir discrétionnaire du Conseil de Sécurité en matière de constatation d'une menace contre la paix, d'une rupture de la paix ou d'un acte d'agression', in R. J. Dupuy (ed.), *The Development of the Role of the Security Council* (Leiden, Brill, 1993), 51, 53; see also N. Krisch, 'Article 39', in B. Simma, D.-E. Khan, G. Nolte et al. (eds.), *The Charter of the United Nations. A Commentary. Volume II* (Oxford University Press, 2012), 1272, 1278 mn. 12–1293 mn. 39.

[42] Individual criminal responsibility of the involved soldier(s) and possibly the commanding officer(s) either on the basis of customary international law or domestic criminal law. Subject to a decision to be taken after 1 January 2017 by a two-third majority of States Parties to the Rome Statute and subject to the ratification of the amendment to the Rome State by thirty States Parties, the ICC will have effective jurisdiction over the crime of aggression. See also Allain, 'The True Challenges', supra note 40, 237, 245.

of the SC to rely on the concept of a 'threat to the peace' to mandate peacekeeping or peace enforcement operations.

The Evolution and Definition of Peacekeeping: Peacekeeping vs Peace Enforcement

An analysis of peacekeeping operations necessitates a definition of peacekeeping and an exploration of its origin.[43] There is no comprehensive definition of peacekeeping which would comprise all operations and functions exercised within an operation, as each operation has its specific mandate and nature,[44] despite good arguments made for such an agreed definition.[45] Likewise, there has been an evolution in the conceptual understanding, as well as in the organisational implementation, of peacekeeping operations since the creation of the first mission.[46] According to the UN itself, peacekeeping operations are,

> [o]perations involving military personnel, but without enforcement powers, undertaken by the United Nations to help maintain or restore international peace and security in areas of conflict. These operations are voluntary and are based on consent and cooperation ... [achieving] their objectives not by force of arms, thus contrasting ... with the 'enforcement action' ... under Article 42.[47]

Peacekeeping operations are traditionally based on the principles of consent of the host-state, neutrality, impartiality of the force and

---

[43] See generally M. W. Doyle, N. Sambanis, 'Peacekeeping Operations', in T. Weiss, S. Daws (eds.), *The Oxford Handbook on the United Nations* (Oxford University Press, 2007), 323, 323–334; K. Annan (with N. Mousavizadeh), *Interventions. A Life in War and Peace* (New York, Penguin Group, 2012), pp. 29–78; J. P. Bialke, 'United Nations Peace Operations: Applicable Norms and the Application of the Law of Armed Conflict', *Air Force Law Review*, 50 (2001), 1, 6–32.

[44] R. Higgins, *United Nations Peacekeeping 1946–1967: Documents and Commentary, Vol I: The Middle East* (Oxford University Press, 1969), ix.

[45] Ralph Zacklin, 'Managing Peacekeeping from a Legal Perspective', in D. Warner (ed.), *New Dimensions of Peacekeeping* (Leiden, Brill, 1995), 159; A. Gillman, W. Johnson (eds.), *Operational Law Handbook, The Judge Advocate General's Legal Center & School* (Charlottesville, The Judge Advocate General's Legal Center & School, 2012), 56, para. IIIA. This is, in addition to the wish of the ILC to follow the pattern of the articles on State Responsibility, also the reason why the ILC decided not to include a specific rule for the attribution of conduct in peacekeeping operations in the articles on the responsibility of international organisations, UN Doc. A/CN.4/541 (2004), 16, para. 34.

[46] For a good overview, see S. Chesterman, 'The Use of Force in UN Peace Operations', External Study, UN Peacekeeping Best Practices (2004).

[47] United Nations, *The Blue Helmets: A Review of United Nations Peacekeeping* (1990), 4.

non-intervention in the state's internal affairs and the non-use of force, except in cases of self-defence.[48] Consent of the host-state is necessary as long as the peacekeeping mission is not established under Chapter VII of the Charter.[49]

Traditionally, the major difference from peace enforcement operations is that the right to the use of force is limited to self-defence.[50] Some confusion has been inserted by the use of certain terminology such as 'robust' or 'muscled or muscular peacekeeping'. The high-level panel gave a very good definition of the distinction between peacekeeping and peace enforcement which is worthwhile citing:

> There is a distinction between operations in which the robust use of force is integral to the mission from the outset (e.g., responses to cross-border invasions or an explosion of violence, in which the recent practice has been to mandate multinational forces) and operations in which there is a reasonable expectation that force may not be needed at all (e.g. traditional peacekeeping missions monitoring and verifying a ceasefire or those assisting in implementing peace agreements, where blue helmets are still the norm).
>
> But both kinds of operations need the authorization of the Security Council (Article 51 self-defence cases apart), and in peacekeeping cases as much as in peace enforcement cases it is now the usual practice for a Chapter VII mandate to be given (even if that is not always welcomed by troop contributors) ... the difference between Chapter VI and VII mandates can be exaggerated: there is little doubt that peacekeeping missions operating under Chapter VI (and thus operating without enforcement powers) have the right to use force in self-defence – and this right is widely understood to extend to 'defence of the mission'.[51]

---

[48] M. Zwanenburg, *Accountability of Peace Support Operations* (Leiden, Brill, 2005), 13, cf. A. Ryniker, 'Quelques commentaires à propos de la Circulaire du Secrétaire général des Nations Unies du 6 août 1999', *Revue internationale de la Croix-Rouge*, 836 (1999), 795, 796. The Peace Support Operations Doctrine of the AU only lists consent and impartiality as criteria distinguishing peace support operations from war, Headquarters of the AU, African Standby Force, Peace Support Operations Doctrine (2006), chapter 3, para. 3, 3-10–3-14; paras. 35–47.

[49] Zwanenburg, ibid., 14, 18; D. Zaum, 'The Security Council, the General Assembly, and War: The Uniting for Peace Resolution', in V. Lowe, A. Roberts, J. Welsh et al. (eds.), *The United Nations Security Council and War* (Oxford University Press, 2008), 154, 171; UN Doc. S/25996 (1993); UN Doc. SG/SM/10250 AFR/1298 (2005).

[50] K. E. Cox, 'Beyond Self-Defense: United Nations Peacekeeping and the Use of Force', *Denver Journal of International Law and Policy*, 27 (1998–1999), 239, 248.

[51] Report of the High-Level Panel, supra note 31, 58, paras. 211–213; cf. the Capstone Doctrine which was not helpful in clarifying the distinction, UN Peacekeeping Operations, Principles and Guidelines (2008), 34–35, 19, para. 2.2. See also R. Zacklin, 'The Use of Force in Peacekeeping Operations', in N. Blokker, N. Schrijver (eds.), *The Security Council and the Use of Force*, 91, 94; cf. C. Tomuschat, 'The European Court of Human Rights and the

Self-defence in peacekeeping operations covers both cases of individual and collective self-defence and may also include 'resistance to attempts by forceful means to prevent it from discharging its duties under the mandate of the Security Council'.[52] The right of collective self-defence in the peacekeeping context could also serve to delimit peacekeeping from peace enforcement operations. Should it be raised as an argument by a state, it indicates – albeit implicitly – that this given operation is to be considered as a peacekeeping operation.

Peacekeeping Post–Cold War: The Ambiguous Practice of the SC: Blurring the Lines between Peacekeeping and Peace Enforcement

The end of the Cold War and the new possibilities for action by the SC transformed peacekeeping as it had been conceived up until then. As Kofi Annan wrote:

> Only with the end of the Cold War did the proliferation in peacekeeping really begin ... In these changed circumstances, the principles and practices which had evolved in the Cold War period suddenly seemed needlessly self-limiting. Within and outside the UN, there is now increasing support for peacekeeping with teeth. When lightly-armed peacekeepers were made to look helpless in Somalia and Bosnia, member states and public opinion supported more muscular action; an increasing number of situations seem to require it, and the Charter of the United Nations provides the legal authority for it.[53]

In addition to 'peacekeeping with teeth', post-1990 peacekeeping operations were often complex and multidisciplinary, including 'civilian police, electoral personnel, human rights experts ... involving nothing less than the reconstruction of an entire society and state'.[54] The multiplication of tasks was attended by a more extensive interpretation of the right to use force in self-defence, especially in the so-called 'third-generation peacekeeping operations', allowing the use of force under Chapter VII of the UN

United Nations', in A. Føllesdal, B. Peters, G. Ulfstein (eds.), *The European Court of Human Rights in a National, European and Global Context* (2013), 334, 344.

[52] UN Doc. S/11052/Rev.1 (1973); United Nations, Memorandum to the Senior Political Adviser to the Secretary-General, *1993 United Nations Judicial Yearbook*, 371, 371–372.

[53] K. Annan, 'UN Peacekeeping Operations and Cooperation with NATO', *Nato Review*, 47(5) (1993), 3–7.

[54] B. Boutros-Ghali, 'Beyond Peacekeeping', *New York University Journal of International Law & Politics*, 25 (1992–1993), 113, 115; Peacekeeping Best Practices Unit, Department of Peacekeeping Operations, *Handbook on United Nations Multidimensional Peacekeeping Operations* (2003), 20.

for other specified purposes than self-defence.⁵⁵ It can also be argued that the penetration of international law by human rights law has contributed to the changing nature of peacekeeping operations.⁵⁶

This progressive complexity and the increasing demands on a peacekeeping operation and peacekeepers since the end of the Cold War have led to mandates of peacekeeping operations blurring the previously comparatively clear line between peacekeeping and peace enforcement⁵⁷; indeed, in this vein, one author refers to these operations as 'militarised peacekeeping' operations.⁵⁸ Gray specifically mentions the cases of Yugoslavia and Somalia when peacekeeping forces were endowed with functions that went beyond the concept of peacekeeping as it had been previously understood.⁵⁹

The vague language of mandates prescribed by the SC in some peacekeeping operations further complicates the distinction between peacekeeping and peace enforcement.⁶⁰ While, on the one hand, this practice might be appropriate and necessary to allow the troops to react to unforeseen

---

⁵⁵ Zwanenburg, *Accountability*, supra note 48, 19. This is also referred to as 'robust peacekeeping' or 'peacekeeping with muscle'. It is argued in the literature that an expansion of the concept of self-defence or a reinterpretation as including the defence of the mandate for the purposes of peacekeeping would be incorrect, N. Krisch, 'Article 42', supra note 39, 1330, 1336 fn. 35. As Cox points out the confusion about the notion of use of force in self-defence in peacekeeping operations is linked to the blurring of the distinction between peacekeeping and peace enforcement operations, Cox, supra note 50, 239, 258.

⁵⁶ Protection of civilians and women and children is increasingly part of the mandate of recent peacekeeping operations. Cf. T. M. Franck, 'Collective Security and UN Reform: Between the Necessary and the Possible', *Chicago Journal of International Law*, 6 (2005–2006), 597, 600–601; J. Sloan, *The Militarisation of Peacekeeping in the Twenty-First Century* (Oxford, Hart Publishing, 2011), 3.

⁵⁷ Hammarskjöld already warned in 1958 that that a wide interpretation of the right of self-defence would blur the distinction between peacekeeping and peace enforcement; see UN Doc. A/3943 (1958), 31, para. 179; T. D. Gill, 'Characterization and Legal Basis for Peace Operations', in T. D. Gill, D. Fleck (eds.), *The Handbook of the International Law of Military Operations* (Oxford University Press, 2010), 135, 136. See also L. Condorelli, 'Pertinence du DIH pour les organisations internationales et les alliances', in S. Kolanowski, Y. Salmon (eds.), *Proceedings of the Bruges Colloquium. The Impact of International Humanitarian Law on Current Security Policy Trends* (2001), 25, 28; Zacklin, 'The Use of Force in Peacekeeping Operations', supra note 51, 91, 91–100. For the fluidity of the distinction between peacekeeping and peace enforcement, see Headquarters of the AU, supra note 48, chapter 3, 3-2, figures 1–3.

⁵⁸ Sloan, *The Militarisation*, supra note 56, 3.

⁵⁹ Gray, *International Law*, supra note 36, 282, also 310. The distinction between peacekeeping and peace enforcement forces was also blurred 'through the establishment of both peacekeeping and enforcement forces to operate at the same time', ibid., 289.

⁶⁰ See, e.g., UN Doc. S/RES/1528 (2004), para. 8; S/RES/1769 (2007), para. 15; S/RES/1996 (2011), para. 4.

circumstances; on the other hand, it simultaneously further obscures the vital difference between peacekeeping and peace enforcement.

This practice is also dubious as it might have a direct impact on the question of international responsibility. Convoluted and vague mandates without clear and defined roles for the involved actors may lead to the authorising entity being considered as responsible for violations of international law. The application of substantive law to peacekeeping forces is also affected. These unclear mandates impede a determination as to whether international humanitarian law could be applicable to a peacekeeping operation.[61] This being the case, peacekeepers would fall under the regime of international humanitarian law, would be bound by these rules and could be attacked from the moment of their participation as combatants.[62]

Yet another aggravating factor is that whereas traditional operations were often regarded as being established under Chapter VI rather than under Chapter VII, the new tasks also mean that the SC is now relying exclusively on Chapter VII for mandating purposes.[63] Some criticism has been made which suggests that the SC sometimes blurs the distinction between Chapters VII and VIII and, indeed, there are resolutions which cannot be classified either into the category of peacekeeping or peace enforcement nor be considered as mandated under Chapter VII *or* Chapter VIII.[64]

---

[61] It is of course correct that the classification as peacekeeping or peace enforcement is of limited use as the application of IHL depends on factual circumstances, but an unclear mandate makes this process more difficult. See C. Greenwood, 'International Humanitarian Law and United Nations Military Operations', *Yearbook of International Humanitarian Law*, 1 (1998), 3, 11.

[62] See Chapter 5.

[63] Cf. Kolb, Porretto, Vité, *L'application du droit international humanitaire*, supra note 28, 38. For Pellet, chapter VII is the 'safer legal ground', with the qualification 'that it must be read in a dynamic perspective and in the light of the development of the law since 1945'; see A. Pellet, 'The Road to Hell Is Paved with Good Intentions – The United Nations as Guarantor of International Peace and Security: A French Perspective', in C. Tomuschat (ed.), *The United Nations at Age Fifty. A Legal Perspective* (Leiden, Martinus Nijhoff, 1995), 113, 130.

[64] For instance, UN Doc. S/RES/1464 (2003), para. 9. Generally, it seems correct to say that the system of delegated enforcement action which developed within the UN due to the lack of implementation of the foreseen agreements and mechanisms under Article 43 and the Charter 'brings military enforcement action under Article 42 ... very close to the system envisaged for regional organisations under Chapter VIII', N. D. White, 'Towards Integrated Peace Operations: The Evolution of Peacekeeping and Coalitions of the Willing', in M. Odello, R. Piotrowicz (eds.), *International Military Missions and International Law* (Leiden, Brill, 2011), 1, 2.

These developments all increase the complexity and the difficulty in legally analysing the phenomenon of peacekeeping operations in the context of the UN[65] from the perspective of the law of international responsibility. Moreover, they conflate the established practice of the SC, which distinguished between peacekeeping operations under UN command and control, and enforcement action or peace enforcement operations as authorised by groups of states or regional organisations.[66]

As such, it is not very surprising that, in practice, there has been a great deal of criticism from within[67] and outside the UN regarding these ambiguous, ambivalent and unclear mandates handed out by the SC which blur the difference between peacekeeping and peace enforcement.

A better criterion to distinguish between peacekeeping and peace enforcement operations would be the 'consent of the host-state'; an operation based on consent is not – per se – violating international law, whereas an operation without consent of the host-state is justified by the power and authority of the SC under the UN Charter. The lack of consent would thereby be an indicator that the operation holds an enforcement character. Nevertheless, the practice of the SC is not absolutely consistent and Secretary-General Boutros-Ghali also acknowledged that in some cases the consent of all parties to the conflict might not be necessary.[68]

---

[65] So it is argued that some UN operations have consisted of a 'combination of traditional peacekeeping, peacekeeping for enforcement purposes, multifunctional peacekeeping, as well as the delegation of the power to use force to member states or regional organisations'. See G. Verdirame, *The UN and Human Rights. Who Guards the Guardian?* (Cambridge University Press, 2011), 197.

[66] On the practice of the UN in this field and international responsibility, see Chapter 2.

[67] UN Doc. A/64/573 (2009), 5–6, paras. 20–26.

[68] UN Doc. S/25859 (1993), 1; UN Peacekeeping Operations, Principles and Guidelines (2008) ('Capstone Doctrine'), supra note 51, 18, para. 2.2. Boutros-Ghali was realistic and acknowledged the blurring of peace enforcement and peacekeeping in his Agenda for Peace. This development was attenuated by his suggestion that peacekeeping would not always need the consent of all parties concerned. See UN Doc. S/25996 (1993), paras. 20, 45. See also H. G. Schermers, N. M. Blokker, *International Institutional Law* (Leiden, Brill, 2011), 945, para. 1495; 947–954, paras. 1501–1512; F. Naert, *International Law Aspects of the EU' Security and Defence Policy, with a particular focus on the Law of Armed Conflict and Human Rights* (Antwerp, Intersentia, 2010), 199–200; Rensmann, 'Reform', supra note 20, 25, 53–54, mn. 96; K. Schmalenbach, *Die Haftung Internationaler Organisationen im Rahmen von Militäreinsätzen und Territorialverwaltungen* (Frankfurt, Peter Lang, 2004), 170.

Lessons Learned from Bosnia and Somalia: The Restoration of Traditional UN Peacekeeping

The failure of the implementation of Article 43 and of the establishment of standing UN forces strengthened cooperation between the UN and regional organisations. This development has also to be set against the background of UN operations in Somalia and Yugoslavia, which led to major criticism and a crisis in UN peacekeeping. The slaughters in Somalia as well as the massacre at Srebrenica gave rise to the question as to why the UN had not acted to prevent these atrocities from happening. Criticism fell upon the lack of an imperative mandate to allow peacekeepers to react with force, as well as a lack of equipment. Higgins, referring to Bosnia and the mandate of UNPROFOR, stated that peacekeepers were put in a place, with a mandate to deliver humanitarian aid and therefore 'all realistic prospect of "enforcing the peace" has [sic] gone. The enforcement of the peace of the victims of violations of Article 2(4) had already effectively been put aside by this selection of method of UN operation.'[69] In fact, the UN troops found themselves in a highly adversarial environment and partly engaged in activities going beyond peacekeeping. Tharoor comments that these activities included, inter alia, the establishment of 'no-fly zones' and 'safe areas', punitive actions against warlords, 'acquiescence in NATO declared "exclusion zones"', and 'peacekeepers mount[ing] anti-sniping patrols and call[ing]in air strikes'.[70] The reaction within the UN was a readjustment of the policy by the Secretary-General and the return to more traditional peacekeeping operations regarding the use of force as explained by the SG in his *Supplement to the Agenda for Peace*.[71]

---

[69] Higgins, 'Peace and Security Achievements', 445, 457. Higgins argues that the more muscular mandates including the protection of safe havens under SC Resolution 836 were only given out in 'sole consideration' of the safety of peacekeeping troops, ibid. This seems rather doubtful as the general practice of the SC and also the infiltration of international law by and the proliferation of human rights law rather point to an explanation of this particular mandate. However, it goes without saying that the protection of peacekeepers was and always has been of concern for the UN as is also illustrated by the Convention on the Safety of United Nations and Associated Personnel; see also Zacklin, 'The Use of Force', supra note 51, 91, 94–95.

[70] S. Tharoor, 'The Changing Face of Peace-keeping and Peace-Enforcement', *Fordham International Law Journal*, 19 (1995), 408, 414.

[71] UN Doc. A/50/60 and S/1995/1 (1995), 8–9, paras. 33–35; More substantiated critique in, B. Boutros-Ghali, *Unvanquished: A U.S.-U.N. Saga* (London, I.B. Tauris Publishers, 1999), 239.

This return to the traditional values of peacekeeping was welcomed by both the General Assembly and the SC.[72] Consequently, these policy intentions led the SC to further institutionalise relations with regional organisations,[73] establishing a general division of labour insofar as the Council would mandate regional organisations to conduct operations which take the nature of enforcement operations.[74] Nevertheless, peacekeeping operations have kept their integrated structures and mandates covering all different kinds of areas and many potential conduits for problems to arise. The problem of imprecise mandates has only been displaced by this shift of practice by the SC from UN operations to UN-mandated operations.[75]

The recent practice of the SC underlines the clear separation between peacekeeping and peace enforcement, despite a general tendency to deploy peacekeeping operations with a rather robust mandate. Reacting to the ongoing security and humanitarian crisis and activities of armed groups in the DRC, the SC adopted Resolution 2098 on 28 March 2013 in which it authorised 'on an exceptional basis and without creating a precedent or any prejudice to the agreed principles of peacekeeping', an 'intervention brigade' with a clear peace enforcement mandate.[76]

Although the Resolution emphasises the exceptional character of this extension of the mandate, it nevertheless proves again that the threshold between peacekeeping and peace enforcement is marginal at most[77] and that the application of international humanitarian law is independent from the classification as a peacekeeping or peace enforcement operation, but

[72] UN Doc. S/PRST/1995/9 (1995), 2. Cf. also Higgins, 'Peace and Security Achievements', 445, 459–460; P. Schori, 'UN Peacekeeping', in A. F. Cooper, H. Heine, R. Thakur (eds.), *The Oxford Handbook on Modern Diplomacy* (Oxford University Press, 2013), 779, 794; also Roberts, 'Proposals for UN Standing Forces', supra note 32, 99, 127; S. Tharoor, 'Should UN Peacekeeping Go "Back to Basics?"', *Survival*, 37 (1995–1996), 52–53.
[73] Cf. A. F. Douhan, *Regional Mechanisms of Collective Security. The New Face of Chapter VIII of the UN Charter?* (Paris, L'harmattan, 2013).
[74] See in particular Chapter 2. Cf. also K. E. Sams, 'IHL Obligations of the UN and Other International Organisations Involved in International Missions', in M. Odello, R. Piotrowicz (eds.), *International Military Missions and International Law* (Leiden, Brill, 2011), 45, 49.
[75] D. Kritsiotis, 'Security Council Resolution 1101 (1997) and the Multinational Protection Force of Operation Alba in Albania', *Leiden Journal of International Law*, 12 (1999), 511, 538–539; cf. also Dinstein, *War, Aggression*, supra note 39, 309.
[76] UN Doc. S/RES/2098 (2013), para. 9. The very same wording was reiterated in SC Resolution 2147, UN Doc. S/RES/2147 (2014), 5, para. 1. See also Statement of the Russian Federation, UN Doc. S/PV.6952 (2013), 2 and UN Doc. S/RES/2148 (2014), 4, para. 9.
[77] The mandate is congruent with the definition of peace enforcement given in the Peace Support Operations Doctrine of the AU, Headquarters of the AU, supra note 48, chapter 3, 3–6, paras. 13–14. See also Statements by the Head of MONUSCO, UN Doc. S/PV.7094 (2014), 3; S/PV.7137 (2014), particularly 3.

based on factual circumstances.⁷⁸ The preparatory report by the Secretary-General for a UN peacekeeping operation in Mali likewise adopts a traditional understanding of peacekeeping:

> At the same time, it is critical that *a clear distinction be maintained between the core peacekeeping tasks of an envisaged United Nations stabilization mission and the peace enforcement and counter-terrorism activities of the parallel force* that will necessarily need to be established to preserve the hard-won security gains achieved so far. Any blurring of this distinction would place severe constraints on the ability of United Nations humanitarian, development and human rights personnel to safely do their work. If this were to happen, the United Nations would find it difficult to mount the kind of comprehensive system-wide response required to address the political, social and economic root causes of the multifaceted crisis in Mali.⁷⁹ [Emphasis added]

This quote is of particular relevance as it highlights the professionalisation⁸⁰ and diversification that has taken place in peacekeeping operations since the end of the Cold War. Part of this development has been economy-driven due to the lack of sufficient funds by the UN and the holding back of payments by certain states.⁸¹ The UN has also developed extensive financial and accountability mechanisms for its activities which have contributed further to the continuing professionalisation of peacekeeping.⁸² Notwithstanding, it cannot be emphasised enough how important it is

---

[78] Paragraph 12(b) of SC Resolution 2098 does not only refer specifically to compliance with international humanitarian law but also speaks of steps normally taken as preparatory steps in military operations before an assault such as information collation and analysis, precautionary measures to protect civilians. The most interesting fact is, however, that – following this Resolution – self-defence in the meaning of defence of the mandate can now include fully scaled military operations to which IHL applies. The intervention brigade, however, poses problems as it is simultaneously a specially protected peacekeeping force and a party directly engaged in hostilities, see L. Müller, 'The Force Intervention Brigade – United Nations Forces Beyond the Fine Line between Peacekeeping and Peace Enforcement', *Journal of Conflict & Security Law*, 20 (2015), 359–380.

[79] UN Doc. S/2013/189 (2013), 19, para. 100; UN Doc. S/2013/338 (2013), 18, para. 83.

[80] Since 2007 the UN relies on its Integrated Missions Planning Process (IMPP) as part of the wider 'Peacekeeping 2010' reform. The IMPP provides a coherent and unified framework for the planning of all multidimensional UN operations covering three stages: advance planning (pre-mission planning), operational planning after authorisation by the SC, review and transition planning. In the advance stage, the Integrated Mission Task Force relies also on in-country planning and consultation with regional and other actors and partners, S. Wiharta, 'Planning and Deploying Peace Operations', *SIPRI Yearbook 2008: Armaments, Disarmament and International Security*, 97, 98, 102.

[81] Department of Peacekeeping Operations and Department of Field Support, The New Horizon Initiative: Progress Report No. 1 (October 2010), 20–21.

[82] See, e.g., UN Doc. A/68/653 (2013), 4, para. 17; 5, para. 19 and especially 6–8, paras. 22–29.

that the SC adopts resolutions with precise mandates.[83] Problems can also arise if the mandate of an operation has to be changed depending on the situation on the ground.[84] The UN operation in Sierra Leone, for example, started as a seventy-strong observer mission (UNOMSIL). After the failure of the peace agreement, the Council authorised the deployment of more than 17,000 troops with a robust mandate adopted under Chapter VII of the Charter, deploying a completely different operation on the ground (UNAMSIL).[85] The lively debate in the SC in June 2014 on new trends in UN peacekeeping illustrates, however, that the issue of peacekeeping operations with more of a peace enforcement mandate is not yet settled.[86] The force commanders of UN operations took a down-to-earth

---

[83] The difficulty of a precise delimitation can also be due to a certain ambiguity of the mandate of the operation, Villani, supra note 5, 225, 398.

[84] Verdirame, supra note 65, 198; R. Dallaire, *Shake Hands with the Devil: The Failure of Humanity in Rwanda* (Boston, Da Capo Press, 2004), 233–238. A deterioration of the security situation might call for an adjustment of the mandate, including enforcement measures (ibid., 398), the same observation was made by the Panel on UN Peace Operations, supra note 33, para. 48. See also Evaluation of the Implementation and Results of Protection of Civilians Mandates in UN Peacekeeping Operations, Report of the Office of Internal Oversight Services, UN Doc. A/68/787 (2014), 11–12, para. 28.

[85] For UNOMSIL, UN Doc. S/RES/1181 (1998), for UNAMSIL, UN Doc. S/RES/1270 (1999); S/RES/1289 (2000).

[86] UN Doc. A/68/899 and S/2014/384 (2014), 3, para. 1. In the ensuing discussion in the Council, it became obvious that the opinion of members is split. The Secretary-General himself called Resolution 2098 for MONUSCO 'a milestone' as an expression of the resolve of the Council to address the changing nature of conflicts and peacekeeping operations, UN Doc. S/PV.7196 (2014), 3. Rwanda (ibid., 3), France (ibid., 9), the UK (ibid., 12), the US (ibid., 19), Jordan (ibid., 16–18) and the EU (ibid., 30) are not opposed to similar future mandates for other operations on the basis of a variety of arguments. France and the US consider the mandates to be effective and they emphasise the need to protect civilians which for the latter is also a 'moral imperative'. In similar fashion, the EU sees MONUSCO as an example that 'peace enforcement where necessary and under defined conditions can support the success and legitimacy of a United Nations operation'. The UK and Jordan do not consider the mandate of MONUSCO to be a radical departure from previous practice, pointing to recent examples of the AU (the UK) or regarding the current UN practice as 'a repetition of previous cycles in peacekeeping'. Jordan goes even so far to call for the establishment of UN standing forces. Several states are opposed to any future similar mandates and they also provide various reasons. Some countries are afraid that this practice might either turn the UN into a party to the conflict (China, ibid., 20), expose peacekeepers to unnecessary risks (India, ibid., 27) or compromise the impartiality of UN peacekeepers (Turkey, ibid., 58), a view which is not shared by Ireland (ibid., 59). Pakistan and Bangladesh believe that peacekeeping and peace enforcement should not be conflated (ibid., 33, 60). The Latin American countries (Guatemala, Peru and Uruguay, ibid., 35, 42, 43) remain apprehensive and emphasise that MONUSCO's mandate should not be a precedent for future operations. Ethiopia shares this view (ibid., 45), but is convinced – as is Chile (ibid., 6–7) that 'some serious thinking' is necessary. Reacting to the developments unfolding in Mali in May 2014, the government also asked for a 'much more robust

approach in their meeting with the SC; one force commander declared frankly that the principles of peacekeeping 'may not always apply against armed criminal groups in contemporary missions'.[87]

An Emerging Division of Labour between International Organisations in Peacekeeping Operations

The multiplication of tasks in peacekeeping operations has been part of the increased inter-institutional cooperation between different international organisations during peacekeeping operations. In 2007, fifty-four peace operations were deployed around the world, of which not less than forty involved an element of cooperation with another international organisation.[88] The practice suggests that there is a general tendency towards the UN focusing on traditional peacekeeping operations regarding the level of the use of force allowed, with an emphasis also on the multi-dimensional and non-military level and that UN-authorised operations will be provided with more robust mandates.[89] The massive presence in the field has also contributed to the overstretching in the capacities of the UN which in 2008 alone deployed 120,000 peacekeepers on the ground.[90]

The organisations thereby use different terminology. Whereas the UN uses the classic terminology of 'peacekeeping operations', the EU refers

---

mandate under Chapter VII' for MINUSCA, UN Doc. S/PV.7179 (2014), 4. To a certain extent that wish was fulfilled by the Council with the adoption of SC Resolution 2164, UN Doc. S/RES/2164 (2014), 6, para. 13(a)(i), (iv). With regard to this issue, cf., ICRC, 'Interview with Lieutenant General Babacar Gaye', *FirstView* article, *International Review of the Red Cross* (2014), 1, 4, 9–10.

[87] UN Doc. S/PV.7275 (2015), 3. See also UN Doc. S/2014/933 (2014), 5, para. 15.
[88] A. S. Bah, B. D. Jones, 'Peace Operations Partnerships: Lessons and Issues from Coordination to Hybrid Arrangements', Center on International Cooperation, New York University (2008), 1.
[89] Besides political and practical reasons, e.g., the military capacity of each organisation is one of the relevant aspects. Secretary-General Annan was very direct in this matter, while addressing NATO Parliamentarians, Secretary-General's opening remarks at meeting with NATO Parliamentarians, New York, 8 March 2004, available at www.un.org/sg/statements/?nid=808.
[90] M. Derblom, E. Hagström Frisell, J. Schmidt, 'UN–EU–AU Cooperation in Peace Operations in Africa', FOI, Swedish Defence Research Agency (2008), 30. The significant engagement of resources also put conflict prevention and early warning systems under the spotlight. The SC adopted, for example, Resolution 1625 aimed at strengthening the effectiveness of the SC's role in conflict prevention, particularly in Africa, UN Doc. S/RES/1625 (2005). See also Department of Peacekeeping Operations and Department of Field Support, A New Partnership Agenda. Charting a New Horizon for UN Peacekeeping (2009), Section 1:4 – A Regional-Global Security Partnership, supra note 26, 18, para. 88.

normally to 'crisis management operations' and the AU speaks of 'peace support operations'. In the present study, the terminology of the UN will be used.[91]

In the past few years, at least three different kinds of cooperation between international organisations in the area of peacekeeping have emerged. They are sequential, parallel and integrated deployment of troops by international organisations.[92] Besides, the strains of international and regional politics are 'pushing global peacekeeping towards a different future, one in which several different organizations – principally the UN, NATO, the EU and the AU – each develop a fuller range of multi-faceted capacities, ranging from rapid, robust response to longer-term, civilian peacebuilding functions.'[93]

(i) Sequential Operations include, inter alia, the 2003 operation of ECOWAS in Liberia which gave way to the long-term presence of the UN Operation in Liberia (UNMIL). Normally peacekeeping operations transit from being an authorised regional or multilateral operation or an ad hoc authorised operation to a UN operation. This is explained by the more effective and faster decision-making process of small actors, and certain other advantages such as geographic proximity, which allow a faster deployment on the ground. However, some recent operations mirror a contrary development, the handover of the NATO operation in Bosnia to the EU, the similar transfer of operational power from the UN to the EU in Kosovo and also the transition from a UN operation into a

---

[91] The importance of a common terminology was stressed by the Study of the Lessons Learned Unit, Lesson Learned Unit, Department of Peacekeeping Operations, Cooperation between the United Nations and Regional Organisations/Arrangements in a Peacekeeping Environment, Suggested Principles and Mechanisms (1999), Part IIA, para. XII.

[92] Bah, Jones, 'Peace Operations Partnerships', supra note 88, 2–3; cf. UN Doc. A/65/762 (2011), 5, para. 5; A/61/204 and S/2006/590 (2006), 8, para. 36; Challenges Project, Meeting the Challenges of Peace Operations: Cooperation and Coordination (2005), 12, para. 5; Department of Peacekeeping Operations and Department of Field Support, supra note 90, 9; Statement by the President of the Security Council, UN Doc. S/PRST/2010/2 (2010), at 3 which calls for coordination of peacebuilding plans and programmes of regional and sub-regional organisations with UN peacekeeping operations and the wider UN presence on the ground. Other classifications mention, e.g., 'subcontracting; bridging operations; joint operations; integrated operations; and evolving operations', W. Pal Singh Sidu, 'Regional Groups and Alliances', in T. Weiss, S. Daws (eds.), *The Oxford Handbook on the United Nations* (Oxford University Press, 2007), 217, 218; Balas speaks of sequential, parallel and hybrid peace operations, A. Ballas, 'It Takes Two (or More) to Keep the Peace: Multiple Simultaneous Peace Operations', *Journal of International Peacekeeping*, 15 (2011), 384, 393–396.

[93] Bah, Jones, 'Peace Operations Partnerships', supra note 88, 1.

Special Task Force of the AU.[94] This development underlines the growth of multifaceted capacities by regional organisations, although one has to keep in mind that many of the member states of these organisations which take part in the new incoming peacekeeping operation had already previously deployed troops as part of the old, outgoing operation. The transfer from one operation to the other is then limited to a 're-hatting' and the transfer of operational command and control.

(ii) In contrast, parallel operations have taken various forms. They include temporary, military, support operations by one organisation for another, for example, operations of the EU in the Democratic Republic of the Congo – Operation Artemis and EUFOR RD Congo. More common is a separation of tasks, from military operations existing alongside observer operations to separated civilian and military operations such as KFOR by NATO and UNMIK in Kosovo.[95]

(iii) UNMIK is also one example of an integrated operation, as UNMIK consisted of four different organisations working together: the UN Secretariat, UNHCR, the EU and the OSCE. The general structure is that either the organisations share the command between themselves or that one organisation subordinates itself to the other.[96] The first example was the International Civilian Mission in Haiti (MICIVIH) which joined the UN operation alongside the operation of the Organisation of American States (OAS). The most integrated operation so far is nonetheless the hybrid UN/AU operation in Darfur whose structure is completely under unified command.

The different forms of cooperation between international organisations in the area of peace and security emphasise anew the complexity of the topic and why an analysis, such as that carried out in the present study, is important. It also highlights some of the underlying advantages and disadvantages. While cooperation allows organisations to build upon the competence of one another,[97] there are also shortcomings such as

---

[94] Ibid., 2. Other recent examples follow the traditional pattern; AFISMA in Mali was transformed in MINUSMA, pending the improvement of security conditions on the ground, AMISOM will most likely be transformed into a UN operation and the operation of ECCAS in the Central African Republic (CAR) was now transformed in an African-led peacekeeping operation.

[95] Bah, Jones, 'Peace Operations Partnerships', supra note 88, 3.

[96] Ibid.,3.

[97] M. Brosig, 'The Multi-Actor Game of Peacekeeping in Africa', *International Peacekeeping*, 17 (2010), 327, 329.

handover challenges and questions of legitimacy and ownership in inter-institutional arrangements.[98]

The increased activism of regional organisations since the end of the Cold War has also led to a reactivation of another Chapter of the Charter, namely Chapter VIII, which had also been impaired during the Cold War.[99]

The New 'Old' Chapter VIII of the UN Charter – Or the Merger of Chapters VII and VIII?

> The ability of the Security Council to become more proactive in preventing and responding to threats will be strengthened by making fuller and more productive use of the Chapter VIII provisions of the Charter of the United Nations than has hitherto been the case.
>
> – Report of the High-Level Panel on Threats, Challenges and Change (2004)[100]

> The principle of establishing stronger partnerships with regional organizations is embedded in the very DNA of the United Nations. With great vision and foresight, Chapter VIII of the Charter of the United Nations lays out the critical role of regional Organizations in maintaining international peace and Security.
>
> – Secretary-General Ban Ki-moon (2014)[101]

The previous two sections have traced the development of peacekeeping within the wider framework of the UN Charter as well as under Chapter VII. They confirmed that the maintenance of international peace and security by the SC cannot be seen in isolation from the larger framework of cooperation with regional organisations. This part, therefore, analyses Chapter VIII of the UN Charter, which applies to relations with regional organisations in the field of the maintenance of international peace and security. Whereas it is generally accepted that peacekeeping is in conformity with the UN Charter, the interpretation of Chapter VIII is rather disputed. This is firstly due to the very vague language used in Chapter

---

[98] Bah, Jones, 'Peace Operations Partnerships', supra note 88, 4–5. One also has to keep in mind that '[r]egional organizations have their own objectives and interests, which do not always coincide with those of the United Nations, and it may be difficult for the United Nations to predict which organizations can and will cooperate and the resources that they will bring to the relationship', UN Doc. A/65/762 (2011), 5, para. 7.

[99] UN Doc. S/25996 (1993), 17, para. 60; Rensmann, 'Reform', supra note 20, 25, 52, mn. 93.

[100] UN Doc. A/59/565 (2004), 70, para. 270. See also Roberts, 'Proposals for UN Standing Forces', supra note 37, 99, 128.

[101] Statement by the Secretary-General, UN Doc. S/PV.7112 (2014), 2.

VIII. Secondly, it is a result of the interests of various actors in interpreting Chapter VIII in their favour, which is once again an expression of the duality between universality and regionalisation: 'total formal control by the UN Security Council to de facto discretion and arbitrariness of... regional organizations; subsidiarity in UN-regional relations to complementarity of intergovernmental tasks'.[102] Chapter VIII is – like Chapters VI and VII – a compromise between universalism and regionalism with regard to the maintenance of international peace and security by the UN and regional organisations.

The Relevance of Practice for the Interpretation of the Charter and a Definition of 'Regional Arrangements and Agencies'

The practice of the UN and the involved regional organisations is particularly relevant for the interpretation of Chapter VIII due to its vague language. This approach has the additional advantage of guaranteeing the flexible interpretation necessary to ensure that the SC can exercise its mandate effectively and efficiently. Being that the SC is a political body, this method might also be better at accommodating the political implications in the activity of the SC. Indeed, the drafters of the UN Charter decided that each organ of the organisation has the primary responsibility for interpreting the parts of the Charter which regulate its competences and functions. Following a proposal by Belgium,[103] the matter was ultimately referred to the Fourth Committee.[104] After a lengthy debate in the subcommittee, the Fourth Committee approved the report in which it declared that

> [i]n the course of the operations from day to day of the various organs of the Organization, it is inevitable that each organ will interpret such parts of the Charter as are applicable to its particular functions. This process is inherent in the functioning of any body which operates under an instrument defining its functions and powers ... Accordingly, it is not necessary

---

[102] Douhan, *Regional Mechanisms*, supra note 73, 22.
[103] United Nations, Documents of the United Nations Conference on International Organisation, San Francisco, 1945, Volume III Dumbarton Oaks Proposals, Comments and Proposed Amendments (1945), 339.
[104] Documents de la Conférence des Nations Unies sur l'organisation internationale, San Francisco, 1945, Tome IX, Commission II Assemblée Générale (1945), 74, 347. The issue was debated extensively in Commission IV and then referred to a subcommittee for further study by an affirmative vote of 16–13, Documents de la Conférence des Nations Unies sur l'Organisation Internationale, San Francisco, 1945, Tome XIII, Commission IV, Organe Judiciare (1945), 633–634, 653–654.

to include in the Charter a provision either authorizing or approving the normal operation of this principle.¹⁰⁵

To safeguard the necessary flexibility for the SC, the drafters of the UN Charter also decided to refrain from defining 'regional arrangements and agencies' for the purposes of Chapter VIII. As stated in the *Agenda for Peace*,

> [t]he Charter deliberately provides no precise definition of regional arrangements and agencies, thus allowing useful flexibility for undertakings by a group of States to deal with a matter appropriate for regional action which also could contribute to the maintenance of international peace and security. Such associations or entities could include treaty-based organizations, whether created before or after the founding of the United Nations, regional organizations for mutual security and defence, organizations for general development or for cooperation on a particular economic topic or function, and groups created to deal with a specific political, economic or social issue of current concern.¹⁰⁶

No further attempts at clarification have been made during the history of the UN. In 1994, the General Assembly adopted a Declaration concerning the enhancement of cooperation with regional entities in the area of international peace and security, but that declaration merely acknowledged the

---

[105] Ibid., Tome XIII, 709–710, 831–832; *Competence of the General Assembly for the Admission of a State to the United Nations, Advisory Opinion of March 3rd, 1950*, 9, second paragraph from the top; *Certain Expenses of the United Nations* (Article 17, Paragraph 2 of the Charter), *Advisory Opinion* (20 July 1962), 10, second-last paragraph. See generally L. B. Sohn, 'Interpreting the Law', in O. Schachter, C. C. Joyner (eds.), *United Nations Legal Order. Volume I* (Cambridge University Press, 1995), 169–230; E. Papastavridis, 'Interpretation of Security Council Resolutions under Chapter VII in the Aftermath of the Iraqi Crisis', *International & Comparative Law Quarterly*, 56 (2007), 83, 91.
[106] UN Doc. S/25996 (1993), 17, para. 61. This lack of definition is also once again a result of the compromise between the regionalists and universalists when the Charter was adopted, E. P. J. Myjer, N. D. White, 'Peace Operations Conducted by Regional Organizations and Arrangements', in T. D. Gill, D. Fleck (eds.), *The Handbook of the International Law of Military Operations* (Oxford University Press, 2010), 163, 164–165. A definition of 'regional organisations' was actually put forward by Egypt, but rejected later on. See United Nations, Documents of the Conference on International Organisation, San Francisco, 1945, Vol. XII, Security Council (1945), 857; Documents de la Conférence des Nations Unies sur l'Organisation Internationale, San Francisco, 1945, Tome XII, Commission III, Conseil de Sécurité (1945), 860. Cf. UN Doc. A/61/204 and S/2006/590 (2006), para. 77; M. Akehurst, 'Enforcement Actions by Regional Agencies with Special References to the Organization of American States', *British Yearbook of International Law*, 42 (1967), 175, 177–178; Walter, 'Chapter VIII Regional Arrangements', supra note 10, 1429, 1439 mn. 16.

'variety of mandates, scope and composition of regional arrangements or agencies'.[107]

It is consequently hard to define the idea and the character of regional arrangements and entities as expressed in Chapter VIII of the Charter. The political arguments which were raised during the preparatory conference of the UN suggest that the concept of 'regional' or 'regional organisation' is a political, and adjustable one, rather than being legal in origin, safeguarding the necessary flexibility to include potentially new regional entities as well.

The Unrelenting Influence of Chapter VII over Chapter VIII

Unfortunately, these political concerns can hardly be reconciled with legal principles such as the principle of legal certainty; however, one can argue that legal principles are intrinsic to Chapter VIII. Chapter VIII can be interpreted as a mechanism to distribute competences, rights and obligations; in other words, it determines whether the UN or a regional organisation is *responsible* for action. Therefore, this Chapter has a direct bearing on the law of international responsibility which determines responsibility on the basis of the attribution of conduct.

Nonetheless, Chapter VIII does not provide the SC with any substantive powers of peace enforcement in addition to the powers the Council holds under Chapter VII of the Charter. Article 53(1) of the Charter only gives the SC the right to delegate Chapter VII powers to regional arrangements; thus '[t]he delegation of Chapter VII powers to a regional arrangement ... takes place by the Council using its specific competences so to delegate under Chapter VIII'.[108] Consequently, there is no legal difference if the SC were to authorise international organisations to use military force under

---

[107] UN Doc. A/RES/49/57 (1994), Annex, 2–3, Preamble. However, in his report of 1995, the Secretary-General interestingly preferred to explain the lack of definition by making the following remark: 'Cooperation between the United Nations and regional organizations must constantly adapt to an ever-changing world situation. The Charter itself anticipated this need for flexibility by not giving a precise definition of regional arrangements and organizations, thus enabling diverse organizations and structures to contribute, together with the United Nations, to the maintenance of peace and security', UN Doc. A/50/1 (1995), 122, para. 930.

[108] D. Sarooshi, 'The Security Council's Authorization of Regional Arrangements to Use Force: The Case of NATO', in V. Lowe, A. Roberts, J. Welsh (eds.), *The United Nations Security Council and War* (Oxford University Press, 2008), 226, 288. This also implies that the SC can only rely on Chapter VIII if the conditions of Article 39 are fulfilled and if the envisaged action has as its aim to restore international peace and security. See Villani, supra note 5, 225, 325.

Article 53 of the Charter or simply under Chapter VII as its powers under Chapter VIII derive from Chapter VII. However, there might be a symbolic importance, given that the use of Chapter VIII amounts to recognising the specific role of regional organisations.[109]

All in all, it appears that Chapter VIII has to be seen as incorporating the conflict between supporters of a universalist and a regionalist view of the system of collective security, as well as an interplay between arguments of law and politics. As a result, any attempt of interpretation of Chapter VIII is highly delicate. Moreover, a joint consideration and analysis of Chapters VII and VIII is necessary. In fact, the influence of universalism versus regionalism as enshrined in the UN Charter is reinforced by the virtue of Chapter VII. While Chapter VII establishes the universalist perception as regards the maintenance of international peace and security – with the SC as the guardian – Chapter VIII establishes the tradition of the regionalistic perspective:

> There was a reason Chapter VIII was drafted by the Charter's framers and that reason is as valid today as it was 61 years ago. It is to ensure that global and regional collective security is mutually complementary and that the total effort of the international community for securing the peace is optimized through the collaboration of our various international organizations.[110]

An analysis of Chapter VIII in the context of peacekeeping is also pertinent as '[a]ny endeavour to enhance [and understand] the relationship between the United Nations and regional organizations under Chapter VIII will need to be based on a clearer definition of the basis and processes of such cooperation'.[111] The Secretary-General proposed that the SC '[d]iscuss[es] the desirability and practicability of partner organizations identifying

---

[109] Gray, *International Law*, supra note 36, 426; C. Walter, *Vereinte Nationen und Regionalorganisationen* (Heidelberg, Springer, 1996), 271. One difference might be that Article 54 foresees that the SC shall at all times be kept fully informed of activities undertaken or contemplated by a regional organisation. However, it is the established practice of the SC that operations conducted on the basis of an authorisation under Chapter VII will report regularly to the SC. Following the decision in *Behrami/Saramati* and the subsequent decisions by the EctHR, it is rather likely that the SC will emphasise the obligation to submit reports in mandates handed out to UN authorised peacekeeping operations. Practice of the SC confirms that assessment, for an extensive analysis, see N. Blokker, 'Outsourcing the Use of Force. Towards More Security Council Control of Authorised Operations?', in M. Weller (ed.), *The Oxford Handbook on the Use of Force in International Law* (Oxford University Press, 2014), 202–226.
[110] UN Doc. A/61/204 and S/2006/590 (2006), 16, para. 80.
[111] UN Doc. S/2008/186 (2008), 6, para. 8.

themselves either as regional organizations acting under Chapter VIII or as other intergovernmental organizations acting under other provisions of the Charter'.[112] But, '[t]he question could be asked, however, whether the partnership would be operationally more effective if each partner knows under which Charter provisions it is functioning'.[113] From a legal point of view, it does not matter whether a regional organisation can be subsumed under Chapter VIII or whether there is acquiescence by the regional organisation to be bound by Chapter VIII and a corresponding agreement by the SC. To offer an example to the contrary, NATO could arguably be considered as a regional organisation under Chapter VIII, but it refuses to be considered as such.[114]

For the purposes of analysing the applicability and the procedural framework of Chapter VIII of the UN Charter to regional organisations, it is firstly necessary to define certain criteria as contained in Articles 52–54 of the Charter.

Defining the Elements in Article 52 of the UN Charter

Article 52 enshrines the priority of regional organisations for matters relating to the maintenance of international peace and security as these are 'appropriate for regional action'. Regional organisations enjoy particular priority for the pacific settlement of 'local disputes' under Article 52(2) and (3).[115] It suggests that the 'regional' criterion is of a geographical nature, meaning that in order to qualify as a regional arrangement or agency under Chapter VIII, the member states of this agency or arrangement need to be in geographical proximity to each other.[116] Such an interpretation is supported by two other aspects; the feeling of solidarity, and the intimate knowledge of the geopolitical conditions in a given situation, which argue both in favour of a geographical interpretation of the 'local disputes' wording in Article 52 as it concerns the meaning of 'regional'.[117]

---

[112] UN Doc. A/61/204 and S/2006/590 (2006), 16–17, para. 82; 21, para. 99.
[113] Ibid.
[114] See Chapter 2.
[115] Cf. Griep, *Regionale Organisationen*, supra note 13, 62, 65–66.
[116] Boisson de Chazournes, supra note 3, 79, 245–246; H. Kelsen, 'Is the North Atlantic Treaty a Regional Arrangement?', *The American Journal of International Law*, 45 (1951), 162, 163.
[117] Cf. Villani, supra note 5, 225, 273; C. Walter, 'Chapter VIII Regional Arrangements. Article 52', in B. Simma, D.-E. Khan, G. Nolte et al. (eds.), *The Charter of the United Nations. A Commentary. Volume II* (Oxford University Press 2012), 1445, 1469 mn. 78–79. See also B. Boutros-Ghali, *Contribution à l'étude des ententes régionales* (Paris, A. Pédone, 1949), 169–173.

The drafting history, however, shows that a large majority of states were against any specification as to the regional criterion.[118] Equally, the existing advantages of geographical proximity for dispute resolution can be offset by the existence of arbitral or judicial proceedings within a regional organisation, and nor is it indispensable that the states intervening in a dispute are located in the same geographic region.[119] Indeed, the SC can use regional organisations under Article 53 'where appropriate' and without any other qualification. The General Assembly has also repeatedly granted the status of observers to organisations based on political, religious or even linguistic ties rather than on geographical ties, such as OSCE, the Commonwealth, the OIC and the Organisation international de la francophonie.[120] Nevertheless, the fact that Chapter VIII speaks of 'regional' agencies and supports an interpretation of the regional specification as meaning that the organisation or its constituent instrument shall concern one specific geographic region; that its rules and competences shall have as their object this zone in order to abet the maintenance of peace and security. Otherwise, one could consider the organisation to be acting outside of Chapter VIII of the Charter.[121] A teleological approach underlines the need of 'some geographical link' as 'activity on the local level, ... pre-existing greater familiarity with the subject-matter of a disputed, enhanced legitimacy, and solidarity are factors favouring a peaceful settlement'.[122]

---

[118] Villani, ibid., 274; Myjer, White, 'Peace Operations', supra note 106, 163, 167; R. Pernice, *Die Sicherung des Weltfriedens durch regionale Organisationen und die Vereinten Nationen. Eine Untersuchung zur Kompetenzverteilung nach Kapitel VIII der UN Charta* (Hamburg, Hansischer Gildenverlag, 1972), 26–29.

[119] Villani, ibid., 274. Walter, 'Article 52', supra note 117, 1445, 1447 mn. 6–7, 1449 mn. 14–15; J. I. Charney, 'The Antarctic System and Customary International Law', in F. Francioni, T. Scovazzi (eds.), *International Law for Antarctica* (The Hague, Kluwer Law International, 1996), 51, 64–65.

[120] The GA, however, does not distinguish between universal and regional organisations. Villani, supra note 5, 225, 275. See also UN Doc. S/25996 (1993), 17, para. 62; 23, para. 83.

[121] Villani, supra note 5, 225, 276. In the case between Cameroon and Nigeria, the ICJ recognised the 'regional' character of the Lake Chad Basin Commission by recognising that it is 'exercising its powers within a specific geographical area', *Case Concerning the Land and Maritime Boundary between Cameroon and Nigeria (Cameroon v. Nigeria)*, Preliminary Objections, Judgment of 11 June 1998, para. 67.

[122] Walter, 'Article 52', supra note 117, 1445, 1448 mn. 11; Boisson de Chazournes, supra note 3, 79, 246. For a general overview of advantages and disadvantages of conflict management on a regional level, see P. F. Diehl, 'New Roles for Regional Organisations', in C. A. Crocker, F. O. Hampson, P. Aall (eds.), *Leashing the Dogs of War: Conflict Management in a Divided World* (Washington, DC, US Institute for Peace, 2007), 537, 540–547.

Other factors, including a shared language or cultural aspects, may contribute to the coherence and common identity of a given organisation strengthening the 'close and reliable ties' between the members of the organisation which generate the expectation that the organisation in question can contribute to the maintenance of peace and security.[123]

One can however infer, from the 'regional criterion' – *argumentum e contrario* – that the membership has to be limited in order to distinguish them from universal organisations falling outside the scope of Chapter VIII.

In academic writing, controversy has also arisen over the question of whether a given regional organisation can be qualified as falling under Chapter VIII if under its constitutive instrument the organisation can take action – whether under Article 52 or Article 53 – against a non-state member (external threat), as these actions are also covered by the right of self-defence as enshrined in Article 51.[124] But there are no indications that such a limitation is imposed by Chapter VIII. Article 53 refers to enforcement action against enemy states 'whether these states are or are not members of the regional organization'.[125] That self-defence, as an exception to the prohibition on the use of force, also applies to Chapter VIII is evident from the introductory words of Articles 51 and 52: 'nothing in this Charter precludes'.[126] Moreover, this approach is not convincing from a functional perspective, since the very same organisation may fulfil quite different tasks according to specific strategic requirements given in precise circumstances. The OAS provided for collective security and collective self-defence,[127] while the re-orientation and expansion of NATO activities

---

[123] Walter, *Vereinte Nationen*, supra note 109, 39–47. For a summary of a functional analysis, see Walter, 'Article 52', supra note 117, 1445, 1450 mn. 16 and especially 1459 mn. 48. For an even more liberal interpretation, cf. N. D. White, 'The EU as a Regional Security Actor within the International Legal Order', in M. Trybus, N. D. White (eds.), *European Security Law* (Oxford University Press, 2007), 329, 332–333.

[124] Boisson de Chazournes, supra note 3, 79, 246. In contrast, the wording of a joint communiqué by the SC and the AU PSC suggests that the dispute settlement role of regional organisations is limited to 'the settlement of disputes among and within their Member States', UN Doc. S/2013/611 (2013), 2, para. 2.

[125] H. Kelsen, 'Is the North Atlantic Treaty a Regional Arrangement?', *The American Journal of International Law*, 45 (1951), 162, 165.

[126] As Kelsen argues, although the 'framers of the Charter did not anticipate that the system of collective security laid down in the Charter will not work at all ... [and although] it may not be in conformity with the intention of the framers of the Charter to organise self-defense by a treaty ... the rule of Article 53, that no enforcement action shall be taken without the authorization of the Security Council ... is restricted by Article 51', ibid., 162, 54.

[127] Articles 28 and 29 of the Charter of the OAS.

following the end of the Cold War is another example of an organisation fulfilling different tasks in a simultaneous manner.[128]

The distinction in Chapter VIII between 'arrangements' (in French: accords) and agencies (organismes) contains, once again, a broad margin for interpretation and the inclusion of regional entities under Chapter VIII. It is probably for this purpose that the distinction was made. However, it is irrelevant in practice as the application of the dispositions of Chapter VIII is identical for both of them.[129] Both require however, that the 'organisation' in question is based on a treaty. Thus, any less developed forms of cooperation, such as the so-called 'coalition of the willing' do not enter the remit of Chapter VIII.

Articles 52 and 53 also imply that organisations subject to Chapter VIII have internal mechanisms to resolve disputes (Article 52(2)) and that they are able to conduct coercive measures (Article 53(1)). In order to enable the UN to 'maintain international peace and security' and 'to take effective collective measures', any interpretation of Chapter VIII has to be done in conjunction with the general rules of the organisation. To guarantee the effective maintenance of international peace and security, it has to be sufficient that a regional organisation disposes of either internal dispute resolution mechanisms or that it is able to carry out coercive measures.[130] As the general requirements for regional organisations are laid down in Article 52(1) it also remains unclear why paragraph 2 should add new requirements; the latter delineates competences between the UN and a regional organisation.[131]

The Relationship between the UN and Regional Organisations under Articles 52 and 53

The effectiveness of the cooperation with regional organisations can, however, be impaired if several organisations deem themselves to be competent in a given situation which is 'appropriate for regional action'. All actions falling short of 'enforcement action' under Article 53, are not

---

[128] See Chapter 2 and also Walter, supra note 109, 1452-1453 mn. 24; R. Wolfrum, 'Der Beitrag regionaler Abmachungen zur Friedenssicherung: Möglichkeiten und Grenzen', *Heidelberg Journal of International Law*, 53 (1993), 576, 579.

[129] Douhan, *Regional Mechanisms*, supra note 73, 46; Villani, supra note 5, 225, 297; Boisson de Chazournes, supra note 3, 79, 248; Myjer, White, 'Peace Operations', supra note 106, 163, 165; Walter, 'Article 52', supra note 117, 1445, 1451 mn. 21.

[130] Cf. Villani, supra note 5, 225, 282-283. The necessary flexible interpretation is confirmed by the practice of the UN, see, e.g., UN Doc. A/RES/49/57 (1994), Annex, para. 2.

[131] Walter, 'Article 52', supra note 117, 1445, 1455 mn. 30-31.

subject to the authorisation of the SC, and thus there can be situations in which a regional organisation is engaged in activities maintaining international peace and security, and the SC simultaneously decides to act or to authorise enforcement action. Generally speaking, Article 52 seems to be inspired by the idea of an alternative rapport between the universal level of the SC and the regional level.[132] An example of joint action by the SC and regional organisations was the crisis within the Democratic Republic of the Congo. In its Resolution 1234, the SC not only expressed its support for the mediation process of the OAU and the Southern African Development Community, but simultaneously, the SC requested all parties to cooperate fully with its special envoy by also reaffirming the readiness of the UN to help with the application of a ceasefire agreement.[133] Generally, the SC is free to decide whether to act itself or whether to delegate and support the actions of a regional organisation.[134]

In comparison to Article 52, the relationship between the UN and regional organisations is reversed in Article 53. The priority of regional organisations as actors under Article 52 is replaced by the priority of the SC.[135]

The SC keeps its broad margin of discretion of which it disposes in maintaining international peace and security under Chapter VII also within Chapter VIII, as it shall utilise 'where appropriate' regional arrangements or agencies. Any other interpretation would only add more than

---

[132] Villani, supra note 5, 225, 318. The practice is unclear as to whether there is a priority for regional action. In several cases, the UN and regional organisations have been active, it 'seems to reject clear alternatives between universal or regional jurisdiction', Walter, 'Article 52', supra note 117, 1445, 1470–1477, 1476 mn. 106; see equally Wolfrum, 'Der Beitrag', supra note 128, 576, 579–580.

[133] UN Doc. S/RES/1234 (1999), paras. 11–15.

[134] In the case of the dispute between Ethiopia and Eritrea, the SC only called upon the parties to fully cooperate with the OAU and expressed its support, Villani, supra note 5, 225, 319; SC Resolution 1177, UN Doc. S/RES/1177 (1998), 2, paras. 4–5. After fights restarted, the SC issued a resolution under Chapter VII demanding the states to resume peace talks under AU auspices and it imposed an embargo on weapons, SC Resolution 1298, UN Doc. S/RES/1298 (2000), 2, paras. 4–8.

[135] Villani, supra note 5, 225, 325. Kelsen said therefore that 'Article 52 and 53 of the Charter refer to regional agencies which may be considered to be – at least indirectly – organs of the United Nations in so far as Members of the United Nations are authorised by the Charter to constitute such agencies for purposes of the United Nations ... Regional agencies are neither principal nor subsidiary organs within the meaning of Article 7' and '[r]egional organisations may act as organs of the United Nations not only in settling local disputes, but also in taking enforcement action under the authority of the Security Council', H. Kelsen, *The Law of the United Nations. A Critical Analysis of its Fundamental Problems* (New York, Praeger, 1950), 145–146, 326.

was intended by the drafters of the Charter.[136] In practice, the SC normally refers to all 'relevant international organisations' in its resolutions rather than specifying a particular one.[137]

The Interpretation of 'Enforcement Action' in Article 53

Another problem of interpretation is the question as to which circumstances the SC can rely upon regional organisations. Article 53(1) speaks of enforcement action, which seems to exclude other coercive measures which can be found in the UN Charter such as 'preventive action' (Article 5) or 'preventive measures' (Article 50).[138] The logical consequence is to presume that the application of Article 53 is limited to cases in which the coercive measures are a *re*action rather than an action, similar in nature to self-defence which is applicable only in cases of an actual armed attack to repel invaders.

However, another argument of systematic interpretation, while referring to Article 1 of the Charter which mentions 'effective collective measures for the *prevention and removal of threats to the peace*' supports the view of a broader interpretation of 'enforcement action'. The powers of the SC under Chapter VIII are derived from Chapter VII and its actions under Chapter VIII are based on the existence of a situation under Article 39, so that a broad interpretation of enforcement action is justified. In practice, the SC has in most cases in its resolutions either referred to a 'threat to international peace and security' or even abstained from giving any determination, but decided 'to act under Chapter VII of the United Nations Charter'. This practice allows the Council to keep a greater margin of discretion and appreciation and this non-distinction between the three different scenarios in Article 39 should accordingly be applied to Article 53 as well.[139]

---

[136] Cf. Villani, supra note 5, 225, 327.
[137] Ibid., 328. However, as always in the context of peacekeeping and peacekeeping operations which are all unique in their individual makeup, it depends on all the relevant circumstances, Resolution 2085 refers expressly to some specific organisations, UN Doc. S/RES/2085 (2012).
[138] Villani, supra note 5, 225, 329. But in the Spanish version of the Charter, Article 42 speaks of *medidas* and not of *acción* and action is equally used in non-military contexts in other articles, e.g., Article 2(5) and Article 11. If one takes into account other differences in the English, French and Spanish versions, no positive conclusion can be drawn from the terminology. C. Walter, 'Article 53', in B. Simma, D.-E. Khan, G. Nolte et al. (eds.), *The Charter of the United Nations. A Commentary. Volume II* (Oxford University Press, 2012), 1478, 1482 mn. 2–3.
[139] See, e.g., UN Doc. S/RES/883 (1993), 1, Preamble; 4, para. 12.

Furthermore, what kinds of measures are comprised by 'enforcement action' under Article 53 should be determined. Article 39 does not distinguish between measures taken under Article 41 and 42 but qualifies both as measures to restore international peace and security. Articles 50 and 5 also show that enforcement measures can be of a non-military nature.[140] Thus, enforcement action under Article 53 comprises all measures which can be coercive upon a state. That interpretation is supported by the principle of effectiveness; in order that the enforcement action is effective, the international organisations have to be able to use all means necessary.[141] Moreover, as established, the power of the SC under Chapter VIII derives from Chapter VII so that they comprise per se all possible forms of enforcement measures under Chapter VII should the SC decide to authorise a regional organisation to act.[142]

This interpretation also finds support in the practice of the SC. In its resolution 757, the SC imposed a ban on the import and export of all goods from Yugoslavia, which was binding for international organisations.[143] Limitations of enforcement action arise in the form of the respective constitutional framework of each regional arrangement or agency which either permits them to carry out a certain action (the action would be *intra vires*) or prohibits them from doing so as this would be tantamount to acts *ultra vires*.[144] This inherent limitation is recognised in the 1994 Declaration according to which '[c]ooperation between regional arrangements or agencies and the United Nations should be in accordance with their respective mandates, scope and composition'.[145]

On the basis of the principle of *pacta tertiis nec nocent nec prosunt* which is enshrined in Article 34 VCLT, the SC likewise cooperates with regional organisations, in the form of recommendations and consultations, as the

---

[140] Including economic measures (under Article 50) or the suspension of rights and privileges of membership (under Article 5).
[141] Against this view, see e.g., Wolfrum, supra note 128, 576, 581–582.
[142] Walter, 'Article 53', supra note 138, 1478, 1497 mn. 53; cf. also Villani, supra note 5, 225, 331–332; UN Doc. A/54/87 (1999), 14, para. 116, 118.
[143] UN Doc. S/RES/757 (1992), para. 11. The resolution contains many other measures which international organisations are asked to apply.
[144] Similarly, Villani, supra note 5, 225, 332. See also Gray, *International Law*, supra note 36, 391–392; comprehensive review of the whole question of peacekeeping operations in all their aspects, Report of the Special Committee on Peacekeeping Operations, UN Doc. A/54/839 (2000), 18–19, paras. 156, 160.
[145] UN Doc. A/RES/49/57 (1994), Annex, 4, para. 4.

SC cannot create obligations for non-members of the UN.[146] D'Aspremont makes a very similar argument with regard to regional organisations which have not submitted themselves at least formally under Chapter VIII of the UN Charter, e.g., NATO.[147]

Another requirement of Article 53 is that the enforcement action is taken under the authority of the SC which corresponds to an adoption of coercive measures by the SC in the form of a resolution.[148] Should the SC authorise enforcement action, it nevertheless keeps control of the activities as it is specified under Article 54 of the Charter. In this way, the SC acts upon its primary responsibility for the maintenance of international peace and security, that is conferred on it by virtue of Article 24 of the Charter.[149]

Various forms of control exist and are used by the SC. The committees created by the SC in order to supervise sanctions are one form of supervision at its disposal, but the Secretary-General can also be included in the control mechanism.[150] With regard to the operational level, the authority of the SC is normally limited to the examination of reports presented to it by states or directly by the regional organisations, as the latter regional organisations conduct the enforcement action.[151]

---

[146] One cannot forget, however, that the organisations are bound indirectly by their respective members which are free to choose in which form they execute the decisions of the SC on the basis of Article 48(2) of the Charter, cf., for instance, UN Doc. S/RES/794 (1992), 4, para. 16; S/RES/770 (1992), 2, para. 2; S/RES/787 (1992), 4, para. 12; S/RES/820 (1993), 4, para. 17; 6, para. 29. In some limits, one could imagine an obligation for regional organisations to carry out decisions of the SC in the form that the SC could impose on its members the need to act through the regional organisations of which they are members, cf. Villani, supra note 5, 225, 345–349.

[147] J. d'Aspremont, 'The Law of International Responsibility and Multilayered Institutional Veils: The Case of Authorized Regional Peace-Enforcement Operations', SHARES Research Paper 24 (2013), ACIL, 2013–10, available at www.sharesproject.nl, 6–7. In his view, such a scenario has also an impact on the law of international responsibility. By the lack of submission to Chapter VIII of the UN Charter by a given regional organisation, the application of Article 17 ARIO to a peace enforcement operation conducted by this organisation authorised by the SC would be precluded if the effect of the authorisation on the law of international responsibility extends only to the fulfilment of the obligations under the UN Charter, ibid., 17–18.

[148] Villani, supra note 5, 225, 349.

[149] Ibid., 225, 349–350.

[150] UN Doc. S/RES/787 (1992), 4, para. 14. Villani, supra note 5, 225, 350–351. In the case of Sierra Leone, the SC attributed the power to the sanction committee to coordinate with its counterpart at ECOWAS, UN Doc. S/RES/1132 (1997), 4, para. 10(h). See also UN Doc. S/RES/1196 (1998), 2, paras. 3–4.

[151] Cf. Villani, supra note 5, 225, 352–353. So, KFOR submitted regular reports directly to the SC.

A Different Interpretation of 'Enforcement Action' for Article 53(1) Second Sentence: The Practice of Sanctions by the UN and Regional Organisations

In the case of regional organisations taking enforcement action under their own initiative, according to Article 53(1), second sentence, 'enforcement action' has to be interpreted more restrictively than in the alternative scenario of the SC utilising regional organisations for enforcement actions under its authority. Otherwise, regional entities would have to ask for the authorisation of the SC for all kinds of acts that were potentially coercive in nature possibly coercive nature, such as diplomatic, economic, political, financial and military measures.

On the basis of Article 31 VCLT, a treaty 'shall be interpreted in good faith in accordance with the ordinary meaning to be given to the terms of the treaty in their context and in the light of its object and purpose'. Taking into account that the terminology is identical to the first sentence of Article 53, not to mention that the first sentence is contextualised by the second sentence, any other interpretation does not seem to be reasonable.

Yet, the object and purpose are different. As explained, in the first sentence, the purpose is to allow the SC to utilise – in an effective way – regional organisations for the maintenance of international peace and security which permits and justifies a broad interpretation, whereas in the second alternative, the authorisation renders an otherwise illegal action legal.[152] Moreover, by applying once more the principle of effectiveness, a stricter interpretation of enforcement action is preferable for the second alternative; otherwise the SC would have to authorise all manners of measures and the resulting workload and delay would not be insignificant. A stricter interpretation further allows the regional entities to keep a certain autonomy, rendering their performance more effective.[153]

---

[152] F. L. Morrison, 'The Role of Regional Organizations in the Enforcement of International Law', in J. Delbrück (ed.), U. E. Heinz (ass. ed.), *Allocation of Law Enforcement Authority in the International System. Proceedings of an International Symposium of the Kiel Institute of International Law, March 23 to 25, 1994* (Berlin, Duncker & Humblot, 1994), 39, 43.

[153] The very same argument was already made by the Columbia Chairman of Committee III/4 in San Francisco, cited in F. V. Garcia-Amador, *The Inter-American System, Its Development and Strengthening* (Dobs Ferry, New York, Oceana Publications, 1966), 190; see also Villani, supra note 5, 225, 356–357. Also in favour of a restricted interpretation, J. Frowein, 'Zwangsmaßnahmen von Regionalorganisationen', in U. Beyerlin, M. Bothe, R. Hofmann (eds.), *Recht zwischen Umbruch und Bewahrung. Festschrift für Rudolf Bernhardt* (Heidelberg, Springer, 1995), 57, 66–67; A. Abass, *Regional Organizations and the Development of Collective Security: Beyond Chapter VIII of the UN Charter* (2004) 43, 45–46, 49, 53–54; N. Tsagourias, 'EU Peacekeeping Operations: Legal and Theoretical

This later interpretation is confirmed by the practice of the SC and the relevant organisations.[154] The EU imposed an embargo on weapons and military equipment against Yugoslavia without asking for the permission of the SC. The European measures were actually more restrictive and went beyond what was required by the resolution of the Council.[155] In 1999, by its own initiative, the EU adopted common position 1999/624/CFSP which imposed a ban on arms, munitions and military equipment against Indonesia.[156] Seven years earlier, ECOWAS had imposed an embargo on weapons on that part of the territory of Liberia which was controlled by the National Patriotic Front of Liberia (NPFL). ECOWAS then proceeded to ask the UN for assistance in the application of the sanctions which was granted by SC Resolution 788.[157] Another important resolution is SC Resolution 841, in which the Council decided to implement the trade embargo recommended by the OAS against Haiti and to make it consequently universally compulsory unless the Secretary-General was to report to the Council that in light of the negotiations conducted by the UN Special Envoy and the OAS Secretary-General, the imposition of sanctions was not warranted.[158]

Thus, the SC can, by its discretionary power, reverse the relationship of Article 53 and act as an executor of decisions taken by a regional organisation of measures not involving the use of force.[159] Whereas this practice underlines the pragmatic approach taken by the SC, it has to be added, however, that the non-application of Article 53 paragraph 1 to

---

Issues', in M. Trybus, N. D. White (eds.), *European Security Law* (Oxford University Press, 2007), 102, 127; M. Roscini, 'L'articolo 17 del Trattato sull'Unione europea...compiti delle Forze di pace', in N. Ronzitti (ed.), *Le Forze di Pace dell'Unione Europea* (Rome, Rubbetino Editore, 2005), 49, 58.

[154] Security Council Official Records, Fifteenth, 893rd meeting, 8 September 1960, 6, para. 32; 13 para. 77; Boisson de Chazournes, supra note 3, 79, 265–266; Gray, *International Law*, supra note 36, 403–404; M. G. Goldman, 'Action by the Organization of American States: When Is Security Council Authorization Required under Article 53 of the United Nations Charter?', *UCLA Law Review*, 10 (1962–1963), 837, 849–851. See also Akehurst, 'Enforcement Action', supra note 106, 175, 195; White, 'The EU as a Regional Security Actor', supra note 123, 329, 340–341.

[155] Villani, supra note 5, 225, 361–362.

[156] Council Common Position (1999/624/CFSP), Preamble, Article 1.

[157] UN Doc. S/24735 (1992), para. 4; S/RES/788 (1992), 3, para. 8; S/PV.3822, 6, 8. See also Walter, 'Article 53', supra note 169, 1478, 1485 mn. 19–22.

[158] UN Doc. S/RES/841 (1993), paras. 1, 3.

[159] Depending on the specific operation, the SC might decide to let a regional organisation intervene and then take over the operation or vice versa. It cannot be strengthened enough that the practice of the SC shows a high degree of flexibility. cf. Griep, *Regionale Organisationen*, supra note 13; Villani, supra note 5, 225, 364.

non-military sanctions by regional entities does not mean that these sanctions or actions are automatically legal. These actions are justified if they have a valid basis under (general) international law.[160] The one exception is that the regional organisation has received an authorisation by the SC.[161]

Recent examples of non-military sanctions by regional organisations not having an authorisation by the SC include those adopted by the Arab League and the EU against Syria in 2011.[162] The SC likewise only took note of the decisions of ECOWAS and the AU to adopt targeted sanctions in Mali.[163]

Should the SC decide to act itself, the legality of actions by regional organisations is more difficult to assess. Measures taken by regional organisations going beyond the measures imposed by the SC could affect the efficiency of the latter and the reestablishment of international peace and security.[164] Additionally, in the event that the Council decides to stop or to lift the imposed sanctions and the regional entities continue to maintain or establish enforcement action under their authority, this would contravene first of all the assessment of the SC of the existence of a situation under Article 39 as well as contravening its primary responsibility for the maintenance of international peace and security on the basis of Article 24 of the Charter.[165]

Concerning Yugoslavia, the EU adopted severe sanctions which went far beyond all measures imposed by the SC. Villani views these sanctions as not legitimate; he considers them to be incompatible with the primary responsibility conferred on the SC by the members of the organisation.[166] It seems nevertheless to be correct to consider them as legitimate under

---

[160] For example, the ban enacted by the EU on Indonesia was justified by the massive violations of international human rights law (*erga omnes* obligations) and IHL by the latter.

[161] Villani, ibid., 225, 364–367.

[162] EU Council Decision 2011/782 CFSP (2011); Walter, 'Article 53', supra note 169, 1478, 1487 mn. 24–25.

[163] UN Doc. S/RES/2056 (2012), 3, para. 6.

[164] It is also in that regard that one can separate 'authorisation' from 'delegation of powers'. Whereas in the case of an authorisation of the use of force, the SC effectively delegates some of its own powers to the regional organisation, in other cases, the SC may authorise or impose measures which if executed by the SC itself would be *ultra vires*, such as the creation of the ICTY, see Boisson de Chazournes, supra note 3, 79, 271–274.

[165] Villani, supra note 5, 225, 367–369.

[166] Ibid. This legal argument is not convincing, as regional organisations have to be distinguished from member states of the UN, the latter ones are bound by the UN Charter. His other arguments are more plausible, and it may, indeed, happen, that certain supplementary or excessive measures adopted by regional organisations could not only affect the effectiveness of the measures by the SC, but that they lead to a resurgence of fighting among parties to a conflict, ibid.

certain circumstances[167] and it is preferable to rely upon the self-regulation mechanisms of the SC. As the primary guardian of international peace and security, there would be a reaction in the form of a resolution, or informal or formal consultations in the case of enforcement measures, contravening the efforts of sanctions by the SC.[168] In practice, there would normally be informal or formal consultations between the UN and regional organisations before the adoption of sanctions by the latter, and even more so in these cases where members of the SC are also engaged in enforcement actions by regional entities given that their dual membership allows them to assess the enforcement actions and to oversee their compatibility.[169]

There may be situations in which a regional organisation recommends the use of force against another state, and in such a case, the authorisation of the SC is also necessary as it would be illogical to require an authorisation by the Council for a binding decision of the regional organisation, but not for recommendations issued by the regional organisation.[170]

The general practice of the UN and the SC regarding the authorisation of the use of force by regional organisations also confirms that the Council continues to exercise its own responsibility to maintain international peace and security by supervising enforcement operations.[171] Resolution 816, for example, authorised member states, 'acting nationally or through regional organizations or arrangements, to take, under the authority of the Security Council and subject to close coordination with the Secretary-General and UNPROFOR, all necessary means in the airspace of the Republic of Bosnia and Herzegovina ... to ensure compliance with the ban on flights'.[172] Although this resolution refers to Chapter VIII in the preamble, it was adopted under Chapter VII and it therefore connects both Chapters of the Charter.[173] Moreover, it effectively blurs the difference between Article 53(1) first sentence and Article 53(1) second

---

[167] See infra 1.3.5, as well as the beginning of this part, 1.3.6.
[168] Villani, supra note 5, 225, 368–369.
[169] But one cannot deduce an authorisation from the silence or inactivity of the Council as silence does not signify consent (*qui tacet neque negat, neque utique fatetur*), cf. Villani, supra note 5, 225, 377–379.
[170] Villani, supra note 5, 225, 369–370; Security Council, UN Doc. S/PV.1022 (1962), 16, para. 81; Boisson de Chazournes, supra note 3, 79, 267.
[171] Villani, supra note 5, 225, 381–389; L.-A. Sicilianos, 'L'autorisation par le Conseil de sécurité de récourir à la force: une tentative d'évaluation', *Revue générale de droit international public*, 106 (2002), 5, 17.
[172] SC Resolution 816, UN Doc. S/RES/816 (1993), 2, para. 4.
[173] Other examples include, e.g., SC Resolution 1744, UN Doc. S/RES/1744 (2007), 2–3, paras. 4(b) and (d); see equally Walter, 'Chapter VIII Regional Arrangements', supra note 10, 1429, 1444 mn. 32.

sentence as any authorisation under Chapter VII can be equated rather to an authorised enforcement action taken by a regional organisation under Article 53(1) second sentence. The repetition of 'under the authority' in the resolution however points towards Article 53(1) first sentence and thereby to an enforcement action by a regional organisation taken under the authority of the SC. Nevertheless, it proves that in practice, the distinction between the two options for enforcement action in Article 53 is less relevant.[174] Thus, this analysis of the practice demonstrates very pragmatic use of the dispositions of Chapter VIII by the SC.

Peacekeeping Operations of Regional Organisations and the Application of Article 53 of the UN Charter

Peacekeeping operations conducted under the auspices of a regional organisation based on the consent of the host-state are exempt from the requirement of an authorisation by the SC.[175] The consent given renders their deployment on the ground legal under international law.[176] Another requirement is that their use of military force is limited to cases of self-defence. The ICJ held in the *Certain Expenses* case that 'the operations known as UNEF and ONUC were not *enforcement* actions within the compass of Chapter VII of the Charter'.[177]

Peacekeeping operations, as classically conceived, which are based on the consent and cooperation of all parties and with a conservative mandate such as the supervision of a ceasefire, only allow for the use of force in cases of self-defence. Self-defence is one of the exceptions to the prohibition of the use of force under the regime of the Charter.[178]

However, the possible coercive nature of recent third-generation peacekeeping operations challenges that premise and an examination of whether Article 53 of the UN Charter is applicable for these operations is thus necessary.[179] Article 53 does not per se apply to peacekeeping operations by regional organisations which were not foreseen during

---

[174] Villani, supra note 5, 225, 355–356; similarly Boisson de Chazournes, supra note 3, 79, 272.
[175] Myjer, White, 'Peace Operations', supra note 106, 163, 169; E. Jimenez de Arachaga, 'International Law in the Past Third of a Century', Recueil des cours de l'Académie de La Haye, Volume 159 (1978), 138; G. Lind, 'Chapter VIII of the UN Charter. Its Revival and Significance Today', in P. Wallensteen, A. Bjurner (eds.), *Regional Organizations and Peacemaking. Challengers to the UN?* (London, Routledge, 2015), 28, 32.
[176] *Certain Expenses*, supra note 105, 170.
[177] Ibid., 165. See also UN Doc. A/3302 (1956), para. 9.
[178] Cf. Villani, supra note 5, 225, 393–395.
[179] Cf. Bothe, 'Peacekeeping', supra note 36, 1171, 1192 mn. 31.

the preparation of the UN Charter; as expressed by Boutros-Ghali, '[p]eace-keeping can rightly be called the invention of the United Nations'.[180] Thus, the precise question is whether regional operations conducting peacekeeping operations, which can include the potential use of military force, need an authorisation or if they can operate independently and autonomously from the SC.[181]

Should an operation include or assume a coercive character, it enters into the field of application of Article 53 and can consequently only be implemented with the authorisation of the SC.[182] The difficulty resides in defining 'coercive' in this context. Obviously, it includes military operations conducted without the consent of the concerned parties, but more often, the operations are established on the basis of consent of the parties and implying a mandate to use force. Notwithstanding the consent of all parties, do these operations nevertheless enter into the field of application of Article 53 or, in other words, does the consent render enforcement action legitimate?[183]

In situations of internal crisis or civil war, it can be difficult, first and foremost, to identify the respective parties and the de facto government. Nevertheless, as it has been highlighted in the Brahimi report, there are no guarantees that the consent will not be revoked or given for insidious reasons.[184] The 1994 Declaration on the Enhancement of Cooperation between the United Nations and Regional Arrangements or Agencies emphasises in this regard that 'peace-keeping activities undertaken by regional arrangements or agencies should be conducted with the consent of the State in the territory of which such activities are carried out' and that regional organisations are encouraged to build up and assemble troops 'for use as appropriate, in coordination with the United Nations and, when necessary, under the authority or with the authorization of the Security Council, in accordance with the Charter'.[185] The reference to 'when necessary' can only be interpreted so that as long as the regional organisation conducts a classic peacekeeping operation which does not involve any form of (military) enforcement action, an authorisation by the SC is not *necessary*; should the regional agency or arrangement however implement

---

[180] UN Doc. S/25996 (1993), 14, para. 46. Cf. also Virally, *L'Organisation Mondiale*, supra note 17, 483–486.
[181] Villani, supra note 5, 225, 392.
[182] Ibid., 225, 407.
[183] Ibid.
[184] UN Doc. A/55/305 and S/2000/809 (2000), 9, para. 48.
[185] UN Doc. A/RES/49/57 (1994), Annex, 2–3, Preamble; 4, paras. 9–10.

an operation with coercive elements, an authorisation under Article 53 is required.[186] The practice of the SC regarding states or groups of states confirms and validates that interpretation, inter alia, in SC Resolutions 940 and 1080.[187] In practice, it can be problematic if there are different interpretations of a mandate provided by the SC for a military operation of a regional organisation. The very recent practice suggests that regional organisations increasingly tend to ask for an authorisation by the SC notwithstanding the qualification of the planned operation as a peacekeeping or peace enforcement operation.[188] Should the SC hand out a rather imprecise mandate which may be interpreted differently by the SC and the regional organisation, the question would arise what consequences this different interpretation could entail in terms of the law of international responsibility if there is a violation of international law occurring during the deployment of the operation. It could be necessary to inquire if the different interpretation of the mandate by the regional organisation would correspond to a failure of supervision by the SC. If that were to be answered in the affirmative, one could at least theoretically also engage the responsibility of the UN and not only the responsibility of the regional organisation conducting the operation.

Towards a Merger of Chapter VII and Chapter VIII in the Practice of the SC

There have been cases when regional peacekeeping operations were conducted without the authorisation of the SC, but the very recent practice shows, indeed, that these operations have been carried out either with a prior authorisation or approbation by the SC in the early stages of the peacekeeping operation.[189] The IFOR operation in Yugoslavia was based on the Annex to the Agreement of Paris and was authorised by a SC Resolution with a mandate to use all means necessary to guarantee the implementation of the Peace Agreements.[190] These examples are very

---

[186] M. N. Shaw, *International Law* (Cambridge University Press, 2008), 1275; Villani, supra note 5, 225, 408–409; C. Walter, 'Security Council Control over Regional Action', *Max Planck Yearbook of United Nations Law*, 1 (1997), 129, 174–175. Another argument one can made is that the consent of the host-state corresponds to the common law doctrine of *volenti fit iniuria*.

[187] UN Doc. S/RES/940 (1994), 2, paras. 1, 4; S/RES/1080 (1996), 2, paras. 1–7.

[188] See in particular Chapter 2.

[189] See, for more details, Villani, supra note 5, 225, 411–416.

[190] UN Doc. S/RES/1031 (1995), 3, paras. 14–15. Similarly, the follow-up operation SFOR was authorised by Resolution 1088 to take all necessary measures for the implementation of

important as the SC considered it to be necessary to give its authorisation, though all the parties had already agreed to the establishment of the peacekeeping operation.[191] Overall, the conclusion is that any assessment will depend on the specific circumstances and the specific mandate given by the SC. Confronted with the situation in Mali, the SC passed Resolutions 2056 (2012), 2071 (2012) and 2086 (2012) of which not one refers to Chapter VIII of the Charter, including Resolution 2086 which established AFISMA, an African-led[192] operation with a clear enforcement mandate.[193] In this regard, Walter argues that

> [w]ith the original concept of using troops under Art. 43 for military enforcement measures having generally been replaced by a concept of authorization, the distinction between Chapter VII and Art. 53(1) as the legal basis for authorizations relating to the use of force by regional organizations has lost its practical relevance.[194]

Other authors offer similar arguments, for example, Boisson de Chazournes sees Article 53 as a precursor of the trend towards the decentralised use of force on the international level.[195] One explanation for the

---

the Peace Agreement, UN Doc. S/RES/1088 (1996), 3, para. 8; 5, paras. 18–21. The same applies for the KFOR operation in Kosovo, UN Doc. S/RES/1244 (1999), 2, para. 7.

[191] Villani, supra note 5, 225, 416.

[192] The operation is implementation on the basis of the African Peace and Security Architecture in coordination between the AU and ECOWAS; see Chapter 4.

[193] UN Doc. S/RES/2056 (2012); S/RES/2071 (2012); S/RES/2086 (2012). That the practice of the SC is accommodating can be seen in other cases. In Resolutions 770 (1992) and 1484 (2003), the Council referred exclusively to Chapter VII. In resolutions 875 (1993) and 1464 (2003), the Council gave references to both chapters, while in Resolution 816 (1993) the Council acted under Chapter VII while equally reaffirming Chapter VIII. Another variation is contained in Resolution 1497 (2003), while acting under Chapter VII, the Resolution contains a reference to Chapter VIII in its preamble. Yet another variation is that the SC will not refer to Chapter VIII but will authorise or encourage states 'acting nationally or through regional agencies or arrangements', UN Doc. S/RES/770 (1992); S/RES/816 (1993); S/RES/875 (1993); S/RES/1464 (2003); S/RES/1484 (2003); S/RES/1497 (2003). For the last scenario, see, e.g., SC Resolution 942, UN Doc. S/RES/942 (1994), 2, para. 5; cf. Boisson de Chazournes, supra note 3, 79, 297; see also S. Paliwal, 'The Primacy of Regional Organizations in International Peacekeeping: The African Example', *Virginia Journal of International Law*, 51 (2010), 185, 195.

[194] Walter, 'Chapter VIII Regional Arrangements', supra note 10, 1429, 1444 mn. 33; also Gray, *International Law*, supra note 36, 426; N. D. White, Ö. Ülgen, 'The Security Council and the Decentralised Military Option: Constitutionality and Function', *Netherlands International Law Review*, 44 (1997), 378, 389.

[195] Boisson de Chazournes, supra note 3, 79, 275. As she observes, the impossibility to implement the system of Chapter VII based on a channelling of the authority to use force through the SC, led to two different reactions. Firstly, the concept of peacekeeping operations under the direct command and control of the UN was created. Secondly, there emerged an tendency towards a decentralised approach within Chapter VII according to

use of Chapter VII rather than Chapter VIII is the fact that many regional organisations are reluctant to be subjected to Chapter VIII and the obligations it entails.[196] From a legal perspective, the shift to Chapter VII does not involve fundamental changes as the practice continues to be based on an authorisation by the SC and as the SC continues to keep global and ultimate control.[197]

As beneficial as this pragmatic approach by the SC may be to prevent tensions arising in its relations with the regional organisations, the potential disadvantages may not be ignored. It may be asked whether this development does not illustrate the gradual impairment of the authority of the SC; the stronger and more resourceful – particularly in a political and economic sense – the regional organisations in question are, the more they can dictate the conditions for the deployment of their troops under the authority of the SC.[198] Furthermore, as pragmatic as the approach of the SC is, these acts of improvisation contribute to the conceptual misunderstandings whose repercussions may influence the legal analysis of the relationship existing between the UN and regional organisations.[199]

Another reason offered for this practice of the SC is to return to the raison d'être of Chapter VIII, which is 'to make available the specific contributions of regional organizations to the maintenance of international peace and security which result from the specific ties which bind their members'. So, if a regional organisation decides to act outside its region as defined in broad terms, 'there are no reasons to assume that such action

---

which the SC authorises and delegates the use of force to the member states. As contrary to the framework of the UN Charter it may appear, it is an expression of the logic of Article 53, ibid., 275–276.

[196] Boisson de Chazournes, supra note 3, 79, 304. One has to note that in practice the SC has also adopted a very flexible approach regarding the qualification of organisations as regional arrangements or agencies, irrespective as to whether the organisation in question falls under Chapter VIII or considers itself to be bound by it, Gill, 'Characterization and Legal Basis', supra note 57, 135, 139. See also Gray, *International Law*, supra note 36, 386.

[197] D. Sarooshi, *The United Nations and the Development of Collective Security. The Delegation by the Security Council of Its Chapter VII Powers* (Oxford University Press, 2000), 248–249; cf. Walter, 'Article 53', supra note 169, 1478, 1499 mn. 58–59; E. de Wet, 'The Relationship between the Security Council and Regional Organizations during Enforcement Action under Chapter VIII of the United Nations Charter', *Nordic Journal of International Law*, 71 (2002), 1, 19–20; Paliwal, 'The Primacy', supra note 193, 185, 195–196. As Naert says, 'Chapter VIII status seems merely to formalize a willingness to integrate in the UN system without any significant rights or obligations under than a reporting duty', Naert, *International Law Aspects*, supra note 68, 239–240.

[198] Cf. Boisson de Chazournes, supra note 3, 79, 305. But see also UN Doc. S/2011/805 (2011), 2, para. 4.

[199] Boisson de Chazournes, supra note 3, 305–306.

occurs within the framework of Chapter VIII'.[200] Such an interpretation opens up the possibility of reliance on Article 48(2) of the Charter.[201] The distinction between Chapter VIII and Chapter VII is even less relevant for Article 53(1), second sentence, which can be equated more closely with authorisations by the SC under Chapter VII.[202]

This evolution has been characterised as a migration of regionalism from Chapter VIII to Chapter VII,[203] but Chapter VIII has, notwithstanding, real relevance in the practice of the SC. As the Secretary-General pointed out: 'The complex challenges in the world today require a revitalized and evolving interpretation of Chapter VIII of the Charter of the United Nations'.[204] Even more striking is the argument made by the President of the SC in the debate on cooperation with regional and subregional organisations:

> More than six decades ago, when the Charter was drafted, there was no practical example of how this cooperation would be structured and executed. However, Chapter VIII of the Charter was groundbreaking in that, in spite of the fact that there were no regional organizations at the time, it

---

[200] It is also suggested that similar considerations apply for measures taken against non–member states of the respective organisation. Walter, 'Article 53', supra note 169, 1478, 1498–1499 mn. 57; Pernice, *Die Sicherung*, supra note 118, 149.

[201] SC Resolutions 770, 781, 787 and 1031 refer all to 'actions be taken nationally or through regional agencies or arrangements' which is very similar to the wording of Article 48(2), UN Doc. S/RES/770 (1992); S/RES/781 (1992); S/RES/787 (1992); S/RES/1031 (1995). In this context, Frowein asserts that there was even confusion among member states of NATO and the WEU as to whether Article 48 or Article 53 would be applicable and thus whether the organisations shall be considered as falling under Chapter VIII, J. A. Frowein, 'Das Verhältnis zwischen den Vereinten Nationen und Regionalorganisationen bei der Friedenssicherung und Friedenserhaltung', Vortrag gehalten am 10. Juli 1996, 11–12.

[202] Walter, 'Article 53', supra note 169, 1478, 1505 mn. 77. Franck argues, however that there is one difference between Chapters VII and VIII which is that the former presupposes the determination of situation constituting a threat to the peace or one of the two other options under Article 39. This argument seems to be rather formalistic and is not convincing if one takes into account that the powers of the Council to act under Chapter VIII are derived from its powers under Chapter VII. Thus, one might reply that they consequently include an implicit assessment under Article 39, T. M. Franck, 'The Emerging Right to Democratic Governance', *American Journal of International Law*, 86 (1992), 46, 84 including fn. 209.

[203] Boisson de Chazournes, supra note 3, 296–304.

[204] UN Doc. A/65/510–S/2010/514 (2010), 14, para. 54. This view is shared by the AU which even calls for a creative reading of Chapter VIII 'to allow the African Union and its regional mechanisms for conflict prevention, management and resolution to fully play their role as integral components of collective security', Statement by the AU, UN Doc. S/PV.6702 (2012), 6–7, 9, 10; AU Doc. PSC/PR/COMM.(CCCVII) (2012), 3; Statement by Ethiopia, UN Doc. S/PV.6702 (Resumption 1) (2012), 7 and by Togo, UN Doc. S/PV.6903 (2013), 11.

provided for flexibility in cases where such regional organizations would be established.²⁰⁵

The reactivation of Chapter VIII following the end of the Cold War has led to flows of activity within the UN but also on an inter-organisational level with the aim to further institutionalise relations via established, permanent organs such as the UN-EU Steering Committee on Crisis Management.²⁰⁶ Various studies and reports on the reform of peacekeeping and the relationship of the UN with regional organisations have been carried out. In 1993, the SC invited, within the framework of Chapter VIII, regional arrangements and organisations to study 'ways and means to strengthen their functions to maintain international peace and security within their areas of competence, paying due regard to the characteristics of their respective regions'. Furthermore, it asked them to analyse ways and means to improve the coordination of their efforts with those of the UN.²⁰⁷ Therefore,

> In all areas not involving the use of force, notably as far as cooperation on matters of peacekeeping in the African context is concerned, Chapter VIII has witnessed an enormous boost, which is largely due to limited resources, both at the regional and the universal levels. It is certainly also favoured by the fact that the antagonism between universalism and regionalism which was formative for the understanding of Chapter VIII during the Cold War period, has today lost much of its significance.²⁰⁸

The aim of all these efforts is to institutionalise relationships, away from relations on an ad hoc, case-by-case basis.²⁰⁹

Conclusions

This chapter began by analysing the thesis that the general framework of the UN Charter for maintaining international peace and security had been

---

[205] Mr. Zuma (South Africa), Security Council, 6702nd meeting, UN Doc. S/PV.6702 (2012), 2; see in contrast G. Ress, 'Article 53', in B. Simma (ed.), *The Charter of the United Nations: A Commentary* (Oxford University Press, 1995), 687.

[206] For each chosen regional organisation and their relations to the UN and among each other, see infra Chapter 2.

[207] UN Doc. S/25184 (1993), 1–2. A similar appeal came from the General Assembly, UN Doc. A/RES/48/42 (1994), 9, paras. 62–65; A/59/565 (2004), 71, paras. 271–272; A/RES/49/57 (1995), 2–5.

[208] Walter, 'Chapter VIII Regional Arrangements', supra note 10, 1429, 1444 mn. 34.

[209] See Chapter 2.

shaped by supporters of both a universalist and a regionalist view of the system of collective security.

Indeed, by examining the documents of the Dumbarton Oaks conference, it became clear that Chapters VII and VIII of the UN Charter were codified by the founders as a compromise between universalism – Chapter VII – and regionalism – Chapter VIII; maintaining the primary responsibility of the SC for the maintenance of international peace and security under Chapter VII while allowing for regional action under Chapter VIII. This dichotomy between universalism and regionalism is mirrored within the specific dispositions of Chapter VIII. Article 52 of the Charter grants, on paper, a high degree of autonomy to regional organisations for the pacific settlement of disputes. In contrast, Article 53 of the Charter retains the primary responsibility of the SC for the maintenance of international peace and security. The Council may look to regional organisations for enforcement actions under its authority, and enforcement actions under the authority of the latter have to be authorised by the SC.[210]

In practice, however, a much more complex picture has emerged of the system for maintaining international peace and security under the UN Charter which, prima facie, is very much removed from the tension characterised by Chapters VII and III. The analysis revealed that the practice of the UN and regional organisations for maintaining international peace and security is very flexible and pragmatic and that, overall, the practice of the UN and regional organisations gravitates around the epicentre of universalism and regionalism and thus cooperation between the UN and regional organisations.[211]

Regarding the specific context of peacekeeping operations, a division of labour is emerging between the UN and regional organisations which, once again, constitutes a compromise between universalism and regionalism. The UN focuses on traditional peacekeeping operations based on the consent of all parties and allowing only a very limited amount of military force whereas peacekeeping operations with a more robust mandate, as well as peace enforcement operations are delegated to and conducted by regional organisations.[212] This practice was possibly also catalysed in

---

[210] This very same dichotomy can be also found within Chapter VI, which grants both rights and obligations to parties in a conflict, and which may, arguably, amount to a group of states all being members of a regional organisation, and to the SC, for the pacific settlement of disputes.

[211] See the Statement of Chile, UN Doc. S/PV.7112 (2014), 15–16. Cf. Lind, 'Chapter VIII of the UN Charter', supra note 175, 28, 30.

[212] Regarding specifically the African continent, the SC has now twice authorised France to act in such a role, in Mali and in the CAR, which does not constitute a change in practice,

response to criticism that the UN would be incapable of mounting 'militarised' peacekeeping operations.[213] As part of the cooperation of the UN with regional organisations in peacekeeping operations, the former would also focus on the broader spectrum of activities surrounding the concept of peacekeeping, e.g., peacebuilding, state-building and the reconstruction of the political system within the state.

Legally speaking, this emerging practice between the organisations led to a shift in the mandating practice of the SC from authorising regional peacekeeping operations solely under Chapter VIII for which there are several reasons. First of all, traditional peacekeeping operations of regional organisations do not require the authorisation of the SC in contrast to robust peacekeeping operations which do require a mandate from the SC. Furthermore, the nature of peacekeeping operations and the nature of 'situations' in which peacekeeping operations are deployed have evolved. In the majority of cases, peacekeeping operations are now deployed in situations of volatile, armed conflicts in which the enduring consent of all parties to the conflict concerning the deployment of a peacekeeping operation is not guaranteed. An authorisation under Chapter VII is therefore preferable as it would enable the peacekeeping operation to respond with military force if unforeseen circumstances make it necessary. The emerging practice of the UN to mandate regional peacekeeping operations under Chapter VII corresponds with the UN's practice as regards its own peacekeeping operations which are now routinely mandated under Chapter VII as well.

Nevertheless, this shift in the mandating practice of the SC does not equate to a convergence of power in the SC at the expense of regional organisations. It has to be emphasised strongly that, in practice, the gap between universalism and regionalism is bridged by cooperation between

---

but rather a pragmatic solution by the SC when a swift intervention was necessary and bearing in mind France's special interests as a former Colonial Power. Nevertheless, also MINUSMA, interestingly, acts under robust rules of engagement. As an analysis of the case studies will illustrate, Mali is however, an exceptional case.

[213] Sloan, *The Militarisation*, supra note 56, 7–8; M. Mandelbaum, 'The Reluctance to Intervene', *Foreign Policy*, 95 (1994), 3, 10–11. It is alleged that past practice of the SC was also to provide understaffed operations with enforcement mandates they were unable to implement as it was perceived to be 'better' than the alternative in which the SC did not act at all, Kofi Annan is quoted saying that '[t]he time has passed when 15 council members can provide themselves with "an alibi" by passing peacekeeping resolutions that cannot be implemented', J. Hoagland, 'Who Wants Peacekeeping? Put Up or Shut Up', *Washington Post/International Herald Tribune*, 3 August 2000, available at www.globalpolicy.org/component/content/article/199/40895.html.

the UN and regional organisations. It has to be further underlined that there is no blueprint to define – including from a legal point of view – the relations between the UN and regional organisations in the exercise of their functions under Chapters VII and VIII of the UN Charter. Indeed, the cooperation arrangements of the involved organisations are solely dependent on the specific circumstances of the situation.

One can draw three conclusions from the analysis carried out in this chapter on the law of the responsibility of international organisations.

Firstly, the emerging practice of the SC and regional organisations which is based on cooperation and the division of labour or an 'institutional balance' is an impetus for a scenario in which the UN and regional organisations might be jointly responsible.

Secondly, any criterion of attributing conduct to international organisations for acts or omissions arising in the context of peacekeeping operations needs to be constructed in such a way so as to take into account the varied nature of cooperation arrangements between the UN and regional organisations in peacekeeping operations. In other words, it must be able to capture the *casuistic approach* used by the UN and regional organisations.

Thirdly, and perhaps most importantly, while examining the attribution of conduct, it is necessary to embark upon an analysis of the legal foundation of the relationship and cooperation between the UN and regional organisations. As was mentioned rather briefly in this chapter, regional organisations are per se not bound by the UN Charter and thereby also not by Chapter VIII which serves as the framework for the relations between the UN and regional organisations for maintaining international peace and security. Therefore, it needs to be analysed if that fact influences the interaction between the regional organisations and the UN, as well as the potential distribution of international responsibility. It is also important, as despite the shift in the mandating practice of peacekeeping operations by the SC to Chapter VII, Chapter VIII is repeatedly invoked in order to legitimate the relations between the UN and regional organisations.

2

The (Emerging) System of Collective Security Consisting of the UN and Regional Organisations

> Now the evolution of United Nations peacekeeping missions is such that the organization, planning and execution of related operations are transcending the primary normative framework mentioned in Chapters VI, VII and VIII of the Charter of the United Nations. Peacekeeping missions, in their multi-dimensional design, now rely on a normative framework that brings together the relevant provisions of the Charter and the international legal instruments for human rights and international humanitarian law, as well as of regional and subregional organizations.
>
> – Statement by Togo in the Security Council[1]

Relations between the UN and Regional Organisations and among Different Regional Organisations

The previous chapter traced the evolution of peacekeeping within the framework of the UN Charter and the general practice of the UN with respect to Chapters VII and VIII of the Charter. It showed that the framework for maintaining international peace and security under the Charter is based on a compromise between a universalist, unipolar and a regionalist, multipolar view, which effectively increases the potential for joint and common action by several entities. This chapter will first of all analyse whether the findings of Chapter 1 can be further corroborated by examining the relations between the UN and regional organisations. Furthermore, such an exercise on the basis of the various cooperation agreements, partnerships and declarations among international organisations can shed light on the potential distribution of responsibility among them or even allow the formulation of a presumption of joint responsibility between two specific organisations. Even if these documents are conceived solely as part of the internal law of the respective organisation(s), they nevertheless '[provide] guidance in determining issues of attribution of conduct and

---

[1] UN Doc. S/PV.6903 (2013), 11.

responsibility' as they define the relational context on whose basis international organisations interact with each other in maintaining international peace and security,[2] as well as in peacekeeping operations. Moreover, their inter-institutional cooperation may also shape financing procedures, command and control arrangements, operational practices, as well as accountability or reporting mechanisms.[3]

Various factors influence the relations between universal and regional organisations. Virally suggests that these relations pivot on three main ideas: collaboration or cooperation, competition, and 'chasse gardée or the safeguarding of respective spheres of action and influence'.[4] Cooperation can be based on formal arrangements and agreements or also simply on practice.[5] Formalised cooperation often implies an orientation of the regional organisations towards the activities of the universal organisation, which may also include the execution of decisions by the latter.[6] Cooperation allows organisations to define their roles as distinct from each other, thereby preventing redundancies and duplications of conduct, according to each organisation's means.

In practice, relations between regional organisations and universal organisations rarely subscribe to one idea alone, but they stretch across various, complex areas while taking into account the specific circumstances in each situation. The network of relations among organisations is normally relatively flexible, practice-driven, and external factors such as lack of resources and means often prompt organisations to seek cooperation rather than confrontation. In addition to burden sharing, cooperation between international organisations can be used as a strategy to allow the development of a holistic or comprehensive approach towards peacekeeping or to enable flexibility and selectivity in engaging in peacekeeping operations.[7]

Moreover, the complexity of the current crises the international community is confronted with has changed, not only in terms of the way in which they are perceived but also in how these crises are understood.

---

[2] L. Boisson de Chazournes, 'United in Joy and Sorrow: Some Considerations on Responsibility Issues under Partnership among International Financial Institutions', in M. Ragazzi (ed.), *Responsibility of International Organizations. Essays in Memory of Sir Ian Brownlie* (Leiden, Brill, 2013), 213, 218.

[3] Cf. T. Tardy, 'Hybrid Peace Operations: Rationale and Challenges', *Global Governance*, 20 (2014), 95, 97.

[4] M. Virally, *L'Organisation Mondiale* (Paris, A. Colin, 1972), 295.

[5] Ibid.

[6] Ibid., 295–296.

[7] Tardy, 'Hybrid Peace Operations', supra note 3, 95, 99–104.

Today, it is generally accepted that one organisation, be it regional or universal, may not be able to tackle a given issue on its own, but that rather cooperation between international organisations and a multi-layered response is necessary.[8]

This chapter introduces the various organisations, their peacekeeping activities, and their normative and political framework. The different organisations introduced in this part are all, in one way, *sui generis* organisations, as they were all created under different political circumstances and considerations and with an individual legal framework. It also analyses the internal and external challenges facing each organisation which affect their ability to carry out peacekeeping activities. It further explores the relations among these organisations. Throughout the past two decades, the UN has continuously strengthened its relations with regional organisations; and in all events many questions remain open. A report of the Secretary-General from 2008 highlights some of the open questions with respect to the relationship between the UN and regional organisations, of which those relevant for the purposes of this thesis shall be addressed in the following analysis.[9]

The report underlines that the cooperation arrangements and methods between the UN and regional organisations are still *in statu nascendi*. The following analysis traces the development of the relations among the UN and the regional organisations, but focuses on the current situation and the current status of relations among these organisations. Past developments might help to give indications for the future and references to specific operations may equally contribute to the assessment; but any such practice merely serves for the purpose of defining the inter-institutional relationship between the two (or more) organisations in question.

As cooperation among international organisations in peacekeeping operations becomes more frequent, the deployment of military troops by one organisation does not 'tak[e] place in a vacuum', but ideally – presupposes coordination and cooperation with other organisations – in a setting of 'reciprocal interaction'[10] – an emerging system of regional security with 'explicit principles, norms, rules, and decision-making procedures around which actors' expectations converge in [this] given area of international relations'.[11]

---

[8] Ibid., 95, 100.
[9] UN Doc. S/2008/186 (2008), 20, para. 71.
[10] M. Brosig, 'The Emerging Peace and Security Regime in Africa: The Role of the EU', *European Foreign Affairs Review*, 16 (2011), 107, 109–110.
[11] S. D. Krasner, 'Structural Causes and Regime Consequences: Regimes as Intervening Variables', in S. D. Krasner (ed.), *International Regimes* (Cornell University Press, 1982), 1, 2.

It cannot be underlined strongly enough that each peacekeeping operation is unique in its mandate, composition and implementation. Many factors, including political factors, combine to determine the way in which an operation is conducted. As the examples mentioned in the previous chapters show, the SC uses its mandate in a very flexible manner so that the relationship between the UN and regional organisations is never static. Whereas the cooperation between the UN and a given regional organisation X might take a relationship in the form of a partnership based on coordination, in another operation Y, coordination might be replaced by the subordination of one organisation to the other.[12] Thus, the relationships are not static in respect of the *mission level*; nor are they static on an inter-organisational or *institutional level* as they continuously develop and evolve. All these factors contribute to raise the level of difficulty in legally assessing the attribution of conduct for violations of international law occurring in peacekeeping operations.

As pointed out, the degree of diversity in terms of institutional structures and capabilities means 'that no simple or singular global pattern for future development can reasonably be proposed'.[13] Nevertheless, it is helpful to distinguish between institutional partnership and operational collaboration, as the former constitutes a long-term effort, whereas the latter is essentially ad hoc.[14]

The present analysis will therefore combine both elements in order to facilitate a thorough examination of the relations existing among the organisations. The focus will nevertheless remain on inter-institutional relations, as operational cooperation will be examined in the case studies in Chapter 4 of this book. It is advantageous to analyse the relationship of the UN with each individual organisation. Following this approach, this study explores two regional organisations from both Europe and Africa,[15] which is beneficial as the links are traditionally particularly strong among regional organisations from the same continent. They often share the very same cultural heritage and as they exercise their activities within the

---

[12] Naturally, the cooperation of the UN with one of these organisations or in between the latter might be different in other areas than in the field of international peace and security.
[13] J. Morris, H. McCoubrey, 'Regional Peacekeeping in the Post-Cold War Era', *International Peacekeeping*, 6 (1999), 129, 147.
[14] H. Yamashita, 'Peacekeeping Cooperation between the United Nations and Regional Organisations', *Review of International Studies*, 38 (2012), 165, 167.
[15] The vast majority of NATO's members are European and the cultural ties are strong with their transatlantic fellow NATO members.

same geographic region, their respective roles are often more defined than towards other international organisations.

NATO: A Euro-Atlantic Pillar for Peacekeeping or a Security Actor with a Broader Agenda?

> NATO possesses unique capabilities to contribute to peacekeeping operations.
> – NATO Defence Planning Committee[16]

The Foundation of NATO

NATO was effectively born out of the power play between the USSR and the US and its allies in the times of the Cold War. The blockade in the SC led to a strange form of regionalism as the two sides attempted to safeguard and expand their spheres of interest and influence by creating regional organisations. The North Atlantic Treaty Organisation was founded in 1949, in the same year as the Council for Mutual Economic Assistance (Comecon). It was clear that international peace and security could not be guaranteed within the SC, and NATO was seen as a way out of the stalemate.[17]

NATO was created with the understanding that it would operate within the framework of the UN and accepts the latter's role in maintaining international peace and security. This role clearly derives from the preamble to the North Atlantic Treaty which says, 'The Parties to this Treaty reaffirm their faith in the purposes and principles of the Charter of the United Nations.'[18] This subordination to the primacy of the UN Charter is mirrored throughout the whole North Atlantic Treaty. For instance, Article 1 reiterates the prohibition of the use of force as enshrined in Article 2(4) of the UN Charter, stating that the parties undertake 'to refrain in their international relations from the threat or use of force in any manner inconsistent with the purposes of the United Nations'.

Article 7 of the North Atlantic Treaty equally refers to the UN Charter and to the primary responsibility of the SC for maintaining

---

[16] Final communiqué of the Meeting of the Defence Planning Committee, 11 December 1992, para. 4.
[17] P. Sands, P. Klein, *Bowett's Law of International Institutions* (London, Sweet & Maxwell, 2009), 195; S. R. Lüder, *Völkerrechtliche Verantwortlichkeit bei Teilnahme an 'Peacekeeping'-Missionen der Vereinten Nationen* (Berliner Wissenschafts-Verlag, 2004), 141.
[18] The North Atlantic Treaty, Washington, DC, 4 April 1949, Preamble.

international peace and security. Despite these close links to the UN system, the question of whether NATO qualifies as a regional arrangement or agency under Chapter VIII of the Charter had been the subject of great controversy.

NATO and Its Formal Submission under Chapter VIII of the UN Charter

NATO is generally considered as an international organisation with separate legal personality under international law[19] and it arguably fulfils the criteria to qualify as a regional organisation under Chapter VIII of the UN Charter,[20] despite some criticism with regard to that qualification.[21] Nevertheless, NATO itself has also always rejected any qualifications as a regional arrangement under Chapter VIII.[22] Until the end of the Cold War this opposition was primarily motivated by NATO's intention not to submit to a SC whose members included the USSR, as well as to the reporting requirements under Article 54 of the UN Charter, than by a position of opposition against cooperation with the UN.[23] Generally, NATO's relations with the UN were limited during the Cold War. This changed in 1992 when 'their respective roles in crisis management led to an intensification of practical cooperation between the two organizations in the field'.[24] In the 1991 Strategic Concept, it was already expressed the idea that 'Allies

---

[19] See, for instance, Plea by France in *Bankovic and others v. Belgium and others*, Admissibility, Decision of 12 December 2001, para. 32, German Constitutional Court, Urteil des Zweiten Senats vom 22. November 2001, 2 BvE 6/99, Fraktion der PDS im Deutschen Bundestag und Bundesregierung, BVerfGE 104, 151, 155. Critics rely in particular on Article 12 of the North Atlantic Treaty.

[20] See Chapter 1.

[21] Critics rely in particular on Article 12 of the North Atlantic Treaty. See, for instance, U. Villani, *Les Rapports entre l'ONU et les organisations régionales dans le domaine du maintien de la paix*, Recueil des cours de l'Académie de La Haye, Volume 290 (2001), 225, 287.

[22] Statement by NATO, UN Doc. S/PV.5007 (2004), 24–25. The Alliance's Strategic Concept, Approved by the Heads of State and Government Participating in the Meeting of the North Atlantic Council in Washington, DC, 24 April 1999, para. 31; M. Zwanenburg, 'NATO, Its Members and the Security Council', in N. Blokker, N. Schrijver (eds.), *The Security Council and the Use of Force: Theory and Reality. A Need for Change?* (Leiden, Martinus Nijhoff, 2005), 189, 195.

[23] D. S. Yost, 'NATO and International Organizations', Forum Paper 3, NATO Defense College, September 2007, 34.

[24] NATO's relations with the UN, available at www.nato.int/cps/en/natolive/topics_50321.htm.

could, further, be called upon to contribute to global stability and peace by providing forces for United Nations missions'.[25]

Another reason for NATO's opposition to a qualification under Chapter VIII was, of course, to safeguard NATO's autonomy of action. NATO's position has changed since the end of the Cold War and this seems to be equally recognised by the UN. So the SC, for instance, referred explicitly to states acting through regional arrangements or agencies in Resolutions 781 (1992) and 787 (1992) upon which NATO acted in Yugoslavia.[26]

NATO: Rising Like a Phoenix Post the Cold War? A New Strategic Alignment

NATO underwent a tremendous transformation and strategic redirection after the end of the Cold War, losing its principal purpose of existence as a Western military alliance against the Soviet bloc.[27] The organisation was forced to transform and to take on new tasks and responsibilities as well as to defend its continuing existence.[28]

NATO declared that for the attainment of its objectives it would no longer act solely through the military dimension, but also in the political field under Article 2 of the North Atlantic Treaty.[29] These political tools and the new agenda of 'comprehensive political guidance' opened up new political courses of action for NATO. They enabled the organisation to expand military crisis management from reaction to action and to include wider elements in its agenda such as conflict prevention. Part of this new comprehensive security notion within NATO was the establishment of

---

[25] The Alliance's New Strategic Concept, Agreed by the Heads of State and Government Participating in the Meeting of the North Atlantic Council, 7–8 November 1991, para. 41.

[26] UN Doc. S/RES/781 (1992), 2, para. 5; S/RES/787 (1992), 4, para. 14; S/25567 (1993), 1, first paragraph; S/25996 (1993), 3 para. 3(d), also pp. 18–19; G. Ress, J. Bröhmer, 'Article 53', in B. Simma (ed.), *The Charter of the United Nations. A Commentary* (Oxford University Press, 2002), 854, 862.

[27] See also The Alliance's New Strategic Concept, supra note 25, para. 1.

[28] Statement by NATO, UN Doc. S/PV.5282 (2005), 25. Cf. A. Hyde-Price, 'NATO's Political Transformation and International Order', in J. Ringsmose, S. Rynning (eds.), *NATO's New Strategic Concept: A Comprehensive Assessment*, DIIS Report (2011), 45–46.

[29] Declaration on a Transformed North Atlantic Alliance, Issued by the Heads of State and Government participating in the meeting of the North Atlantic Council 'The London Declaration', 5–6 July 1990, especially paras. 1–7; J. Woodliffe, 'The Evolution of a New NATO for a New Europe', *The International and Comparative Law Quarterly*, 47 (1998), 174.

regular dialogues with states who were part of the former Soviet Union as well as cooperation with all European states[30] based on the principles contained in the Charter of Paris for a new Europe.[31] On the basis of the partnership for peace and other programmes[32] NATO consequently transformed into an organisation with a broader mandate, 'including fostering peace and stability in the Euro-Atlantic region through crisis management and involvement in peace-keeping operations'.[33] The organisation consequently gained renewed credibility and legitimation as an exporter of stability even outside the North Atlantic area. So in a speech in November 2012 by NATO's Deputy Secretary-General, the core roles of NATO were stated as 'collective defence, crisis management and cooperative security'.[34]

Moreover, the evolving activity outside of the Euro-Atlantic area and beyond the more traditional area in which armed attacks feature, is equally mirrored in the 1991 and the 1999 Strategic Concepts.[35] The interpretation of Article 5 North Atlantic Treaty was further expanded in the latest Strategic Concept, which was issued in November 2010.[36]

---

[30] Declaration on Peace and Cooperation, Issued by the Heads of States and Government Participating in the Meeting of the North Atlantic Council ('The Rome Declaration'), 8 November 1991, para. 4.

[31] Woodliffe, 'The Evolution of a New Nato', supra note 29, 174, 175. See also Charter of Paris for a New Europe, Meeting of the Heads of State or Government of the participating States of the Conference on Security and Co-operation in Europe (CSCE), Paris, 19–21 November 1990; Declaration on Peace and Cooperation, supra note 30, paras. 13–14. The Bucharest summit expanded NATO's reach through 'partnerships across the globe', Bucharest Summit Declaration, Issued by the Heads of State and Government Participating in the Meeting of the North Atlantic Council in Bucharest on 3 April 2008, para. 30.

[32] For instance, Active Engagement in Cooperative Security: A More Efficient and Flexibilie Partnership Policy (2011), para. 2.

[33] Speech by NATO Secretary-General Jaap de Hoop Scheffer at the NATO Defense College, Rome, 28 May 2009; see also Sands, Klein, supra note 17, 195; The Alliance's Strategic Concept, supra note 22, para. 31.

[34] 'NATO in 2020: Strong Capabilities, Strong Partnerships.' Keynote speech by NATO Deputy Secretary-General Ambassador Alexander Vershbow at the international conference 'NATO and the Global Structure of Security: The Future of Partnerships', Bucharest, Romania, 10 November 2012.

[35] Ibid., para. 24. 'The Alliance's New Strategic Concept', supra note 25, para. 12; cf. 'Lisbon Summit Declaration', Issued by the Heads of State and Government participating in the meeting of the North Atlantic Council in Lisbon on 20 November 2010, para. 6; Permanent representative of the US to NATO, Transatlantic Forum, Berlin, 1 July 2009; J. M. Goldgeier, 'The Future of NATO', Council on Foreign Relations, Council Special Report No. 51, February 2010, 8; Speech by NATO Secretary-General Jaap de Hoop Scheffer at the NATO Defense College, Rome, 28 May 2009.

[36] Strategic Concept for the Defence and Security of the Members of the North Atlantic Treaty Organisation, Active Engagement, Modern Defence, 2010, para. 4(a).

Assuming New Tasks of Security Proliferation and Projection: In Accordance with the NAT?

The new Strategic Concept also abdicates the territory requirement in case of an armed attack.[37] The Lisbon Strategic concept thus conveys the collective will of NATO member states to transform NATO into a more globally acting organisation, alone or in combination with the increasing network of partnerships and cooperation arrangements.[38] This transformation is based on three identified core tasks of NATO, 'defence and deterrence', 'security and crisis management' as well as 'promoting international security through cooperation'.[39] This is somewhat astonishing as NATO has not considered it necessary to amend the North Atlantic Treaty accordingly.[40] Consequently, this new Strategy gives NATO a great degree of leeway, if not close to carte blanche to act in matters of international peace and security. Article 5 of the North Atlantic Treaty also provides the legal basis for the peacekeeping operations if NATO is engaged in 'crisis management operations', falling within the scope of the broad interpretation which was given to that article through the practice of the organisation and the recent Strategic Concepts.[41]

---

[37] Ibid. This contrasts with the Alliance Strategy of 1991, The Alliance's New Strategic Concept, supra note 25, para. 35. See also The Bucharest Summit Declaration, supra note 31, para. 44.

[38] J. Ringsmose, S. Rynning, 'Introduction. Taking Stock of NATO's New Strategic Concept', in J. Ringsmose, S. Rynning (eds.), *NATO's New Strategic Concept: A Comprehensive Assessment*, DIIS Report (2011), 7–8, 14. Nonetheless, the main priority is given to the defence of NATO territory, see J. Shea, 'What Does a New Strategic Concept Do for NATO?', in J. Ringsmose, S. Rynning (eds.), *NATO's New Strategic Concept: A Comprehensive Assessment*, DIIS Report (2011), 25, 26.

[39] Cf. K. Wittmann, 'An Alliance for the 21st Century? Reviewing NATO's New Strategic Concept', in J. Ringsmose, S. Rynning (eds.), *NATO's New Strategic Concept: A Comprehensive Assessment*, DIIS Report (2011), 31, 33. See also Wales Summit Declaration, Issued by the Heads of State and Government Participating in the Meeting of the North Atlantic Council in Wales from 4–5 September 2014, para. 3.

[40] Although it is generally accepted that norms and treaties are subject to an evolutionary interpretation, one may question whether an amendment to the North Atlantic Charter might not have been preferable. Two authors suggests that member states have amended the NATO constitution through practice, see E. de Wet, 'The Relationship between the Security Council and Regional Organizations during Enforcement Action under Chapter VIII of the United Nations Charter', *Nordic Journal of International Law*, 71 (2002), 1, 9; N. Blokker, S. Muller, 'NATO as the UN Security Council's Instrument: Question Marks from the Perspective of International Law?', *Leiden Journal of International Law*, 9 (1996), 417, 420–421.

[41] These operations clearly do not fall under the rubric of self-defence, F. Naert, *International Law Aspects of the EU' Security and Defence Policy, with a Particular Focus on the Law of Armed Conflict and Human Rights* (2010), 26.

Although evolutionary interpretation through practice has been recognised in international law,[42] the broadening interpretation raises questions regarding its compliance with other dispositions in the North Atlantic Treaty. Article 7 supports the new interpretation of Article 5 as the establishment of NATO-run operations, such as IFOR and SFOR, is based on resolutions of the SC.[43] Another pertinent norm of the North Atlantic Treaty is Article 4. This article prescribes that NATO members will consult each other in cases of threats to territorial integrity, political independence, or security of any members. In the post–Cold War period, a broader interpretation has been given to that article based on the recognition that threats to members of NATO can arise from other sources than armed attacks by a third state.[44] Consequently, that disposition cannot be interpreted as a limitation of NATO's competences to mere consultations, but it allows other reactions, including the participation of NATO in peacekeeping operations.[45]

NATO, Peacekeeping and Its Relations with Other Organisations

Beginnings/History: NATO and the UN

NATO's engagement in peacekeeping operations commenced in the Yugoslavia crisis. NATO ships were engaged in monitoring operations in the Adriatic in support of the arms embargo which was imposed by the SC against all republics of the former Yugoslavia.[46] Following the conclusion of the Dayton Peace Agreements, NATO deployed its first peacekeeping forces, the Implementation Force (IFOR) under a mandate of the SC.[47] IFOR was replaced a year later by SFOR.[48]

---

[42] *Legal Consequences for States of the Continued Presence of South Africa in Namibia (South West Africa) notwithstanding Security Council Resolution 276 (1970), Advisory Opinion* (21 June 1971), para. 53. See also Pollux, 'The Interpretation of the Charter', *British Yearbook of International Law*, 23 (1946), 54.
[43] B. Dold, *Vertragliche und ausservertragliche Verantwortlichkeit im Recht der internationalen Organisationen* (Zürich, Schulthess, 2006), 36.
[44] S. Trifunovska, *North Atlantic Treaty Organization (NATO) (2010)*, 29–30, para. 26
[45] Dold, *Vertragliche und ausservertragliche Verantwortlichkeit*, supra note 43, 36.
[46] See UN Doc. S/RES/781 (1992), 2, para. 5; S/RES/776 (1992), 2, para. 3; S/RES/787 (1992), 4, paras. 10, 12; NATO, Statement on Former Yugoslavia, 17 December 1992, paras. 6–8; Statement on NATO Maritime Operations (1), 10 July 1992.
[47] UN Doc. S/RES/1031 (1995), 3, paras. 12, 14–16; The General Framework Agreement, Annex 1A, Agreement on the Military Aspects of the Peace Settlement, 14 December 1995, Article I 1.A., Article VI 1.
[48] UN Doc. S/RES/1088 (1996).

NATO is a military organisation so that the range of its activities is clear and defined and cannot be compared with the range of activities of organisations with general competence such as the EU and the AU. It would, however, be short-sighted to consider NATO's potential limited to the military area. As one author argues, NATO combines the military capabilities and the economic power of the US with the collective European political influence and weight, making it a significant global actor.[49]

The ties between NATO and the UN concerning crisis management and maintenance of international peace and security were increased in the following years. NATO cooperated with the UN throughout the Kosovo crisis and on the basis of SC Resolution 1244 it established KFOR. According to the resolution, KFOR was designated as the military component of the broader multidimensional operation, under the authority of the UN special representative and working closely with the civilian component which was set up by the UN (UNMIK).[50]

Between Autonomy and Approximation, NATO and Its Relations with the UN

In 2008, the UN and NATO issued a joint declaration concerning UN/NATO Secretariat Cooperation, 'reaffirming [their] commitment to the maintenance of international peace and security' and providing for further increased but flexible consultation and cooperation between the Secretariats of both organisations.[51] Nevertheless, NATO retains its autonomy with regard to the UN, and there is no institutionalised representation of NATO at the UN through a mission, nor does NATO possess observer status in the General Assembly. The 2008 joint declaration is also a step backwards from the envisaged UN–NATO framework agreement including a joint declaration and a memorandum of understanding, which was drafted in September 2005 by the Alliance. These did not gain approval within the UN before Kofi Annan left his office and no further action has

---

[49] Z. Brzezinski, 'An Agenda for NATO. Towards a Global Security Web', *Foreign Affairs*, 88(2) (2009), 2, 10. However, NATO lacks generally a strong civilian side to peacekeeping; see UN Doc. A/65/762 (2011), 10, para. 28.

[50] UN Doc. S/RES/1244 (1999). As confirmed at the Chicago Summit, NATO remains committed to KFOR, Chicago Summit Declaration, Issued by the Heads of State and Government participating in the meeting of the North Atlantic Council in Chicago on 20 May 2012, para. 12.

[51] Annex to DSG (2008)0714 (INV), Joint Declaration on UN/NATO Secretariat Cooperation, para. 1; Chicago Summit Declaration, ibid., para. 19.

been taken since then in this matter.[52] The 2008 declaration was also only possible after a lengthy struggle between NATO's main contributors in favour of signing the declaration and important states voicing their concern about such a declaration; in the end the UN Secretariat urged NATO not to publish the accord.[53] Nevertheless NATO remains committed to expanding its institutional ties with the UN and its practical support to UN peacekeeping operations as confirmed by the organisation during the Wales Summit 2014.[54]

The relationship between the two organisations has developed along two main lines of cooperation in peacekeeping operations.[55] Under the first option, NATO is subcontracted by the UN and subscribing to its primary responsibility for the maintenance of international peace and security, relying on an authorisation of the SC 'for collective security purposes'. Alternatively, NATO acts on its own without a formal authorisation of the SC, for example the airstrikes in Kosovo in 1999, and in accordance with its primary purpose for which it was established – collective defence against external threats.[56] This did not cause a rift in their relations, largely as a result of their mutual pragmatic approach, nor was there any 'political punishment'.[57] As observed by Griep, NATO and the UN complement each other well: NATO with its unique robust military potential and the UN with the mandate providing globally unique legitimation. NATO also has more than sixty years of experience in preparing and leading complex multinational and inter-service operations.[58] In 2011, NATO contributed through the UN-mandated operation *Unified Protector* to the protection of the civilian population in Libya, an example once again that NATO

---

[52] Yost, 'NATO and International Organizations', supra note 23, 10; K. M. Haugevik, 'New Partners, New Possibilities. The Evolution of Inter-organizational Security Cooperation in International Peace Operations', NUPI Report, Security in Practice 6 (2007), 6.

[53] M. F. Harsch, J. Varwick, 'NATO and the UN', *Survival: Global Politics and Strategy*, 51 (2009), 5, 8–9.

[54] Wales Summit Declaration, supra note 39, 101.

[55] D. Leurdijk, 'NATO and the UN the Dynamics of an Evolving Relationship', *The RUSI Journal*, 149(3) (2004), 24, 26–27.

[56] D. A. Leurdijk, 'The UN and NATO: The Logic of Primacy', in M. Pugh, W. P. Singh Sidhu, *The United Nations and Regional Security. Europe and Beyond* (Boulder, Lynne Rienner Publishers, 2003), 57, 58. Cf. also UN Doc. A/CN.4/637 (2011), 12–13, para. 5.

[57] E. Griep, *Regionale Organisationen und die Weiterentwicklung der VN-Friedenssicherung seit dem Ende des Kalten Krieges* (Baden-Baden, Nomos, 2012), 310.

[58] Yost, 'NATO and International Organizations', supra note 23, 43. After the negative experiences in NATO–UN operational cooperation in Bosnia and Herzegovina, i.e., under the dual-key arrangement, NATO will not commit to any international mission upon which it is decided by the SC in the absence of prior consultations, D. Lightburn, 'Should NATO Support UN Peacekeeping Operations?', *NATO Review*, June 2005.

'can quickly and effectively conduct complex operations in support of the broader international community'.[59] The NATO Operation in Libya, as well as in Afghanistan, further suggest that NATO will in the future always rely on an authorisation of the SC instead of acting on its own. This is, in particular, because NATO's increasing circle of partners will insist on such an authorisation.[60] The organisation learnt – the hard way – in Bosnia as well as in Kosovo 'that it could not win peace on its own, and that success in peace and stabilisation operations ultimately depends on civilian instruments that the Alliance does not possess'.[61] Instead of developing a comprehensive approach of its own, NATO conceptualised its role as that of a catalyst between the various organisations engaged, fostering 'cooperation and coordination between all the relevant actors involved in such operations'.[62] Moreover, it precisely allows NATO to leave the 'driver's seat' to coordinate the needed comprehensive approach to the UN while focusing on its own area of expertise.[63] Nevertheless, NATO continued its 'two-pronged approach' regarding cooperation in peacekeeping operations by enhancing its own capacity to conduct military operations from a comparatively holistic point of view.[64]

NATO and the AU

NATO's relations with the AU are fairly limited, which could be perceived as surprising given that NATO's military capacities could well contribute to the peacekeeping operations undertaken by the AU. One principal

---

[59] Chicago Summit Declaration, supra note 50, paras. 13–14; J. H. Michaels, 'NATO after Libya', *The RUSI Journal*, 156(6) (2011), 56, 57.

[60] Yost, 'NATO and International Organizations', supra note 23, 44; NATO 2020: Assured Security; Dynamic Engagement. Analysis and Recommendations of the Group of Experts on a New Strategic Concept for NATO, 17 May 2010, 10.

[61] P. V. Jakobsen, 'NATO's Comprehensive Approach after Lisbon: Principal Problem Acknowledged, Solution Elusive', in J. Ringsmose, S. Rynning (eds.), *NATO's New Strategic Concept: A Comprehensive Assessment*, DIIS Report (2011), 83–84.

[62] Jakobsen, ibid., 83, 84; cf. Strategic Concept for the Defence and Security, supra note 36, paras. 4(c), 28–33; H. B. Lindbo Larsen, 'Cooperative Security: Warning Influence in the Eastern Neighbourhood', in J. Ringsmose, S. Rynning (eds.), *NATO's New Strategic Concept: A Comprehensive Assessment*, DIIS Report (2011), 91, 92.

[63] Cf. Strategic Concept For the Defence and Security, supra note 36, para. 25 bullet point 3; S. Biscop, 'From Lisbon to Lisbon: Squaring the Circle of EU and NATO Future Roles', in J. Ringsmose, S. Rynning (eds.), *NATO's New Strategic Concept: A Comprehensive Assessment*, DIIS Report (2011), 106, 107–111.

[64] This includes the adoption of the Effects-Based Approach to Operations (EBAO), the Comprehensive Operational Planning Directive (2010), NATO's Counterinsurgency (COIN) Doctrine (2011) as well as the Civilian Advisor (CIVAD) Concept (2010); see also Jakobsen, 'NATO's Comprehensive Approach', supra note 61, 83, 84–85.

reason is that NATO, despite its various partnership programmes with countries outside of the Euro-Atlantic zone, remains primarily committed to this geographic area, as well as the immediate neighbourhood.[65] Therefore, NATO intervened in Libya on the request of the SC but it is not participating in the crisis management in Mali. This is also due to an unwritten rule to grant the former colonial powers in Africa the possibility to intervene on their own – at the request of the respective government.[66] Finally, NATO attempts to avoid duplication with the EU which has institutionalised relationships with the AU. Consequently, NATO is not proactive, but is rather responsive in its relations with the AU, providing the latter 'with operational support, at its request'.[67] This cautious position of NATO is fuelled by internal pressure to justify its operations. Governments of NATO members need to be able to tell their parliaments that they have been asked to assist. In this scenario, a request from the UN is taken very seriously due to its legitimising function. The consequence is 'widespread ignorance in the United Nations, the African Union, and other organizations about NATO's capacities'.[68] Even notwithstanding these explanations of NATO's defensive stand, one may still ask whether such a NATO policy of more or less completely excluding any element of conflict prevention on the African continent is beneficial for the long-term strategy of the organisation.[69] Regarding inter-organisational and intra-operational cooperation, NATO is providing support to the AU Mission in Somalia in providing strategic airlift and sealift support, as well as through the secondment of some experts to the AU's Peace Support Operations Division's desk on AMISOM.[70] Furthermore NATO has been assisting the AU Mission in Sudan (AMIS).[71] During a visit of the AU High Commissioner for Peace and Security to NATO in 2007, he stated that the

---

[65] See, for instance, Active Engagement in Cooperative Security: A More Efficient and Flexible Partnership Policy (2011), para. 4, but also paras. 10, 16; cf. Michaels, 'NATO after Libya', supra note 59, 56.
[66] Yost, supra note 23, 82.
[67] Chicago Summit Declaration, supra note 50, para. 15(3); E. A. Akuffo, 'Human Security and Interregional Cooperation between NATO and the African Union', *Global Change, Peace & Security*, 23 (2011), 223, 232.
[68] Yost, 'NATO and International Organizations', supra note 23, 44–46, 58–59. Cf. Statement of NATO before the Security Council, UN Doc. S/PV.5075 (Resumption 1) (2004), 4.
[69] Cf. Wittmann, 'An Alliance for the 21st Century? Reviewing NATO's New Strategic Concept', supra note 39, 31, 36, 40.
[70] P. D. Williams, 'Somalia', in J. Boulden (ed.), *Responding to Conflict in Africa. The United Nations and Regional Organizations* (London, Palgrave Macmillan, 2013), 257, 275.
[71] NATO assistance to the AU, available at www.nato.int/cps/en/natolive/topics_8191.htm.

AU is looking for long-term cooperation with NATO,[72] but it no further efforts have been undertaken by both organisations regarding such a plan until May 2014 when both organisations signed a technical agreement formalising the status of the NATO liaison office and which is deemed primarily to enhance NATO support to AU peacekeeping operations.[73] Nevertheless, with NATO's distinctive military capacities, it cannot be excluded that – the more violent recent conflicts become – the AU will increasingly also seek the support of NATO.[74]

Conclusions

NATO has evolved from a collective defence organisation to a global security actor, which is independent in its actions, despite maintaining strong connections with the UN and the EU.[75] The analysis of NATO's cooperation with the UN showed that NATO is interested in safeguarding its autonomous role while respecting the primary responsibility of the SC for maintaining international peace and security. The institutionalised arrangements for cooperation between NATO and the UN have not developed further since the joint declaration of 2008.

First, this stagnation might be explained by NATO's impulse for autonomy. Furthermore, NATO–UN relations might not be developing further because NATO appears to prefer fostering relations with a plurality of other partners through its various partnership programmes. NATO's More Efficient and Flexible Partnership Policy foresees the streamlining of its partnership tools, opening all cooperative activities and exercises to all partners as well as harmonising partnership programmes.[76] The consequences are significant also from the perspective of international responsibility as it means that the operational partners will 'be consulted and offered the opportunity to put forward views on all relevant issues and be fully involved in the discussion of documents in particular Concepts of Operations, Operations plans, Rules of Engagements and their revisions'.[77]

---

[72] 'AU looks to long-term cooperation with NATO', 2 March 2007, available at www.nato.int/docu/update/2007/03-march/e0302a.html.
[73] 'NATO and the AU Boost Their Cooperation', available at www.nato.int/cps/en/natolive/news_109824.htm.
[74] E. A. Akuffo, 'The Politics of Interregional Cooperation: The Impact of NATO's Intervention in Libya on Its Relations with the African Union', *African Conflict & Peacebuilding Review*, 4 (2014), 108, 116, 123.
[75] See infra, 2.3.
[76] Active Engagement, supra note 65, paras. 12–13.
[77] Political-Military Framework for Partner Involvement in NATO-led Operations (2011), para. 9–10, 12.

Thus, the input of these partners in the operational activity of NATO will be tremendous. Nevertheless, in its Chicago Summit Declaration, NATO emphasised that it would develop stronger institutionalised relationships with the UN, the EU and the AU and other global and regional actors in the near future.[78]

As regards the general strategic direction of NATO, the organisation appears to oscillate between a broad global outlook on strategic security issues and a narrower Euro-Atlantic–centred one, which attempts to consolidate the status quo of 'an Atlantic alliance focused on the globe'.[79] Other authors submit that the rift within NATO regarding the strategic orientation runs deeper in reality; that it resurfaced and was intensified by NATO's post–Cold War expansion of tasks and missions.[80] This question is even more relevant now after the end of the ISAF operation in Afghanistan. What is the new principal purpose of NATO and what will it entail?[81] One author suggests that due to the geopolitical shift of US interests in the Pacific region, the aftermath of the global economic crisis and NATO's operational experiences, the organisation would be inclined to limit its military operations to smaller scale and short-term missions in the near future, in contrast to the scale and length of the operations such as ISAF and KFOR.[82] Indeed, these operations have drawn strongly on the financial and military reserves of the Alliance and they have only been met with limited success or possibly even failure, thereby 'dampen[ing the] enthusiasm [of NATO members] for undertaking comparatively ambitious and exhausting tasks in the future'.[83]

---

[78] Keynote address by NATO Secretary-General Jaap de Hoop Scheffer at the Youth Forum, 2 April 2009; Chicago Summit Declaration, supra note 50, para. 24.
[79] Ringsmose, Rynning, 'Introduction. Taking Stock of NATO's New Strategic Concept', supra note 38, 7, 8–9; NATO 2020, supra note 60, 20.
[80] Hyde-Price, 'NATO's Political Transformation and International Order', supra note 28, 45–46; Wittmann, 'An Alliance for the 21st Century', supra note 39, 31, 37. But see likewise M. Webber, 'Three Questions for the Strategic Concept', in J. Ringsmose, S. Rynning (eds.), *NATO's New Strategic Concept: A Comprehensive Assessment*, DIIS Report (2011), 99, 101; T. Legendre, 'Military Change – Discord or Harmony', in J. Ringsmose, S. Rynning (eds.), *NATO's New Strategic Concept: A Comprehensive Assessment*, DIIS Report (2011), 137.
[81] Interview with Jaap de Hoop Scheffer in The Hague, 18 April 2013.
[82] M. Madej, 'After the Chicago Summit – The Condition and Prospects for Development', in R. Czulda, R. Łoś (eds.), *NATO towards the Challenges of Contemporary World* (Warsaw, International Relations Research Institute, 2013), 39–45. Simultaneously, NATO will be more disposed to reach out to other international organisations if it decides to deploy military forces, ibid., 51.
[83] Ibid., 44.

In the organisation's latest Strategic Concept, NATO's focus is limited to abstract threats and lacks the political vision necessary to plan for its future.[84] It was suggested by Jaap de Hoop Scheffer, upon his leaving of office, that NATO should focus on 'the new agenda of human security'.[85] The 2010 Strategic Concept is also considered as a tool to re-engage NATO member states with the core principles of the organisation.[86]

Consequently, NATO appears to be currently at the crossroads and it is hard to predict its further development on the international and global security agenda. So, what are the legal implications of NATO's activities in the specific context of cooperation with other international organisations in peacekeeping operations?

In the peacekeeping context and in its relations with the AU and the UN, NATO generally keeps an autonomous role, acting on its own, although in its recent practice with a mandate of the SC or by responding solely to specific requests for support, e.g., by the AU. Even within a framework of cooperation such as KFOR, NATO tends to focus on its own operative role and is not seeking a leadership position. It is therefore not very likely that the activities of NATO in cooperation with the AU and the UN will amount to cases of joint responsibility under international law – at least not beyond a scenario of aid and assistance in terms of international responsibility. It appears more likely that cases of joint responsibility could arise for NATO on the basis of its partnership arrangements.

The EU: An Emerging Strong Actor Within the System of Collective Security?

> The enlarged European Union has the power and the capability to shape global order. During the last fifty years, we built a peaceful Europe based on freedom and solidarity. In the future, to guarantee and to reinforce such achievements, we need to influence and to shape the world around us ...

---

[84] Webber, 'Three Questions for the Strategic Concept', supra note 80, 99, 103. Other authors give a more optimistic assessment, for instance, Biscop, 'From Lisbon to Lisbon: Squaring the Circle of EU and NATO Future Roles', supra note 63, 106–107; K.-H. Kamp, 'The Alliance after Lisbon: Towards NATO 3.0?', in J. Ringsmose, S. Rynning (eds.), *NATO's New Strategic Concept: A Comprehensive Assessment*, DIIS Report (2011), 167.

[85] Speech by NATO Secretary-General Jaap de Hoop Scheffer in Bratislava, Slovakia, 17 July 2009; Webber, ibid., 99, 103–104.

[86] Kamp, 'The Alliance after Lisbon: Towards NATO 3.0?', supra note 84, 167.

We will not live in peace if we do not face the external threats to our security and the instability in the regions close to Europe.
– European Commission President José Manuel Barroso[87]

With the creation of a European military capacity, the question of the EU's possible contribution to UN-mandated peacekeeping and peace-making operations becomes more urgent than ever.
– Communication from the Commission to the Council and the European Parliament (2003)[88]

The European Union (EU) and the United Nations (UN) are natural partners. They are united by the core values laid out in the 1945 Charter of the United Nations.
– The partnership between the UN and the EU[89]

The Foundation of the EU and Its Normative and Political Framework

The Maastricht Treaty, which established the EU, replaced the European Political cooperation with the Common Foreign and Security Policy (CFSP) and paved the way for the development of a European defence policy within the EU.[90] The failure of the member states to agree upon a common stance and to prevent the massacres in the wars in Yugoslavia prompted a change in policy; they increased their activity through the EU in the area of the CFSP.[91]

---

[87] Cited in European Union, Delegation of the European Commission to the US, 'The EU and Peacekeeping: Promoting Security, Stability and Democratic Values' in EU FOCUS (2008), available at www.eurunion.org/News/eunewsletters/EUFocus/2008/EUFocus-Peacekeeping-Nov08.pdf.

[88] Communication from the Commission to the Council and the European Parliament, the European Union and the United Nations: The Choice of Multilateralism, COM (2003) 526 final, 2003, para. 1.1(c).

[89] United Nations, The Partnership between the UN and the EU, the United Nations and the European Commission Working Together in Development and Humanitarian Cooperation (2006), 6.

[90] The Treaty of Maastricht stipulated in Article B the aim of 'the implementation of a common foreign and security policy including *the eventual framing of a common defence policy, which might in time lead to a common defence*' (Maastricht, 7 February 1992). A very similar wording can be found equally in Article J.1(1). On the origins and very early evolution of the CSDP, cf. P. Koutrakos, *The EU Common Security and Defence Policy* (Oxford University Press, 2013), 5–21.

[91] Koutrakos, ibid., 15–16. The wars in the Balkans in the late 1980s and 1990s 'had shocked the system of European integration so profoundly as to create considerable momentum for

The objectives of the CFSP therefore contained, inter alia, 'the safeguard[ing of] the common values, fundamental interests and independence of the Union' as well as the 'strengthen[ing of] the security of the Union and its Member States in all ways'.[92] The Treaty of Amsterdam (1997) introduced further changes to the European security architecture. The framing of a European defence policy became a reality[93] In this treaty, the scope of common defence activities at the disposition of the EU is set out explicitly for the first time under Article 17 of the revised treaty in the form of the so-called *Petersberg tasks*: 'humanitarian and rescue tasks, peacekeeping tasks and tasks of combat forces in crisis management, including peacemaking'.[94]

The EU 'decided to develop a (C)ESDP that should enable it to carry out the Petersberg tasks, either with or without recourse to NATO assets'.[95] The crisis management functions of the WEU were accordingly fully absorbed in the EU in 1999.[96] Similar to the intended arrangements under Article 43 of the UN Charter, the ESDP provides for availability of national military and police forces to the EU so that the latter may carry out 'crisis management' and military actions.

With regard to cooperation with the UN in peacekeeping operations, the 2003 Communication from the Commission to the Council and the European Parliament held that '[g]iven that EU actions in this area will invariably be consistent with, and in many cases complementary to, decisions and frameworks developed by the UN, the need for effective complementarity with the UN is also crucial'.[97]

---

a more active EU in the area of foreign and security policy', ibid., 84; see also, J.-P. Schütze, *Die Zurechenbarkeit von Völkerrechtsverstößen im Rahmen mandatierter Friedensmissionen der Vereinten Nationen* (Berlin, Duncker & Humblot, 2010), 62.

[92] Article J.1(2) TEU (Maastricht).

[93] Cf. Article 17(1) (on the basis of the new numbering, previous article J.7) of the Treaty of Amsterdam, Amending the Treaty on European Union, the Treaties Establishing the European Communities and Certain Related Acts, 2 October 1997.

[94] Article 17(2) of the Treaty of Amsterdam.

[95] The Petersberg Tasks were later complemented in the Treaty of Lisbon (Article 42 TEU) with joint disarmament operations, military advice and assistance tasks as well as post-conflict stabilisation tasks. Peacekeeping operations now include conflict prevention, Naert, *International Law Aspects,* supra note 41, 47.

[96] Council Decision 1999/404/CFSP (1999).

[97] Communication from the Commission to the Council and the European Parliament, the European Union and the United Nations: The Choice of Multilateralism, COM (2003) 526 final, 2003, para. 2.2. See also Articles 21(2) (c), 30(1)(2) of the Treaty on European Union.

Interpreting the Legal Framework of the EU in the Area of the CFSP/CSDP

The legal framework, as amended by the Treaty of Lisbon, regarding the Common Foreign and Security Policy is very short and vague in parts, and, as a result, intrinsically prone to problems of interpretation, which is only heightened by the absence of authoritative interpretation through case law.[98] Article 24(1) provides that

> [t]he Union's competence in matters of common foreign and security policy shall cover all areas of foreign policy and all questions relating to the Union's security, including the progressive framing of a common defence policy that might lead to a common defence.

Whereas, the 'area of foreign policy' is not defined further in the treaty, matters relating to the Union's security are covered in the 'Provisions on the Common Security and Defence Policy' (CSDP)[99] of which Article 42 provides the legal base for EU peacekeeping operations. The following Article 43.1 adds further qualifications:

> The tasks referred to in Article 42(1), in the course of which the Union may use civilian and military means, shall include joint disarmament operations, ... conflict prevention and peace-keeping tasks, tasks of combat forces in crisis management, including peace-making and post-conflict stabilisation.

As such, it appears that, whereas the CSDP objectives are rather precise, the specific CFSP objectives as they existed in the EU treaties *ante*-Lisbon have been replaced by a set of overall objectives for the wide area of EU external action.[100] Moreover, the distribution of competences in the area of CFSP is not clear.[101] Article 2(4) TFEU stipulates simply that the 'Union shall have competence, in accordance with the provisions of the Treaty on

---

[98] The CFSP is expressly excluded from the jurisdiction of the Court of Justice pursuant to Article 24(1) subparagraph 2 TEU and Article 275 TFEU; see also P. Eeckhout, 'The EU Common Foreign and Security Policy after Lisbon: From Pillar Talk to Constitutionalism', in A. Biondi, P. Eeckhout, S. Ripley (eds.), *EU Law after Lisbon* (Oxford University Press, 2012), 265–268; Koutrakos, *The EU Common Security*, supra note 90, 27.

[99] CSDP replaced ESDP as a term.

[100] Article 21(2) TFEU; Eeckhout, 'The EU Common Foreign and Security Policy', supra note 98, 265–267. Furthermore the wording of Article 43(1) 'shall include' underlines that it is a non-exhaustive list, Koutrakos, *The EU Common Security*, supra note 90, 59.

[101] As Craig asserts, the CFSP does not fit really in any of the categories of competences existing under EU law, P. Craig, *The Lisbon Treaty. Law, Politics, and Treaty Reform* (Oxford University Press, 2010), 182.

European Union, to define and implement a common foreign and security policy, including the progressive framing of a common defence policy'. In contrast, the preceding paragraphs of the very same article provide for either shared or exclusive competences. Prior to the Lisbon Treaty, it was never disputed that the CFSP does not fall under the exclusive competence of the EU, but that it is rather in the domain of shared/concurrent competences and these latter concepts were invoked while referring to it.[102] Therefore the silence of the treaties on this particular issue attracts attention. It is suggested that any such characterisation might have had a 'pre-emptive effect'; being seen as falling under the area of 'shared/concurrent competences and thereby trigger action (by member states) accordingly'.[103] A better explanation might be the attempt to safeguard a margin of appreciation not only for member states but also for the EU per se, which has now emerged as even more of an independent legal actor.[104]

According to a similar argument advanced in legal writing the broad wording of these dispositions reflects the 'more ambitious' nature of the CSDP, but it simultaneously acknowledges the central role of member states which 'may draw [on] the policy they want the Union to carry out'.[105] However, there are indeed indications that the CFSP includes elements which hint to an exclusive competence of the EU. One example is the exclusion of the possibility to adopt legislative acts within the scope of the CFSP on the basis of Article 24(1) TEU[106] and the rather

---

[102] Eeckhout, 'The EU Common Foreign and Security Policy', supra note 98, 265, 268; R. G. Bono, 'Some Reflections on the CFSP Legal Order', *Common Market Law Review*, 43 (2006), 337, especially 357–362. Cf. also L. Boisson de Chazournes, 'L'Union européenne en quête d'une politique étrangère et de sécurité commune', in *L'intégration européenne au XXIe siècle, en hommage à Jacques Bourrinet* (Aix-en-Provence, La documentation française, 2004), 237, 245.

[103] Eeckhout, 'The EU Common Foreign and Security Policy', supra note 98, 265, 268; Koutrakos, *The EU Common Security*, supra note 90, 27.

[104] Also because of the clarification about its legal status under international law as an international organisation.

[105] Koutrakos, *The EU Common Security*, supra note 90, 60–61.

[106] The 41st Declaration attached to the Lisbon Treaty prohibits the adoption of legislative acts in the area of CFSP, Declaration on Article 352 of the Treaty on the Functioning of the European Union. The Treaty of Lisbon does not contain the distinction between legislative and non-legislative acts as it was foreseen in the Constitution for Europe, but it retains the distinction between ordinary and special legislative procedures for the adoption of legal acts by the EU all of which involve the participation of the Parliament and the Council, cf. Eeckhout, 'The EU Common Foreign and Security Policy', supra note 98, 265, 279–280. The German Constitutional Court similarly confirmed that the CFSP will not fall under supranational law, 'Lissabon-Urteil', BVerfG, 2 BvE 2/08 vom 30.6.2009, paras. 342, 390.

autonomous administrative structure and development of working methods.¹⁰⁷

Overall, it seems that the regulation of the CFSP and the CSDP within the Treaty of Lisbon was a 'face-saving' compromise to guarantee the autonomy and influence in this area of member states and the EU alike. From a legal point of view, however, it leaves unanswered the question of who is responsible in cases of violations of international law by activities undertaken in this particular field – at least from the internal EU point of view.

The Relevant Organs and the Implementation of the CFSP

This part introduces the relevant organs and the procedures to implement the CFSP of the EU. Concerning the activation and execution of the CFSP according to the EU treaties, the Council is responsible for adopting decisions relating to the task referred to in Article 42(1), and for defining their objectives and scope and the general conditions for their implementation (Article 43.2). The decision-making process is based on unanimity, which increases the challenge to agree upon the deployment of an operation as the twenty-eight Ministers of Foreign Affairs all have to agree.¹⁰⁸ The High Representative of the Union for Foreign Affairs and Security Policy, acting under the authority of the Council and in close and constant contact with the Political and Security Committee (PSC), shall ensure coordination of the civilian and military aspects of such tasks, whereas the PSC exercises the political and strategic direction of the crisis management operations under the responsibility of the Council and of the High Representative.¹⁰⁹

The established chain of command is similar to the one used in UN operations. An appointed EU special representative carries out his

---

[107] Koutrakos, *The EU Common Security*, supra note 90, 64–67. See also especially D. Thym, 'The Intergovernmental Constitution of the EU's Foreign, Security & Defence Executive', *European Constitutional Law Review*, 7 (2011), 453, 460–467.

[108] This can be problematic as the EU's inherent weakness resides in the difficulty of its members to agree upon a common position in the field of foreign and security policy; see M. Derblom, E. Hagström Frisell, J. Schmidt, 'UN–EU–AU Cooperation in Peace Operations in Africa', FOI, Swedish Defence Research Agency (2008), 18.

[109] Article 38 Treaty on the EU. See also Council of the European Union, 'EU Concept for Military Command and Control, Brussels', 24 September 2012, 15–16, para. 16; N. Tsagourias, 'EU Peacekeeping Operations: Legal and Theoretical Issues', in M. Trybus, N. D. White (eds.), *European Security Law* (Oxford University Press, 2007), 102, 114; Koutrakos, *The EU Common Security*, supra note 90, 64; Thym, 'The Intergovernmental Constitution', supra note 107, 453, 465.

mandate under the authority of the High Representative whereas the actual military control of the operation rests with the EU Operation and the EU Force Commanders.[110] In that regard, the decision of the military headquarters is *taken* ad hoc, made among the choice of five locations in five different member states,[111] whereby the state whose headquarters are chosen will act as the framework state for the implementation of the mission.[112] In March 2012, the EU decided to activate for the first time the EU Operations Centre in Brussels which can – by its mandate – act as the headquarters in the case of joint military and civil operations.[113]

The provision of troops to EU military operations resumes the flexible framework for the implementation of the CFSP under the TEU. Generally speaking, member states are obliged under Article 42(1) and (3) to provide military and civilian capabilities for the performance of these tasks.[114] But the EU and the member states have discretion regarding the provision of troops to these operations as the Council under Article 44.1 can also entrust the implementation of a peacekeeping operation to a group of willing and capable member states.[115]

The EU's Security Policy: A Global Actor or Rather a Great Dream?

In 2003, the EU adopted a European Security Strategy. The document clarified that the EU perceives itself as a global actor and even obligated it to act in such a role; thus, it pledges that 'Europe should be ready to share in the responsibility for global security and in building a better world'.[116] This pledge was implemented in practice in the very same year by the deployment of the first peacekeeping operation of the EU in Macedonia. Since then the capabilities of the EU to launch military and civilian crisis management operations have been strengthened extensively.

---

[110] EU Concept, ibid., 9, para. 9(b); Tsagourias, ibid., 102, 114.
[111] The UK, Italy, France, Germany and Greece.
[112] Koutrakos, *The EU Common Security*, supra note 90, 101–102.
[113] Council Decision2012/173/CFSP (2012); Council Decision2008/298/CFSP (2008), 4.
[114] The scope of this disposition also remains vague, Koutrakos, *The EU Common Security*, supra note 90, 63.
[115] Article 44.1 Treaty on European Union. This article therefore corresponds to Article 48(1) of the UN Charter, which authorises the SC to determine a group of states to carry out its decisions for the maintenance of international peace and security. See also, Preparing the December 2013 European Council on Security and Defence, Final Report by the High Representative/Head of the EDA on the Common Security and Defence Policy, Brussels, 15 October 2013, 12.
[116] 'A Secure Europe in a Better World', European Security Strategy (2003).

The Brussels European Council 2008 Presidency Conclusions contain the intent of the EU to augment its capabilities to a level where the EU can deploy 60,000 troops in sixty days for a major operation, as well as to enable the organisation to conduct several operations simultaneously.[117] These pledges sound impressive, but they are, in reality, a reiteration of the policy formulated nine years beforehand. In 1999, the Helsinki Headline Goal envisaged that these troops be operational by the end of 2003.[118] In 2004, however, the deadline was extended to 2010, but was once again not met.[119] In fact, as recently as 2012, the EU was unable to deploy two battlegroups simultaneously and, as a result, not a single battlegroup was deployed.[120] The future of EU battlegroups is generally unclear, as is the political will to deploy them. Whereas Germany proposed to allow the deployment of at least one of the two standing EU battlegroups for other purposes, such as training foreign militaries, other countries prefer the expansion of EU battlegroups and the EEAS proposed even an additional navy and air force component.[121] A month before the European Defence Council of December 2013, the Council of the EU underlined that the 'need for concrete improvements in EU military rapid response capabilities, including

---

[117] Declaration by the European Council on the Enhancement of The European Security and Defence Policy (ESDP), Doc. 17271/1/08 REV 1 (2008), 16, para. 3 and fn. 1.

[118] European Council Meeting, Helsinki Headline Goal, Helsinki, Finland, December 1999. See also A. Roberts, 'Proposals for UN Standing Forces: A Critical History', in V. Lowe, A. Roberts, J. Welsh et al. (eds.), *The United Nations Security Council and War* (Oxford University Press, 2008), 99, 123. The failure to generate the necessary capacities by the end of 2003 led the EU to lower its ambitions and to adopt the EU Battlegroup Concept whereby a Battlegroup will consist of approximately 1,500 personnel, Directorate-General for External Policies of the Union, Directorate B – Policy Department; EU Battlegroups, 12 September 2006, 4–5; EU Council Secretariat ~Factsheet, EU Battlegroups, February 2007, 1–2. See likewise R. Hamelink, 'The Battlegroups Concept: Giving the EU a Concrete "military face"', *Defence and Security* (Winter 2005), 8; M. Hatzigeorgopoulos, 'The Role of EU Battlegroups in European Defence', *European Security Review*, 56 (2012), 1, 2.

[119] Headline Goal 2010 approved by General Affairs and External Relations Council on 17 May 2004, endorsed by the European Council of 17 and 18 June 2004, 1, para. 2

[120] Koutrakos, *The EU Common Security*, supra note 90, 104; M. Norheim-Martinsen, 'Our Work Here Is Done: European Union Peacekeeping in Africa', *African Security Review*, 20 (2011), 17, 20; G. Faleg, A. Giovannini, 'The EU between Pooling & Sharing and Smart Defence. Making a Virtue of Necessity?', *CEPS Special Report* (2012), 3; R. H. Ginsberg, S. Penska, *The European Union in Global Security* (London, Palgrave Macmillan, 2012), 27–28.

[121] C. Hasselbach, 'Military. Debate Surrounds Future of EU Battle Groups', DW, 1 June 2013, available at www.dw.de/debate-surrounds-future-of-eu-battle-groups/a-16852649. See also A. Novosseloff, 'Options for Improving UN-EU Cooperation in the Field of Peacekeeping', in J. Krause, N. Ronzitti (eds.), *The EU, the UN and Collective Security. Making Multilateralism Effective* (London, Routledge, 2012), 150, 154.

the EU Battlegroups' which includes the enhancement of their operational deployability and usability.[122]

In a similar way to NATO, the EU entertains various partnership programmes with other states and regions, e.g., the European Neighbourhood Policy or the Black Sea Synergy within the Union's neighbourhood framework.[123] In 2008, the European Council also issued the Report on the Implementation of the European Security Strategy which – going beyond its title – updated and adapted the main strands of the European Security Strategy.[124] It is suggested that a new security strategy was planned but political pressure by the governments of Germany and the UK prevented it from coming to fruition.[125]

The advantages of the EU are that its broad structure and competences allow it to respond to a multitude of threats and challenges, which require political, economic, judicial, military, etc., responses.[126] Given this flexibility, the EU has been able to carry out thirty-three civilian and military operations since 2003, which nearly amounts to one third of all UN peacekeeping operations since 1945. It proves de novo that the EU will increasingly play a more important role in the field of the maintenance of international peace and security.

The EU and the UN: Submission, Self-reliance and an Emerging Division of Labour

> The UN stands at the apex of the international system. The long standing and unique co-operation between the EU and the United Nations spans many areas, and is particularly vital when it comes to crisis management. At the operational level, cooperation with the UN is dense and fruitful.
>
> – High Representative of the Union for Foreign Affairs and Security Policy, October 2013[127]

---

[122] Council conclusions on Common Security and Defence Policy, Brussels 25–26 November 2013, 5, para. 12(b).

[123] European Council 11 and 12 December 2008 Presidency Conclusions, Doc. 17271/1/08 REV 1 (2008), 11, para. 29.

[124] Report on the Implementation of the European Security Strategy, Doc. S407/08 (2008), 9–12. For the external dimension of security, cf. Communication from the Commission to the European Parliament and the Council, The EU Internal Security Strategy in Action: Five steps towards a more secure Europe (2010).

[125] A. Toje, *The European Union as a Small Power. After the Post-Cold War* (London, Palgrave Macmillan, 2010), 79–80.

[126] 'A Secure Europe', supra note 116, 7. Cf. also 'Preparing the December 2013 European Council', supra note 115, 4, para. II Cluster 1. 1.

[127] Ibid., 5.

> The United Nations and the European Union increasingly work side-by-side on the ground in peacekeeping and civilian crisis-management operations, and through preventive diplomacy.
>
> – Secretary-General Ban Ki-moon, February 2014[128]

The foundations for the institutionalised relations between the EU and UN were first laid down at the European Council of Nice in 2000 and the 2001 Gothenburg Summit.[129] In 2003, the EU and the UN issued the Joint Declaration on EU–UN Cooperation in Crisis Management. Part of this declaration was the establishment of the UN–EU Steering Committee[130] with the mandate to 'examine ways and means to enhance mutual co-ordination and compatibility' in the areas of planning, training, communication and best practices framework for cooperation.[131] The EU, thereby, clearly recognises, that 'the United Nations has the primary responsibility for the maintenance of international peace and security'[132] but it also asserts its willingness to bear its burden, acknowledging that 'Europe should be ready to share in the responsibility for global security'.[133] The EU, as a result, sees its role not only as a partner, but also as an auxiliary organisation for the UN to carry out its mandate effectively.[134] The Security Strategy thus introduced the notion of 'effective multilateralism'

---

[128] UN Doc. S/PV.7112 (2014), 2.
[129] A. Novosseloff, 'United Nations–European Union Cooperation in the Field of Peacekeeping: Challenges and Projects', GGI Analysis Paper No. 4/2012, 8; Council Conclusions 9398/01 (2001); 'Presidency Report to the Götebourg European Council on European Security and Defence Policy', Annex (2001), para. 4; UN Doc. A/65/762 (2011), 18–19, paras. 55–58; cf. also S/PV.6306 (2010); S/PV.6477 (2011).
[130] For more information see, 'EU Presidency Report on ESDP', approved by the European Council, Brussels, 16 December 2005, para. 60; UN Doc. A/60/640/Add.1 (2005), 6, para. 9; Novosseloff, ibid., 15–16; G. De Baere, E. Passivirta, 'Identity and Difference: The EU and the UN as Part of Each Other', in H. de Waele, J.-J. Kuipers (eds.), *The European Union's Emerging International Identity. Views from the Global Arena* (Leiden, Brill, 2013), 21, 28. For a critical view with regard to the Steering Committee, see, Ginsberg, Penska, *The Europea Union*, supra note 120, 167.
[131] 'Joint Declaration on UN–EU Cooperation in Crisis Management' (2003), para. 3; EU–UN Cooperation in Military Crisis Management Operations, Elements of Implementation of the EU–UN Joint Declaration (2004), 2, para. 2. See also United Nations, Department of Peacekeeping Operations, Department of Field Support, United Nations Peacekeeping Operations, Principles and Guidelines (2008), 86; A Secure Europe, supra note 116, 11.
[132] 'A Secure Europe', supra note 116, 9; Joint Declaration on UN–EU Cooperation, ibid., para. 1; Joint Statement on UN–EU cooperation in Crisis Management (2007), para. 1; 'Report on the Implementation', supra note 124, 2.
[133] 'A Secure Europe', supra note 116, 1.
[134] 'Strengthening the United Nations, Equipping It to Fulfil Its Responsibilities and to Act Effectively, Is a European Priority', A Secure Europe, ibid., 9.

which was featured equally in the 2008 *Report on the Implementation of the Security Strategy*.[135]

The Lisbon Treaty followed in the footsteps of this careful balancing act of the EU.[136] On the one hand, the EU is committed to the concept of responsibility within the international security system established under the UN Charter; on the other hand, the EU is committed to effective multilateralism which is perceived as one of the pillars of the EU's international perception and of the understanding of its role in the world.[137] References to the UN and its Charter feature prominently throughout the Treaty of Lisbon[138] prompting some authors to speak of a 'constitutional attitude [of the EU] towards the UN system, rather than an instrumental attitude grounded in traditional foreign policy objectives'.[139] However, the simultaneously existing 'autonomy streak' diversifies the picture.

It is argued by Griep that the quest for autonomy is due to the institutional history of the EU. As an organisation *sui generis*, the EU is a mosaic of competences on the international level.[140] More and more competences of the member states on the internal and external sphere have been transferred to the organisation as otherwise the member states could have damaged the internal process of integration by contracting individually with third states or international organisations.[141] Whereas the European Community and the EU used to act independently, within their respective competences, as entities of distinct legal personality, the Treaty of Lisbon created an entity which has – in comparison to an individual member state – competences in a variety of areas, but on a larger scale.[142]

---

[135] P. Koutrakos, 'The European Union in the Global Security Architecture', in B. Van Vooren, S. Blockmans, J. Wouters (eds.), *The EU's Role in Global Governance: The Legal Dimension* (Oxford University Press, 2013), 81, 82; Report on the Implementation, supra note 124, 2. The emphasis on 'multilateralism' was also an EU response to US 'unilateralism' under the first Bush administration, C. Mace, 'Making Multilateralism Matter: The EU Security Strategy', *European Security Review*, 18 (2003), 1, 2.

[136] See, for instance, TEU, Preamble, 11th Recital, Article 3(5) TEU and Article 21(2)(h) TEU.

[137] Remarks by High Representative Catherine Ashton at United Nations Security Council: Cooperation between the UN and Regional and Sub-regional Organizations, New York, 13 February 2013, 1.

[138] In addition to Article 21, references to the UN Charter are also contained in Article 42(1) and (7) TEU, in the Seventh Recital of the Preamble of the TFEU, Article 208(2) TFEU, Article 214(7) TFEU and Article 220(1) TFEU.

[139] De Baere, Passivirta, 'Identity and Difference', supra note 131, 21, 23.

[140] Griep, *Regionale Organisationen*, supra note 57, 382.

[141] L. Boisson de Chazournes, *Les relations entre organisations régionales et organisations universelles*, Recueil des cours de l'Académie de La Haye, Volume 347 (2010), 79, 184.

[142] Ibid., 79, 185.

Likewise, the EU has refused to submit itself – at least formally – to Chapter VIII of the UN Charter.[143] At the start of the cooperation between the EU and the UN, a number of resolutions referred to Chapter VIII,[144] but now authorisations given to the EU are usually based on Chapter VII.[145] However, one has to interpret this fact with caution as the general mandating practice of the SC for peacekeeping operations in cooperation with regional organisations has moved towards Chapter VII. The EU could, arguably be considered as falling under Chapter VIII of the Charter as a successor to the WEU which was considered to be a regional organisation within the meaning of Chapter VIII.[146] Under Declaration 13 annexed to the Treaty of Lisbon the EU per se, and its member states remain bound by the provisions of the Charter of the UN, including the primary responsibility of the SC for the maintenance of International Peace and Security.[147]

The balanced position of the EU in the perception of its role to maintain international peace and security and in its relations with the UN can be also found in its practice – specifically, in its crisis management operations. In 2004, the EU adopted the 'Elements of Implementation of the EU–UN Joint Declaration' which provides two options for EU–UN cooperation in peacekeeping operations.[148] As the decision to provide military contingents rests with the national states, these could assign forces to UN operations whereby the EU might act as a 'clearing house'

---

[143] Koutrakos, 'The European Union', supra note 135, 81, 83.
[144] UN Doc. S/RES/713 (1991), preamble and para. 1; UN Doc. S/RES/727 (1992), Preamble and para. 5.
[145] UN Doc. S/RES/1671 (2006), 1–2, Preamble; 2, paras. 2–3; 3–4, paras. 6–11; 3, para. 15; S/RES/1778 (2007), 4–5, paras. 6–12.
[146] W. Hummer, M. Schweitzer, 'Chapter VIII: Regional Arrangements. Article 52', in B. Simma (ed.), *The Charter of the United Nations. A Commentary* (Oxford University Press, 2002), 807, 836. Cf. Statement of the President of the Security Council, UN Doc. S/25184 (1993), 3; S/RES/727 (1992), Preamble; S/RES/743 (1992).
[147] Declaration concerning the common foreign and security policy, Declarations annexed to the Final Act of the Intergovernmental Conference which adopted the Treaty of Lisbon, signed on 13 December 2007, 30.3.2010, Official Journal of the European Union, C 83/343, 9.
[148] Also for a list and description of the guiding principles for cooperation, see Actions to enhance EU CSDP support to UN peacekeeping, Brussels, 24 November 2011, 3–4; J. Wouters, 'The United Nations, the EU and Conflict Prevention: Interconnecting the Global and Regional Levels', in V. Kronenberger, J. Wouters (eds.), *The European Union and Conflict Prevention. Policy and Legal Issues* (Heidelberg, Springer, 2004), 369, 388. See generally C. Törő, 'The Practice and Patterns of EU Military Operations in Concert with the United Nations', *Journal of Conflict & Security Law*, 20 (2015), 1–27.

mechanism.¹⁴⁹ The other option is the launching and conducting of an EU operation in support of the UN, under the political control and strategic direction of the EU, and authorised by a SC Resolution.¹⁵⁰ In this context, it is argued that 'there is no legal or political undertaking that the EU will defer to the UN organs. On the contrary, one may trace an independent and assertive streak in EU relations with the UN'.¹⁵¹ There are

> more cogent and political reasons ... subordination to the UN will weaken such control [over EU operations] but also undermine the Union's aim of visibility in security and defence. Secondly, when NATO resources are used, the EU will be even more cautious in submitting to UN control, considering the fact that NATO has resisted such control. Thus, the subcontracting model appears to be the only viable option because it offers flexibility and independence.¹⁵²

In this context, one needs to remember the financial weight of the EU in the UN, providing the largest share of the UN peacekeeping budget (ca. 39 per cent in 2003) and more than half of the world's development assistance (56.9 per cent in 2002).¹⁵³ Thus, it may not be surprising that the UN, in need of external partners, does not hesitate from satisfying the EU in order to ensure their support. In 2008, following the failure of a political settlement on the Kosovo question, doubts arose regarding the legitimacy of the EU's Rule of Law mission. It was suggested that it lacked an express authorisation from the SC.¹⁵⁴ The reaction of the UN was to welcome the mission in two reports.¹⁵⁵

---

[149] EU–UN Cooperation in Military Crisis Management Operations, supra note 131, 2–3 paras. 3–6; Actions to Enhance EU CSDP Support, ibid., 4–6.
[150] EU–UN Cooperation in Military Crisis Management Operations, ibid.; H. Krieger, 'Common European Defence: Competence or Compatibility with NATO', in M. Trybus, N. D. White (eds.), *European Security Law* (Oxford University Press, 2007), 174, 186; C. Major, 'EU–UN Cooperation in Military Crisis Management: The Experience of EUFOR RD Congo in 2006', Occasional Paper, no. 72, September 2008, EUISS, 11; M. Brosig, D. Motsama, 'Modeling Cooperative Peacekeeping. Exchange Theory and the African Peace and Security Regime', *Journal of International Peacekeeping*, 18 (2014), 45, 59–60.
[151] Tsagourias, 'EU Peacekeeping Operations', supra note 109, 102, 129.
[152] Tsagourias, ibid., 102, 129; M. Mubiala, 'Cooperation between the United Nations, The European Union and the African Union for Peace and Security in Africa', *Studia Diplomatica. The Brussels Journal of International Relations*, LX (2007), 111, 116.
[153] European Union, 'The Enlarging European Union at the United Nations: Making Multilateralism Matter' (2004), 5, 7, 28.
[154] Koutrakos, 'The European Union in the Global Security Architecture', supra note 135, 81, 84.
[155] Council Joint Action 2008/124/CFSP (2008); UN Doc. S/2008/211 (2008), 2, para. 5; S/2008/354 (2008), particular 2, para. 8; 3–4, para. 13.

An EU operation in support of the UN includes two further scenarios calling for special attention: rapid response operations in the form of either a 'bridging model' or a 'stand by model'.[156] The bridging model aims at buying time for the UN to mount a new operation or to reorganise an existing one, e.g., Operation Artemis.[157]

The EU and Peacekeeping

When the UN approached the EU to support MONUC during the election process in 2006, the EU did not only insist on political control and strategic direction by the EU, but also requested autonomy to decide upon the use of force.[158] This shift towards more autonomy by the EU is partly based on the expanding autonomous military capabilities of the EU as well as the wish – being the biggest financial contributor for peacekeeping operations – to effectively be involved in shaping the peacekeeping agenda on a global level.[159] The model of sub-contracting was first used outside of Europe in Operation Artemis in the DRC. The departure of Ugandan troops in the North-eastern Province Ituri and the capital led to a void in political power with subsequent violent clashes between Hema and Lendu ethnic groups. Deteriorating human security, a flow of refugees and the inability of UN peacekeepers to stop the violence led to the SC endorsing an additional EU-led intervention. About 1800 troops were deployed in the DRC.

Based on SC Resolution 1484, Operation Artemis was deployed in close coordination with MONUC in anticipation of a strengthened UN military deployment which arrived on 1 September 2003. Several European leaders stressed that the operation constituted the litmus test for the European Security and Defense Policy. It not only proved the military capacities and strength of the EU, but also constituted evidence of emancipation from NATO: 'The EU has a genuine military operational capacity at its disposal.'[160]

---

[156] EU–UN Cooperation in Military Crisis Management Operations, supra note 149, 3–5, paras. 8–14. Statement on behalf of the EU, UN Doc. S/PV.7015 (Resumption 1) (2013), 17–18.

[157] Ibid., 4, para. 9.

[158] UN Doc. S/2006/219 (2006), 4, paras. 1–2; Actions to Enhance EU CSDP Support, supra note 148, 7. Cf. also for a more comprehensive overview of the relations between the EU and the UN, UN Doc. S/PV.6306 (2010), 3; S/PV.6477 (2011); B. Charbonneau, 'What Is So Special about the European Union? EU–UN Cooperation in Crisis Management in Africa', International Peacekeeping, 16 (2009), 546, 549–550.

[159] Major, supra note 150, 13.

[160] Statement by the French defence minister Michèle Alliot-Marie as quoted in R. C. Hendrickson, J. R. Strand, K. L. Raney, 'Operation Artemis and Javier Solana: EU Prospects

However, this appraisal has to be qualified. Indeed, the operation achieved its objectives with only minor casualties, but practical problems persisted throughout the implementation of the operation; the troops had to deal with obsolete equipment, a lack of common communication channels as well as the lack of strategic transport.[161] These problems were not inimitable for Operation Artemis, but also appeared in Operation EUFOR Tchad/RCA, when the EU had to rely on external contributions for strategic airlift by Russia.[162]

In the context of Operation *Artemis*, the EU member states adopted the EU action plan to enhance the Common Security and Defence Policy support for UN peacekeeping activities.[163] The UN, in return, emphasised in the *New Horizon* Agenda, that for any new mission to be deployed in complex situations, it will take into account the capacities of regional actors for supporting action to 'expedite mission deployment, including political measures as well as strategic lift and other operational support'.[164] The UN welcomed the development of EU's peace facility for Africa and encouraged the development of further mechanisms to support the AU.[165] Therefore, it appears that there is a mutual interest for both organisations to cooperate, as well as to increase their cooperation. It is a 'mutually reinforcing link', in

---

for a Stronger Common Foreign and Security Policy', *Canadian Military Review/Revue militaire canadienne*, 8 (2007), 35, 40. See also K. Homan, 'Operation Artemis in the Democratic Republic of Congo', in A. Ricci, E. Kytoèmaa, European Commission (eds.), *Faster and More United? The Debate about Europe's Crisis Response Capacity* (2007), 151, 153; generally S. Duke, 'Consensus Building in ESDP: The Lessons of Operation *Artemis*', *International Politics*, 46 (2009), 395, 397–402.

[161] Koutrakos, *The EU Common Security*, supra note 90, 110; A. Menon, 'Empowering Paradise? The ESDP at Ten', *International Affairs*, 85 (2009), 227, 234.

[162] D. Helly, 'The EU Military Operation in the Republic of Chad and the Central African Republic (Operation EUFOR Tchad/RCA)', in G. Grevi, D. Helly, D. Keohane (eds.), *European Security and Defence Policy. The First 10 Years (1999–2009)* (Paris, European Union International Security Institute, 2009), 339, 349. The number of troops deployed in EUFOR Tchad/RCA also never reached the number originally envisaged, prompting the Operations Commander to comment that 'for a while we were a mission without means', M. Merlingen, *EU Security Policy. What It Is, How It Works, Why It Matters* (Boulder, Lynne Rienner Publishers, 2012), 165.

[163] This document is not available to the public. However, in 2011, the document entitled *Actions to Enhance EU CSDP Support to UN peacekeeping*, Brussels, 24 November 2011, was adopted and in 2012 the *Plan of Action to Enhance EU CSDP Support to UN Peacekeeping*, EEAS 01024/12, Brussels, 13 June 2012.

[164] Department of Peacekeeping Operations and Department of Field Support, 'A New Partnership Agenda. Charting a New Horizon for UN Peacekeeping' (2009), 9. The same applies even more so in cases when UN operations are deploying alongside or in parallel with regional organisations, ibid., 34.

[165] UN Doc. A/58/19 (2004), 13, para. 75; A/59/591 (2004), 4, paras. 14–15.

that the EU can offer both the financial and military support not provided by the UN and thereby 'achieve its ambition to become a central security player'.[166] In exchange, the UN can provide political and legal legitimacy and endorsement of EU operations.[167] In summary, an alternative view to EU–UN relations, is one of 'an affair of transatlantic cooperation' with both the UK and France as the driving forces within the EU and the UN.[168]

A Limited Military Engagement on the African Continent – Or an Emerging Division of Labour?

Following the adoption of the Lisbon Treaty, however, speculations arose whether the aims of the EU might have been too ambitious and if a certain re-evaluation of its active role was necessary. The EU has only launched two training missions since 2007, namely EUTM Somalia, training 2,000 Somali soldiers[169] and EUTM Mali.[170] In January 2014, the EU decided to deploy a small-scale peacekeeping operation in the Central African Republic for a period of up to six months.[171] Plans were established for an EU military operation in support of humanitarian assistance operations in Libya, but the plan was ultimately not implemented.[172] Disagreement within the EU, including the abstention of Germany in the SC might explain why several EU states participated in the airstrikes against Libya outside of the EU framework.[173] Criticism also arose over the EU's passive role in the Arab Spring and its long tolerance of autocratic regimes. Several reasons have been given to explain the passivity of the EU. First of all, it is argued that there was a certain lack of leadership at the top of the CFSP,[174] and second was the focus of member states on the financial crisis, which

---

[166] Koutrakos, 'The European Union', supra note 135, 81, 85. See also UN Doc. S/PRST/2014/4 (2014).
[167] Major, 'EU–UN Cooperation', supra note 150, 9.
[168] Charbonneau, 'What Is So Special', supra note 158, 546, 551–552.
[169] Council Decision 2010/96/CFSP (2010).
[170] Council Decision 2013/34/CFSP (2013); Council Decision 2013/87/CFSP (2013).
[171] Council conclusions 6249/14 (2014); UN Doc. S/RES/2134 (2014), 11, paras. 43–50.
[172] Council Decision 2011/210/CFSP (2011); Council Decision 2011/764/CFSP (2011); Council conclusions on Common and Defence Policy 17720/11 (2011), 2, para. 12.
[173] Koutrakos, 'The European Union in the Global Security Architecture', supra note 135, 81, 85.
[174] Speech of High Representative Catherine Aston on main aspects and basic choices of the Common Foreign and Security Policy and the Common Security and Defence Policy, Brussels, 11 May 2011, A 179/11, p. 3. See also Koutrakos, *The EU Common Security*, supra note 90, 47.

has affected their willingness and capacity to contribute to the implementation of the CFSP.[175]

However, like the UN, and other international organisations, the EU depends on its members for the fulfilment of its mandate, and disagreement among the latter hampers the effective implementation of the EU's mandate.[176] There might also be a preference in some countries to pay for the maintenance of global peace and security rather than to deploy their own troops because of various domestic issues, including pressure by the electorate or the opposition.[177] Syria is another example of the failure of member states to agree upon a common position. Most certainly the principle of unanimity in the Council is not beneficial for the implementation of an effective CFSP and a CSDP. On the macro level, however, one has also to notice the absence of any longer-term reflection on the grand strategy of the CFSP following the entry into force of the Treaty of Lisbon.[178] The 2013 December Defence Council, the first thematic debate on defence since the entry into force of the Lisbon Treaty, also left many of the difficult questions open. These questions include, for example, the funding of CSDP activities or the future of the EU Battlegroups.[179] The Defence Council followed an extensive report by High Representative Ashton which provided more substantial propositions, but nonetheless failed in defining a long-term strategy for the development of the CSDP.[180] Two authors also suggest that the range and number of military operations by the EU has decreased in the past years and will not change in the near future.[181]

---

[175] Koutrakos, ibid., 81, 86. See also Council conclusions 17720/11 (2011), 1, para. 2; 3, para. 18; European Council Conclusions EUCO 205/12 (2012), 10, para. 22.
[176] Cf. Koutrakos, ibid., 81, 88.
[177] B. Franke, R. Esmenjaud, 'Who Owns African Ownership? The Africanisation of Security and Its Limits', *South African Journal of International Affairs*, 15 (2008), 137, 150; E. G. Berman, K. E. Sams, 'Keeping the Peace in Africa', *Disarmament Forum* (2000), 21, 26. See also the remark of Nicholas Sarkozy acknowledging national electoral pressure as not conducive for obtaining consensus within the Council, Y. Devuyst, 'The European Council and the CFSP after the Lisbon Treaty', *European Foreign Affairs Review*, 17 (2012), 327, 342 with reference.
[178] Devuyst, ibid., 327, 332.
[179] N. von Ondarza, M. Overhaus, 'The CSDP after the December Summit', in SWP Comments 7, January 2014, 2.
[180] Among the recommendations are strengthening and ensuring inter-mission cooperation between the different CSDP missions and operations in a region, Preparing the December 2013 European Council, supra note 115, 5. She also recommended the further development of the partnerships with the UN and NATO, ibid., 7.
[181] T. Haesebrouck, M. van Meirvenne, 'EUFOR RCA and CSDP Crisis Management Operations: Back on Track?', *European Foreign Affairs Review*, 20 (2015), 267–286.

Notwithstanding the limited ambition of the EU, refusing to mount fully fledged large-scale peacekeeping operations on the African continent is in fact part of the general strategy of the EU. In practice, EU peacekeeping strategies in Africa have been precisely 'developed around these models of compensating UN shortcomings in the rapid deployment of troops on a short-term basis'.[182] The EU therefore favours 'short-term, geographically limited support operations under its direct political and military control in selected cases'.[183] Also, the EU strategy has to be seen in the wider context of EU–UN, EU–AU and UN–AU relations.[184] The absence of new EU peacekeeping operations on the African continent can consequently be explained by the broader framework of cooperation existing within the organisations. African ownership and the 'primary responsibility of the AU' for the maintenance of international peace and security are key issues in distributing the roles of players on the field on the African continent. Hence, the 2012 Plan of Action to Enhance EU CSDP Support to UN Peacekeeping stipulates that a joint EU–UN coordination mechanism on assistance to the AU and other regional organisations shall be defined through various actions within a year following the adoption of the plan. These actions include:

- Enhanced coordination and information sharing at the operational/technical level in Addis Ababa between the EU Delegation to the AU and the UN Office to the AU (UNOAU);
- A yearly coordination meeting of EU and UN with the AU Peace and Security Department to discuss benchmarks, goals, needs and timelines for operationalisation of the African Peace and Security Architecture (APSA) and possible adjustment of strategies as necessary;
- Possible synergies between the African Peace Facility capacity building program and the technical assistance and training implemented by UNOAU for the African Standby Force (ASF) and within the larger APSA; EU and UN support to the AU for ASF should take into account the results of the Amani Africa cycle;

---

[182] Brosig, 'The Emerging Peace and Security Regime', supra note 10, 107, 115. The EU's decision to deploy troops in the CAR exactly fulfils this role. The EU representative confirmed during a meeting of the SC that the EU's strategy generally consists of deploying bridging operations on the African continent pending an eventual takeover by the UN SC, UN Doc. S/PV.7228 (2014), 6.

[183] Ibid. See also the statement on behalf of the EU, Security Council, UN Doc. S/PV.7015 (2013), 17.

[184] See the other parts in this chapter. See also M. Dembinski, B. Schott, 'Converging around Global Norms? Protection of Civilians in African Union and European Union Peacekeeping in Africa', *African Security*, 6 (2013), 276, 277.

- Cooperation between EU, UN and AU, building on the EU–AU 2010 assessment of the APSA readiness, with an eye to identifying the support required to make the African Standby Force operational;
- Continued EU assistance to AU in the preparation of African forces for deployment on UNPKO.[185]

This framework of cooperation between the EU and the UN therefore suggests that, indeed, a triangular relationship among these two organisations and the AU is emerging for maintaining international peace and security which will be further examined in the parts on EU–AU and on AU–UN relations. Further steps to further institutionalise its relationship with the UN and to foster the triangular relationship with both the UN and the AU were undertaken by the EU in March 2015 with the adoption of the Priorities 2015–2018 to strengthen the UN–EU Strategic Partnership on Peacekeeping and Crisis Management.[186] The document, which was endorsed by the Secretary-General,[187] lists as main priorities the improvement of EU–UN cooperation on rapid response to crises and closer trilateral cooperation with the AU and improvement of the latter's rapid response capacities.[188] Modalities shall be put into place to facilitate the deployment of autonomous EU rapid response forces in parallel to UN forces or as bridging forces.[189]

On 16 March 2015, the Council of the EU also authorised the opening of negotiations for an agreement on cooperation between the UN and the EU in crisis management operations.[190]

The EU and NATO; NATO and the EU: Complementarity, Competition and Compromises

NATO maintains closer relations to the EU than to any other organisation.[191] The overlaps in membership of NATO and the EU have led to a condition of 'cultural symbiosis' and general mutual trust between the two

---

[185] Plan of Action to Enhance EU CSDP Support, supra note 163, 18, para. 58 as well as Actions to enhance EU CSDP support, supra note 148, 11. The two progress reports on the Implementation of the Plan of Action are not available to the public.
[186] Strengthening the UN–EU Strategic Partnership on Peacekeeping and Crisis Management: Priorities 2015-2018, Doc. EEAS 458/15 (2015).
[187] UN Doc. A/70/357 and S/2015/682 (2015), 10, para. 46.
[188] Doc. EEAS 458/15 (2015), 2, 4.
[189] Ibid., 5.
[190] 3796th Council meeting, Foreign Affairs, Brussels, 16 March 2015, 16.
[191] The EU remains a prioritised partner for NATO, cf., e.g., Chatham House, The Future of the Atlantic Alliance, Jaap de Hoop Scheffer, Secretary-General of NATO, 20 July 2009, 6.

organisations. Shared interests and the identity of political and military agendas and objectives[192] have equally contributed to advancing this relationship.[193] The beginnings of NATO and EU cooperation can be traced back for decades. The envisaged European Defence Community Treaty of 1952 included general and specific rules on close cooperation by the inclusion of a mutual defence clause with NATO, as well as an integrated European army.[194] The clauses on cooperation between the EU and NATO in the TEU derive from the treaty on the EDC and are nearly identical.[195] While the incorporation and absorption of the WEU by the EU was slow, this ultimately led to increased interaction between the two organisations. In fact, institutionalised links between NATO and the EU have existed since 2001, but they are based on previous developments in the 1990s. NATO itself recognised the importance of developing the European Security and Defence architecture, and the need for both organisations to develop complementary roles in the security architecture.[196] In subsequent years the cooperation between NATO and EU/WEU increased, further developed,[197] and was fully implemented in 1999[198] after the heads of state and government of NATO decided to develop the arrangements known the 'Berlin-plus agreements'.[199]

In December 2002, NATO and the EU signed the Declaration on ESDP[200] and in March 2003 the Agreement of the Framework on

---

[192] Naturally that the EU is also engaged extensively in the collective defence of the EU-(Atlantic) area.
[193] NATO is committed to the EU; see Statement by the Secretary-General of NATO, UN Doc. S/PV.5529 (2006), 32.
[194] M. Trybus, 'The Vision of the European Defence Community and a Common Defence for the European Union', in M. Trybus, N. D. White (eds.), *European Security Law* (Oxford University Press, 2007), 13, 37. Boisson de Chazournes, 'L'Union européenne', supra note 102, 237, 238.
[195] Article 5 of the Treaty of the EDC, Article 17(1), paragraph 2 of the TEU.
[196] Final Communiqué, North Atlantic Council, Copenhagen, Denmark, 6–7 June 1991, para. 3. The aim was to strengthen European defence capabilities within and outside of NATO.
[197] Ministerial Meeting of the North Atlantic Council/North Atlantic Cooperation Council, NATO Headquarters, Brussels, 10–11 January 1994, Declaration of the Heads of State and Government, paras. 6, 8; Final Communiqué Issued at the Ministerial Meeting of the North Atlantic Council, 10 December 1996, para. 17.
[198] See also Naert, *International Law Aspects*, supra note 41, 34.
[199] 'An Alliance for the 21st Century', Washington Summit Communiqué Issued by the Heads of State and Government Participating in the Meeting of the North Atlantic Council in Washington, DC, on 24 April 1999, paras. 8–10.
[200] According to the Declaration the main principles governing the EU–NATO relationship are partnership, effective mutual consultation, dialogue, cooperation and transparency, equality and due regard to the decision-making autonomy of both organisations.

Cooperation.²⁰¹ These arrangements give the EU assured access to NATO's planning capabilities for EU-led Crisis Management Operations. This includes access to NATO's collective assets and capabilities, including command arrangements and assistance in operational planning; in 'effect they allow the Alliance to support EU-led operations in which NATO as a whole is not engaged'.²⁰² The 'Berlin-plus' agreements comprise various components including:

- Assured EU access to NATO planning capabilities able to contribute to military planning for EU-led operations;
- The presumption of availability to the EU of pre-identified NATO capabilities and common assets for use in EU-led operations;
- Identification of a range of European command options for EU-led operations, further developing the role of DSACEUR in order for him to assume fully and effectively his European responsibilities;
- The further adaptation of NATO's defence planning system to incorporate more comprehensively the availability of forces for EU-led operations.²⁰³

Regarding the early stages planning of EU operations, NATO may contribute to the elaboration of military strategic options via SHAPE in Mons, Belgium. If a decision is taken on the basis of 'Berlin-plus' agreements, operational planning by NATO will be furnished for the implementation of the mission. While NATO military assets are not guaranteed for an EU operation, it is presumed that they are available. Furthermore, NATO should make available a European command option for EU-led operations. The Operation Commander should be NATO's Deputy SACEUR, playing thereby a pivotal role between both organisations.²⁰⁴ From a current perspective, however, the relevance of the agreement has to be

---

[201] EU–NATO Declaration on ESDP, 16 December 2002; Framework Agreement, 17 March 2003. See also, C. Buharalı, 'Better NATO–EU Relations Require More Sincerity', Discussion Paper Series 2010/1, Centre for Economics and Foreign Policy Studies, January 2010, 3; L. Michel, 'NATO and the United States: Working with the EU to Strengthen Euro-Atlantic Security', in S. Biscop, R. G. Whitman (eds.), *The Routledge Handbook of European Security* (London, Routledge, 2013), 255–256.
[202] See, for instance, NATO–EU: A Strategic Partnership, available at www.nato.int/cps/en/natolive/topics_49217.htm.
[203] 'An Alliance for the 21st Century', supra note 199, para. 10. Berlin-plus agreement is a short title for a comprehensive package of agreements between NATO and EU, based on conclusions of the NATO Washington Summit. See also, A Secure Europe, supra note 116, 12.
[204] EU–NATO: The Framework for Permanent Relations and Berlin Plus. See also F. Terpan, 'EU–NATO Relations: Consistency as a Strategic Consideration and a Legal Requirement', in M. Trybus, N. D. White (eds.), *European Security Law* (Oxford University Press, 2007), 270, 284.

relativised. The two organisations did not anticipate that the need may arise to deploy troops cooperatively or even jointly in the same conflict region.[205]

The European Security Strategy (2003) also recognises the important ties with NATO. It states that the transatlantic relationship strengthens the international community as a whole and that 'NATO is an important expression of that relationship'.[206] On a practical level, there are regular meetings of both the EU PSC and the NATO North Atlantic Council. The EU established a small cell at NATO's SHAPE and NATO formed a liaison team at the EU Military Staff.[207]

Nevertheless, the progressing relations between NATO and the EU were not free of competition.[208] Both organisations expanded their competences in various areas in the 1990s which were traditionally within the competences and mandate of the other organisation. The EU was pursuing the development of the CDSP, including the absorption of the WEU, while NATO was transforming in and expanding as a more political organisation.[209] Moreover, the construction of the CSDP was an expression of the political will of the EU to act outside of NATO.[210] This reposition was triggered by the shift of position of the UK government; the 'sea-change' towards EU defence at the Franco–British summit in Saint-Malo in 1998.[211] The US was in favour of a European pillar within NATO,

---

[205] Cf. Ginsberg, Penska, *The European Union*, supra note 120, 188–189, 199.
[206] A Secure Europe, supra note 116, 9. That was reaffirmed in the Report on the Implementation, which called for a deepening of the strategic relationship between the two organisations, Report on the Implementation, supra note 124, 2.
[207] Koutrakos, *The EU Common Security*, supra note 90, 106; cf. Council Joint Action 2003/92/CFSP of 27 January 2003 on the EU military operation in the Former Yugoslav Republic of Macedonia, Article 10.
[208] See generally with regard to the EU and NATO rivalry, R. E. Hunter, *The European Security and Defense Policy. NATO's Companion - or Competitor?* (Santa Monica, Rand, 2002).
[209] Cf. Trybus, 'The Vision of the European Defence', supra note 194, 13, 38–39.
[210] Declaration on a Transformed North Atlantic Alliance, supra note 29, para. 3; The Alliance's New Strategic Concept, supra note 25, para. 2; Cologne European Council, 3–4 June 1999, Conclusions of the Presidency, Annex III – European Council Declaration on Strengthening the Common European Policy on Security and Defence, para. 1. See also Terpan, 'EU–NATO Relations: Consistency as a Strategic Consideration and a Legal Requirement', supra note 204, 270, 272.
[211] Joint Declaration of the British–French summit, Saint-Malo, 3–4 December 1998, in M. Rutten (ed.), *From St Malo to Nice, European Defence: Core Documents*, Chaillot Paper 47 (Paris, European Union Security Institute, 2001), 9 para. 2; Terpan, ibid., 270, 274–275; see also R. Matarazzo, 'Le strutture istituzionali della Pesd', in N. Ronzitti (ed.), *Le Forze di Pace dell'Unione Europea* (Soveria Mannelli, Rubbetino Editore, 2005), 21, 27; Koutrakos, *The EU Common Security*, supra note 90, 18–19.

although the position of its government was ambiguous as it was simultaneously a way 'to hinder the creation of a European defence policy outside NATO'.[212] A compromise was found a year later at the Helsinki European Council where it was decided that the EU could launch and conduct EU-led military operations in response to an international crisis and 'where NATO as a whole is not engaged'.[213] The official positions of NATO and the EU are that the EU is not taking the lead if the US intends to participate; if the US does not want to be involved, the EU may start an operation with recourse to NATO assets if the NATO Council agrees.[214] This safeguarding compromise was also facilitated by increased cooperation between the two organisations following the US government's war against terrorism post–11 September 2001.[215] However, the clause aims primarily at safeguarding the compatibility of the CSDP with NATO: 'The alliance shall not be endangered by some of its Member States which prefer to conduct crisis management operations by excluding other NATO members.' This is emphasised by the formula 'NATO as a whole'.[216] It is important to underline that

> the EU stresses, in principle, its equality as a security actor in ESDP documents. Consequently ... the clause stresses the primacy of NATO missions and contains a prohibition against circumventing NATO. EU Member States shall only use the ESDP as a framework for military operations when NATO agrees or is not willing to act in a manner which is, in principle, consistent with European policy goals or is simply not interested in a mission. Thus ESDP documents show that the ESDP is complementary to NATO and not conceived as a forum for competition.[217]

In practice, controversies have arisen out of these envisaged mechanisms to prevent competition. The EU launched Operation Artemis in the DRC fully independent of NATO, acting with its own facilities and assets, but even further, the EU adopted the decision to deploy troops without

---

[212] Terpan, 'EU–NATO Relations', supra note 204, 270, 277.
[213] Helsinki European Council, 10 and 11 December 1999, Presidency Conclusions, para. 27.; Annex 1 to the Presidency Conclusions, 1, 2; EU–NATO Declaration on ESDP, supra note 201.
[214] Terpan, 'EU–NATO Relations: Consistency as a Strategic Consideration and a Legal Requirement', supra note 204, 270, 286.
[215] M. Szapiro, 'International Organisations' Cooperation in the Field of Conflict Prevention', in V. Kronenberger, J. Wouters (eds.), *The European Union and Conflict Prevention. Policy and Legal Issues* (Heidelberg, Springer, 2004), 347, 365.
[216] Krieger, 'Common European Defence: Competence or Compatibility with NATO', supra note 150, 174, 194.
[217] Krieger, ibid.

previously consulting NATO.[218] One author argues that the following two independent NATO and EU operations in Sudan where a consequence of and a reaction to the lack of NATO consultation for Operation Artemis.[219]

In contrast, other examples underline a good degree of cooperation between the two organisations, also based on the Berlin-plus agreements. EUFOR Althea in Bosnia-Herzegovina took over from NATO's IFOR operation on the basis of SC Resolution 1575. This operation has profited from NATO planning expertise and also drew on other Alliance assets and capabilities and is under the command of the NATO Supreme Allied Commander Europe.[220] In practice, the 'Berlin-plus' agreements were furthermore applied when the EU-led 'Operation Concordia' took over the responsibilities of the NATO-led mission 'Allied Harmony' on the territory of the Former Yugoslav Republic of Macedonia. Regarding future operations, a further use of the Berlin-plus agreements is nevertheless rather implausible as NATO–EU relations continue to be impaired by Turkey and Cyprus over the whole Cyprus issue[221]; NATO has not concluded a security arrangement with Cyprus thereby barring it from meetings and from access to NATO documents, whereas the EU has excluded

---

[218] A. Orakhelashvili, *Collective Security* (Oxford University Press, 2011), 310; see also M. Reichard, *The EU–NATO Relationship: A Legal and Political Perspective* (Farnham, Ashgate, 2006), 267; A. Abass, 'Extraterritorial Collective Security: The European Union and Operation ARTEMIS', in M. Trybus, N. D. White, *European Security Law* (Oxford University Press, 2007), 134, 153; S. Biscop, 'NATO and the EU: A Bipolar Alliance for a Multipolar World', in E. Hallams, L. Ratti, B. Zyla (eds.), *NATO Beyond 9/11. The Transformation of the Atlantic Alliance* (London, Palgrave Macmillan, 2013), 239, 243; F. Faria, 'Crisis Management in Sub-Saharan Africa. The Role of the European Union', Occasional Paper n° 51, European Union Institute for Security Studies, 47; A. Bjurner, 'On EU Peacemaking. Challenging or complementing the UN?', in P. Wallensteen, A. Bjurner (eds.), *Regional Organizations and Peacemaking. Challengers to the UN?* (London, Routledge, 2015), 89, 93–94; Declaration by the European Council on the Enhancement of the European Security and Defence Policy, supra note 117, 17, para. 7.

[219] Buharalı, 'Better NATO–EU Relations', supra note 201, 4. Two other authors suggest the separate provision of the airlift to move AU peacekeeping troops into Darfur was due to the simple fact that neither organisation was willing to defer to the other for leadership, Ginsberg, Penska, *The European Union*, supra note 120, 202–203. A certain rift in NATO–EU relations consisted because of Turkey, NATO member, and, Greece, Cyprus, EU member and the 'Northern Cyprus issue'. It took, for instance, three years for NATO and the EU to finalise the 'Berlin-plus' agreement because the difficulties between Turkey and Greece had to be resolved, Yost, 'NATO and International Organizations', supra note 23, 75.

[220] NATO–EU: A Strategic Partnership, supra note 202. The command arrangement under the Berlin-plus agreements was equally used in Operation Concordia as well as in Operation Althea, Yost, ibid., 79.

[221] Interview with Jaap de Hoop Scheffer in The Hague, 18 April 2003.

Turkey from participating in the European Defence Agency on the basis of the lack of a similar security agreement.[222]

As the US is refocusing its geopolitical interests on Asia and on other challenges predominantly outside of Europe, the US will also play a less dominant role within NATO, prompting an increase in the financial but also logistical burden for the European States within NATO[223] after the percentage of the US contribution to NATO has increased from 63 per cent to 77 per cent in the decade since 2001.[224] However, the EU remains the closest partner for NATO. The financial crisis of the past years, ironically, was beneficial for NATO–EU relations. The decreased military spending by member states fuelled the willingness of NATO members to increase their cooperation in military matters within NATO under the concept of 'Smart Defence'[225] as well as with the EU under its 'Pooling and Sharing initiatives'.[226] The motivation to cooperate is further reinforced by defence cuts in many (European) countries; Germany alone will have reduced its defence budgets by 25 per cent until 2016 while the UK's budget was reduced by 8 per cent until 2015.[227] Many of the initiatives of 'Smart Defence' are carried out, however, on a smaller multinational and not on an Alliance level.[228] An additional incentive is obviously the shift of policy

---

[222] N. H. Hedegaard, 'NATO's Institutional Environment: The New Strategic Concept Endorses the Comprehensive Approach' in J. Ringsmose, S. Rynning (eds.), *NATO's New Strategic Concept: A Comprehensive Assessment*, DIIS Report (2011), 75, 81; Koutrakos, *The EU Common Security*, supra note 90, 106–107; M. Kuhn, *Die Europäische Sicherheits- und Verteidigungspolitik im Mehrebenensystem. Eine rechtswissenschaftliche Untersuchung am Beispiel der Militäroption der Europäischen Union in der Demokratischen Republik Kongo 2003* (Heidelberg, Springer, 2012), 10, 153–154; cf. also NATO 2020, supra note 60, 24.

[223] Department of Defense, Sustaining US Global Leadership: Priorities for 21st Century Defense, January 3, 2012, and letter from President Obama, at p. 1 in the same document. See also Krieger, 'Common European Defence', supra note 150, 174, 176; C. Hagel, 'A Republican Foreign Policy', *Foreign Affairs*, 83 (2004), 64, 73.

[224] Opening Address by High Representative Catherine Aston at the symposium on the Common Security and Defence Policy, Washington, DC, 8 May 2013, 1.

[225] NATO in 2020: 'Strong Capabilities, Strong Partnerships'. Keynote speech by NATO Deputy Secretary-General Ambassador Alexander Vershbow, supra note 34.

[226] Chicago Summit Declaration, supra note 50, para. 20; Wales Summit Declaration, supra note 39, para. 70. S. Mölling, 'Pooling und Sharing in EU und Nato', *SWP Aktuell*, 25 (2012), 1; Council of the European Union, Council conclusions on Common Security and Defence Policy, 3130th Foreign Affairs Council meeting, supra note 172, 6, paras. 34–35; Council of the European Union, Council Conclusions on Pooling and Sharing of Military Capabilities – Foreign Affairs Council (Brussels, 22 March 2012), 2, para. 1; 3, para. 4; Council of the European Union, Doc. 16062/12 (2012), 3, paras. 5–6; 4, para. 9.

[227] J. Gordon et al., 'NATO and the Challenge of Austerity', *Survival*, 54 (2012), 121.

[228] B. Giegerich, 'NATO's Smart Defence: Who's Buying?', *Survival: Global Politic and Strategy*, 54 (2012), 69, 71.

of the US towards a stronger focus on the Pacific area and their decision to decrease their support for Europe within the NATO.[229]

The conflict in Libya created new resentments between the two institutions. In need of swift action, EU member states, i.e., France and the UK chose to rely upon NATO and not upon the EU, prompting some commentators to declare that the EU's security and defence policy is dead or that is has 'failed miserably'.[230] Despite these apparent failures, other authors paint a more optimistic portrait for the EU's future.[231] Indeed, whereas NATO is mostly focused on securing the common defence and security of its own members and becomes involved occasionally in 'international crisis management', the EU's objectives are 'to promote an international system based on strong multilateral cooperation and good global governance'.[232]

The conclusions of the Council of the EU just before and during the European Defence Council 2013 confirm that the EU adheres to its ties and its cooperation with NATO and even intends to strengthen the institutional links. The Council envisaged the development of a proposal for synergies between both organisations for the rapid deployment of troops while safeguarding the institutional decision-making autonomy of both the EU and NATO.[233] It also encouraged 'further implementation of practical steps for effective EU cooperation with NATO while keeping the overall objective of building a true organization-to-organization relationship'.[234] NATO, in its turn reconfirmed its intention at the September

---

[229] Cf. also Mölling, 'Pooling and Sharing', supra note 226, 1, 1. Madej, 'After the Chicago Summit', supra note 82, 39, 41–43; Michaels, supra note 59, 56, 59.

[230] A. Menon, 'European Defence Policy from Lisbon to Libya', *Survival: Global Politics and Strategy*, 53 (2011), 75, 76; J. Larik, 'Arma fero, ergo sum? The European Union, NATO and the Quest for European Identity', in H. de Waele, J.-J. Kuipers (eds.), *The European Union's Emerging International Identity. Views from the Global Arena* (Leiden, Brill, 2013), 43, 57.

[231] Biscop, 'From Lisbon to Lisbon', supra note 63, 106, 107; S. Duke, 'The EU, NATO and the Treaty of Lisbon: Still Divided within a Common City', in P. J. Cardwell (ed.), *EU External Relations Law and Policy in the Post-Lisbon Era* (Heidelberg, Springer, 2012), 335, 354.

[232] Article 21(2)(h) TEU; Larik, 'Arma fero, ergo sum', supra note 230, 43, 58.

[233] Council conclusions on Common Security and Defence Policy, supra note 122, 6, para. 12(b); European Council 19–20 December 2013, Conclusions, 1, Preamble; 2, para. 2; see also Preparing the December 2013 European Council, supra note 115, 6; Council of the European Union, Council conclusions on the EU's comprehensive approach, Foreign Affairs Council meeting, Brussels, 12 May 2014, 4, para. 14. See also Collective Defence and Common Security, Twin Pillars of the Atlantic Alliance, Group of Policy Experts report to the NATO Secretary-General, June 2014, 5, para. 2.3.

[234] Council Conclusions on Common Security and Defence Policy, ibid., 7, para. 15(b).

2014 Wales Summit to 'continue to work side-by-side in crisis management operations' with the EU and to expand political consultations and cooperations.[235]

The EU and the AU: An Effective Partnership

Since the launch of the CSDP in 1999, the EU's strategy towards Africa has been based on the idea of 'African ownership' and the premise that the 'primary responsibility for prevention, management and resolution of conflicts on the African continent lies with Africans themselves', while the SC has the primary responsibility for the maintenance of international peace and security.[236] The EU expressed its intention to work towards more formalised relations with the AU in 2005.[237] Two years later, in 2007, the EU supported its pledge and adopted – with the AU – the Joint Africa–EU strategy in Lisbon.[238]

The Joint Africa–EU strategy consists of eight pillars of which one is devoted to Peace and Security. It provides, inter alia, for financial support in fully implementing and operationalising the APSA.[239] The Action Plan for ESDP support to Peace and Security in Africa of 2004 further mentions that the EU stands ready to consider other forms of support that may include, 'training, the provision of equipment, operational support and possibly even ESDP advisory or executive missions in the framework of African-led operations or United Nations (UN) peacekeeping operations'.[240] The specific goals of the Joint Strategy were laid down in two Actions Plans, covering the years 2008–2010 and 2011–2013. Both recognise and emphasise three items as priority actions: 'Enhanc[ing] dialogue on challenges to peace and security', 'Full operationalization of the African Peace and Security Architecture' and 'Predictable Funding for African-led

---

[235] Wales Summit Declaration, supra note 39, para. 102.
[236] Council Common Position 2004/85/CFSP (2004), Preamble (1), (2); Brosig, 'The Emerging Peace and Security Regime', supra note 10, 107, 111.
[237] Council of the European Union, The EU and Africa: Towards a Strategic Partnership, Brussels, 19 December 2005, 2, paras. 2–4.
[238] Report on the Implementation, Doc. S407/08 (2008), 11.
[239] Council of the European Union, The Africa–EU Strategic Partnership. A Joint Africa–EU Strategy, 16344/07 (Presse 291) (2007), para. 17, also at 26; Fourth EU–Africa Summit, 2–3 April 2014, Brussels, Roadmap 2014–2017, 3, paras. 9, 11–12; Fourth EU–Africa Summit, 2–3 April 2014, Brussels, Declaration, 3, paras. 11–12.
[240] Council of the European Union, Action Plan for ESDP support to Peace and Security in Africa, 10538/4/04 REV 4 (2004), 2; First Action Plan (2008–2010) for the Implementation of the Africa–EU Strategic Partnership, 8.

Peace Support Operations'.²⁴¹ The 2014–2017 Roadmap also identified peace and security as one of five priority areas for the implementation of the 2007 joint strategy.²⁴²

To implement the first priority as contained in the Action Plans, the two organisations sought to develop common positions and implement common approaches on the basis of inter-institutional meetings, regular triennial AU–EU summits, joint annual meetings of the PSC and the EU PSC²⁴³ and meetings at the ministerial and ambassadorial level.²⁴⁴ The second action plan noted positively the progress made on this particular issue.²⁴⁵ Thus a network of cooperation on a political level through meetings has been established, including the appointment of an EU Special Representative to the AU and the establishment of the EU Delegation to the AU in 2008.²⁴⁶ As part of the 2014–2017 Roadmap further efforts are undertaken by both organisations to increase the dialogue and to implement common approaches on challenges to peace and security.²⁴⁷

Regarding the APSA, the EU has undertaken specific steps after the originally envisaged time frame for the operationalisation of the APSA could not be kept; expected to be fully operational in 2010, it is still not fully functional in 2015. The EU appointed a Special Advisor for African Peacekeeping Capabilities in 2008 acting as a focal point in liaison with the EU Delegation and the Special Representative for capacity building programmes.²⁴⁸ The 2011–2013 Action Plan emphasised the need for further

---

[241] First Action Plan (2008–2010), ibid., 2, 5–9; Joint Africa EU Strategy Action Plan 2011–2013, 15. Also Preparing the December 2013 European Council, supra note 115, 6.

[242] Fourth EU–Africa Summit, supra note 239, 2, para. 6.

[243] Council of the European Union, The Africa–EU Strategic Partnership. A Joint Africa–EU Strategy, 16344/07 (Presse 291) (2007); Seventh Meeting of the Joint Coordination Committee of the African Peace Facility, Addis Ababa, 18 October 2011.

[244] First Action Plan (2008–2010), supra note 240, 6. Other meetings include meetings of the established Joint Africa–EU Expert Groups (JEG), meeting biannually, meetings of the Joint Africa–EU Task Force (JTC) as well as meetings of the AU Military Staff Committee (MSC) and the EU Military Committee (EUMC), M. Brosig, 'The African Union a Partner for Peace', in S. Biscop, R. G. Whitman (eds.), *The Routledge Handbook of European Security* (London, Routledge, 2013), 292, 297.

[245] '[T]he structural and systematic linkages between decision making organs, such as the EU PSC and the AU PSC, the EUMC and the AU MSC, Crisis management teams on both sides, have been strengthened. African and EU heads of delegations in Addis Ababa, Brussels and New York are in regular consultation.' Joint Africa EU Strategy, supra note 241, 15. See also pp. 16–20 of the Action Plan.

[246] Delegation of the EU to the A, available at http://eeas.europa.eu/delegations/african_union/about_us/welcome/index_en.htm.

[247] Fourth EU–Africa Summit, supra note 239, 2–3, paras. 9–13.

[248] Council of the European Union, Doc. S091/08 (2008); Brosig, 'The African Union a Partner for Peace', supra note 244, 292, 297.

efforts for the operationalisation of the APSA,[249] following the critique contained in the 2010 Assessment Study, in particular of the 'mandate-resource gap' of the AU.[250] Capacity building through training of groups is also part of the Joint Africa–EU Strategy to operationalise the APSA and to ensure 'its effective functioning to address peace and security challenges in Africa'.[251]

The effective functioning of the APSA includes a further involvement of the regional economic communities, such as ECOWAS, in the process of making the APSA operational whereby the AU will provide the overall leadership.[252] One of the measures which were launched in the support of this purpose is the Euro Recamp–Amani Africa initiative in 2008 with a three-year timeframe. The programme delivered – through civil–military activities – seminars and workshops on strategic planning, particularly on how to establish a decision-making plan for crisis management, and it supports the AU Peace Support Operations Divisions accordingly in the exercise of their activities. Furthermore, it also provided support to the AU Peace Support Operations Division in order to enable it to function and to work effectively from the moment a political decision to deploy military forces is taken up to the commitment of forces.[253] The Amani Africa initiative culminated in a ten-day command post exercise (CPX) in October 2010 involving more than 120 African military components and police forces along with various EU partners, which 'aimed at determining and furthering the force's operational capacity'.[254]

The second three-year cycle covering the period 2011–2014 named Amani Africa II had the overall objective of validating the capacity of the AU to mandate and deploy Rapid Deployment Capability of the ASF and to run multidimensional peace support operations. An EU permanent Planning Team (EUPT) was formed on 23 April 2012 and mandated by the PSC to continue this second cycle of training together with a team

---

[249] Joint Africa EU Strategy, supra note 241, 15.
[250] African Peace and Security Architecture (APSA), 2010 Assessment Study, 26, para. 68.
[251] Information Brief on Amani Africa.
[252] Consultative meeting between the AU - Regional Economic Communities (RECs)/Regional Mechanisms (RMs) for Conflict Prevention, Management and Resolution and the EU on the EU Support to the Operationalization of the African Peace and Security Architecture (APSA), Akosombo, Ghana, 10–11 December 2009, 1, para (a).
[253] European Union, Euro Recamp–Amani Africa (2008–2010); Amani Africa, Implementation Plan, Draft, African Union Peace Support Operations Division, 6–8, paras. 3.1–3.8.
[254] Available at www.africom.mil/Newsroom/Article/7817/in-final-stage-amani-africa-exercise-gauges-africa.

from the AU Commission.[255] Based on lessons learned from the CSDP training missions in Somalia and Mali, the EU is currently preparing to launch a new 'train and equip initiative' to support the operationalisation and independence of regional organisations and countries on the African continent.[256]

The African Peace Facility (APF) was established as a permanent mechanism by the EU to confront the third priority action as identified in the Actions Plans – predictable funding for AU peacekeeping operations – and has provided more than 1.2 billion Euros to date for peacekeeping operations under AU auspices.[257] A further 750 million Euros have been committed for the APF under the new Three-Year Action Programme covering the period from 2014–2017.[258] The AU is not only dependent on financial support of the EU, but it also must submit to the conditions dictated by the EU – under the EU's internal law. Therefore, every AU intervention financed by the African Peace Facility shall be 'subject to prior approval by the Political and Security Committee'.[259] The European External Action Service (EEAS) and the European Commission services prepare – upon the request by the AU or a sub-regional organisation – a joint information note for the responsible Council working groups and seek the approval of the EU PSC.[260]

The AU Commission therefore effectively seeks the approval of the EU PSC 'on the political appropriateness of the intervention requested'.[261] The EU, as an independent actor, will decide upon its own preferences whether to accord further money to the AU or not, thus, it recommended to the AU to make efforts to mobilise alternative sources of funding following

---

[255] African Union, African Standby Force (ASF), Amani Africa II Initial Planning Conference (PSC), Addis Ababa, Ethiopia, 7–9 March 2012, Final Report; Amani Africa II Cycle, Main Events Timeframe (TBC) as at 10 April 2013.

[256] UN Doc. S/2015/229 (2015), 12, para. 41.

[257] Background brief, Foreign Affairs Council, 9 February, Brussels, 3.

[258] Joint Press Release, The African Union Commission and the European Union Hold the Ninth Meeting of the Africa Peace Facility (APF) Joint Coordination Committee, 3 June 2014, 1.

[259] Council Regulation 617/2007 (2007), Article 12. See also K. Aning, K. F. Danso, 'EU and AU Operations in Africa: Lessons Learned and Future Scenarios. An African Perspective', in N. Pirozzi (ed.), *Ensuring Peace and Security in Africa: Implementing the New Africa–EU Partnership* (Rome, Instituto Affari Internazionale, 2010), 47, 48.

[260] C. Rein, 'Enhancing Peace and Security in Africa through Institutional Cooperation', *Contemporary Security Policy*, 36 (2015), 267, 285.

[261] Annual Report, The African Peace Facility (2010), 5, para. 2.5; R. Poulton, E. Trillo, L. Kukkuk, *Part 1 of the African Peace Facility Evaluation: Reviewing the Procedures of the APF and Possibilities of Alternative Future Sources of Funding. Final Report* (2010), 29.

the decision of the SC to increase the number of troops of AMISOM to 12,000.[262]

The APF contains further requirements the AU has to comply with. First of all, the APF contains a reporting requirement for the AU.[263] Secondly, the EU also expects that the AU acts under a UN mandate and as the APF is financed through the European Development Fund (EDF), any financial contribution to the AU cannot be used for military or arms expenditure.[264]

Therefore, the EU could effectively block any AU operation if it so wished. The African Peace Facility also raises issues under the law of responsibility. Under the APF, the EU exercises a high degree of control not only over the financing but also over the envisaged AU operation per se.[265] The EU PSC determines the 'political appropriateness' of the AU operation and the EU could therefore easily demand that various specific, political parameters are fulfilled during the deployment of the operation in order that it grants the AU the necessary funding for the operation.[266] Thus, the question is whether the EU could control the AU to such a degree that its contributions to the AU under the APF regime would fall under the ambit of the

---

[262] Seventh Meeting of the Joint Coordination Committee of the African Peace Facility, Addis Ababa, 18 October 2011, 2.

[263] Council Regulation (EC) No 617/2007, ibid., Article 12. However, the general strategic focus and orientation of the APF is coordinated in the Joint Coordination Committee (JCC) co-chaired by both organisations and as established in 2005, Joint Press Release, supra note 258, 2.

[264] E. Y. Omorogbe, 'Can the African Union Deliver Peace and Security?', *Journal of Conflict & Security Law*, 16 (2011), 35, 43. Non-eligible APF expenditure includes ammunition, arms and specific military equipment, spare parts for arms and military equipment, salaries for soldiers and military training for soldiers. Eligible expenditures include per diems, rations, medical consumables and facilities, transport, fuel, troop allowances and communication equipment. See Annual Report, The African Peace Facility 2010, 5, para. 2.4. According to Rein, African Peace Facility expenditures may also include ammunitions, arms, military equipment and training, Rein, 'Enhancing Peace and Security', supra note 260, 167, 286.

[265] The AU has expressed concern about the influence of its partners, including the EU on the planning of, in particular, AU peacekeeping operations, A. P. Rodt, J. M. Okeke, 'AU–EU Partnership: Strengthening Policy Convergence and Regime Efficacy in the African Peace and Security Complex?', *African Security*, 6 (2013), 211, 226. Even more critical, B. Franke, S. Gänzle, 'How "African" Is the African Peace and Security Architecture? Conceptual and Practical Constraints of Regional Security Cooperation Africa', *African Security*, 5 (2012), 88, 101.

[266] Ninety per cent of the staff within the Peace and Security Department of the AU are actually paid for by the EU which means that '[a]n end to or decrease in EU financial support could thus lead to deep institutional crisi [sic] within the AU', Rodt, Okeke, ibid., 211, 224; see also A. Mattelaer, E. Marijnen, 'EU Peacekeeping in Africa. Towards an Indirect Approach', in M. Wyss, T. Tardy (eds.), *Peacekeeping in Africa: The Evolving Security Architecture* (London, Routledge, 2014), 54, 62, 69.

Articles on the Responsibility of International Organisations.[267] The fact that the EU contributes not only financially to AU operations could, however, also open up the application of other areas of the Articles – aid and assistance as well as the wider issue of joint responsibility. Nevertheless, the controversial issue of financing of peacekeeping operations is not limited to the EU–AU context. Both organisations cooperate on the issue of establishing a UN mechanism, under Chapter VIII, to provide funding for peacekeeping operations undertaken by the AU or under its authority and with the consent of the SC.[268]

The Action Plan (2011–2013) likewise underlined that the AU and regional mechanisms are not yet sufficiently financially independent to conduct peacekeeping operations of their own, necessitating further exchanges and efforts.[269] In this context, the EU emphasises the need for 'more concerted action between the AU, the EU and the UN' on the basis of the recommendations formulated in the Prodi Report.[270]

A Slow Shift Towards an Equal Standing in EU–AU Relations

The current policy of the EU seeks to move away from a donor–receiver relationship towards a relationship of equal standing in which the AU can also fully accept the responsibility for the maintenance of international peace and security on the African continent without being dependent upon financial contributions by the industrialised countries. Although the EU gives priority to 'African ownership', it is nevertheless prepared to become involved, when necessary, with its own troops in crisis management on the African continent.[271] However, the EU's involvement in

---

[267] Article 15 ARIO without prejudice to the question of individual responsibility of the AU.
[268] Council of the European Union, Doc. 16344/07 (Presse 291) (2007), para. 21. Moreover, the UN itself could be responsibility on the basis of its own AU operations finance mechanism based on assessed contributions, cf. the part on UN–AU relations within this chapter.
[269] Council of the European Union, Doc. 16344/07 (Presse 291) (2007), para. 21.
[270] Ibid.
[271] Council Common Position 2004/85/CFSP (2004), Article 1, para. 2; Article 6, para. 1; Council Joint Action 2005/557/CFSP (2005), Article 1. For a critical view of the EU's activities in Africa, see G. R. Olsen, 'The EU and Military Conflict Management in Africa: For the Good of Africa or Europe?', *International Peacekeeping*, 16 (2009), 245, 257; Norheim-Martinsen, supra note 120, 17, 26. Cf. also K. Engberg, 'Trends in Conflict Management. Multilateral Intervention and the Role of Regional Organizations', in P. Wallensteen, A. Bjurner (eds.), *Regional Organizations and Peacemaking. Challengers to the UN?* (London, Routledge, 2015), 72, 82.

peacekeeping operations of its own has very defined limits; the EU prefers limited engagements with its own troops in the form of bridging operations which has prevented joint EU–AU peacekeeping operations or the takeover of one operation by the other organisation.[272] It is, indeed, as it was just argued, more likely that responsibility of the EU in the context of AU peacekeeping operations will arise due its manifold contributions, including on the political level to the AU, rather than on the basis of a joint peacekeeping operation.

As the AU also tends to deploy bridging operations, recent examples include Mali and Somalia, the AU and the EU cooperate more closely with the UN during the deployment of operations than with each other.[273] The lack of resources of the AU means that 'African ownership' can often not be generated,[274] but the EU is forced to step in and engage in capacity building or may be forced to wait for the AU to develop its capacities in this area.[275] The EU's response to the Darfur crisis and the deployment of the EU's Support Operation AMIS II[276] was, in essence, a response to the shortcomings of the AU operation[277] and it sidelined the general capacity building work of the EU, forcing the organisation to do on-the-job capacity building for AMIS.[278] The Support Operation provided planning and technical assistance to AMIS II command, military observers as well as training of African troops and observers and strategic and tactical transportation.[279] Altogether, the EU and its member states spent more than one billion Euros for humanitarian aid and capacity building for AMIS.[280] EU support

---

[272] Brosig, 'The African Union a Partner for Peace', supra note 244, 292, 294.
[273] Cf. Brosig, 'The African Union a Partner for Peace', supra note 244, 292, 294–295. See Article 17 of the PSC Protocol.
[274] See, for example, Amani Africa, Implementation Plan, Draft, African Union Peace Support Operations Division, 8, para. 4.1.1.ii. In addition to 'ownership', the Joint Strategy is based on 'partnership and solidarity'; annual report, The African Peace Facility 2010, 4, para. 2.1.
[275] Brosig, 'The African Union a Partner for Peace', supra note 244, 292, 300; Franke, Esmenjaud, 'Who Owns African Ownership?', supra 177, 137, 149.
[276] Council Joint Action 2005/557/CFSP (2005).
[277] Brosig, 'The Emerging Peace and Security Regime', supra note 10, 107, 117.
[278] International Crisis Group, The EU/AU Partnership in Darfur: Not Yet A Winning Combination, Africa Report N 99, 25 October 2005, 9.
[279] B. Franke, 'The European Union's Supporting Actions to the African Union Mission in Sudan (AMIS) and Somalia (AMISOM)', in G. Grevi, D. Helly, D. Keohane (eds.), *European Security and Defence Policy. The First 10 Years (1999-2009)* (Paris, The European Union Institute for Security Studies, 2009), 255, 260–261; International Crisis Group, ibid., 9–10.
[280] European Union Factsheet, European Union Response to the Darfur Crisis, July 2006, 1.

ended with the transition to the hybrid UNAMID operation, proof once again that the EU's preference is to act on short-term engagements alone with clear exit options.[281] EUFOR Chad/CAR is another example of the EU's political parameters of its peacekeeping strategy on the African continent. The operation was set up for a period of one year, it was based on the consent of the host countries, it included only a limited military contingent,[282] and it was executed in multilateral cooperation with the UN and with a clear exit option.[283]

The cooperation between the EU and the AU in the area of maintaining international peace and security illustrates very well how the CFSP has been stimulated by other areas of the EU's external actions and particularly the broader development agenda.[284]

The institutionalised cooperation agreements between the EU, the UN and the AU were also welcomed by the SC in its Resolution 1809.[285] The engagement of the EU was comparatively more limited regarding AMISOM; it persisted beyond cooperation on a political level and financial support as the EU is also engaged in the training of African troops of the ASF in an operational context, for example in Mali as part of the ESDP support policy.[286]

As the AU is at the head of the African Peace and Security Structure, it is also the point of entry for cooperation between the EU and other organisations with the sub-regional organisations in Africa; the CSDP Policy is therefore to consult with the AU in response to requests from sub-regional organisations on the African continent.[287] Thus, there is no systematic EU

---

[281] Brosig, 'The Emerging Peace and Security Regime', supra note 10, 107, 118.
[282] UN Doc. S/RES/1778 (2007), 4–5, paras. 6–9; S/RES/1834 (2008), 2, para. 4; Council Joint Action 2007/677/CFSP (2007), Article 1.
[283] Brosig, 'The Emerging Peace and Security Regime', supra note 10, 107, 120. But EUFOR Chad was also affected by problems of force generation and equipment. See Norheim-Martinsen, 'Our Work Here Is Done', supra note 120, 17, 24; Menon, 'European Defence Policy', supra note 230, 75, 80.
[284] Cf. Koutrakos, 'The European Union in the Global Security Architecture', supra note 135, 81, 89–90; Joint Statement by the Council and the representatives of the governments of the member states meeting within the Council, the European Parliament and the Commission on European Union Development Policy: 'The European Consensus' (2006/C46/01), especially para. 37.
[285] UN Doc. S/RES/1809 (2008), 3, paras. 5–6.
[286] Council of the European Union, Action Plan for ESDP support to peace and security in Africa, Doc. 10538/04 (2004), 1. Other measures include, for example, capacity building for political and economic analyses, early warning system, negotiation/mediation skills, Doc. 2004/85/CFSP (2004), Article 4, para. 1.
[287] Ibid., 3, 4.B.

strategy to support capacity building for RECs, but the EU has led individual support for specific RECs.[288]

Conclusions

From the early small steps of developing a common foreign security and defence policy, the EU has evolved to become a global actor within the system of collective security with vast military and non-military tools at its disposal. An analysis of the EU's relations with other organisations facilitates a corroboration of some of the findings which were made regarding NATO, as well as the ascertainment of certain general developments.

Firstly, a division of labour or a complementarity of roles has emerged between the EU and NATO regarding their relations with the UN and the AU. It was argued previously[289] that NATO's engagement on the African continent is very limited due to the preference of, in particular, European, NATO members to engage in activities for maintaining international peace and security in Africa through the EU. Furthermore, the analysis of NATO's relations with the AU illustrated that NATO provides principally in-mission support to the AU upon the specific request of the latter. In contrast, the EU has developed an impressive framework of institutional relations with the AU covering an array of areas, including the training of troops and the financing of peace operations. Cooperation between the EU and the AU during the peace operations is a consequence of the institutional cooperation arrangements between the two organisations and has to be assessed accordingly. Generally speaking, 'operational cooperation in peacekeeping missions [between the EU and the AU] is hardly existing'.[290]

Although NATO and the EU therefore seem to have reached a division of labour and an understanding regarding their role on the African continent, it is not clear what the future of their relationship will be, despite their long institutional history and the existing ties and channels. The December 2013 Defence Council emphasised the need to develop a true organisation-to-organisation relationship, but it failed to indicate the necessary steps for such an evolution. It is noteworthy that the conclusions of the Defence Council emphasise the decision-making authority of

---

[288] Brosig, 'The African Union a Partner for Peace', supra note 244, 292, 299.
[289] See the part on NATO and the AU.
[290] Brosig, ibid., 292, 299.

both organisations. This fact could imply a renunciation of the previous policy between the two organisations that the EU would act if NATO as a whole is not engaged or it is recognition of the emerging division of labour between the two organisations. Another interpretation of the decisions making authority of both organisations points towards the termination of the Berlin-plus agreements which were not even mentioned in the documents of the Defence Council. Reichard, however, argues that there has been no reliance on NATO assets by the EU for many years because the recent engagement of the EU with military operations is low-key and the EU distinguishes between two types of military operations, those requiring NATO assets as larger scale operations and those of a lower scale and intensity.[291]

EU–UN relations for maintaining international peace and security have developed along the same institutionalised path as EU–AU relations and they cannot be seen in isolation from the relations of the EU and the UN with the AU. The relations between the EU and the UN comprise an institutional framework on various political levels between the two organisations. Both organisations now interact as partners of equal standing with each other and they have fostered a partnership for maintaining international peace and security on the African continent and for their respective engagement with the AU. A division of roles between the AU, the EU and the UN seems to have emerged, an aspect which will be examined further in the part of this chapter dealing with AU–UN relations.

In another aspect, the EU has followed in the footsteps of NATO. The EU has abandoned the practice of acting as a 'clearing-house mechanism' for a UN peacekeeping operation in favour of launching its own short-term and small-scale operations under a SC mandate in support of UN operations or in the form of a bridging operation until a UN operation can be deployed.

All these specific developments are of course also fuelled by internal constraints such as resource problems. These problems, of which the EU is not spared, are not, once again, the only driving factor in increasing the networks of cooperation between the EU and the other international organisations, but also drive the EU to act in a comprehensive and thorough manner by using other means and tools to remedy for any lack of resources in other areas.[292] According to an estimation in 2008 by the first

---

[291] M. Reichard, 'Some Legal Issues Concerning the EU–NATO Berlin Plus Agreement', Nordic Journal of International Law, 73 (2004), 37, 42.
[292] Council of the European Union, Brussels, 23 July 2012, Council Conclusions, Doc. 12817/12, 2, para. 3; A Secure Europe, supra note 116, 13.

Chief Executive of the EDA, 'the total number of troops deployed today ... constitutes less than one third of one percent of European military manpower'.[293] Nevertheless, the main limiting factors for the engagement of the EU remain an unwillingness to engage[294] and political inactivity among the EU member states to further develop the CSDP.[295]

An analysis of the relations of the EU with other international organisations allows the drawing of two conclusions regarding the assessment of their activities in the peacekeeping context under the law of international responsibility.

Firstly, the criterion for the attribution of conduct has to be constructed in such a way as to take due account of institutionalised cooperation between international organisations; the criterion has to reflect the influence, power and control or the *normative power* that international organisations execute over other international organisations based on their institutionalised cooperation arrangements and even independent of any specific in-mission elements of cooperations. It has already been highlighted that the EU's African Peace Facility, in particular, raises various points under the law of responsibility.

Secondly, the analysis of the EU's relations showed that a certain triangular framework of relations between the AU, the EU and the UN appears to be emerging. It is therefore important that the criterion of attribution allows the attribution of conduct not only to two but also to more international organisations simultaneously.

ECOWAS and Peacekeeping: The Role Model for Other Sub-regional Organisations on the Continent

ECOWAS was set up in 1975 on the basis of the Treaty of Lagos and it is thus the oldest, continuously existing regional organisation on the African continent. Its aims were originally strictly economic; its Constituent

---

[293] N. Witney, *Re-energising Europe's Security and Defence Policy* (2008), European Council on Foreign Relations, 7. See also Koutrakos, *The EU Common Security*, supra note 90, 129.

[294] Apparently there were even instances in which Javier Solana had to '[phone] Defence Ministers in person to secure a single transport plane or field surgeon' as member states were unwilling to provide the necessary troops; see Witney, ibid., 7; Koutrakos, ibid., 154. This trend has also been fuelled by the financial crisis which led to decreased solidarity among EU members, Bjurner, 'On EU Peacemaking', supra note 218, 89, 97.

[295] Cf. Brosig, 'The Emerging Peace and Security Regime', supra note 10, 107, 121; European Council, 13–14 December 2012, Conclusions, Doc. EUCO 205/12 (2012), 9, para. 21; cf. also Generic Standards of Behaviour for ESDP Operations, Doc. 8373/3/05 REV 3(2005), 5.

Treaty of 1975 does not contain any dispositions for collective security. The evolution to include other, non-economic elements in the mandate of ECOWAS started with the adoption in 1978 and 1981 ECOWAS of two protocols on non-aggression, prohibiting cross-border attacks, and on mutual assistance in defence.[296]

In 1990, ECOWAS appointed a Commission of Eminent Persons with the task to submit proposals for a review of the treaty which led to the signature of the revised ECOWAS treaty in Cotonou in 1993, adding security policy elements to the mandate of ECOWAS.[297]

The Normative Framework

Nevertheless, the maintenance of international peace and security remained comparatively unimportant during the treaty revision; in fact it was not even mentioned among the guiding principles of the newly revised treaty. According to Article 3 of the new revised treaty, it was created with the aim

> to promote co-operation and integration, leading to the establishment of an economic union in West Africa in order to raise the living standards of its peoples, and to maintain and enhance economic stability, foster relations among Member States and contribute to the progress and development of the African Continent.[298]

Consequently, it is rather surprising – prima facie – that ECOWAS became involved in peacekeeping activities. However, the revised Treaty follows the road ECOWAS had begun to move along on with the adoption of the two Protocols. Article 58 of the Treaty of ECOWAS entitled Regional Security sets out general objectives concerning the maintenance of peace, stability and security within the region. It provides for the establishment of peacekeeping forces.[299] The Protocol Relating to the Mechanism for

---

[296] Protocol Relating to Mutual Assistance on Defence (1981), Preamble. See also A. T. Soma, 'Les relations entre l'Union Africaine et la Communauté Economique des Etats de l'Afrique de l'Ouest en matière den maintien de la paix', *African Yearbook of International Law*, 18 (2012), 345, 352–353.

[297] Griep, *Regionale Organisationen*, supra note 57, 332–333; International Peace Academy in partnership with Economic Community of West African States, Operationalizing the ECOWAS Mechanism for Conflict Prevention, Management, Resolution, Peacekeeping, and Security (2002), 4.

[298] Article 3 of the Treaty of ECOWAS.

[299] Article 58(2)(f).

Conflict Prevention, Management, Resolution, Peacekeeping and Security of 1999 (MCPMRPS) then established an appropriate framework for conflict resolution.

The Protocol created the Mediation and Security Council and the Council of Elders. Whereas the functions of the Mediation and Security Council are similar to the responsibilities of the SC of the UN, the Council of Elders is a new mechanism unique to ECOWAS. It is a list of eminent personalities who may be asked by the Mediation and Security Council to deal with a given conflict situation.[300] The Authority (of Head of states) remains the highest decision-making body in the domain of peacekeeping and conflict management,[301] but the Mediation and Security Council is mandated by the Authority to take appropriate decisions for the implementation of the Mechanism.[302] Under Article 10 of the Protocol, the Mediation and Security Council shall therefore decide on all matters relating to peace and security, including peacekeeping and the deployment of military missions.[303]

The Protocol also prescribes the composition of the ECOWAS Ceasefire Monitoring Group (ECOMOG) which is 'a structure composed of several Stand-by multi-purpose modules (civilian and military) in their countries of origin and ready for immediate deployment'.[304] ECOMOG or the ECOWAS Standby Force (ESF) as it is also called[305] is charged, inter alia, with peacekeeping and the restoration of peace, humanitarian intervention in support of humanitarian disaster and preventive deployment (Article 22). The ECOWAS Standby Force thereby implements the decisions of the Mediation and Security Council under Article 10 of the Protocol. Similar to the AU, ECOWAS possesses the mandate to intervene to 'alleviate the suffering of the populations and restore life to normalcy in the event of crises, conflict and disaster'.[306] In contrast to the UN which was unable to

---

[300] Article 20 of Protocol Relating to the Mechanism for Conflict Prevention, Management, Resolution, Peacekeeping and Security (1999).
[301] Article 6 of the Protocol.
[302] Article 7 of the Protocol.
[303] Article 10(a)–(d) of the Protocol.
[304] Article 22 of the Protocol: 'Each Member State shall provide ECOMOG with a unit the size of which shall be determined after consultation with each Member State.' Adebayo argues that the refined mechanisms of ECOWAS to manage their own conflicts are in large part due to neglect by the UN SC, A. Adebayo, 'The Security Council and Three Wars in Africa', in V. Lowe, A. Roberts, J. Welsh et al. (eds.), *The United Nations Security Council and War* (Oxford University Press, 2008), 466.
[305] African Peace and Security Architecture (APSA), 2010 Assessment Study, 43, para. 120.
[306] Article 40 of the Protocol.

implement the agreements under Article 43 of the UN Charter, ECOWAS member states make available to ECOMOG composite stand-by units which are under the direct control of the Mediation and Security Council.[307]

Article 52(3) of the Protocol regulates the relationship with the UN, and it stipulates that in accordance with Chapters VII and VIII of the UN Charter, ECOWAS shall inform the UN of any military intervention undertaken which is usually executed by submitting reports.[308] Although Chapter VIII of the UN only refers to of agencies and arrangements, the UN has accepted that this includes sub-regional organisations such as ECOWAS.[309] The organisation has been implicitly recognised by the SC in Resolution 788.[310] It is also argued that the Protocol Relating to Mutual Assistance on Defence made ECOWAS 'both a defense alliance and a regional system of collective security under Chapter VIII of the UN Charter'.[311]

Although the MCPMRPS does not stipulate explicitly that the Mediation and Security Council shall seek the authorisation of the SC before ordering military intervention, other parts of the Protocol state that ECOWAS accepts the primary responsibility of the SC for the maintenance of international peace and security.[312] Article 27 of the Protocol seems to suggest that an authorisation of the SC is not required. Under that disposition, the submission of a report on a situation to the UN or the OAU (now: AU) is only one of six procedures by which the Mechanism may be applied.[313] In contrast to Article 27, Article 26 MCPMRPS submits ECOWAS completely to the authority of the SC as the latter may activate the mechanism upon its request.[314] That article therefore corresponds principally to Article 53(1)

---

[307] Article 28 of the Protocol.
[308] This disposition, as well as Articles 26 and 27, nevertheless refers to the AU as the legal successor to the OAU. The Article also sets out that ECOWAS shall cooperate with the AU and that ECOWAS shall fully cooperate with the AU Mechanism for Conflict Prevention, Management and Resolution. Any military intervention presupposes, of course, an authorisation by the SC.
[309] UN Doc. A/61/204–S/2006/590 (2006), 16, para. 81.
[310] UN Doc. S/RES/788 (1992), 1–2, Preamble; 2, paras. 1–2, 4, 6.
[311] Articles 2–4 of the Protocol Relating to Mutual Assistance on Defence, 29 May 1981; Hummer, Schweitzer, 'Chapter VIII: Regional Arrangements. Article 52', note 146, 807, 838; C. Walter, 'Chapter VIII Regional Arrangements. Article 52', in B. Simma, D.-E. Khan, G. Nolte et al. (eds.), (Oxford University Press, 2012), 1445, 1468 mn. 73.
[312] Preamble and Article 2. See also Articles 83(2)(a) and Article 58(f), Revised ECOWAS Treaty.
[313] Article 27(e). See also Article 27(b).
[314] Article 25 of the Protocol defines the conditions for the application of the mechanism. In the practice of the SC, options (a)–(d) have been and would be considered as fulfilling the

of the UN Charter according to which the SC may utilise regional organisations under its authority for peace enforcement authority.[315] In practice, and as it will be explained in the following part, ECOWAS has intervened twice in conflicts without an authorisation of the SC, but both interventions happened in the period before the Protocol existed. In summary, it is not clear under *ECOWAS law*, whether the organisation is required to seek the authorisation of the SC to intervene militarily in a conflict.[316]

ECOWAS, Peacekeeping and Its Relations with the UN

The relations between ECOWAS and the UN in the area of peacekeeping operations began with a bad start in 1990. Liberia was devastated by a civil war and ECOWAS had requested technical assistance by the UN to establish a peacekeeping force. Although the Liberian Ambassador had tried to bring the conflict to the attention of the SC in June 1990, the SC did not consider the issue until January 1991.[317] The Cold War was just over and the UN and the SC were trying to find and assert their new role in this post-bipolar world. Political implications, national interests as well as procedural traditions hampered any decisiveness, assertiveness and readiness by the Council to take action so that ECOWAS intervened on its own;[318] however, the SC issued a statement commending the efforts of ECOMOG once unity had been reached.[319]

In the absence of a SC mandate, the intervention by ECOWAS occurred in violation of the UN Charter,[320] but it was welcomed by the UN and the

---

criteria under Article 39 of the UN Charter so that any request by the SC under Article 26 of the Protocol would fulfil the conditions for application of the Protocol under Article 25.

[315] The implementation of such a request by the SC would, however, correspond rather to Article 53(2) of the UN Charter as the military intervention would be conducted under the authority of ECOWAS and not under the authority of the UN SC.

[316] For the question of the compatibility of the Protocol with the framework of the UN, it is referred to the analysis of the compatibility of the AU's Legal Framework for Military Intervention with the UN Charter which analyses this question extensively in the part on AU and UN relations within this chapter.

[317] J. Allain, 'The True Challenges to the United Nations System of the Use of Force: The Failures of Kosovo and Iraq and the Emergence of the African Union', *Max Planck Yearbook of United Nations Law*, 8 (2004), 237, 260.

[318] The SC was blocked by three African States, Côte d'Ivoire, Zaire (now the DRC) and Ethiopia which refused any intervention into what they saw as the internal affairs of a member state of the OAU; see Adebayo, 'The Security Council and Three Wars in Africa', supra note 304, 466, 471.

[319] UN Doc. S/22133 (1991); Adebayo, ibid., 466, 471.

[320] Allain, 'The True Challenges', supra note 317, 237, 261; B. Kioko, 'The Right of Intervention under the African Union's Constitutive Act: From Non-interference to Non-intervention',

international community of states.³²¹ For the first time, the UN 'sent military observers to support an already established sub-regional force'³²² and in a statement laid down in a Note by the President of the SC, the SC also commended the efforts of ECOMOG.³²³ This note can be considered as a post facto authorisation to intervene. The relations between the UN and ECOWAS strengthened from 1992 onwards, coinciding with the publication of Boutros-Ghali's report, *An Agenda for Peace*, in which he called for increased cooperation with regional organisations.³²⁴

As ECOMOG continued to struggle with financial difficulties and political divisions, the Secretary-General proposed the establishment of a large UN peacekeeping operation under which ECOMOG would be subsumed. Unfortunately, that proposal was met by 'eloquent silence' as 'the most powerful members of the Council ... [were] increasingly wary of proliferating peacekeeping missions amidst the disasters of Somalia in 1993 and Rwanda in 1994'.³²⁵ The SC then issued Resolution 1001, after receiving the report by the Secretary-General, in which it was stated that the mandate of UNOMIL would not be extended if serious progress would not be made until September 1995. In response, ECOWAS members 'warn[ed] that any UN withdrawal would compromise ECOMOG's efforts and could lead to the further destabilization of the West African sub-region'.³²⁶

The warning by ECOWAS countries was enunciated for reasons of international legitimacy and attention rather than for security concerns as the small UN observation mission of sixty-two persons was largely symbolic. But it underlined the complex relationship existing between the UN and ECOWAS. Whereas the latter wanted the political legitimacy of the UN as well as their greater military and economic resources, they were once again concerned about the UN coming 'late in the day to steal ECOMOG's thunder after several

---

International Review of the Red Cross, 85 (2003), 807, 821. See also Adebayo, 'The Security Council and Three Wars in Africa', supra note 304, 466, 467; UN Doc. A/59/565 (2004), 57, para. 207; 71, para. 272a.

[321] UN Doc. S/RES/788 (1992), 2, Preamble as well as para. 1. Further efforts of ECOWAS in Liberia were, for example, recognised in Resolutions 813, 856 and 866, UN Doc. S/RES/813 (1993), 1, Preamble; 2, para. 2; S/RES/856 (1993), 2, para. 6; S/RES/866 (1993), 1, Preamble. Cf. also Kioko, ibid., 807, 821.

[322] Adebayo, 'The Security Council and Three Wars in Africa', supra note 304, 466.

[323] UN Doc. S/22133 (1991).

[324] Adebayo, 'The Security Council and Three Wars in Africa', supra note 304, 466, 472. See Chapter 1.

[325] Adebayo, ibid., 466, 473–474; UN Doc. S/1995/158 (1995), 3, para. 12; 10–12, paras. 46–55, especially, p. 12, para. 52(b).

[326] Annex to UN Doc. S/1995/701 (1995); S/1995/781 (1995), 2–4; S/RES/1001 (1995); S/1995/781 (1995), 2, para. 7; Adebayo, 'The Security Council and Three Wars in Africa', supra note 304, 466, 474.

years of lonely peacekeeping'.[327] However after the second civil war in Liberia started and ECOWAS intervened again, the UN ultimately established the UN Mission in Liberia (UNMIL) on the basis of Resolution 1509.[328]

In three missions, the UN were forced to take over given that the ECOWAS peacekeepers were logistically ill-equipped and under-resourced. In these scenarios, a partition of labour was finally agreed upon under which ECOWAS provided the core of the UN peacekeepers while the SC took charge of the political oversight and contributed additional troops and financial means.[329] The crisis in Sierra Leone was the second time that ECOWAS intervened without an authorisation of the SC, but as in the previous case in Liberia the non-authorised intervention was not met with any criticism, and rather ECOWAS was commended afterwards by the SC for its role and efforts.[330] The tasks were once again divided, the SC limited itself to travel restrictions and a petroleum and arms embargo on the basis of SC Resolution 1132.[331] This operation is once again a striking example of the interlacement between Chapter VII action of the SC and cooperation under Chapter VIII and the evolutionary practice of the SC regarding this matter.[332] When the failure of the Conakry Peace Agreement became apparent, 13,000 troops were deployed by ECOMOG. As in Liberia, the ECOMOG troops appeared to resent the better equipped and particularly better paid UN military observers.[333]

The UN turned down ECOMOG's request to finance the entire force; however, 4,000 of its peacekeepers were subsumed under the new UN force. ECOWAS and some other sub-regional organisations continued to question why, on the one hand, they should be responsible to the UN, if, on the other hand, the UN does not finance their operations.[334] ECOWAS is nevertheless less dependent on external funding than the AU since about 80 per cent of its budget for conflict prevention and management

---

[327] Adebayo, 'The Security Council and Three Wars in Africa', supra note 304, 466, 474.
[328] UN Doc. S/RES/1497 (2003), 2, para. 1.
[329] Adebayo, 'The Security Council and Three Wars in Africa', supra note 304, 466–468.
[330] UN Doc. S/RES/1162 (1998). See also Kioko, 'The Right of Intervention', supra note 320, 807, 821.
[331] Cf. Allain, 'The True Challenges', supra note 317, 237, 261; UN Doc. S/RES/1132 (1997).
[332] SC Resolution 1132 was adopted under Chapter VII and VIII. The SC effectively combined both chapters to decide upon measures to be implemented by ECOWAS and other actors, ibid, final paragraph of the Preamble, paras. 3, 4, 8, 9, 11, 14; UN Doc. S/RES/1162 (1998), 1–2, para. 5.
[333] UN Doc. S/RES/1181 (1998); Adebayo, 'The Security Council and Three Wars in Africa', supra note 304, 466, 476–477.
[334] Adebayo, ibid., 466, 478. See also International Peace Academy, supra note 297, 14.

is financed through a Community Levy of which a certain percentage is dedicated to the ECOWAS Peace Fund.[335]

One can say that ECOWAS was afflicted with political animosities among its members and that it lacked not only financial resources but also military and other equipment, among other things around the turn of the millennium. In addition, its soldiers were poorly trained and had an insufficient understanding of the applicable law, rules and standards. It is thus not surprising that ECOWAS has sought cooperation with the UN and other international organisations from an early stage. The DPKO reported in 2004 that cooperation with ECOWAS had intensified and that they had, at the request of ECOWAS, provided financial and logistical advice for the deployment of ECOMICI and ECOMIL.[336]

The African understanding was, however, that 'the UN Security Council has primary responsibility for international peace and security and simply shifted its responsibilities to ECOWAS due to the reluctance of the Council, after debacles in Somalia and Rwanda, to sanction UN missions in Africa'.[337] The UN reacted, inter alia, by creating the UN Office in West Africa (UNOWA) whose mandate includes capacity building of regional and subregional mechanisms to address threats to international peace and security.[338]

A New Era of Relations between ECOWAS and the UN

The emergence of the AU in 2002 led, however, to a profound shift in the relations between ECOWAS and other organisations in the area of international peace and security. The continuing operationalisation of the APSA under the AU focused cooperation arrangements as well as communication between the different organisations gradually on the AU as the primary responsible organisation on the African Continent.[339] The same evolution could be seen in the context of other peacekeeping operations in Africa in which the AU slowly gained influence.

In the Côte d'Ivoire crisis, for instance, the AU became increasingly involved as a mediator in the conflict.[340] Following SC Resolution 1633,

---

[335] African Peace and Security Architecture (APSA), 2010 Assessment Study, 66, para. 194. The AU report calls it 'an impressive instrument that undoubtedly enhances ECOWAS' ownership of its peace and security agenda, and should be replicated by other RECs/RM', ibid.
[336] UN Doc. A/59/591 (2004), 2-3, para. 5. See also UN Doc. A/54/839 (2000), 19, 161-166.
[337] Adebayo, 'The Security Council and Three Wars in Africa', supra note 304, 466, 487.
[338] Ibid., 466, 488; UN Doc. S/2001/434 (2001), paras. 6, 11.
[339] See the part on the AU and ECOWAS within this chapter.
[340] UN Doc. S/2005/270 (2005), paras. 1-2, 10, 16; S/RES/1605 (2005), para. 3.

there was increasingly more cooperation among the AU, the UN and ECOWAS in the peace process in Côte d'Ivoire.[341]

Clearly, the AU strengthened its role in the peace process in Côte d'Ivoire, not only in relations with ECOWAS but also in its relations with the UN. For instance, the following peace agreement of Ouagadougou was transmitted to the UN by the AU on the basis of ECOWAS recommendations.[342] Moreover, the AU urged the UN to act 'to expedite the deployment of the UN operation in Côte d'Ivoire'[343] and it mandated ECOWAS 'to take necessary action to ensure full restoration of operations of states in Côte d'Ivoire immediately'.[344] The SC decided then to create an international consultative organ which included among its members, the EU, the AU and ECOWAS.[345]

This partial loss of direct cooperation between ECOWAS and the UN was remedied to a certain extent by the operationalisation of the APSA. The gradual operationalisation of all the five standing brigades of the African Standby Force contributed to an increased cooperation between ECOWAS and the UN and it transformed ECOWAS into a supporter of peace and security beyond their geographic region in Africa,[346] drawing on their strength as the African organisation with the highest degree of experience in peacekeeping operations.[347] Nevertheless, efforts at capacity building are still necessary to improve the functioning of the organisation and communication within its institutions.[348]

Regarding the crisis in Mali, for example, the Support and Follow-up Group on the situation in Mali met under the joint chairmanship of the

---

[341] UN Doc. S/RES/1633 (2005), paras. 5–6; S/RES/1739 (2007), para. 2(i), (j), (m), 8(f). See also Griep, *Regionale Organisationen*, supra note 57, 141; Y. Oke, 'Substitute for the United Nations? Extending the Frontiers of the North Atlantic Treaty Organisation and Implications for African Unity', *African Journal of International and Comparative Law*, 21 (2013), 120, 136.

[342] UN Doc. S/2007/275 (2007), 2, para. 5; AU Doc. PSC/PR/Comm. (2004) (III), paras. 2–3.

[343] UN Doc. S/2007/275 (2007), ibid., para. 5

[344] AU Doc. PSG/AHG/Comm.(X) (2004), para. C. 7. The mandate given to ECOWAS is based on the cooperation with the regional mechanisms as part of the African Peace and Security Architecture, which has its legal basis in Article 16 of the protocol establishing the Peace and Security Council.

[345] UN Doc. S/RES/1765 (2007), paras. 8–9.

[346] Griep, *Regionale Organisationen*, supra note 57, 342; UN Doc. A/58/19 (2004), 12, para. 71; UN Doc. A/59/591 (2004), 2, paras. 3, 5.

[347] Brosig, 'The African Union a Partner for Peace', supra note 244, 292.

[348] A Proactive Mechanism for Change, Strategic Plan 2011–2015, 31; Regional Strategic Plan 2011–2015, 9–10; Regional Strategic Plan, A Proactive Mechanism for Change, 2–4 (of the document).

AU, the UN and ECOWAS and 'ECOWAS, the AU, the UN and the EU [were encouraged] in cooperation with Mali and other stakeholders, to expedite the finalization of the joint planning to respond to the request ... of Mali for an African-led International Force'.[349]

ECOWAS and the EU

The observations regarding the relationship between ECOWAS and the UN are also valid for the relations between ECOWAS and the EU. The latter cooperates nearly exclusively with the 'big brother' of ECOWAS, the AU. One example of direct cooperation between ECOWAS and the EU is the grant agreement of 76 million Euros to support the African-led International Mission in Mali (AFISMA) signed between ECOWAS and the EU.[350]

Conclusions

ECOWAS has generally emerged as a serious actor for maintaining international peace and security. The analysis demonstrates an evolution of the relations ECOWAS entertains with other international organisations. In contrast to EU–NATO, NATO–UN and EU–UN relations, the relations ECOWAS has maintained with these three organisations have not been further institutionalised. This is primarily due to the continuing operationalisation of the APSA of the AU. The focus for cooperational arrangements in maintaining international peace and security is now the AU which under its mandate, has the authority to provide security on the whole African continent.

Nevertheless, an analysis of ECOWAS relations further illustrate that relationships between the UN and regional organisations for maintaining international peace and security, as well as for deploying peacekeeping operations have evolved from the early and also competitive stages to relations based on the principles of collaboration and cooperation.

Regarding the application of the law of international responsibility, the analysis of ECOWAS and its relations with NATO, EU and the UN allows the formulation of three conclusions.

Due to the fact that the relations between ECOWAS and NATO, the EU and the UN have not been further institutionalised, it appears rather likely

---

[349] Meeting of the Support and Follow-up Group on the Situation in Mali, Bamako, 12 October 2012, conclusions, 1, para. 1; 1–3, 4(a), (d), (d)(iii); 4, para. 4(e).

[350] ECOWAS, EU Sign 76 Million-Euro Agreement to Support AFISMA, Free Movement, 9 April 2013, available at http://news.ecowas.int/presseshow.php?nb=095&lang=en&annee=2013.

that internationally wrongful acts committed during the deployment of peacekeeping operations might not be jointly attributable to ECOWAS and these three organisations or only on different legal grounds. Generally, ECOWAS appears to act in a subsidiary – rather than an equal – role in the context of peacekeeping operations, although the example of Mali might suggest that ECOWAS is emerging as an independent actor alongside the AU. Moreover, the analysis of ECOWAS and its institutional relations for maintaining international peace and security further emphasises the need to base the attribution of conduct on a criterion which incorporates the casuistic approach taken to peacekeeping operations as well as in relations among international organisations.

The lack of any substantive relations between ECOWAS and either NATO, or the UN or EU also provides further proof to the thesis that there is a security-facilitating triangle of actors evolving, consisting of the AU, the EU and the UN as will be confirmed in the following part of this chapter analysing the relations of the AU with the other international organisations.

AU Peacekeeping Activities

> [W]hat is happening in Darfur is extraordinary. We see there the African Union, the United Nations and Europe, working for peace. And who here can say that either of those organizations would have succeeded alone? We are able to make progress because we are all together, helping Africa, which will believe once again in its future.
>
> – Statement of H.E. President Sarkozy, during the 5749th meeting, 25 September 2007, of the Security Council on the Head of State/ Ministerial Level (France presiding)[351]

> Africa is no longer a private hunting ground; it is no longer anyone's backyard; it is no longer a part of the Great Game; and it is no longer anyone's sphere of influence: Those are the few simple rules that will allow the continent to shoulder its responsibility and to demonstrate inter-African solidarity.
>
> – Statement of H.E. Mr. Alpha Oumar Konaré, Chairman of the AU Commission, replying (partially) also to the Statement of President Sarkozy, in the very same meeting of the Security Council[352]

---

[351] UN Doc. S/PV.5749 (2007), 15.
[352] Ibid., 17. The quotation should not be interpreted as excluding the willingness of the AU to cooperate with any other (international) actors, but simply of an assertion that African issues shall not be dominated by external actors. Indeed, as he says 'Africa's responsibility ... is essential', ibid. In his statement, Konaré likewise said that 'the partnership between the African Union and the United Nations must be developed. The hybrid operation opens the way for that, and I believe that that indeed is the path to take in the future', ibid.

The AU was established in 2000 succeeding to the OAU and in the consciousness that the armed conflicts on the African soil limit the proper socio-economic development of the continent.[353] The establishment of this new organisation was in particular triggered by the African trauma of the 1994 genocide in Rwanda.[354]

It required the financial backing and guidance of Libya to replace the OAU with the AU which was granted powers going beyond those which had been appropriated by ECOWAS.[355] The objectives of the AU as laid down in Article 3 of the Constitutive Act include the encouragement of international cooperation while taking due account of the UN Charter, and the promotion of peace, security and stability on the African continent.[356] In the Fiftieth Anniversary Solemn Declaration, the member states of the AU reconfirmed their determination to 'end all wars in Africa by 2020'.[357]

The AU's Normative Framework for the Maintenance of International Peace and Security

The AU has established a whole framework for maintaining international peace and security on the African continent (APSA) going beyond the Mechanism for Conflict Prevention, Management and Resolution which already existed in the OAU. Indeed, two years after the foundation of the AU the Constitutive Act was amended by the Protocol establishing the Peace and Security Council, conscious that the previous mechanism with its focus on preventive diplomacy was not sufficient to confront and deal efficiently with security challenges in Africa.[358] The AU PSC sits on top of the

---

[353] Preamble of the Constitutive Act of the African Union (2000). Indeed, the UN system might not be able to prevent the outbreak of internal disturbances or of internal armed conflicts, W. Heintschel von Heinegg, 'The Impact of Law on Contemporary Military Operations – Sacrificing Security Interests on the Altar of Political Correctness?', in H. Hestermeyer, D. König, N. Matz-Lück et al. (eds.), *Coexistence, Cooperation and Solidarity. Liber Amicorum Rüdiger Wolfrum* (Leiden, Brill, 2012), 1177–1178.

[354] Organization of African Unity, *The International Panel of Eminent Personalities to Investigate the 1994 Genocide in Rwanda and the Surrounding Events* (2000), introductory chapter, para. 3; conclusions at chapter 24.

[355] Allain, 'The True Challenges', supra note 317, 237, 264.

[356] Article 1(e), (f).

[357] Fiftieth Anniversary Solemn Declaration by Heads of State and Government of the AU Assembled to Celebrate the Golden Jubilee of the OAU/AU, 5, para. E.

[358] C. R. Majinge, 'Regional Arrangements and the Maintenance of International Peace and Security: The Role of the African Union Peace and Security Council', *Canadian Yearbook of International Law/Annuaire canadien de droit international*, 48 (2010), 97, 114–115.

APSA.[359] The preamble of the Protocol establishing the Peace and Security Council articulates a firm commitment to the principles of the UN, but also to the importance of developing international cooperation between the UN, other international organisations and the AU.[360] The PSC has a fairly broad mandate reaching from anticipation and prevention of conflicts to peace building and post-conflict construction.[361] Its mandate also includes to promote harmonisation and cooperation between the AU and subregional organisations for maintaining international peace and security. For this purpose, the PSC shall develop a strong partnership with the UN and other relevant organisations.[362] The OAU, was explicitly recognised as a regional organisation under Chapter VIII of the UN Charter[363] and there are no contrary arguments why the AU does not fall under Chapter VIII.[364]

Article 4 of the Constitutive Act of the UN and the UN Charter

The objectives of the AU in the domain of peace and security include the defence of 'the sovereignty, territorial integrity and independence of its Member States'. In Article 4 of its Constitutive Act, these broad aims are qualified and specified. So they comprise, inter alia, the establishment of a common defence policy, peaceful conflict resolution, the prohibition of the use of force, non-intervention in the internal affairs of another member state and – in paragraph (h) – the right of the AU to intervene in a member state in grave circumstances, namely war crimes, genocide and crimes against humanity. The codification of these latter principles in Article 4(h) 'provide[s] clear evidence, in the view of African states, that [sic] they should seek to rely on their own forces in such circumstances'.[365]

---

[359] See generally K. Sturman, A. Hayatou, 'The Peace and Security Council of the African Union: From Design to Reality', in U. Engel, J. Gomes Porto (eds.), *Africa's New Peace and Security Architecture: Promoting Norms, Institutionalizing Solutions* (Farnham, Ashgate, 2010), 57–76.
[360] Protocol Relating to the Establishment of the Peace and Security Council of the African Union (2002).
[361] Article 3 of the Protocol.
[362] Article 7(j), (k) of the Protocol.
[363] SC Resolution 199 (1964), Preamble and para. 6.
[364] Hummer, Schweitzer, 'Chapter VIII: Regional Arrangements. Article 52', supra note 146, 807, 828–838.
[365] Sands, Klein, *Bowett's Law*, supra note 17, 250. See also, A. Abass, 'The United Nations, the African Union and the Darfur Crisis: Of Apology and Utopia', *Netherlands International Law Review*, 54 (2007), 415–416; P. M. Munya, 'The Organization of African Unity and Its Role in Regional Conflict Resolution and Dispute Settlement: A Critical Evaluation',

A truly heated debate, particularly within the legal scholarship has however been caused by the question of whether the provisions of Article 4(h) of the Constitutive Act are in conformity with the UN Charter and particularly Article 2(4). It has to be accepted that the constitutional framework of the AU does not expressly refer to the use of force or armed military intervention,[366] but bearing in mind that any intervention under Article 4(h) will respond to war crimes or to the existence of grave circumstances, which is considered to cover similar severe violations of human rights law, one may presume that any such intervention will involve the use of force.[367] Article 4 of the Constitutive Act does not stipulate that an authorisation of the SC is necessary in order for the AU to intervene in a member state on the basis of Article 4(h), nor does it contain an obligation to seek an authorisation after intervening.[368]

One author – referring implicitly to the debate on universalism and regionalism during the drafting of the Charter – states quite harshly that this empowerment of enforcement action by the AU is 'the first true blow to … the ultimate control of the use of force by the United Nations Security Council'.[369] According to this view, the right to intervene of the AU corresponds to the denial of the AU vis-à-vis the SC's primary responsibility for maintaining international peace and security as enshrined in Article 24 of the UN Charter.[370]

Other authors have interpreted this disposition as an internal authorisation clause which establishes the constitutional competence of the AU to

---

Boston College Third World Law Journal, 19 (1999), 537, 543; J.-M. Iyi, 'The AU/ECOWAS Unilateral Humanitarian Intervention Legal Regimes and the UN Charter', *African Journal of International and Comparative Law*, 21 (2013), 489, 491–492. The Amendments to the Constitutive Act of the AU led to the addition of a fourth option and a qualification to Article 4(h) – 'the right of the Union to intervene in a Member state … in respect of grave circumstances, namely … a serious threat to legitimate order'.

[366] Y. G. Muhire, 'The African Union's Right of Intervention and the UN System of Collective Security', unpublished PhD thesis, Utrecht University (2013), 201.

[367] K. Kindiki, 'Intervention to Protect Civilians in Darfur: Legal Dilemmas and Policy Imperatives', ISS Monograph Series, n° 131, 46. However, the application of this norm is difficult in practice, cf. Communiqué of the 12th Session of the PSC, AU Doc. PSC/MIN/Comm.(XII) (2004), para. 2; S. A. Dersso, 'The Role and Place of Human Rights in the Mandate and Works of the Peace and Security Council of the AU: An Appraisal', *Netherlands International Law Review*, 58 (2011), 77, 99.

[368] Boisson de Chazournes, supra note 141, 79, 289.

[369] Allain, 'The True Challenges', supra note 317, 237, 238. Cf. Sands, Klein, *Bowett's Law*, supra note 17, 250, fn. 15.

[370] E. de Wet, 'The United Nations Collective Security System in the 21st Century: Increased Decentralization through Regionalization and Reliance on Self-Defence', in

undertake such an operation in the case of the existence of an authorisation from the SC.³⁷¹

In the specific context of this debate, it is also disputed whether the consent of the state in which intervention takes place, has a bearing upon the legal determination of the intervention as legal or illegal.

On the one hand, Article 3(a) of the African Union Non-Aggression and Common Defence Pact is more restrictive than Article 2(4) of the Charter of the UN, as it covers the prohibition of the use of force 'in matters *between* [states] and *within* them'.³⁷² It so seems that this disposition prohibits the AU from conducting an intervention that is as prohibited under Article 2(7) of the UN Charter, but with the difference that the latter allows for intervention in cases of an authorisation granted by the SC under Chapter VII.³⁷³

On the other hand, it is also argued in legal writings that the AU can intervene, in similar fashion as the UN under Article 2(7) of the UN Charter, in cases of where no consent is given by the concerned state.³⁷⁴ Upon closer inspection, this view cannot, however, withstand legal scrutiny.³⁷⁵ First of all, a distinction of a peremptory and a non-peremptory part of the prohibition of the use of force in this specific case, with the latter being based on consent by being a member of the regional organisation whose charter authorises such an action would exempt all organisations from the requirement of seeking an authorisation by the SC and it would be evidently contrary to Article 53(1) UN Charter.³⁷⁶ Moreover, the AU

H. Hestermeyer, D. König, N. Matz-Lück et al. (eds.), *Coexistence, Cooperation and Solidarity. Liber Amicorum Rüdiger Wolfrum* (Leiden, Brill, 2012), 1553, 1559.

³⁷¹ Boisson de Chazournes, supra note 141, 79, 290.
³⁷² Abass, 'The United Nations', supra note 365, 415, 425.
³⁷³ Ibid., 415, 425; A. Abass, *Regional Organizations and the Development of Collective Security: Beyond Chapter VIII of the UN Charter* (2004), 183–208. See also Muhire, 'The African Union's Right', supra note 366, 229–230.
³⁷⁴ Dersso, 'The Role', supra note 367, 77, 84. So, Yusuf argues that the distinction in Article 13 of the Protocol between peace and support operations and interventions 'implies that the intervention is used … in the sense of coercive action involving armed force in a Member State without the consent of the government of that state'. A. A. Yusuf, 'The Right of Intervention by the African Union: A New Paradigm in Regional Enforcement Action?', *African Yearbook of International Law*, 11 (2003), 3, 9.
³⁷⁵ See, with further references, Iyi, 'The AU/ECOWAS Unilateral Humanitarian Intervention Legal Regimes', supra note 365, 489, 515–516.
³⁷⁶ C. Walter, 'Article 53', in B. Simma, D.-E. Khan, G. Nolte et al. (eds.), *The Charter of the United Nations. A Commentary. Volume II* (Oxford University Press, 2012), 1478, 1491 mn. 37. Cf. Abass, 'The United Nations', supra note 365, 415, 425; Muhire, 'The African Union's Right', supra note 366, 229.

members per se would be violating Article 103 of the UN Charter while intervening in an AU member state on the basis of Article 4(h), without SC authorisation.[377]

Nevertheless, one has to take into account that Article 4 and especially its paragraph (h) are at the core of the system of maintenance of peace and security as set up by the different instruments of the AU. As it is argued by one author, the competences the AU is endowed with under Article 4(h) of the Constitutive Act are broader than the competences of the SC allocated under Chapter VII of the Charter, in the sense that even if the AU were to comply with the UN Charter, it could nevertheless act in that area which is outside the jurisdiction of the SC.[378] Indeed, further dispositions of the legal framework of the AU suggest that a right to intervene without a SC authorisation might have been envisaged by the drafters.[379]

However, this eagerness for independence of the AU vis-à-vis the SC is clearly abdicated in the Protocol establishing the PSC. The Preamble of the Protocol stipulates the determination to enhance the 'capacity to address the scourges of conflicts ... and *to ensure that ... the African Union, plays a central role in bringing about peace, security and stability on the Continent* [emphasis added]'. The intentions of the drafters are made even clearer in Article 16 of the Protocol according to which '[t]he Regional Mechanisms are part of the overall security architecture of the Union, *which has the primary responsibility for promoting peace, security and stability in Africa* [emphasis added]'. This is a blunt and honest contradiction to Article 24 of the UN Charter but it can be questioned whether it truly achieves the displacement of the SC from its primary responsibility for maintaining international peace and security as it is suggested by Allain.[380]

---

[377] But see J. I. Levitt, 'The Peace and Security Council of the African Union and the United Nations Security Council: The Case of Darfur, Sudan', in N. Blokker, N. Schrijver (eds.), *The Security Council and the Use of Force: Theory and Reality. A Need for Change?* (Leiden, Martinus Nijhoff, 2005), 213, 234. His view is not convincing, cf. T. Gazzini, *The Changing Rules on the Use of Force in International Law* (Manchester University Press, 2005), 114.

[378] Allain, 'The True Challenges', supra note 317, 237, 282–283. Cf. also Iyi, 'The AU/ECOWAS Unilateral Humanitarian Intervention Legal Regimes', supra note 365, 489, 497, 500; UN Doc. S/2008/186 (2008), 7, para. 10.

[379] T. Maluwa, 'Reimaging African Unity: Some Preliminary Reflections on the Constitutive Act of the African Union', *African Yearbook of International Law*, 9 (2001), 3, 28. See also AU Doc. Ext/EX.CL/2 (VII) (2005), 6, para. B.ii; L. Gelot, 'African Regional Organizations, Peace Operations and the UN', in P. Wallensteen, A. Bjurner (eds.), *Regional Organizations and Peacemaking. Challengers to the UN?* (London, Routledge, 2015), 137, 143.

[380] Allain, 'The True Challenges', supra note 317, 237, 275.

First of all, the Article refers to the primary responsibility of the AU for the maintenance of international peace and security *only* in the context of its relations with sub-regional organisations on the continent.[381]

This apparent contradiction of Article 4(h) of the AU Constitutive Act with the UN Charter is weakened or even remedied by other clauses in the legal framework of the AU. According to Article 17 of the 2005 African Union Non-Aggression and Common Defence Pact, no position taken by the AU shall be considered as 'derogating in any way from the obligations of Member States contained in the United Nations Charter ... and from the primary responsibility of the United Nations Security Council for the maintenance of international peace and security'.

The Protocol relating to the establishment of the Peace and Security Council also ascertains that the PSC shall cooperate and work closely with the UN SC 'which has the primary responsibility for the maintenance of international peace and security'.[382] Thus, it is argued – on the basis of a harmonious interpretation – that these references to the UN Charter qualify the right of intervention of Article 4(h).[383] While it is unclear whether under *AU law*, the AU has to seek an authorisation from the SC, 'this does not necessarily suggest that the intention was for Article 4(h) to operate outside of the limits set under the UN Charter'.[384]

On the contrary, distinguishing between the internal law of the AU of which the Protocol is part[385] and general international law, it is submitted that the authorisation of the AU to intervene under its internal law is necessary as the AU would be otherwise acting ultra vires under its own law should it be authorised by the SC to resort to enforcement action against one of its members. Without an authorisation of the SC, the AU's right to intervene under Article 4(h) is in violation of Chapters VII and VIII of the UN Charter.[386]

---

[381] Omorogbe, 'Can the African Union Deliver', supra note 264, 35, 41.
[382] Protocol Relating to the Establishment of the Peace and Security Council of the African Union (2002), Article 17. One has to note that the SC has been meeting regularly with the Peace and Security Council since 2007, UN Doc. A/65/762 (2011), 14, para. 44.
[383] Boisson de Chazournes, supra note 141, 79, 290.
[384] Dersso, 'The Role', supra note 367, 77, 85.
[385] At the internal AU law level, the member states of the AU have given their prior consent to any intervention as they have freely signed the treaty. Therefore Naert suggests that there are more compatibilities than tensions with the UN Charter, Naert, *International Law Aspects*, supra note 41, 244.
[386] Muhire, ibid., 237.

The practice of both organisations also illustrates very clearly that an authorisation of the SC for intervention by the AU for measures going beyond traditional peacekeeping operations is considered to be necessary. In a statement by the President of the SC it was also noted that the AU may be authorised by the SC to deal with collective security challenges in Africa.[387] The SC and several of its members have repeatedly emphasised the role that the Council holds at the apex of the collective security system.[388]

Moreover, in practice, Article 4(h) has never been invoked by the AU, not even in Darfur nor in respect of Libya in 2011, despite deliberate and systematic attacks on civilians in both countries.[389] It might be plausible that the inactivity of the AU was due to pragmatic reasons such as political disagreement within the AU or simply the lack of financial and other resources to act independently. Indeed, the financial burden of the AU as well as the troop contributions to peacekeeping operations rest on the shoulders of a few African states.[390] In any case, the practice shows that the African states themselves have defended the view that the SC has the primary responsibility for maintaining international peace and security.[391] In similar fashion, individual African states have expressed the necessity to remain within the ambit of Chapter VIII of the UN Charter with regard to any right of intervention; the extensive analysis by Corten in this context contains references to statements by not less than twenty African states, including some members of ECOWAS.[392] The AU itself states that it acts under Chapter VIII for the purpose of peacekeeping operations.[393] Consequently, despite the apparent contradiction between Article 4(h) of the Constitutive Act of the AU and international law, this appears to

---

[387] UN Doc. S/PRST/2007/7 (2007), 2; S/RES/1631 (2005), Preamble; S/PV.5868 (2008), 11, 20.
[388] See, for example, UN Doc. S/RES/1631 (2005), Preamble; Statement by the President of the Security Council, UN Doc. S/PRST/2009/3 (2009). See also infra Chapter 1.
[389] Rodt, Okeke, 'AU–EU Partnership', supra note 265, 211, 219.
[390] Franke, Gänzle, 'How "African" Is the African Peace and Security Architecture', ibid., 88, 102.
[391] O. Corten, 'L'Union africaine, une organisation régionale susceptible de s'émanciper de l'autorité du Conseil de sécurité? Opinio Juris et pratique récente des Etats', European Society of International Law Conference Paper Series, Conference Paper No. 11/2012, Fifth Biennial Conference, Valencia (Spain), 13–15 September 2012, 6. Among the states which have expressed themselves accordingly are the US, the UK, France, China, Russia, for all references, ibid., 7–8.
[392] Ibid., 8–9. The conclusions of the practice of a general adherence to the system of collective security under the UN Charter are therefore also valid for ECOWAS.
[393] UN Doc. S/2010/392/Add.1 (2010), 2, paras. 1, 3, 7 (b); S/2010/392 (2010), 2, para. 2; S/2007/421 (2007), 29, paras. 1–2; S/2007/421 (2007), 3, para. 12; S/PV.6702 (2012), 8.

have little impact in practice; the latter demonstrates an adherence to the system of collective security as was envisioned by the drafters of the UN Charter in 1945.

The most relevant feature is nevertheless that the AU PSC, in terms of the organisation's internal law and policy, also '*constitutes a legitimate mandating authority under Chapter VIII of the UN Charter. In this regard, the AU will seek UN Security Council authorisation of its enforcements actions. Similarly, the RECs/Regions will seek AU authorisation of their interventions* [emphasis added]'.[394] In this sense, the AU therefore acts as the intermediary between the UN and ECOWAS for the purposes of maintaining international peace and security.[395]

The AU and the UN

The Early Steps: Defining Their Roles in the Relationship

The analysis of the legal framework of the AU showed that the AU's mandate to maintain international peace and security is innovative as well as ambitious. However, whether the ambitions of the AU to be the leading figure in maintaining international peace and security on the African continent can be implemented in practice, and especially vis-à-vis the SC and on the basis of Chapter VIII of the UN Charter, deserves closer examination.

The UN had already cooperated with the OAU from the mid-1990s onwards.[396] This tradition of reliance on the UN was brought within the AU when it was established in 2000. Indeed, the AU adopted a comparable if not parallel attitude to that of ECOWAS towards the UN. The perception

---

[394] Experts' Meeting on the Relationship between the AU and the Regional Mechanisms for Conflict Prevention, Management and Resolution, Addis Ababa 22–23 March 2005, Roadmap for the Operationalization of the African Standby Force (2005), 5, para. 10; Policy Framework for the Establishment of the African Standby Force and the Military Staff Committee (Part I), Document adopted by the Third Meeting of African Chiefs of Defense Staff, 15–16 May 2003, Addis Ababa, 4, para. 2.2; African Standby Force, Peace Support Operations Doctrine (2006), 2–7, para. 22; AU Doc. PSC/PR/2. (CCCVII) (2012), 23, para. 87.

[395] African Union, Memorandum of Understanding on Cooperation in the Area of Peace and Security between the African Union, the Regional Economic Communities and the Coordinating Mechanisms of the Regional Standby Brigades of Eastern Africa and Northern Africa (2008), Article XX, paras. 1–2. This is also in accordance with ECOWAS law.

[396] UN Doc. A/54/839 (2000), 19, 161–166; A/48/475/Add.1 (1993), 7–8, paras. 22–24; S/2008/18 (2008), 2, para. 7; 3, para. 11; 10–11, paras. 45–46; A/59/608 (2004), 17, para. 76. See generally Muhire, 'The African Union's Right', supra note 366.

was that in so far as the AU safeguards the maintenance of international peace and security on the African continent, the UN will provide financial, logistic and military support. The *Declaration on a Common African Defence and Security Policy* sees the UN in a supportive role towards the AU stating that '[w]here necessary, recourse will be made to the United Nations to provide the necessary financial, logistical and military support for the African Union's activities in the promotion of maintenance of peace and security'.[397] This approach illustrates that African leaders were willing to 'push the standards of collective stability and security to the limit'[398] and that they held a somewhat depreciatory view of the SC. In their opinion, the SC was 'meant to assist the African Union's Peace and Security Council [and] not vice versa'.[399]

In contrast to the early AU policy towards the UN, the latter's policy towards the AU has been and remains to support the AU in maintaining international peace and security on the African continent and to further develop the inter-organisational relationship, while nonetheless emphasising the prerogative of the SC for the maintenance of international peace and security.[400] One of the motives for the UN is to prevent the perception that the UN is subcontracting or 'outsourcing' peacekeeping to the AU.[401] A clear expression of this policy is the recognition by the UN of the lack of resources at the disposal of the AU.[402] As several AU or ECOWAS peacekeeping operations have been reassigned to UN peacekeeping operations,[403] there is a conviction within the UN that the AU assumes that it will deploy bridging peacekeeping operations with a view, in due time,

---

[397] Cf. T. Kwasi Tieku, 'The African Union', in J. Boulden (ed.), *Responding to Conflict in Africa. The United Nations and Regional Organizations* (London, Palgrave Macmillan, 2013), 33, 37.

[398] Kioko, 'The Right of Intervention', supra note 320, 807, 821.

[399] Allain, 'The True Challenges', supra note 317, 237, 287; Yamashita, 'Peacekeeping Cooperation', supra note 14, 165, 177–178.

[400] UN Doc. A/63/666 and S/2008/813 (2008), 2, para. 6; A/52/871 and S/1998/318 (1998), 10, para. 44.

[401] UN Doc. A/63/666 and S/2008/813 (2008), 13, para. 39.

[402] UN Doc. S/2008/186 (2008), 11, para. 31; Capacity Survey on Regional and Other Intergovernmental Organizations in the Maintenance of International Peace and Security (2008) produced by the United Nations University – Comparative Regional Integration Studies (UNU-CRIS), 22–23; Peace and Security Architecture (APSA), 2010 Assessment Study, 26, para. 68. Cf. T. Murithi, 'The African Union's Foray into Peacekeeping: Lessons from the Hybrid Mission in Darfur', *Journal of Peace, Conflict and Development*, 14 (2009), 1, 15.

[403] Capacity Survey on Regional and Other Intergovernmental Organizations, ibid., 26.

to handing them over to the UN.⁴⁰⁴ Primarily due to the support of the EU through the African Peace Facility, the African Standby Force attained Initial Operational Capacity in 2010 and was expected to achieve Full Operational Capacity by the end of 2015.⁴⁰⁵

The World Summit as the Catalyser for More Institutionalised Relations

The 2005 World Summit Outcome document laid the basis for more institutionalised relations between the UN and the AU using the cooperation between the UN and the EU as a model.⁴⁰⁶ The UN pledged to 'support the development and implementation of a ten-year plan for capacity-building with the AU'.⁴⁰⁷ The start of this support came in the form of a Framework Declaration which was adopted a year later in 2006.⁴⁰⁸ The main objective is 'to enhance the capacity of the AU ... and African subregional organizations to act as *effective UN partners* [emphasis added]'.⁴⁰⁹ This objective is significant for several reasons. First of all it stressed that the UN and the AU are seen as partners rather than in a subordinate–superior relationship.⁴¹⁰ The SC, in contrast, again demonstrated its flexibility and pragmatic approach in its relations with regional organisations.⁴¹¹

In its report on UN–AU cooperation in peace and security to the SC, the Secretary-General gave a more detailed description of the necessary pragmatic and flexible policy:

> [a]t the operational level, lessons and experience indicate that there is no generic model for cooperation between the two organizations that can be applied to any situation ... It is therefore important to ensure that the conceptualization, mandates, rules of engagement and institutional arrangements for each peacekeeping operation are based on the strategic and operational requirements to support a peace process or the effective

---

⁴⁰⁴ UN Doc. S/2008/186 (2008), 11, para. 29.
⁴⁰⁵ Poulton, Trillo, Kukkuk, *Part 1 of the African Peace Facility Evaluation*, supra note 261, 12; AU Doc. PSC/PR/2.(CCCVII) (2012), 8–9, para. 32.
⁴⁰⁶ UN Doc. A/61/19/Rev.1 (2008), 16, para. 92; A/RES/60/1 (2005), 24, para. 93; A/60/640 (2005), 9–10, paras. 29–31.
⁴⁰⁷ UN Doc. A/RES/60/1 (2005), 23, para. 93(b); Capacity Survey on Regional and Other Intergovernmental Organizations, supra note 402, 26.
⁴⁰⁸ UN Doc. A/61/630 (2006).
⁴⁰⁹ Ibid., para. 2; UN Doc. A/65/510 and S/2010/514 (2010), 4, para. 13.
⁴¹⁰ UN Doc. A/64/359 and S/2009/470 (2009), 2–4, paras. 3–5, 7–10; A/65/510 and S/2010/514 (2010), 2–3, paras. 3–6; A/65/19 (2011), 40, para. 207; S/2008/18 (2008), 11–12, para. 49.
⁴¹¹ UN Doc. A/67/632 (2012), 12, para. 47.

implementation of a peace agreement. Such arrangements should be predicated on a shared vision of the political process and preserve unity of command and strategic direction, while ensuring the provision of critical resource and capability requirements. To ensure a more coherent framework for global peacekeeping, the United Nations is committed to working with the African Union to harmonize peacekeeping standard operating procedures, including with respect to force generation, planning and mission startup.[412]

Moreover, this objective underlines the fact that the UN – just like the AU – has very high incentives for the AU to transform into an organisation which can effectively implement its mandate as the UN was itself overstretched and reaching the limits of its capacities given the volume of peacekeeping operations with which it had been involved.[413] The regional consultative mechanism established between the UN and the AU provides for consultation and cooperation in different clusters within which one is dealing with peace and security.[414]

Aid for Self-Help by the UN

Two years later, in 2008, the UN established a liaison office facilitating support to the AU.[415] Particularly relevant for the context of the present book is that specific priorities within the AU–UN cooperation were given to the development of logistical and financial reserves for the AU's rapid deployment capabilities as well as to help the AU in ensuring a common 'doctrine and procedures for joint planning and operational validation in its coordination with subregional economic communities'.[416] The UN Secretariat also continues

> to provide operational and planning support and long-term capacity-building support to the African Union Commission for its peace support operations ... [which] includes support to the planning and management of ongoing operations such as AMISOM and potential future operations,

---

[412] UN Doc. S/2011/805 (2011), 17, para. 64; S/PV.6178 (2009), 30.
[413] Cf., e.g., UN Doc. A/65/680 (2011), 13, para. 54; Statement by the President of the Security Council, UN Doc. S/PRST/2007/42 (2007); UN Doc. A/63/666 and S/2008/813 (2008), 8, para. 18. See also A. F. Douhan, *Regional Mechanisms of Collective Security. The New Face of Chapter VIII of the UN Charter?* (Paris, L'Harmattan, 2013), 138.
[414] UN Doc. A/66/721 (2012), 21; 61/668/Add.1 (2006), 15, para. 45; see also Yamashita, 'Peacekeeping Cooperation', supra note 14, 165, 180.
[415] UN Doc. S/2008/186 (2008), 9, paras. 19–20; UN Doc. A/61/630 (2006).
[416] UN Doc. A/61/19/Rev.1 (2008), 29 paras. 178–179; see also UN Doc. A/59/591 (2004), 8, para. 35; A/58/694 (2004), 16, para. 84.

as well as technical advice and support in the development of the policies, guidelines, doctrine and training for the African Standby Force.[417]

This fraction of the cooperation between the UN and the AU raises questions from the point of view of responsibility for wrongful acts conducted in peacekeeping operations to be addressed in the following part.

The Policy Framework on the establishment of the ASF and the Military Staff Committee as adopted in 2004 by the Assembly of the AU foresaw the establishment of five standby brigades by 2010 for the five sub-regions on the African continent to be deployed rapidly under the auspices of the AU, ECOWAS or other subregional organisations[418] under one of six conflict scenarios envisaged.[419] The interest of the UN to establish this capacity is particularly profound because regional organisations are better equipped for the rapid deployment of troops.[420] The ASF will comprise a maximum of 25,000 troops and its operationalisation will therefore facilitate the burden of the UN in Africa which deployed 76,029 peacekeepers in Africa alone in November 2015, excluding military observers, police, and other staff.[421] The UN as well as the EU and NATO are also engaged in training of the ASF.[422]

As a result, the UN and other organisations are not only contributing to the mission and operational planning of the AU, but they equally contribute to the training of its troops. Consequently, it has to be examined if and to what extent this part of cooperation between the organisations is relevant for an analysis of the responsibility of the organisations for conduct arising out of peacekeeping operations. It is even more so as the question of financing and financial support to AU peacekeeping operations could

---

[417] For more details, see UN Doc. S/2011/805 (2011), 7, para. 22. Generally on UN partnerships, UN Doc. A/62/19 (2008), 25–26, para. 156; A/66/721 (2012), 20–21, para. 51.
[418] Policy Framework on the establishment of the African Standby Force and the Military Staff Committee, AU Doc. Assembly/AU/Dec.35 (III) (2004); UN Doc. A/59/591 (2004), 3, paras. 8–9, Experts' Meeting on the Relationship, supra note 394, 1, para. 3.
[419] Policy Framework for the Establishment of the African Standby Force, supra note 394, 3, para. 1.6. In the case of scenarios 1–5, which altogether form the potential scenarios of a peacekeeping operation, the mandating authority of the AU derives from both UN law (Chapter VIII) and internal law of the organisation (Article 9(1)(g) of the Constitutive Act, Article 7(1) of the PSC Protocol), cf. also S. A. Dersso, 'The African Union's Mandating Authority and Processes for Deploying an ASF Mission', *African Security Review*, 19 (2010), 73, 80–81.
[420] UN Doc. S/PV.4970 (Resumption 1) (2004), 5–7, 12; S/PV.5776 (2007), 7.
[421] UN Peacekeeping Operations Factsheet, 30 November 2015.
[422] UN Doc. S/PV.6561 (2011), 3–4; S/2008/18 (2008), 11–12, para. 50; African Standby Force, Training Policy, Final Draft, November 2006, 2, para. 14; 5, para. 27(a); 6, para. 34.

also entail the responsibility under international law of the supporting organisations. So far, AU peacekeeping operations authorised by the SC are funded primarily through voluntary contributions, especially the EU's African Peace Facility[423] as well as through UN assessed contributions.[424] Financial problems have so far seriously encroached upon nearly all AU peace operations and hampered the rapid deployment of troops.[425]

Support Packages for AU Peace Operations and the Possibility of Control by the SC

The UN–AU panel was well aware of the fact that the various cooperation packages for the AU raise questions regarding the responsibility and oversight of these operations. Referring to the operations in Somalia and Darfur, the panel stated that '[w]hile the lack of resources put the operations at serious risk of failure, the dependency on external support for deployment and sustainment put the African Union in the position of having the potential responsibility for missions over which it has little institutional or managerial capacity or control'.[426] Although the statements refer rather to political than legal responsibility, it is clear that these cooperation packages also raise questions regarding the international responsibility of the involved organisations.

The UN has generally resisted allowing the distribution of a UN support package financed through assessed contributions to AU peacekeeping operations despite calls by the latter on various occasions.[427] The Secretary-General stressed that the 'current financial framework for partnerships in peacekeeping operations are not conducive to building a sustainable long-term strategy'.[428] The Prodi report called likewise for contributions to AU peacekeeping operations based on assessed contributions[429] and the High-level Independent Panel issued the same recommendation, while alternative financial sources should be also explored.[430] As part of the Common

---

[423] See the previous part on EU–AU relations within this chapter.
[424] UN Doc. A/65/510 and S/2010/514 (2010), 11, para. 42.
[425] Omorogbe, 'Can the African Union Deliver?', supra note 264, 35, 46, 57.
[426] UN Doc. A/63/666 and S/2008/813 (2008), 7, para. 13; S/2011/805 (2011), 17, para. 65.
[427] See, e.g., UN Doc. S/PV.5776 (2007), 8; S/PV.6409 (2010), 7; S/2008/18 (2008), 11–12, para. 52; AU Doc. PSC/PR/Communiqué (II) (2004), paras. 7, 14.
[428] UN Doc. A/65/510 and S/2010/514 (2010)16, para. 61.
[429] UN Doc. A/63/666 and S/2008/813 (2008), 18, paras. 63–66.
[430] UN Doc. A/70/95 and S/2015/446 (2015), 76, paras. 246–248. Yet still in December 2014, the SC emphasised the responsibility of regional organisations to secure their own funding, UN Doc. S/PRST/2014/27 (2014), 2.

African Position on the UN Review of Peace Operations, the AU made anew an advance to canvass for the financing of AU peacekeeping operations by the UN. The AU argued that it is not only providing approximately 45 per cent of the UN's peacekeepers, but that the African capacities have become a critical resource for the success of the UN's operations.[431] The UN should provide support to up to 75 per cent of the costs of the AU-led peacekeeping operations whereas the AU will assume responsibility for at least 25 per cent of the costs.[432]

The implications on a level of the law of responsibility are severe as 'the provision of a United Nations support package financed by United Nations assessed contributions would entail a case-by-case authorization by the United Nations Security Council'.[433] Moreover, the understanding was that UN support packages financed by assessed contributions would be allowed only for short-term periods, ensuring sustainability and for peacekeeping operations of the AU before the eventual transition to a UN operation.[434]

The SC retains a high degree of control over the allocation of a support package, as well as over the to be deployed AU peacekeeping operation since 'United Nations support should only be considered in cases where consultations between the … Security Council and the … Peace and Security Council take place to ensure the political and security objectives of these operations are aligned prior to either body authorizing the establishment and deployment of such an operation'.[435] Therefore, the SC

---

[431] AU Doc. PSC/PR/2(DII) (2015), 9, para. 24. In the AU's view, the UN has a duty to provide assessed contributions to UN-authorised AU peacekeeping operations, ibid., 2, para 6(i). See also UN Doc. S/2014/879 (2014), 2, 4–5.

[432] AU Doc. PSC/AHG/3.(DXLVII), 26 September 2015, 1–2, para. 3; 4–5, para. 15; 5–6, paras. 20–21; PSC/AHG/COMM/2(DXLVII), 3, para. 11.

[433] UN Doc. A/64/359 and S/2009/470 (2009), 10, para. 39. Following an authorisation of the Council, the GA 'would determine the scope of the support package and the level of assessed contributions that would be provided … Funding authorized by the United Nations would be subject to United Nations management regulations and procedures and would therefore have to be accompanied by a United Nations management and accountability structure', ibid.

[434] UN Doc. A/64/359 and S/2009/470 (2009), 9–10, paras. 35–37. Support packages were authorised for AMIS (Light and Heavy Support Packages) and AMISOM (logistics support), ibid., 9, paras. 35–36.

[435] UN Doc. A/64/359 and S/2009/470 (2009), 9–10, paras. 35–37. During the deployment of the operation, the AU would also have to fulfil the regular reporting requirements, either under Article 54 of the Charter or under Chapter VII and as defined in the SC Resolution authorising the operation.

factually retains a certain influence if not a veto about the deployment of an AU operation,[436] whereas a lack of financial means constitutes the main problem preventing the AU from effectively acting upon its mandate.[437] In practice, as it was established the AU seeks authorisation for all its operations, including peacekeeping operations which do not fall under the authorisation requirement of Chapter VIII of the Charter,[438] so that it was suggested that the AU may only anticipate UN support of its envisaged operation if it actually seeks an authorisation of the Council.[439]

A second mechanism in the form of a voluntary funded multi-donor trust fund was established to fund activities in the area of capacity building for conflict prevention and resolution.[440] It is also highly likely that the UN finally gave in for pragmatic reasons and due to self-interest.[441]

All, in all, there are more than '130 different contributions channeled to the African Union – each with its own reporting and monitoring requirements'.[442] Nevertheless, the initial objective 'to financially enable the AU and regional mechanisms to plan and conduct Peace Support Operations' has not been fully achieved, it 'remains a need for more concerted action between the AU, the EU and the UN'.[443] The financial contributions of the UN to the AU in the form of assessed contributions raise the very same questions under the law of responsibility as the contributions of the EU via the African Peace Facility. The UN could also make the provision of financial contributions depending on specific political points or on the inclusion of particular incentives in the concept of operations if it wanted to.

---

[436] Cf. also Griep, *Regionale Organisationen*, supra note 57, 360.
[437] Cf. Derblom, Hagström Frisell, 'UN–EU–AU Cooperation', supra note 108, 24; see also UN Doc. A/65/762 (2011), 9, para. 24.
[438] See Chapter 1.
[439] Dersso, 'The African Union's Mandating Authority', supra note 419, 73, 81.
[440] UN Doc. A/63/666 and S/2008/813 (2008), 4. See also UN Doc. A/59/565 (2004), 71, para. 272 (f); Department of Peacekeeping Operations and Department of Field Support, supra note 164, 6.
[441] UN Doc. A/63/666 and S/2008/813 (2008), 8, para. 16.
[442] Ibid., 17, para. 58.
[443] Joint Africa EU Strategy, Action Plan 2011–2013 introductory part, 15; UN Doc. A/67/280-S/2012/614 (2012), 4, para. 4.

Further Institutionalisation of AU–UN Relations: Moulding the Relations Towards a Division of Labour and Stronger Cooperation

In 2010, a further step was undertaken by the UN and the AU to enhance the strategic partnership with the establishment of the UN–AU Joint Task Force on Peace and Security.[444] Another new mechanism which was created is the desk-to-desk mechanism bringing together the senior leadership and focal points for specific issues of the two organisations.[445] It resorts from recent statements on behalf of the AU and the 2012 Report of the Chairperson of the Commission that the organisation is willing to take on more responsibility for the maintenance of international peace and security on the basis of certain principles including 'African ownership and priority-setting; consultative decision-making, division of labour and sharing of responsibilities' which also requires a flexible interpretation of Chapter VIII of the UN Charter.[446]

Another important principle to foster cooperation for the future is '[d]ivision of labour underpinned by complementarity', establishing a 'mutually-agreed division of labor to foster coherence and limit competition'.[447] The establishment of AFISMA in Mali proves that the AU is committed to live up to its role and to shoulder the primary responsibility for maintaining international peace and security on the African continent. Nevertheless, Mali confirms a certain division of labour in the practice of the AU, the UN and the EU according to which the AU intervenes early in a conflict under conditions in which 'the UN and the EU as well declined to take action', thereby acting as an early responder and in a bridging role for a consecutive deployment of a UN operation.[448] Mali highlighted, however, that the AU still lacks the rapid deployment capacities necessary to respond quickly to a crisis when the armed groups conquered

---

[444] UN Doc. S/2011/805 (2011), 4, para. 12.
[445] AU Doc. PSC/AHG/3.(CCCXCVII) (2013), 1, para. 2.
[446] UN Doc. S/PV.6702 (2012), 7; AU Doc. PSC/PR/COMM.(CCCVII) (2012), para. 11(ii); PSC/PR/2.(CCCVII) (2012), 24–25, para. 91. See also UN Doc. S/2013/611 (2013), 2, para. 2.
[447] AU Doc. PSC/AHG/3.(CCCXCVII) (2013), 2, para. 4(iv).
[448] Brosig, 'The African Union a Partner for Peace', supra note 244, 292, 294; Third African Union High-Level Retreat of Special Envoys and Representatives on the Promotion of Peace, Security and Stability in Africa, AU Doc. HL/Retreat/Decl. (III) (2012), 2, para. 11(b); AU Doc. PSC/Exp/VI/STCDSS/(i-a)2013 (2013), 3, para. 10. Cf. also UN Doc. S/

further territory in Mali, leading to the French intervention in the form of 'Operation Serval'.[449]

The AU therefore decided to improve its quick reaction capacities through the African Immediate Crisis Response Capacity (AICRC).[450] An important reason for the UN not to deploy own troops is the security situation on the ground as well as the set mandate, the UN now generally focuses on traditional peacekeeping and peacebuilding operations.[451] SC Resolution 2100 therefore stipulates that the deployment of MINUSMA 'shall be subject to a further review by the Council ... of the security situation in MINUSMA's area of responsibility, specifically with respect to the cessation of major combat operations by international military forces in the immediate vicinity'.[452] Nevertheless the mandate of MINUSMA is comparatively robust and allows for the use of military force.[453] Part of this division of labour is an extensive interplay on various levels as it facilitates equally the transition from a peacekeeping operation run by one organisation to an operation run by another organisation.[454]

The same interplay can be witnessed in Somalia. The SC agreed in Resolution 2093 with the view of the Secretary-General 'that the conditions in Somalia are not yet appropriate for the deployment of a United Nations Peacekeeping Operation'.[455] In the meantime, the UN Political Office in Somalia was replaced with a new expanded Special Political Mission,[456] which includes the UN Support Office for AMISOM (UNSOA)[457] and

---

2014/172 (2014), 21, para. 78; Securing Peace and Stability for Africa. The EU-Funded African Peace Facility (2004), 8.

[449] W. Lacher, D. M. Tull, 'Mali: Beyond Counterterrorism', SWP Comments, February 2013, 4–5. See infra, Chapter V, 5.1.4.

[450] AU Doc. PSC/Exp/VI/STCDSS/(i-a)2013 (2013), 7, para. 26–28, para. 29. The battlegroups will be not provided by the RECs, but they will be pledged by a lead nation – similarly to the method used by NATO – or by a group of a AU member states, ibid., 8, para. 30.

[451] Cf. also AU Doc. PSC/PR/2.(CCCVII) (2012), 19, para. 71; 29, para. (vii). See also Chapter 1.

[452] UN Doc. S/RES/2100 (2013), 5, para. 8.

[453] Ibid., paras. 16(a)(i), (c)(i), (iii), (d)(i), 17.

[454] UN Doc. S/2014/172 (2014), 21, para. 77; 21–22, paras. 78, 80; S/PV.7128 (2014), 11; S/2014/142 (2014), 12, para. 54; 20–21, paras. 93–94; S/2014/172 (2014), 21, para. 77.

[455] SC Resolution 2093, UN Doc. S/RES/2093 (2013), 5, para. 19. A joint UN–AU mission recommended in July 2015 not to deploy a UN peacekeeping operation due to the high risk posed by Al-Shabaab, UN Doc. S/2015/556 (2015), 2, 5–6, paras. 11–12.

[456] Ibid. 5, para. 18

[457] Ibid., 6, para. 20.

operates alongside AMISOM[458] until conditions permit a peacekeeping operation.[459] The Secretary-General proposed four options for the deployment of such a new operation, either as a Joint AU/UN peacekeeping operation, a fully integrated UN peacebuilding mission, a more limited UN assistance mission or a UN peacebuilding mission separate from UNSOA.[460] Whereas the AU recommended a joint AU–UN operation, the Secretary-General gave a contrary recommendation and it is worthwhile quoting his reasoning:

> My advice remains that the time has not come for these approaches. *In the current context of combat operations, the African Union has comparative advantages as a provider for military support.* Rehatting forces as a United Nations operation would necessitate changes to the concept of operations and rules of engagement that would be likely *to compromise effectiveness of the military campaign* ... A merger of African Union military and United Nations political functions in the current phase would create *constraints to the effectiveness* of both organizations. The option of United Nations or joint African Union/United Nations peacekeeping should be revisited, as conventional combat operations against Al-Shabaab end, in *consultation with the Somali authorities.*[461] [Emphasis added]

Thus, the statement underlines the division of labour between the two organisations on the basis of comparative advantages. The Report of the Chairperson of the Commission draws upon this very same idea recommending that the SC should give 'due consideration to the decisions of the AU and the PSC' because of the proximity and familiarity of the AU with conflict dynamics in its member states.[462] The pledge of the Secretary-General likewise demonstrates that peacekeeping operations have become more professional, and indeed; effectiveness appears to be the key. This division of labour is also enshrined in official AU documents, which likewise underline the need to 'achieve approximate coherence between AU and UN integrated management structures'.[463] Finally, the statement is in line with the traditional doctrine of peacekeeping as any peacekeeping

---

[458] Ibid., 6, para. 21
[459] UN Doc. S/2013/69 (2013), 15, para. 72.
[460] Ibid., 16–17, para. 75(a)–(d).
[461] Ibid., 18, para. 83. See also, UN Doc. S/2013/606 (2013), 1–2; S/2013/620 (2013), 2, and in particular A/70/95 and S/2015/446 (2015), 45, para. 118.
[462] According to the report, such a practice of the SC would be also consistent with Chapter VIII of the UN Charter, AU Doc. PSC/PR/2.(CCCVII) (2012), 12, para. 45.
[463] African Standby Force, Peace Support Operations Doctrine (2006), 4–13, para. 35. See also P. D. Williams, A. Boutellis, 'Partnership Peacekeeping: Challenges and Opportunities in the United Nations–African Union Relationship', *African Affairs*, 113 (2014), 254, 263.

operation will be only deployed in consultation with the Somali authorities. The Secretary-General's recommendation was therefore the creation of a UN assistance mission for the current situation in Somalia.[464] Cooperation and coordination with the AU will be guaranteed, inter alia, through a joint planning team and a joint leadership team comprising.[465]

The remaining challenges for the AU and the UN are how they apply Chapter VIII of the UN Charter without prejudicing the role of the SC, nor undermining or curtailing the efforts undertaken by the AU to develop its own operational crisis response capacities and to provide adequate resources. The key question is:

> What is the appropriate consultative decision-making framework, division of labor and burden-sharing that should be put in place? To date, this question has not been addressed in a consistent manner and, as such, cooperation between the UN and AU has been forced by the exigencies of time.[466]

Some of the relevant aspects to answer this question were provided in the report of the High-Level Independent Panel which also declared that the UN–AU relationship may serve as a blueprint for the relationship of the UN with other regional organisations.[467] In fact, it is envisaged by both organisations to finalise a Joint UN–AU Framework for an Enhanced Partnership in Peace and Security in 2016 as a blueprint for early and continuous engagement between both organisations, before, during and after conflict.[468]

As for now, the lack of resources of the AU does not allow them at this stage to fully engage large-scale operations and for the time being this means that even more operations of the AU might be taken over by the UN.[469] Nevertheless, the UN also remains committed to the operationalisation of the APSA as it was confirmed by the Secretary-General in a meeting of the SC in February 2014: 'The United Nations is keen to deepen the partnership with the AU Peace and Security Architecture.'[470] The UN Office to the AU in particular is working closely with the AU to support

---

[464] Ibid., 19, para. 85: UN Doc. S/2013/239 (2013), 4–8, paras. 10–20; 13, para. 46.
[465] Ibid., 8–9, paras. 21–27.
[466] AU Doc. PSC/PR/2.(CCCVII) (2012), 23–24, para. 88.
[467] UN Doc. A/70/95 and S/2015/446 (2015), 75, para. 104.
[468] UN Doc. A/70/357 and S/2015/682 (2015), 10–11, para. 47.
[469] Cf. Kioko, 'The Right of Intervention', supra note 320, 807, 822. A survey of 198 security experts also painted a rather negative picture of the current capabilities of the AU, M. Brosig, 'The African Peace and Security Architecture and Its partners', *African Security Review*, 23 (2014), 225, 229.
[470] UN Doc. S/PV.7112 (2014), 2.

the operationalisation of the ASF and the conceptualisation, planning and management of AU peacekeeping operations. These tasks include also support in the development and review of key policy and guiding documents, including those issued by the AU Peace Support Operations Divisions.[471] The SC itself decided to hold timely consultations and to conduct collaborative field missions with the PSC to formulate cohesive strategies for conflicts in Africa.[472] The AU itself also suggested regular joint assessment missions, joint planning, joint evaluation, joint benchmark exercises and the strengthening of relations on the political, strategic and mission level.[473]

The AU and ECOWAS

The Normative Framework of the APSA Regulating the Relations between the AU and the Sub-regional Organisations

The relationship between the AU and ECOWAS in the area of the maintenance of international peace and security developed on the basis of the APSA which 'emerged out of a desire by African Leaders to establish an operational structure to execute decisions taken in accordance with the authority conferred by Article 5(2) of the Constitutive Act of the African Union'.[474] The legal framework for the relationship between the AU and subregional African organisations is the Memorandum of Understanding concluded in 2008. The objectives of the Memorandum which is based on the principles of subsidiarity, complementarity and competitive advantage,[475] include a pledge to contribute to the full operationalisation and effective functioning of APSA.[476] In this context, the Memorandum also commits to fostering closer partnerships between the Parties to the Memorandum as well as with the UN, its agencies and other relevant international organisations.[477] All Parties thereby pledge 'scrupulous

---

[471] UN Doc. S/2015/229 (2015), 10–11, para. 36.
[472] UN Doc. S/PRST/2014/27.
[473] AU Doc. PSC/PR/2(DII) (2015), 3, para. 7 (iii); 4–5, paras. 10–11.
[474] African Peace and Security Architecture (APSA), 2010 Assessment Study, 19, para. 48.
[475] E. A. Akuffo, 'Cooperating for Peace and Security or Competing for Legitimacy in Africa? The Case of the African Union in Darfur', *African Security Review*, 19 (2010), 74, 76.
[476] Cf. A. T. Soma, 'Les relations entre l'Union Africaine et la Communauté Economique des Etats de l'Afrique de l'Ouest en matière den maintien de la paix', *African Yearbook of International Law*, 18 (2012), 345, 368–369. Soma concluded that the AU is exercising political control over ECOWAS, ibid.
[477] Article III (2) (i), (iii), (vi), Article VI (1), (3) of the Memorandum of Understanding on Cooperation, supra note 395.

observance' with the Constitutive Act of the AU, the PSC Protocol and 'other related instruments agreed to at continental level' and they thereby recognise the primary responsibility of the AU for the maintenance and promotion of peace, and security and stability in Africa.[478]

Article XX sets out the modalities of interaction for peace support operations. In accordance with the interpretation of the provisions of Chapter VIII of the UN Charter, subregional organisations are encouraged 'to anticipate and prevent conflicts within and among their Member States and ... to undertake ... efforts to resolve them, including through the deployment of peace support operations'.[479] This provision is analogous to Chapter VIII and Article XX(2) prescribes an information requirement for the RECs as regards the Chairperson of the Commission, and through him, the PSC, similar to Article 54 of the UN Charter.

As the use of regional organisations for peace enforcement operations is within the competences of the UN SC alone, paragraphs 3 and 4 allow the Union to have recourse to the resources of the subregional organisations including their regional brigades to facilitate the deployment of a peace support operation or as part of a peace support operation outside their areas of jurisdiction undertaken by the AU. Therefore, in contrast to Chapter VIII of the UN Charter, the element of cooperation is increased within the framework of the APSA as it regulates the relations between the AU and (sub)regional organisations; the former cannot only acquire military contingents to conduct peacekeeping operations under its own leadership, but the AU also has access to all 'assets and capabilities, including planning' to facilitate the deployment of a peacekeeping operation and it can equally request the RECs to make them available to other RECs.

Weak Institutional Links, ECOWAS as the Stronger Actor?

On a political level, the Memorandum also stipulates that the AU shall coordinate the harmonisation of views of the parties in respect of the Memorandum to ensure that African interests and positions as defined at a continental level are effectively pursued in relevant international fora including the UN. In this way, the AU can be also seen as occupying 'a coordinative instead of [an] executive and implementation role' and therefore 'lacking significant executive powers over its member states'.[480] The AU is very keen to establish stronger institutional linkage with ECOWAS

---

[478] Ibid., Article IV(i), (ii).
[479] Ibid., Article XX(1).
[480] Brosig, 'The African Union a Partner for Peace', supra note 244, 292–294.

and other RECs, as evidenced by its 2010 recognition that despite the existence of the Protocol and the MoU, the institutional relationship remains weak, creating 'a critical gap' between the AU and RECs.[481]

This critical gap between the two organisations is strengthened by the fact that ECOWAS' internal structure and resources for maintaining international peace and security are particularly well or even better developed than these of the AU.[482] ECOWAS is comparatively influential within the African Standby Force as three of the centres of excellence are based in its member states[483] and it is well aware of its capacities in comparison to the other RECs, stating that it 'has developed a comparative advantage in the area of peace-keeping and peace enforcement' and that it 'has become a model for the continent... [being] well placed to be the first REC to deliver its brigade' for the ASF.[484] ECOWAS was forced to develop these capacities due to the prevalence of infra-state conflicts and instability within the region and thereby made a virtue out of necessity. The organisation then focused on conflict management and resolution as a key activity of its agenda.[485]

In addition to the fact that Mali is a member of ECOWAS, the latter's well developed capabilities also explain why the AU authorised ECOWAS under the APSA to put in place the required military and security arrangements for a military operation in Northern Mali.[486] This authorisation by the AU was in conformity with AU policy which allows for the deployment of peacekeeping operations on a regional level, whereby the AU and the UN should provide 'direct financial and logistical assistance and assistance

---

[481] African Peace and Security Architecture (APSA), 2010 Assessment Study, 71–72, para. 208; AU Doc. HL/Retreat/Decl. (III) (2012), 2, para. 9. See also A. Vines, 'A Decade of African Peace and Security Architecture', *International Affairs*, 89 (2013), 89, 101; A. van Nieuwkerk, 'The Regional Roots of the African Peace and Security Architecture: Exploring Centre-Periphery Relations', *South African Journal of International Affairs*, 18 (2011), 169, 170; J. Akokpari, S. Ancas, 'The African Union and Regional Economic Communities. A Partnership for Peace and Security?', in T. Murithi (ed.), *Handbook of Africa's International Relations* (London, Routledge, 2014), 73, 76.

[482] ECOWAS is, for example, less dependent on external financial support, cf. the part on ECOWAS within this chapter.

[483] The Kofi Annan International Peacekeeping Training Center in Ghana concentrates on operational issues; the National Defence College in Ajuba/Nigeria offers training to officers on strategic issues; while the Zambakro Peacekeeping School in Côte d'Ivoire focuses on tactical issues.

[484] The ECOWAS Conflict Prevention Framework, Regulation MSC/REG.1/01/08, 11, para. 25.

[485] van Nieuwkerk, 'The Regional Roots', supra note 481, 169, 179.

[486] AU Doc. PSC/PR/COMM. (CCCXXIII) (2012), 3, para. 14.

to mobilise material and financial support'.[487] However, it is suggested that the PSC authorised ECOWAS to intervene after finding itself too slow to respond.[488]

It is also possible that the common efforts made by the two organisations are a reaction of the uncoordinated action by the organisations in Côte d'Ivoire in 2011. ECOWAS envoys issued public warnings that military force would be used if diplomacy did not succeed whereas the AU was holding on to political efforts, leading an ECOWAS spokesman to declare publically that 'African disunity on a solution was undermining the efforts of the regional organization'.[489] Indeed, there seems to be the awareness in both organisations that they need to coordinate more and cooperate better in maintaining international peace and security. In April 2013, the PSC requested the AU Commission, in consultation with the President of the ECOWAS, to take the necessary steps for a Lesson Learnt exercise 'on the African role in the resolution of the Mali crisis, with a view to reinforcing future coordination and facilitating the operationalization ... of the joint AU-ECOWAS office in Mali'.[490]

These contradictions stem from a certain disjuncture in the understanding of the roles of the RECs within the APSA. On the one hand, relations shall be based on the idea of comparative advantages,[491] but on the other hand, the RECs are seen as subsidiary to the authority of the AU.[492] Despite several proclamations in internal documents of the AU that RECs shall seek the authorisation of the PSC for the deployment of peacekeeping operations they are not legally required to do so.[493] Consequently, in practice, the relationship between the AU and ECOWAS is one of equality, in contrast to the normative framework of the AU's relations with the RECs which creates a superior–subordinate relationship. This is confirmed by the last policy documents of the AU which state that the

---

[487] Policy Framework for the Establishment of the African Standby Force, supra note 394, 15, para. 3.6.
[488] Vines, 'A Decade', supra note 481, 89, 104.
[489] Akokpari, Ancas, 'The African Union', supra note 481, 73, 77. See also ECOWAS Peace and Security Report, 1 October 2012, Mali: Making Peace While Preparing for War, 5.
[490] AU Doc. PSC/PR/COMM.(CCCLXXI) (2013), 5, para. 16. See also Press Release N° 009/2014, 5 February 2014, President Ouedraogo Calls for Frank Reflection on ECOWAS Interventions in Mali; Press Release, N°:013/2014, 8 February 2014, Experts Call for an effective ECOWAS Standby Force.
[491] Article 16 of the PSC Protocol, para. 1(b); AU Doc. Assembly/AU/3(XX) (2013), 46–47, para. 170.
[492] Akokpari, Ancas, 'The African Union', supra note 481, 73, 77.
[493] Memorandum of Understanding on Cooperation, supra note 395, Article XX 1).

relationship between the AU and the UN and between the AU and the RECs is a partnership based on consultative decision making, division of labour and burden sharing.⁴⁹⁴ More interesting is however the therein contained statement that the role of the RECs should be 'properly situated in the partnership' with the UN as otherwise efforts to achieve political coherence would be weakened.⁴⁹⁵ So all three organisations should work closer together on the basis of various to be established mechanisms for information and analysis sharing.⁴⁹⁶ This view seems to correspond to the position of the Secretary-General who argued in favour of 'a clear, agreed role for the African Union and subregional organizations' before the SC in December 2014. This would be required to 'increase the predictability of ... cooperation ... and planning exercises ... critical to enhancing joint peace operations'.⁴⁹⁷

Conclusions

The analysis of the relationship between the UN and regional organisations, on the one hand, and among regional organisations, on the other hand, reveals a variety of forms of coordination and cooperation which can hardly be classified.

In many cases, the UN acted before or simultaneously with regional organisations, which have priority for the settlement of local disputes under Article 52 of the UN Charter.⁴⁹⁸ It is again an illustration of the flexibility and pragmatism of the SC in practice. Some authors speak in this context of a true variable geometry and consider it a proof of the difficulty and even the impossibility to systematise the relations between universal and regional organisations.⁴⁹⁹ However, there is a very clear trend or rather a development towards a veritable moulding of relations between the involved organisations in the form of a division of labour benefitting all organisations while simultaneously allowing them to develop further their respective comparative advantages.

The rise of enhanced cooperation between the organisations has changed their relationship in a fundamental way. Whereas some relations

---

⁴⁹⁴ AU Doc. PSC/PR/2(DII) (2015), 2, para. 6 (iii).
⁴⁹⁵ Ibid.
⁴⁹⁶ Ibid., 4, para. 9, para. 9(ii).
⁴⁹⁷ UN Doc. S/PV.7343 (2014), 3.
⁴⁹⁸ One could mention for example UNMIK and the DRC, Griep, *Regionale Organisationen*, supra note 57, 228–229.
⁴⁹⁹ Boisson de Chazournes, supra note 141, 79, 401.

were – in the early stages – not free of certain competitive attitudes, the organisations have now realigned their policies towards cooperation instead of confrontation. As all of the five organisations examined in this study had to confront and face a scarcity of materials, troops and funding, this development might not have been driven entirely by the political will of the organisations, but it does not negate the fact that there is now an increased trend towards cooperation. Part of this development is that all four regional organisations now seek the authorisation of the SC including both the AU and ECOWAS whose constitutional frameworks contain dispositions for military intervention which, if they were to be acted upon without a SC authorisation, were to be in clear violation of the UN Charter and international law.[500]

In the broader context of universalism v. regionalism, it can be argued that the conclusions drawn in Chapter 1 are valid. The two poles of universalism and regionalism within the UN Charter were not only conducive to cooperation, but they have led in the practice of the organisations to a sophisticated framework of relations and cooperation arrangements between all of them in whose context competition has been replaced by cooperation.

Moreover, cooperation now covers all levels from the training of troops to pre-planning to deployment on the ground. UN–AU and EU–AU relations are the most institutionalised, but they have also developed primarily through the practice of the organisations in peacekeeping operations and a clear long-term strategy is only visible to some extent in the EU–AU policy and in the EU–UN policy in support of the AU. For all other relationships, they are entirely based on practice, and the role taken by each organisation has varied depending on the specific conflict situation the organisations were confronted with. The nature of the conflict also determines which actors will be involved; the recent example of Guinea-Bissau demonstrates elements of cooperation between not less than five different

---

[500] For instance, NATO acted upon a mandate of the Council in Libya and the EU, AU and ECOWAS have acted upon a mandate of the SC in Mali and the CAR. See also UN Doc. S/2014/45 (2014), Annex, 2; E. de Wet, 'The Evolving Role of ECOWAS and the SADC in Peace Operations: A Challenge to the Primacy of the United Nations Security Council in Matters of Peace and Security?', *Leiden Journal of International Law*, 27 (2014), 353–354, 368–369; A. Bjurner, P. Wallensteen, 'The Future Relations of the UN and the Regional Organizations', in P. Wallensteen, A. Bjurner (eds.), *Regional Organizations and Peacemaking. Challengers to the UN?* (London, Routledge, 2015), 239, 242; Törő, 'The Practice and Patterns', supra note 148, 1, 21–22.

international organisations in the form of the Joint ECOWAS/AU/CPLP/ EU/UN Assessment mission.[501]

As regards the nature of peace operations in Africa, those following a comprehensive peacekeeping and peace building approach are mostly conducted by the UN.[502] This is because the EU has refused to be engaged with larger scale operations which would definitely overstretch its capacity and the AU has yet been unable to run more demanding operations on its own.[503] Thus, 'reciprocal dependence between them … has triggered the emergence of a loose security system'[504] in the 'triangle of inter-organisational relations between the AU, EU and UN'.[505] But once again,

> looking at all peacekeeping missions deployed in Africa, …a security system is developing between these three actors … that … are dominating this multi-actor game of peacekeeping by forming a variety of different cooperation modes ranging from bridging operations and co-deployment of troops to fully integrated or hybrid missions.[506]

In this triangle, the AU is the primary choice as a first responder, deploying peacekeeping operations in conflict-like situations and the EU acts predominantly as a facilitator, although on different levels. First of all, by deploying bridging operations, secondly by deploying training and civilian missions in support of UN peacekeeping operations, thirdly by providing substantive financial support and support in other forms, including training of troops to the AU.

Thus, whereas the UN–AU and EU–AU relations are predominantly partnerships for African capacity building, the EU–UN partnership is aimed at better operational linkage between the two organisations.[507]

The AU and ECOWAS remain prone to being 'dominated' in their peacekeeping activities – to a certain extent and not only financially – but also in operational matters by the UN and the EU and in a more limited

---

[501] Report of the Joint ECOWAS/AU/CPLP/EU/UN Assessment Mission to Guinea-Bissau (2013), in particular p. 18. See also AU Doc. PSC/AHG/3.(CCCXCVII) (2013), 5, para. 14.
[502] UN Doc. A/61/668 (2007), 12, para. 39; 15, para. 50; S/2014/142 (2014), 13, para. 55.
[503] Cf. Yamashita, 'Peacekeeping Cooperation', supra note 14, 165, 171. See also Bjurner, 'On EU Peacemaking', supra note 218, 89, 95.
[504] Brosig, 'The Emerging Peace and Security Regime', supra note 10, 107, 122; Brosig, 'The African Union a Partner for Peace', supra note 244, 292–293.
[505] Statement of Rwanda, Security Council, 6919th meeting, UN Doc. S/PV.6919 (2013), 21. See also Tardy, supra note 3, 95, 103.
[506] Brosig, 'The African Union a Partner for Peace', supra note 244, 292, 296. See also the Statement of the Foreign Minister of Lithuania, UN Doc. S/PV.7112 (2014), 7.
[507] Yamashita, 'Peacekeeping Cooperation', supra note 14, 165, 182.

way by NATO.⁵⁰⁸ NATO's positioning towards being an active security provider, including the deployment of military operations in the Euro-Atlantic area, while simultaneously acting as a security actor on the global stage through other means such as its various partnership programmes, make it unlikely that NATO will play a more active role in peacekeeping operations on the African continent in the near future.⁵⁰⁹ It can be rather expected that NATO will continue to provide limited support to peace-keeping operations in Africa if actively requested by the UN or a regional organisation.

Despite already quite extensive cooperation activities on the African continent between the UN, the AU, the AU and ECOWAS, a formulation of long-term relationships between all these organisations and based on a clear strategy remains necessary.⁵¹⁰ A number of initiatives have been started since 2013 to achieve that purpose.

The Secretary-General called on the SC to generally define the role of regional organisations with the UN.⁵¹¹ The Argentine Presidency of the SC in August 2013 put the topic anew on the agenda of the Council, emphasising that the topic had not been comprehensively evaluated by the Council since 2010.⁵¹² The ensuing debate in the SC highlighted the need to strengthen relations between the UN and regional organisations in a pragmatic, result-oriented manner, but did not provide any plan of action.⁵¹³ However, the Secretary-General was tasked to provide in his next biannual report recommendations on ways to enhance the cooperation between

---

[508] This means that the EU (indirectly) and the AU (directly) have had to approve the initiation of an ECOWAS peacekeeping operation, Capacity Survey on Regional and Other Intergovernmental Organizations, supra note 402, 28.

[509] UN Doc. S/PV.7228 (2014), 57.

[510] This was emphasised within the SC when it was meeting on the Head of State/Ministerial Level, UN Doc. S/PV.6621 (2011), 5–9, 11, 17, 21; S/PRST/2007/42 (2007) 1; S/RES/1631 (2005); see especially preamble, 1, paras. 1–2; see also statements by other members of the Council, UN Doc. S/PV.4970 (2004); Statement of the Secretary-General, UN Doc. S/PV.5282 (2005), 4–5; S/PV.5529 (2006); Statement by the President of the Security Council, UN Doc. S/PRST/2007/31 (2007); S/PV.5776 (2007); S/PV.6153 (2009); S/PV.6178 (2009); S/PV.6257 (2010; S/PV.6409 (2010).

[511] UN Doc. S/2008/186 (2008), 6–7, para. 8; A/65/510 and S/2010/514 (2010), 24, para. 90; A/65/762 (2011), 11, para. 31; S/PV.7015 (2013), 7. Cf. also J. Boulden, 'The United Nations Security Council and Conflict in Africa', in J. Boulden (ed.), *Responding to Conflict in Africa. The United Nations and Regional Organizations* (London, Palgrave Macmillan, 2013), 13, 25.

[512] UN Doc. S/2013/446 (2013), 4.

[513] See, e.g., the statement on behalf of the EU, UN Doc. S/PV.7015 (2013), 18; statement on behalf of the AU, UN Doc. S/PV.7015 (2013), 7; S/PRST/2013/12 (2013), 3, 5–6.

the UN and regional and subregional organisations.[514] The next initiative under the Rwandan presidency of the Council in July 2014 was more successful.[515] Based on a concept note prepared by Rwanda,[516] the members of the SC, representatives of other member states and international organisations debated about necessary steps for strengthening the relations between the UN and regional organisations with regard to peacekeeping operations and the maintenance of international peace and security.

The unanimously adopted Resolution 2167 – following a long debate in the SC – proved that the SC has truly embraced the loose security system based on the triangle of organisational relations between the UN, the AU and the EU.[517] The Council did not only welcome recent developments regarding operational cooperation between the UN, the AU and the EU but requested the Secretary-General to produce, in close consultation with both the AU and the EU, an assessment report and recommendations on the progress of the partnerships between the UN and relevant regional organisations in peacekeeping operations until 31 March 2015.

The SC underlined that there is a need to enhance the UN and regional organisations' joint planning and joint mission assessment processes. Another measure envisaged was an increased exchange of staff members between the UN and the AU in order to enhance the capacities of the latter, for instance, in mission planning and management.[518]

In his requested report, Ban Ki-moon acknowledged that the simultaneous engagement of all three organisations 'has become a de facto trilateral partnership'[519] but also declared that 'the potential for closer trilateral engagement and cooperation among the United Nations, the African Union and the European Union has yet to be fully explored and exploited'.[520]

However, the common feature of these initiatives is that – overall – they focused on describing the situation as it is, but they did not

---

[514] UN Doc. S/PRST/2013/12 (2013), 6.
[515] Statements by the Secretary-General, the EU, the AU and NATO, UN Doc. S/PV.7228 (2014), 2–9, 56–57. See also M. Brosig, D. Motsama, 'Modeling Cooperative Peacekeeping. Exchange Theory and the African Peace and Security Regime', *Journal of International Peacekeeping*, 18 (2014), 45, 51.
[516] UN Doc. S/2014/478 (2014), see in particular 6–7.
[517] UN Doc. S/RES/2167 (2014), 4, para. 2. See also Secretary-General's remarks at Summit on UN Peacekeeping, available at www.un.org/sg/statements/index.asp?nid=8060.
[518] UN Doc. S/RES/2167 (2014), 4, para. 7; 5, paras. 11, 14; 6, paras. 18–19; 7, para. 28. See also Statement by the SG, UN Doc. S/PV.7228 (2014), 2–3; Statements of the EU and of Ireland, ibid., 4–5, 52.
[519] UN Doc. S/2015/229 (2015), 18, para. 62.
[520] Ibid., 2, para. 6.

formulate the needed long-term strategy or a plan of action to develop such a needed strategy. Things changed with the publication of the High-Level Independent Panel's Report in 2015. The Panel also generally emphasised that '[a] stronger, more inclusive peace and security partnership for the future must be built'.[521] More important is, that the Panel recommended the formulation of a new agenda 'to build a strong global-regional framework to meet those challenges through responsible and principled strategic partnerships'.[522]

The Panel was well aware of the fact that this is a long-term endeavour which should start as soon as possible on the basis of a roadmap of the SG and in close cooperation with regional organisations to realise it within the next decade.[523] Further steps for a real agenda and long-term strategy were made in the follow-up Implementation Report by the Secretary-General. He identified three pillars as essential for priority action: a new focus on prevention and mediation of conflicts, a stronger partnership with regional organisations, and new ways of planning and conducting UN peacekeeping operations to make them not only faster, but also more responsive and accountable to the specific needs in a given conflict.[524]

Bearing in mind of these initiatives on the UN level, it is perhaps less surprising that the AU was calling for a stronger involvement of the RECs in current policy documents and in practice, the trilateral UN, AU and EU relationship might become quadrilateral by including subregional organisations such as ECOWAS.

Therefore, these last initiatives may well be the starting point for further enhanced cooperation between international organisations in peacekeeping operations. This will ultimately also increase the likelihood of joint responsibility of international organisations for violations of international law committed during the deployment of these operations. In fact, the analysis of the relations among the international organisations within this chapter allows the drawing of several conclusions regarding the law of international responsibility and its application to peacekeeping operations conducted in cooperation with international organisations.

First of all, on a general level, the institutionalisation of relations among these international organisations indicates that it is rather likely that conduct arising in the context of a peacekeeping operation and in violation

---

[521] UN Doc. A/70/95 and S/2015/446 (2015), 24, para. 37(c).
[522] Ibid., 28, para. 53.
[523] Ibid., 74, paras. 234–236.
[524] UN Doc. A/70/357 and S/2015/682 (2015), 3, para. 8.

of international law will entail the responsibility of two or more international organisations. In this context, the legal analysis can only be carried out in the form of a casuistic approach – which simultaneously requires that the criterion for attributing conduct to international organisations is defined in a general and abstract way as to include various potential scenarios. Depending on the specific conflict and the involved organisations, the legal significance accorded to specific parts of the cooperation arrangements has to be adapted. In particular, the large degree of control the UN and the EU can exercise over the AU in the form of the financing of AU peacekeeping operations not only raises the question as to whether these actions would be sufficient per se to attribute responsibility to both organisations, but it might simultaneously justify the holding of these two organisations responsible despite a lack of cooperation or an insufficient basis of cooperation in other areas of a given mission. The triangle of relations between the UN, the EU and the AU suggests that it is likely that these three organisations will be jointly responsible in the context of a peacekeeping operation on the African continent. In contrast, ECOWAS and NATO play more of a supporting role in the context of African peacekeeping operations. Outside the framework of the APSA, ECOWAS' relations with the other organisations are so far limited and entirely based on spontaneous practical arrangements. NATO's policy is not to engage on the African continent unless asked to do so.

These predictions are, however, of a general nature, and cooperation in a specific operation is likely to have a variety of consequences with regard to the law of international responsibility as will be illustrated later on in Chapter 5.

Due to the high degree of cooperation between international organisations in peacekeeping operations and their continuously further institutionalising relations, it is necessary to formulate adequate legal rules to hold them effectively responsible if violations of international law occur. Reasons of justice and legitimacy as stressed lastly by the High-Level Panel also dictate that international organisations should not be able to enjoy impunity for their actions.[525] The next chapter will therefore inquire if and to which extent the legal framework for holding international organisations responsible, in the form of the ARIOs of the ILC is appropriate and sufficient or whether a specific legal regime is required for the purposes of holding international organisations jointly responsible in peacekeeping operations.

[525] UN Doc. A/70/95 and S/2015/446 (2015), 30, para. 61(c).

3

From the Broader Legal Framework to International Responsibility

> In law we must beware of petrifying the rules of yesterday and thereby halting progress in the name of process. If one consolidates the past and calls it law, he may find himself outlawing the future.
> – Judge Manfrech Lachs, President of the ICJ[1]

The present study started with an examination of legal framework for the maintenance of international peace and security under the UN Charter. The analysis showed that the legal framework is construed around a careful compromise between a universalist and a regionalist perception of collective security, in which the UN is the central pillar, although, in practice, roles can be reversed. This study inquired into the concept of peacekeeping as it was developed under the UN Charter, as well as cooperation with regional organisations, and it placed emphasis on this 'collective security compromise', as echoed within each of the analysed chapters of the UN Charter.[2] The analysis demonstrated that the Security Council is very adept at handling the legal framework with its corresponding margin of appreciation and has shown a high degree of flexibility and pragmatism in the conduct of peacekeeping operations, as well as in its relations with regional organisations.

Another trend that can be observed with respect to the cooperation between the UN and regional organisations is the increase in the deployment of multiple simultaneous peace operations in the same conflict, which rose from 10 per cent of all peace operations in 1992 to 70 per cent of all peace operations in 2007.[3] The time frame for the evolution of cooperation between the UN and regional organisations in peacekeeping operations has

---

[1] 'The Twenty-Fifth Anniversary of the International Law Commission', speech delivered at a Special Commemorative Meeting of the UN General Assembly (12 October 1973).

[2] It has to be clarified that under Chapter VII it is due to the practice of the Security Council which has established the concept of peacekeeping.

[3] A. Ballas, 'It Takes Two (or More) to Keep the Peace: Multiple Simultaneous Peace Operations', *Journal of International Peacekeeping*, 15 (2011), 384–385. In Bosnia-Herzegovina, for example, four international organisations deployed their own peace operations at overlapping time periods from 1995 onwards: the UN with UNPROFOR and UNMIBH, NATO

been remarkably short, and the facts presented in the past two chapters suggest that cooperation between the organisations will continue to develop at such a pace that the necessity for legal regulation of the joint responsibility of international organisations will be even further enhanced.

Whereas the EU started deploying troops in crisis management operations as recently as in 2003, the AU has existed only since 2000, so that it is to be expected that these two organisations, in particular, will further enhance and institutionalise their cooperational framework with other organisations, as well as start a new wave of activism. This assessment is also made against a background in which one cannot see any trend in international relations towards a decrease of threats to international peace and security, nor a decrease to internal or international armed conflicts. In particular, the African continent unfortunately remains a nursery for conflicts, as the recent examples of Mali and the Sahel Region and the Central African Republic underline.[4] In fact, 62.5 per cent of all UN peacekeeping operations and more than 87 per cent of all UN peacekeepers are in Africa.[5]

The analysis further highlighted the problems and challenges existing in this particular domain of international law. One can truly say that certain areas of international law resemble something of a *terra incognita* when it comes to their application to international organisations.[6] There are several reasons, which include the lack of practice by international organisations in the period of the Cold War. The opposing two blocs in the Security Council prevented the system of global collective security from operating as it was supposed to.

Moreover, the 'humanisation' of international law, in the form of the emergence of international human rights law, expanded the reach of norms protecting the individual to the areas of activities of international organisations.[7] However, these norms were transported from the homogeneous

---

with SFOR and IFOR, the OSCE's Mission to Bosnia-Herzegovina as well as the EU with EUPM and EUFOR.

[4] For instance, in 2014, the SC held ninety-nine meetings on African issues which account for 54.7 per cent of the Council agenda, Highlights of the Security Council Practice 2014, available at www.un.org/en/sc/inc/pages/pdf/highlights/2014.pdf. See also J. Boulden, 'Introduction', in J. Boulden (ed.), *Responding to Conflict in Africa. The United Nations and Regional Organizations* (London, Palgrave Macmillan, 2013), 1, 3.

[5] UN Doc. A/70/95 and S/2015/446 (2015), 74, para. 239.

[6] Cf. I. Brownlie, 'The Responsibility of States for the Acts of International Organizations', in M. Ragazzi (ed.), *International Responsibility Today. Essays in Memory of Oscar Schachter* (Leiden, Brill, 2005), 355.

[7] Cf. generally T. Meron, *International Law in the Age of Human Rights. General Course on Public International Law*, Collected Courses of The Hague Academy of International Law, Vol. 301 (2003), 9–489; T. Meron, *The Humanization of International Law* (Leiden, Brill,

'*contexte étatique*' to the heterogeneous area of international organisations. The lack of adjudicative power by international courts and tribunals over international organisations likewise prevented further elucidation of the applicable legal rules. The consolidation of peacekeeping operations, and the multiplication of tasks, functions and actors, contributed to the difficulty in dismantling and analysing these operations and in determining the applicable legal framework, as well as the responsible entities. A further factor is the uniqueness of each of the organisations; each of them is an organisation *sui generis*. Thus, their relations with other organisations are based on their unique legal make-up, complicating any attempt to draw conclusions of general validity outside of their specific context. The assessment on an inter-organisational level is also true on an operational level for each and every peacekeeping operation.

It is against this comprehensive background that the study approaches the legal framework of international responsibility applicable to international organisations, as well as the practice of the UN therein. It is necessary to address whether the developed rules are appropriate to regulate the specific context of international organisations cooperating in peacekeeping operations. It was concluded in the previous chapter that the cooperation between international organisations in peacekeeping operations has reached a level where cases of joint responsibility are not only likely to occur,[8] but where international organisations are acting as equal partners, and therefore not in a subordinate–superior relationship.

The Law of Responsibility of International Organisations and the Practice of the UN

As peacekeeping was invented by the UN as a tool for conflict regulation, most of the existing practice in this particular area, which has been

---

2006). See letter dated 6 August 1965 from the Secretary-General addressed to the Acting Permanent Representative of the Union of Soviet Socialist Republics, in *United Nations Juridical Yearbook* (1965), 41; C. Tomuschat, 'The European Court of Human Rights and the United Nations', in A. Føllesdal, B. Peters, G. Ulfstein (eds.), *The European Court of Human Rights in a National, European and Global Context* (Cambridge University Press, 2013), 334–335; M. Bothe, 'Security Council's Targeted Sanctions against Presumed Terrorists', *Journal of International Criminal Justice*, 6 (2008), 541.

[8] Cf. A. Clapham, 'The Subject of Subjects and the Attribution of Attribution', in L. Boisson de Chazournes, M. Kohen (eds.), *International Law and the Quest for Its Implementation/Le droit international et la quête de sa mise en oeuvre. Liber Amicorum Vera Gowlland-Debbas* (Leiden, Brill, 2010), 45, 58.

likewise analysed by the ILC for the elaboration of the ARIOs, derives from UN operations.

Activities in the domain of international peace and security and particularly peacekeeping operations, have a great impact on the lives of the people, especially in the case of deployment of troops on the ground. Violations of human rights law and international humanitarian law and international responsibility of international organisations for these acts are consequently not a mere hypothetical possibility, but part of the reality.[9] These acts may be committed in a private or in an official capacity, alone or by a group of individuals and they can include acts such as sexual exploitation, arbitrary detention or murder, or even the unintentional killing of civilians in the exercise of the mandate of an operation.

Sixty-seven UN peacekeeping missions have taken place since the establishment of the UN in 1945. Consequently, there has been a certain practice and some cases dealing with the responsibility arising for peacekeeping missions.[10] The UN declared at an early stage that it would be responsible for all damages occurring during the deployment of peacekeeping forces[11] and that it would pay for any damages caused,[12] despite emphasising that this is only motivated by the 'moral responsibility' of the organisation and underlining that it was not under a legally binding obligation.[13] Although later on certain statements speak of 'liability', others mention that the practice emerged from a 'policy' or from 'considerations of equity and humanity'.[14]

Several arguments can be made against any generally applicable legal rule which could be derived from the practice of the UN. First of all, the practice of one single organisation cannot fulfil the requirements necessary

---

[9] UN Doc. A/70/95 and S/2015/446 (2015), 41, paras. 102–103.
[10] Cf. UN Doc. A/CN.4/541 (2004), 16, fn. 52.
[11] M. Hartwig, *Die Haftung der Mitgliedstaaten für Internationale Organisationen* (Heidelberg, Springer, 1993), 233. Cf. United Nations Treaty Series 388, 144–148.
[12] F. Seyersted, 'United Nations Forces Some Legal Problems', *British Yearbook of International Law*, 37 (1961), 351, 420; also M. Tondini, 'The "Italian Job": How to Make International Organisations Compliant with Human Rights and Accountable for Their Violation by Targeting Member States', in J. Wouters, E. Brems, S. Smis (eds.), *Accountability for Human Rights Violations by International Organisations* (Antwerp, Intersentia, 2010), 169, 180.
[13] International Law Association, New Delhi Conference (2002), Committee on Accountability of International Organisations, Third Report consolidated and enlarged version of recommended rules and practices ('RRP-S'), 10, 16; International Law Association, Berlin Conference (2004), Accountability of International Organisations, 21; Comments by the International Monetary Fund, UN Doc. A/CN.4/582 (2007), 7.
[14] UN Doc. S/6597, Annex 1; A/51/389 (1996), 4, paras. 6–7; Hartwig, *Die Haftung*, supra note 11, 233.

to ascertain a rule of customary law applicable to all international organisations, even if one were to presume that the required element of *opinio iuris* were to be present within the other organisations.[15]

Moreover, the practice of the UN consists mostly of compensation cases under the domestic law of individual states; under which the conditions for a settlement, including the criterion of attribution, may differ from those applying under international law. Many of these cases under domestic law also included qualifications and limitations such as the use of statutes of limitation, restricting the period to present claims.[16] The UN often only assumed responsibility on the international, external level, towards the victims, while recovering the compensation paid from the respective troop-contributing states.

Under circumstances such as 'loss, damage, death or injury [arising] from gross negligence or wilful misconduct of the personnel provided by the Government',[17] one has to distinguish between attribution of conduct and attribution of responsibility; whereas the UN might assume the responsibility on an international level, the conduct would have been attributed to the member state and not the organisation. It is even questionable whether the practice of the UN is in conformity with the rules laid down in the ARIO.[18] The practice is also centred on the relationship between the UN and individual member states.

It has also been pointed out that the lack of practice in a given area may be an indication that a 'particular situation cannot be covered by a general

---

[15] A contrary view on this issue is taken by Larsen who argues that the UN practice has been extensive and consistent enough as well as carried out with *opinio iuris* to qualify as international customary law, K. M. Larsen, *The Human Rights Treaty Obligations of Peacekeepers* (Cambridge University Press, 2012), 101.

[16] UN Doc. A/RES/52/247 (1998), particularly 2-3, paras. 8-11; A/51/903 (1997), particularly 5-11, paras. 12-46; K. Grenfell, 'Effective Reparation for the Victims of Wrongful Acts Committed during UN Peace Operations: How Does It Work Concretely?', in S. Kolanowski (ed.), *Proceedings of the Bruges Colloquium. International Organisations' Involvement in Peace Operations: Applicable Legal Framework and the Issue of Responsibility* (2011), 126, 130-132.

[17] UN Doc. A/50/995 (1996), 6, para. 10; UN Doc. A/51/967 (1997), 7, para. 10.

[18] The Articles limit the responsibility of an international organisation to acts in an official capacity, but *ultra vires* acts in the exercise of an official capacity are covered, cf. Article 8, UN Doc. A/66/10 (2011), 85, para. 3 of the commentary; *mutatis mutandis* also, UN Doc. A/64/10 (2009), 62-63, para. 2 of the Commentary. See also, UN Doc. A/CN.4/637/Add.1 (2011), 15-16, para. 4. Cf. Agreement between the Parties to the North Atlantic Treaty regarding the Status of their Forces, 4 April 1949, Article VIII.

rule due to the diversity of international organizations'.[19] The Special Rapporteur of the ILC himself acknowledged the lack of practice. It is partly in consequence of the fact that only eighteen international organisations reported their practice, and he therefore commented that the practice did not add to the previous knowledge.[20]

The ILC Articles on Responsibility of International Organisations

The following part analyses the question as to whether the articles developed by the International Law Commission are suitable to be applied in the context of peacekeeping operations. Bearing in mind the enhanced cooperation between international organisations, it is important to analyse and to ascertain whether the different possibilities of the attribution of conduct and of responsibility to international organisations as contained in the articles of the ILC are suitable to regulate the conduct of international organisations cooperating in peacekeeping operations. The sixty-five Articles on Responsibility of International Organizations as adopted by the International Law Commission in second reading in 2011 contain several dispositions which set out the various methods to attribute conduct or simply responsibility to international organisations. The first article which will be examined is Article 7 which deals with the attribution of conduct to international organisations in the case of organs of states or organs or agents of international organisations seconded to another international organisation.

Article 7 of the Articles on the International Responsibility of International Organizations

Article 7 prescribes that '[t]he conduct of an organ of a State or an organ or agent of an international organization that is placed at the disposal of another international organization shall be considered under international law an act of the latter organization if the organization exercises effective control over that conduct'.[21]

---

[19] International Law Association, Sofia Conference (2012), Study Group on the Responsibility of International Organizations, 8–11. See comments by Germany, UN Doc. A/CN.4/556 (2005), 47, 63, section D.
[20] UN Doc. A/CN.4/541 (2004), 2, para. 2. See, in particular, UN Doc. A/CN.4/637 (2011), 10–11, para. 2.
[21] See generally B. Montejo, 'The Notion of "Effective Control" under the Articles on the Responsibility of International Organizations', in M. Ragazzi (ed.), *Responsibility of*

States retain a certain amount of control over peacekeepers which are not fully seconded to an international organisation so that peacekeeping operations are deemed to fall under the provision of Article 7.[22] Although this article also covers the conduct of an organ of an international organisation placed at the disposal of another international organisation, the practice in this area is rare; the commentary to the article lists one example.[23] All cases in the context of peacekeeping operations dealing with the international responsibility of a state or an international organisation have been decided on the basis of a criterion of control, but the jurisprudence is varied to say the least.

The controversial *Behrami* case deviated completely from the criterion of 'effective control' but held that 'the United Nations Security Council retained ultimate authority and control so that operational command only was delegated'.[24] In his judgment, the European Court of Human Rights set out the chain of command in detail:

> UNSC Resolution 1244 gave rise to the following chain of command in the present cases. The UNSC was to retain ultimate authority and control over the security mission and it delegated to NATO (in consultation with non-NATO member states) the power to establish, as well as the operational command of, the international security presence, KFOR. NATO fulfilled its command mission via a chain of command ... to COMKFOR, the commander of KFOR. While the MNBs were commanded by an officer from a lead TCN, the latter was under the direct command of COMKFOR. MNB action was to be taken according to an operational plan devised by NATO and operated by COMKFOR in the name of KFOR.[25]

International Organizations. Essays in Memory of Sir Ian Brownlie (Leiden, Brill, 2013), 389–404.

[22] UN Doc. A/66/10 (2011), 85, para. 1; Tomuschat, 'The European Court of Human Rights', supra note 7, 334, 344–350; A. Sari, 'UN Peacekeeping Operations and Article 7 ARIO: The Missing Link', *International Organizations Law Review*, 9 (2012), 77, 78–80; D. Shraga, 'ILC Articles on Responsibility of International Organizations: The Interplay between the Practice and the Rule (A View from the United Nations)', in M. Ragazzi (ed.), *Responsibility of International Organizations. Essays in Memory of Sir Ian Brownlie* (Leiden, Brill, 2013), 202–205.

[23] UN Doc. A/66/10 (2011), 91, para. 16.

[24] *Agim Behrami and Bekir Behrami against France, Ruzdhi Saramati against France, Germany and Norway*, Decision on Admissibility, 2 May 2007, para. 133. Crawford asserts that the Chamber 'seemed to employ more formalistic criteria to determine responsibility', J. Crawford, *State Responsibility. The General Part* (2013), 198. For further critique of the judgment, see the references on p. 199, fn. 174.

[25] Ibid., para. 135.

On the basis of this analysis, the Court concluded that '[t]his delegation model demonstrates that, contrary to the applicants' argument ..., direct operational command from the UNSC is not a requirement of Chapter VII collective security missions'.[26] The Court thus attributed the conduct of a UN-authorised operation to the UN contrary to the *practice* of the UN.[27] The Court confirmed its jurisprudence in *Kasumaj v. Greece*[28] and *Gajic v. Germany*.[29] In *Berić and others v. Bosnia*,[30] the Court, although quoting extensively from *Behrami*, relied on the notion of 'effective overall control'.[31] In yet another case, *Stephens v. Cyprus, Turkey and the United Nations*, the European Court first of all denied the attribution of the alleged violations to the two respective states and then carried on to declare that as to the complaints directed against the UN 'UNFICYP, which has control over the buffer zone, is a subsidiary organ of the UN created under the UN Charter and is under the *exclusive control and command* of the UN'[32] [emphasis added].

In the UK, the House of Lords was seized by a case regarding the actions of British troops after the Iraq Invasion in 2003. In *Al-Jedda*,[33] the Court distinguished the facts of the case presented to it from the *Behrami/Saramati* Decision before the European Court of Human Rights, and held that it could 'not realistically be said that US and UK forces were under the effective command and control of the UN, or that UK forces were under such command and control when they detained the appellant'.[34]

Mr. Al-Jedda then seized the European Court of Human Rights which returned to some extent to the 'effective control' criterion. The Court considered that 'that the United Nations Security Council had neither

---

[26] Ibid., para. 136.
[27] UN Doc. A/66/10 (2011), 89, para. 15 and fn. 115 for selected publications criticising the decision. It will not be dealt with further here, as Behrami is one of the case studies in Chapter 4.
[28] *Kasumaj v. Greece*, first section, Decision as to the Admissibility, 5 July 2007.
[29] *Gajic v. Germany*, first section, Decision as to the Admissibility, 28 August 2007, para. 1.
[30] *Berić and others v. Bosnia*, fourth section, Decision as to the Admissibility, 16 October 2007
[31] Ibid., 15–16, paras. 27–28. Cf. generally C. A. Bell, 'Reassessing Multiple Attribution: The International Law Commission and the *Behrami* and *Saramati* Decision', New York University Journal of International Law and Politics, 42 (2010), 501–548.
[32] *Kyriakoula Stephens against Cyprus, Turkey and the United Nations*, first section, Decision as to the Admissibility, 11 December 2008, 7.
[33] *R (on the application of Al-Jedda) (FC) (Appellant) v. Secretary of State for Defence (Respondent)*, Decision of 12 December 2007.
[34] Ibid., Opinion of Lord Bingham of Cornwall, 17, paras. 23–24; Lord Rodger of Earlsferry, 30, para. 59; 51, para. 113; Baroness Hale of Richmond concurred with Lord Bingham, 54–55, para. 124. So did Lord Carswell, 57, para. 131. See also Lord Brown of Eaton-under-Heywood, 61–64, paras. 141–149.

effective control nor ultimate authority and control over the acts and omissions of troops within the Multi-National Force and that the applicant's detention was not, therefore, attributable to the United Nations'.[35] This approach seems to create yet another test of attribution, a blend of *Berić* with *Behrami/Saramati*.

On the domestic level, the Dutch Courts were engaged with claims against the Dutch Government for conduct arising out of the actions of the Dutch battalion 'Dutchbat' of UNPROFOR in Srebrenica. The District Court in The Hague made only a general reference to the articles on international responsibility of international organisations, and concluded that 'these acts and omissions should be attributed strictly, as a matter of principle to the United Nations'.[36]

In July 2011, the Court of Appeal in The Hague delivered its judgment in the same affair and reversed the attribution of conduct, judging that the Netherlands would be responsible. The Court based its judgment on the notion of 'effective control' as derived from international law literature and the work of the ILC, including Article 7 of the articles on Responsibility of International Organisations.[37] More important however, the Court held that 'the possibility that more than one party has "effective control" is generally accepted, which means that it cannot be ruled out that the application of this criterion results in the possibility of attribution to more than one party'.[38] However, the Court did not substantiate this particular finding.[39] The Court also distinguished between two criteria to determine if an entity exercises 'effective control', first of all 'whether that conduct constituted the execution of a specific instruction' and 'if there was no

---

[35] *Case of Al-Jedda v. The United Kingdom*, Judgment, Grand Chamber, Judgment, 7 July 2011.
[36] *District Court in The Hague, Nuhanović v. The Netherlands*, Judgment, LJN: BF0181, Case No. 265615/HA ZA 06-1671(English translation), 10 September 2008, para. 4.8; see also paras. 4.11, 4.13, 4.15, *District Court in The Hague, Mustafić v. The Netherlands*, Judgment, LJN BF0182, Case No. 265618/HA ZA 06-1672 (English translation), 10 September 2008, para. 4.13, see also paras. 4.10, 4.15, 4.17. See C. Ryngaert, 'Apportioning Responsibility between the UN and Member States in UN Peace-Support Operations: An Inquiry into the Application of the "Effective Control" Standard after Behrami', *Israel Law Review*, 45 (2012), 151, 159.
[37] Court of Appeal in *The Hague, Nuhanović v. The State of the Netherlands*, Judgment, LJN: BR5388, Case No. 200.20.174/01, 5 July 2011, para. 5.8; Court of Appeal in *The Hague, Mustafić v. The State of the Netherlands*, Judgment, LJN: BR5386, Case No. 200.020.173/01, 5 July 2011, para. 5.8. See generally T. Dannenbaum, 'Killings at Srebrenica, Effective Control, and the Power to Prevent Unlawful Conduct', *International and Comparative Law Quarterly*, 61 (2012), 713–728.
[38] Ibid., para. 5.9 in both judgments.
[39] Ibid.

such instruction, the UN or the State had the power to prevent the conduct concerned'.[40]

On 6 September 2013, the Supreme Court of the Netherlands rendered its judgment in the two affairs, confirming the judgments of the Court of Appeal. The Supreme Court confirmed not only that conduct can be attributed to both an international organisation and a state if they 'exercise effective control',[41] but also that 'all factual circumstances and the special context of the case must be taken into account'.[42]

The Court of First Instance of Brussels was seized in a civil law case for compensation for acts of war crimes in the conduct of operation UNAMIR in Rwanda. The Court attributed the conduct to the Belgian State and not to the UN. The Belgian soldiers were withdrawn from UNAMIR and were therefore under the authority of the Belgian state. The Court did not itself pronounce on any rule of attribution applicable under international law.[43]

This overview of jurisprudence shows that there is no discernible rule under international law for the attribution of responsibility of an organ seconded to an international organisation by another state or another international organisation. In other words, there is no consensus regarding the variant of control required to attribute conduct to an international organisation. The European Commission expressed a similar view:

> The question must be asked whether the international practice is presently clear enough and whether there is identifiable opinio juris that would allow for the proposed standard of the International Law Commission ... to be codified in the current draft. There is no doubt that this remains a controversial area of international law, in relation to which one can expect a

---

[40] Ibid.
[41] Supreme Court of the Netherlands, *The State of the Netherlands (Ministry of Defence and Ministry of Foreign Affairs) v. Hasan Nuhanović*, Judgment, First Chamber, 12/03324, LZ/TT, 6 September 2013, 22–23, para. 3.11.2; Supreme Court of the Netherlands, *The State of the Netherlands (Ministry of Defence and Ministry of Foreign Affairs) v. Mehida Mustafić, Damir Mustafić, Alma Mustafić*, Judgment, First Chamber, 12/03329, LZ/TT, 6 September 2013, 21–22, para. 3.11.2.
[42] Ibid., 22–23, para. 3.11.3. In July 2014, the District Court in The Hague reconfirmed the application of the 'effective control' criterion in a civil law suit against the Netherlands, *District Court in The Hague, Stichting Mothers of Srebrenica and Others v. The Netherlands*, Judgment, Case No. C/09/295247/HA ZA07-2973, 16 July 2014, paras. 4.33–4.34, para. 4.87.
[43] Tribunal civil de Bruxelles (71e chambre), M. et autres / Etat belge, ministre de la Défense nationale et A. et autres, 8 décembre 2010, paras. 38, 40; cf. also N. Gal-Or, C. Ryngaert, 'From Theory to Practice: Exploring the Relevance of the Draft Articles on the Responsibility of International Organizations (DARIO) – The Responsibility of the WTO and the UN', *German Law Journal*, 13 (2012), 511, 534–536.

steady stream of case law not only from the European Court of Human Rights, but also from domestic courts, in addition to voluminous academic writings.[44]

Further critique came from the UN which emphasised that the test of 'effective control' has never been used to determine the division of responsibility between the organisation and its troop-contributing states[45] but that the test of effective control is used on a horizontal level in joint operations to distinguish between a UN operation under UN command and control and a UN-authorised operation conducted under national or regional command and control.[46]

It is even less clear – in the framework of the articles – under which conditions international organisations could be jointly responsible. The Special Rapporteur remarked that there are cases of joint attribution of conduct, but one could also consider 'that the infringing acts are attributed to either the State or the United Nations, while omission, if any, of the required preventive measures is attributed to the other subject. Similar conclusions may be reached with regard to infringements by members of peacekeeping forces that affect other areas of the protection of human rights'.[47]

Dealing with the particular case of the European Community, he expressed the view that 'joint, or joint and several, responsibility does not necessarily depend on dual attribution ... in case of an infringement... that does not distinguish between the respective obligations of the EC and its member States – either directly, or by referring to their respective competencies – responsibility would be joint towards the non-member State party to the agreement'.[48] Specifically referring to

---

[44] UN Doc. A/CN.4/637 (2011), 22. Cf. also K. M. Larsen, 'Attribution of Conduct in Peace Operations: The "Ultimate Authority and Control" Test', *European Journal of International Law*, 19 (2008), 509, 518; EU/Council of Europe, Fifth Negotiation Meeting between the CDDH Ad Hoc Negotiation Group and the European Commission on the Accession of the European Union to the European Convention on Human Rights, Final Report to the CDDH, Strasbourg, 5 April 2013, 19, para. 24.

[45] UN Doc. A/CN.4/637/Add.1 (2011), 13–14, paras. 1–3; 14, para. 6; S/2008/354 (2008), 4 para. 16; A/51/389 (1996), 6, paras. 17–18; A/CN.4/545 (2004), 18. See generally UN Doc. A/CN.4/637/Add.1 (2011), 10–12, paras. 2–10.

[46] UN Doc. A/CN.4/637/Add.1 (2011), 13, para. 2; A/51/389 (1996), 6, paras. 17–18; A/66/10 (2011), 88, para. 9.

[47] UN Doc. A/CN.4/541 (2004), 20, para. 42.

[48] Ibid., 4–5, para. 8. In his report he referred to C-316/91, *European Parliament v. Council of the European Union*, Judgment of the Court of 2 March 1994, I-664–I-665, para. 29. It is thus a legal rule derived from the internal European legal order, but it does not diminish the potential to draw upon the reasoning as a model for attribution in other circumstances.

military operations, he declared that 'one may argue that attribution of conduct to an international organization does not necessarily exclude attribution of the same conduct to a State, nor does, vice versa, attribution to a State rule out attribution to an international organization. Thus, one possible solution would be for the relevant conduct to be attributed both to NATO and to one or more of its member States, for instance because those States contributed to planning the military action or to carrying it out'.[49]

One other author even suggests that the UN has no 'real authority or means to control the peacekeepers, absent the TCC's concurrence'.[50] It is also questionable whether the distinction between organs made available under Article 6 and organs seconded under Article 7 is not simply artificial and somehow redundant. Article 6 stipulates that the

> conduct of an organ or agent of an international organization in the performance of functions of that organ or agent shall be considered an act of that organization under international law, whatever position the organ or agent holds in respect of the organization.

The ILC relied on the jurisprudence of the ICJ, making reference to the UN, to define the content of agent under this article. In this context, *agent* has to be interpreted 'in the most liberal sense' as it was held by the ICJ in the *Reparation* case[51] and the notion 'refers not only to officials, but also to other persons acting for the United Nations on the basis of functions conferred by an organ of the organization'.[52] Therefore this disposition is

---

In the same way, UN Doc. A/64/10 (2009), 56, para. 4 of the commentary; UN Doc. A/66/10 (2011), 81, para. 4 of the commentary; see generally S. Talmon, 'Responsibility of International Organizations: Does the European Community Require Special Treatment', in M. Ragazzi (ed.), *International Responsibility Today. Essays in Memory of Oscar Schachter* (Leiden, Brill, 2005), 405–421.

[49] UN Doc. A/CN.4/541 (2004), 4, para. 7.
[50] C. Leck, 'International Responsibility in United Nations Peacekeeping Operations: Command and Control Arrangements and the Attribution of Conduct', *Melbourne Journal of International Law*, 10 (2009), 346, 360–361; UN Doc. A/CN.4/541 (2004), 23, para. 48. For a general critique of the criterion of 'effective control' as formulated in Article 7, see F. Messineo, 'Attribution of Conduct', SHARES Research Paper 32 (2014), available at www.sharesproject.nl, 30–34.
[51] Reparation for Injuries Suffered in the Service of the United Nations, Advisory Opinion (11 April 1949), p. 177; UN Doc. A/66/10 (2011), 84–85.
[52] Difference Relating to Immunity from Legal Process of a Special Rapporteur of the Commission on Human Rights, Advisory Opinion of 29 April 1999, 88–89, para. 66; UN Doc. A/66/10 (2011), 85.

supposed to cover also organs of states which are 'absorbed' by the organisation to the extent that the sending State does not retain any form of control.

Nevertheless, any transferring entity, be it a state or an international organisation, will always retain a 'substantial degree of authority over any organ' as they would otherwise cease to be organs of the transferring entities. Thus there is a necessity for the transferring entities under their domestic or internal law to keep a certain oversight over their transferred organs.[53] Therefore, the difference between the two articles is 'at best one of degree [of retained and transferred control], but not of principle'.[54]

The ILA recognises the possibility of joint responsibility and differentiates between joint responsibility per se and cases of aid and assistance of an international organisation in the commission of other wrongful acts.[55] The ILC commentary does not state whether cases of joint responsibility could fall under Article 7, but it seems to suggest that Article 7 is a disposition which decides whether conduct has to be attributed to the contributing State or organisation or to the receiving organisation[56] which implicitly excludes joint responsibility under this article.[57] In contrast, an application of Article 14 normally leads to two or more international organisations being responsible, regulating cases in which one international organisation aids or assists another international organisation in the commission of an internationally wrongful act.

---

[53] Cf. A. Sari, R. A. Wessel, 'International Responsibility for EU Military Operations: Finding the EU's Place in the Global Accountability Regime', in B. Van Vooren, S. Blockmans, J. Wouters (eds.), *The EU's Role in Global Governance: The Legal Dimension* (Oxford University Press, 2013), 126, 132.

[54] Ibid., 132; B. Boutin, 'Responsibility of the Netherlands for the Acts of Dutchbat in *Nuhanović* and *Mustafić*: The Continuous Quest for a Tangible Meaning for "Effective Control" in the Context of Peacekeeping', *Leiden Journal of International Law*, 25 (2012), 521, 527. Further critique came by Larsen who considers the complexities of practice not to be fully reflected by the criterion of effective control, Larsen, 'Attribution of Conduct in Peace Operations', supra note 44, 518.

[55] The ILA distinguishes between joint responsibility per se and aid and assistance by other international organisations: '*The responsibility of an IO does not preclude any separate or concurrent responsibility of a State or of another IO which participated in the performance of the wrongful act or which has failed to comply with its own obligations concerning the prevention of that wrongful act. There is also an internationally wrongful act of an IO when it aids or assists a State or another IO in the commission of an internationally wrongful act by that State or other IO*': Berlin Conference (2004), supra note 13, 28.

[56] UN Doc. A/66/10 (2011), 86, para. 5.

[57] One could ask under which article UNAMID would fall.

Aid and Assistance – Compatible with Cooperation in Peacekeeping Operations?

Article 14 of the ARIO states as follows:

> An international organization which aids or assists a State or another international organization in the commission of an internationally wrongful act by the State or the latter organization is internationally responsible for doing so if:
>
> (a) the former organization does so with knowledge of the circumstances of the internationally wrongful act; and
> (b) the act would be internationally wrongful if committed by that organization.

The commentary by the ILC does not provide a single example of a case in which an international organisation has aided or assisted another international organisation and incurred responsibility under international law.[58] However, it refers to the example of MONUC, the previous peacekeeping operation in the DRC, assisting the security forces of the government, and thereby a state.[59]

MONUC was told to stop all support to the armed forces of the DRC in the case of violations of IHL, human rights or refugee law, including logistic or service support. The UN specified that MONUC was a case where (solely) 'the possibility of United Nations aid or assistance being used to facilitate the commission of unlawful acts arose ... [a]nd [that] it remains a unique example'.[60] As emphasised by the UN, it must be made clear that responsibility for aid and assistance is entailed not for the wrongful act itself, but for the organisation's own conduct, which has been the cause of or contributed to that wrongful act.[61] Nevertheless, as it was also declared by the UN in its comments upon the ARIO: '[T]he Secretariat wishes to underscore the fundamental difference between States and international organizations, whose aid and assistance activities in an ever-growing

---

[58] UN Doc. A/66/10 (2011), 104–105. The Commentary only refers to the mentioned example of MONUC.
[59] Ibid., 102, para. 6. Note to Mr. Le Roy, MONUC – Operation Kimia 2, 1, para. 7; 2, para. 10. Attachment to Ms. O'Brien's Note of 12 October 2009 to Mr. Le Roy, 3–4, paras. 11–12. All documents were published by the *New York Times* on 9 December 2009. See also Shraga, 'ILC Articles on Responsibility', supra note 22, 201, 205–206.
[60] UN Doc. A/CN.4/637/Add.1 (2011), 17–19, main paras. 1, 5. For more information on MONUC and the UN reaction, ibid., paras. 2–5.
[61] Ibid., 17–19, para. 7.

number and diversity of areas, often constitute their core functions.'[62] Following the MONUC incident, the UN adopted the human rights due diligence policy on UN support to non-UN security forces, which includes peacekeeping operations deployed by other international organisations. It was further elaborated upon in a seventy-eight-page aide-memoire adopted by the Security Council in February 2014.[63]

Thus, whereas cooperation may be one of the core functions of international organisations, it is highly questionable whether the application of this article properly reflects the reality of cooperation between international organisations in peacekeeping operations which goes beyond cases of mere assistance. Assistance implies that an organisation acts in an auxiliary function to another organisation.[64] Subject to the specific arrangements in each operation,[65] the reality of cooperation between international organisations in recent peacekeeping operations is reminiscent of co-perpetration of these internationally wrongful acts rather than of cases in which an international organisation is subordinated to another one. Furthermore, it is necessary according to Article 14 that the aiding or assisting organisation has 'knowledge of the circumstances of the internationally wrongful act' and that the organisation intended 'by the aid or assistance given, to facilitate the occurrence of the wrongful conduct and the internationally wrongful conduct is actually committed'.[66] These strict requirements regarding the intention of the aiding or assisting organisation also do not reflect the reality of cooperation between international organisations in peacekeeping operations.[67] On the contrary, there are

---

[62] Ibid., 19, main para. 7, sub-para. 5.
[63] UN Doc. S/PRST/2014/3 (2014); A/67/777 &S/2013/110 (2013). See generally H. P. Aust, 'The UN Human Rights Due Diligence Policy: An Effective Mechanism against Complicity of Peacekeeping Forces', *Journal of Conflict and Security Law*, 20 (2015), 61–73; J. Labbé, A. Boutellis, 'Peace Operations by Proxy: Implications for Humanitarian Action of UN Peacekeeping Partnerships with Non-UN Security Forces', *International Review of the Red Cross*, 95 (2013), 539–559.
[64] So the UN acknowledges that 'aid and assistance activities in an ever-growing number and diversity of areas often constitute ... core functions of international organisations', UN Doc. A/CN.4/637/Add.1 (2011), 19, para. 5.
[65] Of course, there may be cases of pure aid and assistance by an international organisation, even in peacekeeping operations, General Assembly, 58th session, Official Records, Sixth Committee, Summary Record of the 15th Meeting, UN Doc. A/C.6/58/SR.15 (2003), 7, para. 27. In these cases, Article 14 would be applicable and Article 7 would arguably be applicable for the organisation committing the internationally wrongful act.
[66] UN Doc. A/66/10 (2011), 104, paras. 3–4.
[67] Cf. also V. Lanovoy, 'Complicitiy in an Internationally Wrongful Act', in A. Nollkaemper, I. Plakokefalos, J. N. M. Schechinger (eds.), *Principles of Shared Responsibility in International Law. An Appraisal of the State of Art* (Cambridge University Press, 2014), 134, 162–163, 166.

no cases in which international organisations cooperate intentionally in peacekeeping operations to commit violations of international law, but the cooperation agreements and particularly the existing control arrangements, such as the reports to be submitted to the Security Council, seek to prevent or at least minimise the risk of violations of international law. In the majority of academic writings, this intent requirement has also been criticised as 'unwarranted'.[68]

The comments and observations received by international organisations focused on the practice of International Financial Institutions of lending funds to states,[69] especially in the context of development assistance.[70] In Chapter II an inquiry was made into the financing of AU peacekeeping operations by the EU and the UN. It was stressed that the element of control exercised by both the UN and the EU on the basis of these financial arrangements is substantial. Both organisations could actually block the deployment of an AU peacekeeping operation by refusing to provide funds or at least by demanding that certain specific requirements are fulfilled. So, on the one hand, they would arguably facilitate the occurrence of an internationally wrongful act, but on the other hand, the amount of the control they are able to exercise, seems to surpass a case of aid or assistance and thereby the application of Article 14. In fact, one can say, that they actually are dominating the relationship with the AU if they decide to provide funds. Consequently, as international organisations cooperate in various areas in peacekeeping operations and if financial assistance provided in the peacekeeping context could already surpass the application of Article 14, it results, *a fortiori*, from their cooperation on various other levels that their interaction does not correspond to 'aid and assistance' and cannot legally be regulated by the application of Article 14.[71]

Article 15: Direction and Control

Another article which has to be mentioned is Article 15, which deals with the direction and control of an international organisation over the commission of an internationally wrongful act by another international

---

[68] Aust, 'The UN Human Rights Due Diligence Policy', supra note 59, 68, with further references.
[69] Criticism came from the EU: '[s]ince aid or assistance is often used in a financial context, it would seem desirable that this draft article and its interpretation be kept as narrow as possible', Responsibility of International Organizations, Comments and Observations Received from International Organizations 2, supra note 20, 27.
[70] International Law Association, Sofia Conference (2012), supra note 19, 29.
[71] Cf. also again, UN Doc. A/CN.4/541 (2004), 4, para. 7, regarding joint military planning.

organisation. The only example the ILC refers to in its commentary is KFOR – based on a submission by the French government. Based on this submission, the ILC commented upon the KFOR operation, while assuming that KFOR is an international organisation, that it is 'an example of two international organizations allegedly exercising direction and control in the commission of a wrongful act',[72] whereas according to France 'NATO is responsible for the "direction" of KFOR and the United Nations for "control" of it'.[73] The ILC also remarked in this context that '[a] joint exercise of direction and control was probably envisaged'.[74] The UN Secretariat itself states that it 'knows of no practice supporting the rule on "direction and control" … and doubts the propriety of applying it by analogy from the articles on the responsibility of States' as also '[m]any aspects of this rule, the threshold …, its nature … remain unclear'.[75]

It is also questionable if this article can be applicable to international organisations cooperating in peacekeeping operations besides the alleged example of KFOR. This article presupposes a very one-sided relationship between two international organisations, namely, 'cases of domination over the commission of wrongful conduct and not simply the exercise of oversight, still less mere influence or concern'.[76] In that context, 'the word "directs" does not encompass mere incitement or suggestion but rather connotes actual direction of an operative kind'.[77] The directed or controlled organisation has to be seen as being given no discretion to conduct itself in a specific manner.[78] Thus, the cooperative nature and framework of international organisations in peacekeeping operations does not fit either under this article of the ARIOs.

---

[72] UN Doc. A/66/10 (2011) 103, paras. 3–4.
[73] *Case Concerning Legality of Use of Force (Yugoslavia v. France)*, Preliminary Objections of the French Republic, 5 July 2000, 33, para. 46.
[74] Report of the International Law Commission, 63rd session, supra note 18, 103, para. 3; A. Reinisch, 'Aid or Assistance and Direction and Control between States and International Organizations in the Commission of Internationally Wrongful Acts', *International Organizations Law Review*, 7 (2010), 63, 75.
[75] UN Doc. A/CN.4/637/Add.1 (2011), 19–20, para. 3; Shraga, 'ILC Articles on Responsibility', supra note 22, 201, 208.
[76] The ILC relies on the commentary to the articles on state responsibility, UN Doc. A/66/10 (2011), 103–104, para. 4.
[77] Ibid.
[78] Ibid. See, in contrast, International Law Association, Berlin Conference (2004), supra note 13, 29; UN Doc. A/53/10 (1998), 160, para. 395; 164, para. 422.

Assessing the ARIO

Consequently, the analysis of the relevant Articles from the ILC leads to the conclusion that the concept of joint responsibility is only covered in the form of auxiliary functions by one organisation – aid and assistance – or for situations in which one organisation is clearly dominating the conduct of another through direction and control. For any other potential cases, the concept of joint responsibility does not fit under the articles of the ILC.[79] The articles therefore contain a *lacuna* or a 'responsibility gap' with respect to cases of joint responsibility. Indeed, although Article 48 holds that one or several international organisations may be responsible for the same wrongful act, it 'fails to define when and how this would operate'.[80] The ILC has even specifically mentioned – early in the process of elaborating the articles – the possibility that two international organisations will be simultaneously responsible as equals, but once again without providing any indication of the applicable criterion of attribution.[81] The reason may be that the current view in legal doctrine, and in at least some parts of judicial practice, is still that cases of dual or multiple attribution are rare, so that 'the system of international responsibility would be fundamentally ill-equipped to deal with issues of shared responsibility'.[82] Furthermore, as the system of international responsibility was originally conceptualised with bilateral

---

[79] Other relevant articles for the analysis of responsibility for a specific case will be examined in the case studies, e.g., self-defence.

[80] J. D'Aspremont, 'The Articles on the Responsibility of International Organizations: Magnifying the Fissures in the Law of International Responsibility', *International Organizations Law Review*, 9 (2012), 15, 24.

[81] UN Doc. A/59/10 (2004), 101 para. 4. See also J. Saura, 'Lawful Peacekeeping: Applicability of International Humanitarian Law to United Nations Peacekeeping Operations', *Hastings Law Journal*, 58 (2007), 479, 521; D. Stephens, 'The Lawful Use of Force by Peacekeeping Forces: The Tactical Imperative', *International Peacekeeping*, 12 (2005), 157, esp. 161–162; A. Sari, 'Jurisdiction and International Responsibility in Peace Support Operations: The *Behrami* and *Saramati* Cases', *Human Rights Law Review*, 8 (2008), 151, especially 150–160; Larsen, 'Attribution of Conduct in Peace Operations', supra note 44, 509, 517, 524; A. Nollkaemper, 'Dual Attribution: Liability of the Netherlands for Conduct of Dutchbat in Srebrenica', *Journal of International Criminal Justice*, 9 (2011), 1143–1157.

[82] F. Messineo, 'Multiple Attribution of Conduct', SHARES Research Paper No. 2012-11, available at www.sharesproject.nl, 3. See in particular A. Nollkaemper, D. Jacobs, 'Shared Responsibility in International Law: A Concept Paper', ACIL Research Paper No 2011-07 (SHARES Series), finalised 2 August 2011 (www.sharesproject.nl), 10, 14. Cf. also Ö. F. Direk, 'Responsibility in Peace Support Operations: Revisiting the Proper Test for Attribution Conduct and the Meaning of the "Effective Control" Standard', *Netherlands International Law Review*, 61 (2014), 1, 9.

relations and obligations in mind, it would be therefore also 'ill-equipped to deal with the multiple attribution of conduct to more than one actor at once'.[83] It is true that the idea of a breach of an obligation owed to the whole community (*erga omnes*) was not foreseen, but developed in practice in the progress of the rise of international human rights law and the increased recognition of the individual in international law.[84] Nevertheless, it does not pose a problem as the invocation of responsibility towards each party to which the alleged conduct is attributed, remains possible.[85] It is therefore necessary to look beyond the law of responsibility for inspiration.[86]

The Quest for a New Criterion of Attribution

Instances of joint responsibility of international organisations may have been rare thus far in practice; nevertheless this does not mean that they do not arise or that they will not arise more often in future. The articles of the ILC hold on to the traditional understanding of the law of international responsibility as being derived from bilateral relations existing between entities possessing international legal personality.[87] However, this study has shown that in the specific area of peacekeeping operations, international organisations engage in cooperation arrangements which derogate from the general rules that the ARIO seek to codify as they are outside the scope of the scenarios of joint responsibility regulated in the articles. In short, legal regulation of peacekeeping operations from the point of view of international responsibility requires a new criterion of attribution to allocate responsibility to two or more international organisations.

Article 64 of the ARIOs contains the possibility to derogate from the articles in the case of an existing rule of *lex specialis*. Such special rules

---

[83] Messineo, ibid., 23–24; *Yearbook of the International Law Commission* (1978), Volume I, summary records of the thirtieth session, 233, para. 7. See in particular L. Boisson de Chazournes, V. Pergantis, 'À propos de l'arrêt Behrami et Saramati: Un jeu d'ombre et de lumière dans les relations entre l'ONU et les organisations régionales', in M. Kohen, R. Kolb, D. L. Tehindrazanarivelo (eds.), *Perspectives of International Law in the 21st Century/ Perspectives du droit international au 21e siècle* (Leiden, Brill, 2011), 191, 222. Cf. also L. Boisson de Chazournes, 'United in Joy and Sorrow: Some Considerations on Responsibility Issues under Partnership among International Financial Institutions', in M. Ragazzi (ed.), *Responsibility of International Organizations. Essays in Memory of Sir Ian Brownlie* (Leiden, Brill, 2013), 213–214.
[84] See, e.g., *Barcelona Traction, Light and Power Company, Limited (Belgium v. Spain)* (New Application 1962), Judgment of 5 February 1970, second phase.
[85] Cf. Messineo, 'Multiple Attribution of Conduct', supra note 82, 24.
[86] This includes the danger that the Articles will be demoted 'to a cosmetic instrument', D'Aspremont, supra note 80, 15, 24.
[87] Cf. Crawford, *State Responsibility*, supra note 24, 331.

'may be contained in the rules of the organization applicable to the relations between an international organization and its members'. As the wording shows, these special rules[88] are not limited 'to rules contained in the internal law of the organisations and applicable to the relations of the organisations and its members'.[89] Furthermore, Article 65 provides that 'the applicable rules of international law continue to govern questions concerning the responsibility of an international organization ... for an internationally wrongful act to the extent that they are not regulated by these draft articles'. The rules of an organisation include its practice.[90] The practice of cooperation in peacekeeping operations can therefore constitute a rule of *lex specialis* according to Article 64 ARIO, drawing inspiration from and being based on other existing rules of international law. It is therefore in line with both Articles 64 and 65.[91] Moreover, as it was pointed out in the General Commentary to the ARIO:

> The fact that several of the present draft articles are based on limited practice moves the border between codification and progressive development in the direction of the latter. It may occur that a provision in the articles on State responsibility could be regarded as representing codification, while the corresponding provision on the responsibility of international organizations is more in the nature of progressive development. In other words, the provisions of the present draft articles do not necessarily yet have the same authority as the corresponding provisions on State responsibility.[92]

With regard to Article 7 ARIO, in particular, there seems to be 'a certain level of consensus' that the test adopted by the ILC constitutes progressive development and should be applied on a case-by-case basis.[93] In the

---

[88] See generally K. E. Boon, 'The Role of *Lex Specialis* in the Articles on the Responsibility of International Organizations', in M. Ragazzi (ed.), *Responsibility of International Organizations. Essays in Memory of Sir Ian Brownlie* (Leiden, Brill, 2013), 135, 141.

[89] J. D'Aspremont, 'A European Law of International Responsibility: The Articles on Responsibility of International Organizations and the European Union', SHARES Research Paper 22 (2013), ACIL 2013–2014, available at www.sharesproject.nl, 10.

[90] Article 2b of the articles; cf. S. P. Sheeran, 'A Constitutional Moment? United Nations Peacekeeping in the Democratic Republic of Congo', *International Organizations Law Review*, 8 (2011), 55, 66.

[91] An application of Article 64 in the peacekeeping context is also advocated by several experts, B. Boutin, 'Responsibility in Multinational Military Operations: A Review of Recent Practice", SHARES Expert Seminar Report (16 December 2010, Amsterdam), published in December 2011, available at www.sharesproject.nl, 17; cf. F. Salerno, 'International Responsibility for the Conduct of "Blue Helmets": Exploring the Organic Link', in M. Ragazzi (ed.), *Responsibility of International Organizations. Essays in Memory of Sir Ian Brownlie* (Leiden, Brill, 2013), 415, 418–419; UN Doc. A/66/10 (2011), 86, para. 9.

[92] UN Doc. A/66/10 (2011), 67–68, para. 5.

[93] Montejo, 'The Notion of "Effective Control"', supra note 21, 404.

end, the attribution of acts of peacekeepers to the international organisation they are seconded to as enshrined in Article 7 ARIO is also based on considerations of practice. Due to their institutional status as a subsidiary organ of the respective organisation, their conduct is generally deemed to be attributable to the latter. The transfer of operational command over the troops, however, leads to the formulation of another presumption which is that the international organisation is exclusively responsible for their conduct.[94] Thus, nothing in the articles contravenes an articulation of a specific criterion of attribution in the context of cooperation of international organisations in peacekeeping operations.

The Need for a Special Rule on Attribution for Peacekeeping Operations and Discussions to this Effect

Due to the specific context of peacekeeping operations, it is suggested that the new criterion of attribution will be used exclusively for the purposes of this present study. In contrast, it is not submitted that the articles of the ILC are inappropriate to the regulation of any conduct of international organisations outside of the specific context of peacekeeping operations and particularly cooperation between international organisations during peacekeeping operations. Indeed, as the ICJ stated in the *Genocide* case 'logic does not require the same test [on attribution] to be adopted in resolving ... issues which are very different in nature'.[95] In fact, a variety of concepts of control have been developed in other fields of international law for regulating internationally wrongful conduct, including terrorism and investor state arbitration.[96] It is also not even argued that any future peacekeeping operation which is conducted under the auspices of one international organisation without any external participation by other organisations will not fall under the Articles of the ILC.[97]

Regarding the present subject matter, the suggestion that a specific rule or even a regime *sui generis* is necessary is not new. Article 7 of the articles of the ILC was drafted in recognition of the need to create a separate

---

[94] Sari, Wessel, 'International Responsibility for EU Military Operations', supra note 53, 133–134.

[95] *Application of the Convention on the Prevention and Punishment of the Crime of Genocide (Bosnia and Herzegovina v. Serbia and Montenegro)*, Judgment of 26 February 2007, para. 405. Cf. N. Tsagourias, N. D. White, *Collective Security. Theory, Law and Practice* (Oxford University Press, 2013), 373.

[96] K. E. Boon, 'Are Control Tests Fit For the Future? The Slippage Problem in Attribution Doctrines', *Melbourne Journal of International Law*, 15 (2014), 1, 7, also pp. 17, 19–20.

[97] The development of practice does not, however, suggest that any such scenario will still occur.

article, and thus a specific rule of attribution, applicable to situations such as peacekeeping operations.[98] The ILA remarked that '[i]n some areas, such an attempt [of attribution of conduct to an international organisation] can only be undertaken on a case-by-case basis, e.g. incidents occurring during operations of peacekeeping and peace enforcement'.[99] Moreover, several members of the International Law Commission raised the question of whether, given the difficulties encountered in the area of peacekeeping operations, it would not be preferable to either study further the practice of the UN or to codify a separate rule applicable to peacekeeping operations.[100] Other authors suggest an application of Articles 64 or 44 ASR generally for the conduct of armed forces based on considerations arising under international humanitarian law.[101]

The recommendation of a special rule for peacekeeping operations was to a certain extent examined as the ILC considered the inclusion of a specific disposition specifying that a contributing state or organisation could derogate from the general rule of attribution in its relations with the host organisations under the form of an agreement.[102] However, in the end, the Commission decided against it, following the opinion of the Special Rapporteur Giorgio Gaja, who was opposed to a specific rule for peacekeeping operations for two reasons, the first one being purely methodological – namely that such a specific rule would have been 'at odds with the pattern of the articles on State responsibility'.[103] Secondly, any such rule would be difficult to establish due to the lack of an agreed definition of 'peacekeeping operation'.[104]

---

[98] UN Doc. (A/59/10) (2004), 99, 110, para. 1; Leck, 'International Responsibility', supra note 50, 346, 349.

[99] International Law Association, New Delhi Conference (2002), supra note 13, 16. Generally, the ILA agrees with the application of the 'effective control' test to international organisations, but it highlights again that the 'test of effective control should be further specified based on the available practice, and in relation to the test of effective control as applied in the law of State responsibility', International Law Association, Sofia Conference (2012), supra note 19, 25.

[100] UN Doc. A/CN.4/SR.2800 (2004), paras. 16, 19; A/CN.4/SR.2801 (2004), para. 70; A/CN.4/SR.2802 (2004), paras. 12–13, 19; A/CN.4/SR.2803 (2004), para. 34; A/CN.4/650/Add.1 (2012), 6, para. 14.

[101] B. Stern, 'The Elements of an Internationally Wrongful Act', in J. Crawford, A. Pellet, S. Olleson (eds.), *The Law of International Responsibility* (Oxford University Press, 2010), 193, 203; B. Kondoch, 'The Responsibility of Peacekeepers, Their Sending States, and International Organizations', in T. D. Gill, D. Fleck (eds.), *The Handbook of the International Law of Military Operations* (Oxford University Press, 2010), 515, 529; R. Burke, 'Attribution of Responsibility: Sexual Abuse and Exploitation, and Effective Control of Blue Helmets', *Journal of International Peacekeeping*, 16 (2012), 1, 42.

[102] UN Doc. A/CN.4/SR.2810 (2004), para. 17.

[103] UN Doc. A/CN.4/541 (2004), 16, para. 34.

[104] Ibid., 16, para. 34.

In doctrine it is, inter alia, argued that it is impossible to construe a general rule for attribution of conduct in UN peacekeeping operations.[105] The difficulty with which the ILC was faced in developing the articles was that the rules needed to be wide enough to take into account the diversity of international organisations, while simultaneously being universally applicable.[106]

Defining the New Rule of Attribution

Two main points have to be addressed for the establishment of a new criterion of attribution. First of all, it would be preferable if the new criterion were to have an ascertainable legal basis. Secondly, the threshold of control over the conduct has to be determined.[107] In this regard, one has to distinguish between the levels in the chain of command for the attribution of conduct to two or more international organisations. As the present study examines the possibility of joint responsibility of international organisations, it is concerned with the highest level in the chain of command within the organisations, the organisations to which responsibility is ultimately attributed. Thus, force commanders of a peacekeeping operation might exercise 'effective control' over a given specific act, while the Security Council as the organ on top of the chain exercises a different kind of control, which also has political connotations. In UN peacekeeping operations, one distinguishes, for instance, between three levels of command: 'overall political direction, the purview of the Security Council ..., executive direction and control, provided by the Secretary-General; and ... command in the field, residing in the chief of mission'.[108] This argument is even more relevant in the context of two or more international organisations.[109] The criterion needs to be construed in such a way as to reflect the 'equal standing' of two or more international organisations.

---

[105] G. Verdirame, *The UN and Human Rights. Who Guards the Guardian?* (Cambridge University Press, 2011), 201.
[106] J. Wouters, J. Odermatt, 'Are All International Organizations Created Equal?', *International Organizations Law Review*, 9 (2012), 7, 12.
[107] N. Tsagourias, 'The Responsibility of International Organisations for Military Missions', in M. Odello, R. Piotrowicz (eds.), *International Military Missions and International Law* (Leiden, Brill, 2011), 245, 248.
[108] UN Doc. A/49/681 (1994), 2, para. 4.
[109] Ibid., 2, para. 5. See also Department of Peacekeeping Operations and Department of Field Support, Policy, February 2008, Authority, Command and Control in United Nations Peacekeeping Operations, 3–4, paras. 7–11. For the EU, see Council of the European Union, EU Concept for Military Command and Control, Brussels, 24 September 2012.

A new criterion of attribution has to take into account particularly the *organisational element*. International organisations are complex entities with different organs, chains of command and control mechanisms, and this also affects peacekeeping operations carried out by international organisations, especially modern, integrated operations. If two or more organisations then decide to cooperate in this complex matter, it is evident that these internal organisational arrangements, as well as the inter-organisational arrangements, do not only have to be taken into account, but they also have to be part of the basis of the criterion of attribution. An excellent observation was made by Bodeau-Livinec in this context. Commenting on the position of the ILC regarding the notion of 'control', he stated:

> La position de la CDI paraît plus conforme aux prescrits classiques du droit international en la matière, qui se fondent sur l'emprise exercée sur un comportement plutôt que sur l'autorité exercée sur une personne ou une entité: la responsabilité est déterminée à raison de faits, et non de liens entre sujets.[110]

This is exactly the crux of the problem with the current notion of 'control'. It still adheres to this very limited view of control over the specific conduct in a specific moment, while completely ignoring the fact that such a notion cannot be operational in a system which becomes gradually more institutionalised and complex.[111] In fact, although the notion of 'control' is well established in international law, it has not been fully explored yet in a theoretical manner.[112] Control is also a requirement of the internal law of an international organisation, e.g., the UN, 'and must not be confused with control as a distinct basis of attribution of conduct'.[113] But it is exactly through these institutionalised mechanisms and channels that

---

[110] P. Bodeau-Livinec, 'Le cadre juridique général de la détermination de la responsabilité pour faits illicities commis au cours d'opérations de maintien de la paix: les principles d'attribution et leurs implications', in S. Kolanowski (ed.), *Proceedings of the Bruges Colloquium. International Organisations' Involvement in Peace Operations: Applicable Legal Framework and the Issue of Responsibility* (2011), 83, 93. Cf. C. Eagleton, *International Organization and the Law of Responsibility*, Collected Courses of the Hague Academy of International Law, Vol. 076 (1950), 320, 385.

[111] Cf. Sari, Wessel, 'International Responsibility for EU Military Operations', supra note 53, 126, 132; C. Major, 'EU-UN Cooperation in Military Crisis Management: The Experience of EUFOR RD Congo in 2006', Occasional Paper, n°72, September 2008, EUISS, 7; Direk, 'Responsibility in Peace Support Operations', supra note 82, 1, 19.

[112] Gal-Or, Ryngaert, 'From Theory to Practice', supra note 43, 511, 529.

[113] Sari, Wessel, 'International Responsibility for EU Military Operations', supra note 53, 126, 133.

international organisations also contribute to, and exercise control over, conduct amounting to a violation of a rule under international law.[114]

Furthermore, the importance of the element of control has to be questioned particularly in the context of the responsibility of international organisations, which operate as international legal entities without being sovereigns of any territory. As explained by Eagleton: '[R]esponsibility derives from control. The responsibility of a state rests largely upon a territorial basis, but behind this territorial basis lies the broader concept of control.'[115] The attribution of extra-territorial conduct to a state developed later, particularly also in the practice of the European Court of Human Rights, and is limited to specific circumstances. International organisations, however, neither act territorially nor extraterritorially, but 'unterritorially' from their point of view and 'territorially' from the point of view of the state in whose territory they are engaged. Therefore it is important that the criterion of control in its traditional understanding is less decisive in determining the responsibility of an international organisation.[116]

Indeed, even in the early writings of modern international law, one can find arguments for taking into account other factors for the attribution of conduct and responsibility. Grotius not only acknowledged the possibility of the attribution of conduct to several actors,[117] but he also emphasised as a determinative factor that their action gave a determinative cause to the whole violation and the resulting damage or parts of both.[118] Emphasising the element of contribution to injury instead of the very same wrongful act, would allow one to articulate responsibility based on the idea of a single, undivided injury, an avenue which was closed in the articles of the ILC.[119]

---

[114] Meeting Summary, Legal Responsibility of International Organisations in International Law, Summary of the International Law Discussion Group meeting held at Chatham House on Thursday, 10 February 2011, 7. Cf. *Stichting Mothers of Srebrenica and Others v. The Netherlands*, supra note 42, para. 4117.

[115] Eagleton, *International Organizations*, supra note 110, 320, 386; G. Jellinek, *Allgemeine Staatslehre* (Darmstadt, Wissenschaftliche Buchgesellschaft, 1900), 396.

[116] Cf. Eagleton, ibid., 386, 403. See also Report of the International Law Commission, sixty-third session, supra note 18, 88, para. 5; Dannenbaum, supra note 37, 713, 724.

[117] H. Grotius, *De jure belli ac pacis, Libri tres* (1625), in the German version by Dr. W. Schätzel (Frankfurt am Main, Textor Verlag, 2008), 304, paras. VI–VII.

[118] Ibid., 305, para. X.

[119] N. Nedeski, A. Nollkaemper, 'Responsibility of International Organizations in Connection with Acts of States', *International Organizations Law Review*, 9 (2012), 33, 50.

The following example – based roughly on AFISMA – may helpfully illustrate the issues at stake:

An ECOWAS peacekeeper, in an operation XY with the authorisation to use all necessary means to defend the mandate, due to misinterpreting the ROEs and unclear circumstances on the ground and faulty communication equipment, shoots and kills a civilian on the ground. The operation was paid for by the EU through the African Peace Facility Fund. The soldier was trained as part of the ASF in a joint training exercise of the AU in cooperation with ECOWAS and in coordination with the EU and NATO. Logistical support to the operation was provided by the UN in the form of a Support package based on assessed contributions. The mission plans were developed in cooperation among the AU, ECOWAS and the UN. The mandate of this operation is based first of all on the implementation of the ECOWAS Mechanism, which was authorised by the AU, which itself was authorised by the UN Security Council.

So, why would one break down this whole structure and simply look at which entity was exercising 'effective control' over a specific act if the whole mission is based on cooperation and interaction among several actors? Even the ICJ in its *Nicaragua* decision spoke of 'effective control of the ... operations in the course of which the alleged violations were committed'.[120] The more complex the situation in which responsibility for an internationally wrongful act arises, the more artificial it becomes to ignore all pertinent circumstances for the establishment and execution of the peacekeeping operation, and it would become even more important to respond to and to develop a norm which takes into account these complex circumstances. Arguments of justice and equity likewise support this view.[121] The very same argument is made for the responsibility of troop-contributing countries (TCCs) and international organisations for peacekeeping operations.[122] Tomuschat argues similarly on the organisational level, and contends that the UN may also entail responsibility for an authorised operation (of several states) if 'the Security Council may be so tightly involved in the activities endorsed

---

[120] *Military and Paramilitary Activities in and against Nicaragua (Nicaragua v. United States of America)*, Merits, Judgment (27 June 1986), 14, para. 115.
[121] For example, R. G. Teifel, *Humanity's Law* (Oxford University Press, 2011), 141–164; D'Aspremont, 'The Articles on the Responsibility', supra note 80, 15, 22–23; Tomuschat, 'The European Court of Human Rights', supra note 7, 334, 357–358; Direk, 'Responsibility in Peace Support Operations', supra note 82, 1, 15.
[122] Leck, 'International Responsibility', supra note 50, 346, 359.

by it that the operation concerned may become legally attributable to the UN'.[123]

Consequently, in order to further define the new criterion of attribution it appears necessary to look to other areas of law for inspiration. Judge Simma, in his separate opinion in the *Oil Platforms* case, described the difficulty of establishing the responsibility of multiple tortfeasors as a 'textbook situation calling for ... an exercise in legal analogy'.[124] In particular, criminal law and international criminal law may provide useful guidance for the present purposes.[125]

Drawing Inspiration from Other International Legal Rules: (International) Criminal Law

As with international criminal law, the law of international responsibility can also only promote compliance and exude a deterrent effect if responsibility is attributed to those entities which are truly responsible, thereby preventing an actor from taking a free ride on account of another entity being held responsible unjustly on its own.[126] Taking a wider perspective, there are other undertakings on the international level that have the aim of limiting the exercise of powers on an international level and by international organisations, for example, the emergence of global administrative law.[127] There are also arguments put forward for a constitutionalisation of international law, according to which acts need to be in conformity with the constitutional values of the international legal order which includes, for example, human rights, and are therefore also binding international organisations in their actions.[128]

---

[123] C. Tomuschat, 'Case Note. R *(on the Application of Al-Jedda) v. Secretary of State for Defence*. Human Rights in a Multi-Level System of Governance and the Internment of Suspected Terrorists', *Melbourne Journal of International Law*, 9 (2008), 391, 394; also J.-P. Schütze, *Die Zurechenbarkeit von Völkerrechtsverstößen im Rahmen mandatierter Friedensmissionen der Vereinten Nationen* (Berlin, Duncker & Humblot, 2010), 137.

[124] *Case Concerning Oil Platforms (Islamic Republic of Iran v. United States of America)*, Judgment of 6 November 2003 (Judge Simma, Separate Opinion), 354, para. 66.

[125] See also Crawford, *State Responsibility*, supra note 24, 328–329, with further references.

[126] Cf. Ryngaert, 'Apportioning Responsibility', supra note 36, 151, 154.

[127] Cf., for example, S. Cassese, B. Carotti, L. Casini et al. (eds.), *Global Administrative Law: The Casebook* (New York, IRPA-IILJ, 2012) and especially J. Arato, 'Material Limits to the Power of the United Nations Security Council: Between Law and Politics', ibid., 59, 65–67.

[128] J. Klabbers, 'Controlling International Organizations: A Virtue Ethics Approach', *International Organizations Law Review*, 8 (2011), 285–287; A. von Bogdandy,

In its *Tadić* decision, the ICTY stated:

> In order to attribute the acts of a military or paramilitary group to a State, it must be proved that the State wields overall control over the group, not only by equipping and financing the group, but also by coordinating or helping in the general planning of its military activity.[129]

The clear chain of command in peacekeeping operation, as in any military operation, appears in that context as beneficial for the exercise of command and control in the complex circumstances of peacekeeping operations. Consequently, it seems to be justified, as it was ultimately held by the ICTY to inquire whether the nature and degree of organisation of an organ, over which control is exercised, is relevant for the purposes of attributing control and justifies adapting the required degree of control.[130]

But *Tadić* is also a good example of being aware of the interweaving (*Verpflechtung*) of international actors in their activities for the purposes of the attribution of conduct.[131] This case is even more relevant as it also established the notion of 'joint criminal enterprise' under international law.[132]

The aim of this concept of liability in criminal law is to prevent crimes from going unpunished which have been committed in very complex organisational settings. As explained in the *Amicus Curiae* brief in the *Duch* case:

> When such crimes are committed, it is extremely difficult to point out the specific contribution made by each individual participant in the collective criminal enterprise because (i) not all participants acted in the same

---

M. Steinbrück Platise, 'ARIO and Human Rights Protection: Leaving the Individual in the Cold', *International Organizations Law Review*, 9 (2012), 67–68, 70.

[129] *Prosecutor v. Duško Tadić a/k/a 'Dule'*, Judgment, Case No. IT-94-1, Ap. Chamber, 15 July 1999, 56, para. 131; 58–59, para. 147. See also J. Cerone, 'Human Dignity in the Line of Fire: The Application of International Human Rights Law During Armed Conflict, Occupation, and Peace Operations', *Vanderbilt Journal of Transnational Law*, 39 (2006), 1447, 1460.

[130] See, for example, *Velásquez Rodríguez v. Honduras*, Judgment of 29 July 1988, Inter-Am Ct. H.R., para. 172; Sari, Wessel, 'International Responsibility for EU Military Operations', supra note 53, 126, 138–139; A.-M. Slaughter, W. Burke-White, 'An International Constitutional Moment', *Harvard International Law Journal*, 43 (2002), 1, 19–20. See also K. N. Trapp, *State Responsibility for International Terrorism* (Oxford University Press, 2011), 44–45.

[131] This is without prejudice to the decisions of the ICJ in the *Nicaragua* Case and in *Congo v. Uganda*. But see T. Dannenbaum, 'Translating the Standard of Effective Control into a System of Effective Accountability: How Liability Should be Apportioned for Violations of Human Rights by Member State Troop Contingents Serving as United Nations Peacekeepers', *Harvard International Law Journal*, 51 (2010), 113, 155; R. Buchan, 'UN Peacekeeping Operations: When Can Unlawful Acts Committed by Peacekeeping Forces Be Attributed to the UN?', *Legal Studies*, 32 (2012), 282, 288, 298, 301.

[132] *Prosecutor v. Duško Tadić a/k/a 'Dule'*, supra note 129, 82–83, para. 192; see also Nollkaemper, Jacobs, 'Shared Responsibility', supra note 82, 15.

manner, but rather each of them may have played a different role in planning, organizing, instigating, coordinating, executing, or otherwise contributing to the criminal conduct, and (ii) the evidence related to each individual's conduct may prove difficult if not impossible to find ... To obscure responsibility in the fog of collective criminality and let the crimes go unpunished would be immoral and contrary to the general purpose of criminal law.[133]

Particularly in domestic law, one can compare it with the notion of 'co-perpetration' as it exists in various domestic laws, including German and Swiss law.[134] However, the concept of co-perpetration is also another method of weighing criminal responsibility under international criminal law.[135] In international criminal law, yet another concept is derived particularly from German criminal law. According to this concept, an individual can be held legally responsible for inducing others to commit crimes through a hierarchically structured organisation under his or her control, thereby acting as '*der Täter hinter dem Täter*' (the perpetrator behind the perpetrator)[136] and it has been applied in practice by the ICC.[137] Especially relevant for the present purposes are the instances in which the individual acts by means of 'control over an organisation' (*Organisationsherrschaft*), often also in a military context.[138] As pointed

[133] A. Cassese and Members of the Journal of International Criminal Justice, 'Amicus Curiae Brief of Professor Antonio Cassese and Members of the Journal of International Criminal Justice on Joint Criminal Enterprise Doctrine', *Criminal Law Forum*, 20 (2009), 289, 301; H. Olasolo, 'Joint Criminal Enterprise and Its Extended Form: A Theory of Co-perpetration Giving Rise to Principal Liability, a Notion of Accessorial Liability, or a Form of Partnership in Crime?', *Criminal Law Forum*, 20 (2009), 263, 265.

[134] § 25 of the German Criminal Code (StGB), under Swiss Criminal Law it is not explicitly provided for in the Swiss Penal Code, but derived from customary law. The Swiss Penal Code only contains dispositions with regard to aid and assistance and incitement.

[135] For instance, Article 25(3)(a) second alternative of the Rome State of the ICC.

[136] Decision on the Confirmation of Charges, *Prosecutor v. Germain Katanga and Mathieu Ngudjolo Chui* (ICC-01/04-01/07), Pre-Trial Chamber I, 30 September 2008, 167, para. 496. See generally T. Weigend, 'Perpetration through an Organization. The Unexpected Career of a German Legal Concept', *Journal of International Criminal Justice*, 9 (2011), 91, 94–111; C. Roxin, 'Organisationsherrschaft und Tatentschlossenheit', *Zeitschrift für internationale Strafrechtsdogmatik*, 1 (2006), 293–300; S. Eldar, 'Exploring International Criminal Law's Reluctance to Resort to Modalities of Group Responsibility', *Journal of International Criminal Justice*, 11 (2013), 331–349.

[137] Decision on the Confirmation of Charges, *Prosecutor v. Thomas Lubanga Dyilo* (ICC-01/04-01/06), Pre-Trial Chamber I, 29 January 2007, paras. 322–367, 488. See especially Decision on the Confirmation of Charges, ibid., paras. 487–518; Judgment pursuant to Article 74 of the Statute, *Prosecutor v. Thomas Lubanga Dyilo* (ICC-01/04-01/06), Trial Chamber I, 14 March 2012, 423, para. 978; 433, para. 1003.

[138] Decision on the Confirmation of Charges, ibid., 167–168, para. 498; Olasolo, 'Joint Criminal Enterprise', supra note 133, 263, 269. Generally K. Ambos, 'Command

out by the ICC, this approach can be distinguished from the notion of joint criminal enterprise.[139] Moreover, it covers cases of 'political and military leaders, who are each of them in control of a different hierarchical organisation ... [and who] direct their different organisations to implement in a coordinated manner a common criminal plan'.[140] Interestingly, it was even held in the *Eichmann* trial that the blameworthiness and responsibility of an individual increases depending on his or her position within the organisation and thus, the complexity of the structure of the latter.[141]

A New Notion of Control: *Normative Control*

It is not to suggest that the new notion of control for the purposes of attribution is based on something similar to the idea of a 'crime of states.'[142] However, the new notion of attribution is derived from the idea that international organisations are jointly responsible in peacekeeping operations because they cooperate in various areas and that this 'cooperative effort' is simultaneously causal for violations of international law in a given case. This is precisely why the notion of control has to be broader than 'factual control'.[143] As explained, factual control alone is not sufficient due to the territorial differences between states and international organisations. On the contrary, also important is 'normative control' based on institutionalised relations between the international organisations, including any form of 'political' influence over the decision making of the other organisation.[144]

Responsibility and *Organisationsherrschaft*: Ways of Attributing International Crimes to the "Most Responsible"', in A. Nollkaemper, H. van der Wilt (eds.), *System Criminality in International Law* (Cambridge University Press, 2009), 127–157.

[139] Decision on the Confirmation of Charges, *Prosecutor v. Thomas Lubanga Dyilo* (ICC-01/04-01/06), ibid., para. 338–341.

[140] Olasolo, 'Joint Criminal Enterprise', supra note 133, 263, 269; Decision on the Confirmation of Charges, supra note 136, paras. 540–582; Decision on the Prosecutor's Application for a Warrant of Arrest against Jean-Pierre Bemba Combo (ICC-01/05-01/08), Pre-Trial Chamber III, 10 June 2008, paras. 69–84; *Prosecutor v. Milomir Stakić*, Judgment, Case No. IT-97-24-T, T. Ch. II, 31 July 2003, paras. 738–744, 774, 818, 822 and 826.

[141] Jerusalem District Court, *The Attorney General v. Eichmann*, Case No. 40/61, Judgment, 36 I.L.R. 5–14, 18–276, 12 December 1961, para. 197.

[142] *Yearbook of the International Law Commission* (1976), Volume II, Part Two, Report of the Commission to the General Assembly on the Work of Its Twenty-Eighth Session, 95–112. Cf. G. Nolte, 'From Dionisio Anzilotti to Roberto Ago: The Classical International Law of Responsibility and the Traditional Primacy of a Bilateral Conception of Inter-state Relations', *European Journal of International Law*, 13 (2002), 1083–1098.

[143] Cf. UN Doc. A/CN.4/637/Add.1 (2011), 20, para. 3 under draft article 8.

[144] Some elements can be both normative and factual; see J. D'Aspremont, 'The Law of International Responsibility and Multi-layered Institutional Veils: the Case of Authorized Regional Peace-Enforcement Operations', SHARES Research Paper 24 (2013), ACIL

In the WTO *Geographical Indications Dispute*, for instance, the Panel accepted the view of the EC that member states were to act as de facto organs of the Community for the implementation of its law. The dependence of the states on the EU and the control of the latter are based on a transfer of competences to the EC and thus on control derived from legal instruments, which amounts to normative control.[145] This case is particularly relevant as it involves normative control based on the transfer of competences over other entities possessing independent legal personality, *a fortiori*, it should even more be applicable to the transfer of competences by the Security Council to a UN Peacekeeping operation which as a subsidiary organ does not possess independent legal personality.

The ICJ, in the *Genocide Case* took into account these alternative bases for establishing control, declaring that 'the physical acts constitutive of genocide ... have been committed by organs ... [and] were carried out, *wholly or in part*, on the instructions or directions of the State, *or* under its effective control'.[146] Effective control pervades as an alternative through the whole judgment[147] and the 'wholly or in part' also suggests that other criterion are determinative for the attribution of conduct.

The new proposed criterion does not touch upon the question of whether member states could, in individual cases, also be (jointly) responsible, which is outside of the focus of the present study.[148] As states equally increase coordination on a bi- and multinational level outside of an international organisation, the complexity of an examination of attribution of conduct to states will increase, as well as the number of cases of joint

---

2003–10, available at www.sharesproject.nl, 4. See also UN Doc. A/CN.4/SR.2803 (2004), 86–87, para. 8; 90, para. 36; A. Nollkaemper, 'Power and Responsibility', SHARES Research Paper 42 (2014), ACIL 2014–22, available at www.sharesproject.nl, in particular p. 12.

[145] WTO Panel Report, European Communities – Protection of Trademarks and Geographical Indications for Agricultural Products and Foodstuffs, DS174, 15 March 2005, paras. 7.98 and 7.269; cf. Sari, Wessel, 'International Responsibility for EU Military Operations', supra note 53, 126, 139.

[146] *Application of the Convention*, supra note 95, para. 401.

[147] Ibid., e.g., paras. 400, 406, 412–413; cf. also Dannenbaum, 'Translating the Standard', supra note 131, 113, 154.

[148] Cf. UN Doc. S/RES/1528 (2004), para. 16; Briefing by the Force Commander of MONUSCO, UN Doc. S/PV.6987 (2013), 2–3; Ryngaert, 'Apportioning Responsibility', supra note 36, 151, esp. 155–158, 165–166. Increasingly, tasks of peacekeeping operations are also outsourced to private security contractors which also raises questions of responsibility; see R. Buchan, H. Jones, N. D. White, 'The Externalization of Peacekeeping: Policy, Responsibility and Accountability', *Journal of International Peacekeeping*, 15 (2011), 281, 286, 293–296; A. G. Østensen, 'In the Business of Peace: The Political Influence of Private Military and Security Companies on UN Peacekeeping', *International Peacekeeping*, 20 (2013), 33–47.

responsibility of states.¹⁴⁹ In contrast to these cases, however, it should not be apprehended that the attribution of responsibility to two or more international organisations instead of one will diminish the willingness of member states to contribute troops to military operations of international organisations.¹⁵⁰ In contrast, the benefit of a regime of shared responsibility is that it prevents 'behavioural externalities and other undesirable consequences'.¹⁵¹

Responsibility under criminal law necessitates an element of intent (*mens rea*) which can also be found in the articles of the ILC which presuppose 'knowledge' by the organisation in aiding or abetting another international organisation. But one cannot completely reconcile the law of responsibility and international criminal law as regards their inherent systemic functions. Both bodies of law contain an inherent aspect of deterrence to prevent further violations of norms, but whereas criminal law sanctions individuals to serve a sentence in prison, the law of responsibility allows for different forms of reparation as one finds in domestic civil law.¹⁵² It is actually, the requirement or non-requirement of 'intent' which circumscribes the two fields of law. Whereas wilful damage of property falls under criminal law and is appropriate for claims of compensation under civil law, as regards unintentional damage of property, compensation is only possible under civil law.¹⁵³ Moreover, one can distinguish between 'intent' and 'wrongful intent' and the law of responsibility is simply neutral regarding the requirement of the latter.¹⁵⁴ It so appears that despite the possibility of drawing inspiration from criminal law in the form of a criterion of attribution, one has nevertheless to differentiate between the two bodies of law in respect of the element of 'intent'.¹⁵⁵ It could

---

¹⁴⁹ For instance, Declaration of Intent on 28 May 2013 between Germany and the Netherlands, covering thirty-eight specific points under which the cooperation between the two countries in the field of defence will be increased.
¹⁵⁰ Ryngaert, 'Apportioning Responsibility', supra note 36, 151, 164. Nevertheless, States also have a legitimate interest in accepting responsibility, the refusal of which would be tantamount to admitting that the State in question has no control whatsoever of its troops placed at the disposal of an international organisation, ibid., 165.
¹⁵¹ Leck, 'International Responsibility', supra note 50, 346, 364.
¹⁵² See Articles 34–38 ARIO.
¹⁵³ See, e.g., under German law, §§ 303 and 15 StGB and § 823 BGB.
¹⁵⁴ Sheeran, 'A Constitutional Moment', supra note 90, 55, 76.
¹⁵⁵ In other instances, the law of responsibility is, of course, synonymous with ideas and concepts of (international) criminal law. The institution of 'aid and assistance' can be found in most criminal legal systems.

be argued that the UN and regional organisations have voluntarily entered into various agreements of cooperation for the purposes of the conduct of peacekeeping operations, in the knowledge that despite all efforts, violations of human rights, humanitarian law and other potentially applicable norms by peacekeepers may occur and, as a result, they therefore possess the necessary degree of *mens rea*.[156] However, it would be required that they have provided assistance or rather cooperated with a specific purpose in mind and with the knowledge that violations of international law are committed in the execution of that given specific purpose.[157]

Moreover, the framework of the ARIOs as developed by the ILC is generally based on the idea of objective responsibility[158] and it would be simultaneously very difficult to prove that an international organisation was acting with the aim to facilitate violations of international law. The criterion of normative control as developed in this chapter and as further defined in Chapter 4 will therefore be based on objective criteria for the attribution of conduct similar to Article 7 ARIO.

Yet another advantage of the proposed criterion of normative control is that it disposes of the distinction between UN-authorised and UN operations,[159] as cooperation between the organisations is independent of the question whether it is an authorised or a UN operation.[160] Article 17 equally allows for an international organisation to be responsible for any binding decisions it has adopted which were implemented by its member states or international organisations (para. 1), as well as for authorisations acted upon accordingly (para. 2).

---

[156] Cf. Tomuschat, 'The European Court of Human Rights', supra note 7, 334, 357.
[157] P. Klein and O. Corten, 'The Limits of Complicity as a Ground for Responsibility: Lessons Learned from the Corfu Channel Case', in K. Bannelier, T. Christiakis, S. Heathcote (eds.), *The ICJ and the Evolution of International Law: The Enduring Impact of the Corfu Channel Case* (London, Routledge, 2012), 315, 330; Lanovoy, 'Complicity', supra note 67, 18; J. Quigley, 'Complicity in International Law: A New Direction in the Law of State Responsibility', *British Yearbook of International Law*, 57 (1987), 77, 110–113.
[158] Cf. G. Nolte, H. P. Aust, 'Equivocal Helpers – Complicit States, Mixed Messages and International Law', *International and Comparative Law Quarterly*, 58 (2009), 1, 13.
[159] The UN accordingly criticised the Behrami/Saramati decision, Responsibility of International Organizations, Comments and Observations Received from International Organizations, supra note 18, 10–12, paras. 9–10; P. Klein, 'The Attribution of Acts to International Organizations', in J. Crawford, A. Pellet, S. Olleson (eds.), *The Law of International Responsibility* (Oxford University Press, 2010), 297, 299–300.
[160] UN Doc. A/CN.4/553 (2005), paras. 41–42. See also UN Doc. A/CN.4/SR.2802 (2004), paras. 21–22.

Distinguishing the New Criterion of Attribution from Cases of Other Forms of Responsibility (e.g., Aid and Assistance)

A clear line of distinction is necessary between cases falling under the new criterion of attribution for cases of joint responsibility and cases of auxiliary responsibility. It is suggested that the distinction between these two notions can be best achieved by the form of a causal, cumulative criterion; if the cooperative involvement of one organisation in the peacekeeping operation of another organisation penetrates the operation on all structural levels and over the whole period of time, thereby including planning, pre-deployment and deployment, the two organisations should be held jointly responsible on the basis of this new specific criterion of attribution which includes elements used in *Nicaragua* and *Tadić*. Causality is included insofar as this involvement of the contributing organisation allows a piercing of the institutional veil of the control of the other organisation under whose *aegis* the operation is conducted. The contributing organisation would be responsible by virtue of its position or functions – on the basis of the new criterion of attribution and similar to the principle of joint criminal enterprise and co-perpetration as developed in international criminal law.

The cumulative criterion shall include, for example, contributions of a normative and factual nature: normative and legal control also through the exercise of political 'soft power' which cannot be truly legally ascertained, factual elements such as support in the training of troops, financing, logistical and other operational support, mission planning and the operation plan, and general involvement in the oversight and implementation of the operation. Bearing in mind the complexity of the topic and the fact that each organisation and each peacekeeping operation is unique, a clear-cut distinction will not be legally feasible, and the particularly strong involvement of one organisation through one specific element such as financing may remedy weaker involvement in another area.

Two authors suggest that the impact of the theory of the delegation of powers on the law of responsibility merits further exploration.[161] Indeed, it is also possible to partially conceptualise this new notion of attribution from the perspective of other international organisations as a contribution to implementing the powers of the Security Council. Implementation

---

[161] Boisson de Chazournes, Pergantis, 'À propos de l'arrêt Behrami et Saramati', supra note 83, 191, 220.

through the various cooperation mechanisms in peacekeeping operations would constitute a method of delegation.

The case studies will therefore not only serve to verify the need for and the relevance of such a new criterion of attribution, but they will also help to further delimit it from other cases of attribution of conduct and/or responsibility.

The difficulty resides in conceptualising a rule which is both defined and confined enough to qualify as a 'rule' in a legal understanding, but simultaneously flexible enough to accommodate the different and unique cooperation arrangements and mechanisms in peacekeeping operations. As with any other legal rule, the only possibility to correspond to these requirements is in the form of a general and abstract rule.[162]

Moreover, any wide interpretation might lead to more international organisations becoming implicated in internationally wrongful acts. Participation in internationally wrongful acts might appear as the norm rather than the exception which reduces the respect for international law and the willingness of international organisations to obey international rules.[163]

The conceptual nature of the new criterion of attribution adds another layer of difficulty. Similarly to the rules of complicity such as aid and assistance under Article 14,[164] it has some features of primary rules; it does not only address the consequences of an internationally wrongful act, but it extends their application to international organisations which would – in other circumstances – not incur responsibility.[165]

It could be helpful to resort to a negative definition similar to that of 'civilian' in IHL to distinguish between acts falling under the new joint criterion of attribution and cases of complicity. Any cooperative interaction between two or more international organisations which exceeds an act of complicity would be falling under the new criterion of attribution.[166] In

---

[162] Cf. M. Koskenniemi, 'International Law in the World of Ideas', in J. Crawford, M. Koskenniemi (eds.), *The Cambridge Companion to International Law* (Cambridge University Press, 2012), 47, 60–61.

[163] Cf. H. P. Aust, *Complicitiy and the Law of State Responsibility* (Cambridge University Press, 2011), 89–90. However, as the proposed new criterion amounts to the most 'severe' form of responsibility as international organisations are treated as equal partners, their conduct would – possibly or even most likely – fall under one of the other forms of responsibility under the ARIO.

[164] Cf. *Application of the Convention*, supra note 95, para. 419.

[165] Aust, *Complicity*, supra note 163, 188.

[166] In this context, 'complicity' is just another term for the neutral concept of 'aid and assistance', cf. Crawford, supra note 24, 329.

other words, a contribution of such substantial character that it oversteps the threshold for joint commission would be necessary.[167] This matter was actually debated within the ILC during its 1978 session in the context of the definition of 'aid and assistance'. Ushakov described the problem of definition in the following terms:

> [P]articipation must be active and direct. It must not be too direct, however, for the participant then became a co-author of the offence, and that [goes] beyond complicity. If, on the other hand, participation [is] too indirect, there might be no real complicity.[168]

However, the exact contours of complicity in international law remain equally unclear.[169] In his extensive treatise, Aust concludes that 'aid and assistance' is a normative and case-specific concept, meaning that its content will have to be determined in the specific situation.[170]

Another helpful way of narrowing the distinction between aid and assistance and joint responsibility could be to analyse which 'entity ... is best positioned to act effectively and within the law to prevent the abuse in question'.[171]

Application of the New Criterion of 'Normative Control' in Practice: Problems and Obstacles

Chapter I of the ARIOs contains the provisions pertaining to the invocation of responsibility. Article 48, which is not a substantive rule of responsibility,[172] stipulates the principle of separate or individual responsibility: 'Where an international organization and one or more ... other international organizations are responsible for the same internationally

---

[167] Aust, *Complicity*, supra note 163, 216–217.
[168] *Yearbook of the International Law Commission* (1978), Volume I, summary records of the thirtieth session, 239, para. 11.
[169] Aust, *Complicity*, supra note 163, 193–194. There are, indeed, various forms of complicity which can be found in different areas of international, for an overview; see, e.g., A. Clapham, S. Jerbi, 'Categories of Corporate Complicity in Human Rights Abuses', *Hastings International and Comparative Law Review*, 24 (2001), 339, 342–349.
[170] Given that the practice is even scarcer for international organisations than for states, there are no reasons why his conclusions cannot be applied in the context of international organisations. Aust, ibid., 230; Crawford, *State Responsibility*, supra note 24, 405.
[171] Dannenbaum, 'Translating the Standard', supra note 131, 113, 157; Crawford, ibid., 209, see also pp. 206–208.
[172] Pierre d'Argent, 'Reparation, Cessation, Assurances and Guarantees of Non-Repetition', in A. Nollkaemper, I. Plakokefalos, J. N. M. Schechinger (eds.), *Principles of Shared Responsibility in International Law. An Appraisal of the State of Art* (Cambridge University Press, 2014), 208, 238.

wrongful act, the responsibility of each ... organization may be invoked in relation to that act.' Thus, this article accommodates the primarily bilateral nature of international dispute settlement; the 'plurality [of responsible actors] is reduced to bilateral relationships where issues of invocation of responsibility are concerned'.[173]

Paragraph 2 further stipulates that '[s]ubsidiary responsibility [of another international organisation] may be invoked insofar as the invocation of the primary responsibility has not led to reparation'. The Commentary fails to define precisely which categories of states and international organisations would fall under the notion of subsidiary responsibility, but it states that the responsibility of a state member of an international organisation according to Article 62 ARIO belongs in this category.[174] It is rather likely that cases of aid and assistance and of direction and control would also fall into this category as they presuppose the breach of an international obligation by another organisation. Thus, their responsibility cannot be invoked without a previous determination as to the breach of an international obligation by the other international organisation(s). The vague framework providing for the invocation of international responsibility in the ARIOs therefore allows an accounting for the different arrangements of international dispute settlement in cases involving a plurality of actors.

In the literature, this article has been criticised as failing to provide for 'inherent differences that exist between situations with one responsible ... international organisation and situations involving a plurality of responsible ... organisations'.[175] Indeed, '[r]equiring the individualisation of responsibility leads to particular complexities in cases involving aid and assistance, coercion, the creation of joint organs, direction and control'.[176] Nevertheless, these are problems which are intrinsic to and inherent in the different systems for the settlement of international disputes, for whose application the ARIOs only provide a general and vague framework.

Article 49 ARIO increases the circle of international organisations and states which may invoke international responsibility beyond injured states or international organisations. In the case of *erga omnes* violations, all states are entitled to invoke international responsibility, whereas only

---

[173] Messineo, 'Attribution of Conduct', supra note 50, 19–20.
[174] UN Doc. A/66/10 (2011), 142, para. 2 of the commentary.
[175] A. Vermeer-Künzli, 'Invocation of Responsibility', in A. Nollkaemper, I. Plakokefalos, J. N. M. Schechinger (eds.), *Principles of Shared Responsibility in International Law. An Appraisal of the State of Art* (Cambridge University Press, 2014), 251, 255.
[176] Ibid., 10.

the international organisations can invoke responsibility in the case of a breach of an *erga omnes* violation if 'safeguarding the interest of the international community as a whole underlying the obligation breached is within the functions of the international organisations invoking responsibility' (Article 49(3)). Such a limitation upon international organisations is in conformity with the principle of speciality,[177] but it could be questioned whether it is appropriate within the context of the present study. Unless one were to argue that the maintenance of international peace and security by regional organisations, such as those examined in this study, is also in the interests of the international community, regional organisations such as the AU or the EU would be precluded from invoking the international responsibility of the UN, whereas the latter could invoke the responsibility of the regional organisations.

In practice, several problems would arise if one were to attempt the invocation of international responsibility in respect of a plurality of actors. These problems relate to the procedural and the substantive law applicable in international dispute settlement, and in particular to the admissibility of claims, issues of jurisdiction and standing, as well as the applicable substantive law.

Taking up the sketch of a breach of an international obligation arising during the deployment of a peacekeeping operation as it was just presented, the following analysis will briefly address the main obstacles encountered, as well as suggest potential solutions and remedies with regard in particular to the application of the criterion of normative control.

Generally speaking, any international organisation that is part of a group of responsible actors, but not part of the judicial proceedings invoking international responsibility, finds itself simultaneously both at an advantage and a disadvantage:

> The advantage is that its responsibility and its contribution to the injury will not be identified. The disadvantage, though, is that it will be unable to argue its position, or bring additional evidence, and so on, to clear its name without compromising its position as a non-participant in the procedures.[178]

As mentioned earlier, the system of international dispute settlement is essentially bilateral in character, involving a claimant and a respondent. It is also derived from a conceptualisation of international law as a system of independent, sovereign actors whose consent is a requirement for the exercise of jurisdiction over them. To this end, the ICJ formulated the

---
[177] See Chapter 5.
[178] Vermeer-Künzli, 'Invocation of Responsibility', supra note 175, 27.

famous *Monetary Gold* principle.[179] It is however doubtful whether the *Monetary Gold* principle is also applicable to international organisations. Indeed, the explicit reference to a third state suggests an application of that principle solely to states.[180] Nevertheless, such an application of the principle was acknowledged by Judge Schwebel in his dissenting opinion in the *Lockerbie case*.[181] In the case relating to the *Application of the Interim Accord*, the ICJ did not immediately reject the application of the principle to NATO, but distinguished the facts from those in the *Monetary Gold* case, thereby leaving the door open to its application to international organisations.[182] Nollkaemper nevertheless argues against an application of the principle to international organisations; he perceives the principle as deriving from consent. Consequently, in his view, it can only apply to these entities that have consented to the ICJ's jurisdiction. If the Court does not exercise jurisdiction over an entity, it can also not pronounce itself – from a technical point of view – upon the rights and obligations of that given entity. Moreover, he sees the risk that an application to international organisations could be the first step to a wider application of the principle beyond states and international organisations.[183]

In the European Court of Human Rights (ECtHR) Statute and rules of procedure, there is no inherent prohibition on claims against more than one state. The ECtHR has decided cases against more than one state and even held one or both states responsible.[184] But the ECtHR always follows

[179] *Case of the Monetary Gold Removed from Rome in 1943*, Preliminary Question *(Italy v. France, United Kingdom of Great Britain and Northern Ireland and United States of America)*, Judgment of 15 June 1954, 32–33. See also case concerning *East Timor (Portugal v. France)*, Judgment of 30 June 1995, 102, paras. 28–29; case concerning certain phosphate lands in Nauru *(Nauru v. Australia)*, Preliminary Objections, Judgment of 26 June 1992, 261, para. 55; *Application of the Interim Accord of 13 September 1995 (The Former Yugoslav Republic of Macedonia v. Greece)*, Judgment of 5 December 2011, 659–660, para. 43; A. Nollkaemper, 'Concerted Adjudication in Cases of Shared Responsibility', SHARES Research Paper 40 (2014), ACIL 2014–17, available at www.sharesproject.nl, 9.
[180] *Monetary Gold*, supra note 179, 32–33. Nollkaemper, 'Concerted Adjudication', supra note 179, 10.
[181] Questions of Interpretation and Application of the 1971 Montreal Convention arising from the Aerial Incident at Lockerbie *(Libyan Arab Jamahiriya v. United States of America)*, Preliminary Objections, Judgment of 27 February 1998 (Dissenting Opinion of President Schwebel), 172.
[182] Application of the Interim Accord of 13 September 1995 *(The Former Yugoslav Republic of Macedonia v. Greece)*, Judgment of 5 December 2011, paras. 43–44.
[183] Nollkaemper, 'Concerted Adjudication', supra note 179, 10–11.
[184] See, for example, *Bankovic and others v. Belgium and others*, Admissibility, Decision of 12 December 2001; *Behrami*, supra note 24; *Case of Ilaşcu and Others v. Moldova and Russia*, Judgment of the Grand Chamber, 8 July 2004; *Case of Rantsev v. Cyprus and Russia*,

the law of international responsibility approach by isolating the conduct of each state and trying to establish its individual responsibility. The analysis in the previous chapters demonstrated that such a breakdown of responsibility is precisely not possible in the circumstances of cooperation between international organisations in peacekeeping operations. Moreover, on the basis of the principle of the relativity of treaties, the ECtHR can not, in any case, exercise jurisdiction over states or international organisations which are not parties to the Convention.[185] The *Monetary Gold* principle is generally not applied by the ECtHR,[186] but an application of the principle would also, arguably, preclude the European Court of Human Rights from rendering a judgment with regard to the sketch of a fictitious case scenario and the possible responsibility of the EU,[187] unless the other, involved international organisations were also part to the proceedings.

There is only one feasible and legal option that allows not only accommodation of the (legal) interests of other international organisations involved, but also consideration of their contributions to the internationally wrongful act in question – a third-party intervention by these organisations under Article 36(2) of the Convention. Intervenors can thereby present evidence and defend their legal interests. In the *Behrami/Saramati* case, the UN intervened as a third party[188] and the Draft Accession agreement of the EU likewise foresaw such a possibility for other international actors.[189] Nevertheless, the ECtHR could only pronounce, even in the case of a third-party intervention, upon the individual responsibility of the EU, unless the intervening involved international organisations were also to become members to the ECHR, a situation which would be not possible without further major changes to the Convention, in particular with regard to the *espace juridique* of the Convention, at least for the AU and ECOWAS.

International organisations could contribute to reach a halfway satisfactory solution – in terms of transparency in global governance, the

---

Judgment of 7 January 2010. For further references, see M. den Heijer, 'Procedural Aspects of Shared Responsibility in the European Court of Human Rights', *Journal of International Dispute Settlement*, 4 (2013), 361, 381.

[185] Cf. also Nollkaemper, 'Concerted Adjudication', supra note 179, 4.

[186] Ibid., 11. It is, as, indeed, the parties to the Convention have given their prior consent to the exercise of jurisdiction by the Court by becoming parties to the ECHR.

[187] Presupposing the EU will become a contracting party to the ECHR in the end after the negative votum of the Court of Luxemburg.

[188] *Behrami*, supra note 24, paras. 118–120; den Heijer, 'Procedural Aspects', supra note 184, 361, 377.

[189] Fifth Negotiation Meeting, supra note 44, 23, para. 45.

rule of law, and the sanctity of international obligations. An international organisation under the jurisdiction of an international court or tribunal could assume the international responsibility within the proceedings; the other international organisations involved in the peacekeeping operation would intervene as third parties; and the intervening organisations and the organisation which is a party to the case would agree that the respondent organisation could recover an equal share of any reparation paid on the basis of a separate agreement concluded between all organisations or on the basis of a specific disposition in the SOMA in conformity with Article 48(3) ARIO.[190]

This assumption of responsibility by one international organisation on the external sphere would operate similar to the practice of the UN, which generally assumes international responsibility for the conduct of UN peacekeeping operations on the external level with regard to the troop-contributing countries. Thus, if the degree of cooperation between international organisations during a peacekeeping operation is of such a degree as to fall under the criterion of normative control, it would be automatically assumed that one international organisation should assume the responsibility, on behalf of the involved organisations, in any case pending before a competent international body.

Generally speaking, the UN should assume a leading role. The analysed practice of the regional organisations has demonstrated that they increasingly seek authorisation for the deployment of a peacekeeping operation from the Security Council which is the ultimate guardian for the maintenance of international peace and security, thus it is highly unlikely that a peacekeeping operation which contains elements of cooperation with other international organisations will be deployed without any contribution by the UN.

Another theoretical option would be to use cross-judging in situations of shared responsibility.[191] This technique also presupposes that several courts and tribunals can exercise jurisdiction over the international organisations involved in the fictitious case scenario. But despite the benefits that this option presents – such as the prevention of double-dipping, access to evidence, and the prevention or mitigation of jurisdictional disputes[192] – it

---

[190] The EU and the UN are currently negotiating a Framework agreement for future peacekeeping operations which will most likely also contain a clause with regard to respective claims by the organisations against each other, Presentation by Katarina Grenfell of the Office of Legal Affairs at the UN at the SHARES Seminar in Amsterdam on 3 October 2014.
[191] See generally Nollkaemper, 'Concerted Adjudication', supra note 179.
[192] Ibid., 35.

creates problems of its own.[193] International organisations are also reluctant to accept any form of responsibility, despite of or perhaps because of a number of court cases in the past few years in which the responsibility of in particular the UN was at least implicitly invoked. However, the public perception sees immunity increasingly as meaning impunity under international law as alternative ways of settlement provided for by international organisations are often unsatisfactory[194] and it might therefore be advisable for international organisations to engage in the debate on responsibility and to accept responsibility on the international level.[195]

In summary, the invocation of international responsibility in the context of cooperation of international organisations in peacekeeping operations raises several problems, which, however, do not only derive from the specific context of the present study, but primarily from the inherent inaptitude of the system for the settlement of international disputes to accommodate sufficiently for the intrinsic specific features of cases involving a plurality of actors.

Outlook for the Case Studies

The case studies in the next chapter will explore and define this new notion of 'normative control', on the firm general foundation of the Articles of the International Law Commission. The focus of the case studies is on recent and ongoing peacekeeping operations for two reasons. First of all, they display a higher degree of cooperation between international organisations, and they continue to evolve. Secondly, ongoing peacekeeping operations allow the application of the law as it is and stands nowadays. Bearing in mind the findings in particular of Chapter 2, as well as taking into account the nature of the specific peacekeeping operations whose geographical focus is the African continent, the following propositions can be made the validity of which will be examined in the next chapter.

NATO, with the exception of KFOR, might find itself in an auxiliary role regarding the attribution of conduct and/or responsibility. The EU entertains strong institutional ties with both the AU and the UN, but its engagement on the African continent is more limited. Nevertheless, these three organisations might be jointly responsible. ECOWAS could be jointly

---

[193] Ibid., 19–24.
[194] O. Crellin, 'Haiti Cholera Victims Get a Hearing in US Court', *Aljazeera America*, 22 October 2014, available at http://america.aljazeera.com/articles/2014/10/22/cholera-lawsuit-un.html
[195] See Chapter 6.

responsible with these three organisations for these operations in which it is actively involved on the African continent, as despite the limited institutional relations ECOWAS entertains with the EU, NATO and the UN, it is part of the African Peace and Security Architecture.

Peacekeeping operations are all *sui generis* as are the international organisations so the latter might display a different kind of cooperation in peacekeeping operations in other geographical and political settings and they would then potentially, also be held responsible differently.

4

The Case Studies

This chapter introduces the five different case studies which are part of this study. They analyse the attribution of conduct to international organisations for internationally wrongful conduct committed by peacekeepers in Kosovo (KFOR), Darfur (UNAMID), South Sudan (UNMISS and UNISFA), Mali (AFISMA and MINUSMA) and in the Central African Republic (MISCA and MINUSCA). The chronological order of their examination was chosen as it allows us to highlight once again the continuously developing character of the relations among these organisations which are becoming increasingly institutionalised. In addition, this approach might also be beneficial for the purpose of further defining the criterion of attribution as the development towards more cooperation simultaneously takes place on the intra-mission level. Therefore, whereas the framework for coordination is rather limited in the case of KFOR and UNMIK, the case studies of Mali and the CAR demonstrate the full integration of the entire mission within a cooperative framework. On the one hand, the case studies serve as representative examples of peacekeeping operations; on the other, they provide a basis for a circumscription of the criterion of normative control. Furthermore, they might allow a certain generalisation of the criterion for future peacekeeping operations.

On the basis of the chronological approach, it is possible not only to trace the development of intra-mission cooperation but also to identify these particular features which constitute the required nexus justifying the attribution of conduct to two or several international organisations. Nevertheless, the analysis will also demonstrate that intra-mission cooperation is unique in each case and that there is no tangible blueprint for categorising it. Any application of law requires an analysis of the specific circumstances of a given case. The fact that there is a vast diversity of intra-mission cooperation arrangements underlines the necessity to thoroughly analyse the individual circumstances in each and every case study with the aim to further circumscribe the suggested special criterion of attribution.

The Attribution of Conduct and the Difficulty to Classify Intra-mission Cooperation

Attribution of Conduct of KFOR

> Throughout Kosovo, and bearing in mind its operational Mandate, KFOR is cooperating with and assisting the UN, the EU and other international actors, as appropriate, to support the development of a stable, democratic, multi-ethnic and peaceful Kosovo.
>
> – KFOR official homepage[1]

KFOR is the subject of the first of five case studies of this chapter. The decision of the European Court of Human Rights in *Behrami/Saramati* to attribute the conduct of KFOR troops to the UN, despite the operation being NATO-led, implicitly raises the question whether the conduct of KFOR troops could not have been attributed both to the UN as well as to NATO.[2] Indeed, some authors suggest that the conduct of KFOR could generally be attributed to the UN and NATO: 'Nato [*sic*] is responsible for the "direction" of KFOR and the United Nations for "control" of it.'[3] Another author suggests, '[t]he Court could have examined in the first place KFOR's legal status and, had it satisfied itself that KFOR was

---

[1] NATO's Role in Kosovo, available at www.aco.nato.int/kfor/about-us/natos-role-in-kosovo.aspx.

[2] The ECtHR, however, reiterated its view in the follow-up decisions of *Kasumaj v. Greece* and *Gajić v. Germany*, attributing the conduct of national contingents of KFOR to the UN. UN Doc. A/64/10 (2009), 68, para. 10 of the commentary; UN Doc. A/66/10 (2011), 89, para. 11 of the commentary.

[3] UN Doc. A/CN.4/553 (2005), 12, para. 28; A/C.6/60/SR.13 (2005), 3, para. 12. See also *Case Concerning Legality of Use of Force (Yugoslavia v. France)*, Preliminary Objections of the French Republic, 5 July 2000, 29, para. 25; 33, para. 46; A. Pellet, 'L'imputabilité d'éventuels actes illicites. Responsabilité de l'OTAN ou des Etats membres' in C. Tomuschat (ed.), *Kosovo and the International Community: A Legal Assessment* (Leiden, Martinus Nijhoff, 2002), 193, 199. Cf. H. G. Schermers, N. M. Blokker, *International Institutional Law* (Leiden, Brill, 2011), 1016, para. 1590; U. Häußler, 'Human Rights Accountability of International Organisations in the Lead of International Peace Missions', in J. Wouters, E. Brems, S. Smis (eds.), *Accountability for Human Rights Violations by International Organisations* (Antwerp, Intersentia, 2010), 215, 240; European Commission for Democracy through Law (Venice Commission), Opinion on Human Rights in Kosovo: Possible Establishment of Review Mechanisms, CDL-AD 033 (2004), 18, para. 79; F. Naert, *International Law Aspects of the EU Security and Defence Policy, with a Particular Focus on the Law of Armed Conflict and Human Rights* (Antwerp, Intersentia, 2010), 518.

a subsidiary organ of NATO, perhaps attributed its conduct to NATO'.[4] Tomuschat asserts that

> [t]here could be no doubt that the political direction of the operation in Kosovo remained in the hands of the UN. KFOR was meant to ensure public safety and order until UNMIK could take responsibility for that task. It was enjoined to support UNMIK and cooperate with it; thus, it was part of a concerted action by the UN.[5]

This quick overview shows that several arguments are made to determine the legal status of KFOR, as well as which entity is responsible for the conduct of KFOR: political control vs. operational control, direction vs. control, as well as arguments pertaining to the legal status of KFOR. As argued in this book, acts committed in a peacekeeping operation under the operational command and control of one organisation can be also attributed to another organisation outside of the military chain of command of the former. For determining the responsibility of this organisation, the element of 'political control' or 'normative control', based on the exercise of influence through institutional relations, is particularly important. Moreover, it is important as the conduct is ultimately attributed to the organisations through their respective organic structure and their political organs are at the top of the echelons. In this regard, it is preferable to focus primarily on the first phase of the provision of security in Kosovo in which 'KFOR was responsible for ensuring public safety and order until the international civil presence could take responsibility for this task. Until the transfer of that responsibility, UNMIK's civilian police advised KFOR on policing matters and established liaison with local and international counterparts'.[6] The incentives for cooperation between KFOR and UNMIK were the greatest in this first phase of deployment and it is thereby most interesting for the purpose of analysing the distribution of international responsibility.

The European Court of Human Rights' judgment in *Behrami* seems to have been inspired by the writings of Sarooshi.[7] In his book, Sarooshi

---

[4] N. Tsagourias, 'The Responsibility of International Organisations for Military Missions', in M. Odello, R. Piotrowicz (eds.), International Military Missions and International Law (Leiden, Brill, 2011), 245, 252. The Venice Commission likewise considered KFOR as an organ of NATO, European Commission for Democracy through Law, ibid., para. 63.
[5] C. Tomuschat, 'The European Court of Human Rights and the United Nations', in A. Føllesdal, B. Peters, G. Ulfstein (eds.), *The European Court of Human Rights in a National, European and Global Context* (Cambridge University Press, 2013), 334, 353.
[6] UN Doc. CCPR/C/UNK/1 (2006), 8, para. 30.
[7] D. Sarooshi, *The United Nations and the Development of Collective Security. The Delegation by the Security Council of Its Chapter VII Powers* (Oxford University Press, 2000), 163. Cf.

argued that the adoption of resolution by the Security Council authorising the use of military force by an international organisation amounts to a delegation of powers of the Security Council to this particular organisation. Thus, in his view, the Council would have temporarily given away some of its own powers, instead of having simply authorised the use of force, a view which is taken by other scholars.[8]

The distinction between the two concepts has been highly debated in legal scholarship,[9] but it appears in any case correct that the Court failed to distinguish between the act conferring authority to act, Security Council Resolution 1244, and the actual exercise of authority by KFOR and UNMIK.[10] If the Security Council decides to authorise a peacekeeping operation under the authority of another international organisation and then 'retreats into its shell' and abstains from exercising from any form of supervisory control or influence over the execution of the mandate by the peacekeeping operation, there would be no nexus at all to attribute conduct and/or responsibility to the UN.

Apart from the scenario in which the Security Council does not exercise any supervision over a peacekeeping operation deployed by a regional organisation, circumstances may even arise under which there would be de facto no delegation of powers by the Security Council. If one bears in mind that regional organisations are allowed under Article 53 of the UN Charter to deploy peacekeeping operations without an authorisation of the Security Council, provided that the use of force is limited to cases of self-defence,[11] in such circumstances any authorisation of the Security Council would not add or transfer any additional powers to the regional organisation, at least from the perspectives of the internal law of the regional organisation and from the perspective of international law.[12] However,

---

Agim Behrami and Bekir Behrami against France, Ruzdhi Saramati against France, Germany and Norway, Decision on Admissibility, 2 May 2007, paras. 129, 135.

[8] L. Boisson de Chazournes, *Les relations entre organisations régionales et organisations universelles*, Recueil des cours de l'Académie de La Haye, Volume 347 (2010), 79, 322, 324–335; M. Milanović, T. Papić, 'As Bad as It Gets: The European Court of Human Rights' *Behrami and Seramati* Decision and General International Law', *International and Comparative Law Quarterly*, 58 (2009), 267, 278–279; Häußler, 'Human Rights Accountability', supra note 3, 215, 241.

[9] See, for instance, E. de Wet, *The Chapter VII Powers of the United Nations Security Council* (Oxford, Hart Publishing, 2004).

[10] Häußler, 'Human Rights Accountability of International Organisations', supra note 3, 215, 241.

[11] See Chapter 1.

[12] This argument could also be used to distinguish further between authorisation and delegation of powers as it is debated in academic writings.

under internal UN law, one could arguably consider the Security Council authorisation as effectively delegating some of the powers of the Council to these member states of the UN who are simultaneously members of the authorised regional organisation.[13]

The degree of force authorised by the Security Council would then actually be decisive to determine if powers of the Security Council have been delegated to the regional organisation or not. In this context, one also has to recall that in practice there have been cases in which the distinction between peacekeeping and peace enforcement has been effectively blurred.[14] Thus, any attempt to determine as to whether powers of the Security Council have been effectively delegated to a regional organisation on the basis of the use of force authorised appears at least to be questionable.

The law of international responsibility has also adopted a different approach to determine if an authorisation by an international organisation will give rise to international responsibility of the organisation.[15] It is very unlikely that the Security Council will adopt a resolution authorising conduct which would be internationally wrongful if committed by it.

On the contrary, as the previous chapters of this thesis illustrated and as the other case studies will further demonstrate, the recent practice of the UN and regional organisations show that the UN is not limiting its role to solely handing out authorisations without any element of cooperation in the planning or deployment of the operation. This enhanced input of the UN, in the form of cooperation arrangements and mechanisms, in peacekeeping operations operated by regional organisations is also possibly precisely a reaction to judicial decisions with regard to peacekeeping forces, including the judgments from Dutch courts and the *Behrami/Saramati* decision of the ECtHR. In fact, it is rather ironic that the criticised decision in particular of the ECtHR in *Behrami/Saramati*, which arguably might not have involved any delegation of powers by the Security Council, has boosted an increase in cooperation between the UN and regional organisations which might justify holding the organisations jointly responsible on the basis of their framework of cooperation.

Nevertheless, as was pointed out in the previous chapter, there may of course be cases in which the amount of cooperation by the UN in the deployment of a peacekeeping operation by a regional organisation

---

[13] Cf. for instance de Wet, *The Chapter VII Powers*, supra note 9, 260.
[14] See Chapter 1.
[15] Article 17 ARIO.

would not justify considering it jointly responsible under the criterion of normative control. The basis to determine whether the normative control criterion is applicable is if the involvement of the respective 'external organisations' – the organisations cooperating with the organisation which was entrusted with the mandate by the Security Council – is of such an intensity as to justify the application of the normative control criterion. If the analysis leads to the conclusion that the normative control criterion is not applicable, there is, indeed, a lacuna in the ARIO, as acts of aid and assistance require the element of intent, which under normal circumstances could not be established on behalf of the UN.[16]

Should the ECtHR, however, continue to rely on its approach as developed in *Behrami/Saramati* and further developed in *Al-Jedda*, the UN would possibly even then not be able to escape responsibility.[17]

Generally with regard to the distinction between UN and UN-authorised operations, it has been argued in the previous chapters that this distinction is not really relevant as cooperation between the UN and regional organisations has generally emerged as part of the division of labour between these organisations. Therefore, the case study analyses whether the conduct of KFOR troops can be attributed to both the UN and NATO on the basis of the newly proposed criterion of attribution. The following section introduces the application of the law of international responsibility.

The Attribution of Conduct of Acts and Omissions of KFOR under the Law of International Responsibility of International Organisations

The Application of the Law of International Responsibility

The law of international responsibility operates following a two-step procedure. According to Article 4 of the ARIO, there is an internationally wrongful act of an international organisation when conduct consisting of an action or omission:

(a) is attributable to that organisation under international law; and
(b) constitutes a breach of an international obligation of that organisation.

The analysis will therefore start with the question as to which international organisation(s) the conduct of KFOR is attributable. As a

---

[16] See Chapter 3.
[17] At least indirectly, as the UN is not a contracting party of the ECHR.

principle, 'the command and control framework of all peacekeeping operations is similar, no matter whether under OPCON of the United Nations, NATO, the European Union, ... accordingly, equivalent legal considerations apply'.[18]

Relevant for the analysis are resolutions of the Security Council and other documents pertaining to the mandate, structure and functioning of the operation, e.g., the rules of engagement,[19] as well as documents being part of the internal law of the respective organisations.

Attribution of Conduct of KFOR – The Institutional and Normative Framework

KFOR Mandate KFOR's mandate is derived from Security Council Resolution 1244. NATO was not directly authorised to establish 'the international security presence' which would become KFOR, but the Council authorised 'Member States and relevant international organizations to establish the international security presence in Kosovo ... with all necessary means to fulfil its responsibilities'.[20] One day prior to the adoption of Security Council Resolution 1244, the North Atlantic Council (NAC) had decided to implement the 'Joint Guardian' operation order concerning the deployment of KFOR; the deployment was authorised on 11 June 1999, the day following the adoption of the resolution by the Security Council.[21] Paragraph 9 stipulates that the responsibility of the international security presence (KFOR) include:

> (a) Deterring renewed hostilities, maintaining and where necessary enforcing a ceasefire, and ensuring the withdrawal and preventing the return into Kosovo of Federal and Republic military, police and paramilitary forces, except as provided in point 6 of annex 2; ...
> (c) Establishing a secure environment in which refugees and displaced persons can return home in safety, the international civil presence can operate, a transitional administration can be established, and humanitarian aid can be delivered;
> (d) Ensuring public safety and order until the international civil presence can take responsibility for this task; ...

---

[18] Häußler, 'Human Rights Accountability', supra note 3, 215, 236 fn. 70.
[19] Regarding the rules of engagement, it can be problematic to interpret and apply these rules during the deployment on the ground, cf. B. Klappe, 'Rules of Engagement', in M. Odello, R. Piotrowicz (eds.), International Military Missions and International Law (Leiden, Brill, 2011), 145; see especially the examples of Rwanda, 150–152 and the DRC, 154–156.
[20] UN Doc. S/RES/1244 (1999), 2, para. 7.
[21] *Case Concerning Legality*, supra note 3, 32, para. 42. For the process of deploying a NATO operation, cf. also UN Doc. A/CN.4/637 (2011), 12–13, para. 5.

(h) Ensuring the protection and freedom of movement of itself, the international civil presence, and other international organizations.[22]

According to point 4 of Annex 2 to the Resolution, '[t]he international security presence with substantial North Atlantic Treaty Organization participation must be deployed under unified command and control and authorized to *establish a safe environment for all people in Kosovo*'.[23] In addition, NATO concluded a military technical agreement (MTA) with the Federal Republic of Yugoslavia which further defines the powers and competences of KFOR.[24] The MTA contains an authorisation also by the governments of the Federal Republic of Yugoslavia and of the Republic of Serbia to use all necessary action to establish and maintain a secure environment for all citizens of Kosovo.[25]

Military command of KFOR was initially conferred on the Supreme Allied Commander Europe (SACEUR) who delegated it to the Commander in Chief Allied Forces, Southern Europe (CINCSOUTH), the former was responsible to the NAC. The KFOR commander was appointed by NATO and he is responsible to CINCSOUTH.[26] The operation per se is not part of the NATO military command structure but rather resembles an ad hoc force, comprising thirty-five states, including twelve non-NATO members, whereas the majority of positions at KFOR headquarters are held by personnel from NATO member states. As mentioned, KFOR is NATO-led and a de facto NATO-commanded operation.[27]

Cooperation between UNMIK (UN) and KFOR (NATO) The following parts analyse the cooperation between UNMIK (UN)[28] and KFOR (NATO) on various levels to ascertain whether the cooperation arrangements on a practical and an operational level justify a joint attribution of

---

[22] Ibid., 3, para. 9.
[23] Ibid., 6, para. 4.
[24] UN Doc. S/1999/682 (1999), 3–10.
[25] Ibid., 3, para. 2; 9, paras. 1–2, 4.
[26] M. Zwanenburg, *Accountability of Peace Support Operations* (Leiden, Brill, 2005), 47.
[27] R. Murphy, *UN Peacekeeping in Lebanon, Somalia and Kosovo. Operational and Legal Issues in Practice* (Cambridge University Press, 2007), 146–147; R. Kolb, G. Porretto, S. Vité, *L'application du droit international humanitaire et des droits de l'homme aux organisations internationales. Forces de paix et administrations civiles transitoires* (Brussels, Bruyant, 2005), 287. See also Statement of Russia, UN Doc. S/PV.4288 (Resumption 1) (2001), 13; German Supreme Court, III ZR 190/05, Urteil, 2 November 2006, 15, para. 23.
[28] See generally, R. Caplan, 'United Nations Interim Administration Mission in Kosovo', in J. A. Koops, N. Macqueen, T. Tardy et al., *The Oxford Handbook of United Nations Peacekeeping Operations* (Oxford University Press, 2015), 617–628.

conduct to both organisations or whether the UN might rather be held responsible as an accessory.

Political Level KFOR and UNMIK established various consultation mechanisms on the political level to ensure the coordination and cooperation of the international civil and the international military presence.

On the echelon of the Special Representative of the Secretary-General,[29] the Joint Planning Group of the Executive Committee of the Special Representative of the SG works with a Senior Representative of KFOR on military–civilian issues.[30] The Special Representative him- or herself also oversees coordination with KFOR directly through the Executive Committee.[31] The Joint Planning Group Secretariat serves to provide political guidance to KFOR and the four components, whereas working-level staff from KFOR and the four components 'provide operational requirements for planning and policy implementation ..., the political officers from the Office of the Special Representative contribute political guidance'.[32] Meetings cover a wide range of issues, promoting and enhancing cross-competent coordination, including 'information management, border control ... and joint UNMIK/KFOR security issues'.[33] The Secretariat is the main mechanism responsible for the formation of task forces and workings groups 'which develop strategy and policy recommendations and plans for the implementation of mission priorities'.[34]

On 5 December 1999, the Special Representative of the Secretary-General issued the first version of the UNMIK Strategic Planning Document which provided 'a basis for periodic joint UNMIK-KFOR Strategic Planning Conferences, where the Special Representative, the Commander of KFOR and their respective Deputies synchronise aims,

---

[29] See generally Note of Guidance on Integrated Missions; Clarifying the Role, Responsibility and Authority of the Special Representative of the Secretary-General and the Deputy Special Representative of the Secretary-General/Resident Coordinator/Humanitarian Coordinator, 17 January 2006, 2, paras. 5, 7, 8.

[30] Financing of the United Nations Interim Administration Mission in Kosovo, Report of the Secretary-General, UN Doc. A/54/494 (1999), 5, para. 10; Financing of the United Nations Interim Administration Mission in Kosovo, Report of the Secretary-General, UN Doc. A/54/622 (1999), 2, para. 9.

[31] UN Doc. A/54/807 (2000), 5, para. 7.

[32] Ibid., 5, para. 8; UN Doc. A/55/833 (2001), 6, para. 9.

[33] UN Doc. S/1999/1250 (1999), 5, para. 20.

[34] UN Doc. S/1999/779 (1999), 5, para. 17; 6, para. 24.

capabilities and support'.³⁵ The Advisory Unit on Security, established in March 2001 is, inter alia, 'directly involved in the coordination of policy issues in respect of KFOR and UNMIK Police'.³⁶ Liaison and exchange of information on security-related measures between the UN and KFOR occurs on a daily basis.³⁷

On the lower regional level, the Regional Security Supervisor who acted as the principal security advisor to the Regional and Municipal Administrators was responsible for liaising with the KFOR multinational brigade, which is in charge of the Region Centre.³⁸

On a local level, UNMIK municipal administrative teams coordinated the activities of UNMIK components and 'maintain[ed] close liaison with KFOR with respect to security and law and other matters, at the municipal level'³⁹ during the first phase of the mission.⁴⁰

The Security Council itself is the recipient of monthly reports of the activities of KFOR on the basis of Resolution 1244. The reports with an average length of three to four pages provide only a summary of the activities of KFOR within the past month for the Security Council's information. However, it should be noted that there were at least instances in which the Security Council was kept very well informed of KFOR's activities. The Russian member of the Council, for example, mentioned in a statement on 6 April 2001 the arrest of Major Saramati, 'the commander of a KPC brigade accused of undertaking activities threatening the international presences in Kosovo'.⁴¹ Nevertheless, it is not evident from his statement how he had become aware of that arrest.⁴²

UNMIK Regulation No. 2000/47 ordered KFOR personnel to respect 'the laws applicable in the territory of Kosovo and regulations issued by the Special Representative of the Secretary-General insofar as they do not conflict with the fulfillment of the mandate given to KFOR under Security Council resolution 1244 (1999)'⁴³ which suggests, on the one hand, a more profound subordination of KFOR under the authority of the

---

³⁵ UN Doc. A/54/807 (2000), 5, para. 8; A/55/477 (2000), 5, para. 8. See also the remarks by the President of the Security Council, UN Doc. S/PV.4309 (2001), 24.
³⁶ UN Doc. A/56/802 (2002), 6–7, para. 9, 15, para. 49.
³⁷ UN Doc. A/65/711 (2011), 10; S/1999/868 (1999), 4, para. 17.
³⁸ UN Doc. A/55/477 (2000), 50, para. 236.
³⁹ UN Doc. A/54/494 (1999), 17, para. 63; A/54/807 (2000), 16, para. 60.
⁴⁰ UN Doc. A/56/802 (2002), 29, para. 125.
⁴¹ UN Doc. S/PV.4350 (2001), 6. See also Schermers, Blokker, *International Institutional Law*, supra note 3, 1016, para. 1590.
⁴² The short summary reports of KFOR do not contain any information about this incident.
⁴³ UN Doc. UNMIK/REG/2000/47 (2000), para. 2.2.

UN. On the other hand, this regulation also indicates that KFOR enjoyed some form of autonomy from the UN as the Special Representative was only authorised to issue directives to KFOR as long as they did not contravene KFOR's mandate.[44] Stahn consequently concludes that the role of the Special Representative of the Secretary-General towards KFOR was limited to mere tasks of coordination.[45] Indeed, an analysis of the available documents on KFOR and UNMIK does not suggest that the cooperation on the political level surpassed the level of coordination and included essential elements of control by UNMIK and thereby the UN over KFOR.[46]

Strategic Level On a strategic level, an UNMIK liaison officer was deployed as the strategic and operational planner and liaison officer with the KFOR planners.[47] Furthermore, UNMIK had deployed military liaison officers to the headquarters of KFOR, at regional and at the five KFOR multinational brigades level.[48] KFOR representatives took part, 'as necessary, in the work of UNMIK', and UNMIK, in turn, participated in KFOR's Joint Implementation Commission (JIC), which liaised with both the FRY's Armed Forces and the Kosovo Liberation Army (KLA).[49] As there are no further documents publicly available, it is difficult to assess whether these liaison officers exercised any form of control on the strategic level over the conduct of KFOR troops.

Operational/Mission Level Operational cooperation between UNMIK and KFOR was centred on the conducting of joint patrols between UNMIK (police) and KFOR troops. In the period until 30 June 2002, UN Civilian Police alone had conducted 11,161 joint patrols with KFOR.[50] In 2000, KFOR decided to establish joint operations centres with UNMIK police at brigade and battalion levels, with 'the aim of fostering closer cooperation

---

[44] KFOR nevertheless enjoys the same privileges and immunities as UNMIK under the mentioned regulation.
[45] C. Stahn, *The Law and Practice of International Territorial Administration. Versailles to Iraq and Beyond* (Cambridge University Press, 2008), 330.
[46] For a contrary view, see C. Tomuschat, 'Attribution of International Responsibility: Direction and Control', in M. Evans, P. Koutrakos (eds.), *The International Responsibility of the European Union* (Oxford, Hart Publishing, 2013), 7, 28–29 and in particular 31.
[47] UN Doc. A/55/477 (2000), 66, para. 3.
[48] UN Doc. S/1999/779 (1999), 11, para. 50.
[49] Ibid., 6, para. 25.
[50] UN Doc. A/57/678 (2002), 9; S/1999/1185 (1999), 3, para. 9.

between both organizations'.[51] In this context, a Political Violence Task Force staffed by senior staff of UNMIK police and KFOR was established to coordinate activities at the local, regional and central levels. On 2 July 2002, UNMIK police and officials of KFOR signed a memorandum of understanding which established a process to transfer to UNMIK the responsibility of KFOR over general public security, management of demonstrations and other related tasks in the Mitrovica region.[52]

Therefore the analysis of the cooperation on the operational level does not allude to any exercise of control by UNMIK over the operation of KFOR on the ground. However, it cannot be excluded that the UN and NATO could have been jointly responsible, under specific circumstances, for the conduct of UNMIK (police) and KFOR troops during their joint patrols. One specific joint patrol which gave reason to serious criticism by Serbia underlines this assessment. A monthly report of KFOR to the UN Security Council notes the following:

> On 17 March, after a formal request for support from UNMIK to KFOR, an operation to retake the courthouse was launched by UNMIK police supported by KFOR ... UNMIK police arrested 35 Kosovo Serb protesters, while KFOR blocked off nearby roads. With KFOR assistance to clear the route, UNMIK police delivered the detainees to the detention facility in Pristina. However, as UNMIK attempted to transport the detainees to Pristina for processing, a large crowd gathered and started to throw stones, Molotov cocktails, grenades and other objects at the security forces; AK-47 rifles and pistols were also fired. UNMIK police and KFOR responded to the violence using tear gas, baton rounds and warning shots using live rounds in accordance with the agreed rules of engagement. In the end, 48 KFOR soldiers, 7 officers of the Kosovo Police Service and 35 UNMIK police officers were wounded, including a Ukrainian police officer who later died of his wounds.[53]

Indeed, as written by the Secretary-General in his report from 18 September 2000, 'the level and sophistication of the joint security operations conducted by UNMIK police and KFOR continued to develop in many regions'.[54] The Security Council Mission to Kosovo reported likewise that '[t]he level of cooperation and coordination between UNMIK Police and KFOR is extremely high'.[55] UNMIK police also arrested Mr. Saramati

---

[51] UN Doc. S/2000/634 (2000), 3 para. 14.
[52] UN Doc. S/2002/984 (2002), 4, para. 19; Statement by the Assistant Secretary-General for Peacekeeping Operations, UN Doc. S/PV.4249 (2000), 3.
[53] UN Doc. S/2008/362 (2008), 2–3, para. 14. Serbia recalled the events differently, UN Doc. S/2008/260 (2008), 10–11, para. 14.
[54] UN Doc. S/2000/878 (2000), 5, para. 26.
[55] UN Doc. S/2000/363 (2000), 5, para. 18; UN Doc. A/55/624 (2000), 9, para. 45.

on KFOR orders, and, as a result, it is worthwhile to inquire whether UNMIK could not have aided and assisted KFOR for the purposes of the law of international responsibility.

Assessment of the Cooperation Arrangements and Implications for the Attribution of Conduct

It has been stressed previously that the element of 'normative control' based on institutional relations between the involved organisations is particularly important in the determination of the attribution of conduct and responsibility.[56] The analysis showed that the degree of cooperation on a political level between KFOR and UNMIK is certainly high and that arguably UNMIK is exercising some form of control on a political level via 'political guidance', but that element of control has not penetrated the strategic or operational level of cooperation.

Bearing in mind that joint responsibility as envisaged for the purposes of this book presupposes that one organisation makes more than a 'substantial contribution' to surpass aid and assistance under Article 14 ARIO, any attribution of conduct of KFOR to the UN would require that there is a strong nexus between the control exercised on a political level, outside the military chain of command, and the control exercised on strategic and operational levels.

There must be an *intimate link* between the control exercised on a political level and on the other levels to justify holding both organisations jointly responsible, precisely because the UN is not part of the chain of command of NATO. Otherwise, one could hold both organisations jointly responsible, at least on the basis of the suggest criterion of normative control. The disjuncture between these elements in the present case of KFOR is underlined by the hybrid base of authority of KFOR; on the one hand, its authority is derived from Security Council Resolution 1244, and on the other hand, it stems from the MTA. Moreover, the cooperation arrangements on the different levels between KFOR and the UN do not appear to be part of an overall strategy of cooperation and coordination. Such a strategy would also be a further indication for a high degree of cooperation as

---

[56] One could also use the term 'normative power' as it is used by Boisson de Chazournes regarding partnerships among International Financial Institutions, L. Boisson de Chazournes, 'United in Joy and Sorrow: Some Considerations on Responsibility Issues under Partnership among International Financial Institutions', in M. Ragazzi (ed.), *Responsibility of International Organizations. Essays in Memory of Sir Ian Brownlie* (Leiden, Brill, 2013), 213, 215.

it would imply an element of pre-deployment planning between the UN and NATO.

One therefore has to conclude that the responsibility for the conduct of KFOR lies at least primarily with NATO and to a lesser extent with the UN.[57] There are, indeed, instances, in which KFOR and, consequently, NATO acted independently from any UN involvement by virtue of its powers granted under the MTA. For example, the Security Council welcomed the decision by NATO 'to authorize the commander of KFOR to allow the controlled return of forces' of the FRY to the ground safety zone as defined in the MTA.[58]

In conclusion, the conduct of KFOR troops can generally not be attributed jointly both to the UN and NATO on the basis of an analysis of the cooperation arrangements. As the Articles of the ILC articulate the requirement of intent for one organisation to be aiding and assisting another, UNMIK could also not be responsible for having aided or assisted KFOR. Nevertheless, there may be specific circumstances which warrant the attribution of conduct to both the UN and NATO. The question to ask now is how this second *lacuna* in the Articles of the ILC regarding cases which fulfil the objective requirements of aid and assistance, but where the element of intent is missing, should be remedied. Clearly, international organisations should also not be exempt from responsibility for such cases of aiding and assistance without the intent to commit an internationally wrongful act, but a determination if one organisation is responsible for having aided and assisted simply on the basis of a test of causality is too broad. This is exactly, why for the purposes of joint responsibility of international organisations under the normative control criteria, the threshold for the attribution of conduct is very high.

This first case study also proves that it is at least highly questionable whether the focus on individual acts and intent and knowledge for the purposes of the attribution of conduct to cooperating international organisations is always appropriate in an era when cooperation is the lingua franca of interaction between international organisations. The next case study, UNAMID illustrates that particular point as well. The wider political process to resolve the conflict in Darfur is intrinsically linked to the deployment of the peacekeeping operation and so is the control of the political actors over the operation.

---

[57] Cf. *Case Concerning Legality*, supra note 3, 33, para. 45.
[58] UN Doc. S/PRST/2001/8 (2001), 2.

Attribution of Conduct of UNAMID

> The Hybrid Operation is not a joint force. Let there be no confusion about it. We are not talking about any joint force by the United Nations and the African Union.
>
> – Ambassador Abdalmahmood Abdalhaleem of Sudan[59]

> In fact, the hybrid nature of the Mission has optimized the level of complementarity between the UN and AU.
>
> – Report of the Chairperson of the Commission of the AU, 23 September 2013[60]

The deployment of AMIS and later on UNAMID[61] came as the reaction of the international community to military clashes between the Sudanese government and the Arab *Janjaweed* militia against the Sudanese Liberation Movement/Army (SLM/A) and the Justice Equality Movement (JEM) who claim to represent the black Darfurians.[62] It is undisputed that the situation in Darfur amounts to an armed conflict for the purposes of international law. In fact, there was no operative peace agreement in Darfur when AMIS formally handed over to UNAMID, meaning the operation was deployed in an 'as-yet-unresolved war'.[63]

The Peace and Security Council of the AU decided 'to endorse the conclusions of the Addis Ababa High Level Consultation on the Situation in Darfur ... which provided for a three-phased support to the African Union Mission in Sudan'[64] at its meeting in November 2006. The foreseen three-phased support included in addition to a light and a heavy support package a hybrid operation with the UN.[65] As the AU operation evolved into a complex peacekeeping operation and owing to 'uncertainty regarding its financial sustainability', the AU supported the transition

---

[59] Cited in A. Abass, 'The United Nations, the African Union and the Darfur Crisis: Of Apology and Utopia', *Netherlands International Law Review*, 54 (2007), 415–416, fn. 2.
[60] Report of the Chairperson of the Commission, AU Doc. PSC/AHG/3.(CCCXCVII) (2013), 4, para. 10.
[61] See generally, D. Lanz, 'African Union–United Nations Hybrid Operation in Darfur (UNAMID)', in J. A. Koops, N. Macqueen, T. Tardy et al. (eds.), *The Oxford Handbook of United Nations Peacekeeping Operations* (Oxford University Press, 2015), 779–790.
[62] Z. Yihdego, 'Darfur and Humanitarian Law: The Protection of Civilians and Civilian Objects', *Journal of Conflict & Security Law*, 14 (2009), 37–38.
[63] A. de Waal, 'Sudan: Darfur', J. Boulden (ed.), *Responding to Conflict in Africa. The United Nations and Regional Organizations* (London, Routledge, 2013), 283, 293.
[64] Peace and Security Council, AU Doc. PSC/AHG/Comm(LXVI) (2006), para. 2 chapeau.
[65] UN Doc. S/2007/307/Rev.1 (2007), 3, para. 8; 10–17, paras. 40–63.

to a UN operation.⁶⁶ The envisaged three-phased plan was preceded by the vigorous opposition of the Sudanese government to an autonomous UN peacekeeping operation in Darfur as envisaged in Security Council Resolution 1706.⁶⁷ The found compromise was a UN–AU hybrid operation.⁶⁸ UNAMID is a particularly important case study as it is not only the first hybrid peacekeeping operation deployed by international organisations, but the findings regarding UNAMID could also help in the analysis of a potentially envisaged hybrid AU–UN operation for Somalia.⁶⁹ Furthermore, as a hybrid operation, on a first glance, at least, one would presume that its acts are attributed jointly to the UN and the AU.⁷⁰ Besides, UNAMID is an interesting experiment of 'marrying universalism and regionalism'⁷¹ and can therefore also serve to elaborate further upon the wider debate previously addressed in this book which is the relationship between universalism and regionalism under the framework of the UN Charter.⁷²

This intervention by invitation also leads to questions concerning the existing or non-existing enforcement character of Security Council Resolution 1769 which constitutes the legal basis for UNAMID. The resolution was adopted under Chapter VII, but the records of the meeting leading to the resolution suggest that there was a clear majority for the position that the mandate of the force would not be of an enforcement nature which corresponds to the Chinese statement that 'the purpose of the resolution is to authorize the launch of the hybrid operation, rather than to exert pressure or impose sanctions'.⁷³ In the rare cases of intervention by invitation with the right to enforcement action by the intervening party this right was formally granted through treaty ratifications as in

---

⁶⁶ Ibid., 2, para. 4; Report of the Chairperson of the Commission, AU Doc. PSC/AHG/3(LXVI) (2006), 7, para. 29.
⁶⁷ UN Doc. S/RES/1706, especially 3, para. 5; Report of the Chairperson of the Commission, AU Doc. PSC/AHG/3(LXVI) (2006), 15–20 paras. 63–79.
⁶⁸ Abass, 'The United Nations', supra note 59, 415, 434. But see, C. Walter, 'Hybrid Peacekeeping: Is UNAMID a New Model for Cooperation between the United Nations and Regional Organizations?', in H. Hestermeyer, D. König, N. Matz-Lück et al. (eds.), *Coexistence, Cooperation and Solidarity. Liber Amicorum Rüdiger Wolfrum* (Leiden, Brill, 2012), 1327, 1337; Comments by the US, UN Doc. S/PV.6702 (2012), 16.
⁶⁹ UN Doc. S/2013/239 (2013), 13, para. 46.
⁷⁰ Tsagourias, 'The Responsibility of International Organisations for Military Missions', supra note 4, 245, 254.
⁷¹ Report of the Chairperson of the Commission, AU Doc. PSC/PR/2.(CCCVII) (2012), 16, para. 61.
⁷² See Chapter 1.
⁷³ UN Doc. S/PV.5727 (2007), p. 10. Cf. Statement of the USA, ibid., 7.

the cases of the ECOWAS intervention in Sierra Leone (2000) and Togo (2005–2006).[74]

Attribution of Conduct

Establishment of UNAMID The establishment of UNAMID was already preceded by a high level of cooperation between the UN and the AU, including joint technical assessment missions, joint reports to both the UN SC and the AU PSC and the establishment of an assistance mission to the AU.[75] The UN had previously already provided support packages to AMIS to allow a smoother transition to UNAMID.[76]

Mandate of UNAMID According to Security Council Resolution 1769, the mandate of UNAMID is as set out in paragraphs 54 and 55 of the report of the UN SG and the Chairperson of the AU Commission on UNAMID.[77] The report stipulates that UNAMID has a broad mandate covering the improvement of security conditions in Darfur, thereby allowing the deliverance of humanitarian assistance, as well as the protection of civilian populations under imminent threat of physical violence. These tasks are supposed to be carried out in support of the political process and the AU–UN joint meditation.

Acting under Chapter VII of the Charter,[78] UNAMID was provided with a mandate to protect civilians under paragraph 15 of Resolution 1769.[79] The Security Council further elaborated upon the 'protection of civilians' mandate in the follow-up Resolutions 2003 and 2113.[80] The Council likewise urged UNAMID to deter any threats against itself and its mandate.[81] Reviews of UNAMID's mandate are conducted by the Secretary-General,

---

[74] Abass, 'The United Nations', supra note 59, 415, 434. Another potential problem is whether UNAMID can be considered under UN law as a UN operation regarding the expenses for the operation, ibid., 438.
[75] C. Hull Wiklund, G. Ingerstad, *The Regionalisation of Peace Operations in Africa. Advantages, Challenges and the Way Ahead* (2015), FOI, 26–27.
[76] Ibid. See also Chapter 2.
[77] UN Doc. S/RES/1769 (2007), 3, para. 1; S/2007/307/Rev.1 (2007), para. 54(b), (d), (f); 13–15, para. 55(a)(i), (b)(i), (vii).
[78] The Security Council emphasised UNAMID's Chapter VII mandate in Resolution 2003, UN Doc. S/RES/2003 (2011), 3, para. 5.
[79] UN Doc. S/RES/1769 (2007), 5, para. 15. See also UN Doc. S/RES/1809 (2008), 3, paras. 7, 11; S/RES/1881 (2009), 2, para. 2; S/RES/1935 (2010), 2, para. 2; 3, para. 4; S/RES/2063 (2012), 3–4, para. 3; S/RES/2113 (2013), 4–5, para. 4.
[80] UN Doc. S/RES/2003 (2011), 3, para. 3(a); S/RES/2113 (2013)4, para. 4.
[81] Ibid., 5, para. 5; 6, para. 11.

in close consultation with the AU.[82] Accordingly, UNAMID military and police units are operating on the basis of a very robust mandate regarding the use of military force. Both components of the operation were instructed that attacks upon UNAMID patrols 'are to be responded to robustly and in accordance with the rules of engagement, proactive measures are to be taken to protect civilians'.[83] The updated strategy for the protection of civilians outlines among the four main objectives the protection of civilians from physical acts of violence.[84]

The Political Process to Resolve the Conflict in Darfur and Political Oversight of UNAMID The deployment of UNAMID is directly linked to the political process to resolve the conflict in Darfur under the leadership of both the AU and the UN. The political process is managed by Joint AU and UN Mediation Activities in respect of talks between the Government of Sudan and non-signatory movements[85] on the basis of the AU–UN Roadmap[86] which was later replaced by the Framework for African Union and United Nations facilitation of the Darfur peace process.[87] In 2011, the Government and the Liberation and Justice Movement (LJM) signed the Agreement for the Adoption of the Doha Document for Peace in Darfur.[88]

The Joint Chief Mediator reports to both the UN Secretary-General and the Chairperson of the AU Commission through the Under-Secretary-General of the DPKO and the Commissioner for Peace and Security. According to his mandate he is entrusted with the AU/UN-led political process and mediation efforts between the parties to the Darfur Conflict, in the exercise of which he maintains 'close liaison' with the Joint Special Representative.[89]

---

[82] See, e.g., UN Doc. S/RES/2113 (2013), 4, para. 3.
[83] Report of the Chairperson of the Commission, AU Doc. PSC/PR/2(CCLVIII) (2011), 1, para. 3.
[84] Ibid., 3, para. 13. Statement by the Under-Secretary-General for Peacekeeping Operations, UN Doc. S/PV.6170 (2009), 3.
[85] Report of the Chairperson of the Commission, AU Doc. PSC/PR/2.(CCCXLVIII) (2012), 3, para. 11.
[86] Joint AU–UN Roadmap for Darfur Political Process, 8 June 2007.
[87] UN Doc. S/2012/166 (2012), 2–10. See, e.g., UN Doc. S/2009/173 (2009), 2, para. 2; 4, para. 6.
[88] UN Doc. S/2011/814 (2011), 1–4, paras. 2–17; 14, para. 75. Following this adoption, the Joint Special Representative and Joint Chief Mediator ad interim of the AU and the UN promoted further talks between non-signatory movements and the Government of Sudan with the aim of reaching an inclusive peace agreement through their participation, UN Doc. S/2012/231 (2012), 2, para. 11.
[89] UN Doc. A/64/685 (2010), 5–6, para. 7.

The most interesting feature is, however, that the implementation of the political process is generally managed directly by UNAMID. The Darfur political process secretariat, which was established at UNAMID headquarters, is responsible for 'strategic planning and management of the Darfur political process, overseeing its implementation ... and monitoring and maintaining an overview of substantive discussion during the process'.[90] For that purpose, Darfur political process sub-units were established at each sector office. In the exercise of its duties, the secretariat directly reports to the Joint Special Representative and the chair of the AU High-level Implementation Panel.[91]

As to the political oversight by the respective organs of the AU and the UN, the AU Peace and Security Council requested the AU Commission to ensure that there is regular interaction with UNAMID, including briefings to the Peace and Security Council every ninety days.[92] A review exercise of UNAMID uniformed personnel by the AU Commission and the UN Secretariat was conducted in February 2012, in accordance with Security Council Resolution 2003.[93] The Mandate of UNAMID is extended by both organisations through decisions of the AU PSC and the UN Security Council.[94]

The Tripartite Coordination Mechanism on UNAMID which includes representatives of both the AU and the UN as well as of the Government of Sudan serves as another instrument to resolve issues and challenges related to UNAMID deployment and operations.[95]

Strategic Control   Strategic guidance of UNAMID is provided from New York by both the UN and the AU.[96] The military concept of operations was developed jointly by the AU and the UN focusing on three core

---

[90] UN Doc. S/2011/252 (2011), 5, para. 18. The secretariat comprises representatives of several UNAMID sections, including political affairs, human rights, humanitarian liaison, legal affairs, rule of law, the joint mission analysis centre, security, the joint logistics operation centre, mission support, as well as staff of the AU, UN Doc. A/64/685 (2010), 5–6, para. 7.
[91] UN Doc. S/2011/252 (2011), 2, para. 6. See also UN Doc. S/2010/543 (2010), 2, para. 7; 4–5, paras. 15–19; S/2011/244 (2011), 3, paras. 9–11.
[92] Peace and Security Council, AU Doc. PSC/PR/COMM.3(CCCLXXI) (2013), 2, para. 13.
[93] Peace and Security Council, AU Doc. PSC/PRC/COMM.(CCCXXVIII) (2012), 2, para. 11.
[94] Ibid., 3, para. 14; UN Doc. S/2011/466 (2011), 2, second para; 5–6, para. 12.
[95] See, e.g., press release, 16 Apr 2013, Tripartite Meeting on UNAMID Focuses on Darfur Security, Access.
[96] Opening Remarks by Ambassador Ramtane Lamamra, AU Commissioner for Peace and Security, on the occasion of the fifteenth session of the UNAMID Tripartite Coordinating Mechanism Meeting, 15 April 2013, Addis Ababa, 3.

complementation functions: protection, liaison, and monitoring and verification.[97] The same procedure was used for the elaboration of various other strategic and legal documents, including the military command directive for the Force Commander of UNAMID and the UNAMID rules of engagement.[98] The envisaged exit strategy for UNAMID is also developed in a cooperative manner by the AU and the UN and as mandated by the UN Security Council and the AU Peace and Security Council.[99]

The Chain of Command and Operational Control The distribution of tasks between the two organisations foresees that whereas 'the [m]ission shall benefit from United Nations backstopping and command and control structures and systems',[100] the AU shall merely decide upon the size of the force and should also appoint the force commander.[101]

As support, command and control structures for UNAMID are provided by the UN alone, the overall management of the operation is likewise based on UN standards, principles and established practices. To compensate the AU for the UN's dominance in that area, it was agreed between both organisations that 'all efforts will be made to ensure that the peacekeeping force will have a predominantly African character' regarding the force and personnel generation.[102] In order 'to maintain the joint nature of the mission, and to ensure joint decision-making and input into operational decisions and procedures for UNAMID', the UN and the AU agreed to appoint a joint special representative and that strategic guidance would be jointly provided by both organisations.[103] This decision was also taken as a reaction to the fact that the daily operational command and control of the mission, however, resides with the UN.

The Joint Special Representative of the Chairperson of the AU Commission and the Secretary-General of the UN has overall authority over UNAMID, overseeing the implementation of its mandate and

---

[97] UN Doc. S/2007/307/Rev.1 (2007), 18, para. 73; S/2007/517 (2007), 2, para. 7; 4, para. 13.
[98] UN Doc. S/2007/596 (2007), 3–4, para. 13.
[99] Statement by the UN, UN Doc. S/PV.7608 (2016), 4.
[100] Peace and Security Council, AU Doc. SC/AHG/Comm (LXVI) (2006), para. 2(c).
[101] Ibid., paras. 2b, d.
[102] UN Doc. S/2007/307/Rev.1 (2007), 27, para. 113; S/RES/1769 (2007), 4, para. 8. Interestingly, though, the Convention on the Privileges and Immunities of the United Nations applies to the whole operation; see Agreement between the United Nations and the African Union and the Government of Sudan Concerning the Status of the African Union/United Nations Hybrid Operation in Darfur (2008), 1, para. 1(f); 2, para. 2.
[103] UN Doc. S/2011/805 (2011), 11–12, para. 39.

being responsible for the operation's functioning and management.[104] He or she is in charge of analysing and implementing the strategic directives issued by the Under-Secretary-General of the DPKO of the UN and the AU Commissioner for Peace and Security, and he reports, through them, to the UN Secretary-General as well as to the Chairperson of the AU Commission.

The Force Commander and the Police Commander were both appointed by the AU in consultation with the UN and report to the Joint Special Representative while exercising command and control over the military and police activities, respectively.[105]

An important feature of the command and control arrangements on an operational level is that the deployment of UNAMID is coordinated through the Joint Support and Coordination Mechanism (JSCM) established in Addis Ababa and 'tasked with empowered liaison' between the DPKO and the AU Peace and Security Department.[106] Another part of the mandate of the JSCM is the coordination and support of the implementation of the mandate of UNAMID in the form of operational directives as well as deepening 'the current collaboration between the two institutions'.[107]

Assessment of the Control Arrangements

The analysis of the command and control structures of UNAMID on the basis of the available documents showed that in contrast to the previous case study, the deployment of UNAMID as a peacekeeping operation is directly included in and part of the wider political framework for a peaceful resolution of the Darfur crisis. In fact, the political process is not only intrinsically connected to the deployment of UNAMID, but the latter is actually steering the implementation and management of the process. The cited report of the Secretary-General indicates that the strategic planning of the peace process is also part of the therefore established secretariat at

---

[104] UN Doc. A/64/685 (2010), 5, para. 5; A/65/740 (2011), 5, para. 4; A/62/791 (2008), 5–6, para. 10.
[105] UN Doc. A/64/685 (2010), 5–6, paras. 6–7.
[106] UN Doc. S/RES/1769 (2007), 4, para. 7; A/64/685 (2010), 6, para. 8. The review of UNAMID by the UN found that the JSCM 'performs important coordination, support and liaison functions effectively', despite the challenges the UN and the AU are faced with to coordinate with one another on joint strategic guidance to UNAMID, UN Doc. S/2014/138 (2014), 10, para. 38; S/RES/1769 (2007), 12, para. 39; 13, para. 44; A/67/806 (2013), 7, para. 8. See also UN Doc. A/66/596 (2011), 9, para. 34.
[107] UN Doc. A/64/685 (2010), 7, para. 13; A/66/596 (2011), para. 37. See also UN Doc. S/2009/388 (2009), 5, para. 18; S/2007/307/Rev.1 (2007), 16, para. 57.

UNAMID headquarters. Then again, the overall authority over UNAMID is exercised by the Joint Special Representative whose functions include the supervision of UNAMID's mandate and the implementation of strategic directives issued by the AU and the UN.

It was stressed in the previous case study that in order to justify that two international organisations are held jointly responsible on the basis of the proposed criterion of attribution, there has to be a strong nexus between the control exercised on the political level by the organisations and the control performed by the responsible organs in the peacekeeping operation. In the present context of UNAMID, it appears that the set-up of the operation actually transcends the required intimate link; part of the wider political control has been allocated to the peacekeeping operation itself, although ultimately under the authority of both organisations. UNAMID can, to a certain extent, navigate the political process autonomously. This fact also raises the question as to whether there is a heightened responsibility of the UN and the AU. The attribution of responsibility to international organisations cannot only be seen as a sliding scale upon which the amount of control exercised by international organisations reflects the likelihood of the attribution of conduct to that organisation. In contrast, another factor is the autonomy of the respective organ (the peacekeeping operation); not autonomy in the sense of a lack of control by the organisation, but autonomy due to a transfer of certain tasks to the organ whose implementation by the organ binds the organisation. This corresponds to a more mature relationship between the organ and the organisation, as the latter has actually done more by entrusting certain specific functions to that organ. One author speaks in this context of the 'hierarchy of influence' which is more about *auctoritas* than *potestas*, a very fitting description for this particular cooperation arrangement in UNAMID.[108] Future UN peacekeeping operations will all enjoy more autonomy with regard to overall mission planning in order to allow the formulation of coherent, interoperable and tailored missions plans which might also shift more responsible towards the organisations involved.[109]

One can draw two conclusions here. Firstly, UNAMID reconfirmed the particular relevance of political control, as well as of the translation of that control over the mission. Secondly, it became evident that a comprehensive approach towards the political peace process and the deployment of

---

[108] J. J. Piernas López, 'Regionalism in the Field: The Case of South Sudan', *European Society of International Law, Conference Paper Series*, Conference Paper No. 7/2012, 14.

[109] UN Doc. A/70/357 and S/2015/682 (2015), 12–13, para. 55.

a peacekeeping operation, involving the same institutional actors, reinforces the control and oversight executed over the operation.

Regarding the distribution of responsibility between the UN and the AU, the analysis highlighted that, notwithstanding the provision of backstop and command and control structures solely by the UN, all decisions regarding the deployment, the operations on the ground, the appointment of personnel, the revision of operational directives and other issues are taken jointly by both organisations. Therefore, even if the UN enjoys greater control and influence over UNAMID than the AU due to an advantage in resources and experience,[110] it does not compromise the fact that all decisive strategic and operational decisions are taken jointly by both operations.[111] Thus, the daily operational command and control of the mission by the UN does not impair the essential and predominant hybrid character of the operation.

The available documents do not give any indication that the UN exercises any more supplementary control by paying for the budget of the operation; neither does the financing of the operation by the UN affect the decision-making processes within the operation.

The UN and the AU are not only acting together in the operation of UNAMID, but all political activities are equally steered jointly by the two institutions, through their joint Chief Mediator and in coordination – when necessary – with the Government of Sudan.

Naturally, the UN is in a slightly stronger moral position than the AU due to the Security Council being at the forefront of the international system of collective security. Another factor is the extensive experience of the organisation in the deployment of peacekeeping operations. In the end, the UN and the AU cooperate on the political, strategic and operational levels as equals so that any conduct of UNAMID personnel, in violation of international law is to be attributed jointly to the AU and to the UN.

The next section, on South Sudan, will highlight in particular the relevance of not only the political process but also of inter-mission cooperation as another contributing factor to the analysis of the responsibility of international organisations in the context of peacekeeping operations.

---

[110] A. Bashua, 'Challenges and Prospects of AU–UN Hybrid Operations', *Journal of International Peacekeeping*, 18 (2014), 92, 99–100.
[111] The SOFA of UNAMID also stipulates that the AU and the UN shall ensure that UNAMID conducts its operations in full conformity with international humanitarian law, Agreement between the United Nations and the African Union and the Government of Sudan, supra note 102, 3, para. 6a.

Attribution of Conduct of UNISFA and UNMISS

Since the beginning of the Sudan and Darfur crisis, the AU has led the international community to find a political solution for this situation.[112] That leadership of the AU on the political level is undisputed by all other international actors; the AU Roadmap for the settlement of the unresolved issues between Sudan and South Sudan of April 2012, following hostilities between the two states along the border, and as adopted by the AU Peace and Security Council was not only accepted by the Parties, but endorsed by the Security Council just one week later in Resolution 2046.[113] In that Resolution the Council, while determining that the prevailing situation along the border between Sudan and South Sudan constitutes a serious threat to international peace and security, decided that both states shall, inter alia, immediately cease all hostilities, including aerial bombardments and withdraw all of their armed forces to their side of the border.[114] The Council also legally obliged both governments to resume negotiations under the African Union High-Level Implementation Panel on Sudan (AUHIP).[115]

The Agreements signed between the Governments of Sudan and South Sudan on 27 September 2012 support the primacy of the political role of the AU in dealing with the crisis involving the two states.[116] The Security Council in a press release, following the conclusion of the agreements, stated that it 'look[s] forward to President Mbeki's recommendations on

---

[112] Ibid., 7.
[113] UN Doc. S/2012/486 (2012), 4, para. 17; Report of the African Union High-Level Implementation Panel, AU Doc. PSC/PR/COMM.1 (CCCLIII) (2013), 1, para. 2; Peace and Security Council, AU Doc. PSC/MIN/COMM/3.(CCCXIX) (2012), 3–4, para. 12; 5, para. 18; Report of the Chairperson of the Commission, AU Doc. PSC/AHG/3.(CCCXCVII) (2013), 3, para. 8. The EU is fully supportive of the roadmap; see Council of the European Union, Council conclusions on the Roadmap for Sudan and South Sudan, 3183rd Foreign Affairs Council meeting, Brussels, 23 July 2012, 1, paras. 1–3; 2, para. 6; Statement by the High Representative Catherine Aston on the agreements concluded between Sudan and South Sudan in Addis Ababa, Brussels, 27 September 2012, A 425/12, 1; Council conclusions on Sudan and South Sudan, Foreign Affairs Council meeting, Brussels, 22 July 2013, 1, paras. 1–2; 2, para. 4.
[114] UN Doc. S/RES/2046 (2012), 3, para. 1(i), (ii).
[115] Ibid., 4, paras. 2–3. The Security Council likewise requested the Secretary-General to consult with the AU regarding the implementation of the resolution and the decisions of the AU PSC as well as to work closely with the AUHIP, ibid., 4, para. 6.
[116] The Cooperation Agreement between the Republic of the Sudan and The Republic of South Sudan, 27 September 2012, p. 2, Preamble; 3, Preamble; 4, para. 1; 6, para. 4; Agreement on Security Arrangements between The Republic of the Sudan and The Republic of South Sudan, 27 September 2012, 2–3, para. 3.

these matters after he reports to the African Union Peace and Security Council and to the report of the Secretary-General'.[117]

A division of labour between the AU and the UN has been established, whereas the former focuses on direct interaction with the two governments and the facilitation of new agreements between them, the UN concentrates on the correct implementation of the Comprehensive Peace Agreement.[118]

The UN is engaged with two operations in South Sudan, UNISFA and AFISMA which have different tasks and responsibilities under their mandate. As the available documents demonstrate, there is a rather close linkage between the deployment and execution of their mandates between the two operations as well as other peacekeeping operations in the area. The main problem of those available documents is that they only contain very limited information with regard to cooperation arrangements between the UN and the AU which makes a legal assessment for the purposes of attributing conduct to the UN and/or the AU quite hard.

UNISFA

Mandate UNISFA was established on the basis of Security Council Resolution 1990 in 2011 in order to support the implementation of the Agreement between the Government of Sudan and the Sudan's People Liberation Movement on temporary arrangements for the disputed Abyei area, including the protection of civilians and the peaceful administration of that area.[119] The Security Council acted in that instance under Chapter VII of the UN Charter.[120] Referring explicitly to Chapter VII later in the Resolution, UNISFA is authorised, 'within its capabilities and its area of deployment to take the necessary actions to' protect UNISFA and UN personnel, installations and equipment as well as to protect civilians and to ensure security in the Abyei area.[121] UNISFA's protection of civilians mandate 'includes taking the necessary actions to protect civilians under

---

[117] UN Doc. SC/10779 (2012), second paragraph.
[118] Piernas López, 'Regionalism in the Field', supra note 108, 9.
[119] UN Doc. A/66/526 (2011), 4, para. 2; S/RES/1990 (2011), 2, para. 1.
[120] The Council abstained from referring explicitly to Chapter VII but recognised in the last paragraph of the preamble of Resolution 1990 that the situation in Abyei constitutes a threat to international peace and security, ibid., 2.
[121] UN Doc. S/RES/1990 (2011), 3, para. 3. As emphasised in Resolution 2126, 'UNISFA's protection of civilians' mandate ... includes taking the necessary actions to protect civilians under imminent threat of physical violence, irrespective of the source of such violence', UN Doc. S/RES/2126 (2013), 4, para. 5.

imminent threat of physical violence, irrespective of the source of such violence'.[122]

Political Control/Chain of Command The Temporary Arrangements Agreement for the Administration and Security of the Abyei Area signed in June 2011 established various mechanisms 'which hinge on the effective and efficient cooperation between the AU and the UN'.[123] It is particularly important to mention the Abyei Joint Oversight Committee (AJOC) consisting of an AU official, the UNISFA Force Commander and representatives of the two countries.[124] In this regard, the AU commended the UN and in particular its Special Envoy and as well as UNISFA for their continued support to AU-led efforts.[125]

UNISFA was deployed consisting of Ethiopian soldiers under its own command structure on the insistence of Ethiopia which was represented the only third party that both sides would accept as an intervening agent.[126]

Inter-mission Cooperation Following the adoption of the Joint Border Verification and Monitoring Mechanism implementation plan by the Joint Political and Security Mechanism, UNISFA, UNMISS and UNAMID held a joint meeting in Juba on 30 November 2012 '[f]or the purpose of establishing necessary operational and strategic mechanisms'.[127] In this context, UNISFA also conducted a series of reconnaissance missions with UNMISS support.[128] UNISFA draws 'significantly on existing logistical arrangements and support structures in UNMISS'.[129] UNMISS provided UNISFA 'with aviation support, spare parts, accommodations for personnel in transit, cargo movement services and full communications and information technology support while ... [UNAMID] has provided UNISFA with staff on temporary assignment, surplus vehicles ..., and customs clearance services ..., and has facilitated inter-mission transfer and transportation

---

[122] UN Doc. S/RES/2104 (2013), 4, para. 4.
[123] Report of the Chairperson of the Commission, AU Doc. PSC/AHG/3.(CCCXCVII) (2013),4, para. 9.
[124] Ibid.
[125] Peace and Security Council, AU Doc. PSC/MIN/COMM.1/CCCLXXXVII) (2013), 1, para. 4.
[126] A. M. Fitz-Gerald, 'South Sudan', in J. Boulden (ed.), *Responding to Conflict in Africa. The United Nations and Regional Organizations* (London, Routledge, 2013), 307, 318.
[127] UN Doc. S/2013/59 (2013), 5, paras. 20–22.
[128] Ibid., 5, para. 22.
[129] UN Doc. A/66/526 (2011), 8, para. 27.

of critical stores'.¹³⁰ Inter-mission cooperation has further increased in the past few years, for instance, the SC urged close coordination among the UN missions in the region and requested the Secretary-General to 'ensure effective inter-mission cooperation'.¹³¹

Bearing in mind that the deployment of UNISFA is coordinated with the deployment of UNMISS, it seems preferable to analyse the question of attribution of conduct following the analysis of UNMISS.

UNMISS

Mandate The UN Mission in the Republic of South Sudan (UNMISS) was established as the follow-up operation to UNMIS. As its name mission instead of operation suggests, it is an integrated operation whose head the Special Representative for the Republic of South Sudan coordinates all activities of the whole UN system in the Republic of South Sudan.¹³² The overall mandate is to consolidate peace and security and to help establish the conditions for development in South Sudan.¹³³

The government of South Sudan protested in a letter to the Security Council that the adoption of the mandate for UNMISS in 2011 under Chapter VII was not appropriate,¹³⁴ but as it was established in Chapter 1, the recent practice of the Security Council has been to resort to Chapter VII for mandating peacekeeping operations. The mandate includes a strong 'protection of civilians' component, which might also explain and justify the adoption under Chapter VII by the Council despite the criticism of the South Sudanese government.

According to paragraph 3, UNMISS shall support the South Sudanese government in a twofold manner to protect civilians. First of all, UNMISS is charged with the responsibility to advise and assist the Government, including the military and police at national and local levels, in order to protect civilians in compliance with international humanitarian, human rights and refugee law. As such, the language used in the resolution

---

[130] UN Doc. A/66/576 (2011), 3–4, para. 12.
[131] UN Doc. S/RES/2228 (2015), 8, paras. 21–22.
[132] UN Doc. S/RES/1996 (2011), 3, paras. 1–3.
[133] UN Doc. A/67/716 (2013), 4, para. 2.
[134] The government alleged that the safety conditions did not warrant any further qualification of the situation in the South Sudan as falling under Chapter VII of the Charter, UN Doc. S/2012/429 (2012), 2. The Secretary-General had proposed that the mandate of the operation should be adopted under Chapter VI of the Charter, UN Doc. S/2011/314 (2011), 8, para. 41.

resembles strongly 'the responsibility to protect' concept.[135] Moreover, UNMISS is authorised to deter the conduct of violence including through proactive deployment and patrols 'in areas at high risk of conflict, within its capabilities and in its areas of deployment, protecting civilians under imminent threat of physical violence'.[136] Paragraph 4 authorises UNMISS to 'use all necessary means, within the limits of its capacity and in the areas where its units are deployed to carry out its protection mandate'.[137] In the follow-up resolution 2057, the Security Council emphasised the importance of UNMISS' mandated tasks for the protection of civilians.[138] The political and security crisis which broke out in December 2013 led to a temporary shift of the mandate of UNMISS on more peacebuilding activities.

The Political Level and the Political Process The political process between South Sudan and Sudan is led by the AU.[139] Under the auspices of the AUHIP, both governments signed a memorandum of understanding on non-aggression and cooperation.[140] The AU cooperates in its political mediation activities regarding these two countries with the UN.[141] According to the Report of the Chairperson of the AU Commission of 23 September 2013, a close working relationship has therefore been forged with then UN through the Secretary-General's Special Envoy.[142] The political and security crisis in South Sudan also led to changes in the political framework and with regard to the group of involved actors for conflict resolution in South Sudan.

---

[135] Security Council Resolution 2057 supports such a view; UN Doc. S/RES/2057 (2012), 5, paras. 13, 16–17.
[136] UN Doc. S/RES/1996 (2011), 3–4, para. 3(b) (iv), (v).
[137] The Security Council confirmed this authorisation its resolution 2057, UN Doc. S/RES/2057 (2012), 4, para. 5. UNMISS is allowed to use all necessary to protect civilians under imminent threat or physical violence, irrespective the source of such violence which translates to an authorisation to act even against agents of the Government of South Sudan, UN Doc. S/RES/2109 (2013), 4, paras. 3–4; 5, para. 8.
[138] UN Doc. S/RES/2057 (2012), 3–4, paras. 3–4.
[139] Peace and Security Council, AU Doc. PSC/MIN/COMM.1(CCCLXXXVII) (2013), 1, para. 4; 3, para. 14.
[140] UN Doc. S/2012/135 (2012), 2–3; S/2015/700 (2015), 6, para. 28; 10, para. 44.
[141] UN Doc. S/PRST/2012/5 (2012), 3; S/PRST/2012/12 (2012), 2. The Cooperation is based on the AU's Roadmap and Security Council Resolution 2046, UN Doc. S/PRST/2012/19 (2012), 1. See especially Doc. S/PRST/2013/14 (2013), 1–2 and UN Doc. S/PV.6583 (2011).
[142] Report of the Chairperson of the Commission, AU Doc. PSC/AHG/3.(CCCXCVII) (2013), 3, para. 8.

Following the signing of the Cessation of Hostilities Agreement in January 2014 between the government and opposition forces and the deteriorating security situation in South Sudan, the AU decided that the conflict resolution process for South Sudan should be led by the regional East African Intergovernmental Authority on Development (IGAD) which deployed a monitoring and verification mission within UNMISS for that purpose. IGAD even deployed an own deterrent force to provide protection to its force and installations.[143] The strengthening of the mandate of UNMISS included the absorption of the monitors and force protectors by the UN.[144] On 17 August 2015 an agreement on the resolution of the conflict in South Sudan, mediated by IGAD was signed by the Government and Opposition forces.[145] This success was also due to increased political pressure and the involvement of a bigger group of actors after the suspension of the peace talks in March 2015. The IGAD mediation team was expanded to incorporate other key regional and international stakeholders, including the EU and the UN in order 'to collectively exert the necessary pressure on the South Sudanese parties ... so that an inclusive ... peace agreement can finally be reached'.[146]

UNMISS ensures strategic and operational coordination with other international partners, 'in particular the African Union ... the European Union and the World Bank'; on a political level UNMISS is charged with 'bringing together international actors to speak with one voice in helping the new Government to address its peace consolidation challenges'.[147] Under its mandate UNMISS is also obliged to provide a summary of cooperation and to share information with UNAMID, MONUSCO and regional and international partners in addressing the threat posed by the Lord's Resistance Army (LRA).[148] In that context, one could ask whether the sharing of information which might be used to facilitate military attacks against the LRA could engage the responsibility of UNMISS.

---

[143] C. Hull Wiklund, G. Ingerstad, *The Regionalisation of Peace Operations in Africa. Advantages, Challenges and the Way Ahead* (2015), FOI, 34.
[144] UN Doc. S/RES/2155 (2014), 4–5, para. 4.
[145] UN Doc. S/2015/654 (2015); S/2015/899 (2015), 3, para. 4; S/2015/899 (2015), 6–7, paras. 26–27.
[146] UN Doc. S/2015/655 (2015), 1, para. 2. Other – parallel – mediation and diplomatic efforts were helpful for the signing of the agreement, ibid., 1–2, paras. 3–7.
[147] UN Doc. S/2011/314 (2011), 8, para. 39. See, e.g., UN Doc. S/RES/1996 (2011), 6–7, paras. 18, 20.
[148] UN Doc. S/RES/1996 (2011), 6, paras. 15, 17; S/RES/2057 (2012), 1, Preamble; S/RES/2109 (2013), 7, paras. 25–6; S/RES/2047 (2012), 4, para. 16; S/RES/2075 (2012), 5, para. 18.

Inter-mission Cooperation Under its mandate, UNMISS shall share information with UNAMID, MONUSCO and regional and international partners in support of addressing threats.[149] Following the escalation of combats in South Sudan, the Secretary-General decided to transfer troops to UNMISS from MONUSCO, UNAMID, UNISFA, UNOCI and UNMIL, including five infantry battalions and three attack helicopters,[150] a decision which was approved by the Security Council in resolution 2132.[151]

Assessment

Despite the scarcity of available documents providing information with regard to the cooperation arrangements in place for UNISFA and UNMISS several conclusions regarding the attribution of conduct can be drawn. First of all, whereas the AU is the leading political actor in South Sudan, its political influence on the peace process and on the peacekeeping operations, especially on UNISFA, is not mirrored in the strategic and operational control arrangements. In contrast, the division of labour between the UN and the AU is quite distinct. The lack of any 'input' or 'control' of the AU on the strategic or operational level of both operations is rather surprising. A possible explanation might be that the UN as the ultimate authority for maintaining international peace and security is unwilling, on the basis of its special position, to allow any external contribution by the AU towards the operations under its authority, outside of the political framework and the context for conflict resolution. The civil war in South Sudan illustrated that the AU on its own is not yet capable to resolve complex political and security crises, but that it requires concerted international efforts – including the EU and the UN to find political solutions. The following case study of Mali will allow a verification as to whether this hypothesis is true or not. Another possible explanation for the limited degree of operational cooperation between the AU and the UN in South Sudan is based on the fact that the political process was predominantly steered by the AU and later on by IGAD, an external actor, whereas the deployment of the peacekeeping operations was executed by the UN. Consequently, there was no comprehensive approach with regard to both the political process and the deployment of peacekeeping operations which resulted in cooperation between the AU and the UN in the deployment of UNISFA and UNMISS to be restricted. This changed to

---

[149] UN Doc. A/66/532 (2011), 7, para. 17.
[150] UN Doc. S/2013/758 (2013), 1.
[151] UN Doc. S/RES/2132 (2013), 2, paras. 3, 5.

some extent with the intervention of IGAD and the political initiatives up to the conclusion of the Cessation of Hostilities Agreement in January 2014. Two months later, the Security Council then authorised the deployment within UNMISS of the IGAD taskforce in support of the protection of civilians and the Monitoring and Verification Mechanism which was established as part of the Cessation of Hostilities Agreement.

One other particular feature of UNISFA and UNMISS is the emphasis on inter-mission cooperation. However, the lack of further information and the extent of inter-mission cooperation do not justify any suggestion that the AU could be jointly responsible with the UN for the conduct of AFISMA and/or UNMISS via the back door of inter-mission cooperation with UNAMID. Nevertheless, it underlines that for future peacekeeping operations, the network of cooperation between the involved actors is enriched by another layer. Consequently, it proves that the main hypothesis of this present study, the need for a criterion of joint attribution is valid and warranted. Furthermore, it cannot be excluded that during the deployment of future peacekeeping operations, responsibility may also arise on the basis of inter-mission cooperation.[152]

Attribution of Conduct of AFISMA and MINUSMA

> In Mali, the efforts by the two organizations [the AU and the UN] have focused both on the political and the peacekeeping aspects of the crisis
>
> Report of the Chairperson of the AU Commission,
> 23 September 2013[153]

In January 2012, a Tuarag rebellion began in Northern Mali, led by the National Movement for the Liberation of Azawad (NMLA) which quickly took over control of the Northern part of the country. Islamist groups saw their chance to take over control of a part of the country themselves and turned against the NMLA, after having helped to defeat the Malian government, and started to introduce the Sharia law in the territory under their control.

---

[152] It should, of course, be noted that inter-mission cooperation is not a new feature; one could, for example, refer to the Liberia crisis and cooperation between the parallel UN and ECOWAS operations. The difference is that inter-mission cooperation in South Sudan is an explicit mandate of the operations and it is executed in the form of a continuing, permanent, institutionalised mechanism and not in the form of ad hoc cooperation in the field.

[153] Report of the Chairperson of the Commission, AU Doc. PSC/AHG/3.(CCCXCVII) (2013), 5, para. 15.

A coup d'état against the legitimate Malian government increased the anxiety of the international community that the situation in Mali would spin completely out of control and threaten international peace and security within the whole region. A major concern was the fact that the Sahel region extends over the Northern part of Mali which has been used for a longer period for 'drug cartel operations, cross-border banditry, smuggling, human trafficking, kidnapping-for-ransoms and money-laundering'[154] as well as a hide-out for Al-Qaida's Northern African branch which is active within the region. The prospects of increased terrorism, migration and destabilisation led the international community to adopt a harmonised approach from the very beginning to confront the political as well as the security crisis in Mali: 'advocat[ing] a double strategy based on two axes of action, one a political process and the other military action, if necessary'.[155] In this context, it was emphasised that the UN and other international organisations operate, indeed, 'in a new geopolitical context … fac[ing] threats that have not been encountered before in a peacekeeping context'.[156] The Under-Secretary-General for Peacekeeping Operations spoke in a similar vein of 'a peacekeeping operation in a geopolitical context characterized by asymmetrical threats not previously encountered in a United Nations peacekeeping environment'.[157]

The response of the international community to the coup d'état in Mali and the wider security crisis was coordinated from the early hours, primarily between the UN, the AU and ECOWAS.[158] Following the gain of territory by the Islamist armed groups in Northern Mali, it was decided to curtail the mandate and the deployment of AFISMA in favour of the quickest possible deployment of MINUSMA. The analysis of the attribution of conduct starts with AFISMA, followed by an examination of MINUSMA.

AFISMA

Establishment and Elaboration of the Mandate The occupation of the North of Mali by armed groups, 'including terrorists, drug traffickers and criminals of every sort' led to a severe security crisis in Mali, prompting

---

[154] UN Doc. S/2013/189 (2013), 11, para. 61
[155] Statement by the AU, UN Doc. S/PV.6952 (2013), 4.
[156] Statement by the Under-Secretary-General for Political Affairs, UN Doc. S/PV.6944 (2013), 5.
[157] Statement by the Under-Secretary-General for Peacekeeping Operations, UN Doc. S/PV.6985 (2013), 7.
[158] Mediation efforts in the Mali crisis were made by the UN, the AU and ECOWAS, UN Doc. S/2012/444 (2012), 5, para. 22.

the Government to request help from ECOWAS, as well as to request the adoption of a UN Security Council Resolution authorizing the intervention of an international military force under Chapter VII.[159]

Originally, ECOWAS and the AU had requested a Security Council mandate authorising the deployment of an ECOWAS stabilisation force and the Council expressed its readiness to further examine the request once additional information had been provided. This decision followed the positive response of the AU PSC to a request by ECOWAS to deploy elements of its Standby Brigade in Mali.[160] The Security Council then requested that the Secretary-General supports the Commissions of ECOWAS and AU in 'preparing such detailed options'.[161] The plans for the ECOWAS operation MICEMA, however, never went beyond the planning stage, due in particular to the absence of consensus within ECOWAS on the approach to be taken for resolving the crisis and particularly also with regard to financial and logistical constraints.[162] The Secretary-General also initially remained unconvinced by the plans for the deployment of AFISMA and recommended that the SC imposes conditions on the deployment of such an operation which included conditions on further planning, mission management and command and control arrangements.[163]

An initial planning conference was held in Abidjan from 11 to 15 June 2012 for which the UN provided advisory and planning support.[164] The following technical assessment mission with representatives of ECOWAS and the AU – under ECOWAS leadership – also included a multidisciplinary UN team in advisory capacity as well.[165] A further planning conference, held from 9 to 13 August 2012 – including representatives of the AU,

---

[159] UN Doc. S/2012/727 (2012), 2.
[160] Report of the Chairperson of the Commission, AU Doc. PSC/PR/3.(CCCXXXIX) (2012), 1, para. 2; Statement by ECOWAS, UN Doc. S/PV.6903 (2013), 51–52.
[161] UN Doc. S/RES/2056 (2012), 4, paras. 17–18; S/RES/2071 (2012), 2, Preamble; 3–4, para. 7.
[162] L.-A. Théroux-Bénoni, 'The Long Path to MINUSMA: Assessing the International Response to the Crisis in Mali', in M. Wyss, T. Tardy (eds.), *Peacekeeping in Africa: The Evolving Security Architecture* (London, Routledge, 2014), 171–172.
[163] W. Lotze, 'United Nations Multidimensional Integrated Stabilization Mission in Mali (MINUSMA)', in J. A. Koops, N. Macqueen, T. Tardy et al., *The Oxford Handbook of United Nations Peacekeeping Operations* (Oxford University Press, 2015), 854, 858.
[164] Report of the Secretary-General on the Situation in Mali, UN Doc. S/2012/894 (2012), 11, para. 46. The UN also provided further support to ECOWAS and the AU 'in developing the objectives, means and modalities of the envisaged deployment', ibid.
[165] Ibid., 11, para. 47.

the UN and the EU – further developed the concept of operations for the ECOWAS force which was envisaged to be deployed in Mali.[166]

At yet another joint planning conference with participants of all four organisations, a harmonised joint concept of operations was developed and subsequently endorsed by both ECOWAS and the AU.[167] Thus, the concept of operations for the envisaged operation, which would ultimately become AFISMA, was developed in cooperation among four international organisations: the AU, the UN, the EU and ECOWAS.[168] The late reaction of the Security Council with regard to authorising the deployment of such an operation led to criticism from ECOWAS[169] and ultimately to the French intervention with 'Operation Serval' for which France was applauded by the Secretary-General.[170]

The concept of operations (CONOPS) was revised in mid-February 2013 upon a request of the AU PSC[171] following developments on the ground by military and civilian experts of the AU and ECOWAS Commissions, Mali and other bilateral and multilateral partners.[172]

The troop strength of AFISMA was increased[173] and the leadership of AFISMA was entrusted to the AU which 'had overall authority over the Mission'.[174] The UN was heavily involved by not only providing planning support through UN military planners, but also by helping to establish

---

[166] Ibid., 11, para. 48; also Report of the Chairperson of the Commission, AU Doc. PSC/PR/3.(CCCXXXIX) (2012), 3, para. 9.
[167] UN Doc. S/2012/894 (2012), 12, paras. 50–51; 20, para. 85; S/2012/825 (2012), 14, para. 15. See generally Peace and Security Council, AU Doc. PSC/AHG/COMM/1.(CCCXCVII) (2013), 3, para. 8.a.v.
[168] The High-level Independent Panel recommended that the UN should consult closely with regional organisations in planning operations and thereby also define the role nature of the partnership in the mission, UN Doc. A/70/95 and S/2015/446 (2015), 58, para. 176; 62, para. 192.
[169] UN Doc. S/2012/905 (2012), 3, para. 2. See also ibid., 3, para. 7; 4, para. 9.
[170] Statement by the Under-Secretary-General for Political Affairs, UN Doc. S/PV.6905 (2012), 2; S/2013/189 (2013), 1–2, para. 4.
[171] Ibid., 8, para. 45.
[172] Progress Report of the Chairperson of the Commission, AU Doc. PSC/PR/2(CCCLVIII) (2013), 3, para. 9; Solemn Declaration of the Assembly of the Union on the Situation in Mali, Addis Ababa, 27 and 28 January 2013, 3, para. 7(a); Peace and Security Council, AU Doc. PSC/PR/COMM.(CCCLVIII) (2013), 2, paras. 10–12.
[173] UN Doc. S/2013/189 (2013), 8, para. 45.
[174] Sixth Ordinary Meeting of the Specialised Technical Committee on Defence, Safety and Security, Preparatory Meeting of Chiefs of Staff, Addis Ababa, Ethiopia, 29–30 April 2013, AU Doc. RPT/Exp/VI/STCDSS/(i-a) (2013), 5, para. 20; 6, para. 23. See also ECOWAS Peace and Security Report, Issue 1 October 2012, Mali: Making Peace While Preparing for War, 5.

coordination mechanisms as well as supporting the development of key documents for AFISMA, including 'operational directives, guidelines for the protection of civilians, rules of engagement and a code of conduct'.[175] The Conclusions of the Meeting of the Follow-up and Support Group and an AU report suggest that the EU was also involved in the joint planning, in cooperation with the three other international organisations, Mali and other stakeholders, but in a subsidiary role to the three other organisations.[176] The previously existing concept of operations for the international military mission, which would become AFISMA, was transmitted to the Security Council 'to seek the latter's total support for its effective implementation'.[177]

Mandate AFISMA was endowed with a robust, coercive mandate involving an authorisation of offensive combat operations, together with the Malian Defence Forces, including simultaneously the strong protection of civilians.[178] According to the joint strategic concept of operations, the strategic objectives include, inter alia, the protection of 'the population with respect to international human rights and international humanitarian and refugee law' as well as the reduction of threats posed by terrorist and transnational criminal groups and the establishment of a safe and secure environment in Mali.[179] The Security Council authorised AFISMA to 'take all necessary measures, in compliance with applicable international humanitarian law and human rights law'.[180]

---

[175] Statement by the Under-Secretary-General for Political Affairs, UN Doc. S/PV.6944 (2013), 4; UN Doc. S/2013/189 (2013), 9, para. 47. See also Security Council Resolution 2085, UN Doc. S/RES/2085 (2012), 5, para. 11.

[176] Meeting of the Support and Follow-up Group on the Situation in Mali, Bamako, Mali, 19 October 2012, Conclusions, 3, para. (iii); Report of the Chairperson of the Commission, AU Doc. PSC/PR/3.(CCCXXXIX) (2012), 1, para. 2; 3, para. 10. See also Assembly of the Union, Twentieth Ordinary Session, 27–28 January 2013, Addis Ababa, Ethiopia, Report of the Peace and Security Council on Its Activities and the State of Peace and Security in Africa, AU Doc. Assembly/AU/3(XX) (2012), 35, 121.

[177] UN Doc. S/2012/825 (2012), 4, para. 7. ECOWAS had requested the AU PSC to endorse the Concept and to ensure its transmission, together with the Strategic Concept to the United Nations Secretary-General within the deadline under SC Resolution 2071, Extraordinary Session of the Authority of ECOWAS Heads of State and Government, Abuja, Federal Republic of Nigeria, 11 November 2012, 3, para. 9; UN Doc. S/2012/876 (2012), 2.

[178] Council Decision 2013/34/CFSP (2013); Council Decision 2013/178/CFSP (2013); Council Decision 2013/87/CFSP (2013); UN Doc. S/2012/876 (2012), 11, para. b (phase 2).

[179] UN Doc. S/2013/163 (2013), 7, para. 11(d), (e), (f).

[180] UN Doc. S/RES/2085 (2012), 4, para. 9; 6, para. 18; 7, para. 23.

Political and Strategic Control of AFISMA Cooperation on a strategic level is exercised through the established Mali Integrated Task Force (MITF) based at the AU Commission[181] in Addis Ababa which is composed of representatives of the AU, ECOWAS and the UN and is 'responsible for coordination at the strategic level of AFISMA'[182] in the form of 'strategic guidance and advice for AFISMA'.[183] It is furthermore responsible to 'ensure coordinated strategic implementation of the relevant decisions of the three organizations on the situation in Mali'.[184] The Secretary-General also recommended that the Security Council plays an active role in ensuring that the African-led international military operation is 'held fully accountable'.[185] The Security Council encouraged the AU, ECOWAS, the EU and the UN to maintain coordination through the task force in its Resolution 2100 establishing MINUSMA,[186] as well as through the Support and Follow-up Group and it stressed 'the importance of continued coordination' between the UN, the AU and ECOWAS.[187]

Operational Control A joint coordination mechanism (JCM) for the implementation of Security Council Resolution 2085 was established in Bamako at the operational coordinational cell, under the leadership of the AU High Representative for Mali and the Sahel, President Pierre Buyoya who was appointed as the Special Representative and Head of AFISMA,[188] following consultations with ECOWAS.[189] It is co-chaired by the AU and the UN.[190] Its tasks are to facilitate 'regular consultations on political leadership, resource mobilization and accountability as well as the monitoring and assessment of expenditures',[191] thereby coordinating support to the mission.[192] The ECOWAS Special Representative in Mali,

---

[181] UN Doc. S/2013/163 (2013), 14, para. 33.
[182] Progress Report of the Chairperson of the Commission, AU Doc. PSC/PR/2(CCCLVIII) (2013), 2, para. 6; Statement by the Under-Secretary-General for Political Affairs, UN Doc. S/PV.6944 (2013), 4.
[183] Statement by the AU, S/PV.6905 (2013), 8.
[184] Solemn Declaration of the Assembly of the Union, supra note 172, 3, para. 7(c).
[185] UN Doc. S/2012/894 (2012), 21, para. 89.
[186] Security Council Resolution 2100, UN Doc. S/RES/2100 (2013), 3, Preamble.
[187] Ibid., 5, para. 5.
[188] He was appointed after consultations between the AU and ECOWAS, UN Doc. S/2012/894 (2012), 12, para. 52; Peace and Security Council, AU Doc. PSC/PR/2(CCCLVIII) (2013), 1, para. 3.
[189] UN Doc. S/2013/163 (2013), 14, para. 32.
[190] UN Doc. S/2013/189 (2013), 6, para. 29.
[191] Statement by ECOWAS, UN Doc. S/PV.6905 (2013), 9.
[192] UN Doc. S/2012/876 (2012), 14, para. 33. See also UN Doc. S/RES/2085 (2012), 5, paras. 13–14.

Ambassador Cheaka Touré of Togo, was appointed to his Deputy position.[193] It includes representatives of the AU, ECOWAS and the UN as well as members from Mali and other partners.[194] One can only speculate as to why the early plans of an ECOWAS Mali force[195] were changed to an AU-led international military force, but it is reasonable to presume that a wider range of capacities and resource acquirement by the AU were a determinative factor. Moreover, the Memorandum of Understanding between the AU and the RECs as part of the African Peace and Security Architecture might have triggered this development.

Chain of Command   The Chain of Command of AFISMA is headed by the Chairperson of the AU Commission who has delegated 'overall responsibility' for all AU(-led) organisations to the Commissioner for Peace and Security. The AU exercises 'operational authority' of AFISMA.[196] The Special Representative as Head of the Mission exercises 'overall AUC authority over civilian, police and military components of AFISMA' whereas the Force Commander and the Police Commander have 'operational control over assigned forces'.[197]

Operational/Financial Support   The Secretary-General emphasised in his report that the UN does not possess the capability to provide logistical support to international military forces deployed in the context of offensive combat operations against hostile armed forces.[198] He therefore suggested the provision of logistical support based on three possible alternatives which would be funded through UN-assessed contributions and comprise the equipment and support services as they would be provided to

---

[193] Progress Report of the Chairperson of the Commission, AU Doc. PSC/PR/2(CCCLVIII) (2013), 2, para. 6. Previously the Chairperson of the AU Commission received the request by the PSC to initiate consultations with ECOWAS on the command and control of AFISMA, AU Doc. PSC/PR/COMM.2(CCCXLI) (2012), 3, para. 10. The Joint Strategic Concept of Operations foresaw that ECOWAS would, in consultation with the AU, appoint a Special Representative as Head of the Mission, UN Doc. S/2012/876 (2012), 13, para. 36.
[194] Progress Report of the Chairperson of the Commission, AU Doc. PSC/PR/2(CCCLVIII) (2013), 2, para. 6; Statement by the Under-Secretary-General for Political Affairs, UN Doc. S/PV.6944 (2013), 4; S/2012/894 (2012), 12, 15, para. 64.
[195] UN Doc. S/2012/739 (2012), 3.
[196] UN Doc. S/2013/163 (2013), 14, para. 32.
[197] Ibid.
[198] The AU had officially requested the authorisation of a support package funded by UN-assessed contributions, Report of the Chairperson of the Commission, AU Doc. PSC/PR/3.(CCCXXXIX) (2012), 1, para. 2.

a UN operation.¹⁹⁹ The UN Security Council did not authorise the financing of AFISMA itself through assessed contributions,²⁰⁰ but requested the Secretary-General in Resolution 2085 to establish a Trust Fund for the operation.²⁰¹ A donor's conference was convened by the AU in close consultation with ECOWAS in January 2013.²⁰²

The EU committed 50 million Euros through the African Peace Facility for AFISMA²⁰³ and promised further financial and logistical support in close coordination with the AU and ECOWAS²⁰⁴ following the activation of the 'Clearing House' mechanisms to support AFISMA,²⁰⁵ under the guidance of the AU High Representative for Mali and the Sahel.²⁰⁶ The AU decided to contribute 50 million US dollars to the budget of AFISMA which amounts to 460 million US dollars.²⁰⁷

AFISMA also received logistical support from bilateral and multilateral donors 'providing funding and reimbursement for operations, critical life support (rations, water and fuel), logistical support for strategic and in-theatre movements, direct materiel support and the training of enabling units'.²⁰⁸

EUTM Mali is supporting the training and reorganisation of the Malian Armed Forces.²⁰⁹ The training includes sessions on gender and human rights.²¹⁰

---

[199] UN Doc. S/2012/926 (2012), 1, second paragraph; 3, first paragraph.
[200] The Security Council considered such an option in the Resolution and charged the Secretary-General to refine options within a report. Following the report and the development of events in Mali calling for the French intervention and a transfer from AFISMA to MINUSMA after six months, the Security Council did not authorise the funding by assessed contributions, UN Doc. S/RES/2085 (2012), 6, paras. 21–22.
[201] See also UN Doc. S/RES/2100 (2013), 6, para. 10.
[202] Conclusions of the Donors' Conference for the African-led International Support Mission in Mali and the Malian Defense and Security Forces (2013), 1, paras. 2–3.
[203] Background, Foreign Affairs Council, Monday, 18 February 2013, in Brussels; UN Doc. S/RES/2085 (2012), 6, para. 20.
[204] Statement by the EU, UN Doc. S/PV.6905 (2013), 18.
[205] EEAS provides a 'Clearing House' mechanism to support AFISMA mission in Mali, Brussels, 21 January 2013, A/30/13, 1–2.
[206] Council conclusions on Mali, 3222nd Foreign Affairs Council meeting, Brussels, 18 February 2013, 3, para. 8.
[207] Solemn Declaration of the Assembly of the Union, supra note 172, 5, para. (B)(i).
[208] Report of the Secretary-General on the situation in Mali, UN Doc. S/2013/338 (2013), 14, para. 66.
[209] Statement by Under-Secretary-General for Political Affairs, UN Doc. S/PV.6905 (2013), 3. The Security Council took note of the (then) planned operation in its Resolution 2085, UN Doc. S/RES/2085 (2012), 4, para. 8.
[210] Statement by the EU, UN Doc. S/PV.6948 (2013), 33.

THE ATTRIBUTION OF CONDUCT 241

Coordination and Cooperation between the International Organisations Regarding the Political Process The PSC of the AU established the Support and Follow-up Group at its meeting in Banako, on 20 March 2012, to facilitate the resolution of the crisis in the North of Mali.[211] Early meetings of the Support and Follow-up Group on the situation in Mali were hosted by the EU, co-chaired by the AU, ECOWAS and the UN.[212] Later meetings of the Support and Follow-up Group were convened by the AU. The Group brings together ECOWAS, its member states, the AU, the UN, the EU, the International Organisation of *La Francophonie* (OIF), the Organisation of the Islamic Conference (OIC), all neighbouring countries, countries of the region, all permanent members of the Security Council and other bilateral partners.[213]

Whereas the group should remain 'at the heart of international coordination on the situation in Mali',[214] the international efforts are mainly coordinated by the triumvirate of ECOWAS, the AU and the UN,[215] also via the High/Special Representatives for the Region of the involved organisations.[216] The UN favoured this close interaction as it 'allow[s] the United Nations to focus on its core responsibilities', but it is also due to this close interaction and 'the large numbers of actors involved, [that] the United Nations mission [MINUSMA] should provide a strong coordination mechanism'.[217] Generally, there is a lot of coordination among the AU,

---

[211] Report of the Chairperson of the Commission, AU Doc. PSC/PR/3.(CCCXXXIX) (2012), 11, para. 28.

[212] Remarks to the press by High Representative Catherine Ashton following the meeting of the support and follow-up group on the situation in Mali, Brussels, 5 February 2013, 1; EU host a ministerial meeting of the Support and Follow-up Group on the situation in Mali, Doc. A/60/13 (2013), 1; Progress Report of the Chairperson of the Commission, AU Doc. PSC/PR/2.(CCCLVIII) (2013), 2, para. 8; 3183rd Council meeting, Foreign Affairs, Brussels, 23 July 2012, 15, para. 7. Some of the later meetings of the Support and Follow-up Group were under the joint chairmanship of the AU, the UN and ECOWAS, Meeting of the Support and Follow-up Group on the Situation in Mali, supra note 176, 1, para. 1.

[213] Report of the Chairperson of the Commission, AU Doc. PSC/PR/3.(CCCXXXIX) (2012), 2, paras. 11, 28.

[214] Ibid., 11, para. 29; see also Statement by the Secretary-General, UN Doc. S/PV.6820 (2012), 3.

[215] Report of the Chairperson of the Commission, AU Doc. PSC/PR/3.(CCCXXXIX) (2012), 11–12, para. 29. The Strategic Concept nevertheless also foresees the establishment of a working-level mechanism among the UN Secretariat, The AU and ECOWAS Commissions, the EU and the OIF, and other international stakeholders as required, ibid. The Security Council requested in Resolution 2056 the Secretary-General to support the efforts of international and regional actors, including the Follow-up and Support Group, UN Doc. S/RES/2056 (2012), 5, para. 25.

[216] UN Doc. S/2012/825 (2012), 2.

[217] UN Doc. S/2012/894 (2012), 16, para. 84.

ECOWAS, UN and the EU also through the exchange of documents[218] and through meetings on various levels.[219]

The UN supported the mediation efforts of ECOWAS through the UN Office in Mali (UNOM) and the Office of the Special Representative of the Secretary-General for West Africa (UNOWA).[220]

Assessment The unprecedented peacekeeping context and the complexity of the security crisis in Mali have not triggered, on their own, such a concerted approach by the involved international organisations. External constraints, in the form of a lack of financial and logistical resources particularly, were influential in the change of plans from an ECOWAS to an African-led operation.[221] It is also plausible that the lack of time for long-term mission planning for Mali due to the land gain by the Islamist armed groups has forced the UN to interact so intensively with regional organisations which are better equipped to rapidly deploy troops than the UN. Generally speaking, one can conclude that the standard of cooperation of international organisations in the mandating, planning, deployment and supervision of AFISMA is, indeed, unprecedented.

Surprisingly, the level of cooperation is actually even higher than for the deployment of UNAMID in Darfur. The analysis of the various elements of cooperation has demonstrated that one can speak nearly of a 'monolithic' peacekeeping operation, excluding the chain of command which is directed by the AU; all other elements of the operation were determined on the basis of cooperation and coordination arrangements among the AU, ECOWAS and the UN. Regarding the attribution of conduct, there is consequently no doubt that conduct arising during the deployment of AFISMA, and in violation of international law, would have to be attributed to all three organisations.

As regards the EU, it is suggested that its contributions to the deployment are also more than substantial, resulting in responsibility for the EU in partnership with the three other organisations. The EU's role in Mali has focused particularly on the purely political process of resolving the crisis in Mali, as well as on the political level of the peacekeeping operation, remaining true to its policy on the African continent. Then again,

---

[218] Peace and Security Council, AU Doc. PSC/PR/COMM.(CCCXVI) (2012), 1, para. 5; 4, para. 16; UN Doc. S/RES/2056 (2012), 2, para. 1.
[219] See, e.g., UN Doc. S/2012/894 (2012), 12, 8, paras. 32–33.
[220] Statement by the Under-Secretary-General for Political Affairs, UN Doc. S/PV.6944 (2013), 2.
[221] Théroux-Bénoni, 'The Long Path to MINUSMA', ibid., 171–172, 175–177.

the EU has not only contributed a major part to the budget of AFISMA, but deployed a training mission (EUTM Mali) on the ground to train the Malian Armed Forces. It may be recalled that AFISMA, under its mandate, is acting also in support of the Malian Armed Forces. Furthermore, the EU has made a more than substantial contribution to the continuing operationalisation of the African Peace and Security Architecture of the AU – on the interinstitutional and not the mission level – which is the leading organisation, in terms of the chain of command of AFISMA. Therefore, these contributions of the EU remedy its more limited role in the other areas and, consequently, the EU has to be considered responsible for the conduct of AFISMA jointly with the AU, ECOWAS and the UN. However, it could be possible to retain a certain distinction between the EU and the AU, ECOWAS and the UN. The different input of the EU towards the command and control arrangements of AFISMA could be mirrored in the exercise of jurisdiction under human rights law. Whereas the three other organisations could possibly exercise jurisdiction on the basis of the spatial model of jurisdiction, the EU could be found to solely exercise jurisdiction on the basis of the personal model.[222]

MINUSMA

ECOWAS recommended the transformation of AFISMA in a UN stabilisation operation, 'with a robust mandate and a parallel rapid reaction force' based on one of two alternatives proposed by the Secretary-General.[223] The AU similarly requested such a transition.[224] According to a report by the International Crisis Group, 'the fear of sending an under-equipped African force into an extremely difficult environment requiring costly logistical support, because of the lack of reliable support', led the Security Council to quickly transform AFISMA into MINUSMA.[225] The authors of the ECOWAS report assert that the transformation was 'primarily driven by France's concern', while taking into account of the logistical and financial constraints encountered by AFISMA.[226]

---

[222] See Chapter 5.
[223] Mr. Bamba, Côte d'Ivoire, speaking on behalf of ECOWAS, Security Council, UN Doc. S/PV.6944 (2013), 8.
[224] Statement by the AU for Mr. Pierre Buyoya, Special Representative of the AU and Head of AFISMA, UN Doc. S/PV.6952 (2013), 4.
[225] International Crisis Group, Mali: Security, Dialogue and Meaningful Reform, *Africa Report N 201*, 11 April 2013, 38.
[226] *ECOWAS Peace and Security Report*, 5 July 2013, A Tenuous Solution in Mali: Between Internal Constraints and External Pressures, 6.

(Elaboration of the) Mandate   It was desired by the AU and ECOWAS to transform AFISMA into a UN operation 'with an appropriate mandate'; in other words, 'it should be a peace enforcement mission based on Chapter VII of the United Nations Charter'.[227]

The mandate of MINUSMA was developed in cooperation with the AU.[228] Both organisations noted 'that the content of the draft resolution broadly reflects the desire of both organizations, as contained in the relevant decisions' of the AU PSC and the ECOWAS Authority.[229] They emphasised that the anticipated resolution should 'fully incorporate the contributions that the two organizations will continue to make towards the definitive resolution of the security and institutional crisis facing Mali'.[230]

As noted by the Support and Follow-up Group, the SC should 'ensure that the envisaged operation ... build[s] on the achievement made with ECOWAS and AU support, and foster[s] enhanced and coordinated African and international engagement in support of peace and security in Mali'.[231] However, following the adoption of the Resolution establishing MINUSMA, the AU criticised the lack of consultation by the Security Council and noted that its concerns were not taken into account.[232] The Security Council, in turn, noted that the AU, ECOWAS, the Secretary-General and other international partners did not report back to the Security Council every sixty days as requested in its previous Resolution 2085.[233] Some members of the Security Council felt that the AU has been slow on occasions to act on urgent matters. Indeed, the limited AU representation in NY and the lack of meetings of the AU PSC members in New York mean that the African countries in the Security Council and

---

[227] UN Doc. S/2013/231 (2013), 2; Progress Report of the Chairperson of the Commission, AU Doc. PSC/PR/2(CCCLVIII) (2013), 3–4, paras. 12–13.
[228] Statement by the AU, UN Doc. S/PV.6952 (2013), 4.
[229] UN Doc. S/2013/265 (2013), 2.
[230] Ibid. This included that the SC undertakes 'appropriate consultations' with the AU and ECOWAS, 'including on the leadership and the composition of the envisaged mission in a spirit of continuity'. UN Doc. S/2013/163 (2013), 2–3.
[231] Fourth Meeting of Support and Follow-up Group on the Situation in Mali, Bamako, Mali, 19 April 2013, Conclusions, 4, para. 14.
[232] Peace and Security Council, AU Doc. PSC/PR/COMM.(CCCLXXI) (2013), para. 10. Nevertheless, the AU also accepted that its actions were limited by its own constraints, Seventh Meeting of the Specialized Technical Committee on Defense, Safety and Security, Addis Ababa, 14 January 2014, Opening Remarks by Ambassador Smaïl Chergui, AU Commission for Peace and Security, 2.
[233] UN Doc. S/RES/2100 (2013), 3, Preamble.

the Council itself may not always be informed and aware of the AU PSC's decisions.[234]

MINUSMA operates in a similar way to AFISMA under robust rules of engagement and most of the military and police forces of AFISMA have been absorbed.[235] Under the mandate, MINUSMA troops deploy from major cities in Northern Mali, conducting patrols both alone and with the Malian defence and security forces whereby all MINUSMA operations 'will take into account the need to minimize the risk to civilians'.[236]

In this context,

> MINUSMA has a mandate to use all necessary means to ensure the implementation of many elements of its mandate, including taking active steps to deter and prevent the return of armed elements to key population centres. *While that does not describe a peace-enforcement or counter-terrorism role, which will be undertaken by others who have capacities beyond the scope of and means of the United Nations mandate and capabilities, it will require the United Nations to be as robust as possible in implementing that mandate in an environment characterized by threats.*[237] [Emphasis added]

All AFISMA troops which were rehatted under MINUSMA underwent 'predeployment training and vetting procedures, including in accordance with the requirements of the United Nations human rights screening policy, so as to ensure that they ... have the necessary skills to implement the mandate'.[238] The transfer of AFISMA personnel to MINUSMA should be accomplished in close coordination with the AU and ECOWAS.[239] Other UN operations in the region were required to share logistic and administrative support with MINUSMA to the extent possible.[240]

The mandate allows implicitly and expressly for the use of military force. First of all, the Resolution states that the mandate of MINUSMA shall be 'to stabilize the key population centres, especially in the North

---

[234] P. D. Williams, A. Boutellis, 'Partnership Peacekeeping: Challenges and Opportunities in the United Nations–African Union Relationship', *African Affairs*, 113 (2014), 254, 260–261, 278. Cf. UN Doc. S/2014/341 (2014), 21–22, para. 11.
[235] Statement by Mr. Hervé Ladsous, Under-Secretary-General for Peacekeeping Operations, UN Doc. S/PV.6985 (2013), 5.
[236] Ibid., 6.
[237] Ibid., 7. See also UN Doc. S/2013/189 (2013), 14, para. 75. These tasks include, e.g., maintaining checkpoints, conducting patrols and contributing to de-escalation of tensions, UN Doc. S/2013/582 (2013), 5, para. 24.
[238] Statement by Ms. Leila Zerrougui, Special Representative of the Secretary-General for Children and Armed Conflict, UN Doc. S/PV.6980 (2013), 6.
[239] UN Doc. S/RES/2100 (2013), 5, para. 7.
[240] Ibid., 7, para. 15.

of Mali, and, in this context, to deter threats and take active steps to prevent the return of armed elements to those areas'.[241] In paragraph 17 of the Resolution, however, the Security Council returns to the traditional formula explicitly authorising 'MINUSMA to use all necessary means'.[242] The mandate further specifically includes the protection of civilians and UN personnel.[243]

MINUSMA shall also 'monitor, help investigate and report to the Council on any abuses or violations of human rights or violations of international humanitarian law committed throughout Mali and to contribute to efforts to prevent such violations and abuses'.[244]

Appointment of the Force Commander ECOWAS and the AU also requested that the Special Representative leading MINUSMA be appointed after 'appropriate consultations' with both organisations to contribute to the 'African ownership of this effort and to optimize the efficiency of the Mission'.[245] It could not be verified whether this request was approved by the UN.

Political Control The AU emphasised strongly that the central political roles both of the AU and ECOWAS should be recognised 'in full partnership with the United Nations Mission' and that these two organisations 'would maintain a strong presence in Bamako to pursue their political commitment in Mali. Secondly, the practice of consultations that has characterized all our joint action on Mali to date should continue, especially with respect to major decisions, such as choosing contingents and selecting military and civilian leadership'.[246] Both organisations have, in pursuance of their political commitment, 'engaged the United Nations on possible areas of support in terms of strategic and operational-level communication, in theatre movement, accommodation, medical care and security for their personnel'.[247] The AU accordingly established the AU Mission for Mali and the Sahel (MISAHEL) which was also mandated to

---

[241] Ibid., 7, para. 16(a), (i).
[242] Ibid., 9, para. 17.
[243] Ibid., 8, para. 16(c), (i), (iii).
[244] Ibid., 8, para. 16(d)(i).
[245] Progress Report of the Chairperson of the Commission, AU Doc. PSC/PR/2(CCCLVIII) (2013), 4, para. 16.
[246] Statement by the AU for Mr. Pierre Buyoya, Special Representative of the AU and Head of AFISMA, UN Doc. S/PV.6952 (2013), 4.
[247] UN Doc. S/2013/338 (2013), 16, para. 75.

promote regional security and cooperation.²⁴⁸ On 4 November 2013, the AU affirmed at the ministerial meeting held in Bamako 'its readiness to work for the establishment of a joint secretariat' on the basis of the UN integrated strategy for the Sahel.²⁴⁹ This 'flexible technical Secretariat' serves to support coordination efforts within the region, co-chaired by the UN and the AU and also comprising the Arab Maghreb Union (AMU), ECOWAS, ECCAS, the Community of Sahelo-Saharan States (CENSAD), the World Bank Group, the African Development Bank (ADB), the Islamic Development Bank (IDB), the EU and the OIC.²⁵⁰

The Security Council sent a mission to Mali in early 2014 which was not only an expression of the full support of the Council for the peace process, but also a way of gathering information in order to exercise political control.²⁵¹ The AU and the EU have both developed own strategies for the Sahel aimed at increasing the cooperation with the other international actors; similar efforts have been undertaken by ECOWAS.²⁵² In its resolution renewing the mandate of MINUSMA, the Security Council also called upon the AU, ECOWAS, the EU and other key actors to coordinate their efforts for the promotion of lasting peace with the Special Representative of the Secretary-General and MINUSMA.²⁵³ The Peace Agreement concluded in Summer 2015 underlines this unified approach towards the steering of the political process by the UN, the AU, the EU and ECOWAS which continue jointly to grant their full support to its implementation.²⁵⁴

Strategic and Operational Level   The UN Secretariat deepened its cooperation with the AU and ECOWAS regarding the transition from AFISMA to MINUSMA through meetings of multidisciplinary teams including 'the

---

²⁴⁸ Sixth Meeting of the Support and Follow-up Group on the Situation in Mali, Bamako, 2 November 2013, Opening remarks by Dr. H. E. Nikosazana Diamini Zuma, Chairperson of the Commission of the AU, 3–4; Third Ministerial Meeting on the Enhancement of Security Cooperation and the Operationalisation of the African Peace and Security Architecture in the Sahelo-Saharan Region, Niamey, Niger, 19 February 2014, Second Progress Report of the Commission on the Implementation of the Conclusions of the Ministerial Meeting Held on 17 March 2013 and Prospects for the Enhancement of the Nouakchott Process, 1, para. 5; 3, para. 9.
²⁴⁹ Statement by the AU, UN Doc. S/PV.7081 (2013), 7.
²⁵⁰ UN Doc. S/PRST/2013/20 (2013), 2.
²⁵¹ UN Doc. S/2014/72 (2014), 2, para. 5; 3, para. 9.
²⁵² Third Ministerial Meeting on the Enhancement of Security Cooperation, supra note 248, 3, paras. 9–10.
²⁵³ UN Doc. S/RES/2164 (2014), 5, para. 10.
²⁵⁴ UN Doc. S/2015/364 (2015), 14, Articles 54, 58; 15, Article 61.

conduct of a joint planning session and the subsequent establishment of a joint AFISMA-MINUSMA mechanism in Bamako'.[255] Cooperation and coordination is also continued through the Mali Integrated Task Force which was established for AFISMA.[256]

Cooperation with the EU/EUTM Mali Regarding EUTM, the Security Council called upon the EU, notably its Special Representative for the Sahel, 'to coordinate closely with MINUSMA ... to assist the transitional authorities of Mali in the Security Sector Reform'.[257] In February 2014, the EU announced to deploy a civilian mission in Mali.[258] Having been deployed in January 2015, EUCAP Mali has the mandate to support the Malian government in the implementation of its security reform, in particular for the international security forces.[259]

Assessment The analysis of the structure of MINUSMA, from the point of view of control via and by other international organisations than the UN, reaffirms the assessment made regarding the UN operations in South Sudan. Indeed, it appears that the influence, control and input of other international organisations in UN-mandated peacekeeping operations is more limited than the respective control and influence exercised by the UN over authorised operations.

In comparison to AFISMA, the inter-institutional control and cooperation arrangements are by far more constricted. The complaints raised by the AU about the lack of inclusion in the elaboration and formulation of the mandate and the reply by the Security Council relating to the non-submission of reports, indicates that there are inter-institutional tensions which might derive from the AU and ECOWAS not being willing to limit their engagement immediately after the transfer of authority from AFISMA to MINUSMA. Despite these problems, Mali may represent the beginning of a new era in peacekeeping operations in which the political process for conflict resolution and the deployment of a peacekeeping operation are included within a wide concerted approach by two or more

---

[255] UN Doc. S/2013/338 (2013), 14, para. 67.
[256] UN Doc. S/RES/2100 (2013), 3, Preamble, third paragraph.
[257] Ibid., 9, para. 22.
[258] Address by EU High Representative Catherine Ashton at the UN Security Council, Doc. 140214/02 (2014). The mandate of the training mission was extended until 18 May 2016, Council of the European Union, Doc. 8775/14 (2014), 1.
[259] Council Decision 2014/219/CFSP (2014), Articles 1 and 2; Council Decision 2015/76 (2015); Political and Security Committee Decision, Doc. 2015/67 (2015).

international organisations. The political process and political consultation serve thereby as the 'focus point' for the development of the strategy for the to-be-deployed peacekeeping operation.

It is also noticeable that the EU has been completely marginalised in the debate on and in the documents relating to MINUSMA. Bearing in mind the general concept of division of labour as it has emerged among the AU, the EU and the UN on the African continent, it corresponds to the limited engagement the EU plays in peacekeeping operations on the African continent when it comes to direct (military) involvement in peacekeeping operations.

The overwhelming control exercised by the UN over MINUSMA prevents any contribution by and any cooperation with other international organisations from reaching such a degree that it surpasses the level required for aid and assistance, leading to the application of the normative control criterion. Consequently, there is no joint responsibility of the UN in union with the other organisations for the conduct of MINUSMA. Naturally, it does not touch upon the question whether the AU and ECOWAS could not be responsible as accessories, but as was established earlier on,[260] the lack of the intent required for aiding and assistance under the ARIOs means that any violation of international law based on cooperation between international organisations which does not surpass the threshold for the application of the normative control criterion will not lead to any attribution of responsibility under the ARIOs in their current form.

Attribution of Conduct for MISCA and MINUSCA

After decades of instability and fighting, the Central African Republic (CAR) witnessed a resumption of violence in December 2012 when the mainly Muslim Séléka rebel coalition launched a series of attacks. A peace agreement (Libreville Agreement) was reached in January 2013, but the rebels seized the capital, in March, forcing the President to flee. The conflict took on increasingly sectarian overtones by December 2013 as the mainly Christian anti-Balaka movement took up arms and inter-communal clashes erupted again in and around Bangui.

The self-declared President Djotodia bowed to international and domestic pressure and stepped down in January 2014. A transitional assembly elected Mrs. Samba-Panza as interim president pending the

---

[260] See the case study of KFOR.

organisation of elections which are now scheduled for 27 December 2015 and 31 January 2016. The worsening security situation up to December 2013 led the Security Council to ultimately authorise the deployment of the African-led International Support Mission in the Central African Republic (MISCA). MISCA was preceded by ECCAS' operation MICOPAX which had been already established in 2008. This AU-led operation was ultimately transformed into MINUSCA, a UN-led peacekeeping operation. Consequently, in contrast to the previous case studies, in the CAR there were two transitions: first from a sub-regional peacekeeping operation to a regional AU-led operation and secondly from the regional to the international – UN – level.

MISCA

The AU PSC decided on 17 June to support, in principle, the deployment of an AU-led operation (MISCA) and requested the AU Commission to develop the mandate with ECCAS, TCCs and relevant international partners.[261] On 19 July 2013, MISCA was authorised by the PSC, with the MICOPAX troops to be rehatted until 1 August 2013.[262] The PSC of the AU requested the SC to authorise the deployment (MISCA) for initially six months. The Security Council itself did not authorise the deployment of MISCA until 5 December 2013 when it adopted Resolution 2127. The authorisation by the SC which followed nearly five months after the authorisation by the AU PSC does not mean that the AU decided to deploy MISCA on its own.

On the contrary, the adoption of Security Council 2127 was the result of several months of joint planning and coordination between all organisations. The UN and the AU thereby benefitted from lessons drawn from the transition from AFISMA to MINUSMA when both ECOWAS and the AU had already started to develop distinct concept of operations once the UN deployed military and security planners.[263] With regard to the CAR, the UN 'worked from the outset to support the transition from … [MICOPAX] to the African-led operation MISCA'.[264] The UN explicitly welcomed the authorisation of MISCA by the PSC in Resolution 2121.[265]

---

[261] UN Doc. S/2013/677 (2013), 4, para. 14.
[262] AU Doc. PSC/PR/COMM.2(CCCLXXXV) (2013), 2, para. 6.
[263] UN Doc. S/2015/3 (2015), 4.
[264] Ibid., 4–5.
[265] UN Doc. S/RES/2121 (2013), 2. In contrast the AU had already called on the SC in September to adopt a resolution on MISCA, AU Doc. PSC/AHG/BR/1(CCCXCVII) (2013), 2.

In fact, the UN participated in AU-led assessment missions from April 2013 on, supporting the development of the MISCA concept of operations. As called for in SC Resolution 2127, authorising MISCA and adopted two weeks before the transfer of authority from MICOPAX to MISCA, the SC also called upon the Secretariat to provide 'technical and expert advice to support the planning and deployment of MISCA and to strengthen its command and control, including through the mobile training team designed and delivered in a coordinated fashion by the UN and the AU'.[266] This included support on the implementation on the MISCA concept of operations.[267]

The transformation of MICOPAX into MISCA was steered by ECCAS and AU in consultation with experts from UN, EU and other partners and included also various rounds of expert meeting to assess the logistical and other resources needed by MISCA and to work on the establishment of MISCA headquarters.[268] The AU agreed with ECCAS after a consultative meeting on 2 and 3 September on the specific modalities of the transfer of authority.[269] The concept of operations for MISCA was finalised during an operational planning meeting from 7 to 10 October 2013 between AU and ECCAS with support by the UN and the EU.[270] The UN Special Representative also facilitated talks between AU and ECCAS to harmonise their views on the deployment of MISCA.[271]

The International Contact Group on the CAR encouraged the consultations between ECCAS, AU and, particularly the EU and UN for the preparation of a concept of operations and a concept of logistical Support for MISCA and for the transformation of MICOPAX into MISCA.[272] A better coordination in planning and long-term conflict resolution planning was one of main strategic aims and key features of the coordination between the AU and the UN in the CAR.

However, MISCA's deployment did not go as swiftly as planned, African countries did not provide enough personnel to meet MISCA's authorised force size and the SC first failed to reach consensus on endorsing the mission and on authorising a support package as envisaged in the concept of operations. SC Resolution 2121 therefore postponed a decision on the type

---

[266] UN Doc. S/2015/3 (2015), 5; S/RES/2121 (2013), 6, paras. 20–22; S/2013/677 (2013), 4, para. 16; AU Doc. PSC/PR/COMM.1(CDVI) (2013), 2, para. 9.
[267] UN Doc. S/RES/2127 (2013), 8, para. 37.
[268] UN Doc. S/2013/677 (2013), 5, paras. 19–20; AU press release, 30 August 2013.
[269] UN Doc. S/RES/2121 (2013), 2.
[270] UN Doc. S/2013/677 (2013), 4, para. 16; 6, para. 23; UN Doc. S/2014/172, 7, para. 17; 9, para. 25; AU Doc. PSC/PR/COMM.1(CCCLXXX) (2013), 3, para. 6.
[271] UN Doc. S/2013/671, 5, para. 22.
[272] Second Meeting of the International Contact Group on the Central African Republic (ICG-CAR), 8 July 2013, Communiqué, 2, paras. 9–10.

of support provided and requested the SG to report to the SC on options for international support to MISCA.²⁷³

Thus, pending the adoption of Resolution 2127, the report by the Secretary-General foresaw five options for the provision of international support to MISCA, of which was the transformation of MISCA into a UN operation at a later stage.²⁷⁴ The majority of partners and international and civil organisations the joint assessment missions had met with during the summer of 2013, favoured this option and so did the UN Secretariat.²⁷⁵ Consequently in Resolution 2127 the Security Council took the first step for the planning of a follow-up UN operation, taking note of the general agreement on the issue, by requesting the SG to undertake contingency preparations and planning for the possible transformation of MISCA into a UN operation. He was asked to report back no later than in three months, in consultation with the AU.²⁷⁶ This 'strategic convergence among the partners involved was facilitated to a large extent by the common vision that was provided by the Security Council at an early stage and in several resolutions'.²⁷⁷

Mandate The Mandate of MISCA included specific dispositions on the protection of civilians.²⁷⁸ The high degree of cooperation between the AU, ECCAS, the EU and other international stakeholders in planning and developing the concept for MISCA up to its deployment was mirrored in the unique reporting requirement under Resolution 2127. The SC requested 'the African Union, in close coordination with the Secretary-General and other international organizations and bilateral partners, involved in the crisis' to report to it.²⁷⁹

Political Process and Control The settings in the CAR where a subregional peacekeeping operation was already deployed once the civil war started, induced that the political process – and thereby the political

---

²⁷³ P. D. Williams, S. A. Dersso, *Saving Strangers and Neighbors: Advancing UN–AU Cooperation on Peace Operations* (New York, International Peace Institute, 2015), 8–9; UN Doc. S/RES/2121 (2013), 6, para. 22.
²⁷⁴ UN Doc. S/2013/677 (2013), 6–11, paras. 26–47.
²⁷⁵ Statement by the Deputy Secretary-General, UN Doc. S/PV.7069 (2013), 4.
²⁷⁶ UN Doc. S/RES/2127 (2013), 9, paras. 46–48; AU Doc. PSC/PR/2.(CDXXII) (2014), 1–2, paras. 3–5; 4, para. 16.
²⁷⁷ UN Doc. S/2015/229 (2015), 4, para. 12.
²⁷⁸ UN Doc. S/RES/2127 (2013), 7, para. 28.
²⁷⁹ Ibid., 7, para. 32.

control – for the resolution of the conflict was at least primarily steered by the AU and ECCAS.

The AU Special Representative and Head of MISCA and the ECCAS Mediator and Chairman of its Follow-up Committee on the CAR were in fact steering the political process in coordination 'with members of the international community'.[280] The UN deployed a mediation support team in support of the ECCAS mediation which provided advice on the process, help in drafting of the outcome document, as well as logistical support to rebel groups to ensure their participation in the peace talks held in Libreville.[281] Further support was provided *in loco* by the UN Integrated Peacebuilding Office in the Central African Republic (BINUCA).[282] The mandate of BINUCA was updated and expanded in Resolution 2121. The SC decided to include in its mandate support for the implementation of the transition process and for the coordination of the international actors involved.[283]

UN-Assessed Contributions The AU called for a UN logistical support package for MISCA financed by UN-assessed contributions on several occasions, as well as for a fully fledged support package.[284] Before the AU had already issued calls to the international community to support the ECCAS operation MICOPAX financially.

In Resolution 2127, the Security Council decided to deploy UN experts to support MISCA by providing additional technical surge capacity, including in the areas of mission support, communications and military and police planning.[285] Nonetheless, the Council underlined again that regional organisations are responsible to provide their own funding for peacekeeping operations under their authority.[286] However, the Council called on other international organisations and states to provide funding and welcomed the willingness of the EU to provide funding for that purpose.[287] Following the adoption of Resolution 2127 and the transfer of authority to MISCA, the UN Secretary-General intended to advocate for a

---

[280] PSC/AHG/4(CDXVI) (2013), 1, para. 4.
[281] UN Doc. S/2013/261 (2013), 4, para. 18; S/RES/2121 (2013), 3, para. 4.
[282] UN Doc. S/RES/2088 (2013), 1, Preamble.
[283] UN Doc. S/RES/2121 (2013), 4, para. 10.
[284] Statement by Ambassador Tete Antonio, African Union Permanent Representative to the United Nations, Security Council, 6 March 2014, 3.
[285] UN Doc. S/RES/2127 (2013), 8, para. 37; UN Doc. S/2015/3 (2015), 7.
[286] UN Doc. S/RES/2127 (2013), 8, para. 41.
[287] Ibid., 8, para. 42.

support package for MISCA which prompted the AU to suggest the development of a strategic concept to provide a comprehensive and integrated approach in this matter.[288] These plans were once again not fruitful, but financial support was provided by the EU.

EU Support Missions and Financial Support   The Council of the EU agreed on 20 January 2014 that it would deploy a military operation to contribute to the protection of civilians in coordination with the French forces and the AU and for that purpose asked for a SC mandate.[289] The decision was welcomed by AU[290] which had previously noted positively the consultations between the EU and the UN about where an EU military operation could effectively support MISCA.[291] EUFOR RCA was deployed as a bridging operation with the view to hand it over to MISCA or a UN peacekeeping operation.[292] The CAR also granted its consent to the deployment of EUFOR RCA.[293] The military and police concepts of operation of MINUSCA were actually reviewed together with those of EUFOR RCA and Operation Sangaris, which was deployed by France.[294]

The EU provided 125 million Euros to MISCA under the African Peace Facility which covered the cost of allowances, accommodation, nutrition. Salaries of Civilian MISCA personnel and operational costs such as transport, communication and medical services were also supported.[295] The EU had already worked in a 'close and action-oriented partnership' with the AU for the provision of funding for MICROPAX.[296]

EUFOR RCA provided one liaison officer to MISCA and later on two to MINUSCA. The EU troops conducted joint patrols with MINUSCA military forces.[297] Following the transfer of authority from MISCA to MINUSCA and thus the successful completion of EUFOR RCA as a bridging operation, the EU deployed a new military advisory operation (EUMAM RCA) to help the CAR in the reform of its security

---

[288] UN Doc. S/2014/117 (2014), 5.
[289] UN Doc. S/2014/45 (2014), 2.
[290] UN Doc. (S/2014/99) (2014), 5, para. 15.
[291] AU Doc. PSC/AHG/COMM.2(CDXVI), 4, para. 15.
[292] Council Conclusions 8651/14 (2014), 2, para. 2.
[293] UN Doc. S/2014/34 (2014).
[294] Statement by the UN, UN Doc. S/PV.7329 (2014), 3; AU press release, 24 May 2014.
[295] EU Commission Fact Sheet, The EU Engagement with the CAR, 26 May 2015, 1.
[296] AU Doc. PSC/PR/2.(CCCXLV) (2012).
[297] UN Doc. S/2014/858 (2014), 6, para. 14.

forces.[298] For that purpose, the EU acts in cooperation and coordination with the UN.[299]

Assessment The analysis of AFISMA demonstrated such a high degree of cooperation on all levels that it was called a truly 'monolithic' peacekeeping operations. In contrast to AFISMA, MISCA, can only be seen as monolithic with regard to the planning, mandating and establishment of the operation which was a concerted approach by the AU, ECCAS, the UN and – in a more limited role – the EU. Due to the transition from a subregional operation into a regional – AU-led – operation, the AU was the main political actor steering the political process right from the beginning, jointly with ECCAS.

There was consequently nearly no room for the UN to get involved on its own and to shape the political process or to exercise influence on MISCA during its deployment. The biggest surprise in comparison with the previous case study of Mali is that there is virtually no input and shared command and control on the mission level between the AU, the UN and the EU. Therefore, the conduct of MISCA cannot be jointly attributed to the UN, the EU and the AU.

Two reasons might explain why on the one hand, there is a truly this abundance of cooperation with regard to the planning, mandating and establishment of MISCA, and on the other hand no real external contribution or shared command and control on the mission level.

First of all, MISCA was deployed with the clear understanding between all organisations that it will be transformed into a UN Peacekeeping operation sooner or later. Secondly, learning from Mali where the relationship between the AU and the UN was slightly affected by what the AU considered to be not a sufficient degree of consultation for the transition of AFISMA to MINUSA, MISCA was planned and coordinated from the earliest stages on between ECCAS, the AU, the UN and also the EU. All these organisations contributed to the concept of operations, the mandate of the operation and cooperated through the transition phase. Consequently the transition was comparatively smoothly and there was afterwards no necessity for the UN to cooperate with the AU in-mission as it had effectively determined the 'design' of MISCA as much as the AU. The EU provided extensive funding to MISCA under the AFP and could thereby further

---

[298] Council Conclusions 6044/15 (2015), 19; Council Decision 5024/15 (2015).
[299] Council Decision 2015/78/CFSP, 1, para. 2; 2, Article 1.

influence the mandate and deployment of MISCA. Generally, all three organisations were acting in their respective roles as they have developed in practice, based on the idea of a division of labour for the mutual advantage of all organisations.

MINUSCA

The AU had 'from the outset, envisaged the transformation, at the appropriate time of [MISCA] into a UN peacekeeping operation'.[300] The CAR called on the SC in January 2014 to deploy a UN peacekeeping operation. The AU expressed its support for that idea once the required conditions had been met.[301] This view was echoed by the Secretary-General.[302] He therefore recommended the immediate deployment of a transition team, in coordination with the AU and MISCA and BINUCA participation which should develop strategic plans, 'most importantly a mission concept and related concepts of operation' and initiate the construction of necessary facilities.[303]

In order to facilitate the transition, the AU also asked for more international support, including the provision of additional financial and logistical resources and technical expertise and provision of support in other specific areas.[304] The Security Council then requested the Secretary-General to report back, after a joint assessment mission with the AU, on the state of preparation for the joint transition.[305]

As one of the lessons learned from the transition of AFISMA to MINUSA, the AU called very early on the UN and stated that it 'would welcome the co-authoring of the draft resolution with one of the African members of the UN Security Council' in line with a previously adopted AU communiqué and in the form of 'the designation of African states as penholders/co-penholders of draft resolution [sic] that concern the continent'.[306] Later on the AU noted with satisfaction the close consultation between the penholder (France) and the African side throughout the drafting of SC Resolution 2149 authorising the deployment of MINUSCA.[307]

---

[300] UN Doc. S/2014/172 (2014), 21, para. 77; PSC/PR/2.(CDXXII) (2014), 5, para. 20.
[301] UN Doc. S/2014/142 (2014), 12, paras. 53–54.
[302] Ibid., 13, para. 55; 22–23, para. 103.
[303] Ibid., 20, para. 93.
[304] UN Doc. S/2014/172 (2014), 21, para. 76.
[305] Un Doc. S/2014/149 (2014), 8, para. 27.
[306] AU Doc. PSC/PR/2.(CDXXII) (2014), 6, para. 20(v); PSC/AHG/COMM/1.(CCCXCVII) (2013), 3, para. 8a, v; C. Hull Wiklund, G. Ingerstad, *The Regionalisation of Peace Operations in Africa. Advantages, Challenges and the Way Ahead* (2015), FOI, 30–31.
[307] AU press release 12 April 2014.

As part of the authorisation for the deployment of MINUSCA, BINUCA was absorbed into MINUSCA.[308] Similar to Resolution 2127 establishing MISCA, Resolution 2149 authorising the deployment of MINUSCA foresaw the deployment of military enablers to MINUSCA before the transfer of authority from MISCA to MINUSCA.[309]

Generally the SG declared that the SC could consider the authorisation of 'soft' logistical support packages or technical support teams for AU operations or even the 'early deployment of UN expertise and military enablers, including engineering assets and tactical lift capabilities' which would enhance the capacity and effectiveness of AU operations and facilitate a seamless transfer of authority.[310]

Generally, the AU emphasised that following the transfer of authority to a UN peacekeeping operation, the AU and ECCAS must continue to play a crucial role in the political and other fields of MINUSCA.[311]

Mandate Similar to MISCA, MINUSCA was established with an explicit protection of civilian mandate.[312] An interesting feature of MINUSCA's mandate which was the first for a peacekeeping operation was that due to the complete breakdown of law, order and justice in the Central African Republic, part of its mandate included law enforcement tasks on an exceptional basis and 'without creating a precedent and without prejudice to the agreed principles of peacekeeping'.[313]

Political Process and Political Control There were 'intensive consultations on the political process ... and joint planning and coordination processes to ensure smooth transition' from MISCA to MINUSCA among the UN, the AU and the EU.[314] Strong engagement took place by the UN with the EU throughout the planning and start-up phases of the mission in the CAR and in the transition phases; at political and strategic levels cooperation between the SC and the EU PSC continue to grow.[315] On a broader scale, the transition to MINUSCA and coordination of international

---

[308] UN Doc. S/RES/2149 (2014), 7, para. 19.
[309] Ibid., 8, para. 23.
[310] UN Doc. S/2015/3 (2015), 10.
[311] UN Doc. S/2014/172 (2014), 22, para. 80.
[312] UN Doc. S/RES/2149 (2014), 9, para. 30.
[313] Ibid., 12–13, para. 40.
[314] UN Doc. A/69/642 (2014), 28, paras. 108–109.
[315] UN Doc. A/69/642 (2014), 29, para. 112.

efforts occurred through the International Contact Group on the CAR, co-chaired by the AU and the Republic of Congo as chair of the ECCAS Follow-up Committee on the CAR.

A rather self-confident AU – and once again relying on the lessons learned from Mali – therefore also called on the UN to acknowledge and 'strongly support the role of the region, and the AU in the post-MISCA phase' so that MINUSCA will be anchored on strong regional and continental support, thus the UN was asked to support efforts by ECCAS and AU for the political process.[316] From that perspective, the AU effectively conditioned its approval to a UN follow-up operation to MISCA as the UN Security Council was asked to acknowledge and support the leading role of the region and the AU in the post-MISCA phase. On the other hand, it should not be forgotten that the AU is dependent on external support so that the role of these statements needs to be relativised. They can equally be seen as a defence of the AU's legitimacy towards ECCAS and the other international actors being part of the contact group. Just a few weeks later, an International Mediation group was established under the authority of the EECAS Mediator and comprising UN and AU representatives as Deputy Mediators.[317] Another arrangement needs to be mentioned with regard to the steering of the political process and political control (over MINUSCA), which is the Group of Five (UN, AU, EU, US and France) who conducted weekly meetings and conference calls as part of finding a political solution to the crisis in the CAR.[318] It was later expanded to the Group of Eight with MISCA, MINUSCA and ECCAS as additional members.[319] The Mediators work in close support with the Group of Eight for which MINUSCA also provides secretariat support.[320] In fact, MINUSCA 'played a central role in the activities of the so-called "G8-Forum" of the International Contact Group'.[321] The Security Council recognised the important role of the region in mediation under the active leadership of ECCAS and requested MINUSCA to support the AU and ECCAS for that purpose.[322]

---

[316] Statement by the AU, UN Doc. S/PV.7128 (2014), 11. See also S/RES/2149 (2014), 12, para. 36.
[317] Fifth Meeting of the International Contact Group on the Central African Republic (ICG-CAR), 7 July 2014, Conclusions, 3, para. 13 (iii); UN Doc. S/RES/2149 (2014), 5, para. 4; S/2014/812 (2014), 2, para. 4.
[318] UN Doc. S/2013/787 (2013), 5, para. 21.
[319] Statement by the Head of MINUSCA, UN Doc. S/PV/7246 (2014), 2.
[320] UN Doc. S/2015/227 (2015), 6, para. 29.
[321] UN Doc. A/69/633 (2014), 7, para. 14.
[322] UN Doc. S/RES/2217 (2015), 6, para. 4; 14, para. 41.

Strategic Control Control on the strategic level of MISCA and MINUSCA also profited from lessons learned from the previously deployed operation in Mali. In Mali, the Joint Operations Centre of AFISMA was dissolved pending the transition to MINUSMA. In the CAR, the previous two joint operation centres of MISCA and MINUSCA were combined in order to facilitate the transition from MISCA to MINUSCA.[323] The UN also provided training to those trainers for MISCA military and police personnel which would be rehatted.[324]

Assessment In a letter to the Security Council, the Secretary-General stated that the lessons learned exercise of Mali and the CAR generally underlined the necessity to ensure that mandates by the SC and the AU PSC for 'operations supported by both operations are developed through close consultations'.[325] The deployment of MISCA and MINUSCA can be seen as the prime example for close cooperation in planning and mandating peacekeeping operations. Whereas in Mali, the UN ultimately had to take over sooner from AFISMA as planned, MISCA was deployed in the clear understanding that it would be transformed into a UN operation. The key for the transitions in both Mali and the CAR were specific instructions by the SC on the conduct of joint strategic assessments and planning processes.[326] The close cooperation of the UN, the AU, ECCAS and the EU in planning and mandating both operations is mirrored on the political level and in the political process for peace. However, there is no real inter-organisational cooperation on the strategic and tactical mission level of MINUSCA.

There are several reasons which could explain this surprising duality of full cooperation on the one hand, and no cooperation among international organisations on the other. First of all, from the outset the conflict in the CAR was dealt with on a subregional and a regional level. MICOPAX had been deployed in the CAR since 2008. From the perspective of ECCAS and the AU they were therefore in charge with regard to finding a peaceful solution to the conflict in the CAR. The transfer of authority from a subregional to a regional African peacekeeping operation also limited the possibility of external actors to contribute to and to cooperate in the operationalisation of MISCA. African boots and command structures were already on the ground and subsequently rehatted from MICOPAX

---

[323] UN Doc. S/2015/3 (2015), 5; S/2014/562 (2014), 15, para. 64.
[324] UN Doc. S/2014/562 (2014), 15, para. 64.
[325] UN Doc. S/2015/3 (2015), 3.
[326] Ibid.

to MISCA. Another aspect is the growing maturity of the AU which is seeking more of a leadership role for maintaining international peace and security on the African continent and the understanding within the international community of African ownership for African problems.

The multiplication of actors on the political level in the form of the International Contact Group, the Group of Five and later on the Group of Eight might also have prevented the UN, the EU and the AU to develop strong cooperation arrangements on the mission level of MISCA and MINUSCA respectively. Bearing in mind that all three organisations cooperated very closely in the mandating and planning process of MISCA and MINUSCA, they might not have considered it necessary to be actively involved on the strategic and tactical mission level. Both peacekeeping operations were effectively formed from the very outset, according to the wishes of all three organisations and with the perspective that MISCA would be transformed into a UN operation.

What is evident following the analysis of the case studies of Mali and the CAR is that future peacekeeping operations will involve even more planning and cooperation before the deployment of an operation by the involved international organisations. In that regard, the case study of MISCA and MINUSCA can be called a harbinger of the recommendations for the future of cooperation in peacekeeping operations by the High-Level Independent Panel, as well as in the Implementation Report of the Secretary-General.

Another consequence of the focus of the three international organisations on cooperation in the planning and mandating of MISCA and MINUSCA is that they cannot be seen as jointly responsible for the conduct of both operations on the basis of the normative control criterion. The very limited input or rather the lack of cooperation on the tactical and strategical level of both operations does not justify also attributing the conduct of MISCA to the UN and the EU, nor the attribution of the conduct of MINUSCA to the AU, the EU in addition to the UN. It was argued previously that the lack of cooperation between international organisations in one aspect may be remedied – for the purposes of the attribution of conduct – by increased cooperation in other areas. It was also emphasised that the nexus of the political level of control and control over the mission is the key element to allow the joint attribution of conduct in peacekeeping operations. Future peacekeeping operations might become more integrated in the sense that their deployment and the steering of the political process will be steered even more by a plurality of international organisations than in the cases of Mali and the CAR. Consequently, the constant evolution of the cooperation of international organisations in peacekeeping operations might necessitate an adjustment of the criterion of normative control in the future in order to further guarantee the effective administration of justice. International Law is constantly evolving and reasons of justice, legitimacy and credibility dictate that the rules regulating the conduct of international organisations and states develop accordingly.

The Attempt of a Typology of Intra-mission Relationships, Its Implications on International Responsibility and a Clarification of the Normative Control Criteria

The inquiry into the eight different peacekeeping operations allowed defining further the contours of the suggested criterion of attribution in the context of cooperation in peacekeeping operations. The analysis also showed that the cooperation arrangements existing in each peacekeeping operation are unique for a variety of reasons, including political and security interests of the involved actors, the availability and lack of resources and institutional cooperation agreements.

Nevertheless, this part of the chapter will now attempt to establish a typology of possible relationships in intra-mission cooperation, based on the different levels of control and cooperation, as part of the operational framework of a peacekeeping operation. Naturally, such an exercise would be more probative where an analysis was conducted of all peacekeeping operations of the organisations which include a cooperative element, but such an exercise would go beyond the scope of the present study.

The examination of the eight operations showed that the mandate of the operations was developed on the basis of cooperation in all operations, aside from UNMISS and UNISFA.[327] Regarding the political level, seven operations, excluding UNMISS, included cooperation arrangements on the political level, partially stretching over to the strategic level. Once again, the degree of cooperation in this particular field varies, from limited support by the AU and ECOWAS to MINUSMA over equal participation of both the AU and the UN on the political level, exclusive strategic control of the UN to joint strategic planning of the UN and KFOR or even the exercise of a high amount of strategic control directly by the peacekeeping

---

[327] In addition to Security Council Resolution 1244, KFOR's powers are also derived from the MTA concluded.

operation, as in the case of UNAMID. Regardless of these differences, this comparison confirms the particular relevance of cooperation and control on a political level for the attribution of conduct.

On the operational level, UNMISS and UNISFA are under the exclusive control of the UN and KFOR is under the exclusive control of NATO. Operational control over AFISMA was effectively executed by all four organisations, whereas MINUSMA is under UN control, but supported by the AU and ECOWAS. Bearing in mind the debate surrounding the adoption of MINUSMA's mandate, when the AU ultimately complained of the lack of consultation in the adoption of the mandate, one could prima facie reason that this debate has diminished the involvement of both organisations on the operational level. MISCA was under AU operational control and MINUSCA is under operational control of the UN.

However, the analysis showed that the AU and the ECOWAS were eager to contribute to MINUSMA on an operational level and this fact rather points towards a general distinction between UN and UN-mandated operations. It appears that the UN is less willing to incorporate the contribution of other actors in its own operations than it is willing to participate itself in UN-authorised operations. This particular behaviour is, of course, conditioned also by the role of the UN in maintaining international peace and security and its long experience, but nevertheless, it could also be an expression of a certain *chasse gardée* the UN maintains, in practice. The case study of the CAR confirms this hypothesis, at least to a certain extent, as in both operations the input of the respective external operations on the operational level was very limited.

Consequently, a first clarification to identify a case of normative control triggering the joint responsibility of international organisations can accordingly be formulated. If the peacekeeping operation is a UN operation, the amount and level of intra-mission cooperation is likely to be more limited than in the case of a non-UN operation, so that it is consequently also less likely that the required threshold of cooperation will be surpassed to justify an application of the normative control criteria.[328] Furthermore, one can formulate a general presumption that a partially competitive relationship between two international organisations will translate into political cooperation in a peacekeeping operation and less operational cooperation. This nexus between political control and control on other operational levels is required to trigger and justify the application of the criterion of normative control. In this regard, one can

---

[328] Cf. in this regard UN Doc. A/70/95 and S/2015/446 (2015), 27, para. 47.

formulate another general presumption. If the deployment of the peacekeeping operation and the political process is based on a comprehensive approach steered by the same institutional actors, it reinforces the control and oversight executed over the operation by all these institutional actors, increasing thereby the likelihood of a case of joint responsibility. The findings of the previous chapters, as in this chapter, further allow writing in full a definition of the normative control criterion as developed throughout this study:

(1) Internationally wrongful acts committed during the deployment of a peacekeeping operation may be jointly attributed to two or several international organisations if:

  a) the international organisation(s), other than the international organisation(s) under whose auspices the peacekeeping operation is deployed, effectively exercise the same degree of control over the conduct of the peacekeeping operation as the deploying organisation(s) on the basis of:

    (i) existing cooperation arrangements and mechanisms on an inter-institutional level between the external organisation(s) and the deploying operation(s) with regard to peacekeeping operations and;
    (ii) existing cooperation arrangements and mechanisms on the mission level between the external organisation(s) and the deploying organisation(s); and
    (iii) a direct and immediate link between these cooperation arrangements and mechanisms on a political level and those cooperation arrangements and mechanisms on a tactical and strategic level in existence between the external organisation(s) and the deploying organisation(s) so that command and control over the operation is effectively shared (normative control).

  b) That article is without prejudice to the question if one or several member states of the international organisation(s) under whose auspices the peacekeeping operation is deployed may be also responsible for internationally wrongful acts occurring during the deployment of the operation on the basis of the relevant dispositions of the Articles on the Responsibility of International Organisations.

In this context, a direct and immediate link has to be interpreted in the sense that the exercise of political control is in fact indivisible from the exercise of control on both strategic and tactical levels of command and control.

To return to Virally's classification of relations between international organisations,[329] all the peacekeeping operations, which were used as case studies, show that the relations between these organisations are based on coordination and cooperation, rather than confrontation. A variety of reasons were established throughout this study for this development which is even more evident on the institutional level. The lack of resources in various areas is one main reason and it also explains why the relations among the organisations are not completely free of competition. However, one can even go so far to ask as to whether regional organisations are not even obliged to carry out the decisions of the Security Council with regard to the deployment of a peacekeeping operation.

Chapter 1 traced the mechanisms for cooperation with regional organisations under the UN Charter, but *en passant* it mentioned the basic fact that regional organisations per se as non-members of the UN are not directly bound by the Charter. In the analysis presented in this book, we have seen the development of institutionalised relations between the UN and regional organisations, both on the institutional level, as well as in the operational context so that it does not '[seem] to be sufficient' to consider only member states bound by the UN Charter, but also certain regional organisations, contrary to what is asserted in the Commentary to Article 48(2) of the UN Charter.[330]

Therefore, on the basis of an analysis of the potential legal foundations, it might be possible to shed even more light upon the application of the normative control criterion to peacekeeping operations. If regional organisations were obliged to cooperate or even to implement decisions of the Security Council, it would raise questions with regard to direction and control in the context of cooperation in peacekeeping operations. Could the UN be responsible on the basis of the fact that regional organisations were obliged to carry out its decision regarding the deployment of a peacekeeping operation and how would that impair the responsibility of these regional organisations?

---

[329] See Chapter 2.
[330] A. Reinisch, G. Novak, 'Article 48', in B. Simma, D.-E. Khan, G. Nolte et al. (eds.), *The Charter of the United Nations. A Commentary*, Volume I (Oxford University Press, 2012), 1376, 1381 mn. 10.

Chapter VIII Revisited – Regional Organisations as Being Bound by the System of Collective Security

Regarding the question of whether the UN Charter and particularly decisions of the Security Council are binding upon entities which are non-members of the UN, Article 2(6) of the Charter comes to mind. According to that disposition, the organisation 'shall ensure that states which are not Members of the United Nations act in accordance with these Principles so far as may be necessary for the maintenance of international peace and security'. In addition, Article 48(2) of the UN Charter stipulates that decisions of the Security Council for maintaining international peace and security shall be carried out by the Members of the UN 'directly and through their action in the appropriate international agencies of which they are members'.

The wording and the context of Article 2(6) do not suggest that the obligations therein do extend to other international organisations.[331] However, in the Commentary it is argued that the limited scope of Article 2(6) does not allow the organisation to adequately address external threats to international peace and security and accordingly it has been 'superseded by a universal system of collective security which is based upon the relevant Charter provisions but does not derive its legal force from the Charter as a treaty ... [i]t subjects all relevant international actors to the authority of the UN, and in particular the SC, with regard to measures necessary for the maintenance of international peace and security'.[332] They are all 'under an obligation to give the UN every assistance in any action it takes in accordance with the Charter; and in particular to accept and carry out the decisions of the SC'.[333] The practice of the UN and states and non-member states confirms that the UN is competent to create obligations for members and non-members alike.

In 1953, the Security Council had already expressed the view that it can create obligations for non-members; in Resolution 101 the Council recalled 'to the Governments of Israel and Jordan', non-members at that time, their obligations under Security Council Resolutions and reaffirmed 'that it is essential ... that the parties abide by their obligations under ... the resolutions of the Security

---

[331] S. Talmon, 'Article 2(6)', in B. Simma, D.-E. Khan, G. Nolte, et al. (eds.), *The Charter of the United Nations. A Commentary*, Volume I (Oxford University Press, 2012), 252, 262 mn. 32.
[332] Ibid., 252, 265, mn. 39–41.
[333] Ibid., 252, 265, mn. 40.

Council'.³³⁴ Since the adoption of Resolution 418 in 1977, the Security Council has addressed all resolutions containing binding obligations regarding sanctions to all states, although at that time, there were still more than ten states which were not members of the organisation.³³⁵ The Security Council made clear in that resolution that it is binding upon all states.³³⁶

The reference to non-members of the organisation has been continuously replaced over the years with references to all international and regional organisations, starting in 1991. Organisations such as the EU 'have consistently implemented economic and other sanctions decisions of the SC, indicating an intention to be bound'.³³⁷ Talmon argues that, although the EU is not bound by the UN Charter per se, it is 'subject to the universal system of collective security and thus bound to comply with the decisions of the SC',³³⁸ a view which seemed to be confirmed in Declaration 13 annexed to the Treaty of Lisbon, according to which the EU per se, as well as its member states remain bound by the provisions of the Charter of the UN, including the primary responsibility of the Security Council for the maintenance of international peace and security.³³⁹

Member states of the UN have expressed repeatedly over the years the opinion that the powers of the UN with respect to maintaining international peace and security apply also to non-members.³⁴⁰ The ICJ in the *Namibia* advisory opinion held that non-members of the UN were not bound by Article 24 and 25 of the Charter, but that certain decisions of the SC are 'opposable to all States ... [and] that it is for non-member States to

---

³³⁴ UN Doc. S/RES/101 (1953), paras. B2, C1. Cf. also SC Resolutions 50 and 54 which were also addressed at Israel and Jordan when they were non-members of the organisation, UN Doc. S/RES/50 (1948); S/RES/54 (1948).

³³⁵ Talmon, 'Article 2(6)', supra note 331, 252, 268, mn. 46; 268–269, mn. 47–48.

³³⁶ C. Tomuschat, 'Obligations Arising for States Without or Against Their Will', *Recueil des cours de l'Académie de La Haye*, Volume 241 (1993), 195, 245.

³³⁷ Talmon, 'Article 2(6)', supra note 331, 252, 269, mn. 49; see also D. Bethlehem, 'The European Union', in V. Gowlland-Debbas (ed.), *National Implementation of United Nations Sanctions. A Comparative Study* (Leiden, Brill, 2004), 123–165.

³³⁸ Talmon, 'Article 2(6)', supra note 331, 252, 269 mn. 50.

³³⁹ Declaration concerning the common foreign and security policy, Declarations annexed to the Final Act of the Intergovernmental Conference which adopted the Treaty of Lisbon, Signed on 13 December 2007; 30 March 2010, Official Journal of the European Union, C 83/343, 9.

³⁴⁰ Several members, for example, expressed the view that Indonesia would remain 'amenable to the jurisdiction of the Security Council', when the country decided to withdrew from the UN. Also for further references Talmon, 'Article 2(6)', supra note 331, 275, mn. 64.

act in accordance with those decisions'.³⁴¹ Although the Court's advisory opinion was given within the specific circumstances of the *Namibia* case, the termination of the mandate, it nevertheless shows that non-member states are supposed to assist actions taken by the UN.

In the *Kosovo* advisory opinion, the ICJ had another opportunity to express its views on the issue and the judges declared that 'it has not been uncommon for the Security Council to make demands *on actors other than* United Nations Member States and *inter-governmental organizations*' [emphasis added].³⁴² So it appears, the ICJ considered it to be existing practice that the Security Council would adopt resolutions binding also upon international organisations.

Nevertheless, it raises questions about the legal basis of such a binding regime of collective security which transcends the boundaries of the UN Charter. One possibility would be to rely on the dictum in the *Reparations* judgment of the ICJ regarding 'the objective international personality' with which the UN was created and to argue that the majority of the international community could create an objective and universal system of collective security.³⁴³ However, as rightly pointed out by Talmon, it is very unlikely that the ICJ intended to attribute general law making power to the UN in its advisory opinion.³⁴⁴ Moreover, such an interpretation does not provide an answer regarding a valid source of international law for such a system. The lack of a legitimate basis in international law is the same problem encountered by arguments of constitutionalism which perceive the Charter as the constitution of the international community. Under this theory, the rules of the Charter supersede ordinary rules and are binding on all members of the international community.³⁴⁵ The problem with this theory is that its legal source is the preconceived idea on which it is based, so that in the end it is a circular argument.

The only realistic and legally sound argument is that on the basis of practice of the UN and the SC, the opinions expressed by member states

---

[341] Legal Consequences for States of the Continued Presence of South Africa in Namibia (South West Africa) Notwithstanding Security Council Resolution 276 (1970), Advisory Opinion (21 June 1971), paras. 126, 133.
[342] Accordance with International Law of the Unilateral Declaration of Independence in Respect of Kosovo, Advisory Opinion of 22 July 2010, para. 116.
[343] Reparation for Injuries Suffered in the Service of the United Nations, Advisory Opinion, 11 April 1949.
[344] Talmon, 'Article 2(6)', supra note 331, 252, 277 mn. 70. As quasi all states are now members of the UN, the argument of the objective international personality has also lost quite some value.
[345] Ibid., 252, 278, mn. 72–73.

and the practice of non-member states and regional organisations, 'at least since the 1990s, the provisions of the Charter dealing with international peace and security have acquired the status of customary international law that are binding on non-members, both States and non-State actors alike, independently of the Charter'.[346]

The present study has demonstrated that there is an abundance of interaction, practice and cooperation between the UN and regional organisations. In this context, the primary responsibility for maintaining international peace and security of the Security Council has been emphasised by all regional organisations which are part of this study in official documents, as well as in practice. The clear trend of regional organisations to seek the authorisation for the deployment of peacekeeping operations also suggests that regional organisations consider themselves to be bound by the provisions of the UN Charter, on a customary law basis.[347] One could therefore say that regional organisations have voluntary submitted themselves to the legal obligations which exist under the collective system for maintaining international peace and security.

Are there any implications for the attribution of conduct to international organisations for the purpose of the present study?

The short answer is yes. Considering regional organisations as being directly bound by the provisions of the UN Charter affects the attribution of conduct on a variety of levels.

Generally, the first question to ask is to what extent regional organisations can be seen as being directly bound by the UN Charter. The practice of an organisation does not only determine the interpretation of the constituent instrument of an international organisation and vice versa, but it can also shape the form and content of a developing customary norm to the extent that it is different from the corresponding written or codified rule. Thus, the customary rules for the maintenance of international peace and security by which regional organisations are bound do not necessarily entirely correspond to these obligations as laid down in the UN Charter.

---

[346] Ibid., 252, 279 mn. 75. See also A. Tzanakopoulos, *Disobeying the Security Council. Countermeasure against Wrongful Sanctions* (Oxford University Press, 2011), 78; T. M. Franck, 'Is the U.N. Charter a Constitution?', in J. A. Frowein, K. Scharioth, I. Winkelmann et al. (eds.), *Verhandeln für den Frieden – Negotiating for Peace. Liber Amicorum Tono Eitel* (Heidelberg, Springer, 2003), 95, 97. Klein, writing in 1992, stated that 'it is unanimously held today that the United Nations may direct sanctions against non-members as well as against members', E. Klein, 'Sanctions by International Organizations and Economic Communities', *Archiv des Völkerrechts*, 30 (1992), 101, 104.

[347] Cf. Article 38 of the 1986 VCLT between States and International Organizations or between International Organizations.

Moreover, due to the limited competences of international organisations which are unlike states, the analysed regional organisations are only bound by these customary rules which concern the area of international peace and security.

Under Chapter VIII, the SC may use regional organisations for peace enforcement operations. Presuming that the corresponding customary rule were to be identical, the Security Council could thereby directly oblige regional organisations to deploy peace enforcement operations. However, peacekeeping itself has developed in practice and is not explicitly provided for in the UN Charter. The analysis of the practice of the UN showed that mandates for peacekeeping operations are handed out to these states or groups of states and/or regional organisations which are willing to undertake the peacekeeping operation. Its mandating nature is therefore essentially voluntary, failing the implementation of Article 43 of the Charter.

Consequently, the Security Council could not oblige regional organisations under customary law to deploy a peacekeeping operation, unless it were to be argued that regional organisations are not only directly bound by the UN Charter (on a customary law basis), but that due to this submission under the UN Charter they are obliged to execute the decisions of the Security Council. In such a scenario, the UN would automatically assume responsibility on the international level as it would effectively direct and control – in terms of the ARIO – the regional organisation which would be bound to deploy the peacekeeping operation. However, it appears very unrealistic that these regional organisations would have wanted to submit themselves to such a degree under the authority of the UN, when they simultaneously emphasise their autonomy. In fact, one motivating factor for regional organisations to seek the authorisation of the Security Council is simply the consciousness that cooperation with the UN and division of labour are required.

From the perspective of the internal law of the UN, there is also an argument against this hypothesis. If one subscribes to the view, which was previously established, that the degree of the use of force authorised in a mandate handed out by the Security Council to a regional organisation determines if powers of the UN have been effectively transferred to the regional organisation,[348] only in such a case could one consider the UN directly responsible for the conduct of that peacekeeping operation.[349]

---

[348] See the case study of KFOR.
[349] By this logic, any authorisation by the Security Council addressed to a regional organisation going beyond the competences of the SC would not only be *ultra vires*, but it would also never entail a transfer of powers.

Theoretically, one could attempt to argue that the UN could simply oblige its members to adopt a decision in the regional organisation of which they are members to deploy a peacekeeping operation with a specific mandate, but as valid as this argument might appear from the perspective of UN internal law, on the level of international law, the independent legal personality of an international organisation would generally prevent such a possibility. Nevertheless, the fact that a mandate was handed out by the SC to a given regional organisation makes it more likely that this organisation will be jointly responsible with the UN than a third organisation which might be cooperating with this UN-authorised operation.[350]

Assessment

Starting with the different case studies with regard to the attribution of conduct, followed by an analysis of breach of an international obligation and an examination of relevant circumstances precluding wrongfulness, this chapter highlighted the complexity of the topic of the present study, as well as the legal uncertainties associated with many aspects, e.g., the question if and under which conditions regional organisations are directly bound by the UN Charter.

The case studies confirmed the previously formulated view that any appraisal of the attribution of conduct hinges on the specific circumstances of the case. In this context, in order to attribute the conduct of a peacekeeping operation to organisation(s) that are not part of the chain of command, an intimate link is necessary in the form of a strong nexus between the political control they exercise and control over the operational conduct of the operation. The existence of such a link could also serve as a main sign that the required threshold for an application of the criterion of normative control has been reached and that one of the involved organisations would assume the responsibility on behalf of the other involved organisations in any possibly existing case in court.[351]

The case studies confirmed furthermore that there is, indeed, a division of labour emerging between the different organisations regarding the deployment of peacekeeping operations, particularly with regard to the African continent. Depending on the specific situation, the involvement of each organisation varies in conformity with its defined niche within the established division of labour. With regard in particular to AFISMA,

---

[350] See Chapter 5, breach of an international obligation.
[351] Unless the Court would have jurisdiction over all involved organisations.

the question is also raised of whether the traditional distinctions between not only peacekeeping and peace enforcement operations, but also UN and UN-authorised operations are still valid or already out of date.[352] The cooperation mechanisms in AFISMA illustrated an involvement of the UN, and also other organisations, on various levels of command and control. MISCA and MINUSCA simultaneously confirm and relativise this assessment. On the one hand, the degree of cooperation on the political level was very high for both MISCA and MINUSCA, but on the other hand, the amount of cooperation on the strategic and operational level was rather limited.

The analysis demonstrated that there are good reasons to consider regional organisations being directly bound by the UN Charter on a customary law basis. It further showed that it would – at least theoretically – have an effect upon the attribution of conduct to international organisations. Nonetheless, one can hardly pinpoint the exact obligations which would arise for regional organisations directly under the UN Charter. This is not only due to the generally vague nature of customary law, but also due to the fact that peacekeeping operations themselves were not even explicitly provided for in the UN Charter and their exact origin under the Charter has been disputed ever since.

Attributing conduct to international organisations is the first step for establishing their responsibility under international law. Only if the conduct of the international organisation(s) gives rise to a breach of an international organisation will the international organisation(s) be responsible under international law. The next and final chapter will therefore analyse the rules of material law applicable to international organisations. As we will see the different sources and layers of international obligations in the context of this book further increase the likelihood of international organisations being jointly responsible, but they also create further problems.

---

[352] Cf. N. Blokker, 'The Security Council and the Use of Force: On Recent Practice', in N. Blokker, N. Schrijver (eds.), *The Security Council and the Use of Force: Theory and Reality. A Need for Change?* (Leiden, Martinus Nijhoff, 2005), 1, 15–17, 28.

5

The Law Applying in Peacekeeping Operations

This chapter explores the law applying to the conduct of peacekeeping operations during deployment in a conflict situation. The multidimensional nature of current peacekeeping operations means that peacekeeping troops engage in a variety of different activities of which many involve direct interaction with the local population. It was established in the previous chapters that current peacekeeping doctrines emphasise the protection of individuals as well as their basic rights, particularly under human rights and humanitarian law. Nevertheless, violations of international law occur during the deployment of peacekeeping operations.

The law applicable to the conduct of peacekeeping operations constitutes the primary rules upon which the law of international responsibility, as a system of secondary rules, is based. Therefore, any analysis of the international responsibility of a state or an international organisation requires an examination of the applicable primary rules. Consequently, this chapter examines the specific bodies of law applicable in peacekeeping operations and some of the intrinsic problems regarding their application.

On the basis of the fact that the UN and the four regional organisations which are part of this study possess international legal personality,[1] the following parts will examine the extent to which and in what ways they are bound by international norms during the deployment of peacekeeping operations.

The Applicable International Law to Peacekeeping Operations of International Organisations

In the case of peacekeeping and peace enforcement operations under the authority of international organisations, members of the military personnel are under 'double control' as troop-contributing states retain their control and authority regarding matters of discipline, finances, promotions

---

[1] See Chapter 2.

and punishment, despite having transferred operational command and control over their troops for the conduct of the operation to the respective international organisation. Therefore, the 'organic link' between the peacekeeping forces and their sending states is normally not completely dissevered and the troops remain bound by the international law obligations of their state even while exercising functions of the international organisation, as long as the former continues to exercise this form of limited control.[2]

Consequently, it is not surprising that several arguments brought forward and theories developed to determine the law applicable to international organisations, particularly in the human rights law context, rely on derivation or analogy, binding the international organisation indirectly through the obligations of states. Other approaches seek to bind international organisations directly, on the basis of their own international legal personality. In addition to human rights law, International Humanitarian Law (IHL) is also relevant insofar as it may be applicable during the specific context of a peacekeeping operation. The next part examines the application of human rights law to international organisations.

Application of International Human Rights Law to International Organisations

International Organisations as Bound by the Human Rights Obligations of Their Members

There are different doctrinal approaches used to argue for international organisations to be bound by the human rights of their member states' obligations. The majority of states have ratified international and regional human rights treaties, including the ICCPR, the ECHR, the Inter-American Convention on Human Rights and the African Charter on Human and Peoples' Rights.[3] The abovementioned doctrinal approaches seek to overcome the principle of relativity as it applies to international treaties on the basis of Article 34 VCLT and thus also for the various human rights treaties of which states exclusive are members.[4] One doctrinal approach is to

---

[2] R. Kolb, G. Porretto, S. Vité, *L'application du droit international humanitaire et des droits de l'homme aux organisations internationales. Forces de paix et administrations civiles transitoires* (Brussels, Bruyant, 2005), 252.

[3] Another relevant instrument is the Universal Declaration of Human Rights which, although it is not a treaty, has at least partially become customary international law.

[4] As a fundamental principle of international law, it is also arguably in any case valid on a customary law basis.

consider international organisations as successors or substitutes for the international human rights instruments to which their member states are parties.[5] In other words, the question is whether international organisations can be and are bound by the existing international obligations of their members or 'whether, since they are separate subjects of international law, they may in principle disregard any such pre-existing obligations'.[6] In its judgments in the cases of *Kadi* and *Yusuf*, the Court of First Instance ruled on this very specific question and held that the EC is not directly bound by the UN Charter and thereby not required to carry out – under general international law – decisions of the SC.[7]

The Court then concluded that the obligation to implement the Security Council Resolutions is not derived from the basis of general international law, but from internal EU law.[8] Another problem with the theory of succession is that it requires all member states of a given organisation to be bound by the very same obligations which are supposed to be imposed on the organisation; a requirement which becomes more and more theoretical, the more members a given organisation has.[9] Otherwise, there might be cases in which the nationality of the peacekeeper, be it for example French or Nigerian, would determine the applicable law. This theory is

---

[5] T. Ahmed, I. de Jesùs Butler, 'The European Union and Human Rights: An International Law Perspective', *The European Journal of International Law*, 17 (2006), 771–801; Critical of this theory, F. Naert, 'Binding International Organisations to Member State Treaties or Responsibility of Member States for Their Own Actions in the Framework of International Organisations' in J. Wouters, E. Brems, S. Smis (eds.), *Accountability for Human Rights Violations by International Organisations* (Antwerp, Intersentia, 2010), 129, 132.

[6] O. De Schutter, 'Human Rights and the Rise of International Organisations: The Logic of Sliding Scales in the Law of International Responsibility' in J. Wouters, E. Brems, S. Smis (eds.), *Accountability for Human Rights Violations by International Organisations* (Antwerp, Intersentia, 2010), 51, 58.

[7] T-135/01, *Yassin Abdullah Kadi v. Council of the European Union and Commission of the European Communities* [2005], para. 192; T-306/01, *Ahmed Ali Yussuf and Al Barakaat International Foundation v. Council of the European Union and Commission of the European Communities* [2005], para. 242.

[8] *Yassin Abdullah Kadi*, ibid., paras. 204, 207; *Ahmed Ali Yussuf*, ibid., paras. 254, 257.

[9] P. Klein, *La responsabilité des organisations internationales dans les ordres juridiques internes et en droit des gens* (Brussels, Bruylant, 1998), 342: In favour of this view, see M. Forteau, 'Le droit applicable en matière de droits de l'homme aux administrations territoriales gérées par des organisations internationales', in Société française pour le droit international/ Institut International des droits de l'homme, Journée d'études de Strasbourg. La soumission des organisations internationales aux normes internationales relatives aux droits de l'homme (2009), 7, 25–28; an opposing opinion was issued, e.g., by the Venice Commission, European Commission for Democracy through Law (Venice Commission), Opinion on Human Rights in Kosovo: Possible Establishment of Review Mechanisms, Opinion no. 280/ 2004, CDL-AD (2004) 033, 15, para. 78.

also problematic as it does not resolve the problem of international organisations not possessing territories of their own.[10]

Another attempt to make the obligations of member states applicable to international organisations is on the basis of the principle of *nemo plus juris transferre potest quam ipse habet*.[11] The idea is that 'as no one can transfer more powers than he has, the Member States were not competent to transfer any powers conflicting with ... treaties' concluded prior to the establishment of the international organisation.[12] As such international organisations never had the power to contravene the respective treaty or to act against it.[13] However, this argument fails to convince for the following reasons. First of all, it applies only when the respective international organisation is established after the ratification of the treaty in question.[14] Even more crucial is that this doctrine 'should correspond to any international obligation of any Member State of the organisation, without it being necessary that all Member States are bound by the said obligation'.[15] It is, as

---

[10] L. Cameron, 'Human Rights Accountability of International Civil Administrations to the People Subject to Administration', *Human Rights & International Legal Discourse*, 1 (2007), 267, 279.

[11] Forteau, 'Le droit applicable en matière de droits de l'homme', supra note 9, 7, 24. See also De Schutter, 'Human Rights and the Rise of International Organisations', supra note 6, 51, 62; B. Dold, *Vertragliche und ausservertragliche Verantwortlichkeit im Recht der internationalen Organisationen* (Zürich, Schulthess, 2006), 53–54; A. Peters, 'Article 25', in B. Simma, D.-E. Khan, G. Nolte et al. (eds.), *The Charter of the United Nations. A Commentary, Volume I* (Oxford University Press, 2012), 787, 820 mn. 105.

[12] Legal Consequences for States of the Continued Presence of South Africa in Namibia (South West Africa) Notwithstanding Security Council Resolution 276 (1970), Advisory Opinion (21 June 1971) (Judge Fitzmaurice, Dissenting Opinion), para. 65; H. G. Schermers, 'The European Communities Bound by Fundamental Human Rights', *Common Market Law Review*, 27 (1990), 249, 251.

[13] M. Tondini, 'The "Italian Job": How to Make International Organisations Compliant with Human Rights and Accountable for Their Violation by Targeting Member States' in J. Wouters, E. Brems, S. Smis (eds.), *Accountability for Human Rights Violations by International Organisations* (Antwerp, Intersentia, 2010), 169, 192–193; E. Abraham, 'The Sins of the Savior: Holding the United Nations Accountable to International Human Rights Standards for Executive Order Detentions in its Mission in Kosovo', *American University Law Review*, 52 (2002–2003), 1291, 1312–1313; H. Ascensio, 'Le Règlement des différents liés à la violation par les organisations internationales des normes rélatives aux droits de l'homme', in Société française pour le droit international/Institut International des droits de l'homme, Journée d'études de Strasbourg. *La soumission des organisations internationales aux normes internationales relatives aux droits de l'homme* (2009), 105, 119–120; L. Condorelli, 'Conclusions générales', in Société française pour le droit international/Institut International des droits de l'homme, ibid., 127, 129.

[14] Forteau, 'Le droit applicable en matière de droits de l'homme', supra note 9, 7, 25.

[15] De Schutter, 'Human Rights and the Rise of International Organisations', supra note 6, 51, 64; F. Naert, 'Binding International Organisations to Member State Treaties', supra note 5,

a result, not applicable in practice, especially for those organisations with an evolving membership such as the EU.[16] Supporters of this theory argue, however, that international organisations – as entities of delegated power – cannot dispose of a decision-making authority to define autonomously their position regarding the application of general international law.[17]

In the *Reparations* case, the ICJ also held that 'the subjects of law in any legal system are not necessarily identical in their nature or in the extent of their rights'.[18] Moreover, on the basis of the principle of speciality there will be cases in which international organisations simply lack the competence to act in the field of human rights.[19] Finally, this theory is completely impractical in its concrete application, as the nationality of a peacekeeper would also determine the applicable law.[20]

The problems related to these particular theories support the analysis of the obligations of international organisations by human rights obligations through other methods.

The Specific Case of Accession to Human Rights Treaties

The potential accession of international organisations to human rights treaties[21] also raises its own problems.

The absence of a real territorial basis, and of an administrative structure similar to governmental structures and the general limitation of powers of international organisations to those necessary for the fulfilment of their mandates, renders the conformity of action by the international

---

129, 134; Forteau, ibid., 7, 25. Forteau also points out that this theory has not been accepted in jurisprudence so far (ibid., 24).

[16] De Schutter, 'Human Rights and the Rise of International Organisations', supra note 6, 51, 65–66.

[17] Klein, *La responsabilité des organisations internationales*, supra note 9, 346; B. Rouyer-Hameray, *Les compétences implicites des organisations internationales* (Paris, Librairie générale de droit et de jurisprudence, 1962), 12; N. B. Krylov, 'International Organizations and New Aspects of International Responsibility', in W. E. Butler (ed.), *Perestroika and International Law* (Leiden, Martinus Nijhoff, 1990), 221–222. Also for a broader discussion of sovereignty of international organisations, M. Singer, 'Jurisdictional Immunity of International Organizations: Human Rights and Functional Necessity Concerns', *Virginia Journal of International Law*, 36 (1995), 53, 61–65.

[18] Reparation for Injuries Suffered in the Service of the United Nations, Advisory Opinion (11 April 1949), 8.

[19] Legality of the Use by a State of Nuclear Weapons in Armed Conflict, Advisory Opinion (8 July 1996), para. 25.

[20] Cameron, 'Human Rights Accountability', supra note 10, 267, 279.

[21] So far, it is only generally possible for the EU under the European Convention on Human Rights.

organisation with conventional requirements very difficult, if not impossible.[22] It means that 'whereas the organisation may be obliged to adopt certain measures, to the extent that human rights treaties impose certain positive obligations, it would only have to do so to the extent that this does not lead the organisation to go beyond the principle of speciality'.[23] It is debated in the doctrine what kind of obligations an accession to an international human rights treaty would entail for an international organisation.

On the one hand, it is suggested that accession to an international human rights instrument would not lead to a transfer of additional powers to the international organisation, however it could affect the exercise of any powers which had been attributed by the states to the extent that the organisation has positive obligations to protect the human rights which are enshrined in the treaty.

The other view is that due to the principle of specialty, the accession to human rights treaties would only impair negative obligations on the acceding international organisation as it should not lead to the transfer of additional powers to the organisation.[24] The argument made for the second view is that otherwise the international organisation would exercise powers which were not attributed to it, and that it should also only use the powers for the purposes for which they have been attributed. According to this view, the accession is equivalent to a change of the mandate of the organisation.[25]

---

[22] Klein, *La responsabilité des organisations internationales*, supra note 9, 319. This is also an argument raised by the UN against its non-accession to the Geneva Conventions, notwithstanding the question of the possibility for non-states to accede to these instruments (ibid.). A specific argument raised by the UN is its incapacity to satisfy the requirement as regards the repression of grave violations of the Conventions, however as argued also by other authors, the United Nations could establish a judicial organ charged with that function similarly to the ICTY and the ICTR (ibid., 320); see R. D. Glick, 'Lip Service to the Laws of War: Humanitarian Law and United Nations Armed Forces', *Michigan Journal of International Law*, 17 (1995), 53, 68–69.

[23] De Schutter, 'Human Rights and the Rise of International Organisations', supra note 6, 51, 114. On this specific point see also, infra 3.2.2.6.

[24] The European Convention, The Secretariat, Report from Chairman of Working group II 'Incorporation of the Charter/accession to the ECHR to Members of the Convention', CONV 354/02 (2002), 115.

[25] De Schutter, 'Human Rights and the Rise of International Organisations', supra note 6, 51, 115–116; Similarly, while referring explicitly to the EU, A. von Bogdandy, 'The European Union as a Human Rights Organization? Human Rights and the Core of the European Union', *Common Market Law Review*, 37 (2000), 1307, 1317. One has, however, to keep in mind that in order to accede to a Human Rights treaty, the international organisation does not need to possess competence in this specific area. Moreover, this argumentation fails to oversee the principle of implied powers as applicable to international organisations.

Should the EU still accede to the ECHR, it could be expected that the jurisprudence of the European Court of Human Rights would shed some light on these briefly mentioned and other related issues.

Human Rights Obligations of International Organisations as Part of General International Law

Apart from the theories which rely on binding international organisations through the obligations of their respective members, international organisations can be bound directly by human rights obligations as part of general international law. This includes 'general principles of (international) law' as well as customary international law. In contrast to the previously analysed theories, this approach has the advantage that the respective norms are directly applicable and that there is no need to use analogies or other legal methods. In contrast to the bulletin on IHL issued by the Secretary-General, there is not such a bulletin on human rights law which would have also facilitated the identification of certain human rights norms which could be applicable to peacekeeping forces.[26]

Human Rights Obligations of International Organisations on the Basis of Customary International Law

The existence of a rule of customary law presupposes the existence of state practice and *opinio iuris*.[27] Specifically in the field of human rights, it has been suggested that official declarations and participation in the negotiation of human rights conventions should be included as practice of states.[28] In favour of this proposition, it is suggested that one can hardly distinguish between the state practice and *opinio iuris*; the relevant state practice is legally significant as testifying to the emergence of a rule and the *opinio iuris* can only be detected and recognised on the basis of the state practice.[29]

---

[26] K. Grenfell, 'Applicability/Application of Human Rights Law to IOs involved in Peace Operations', in S. Kolanowski (ed.), *Proceedings of the Bruges Colloquium. International Organisations' Involvement in Peace Operations: Applicable Legal Framework and the Issue of Responsibility* (College of Europe, Bruges, 2011), 57–58; UN Doc. A/55/305 and S/2000/809 (2000), 14, para. 81.

[27] *North Sea Continental Shelf Cases (Federal Republic of Germany v. Denmark and Federal Republic of Germany v. the Netherlands)*, Judgment (20 February 1969), para. 77.

[28] Cf. Tondini, 'The "Italian Job"', supra note 13, 169, 191–192.

[29] De Schutter, 'Human Rights and the Rise of International Organisations', supra note 6, 51, 69; P.-M. Dupuy, 'L'unité de l'ordre juridique international, Cours général de droit international public', *Recueil des cours de l'Académie de La Haye*, 297 (2002), 9, 166; H. Charlesworth, 'Law-Making and Sources', in J. Crawford, M. Koskenniemi (eds.), *The Cambridge Companion to International Law* (Cambridge University Press, 2012), 187, 194.

Besides, human rights are traditionally concerned with the relationship between states and their nationals. The international community, and thereby the other states, have therefore normally reacted less frequently to violations of these rights than to violations of rules directly pertaining to inter-state relations as the latter directly touch upon their interests.[30] This argument might, however, have lost a degree of its pertinence due to the development of the concepts of humanitarian intervention and the responsibility to protect.

Other authors argue for a shifting of the importance of state practice or *opinio iuris*; the more strongly one is identified, the weaker the other may be.[31]

The proof of an existing customary norm on the basis of state practice and *opinio iuris* is nevertheless problematic in the context of the present study. As human rights primarily address states and have attained customary status because of State practice and *opinio iuris*, 'the question ... remains whether an international organisation can be bound by customary norms, which have become binding because of *State* practice'.[32] One can argue that the substance of each customary norm indicates its addressees; human rights law was conceived as binding states in the exercise of their power towards their citizens so that it would be – following this doctrine – not applicable to international organisations which are not in direct contact with human beings.[33] In response, it can be said that this doctrine blurs the difference between customary and treaty norms, as it applies the principle of relativity de facto to the formation of customary law. It therefore appears that, in practice, customary law is binding on all legal entities, including international organisations as long as there is no formal objection.[34]

---

[30] O. Schachter, *International Law in Theory and Practice. General Course on Public International Law*, Recueils des cours de l'Académie de La Haye, Volume 178 (1982), 12, 334. See also C. Tomuschat, *Human Rights. Between Idealism and Realism* (Oxford University Press, 2003), 34–35.

[31] F. Kirgis, 'Customs on a Sliding Scale', *The American Journal of International Law*, 81 (1987), 146, 149.

[32] B. Fassbender, 'Sources of Human Rights Obligations Binding the UN Security Council', in P. H. F. Bekker, R. Dolzer, M. Waibel (eds.), *Making Transnational Law work in the Global Economy* (Cambridge University Press, 2010), 71, 79–80.

[33] A. Bleckmann, 'Zur Verbindlichkeit des allgemeinen Völkerrechts für internationale Organisationen', *Heidelberg Journal of International Law*, 37 (1977), 107, 110–113.

[34] Cf. E. De Brabandere, 'Human Rights Accountability of International Administrations: Theory and Practice in East Timor', in J. Wouters, E. Brems, S. Smis (eds.), *Accountability for Human Rights Violations by International Organisations* (Antwerp, Intersentia, 2010), 331, 337; C. Tomuschat, *International Law: Ensuring the Survival of Mankind on the Eve of a New Century. General Course on Public International Law*, Recueil

Moreover, evolutionary interpretation has always been used in international law and it is now accepted that international organisations are bearers of rights and obligations under international law and this includes customary international law.[35] The fact of their coming into being later than states, and their resulting non-participation in the formation of certain rules, should not be decisive.[36] Any newly created state, such as the recent example of South Sudan shows, would be deemed bound by the whole body of customary law and there is no reason why it should be different for an international organisation.[37] The only legitimate argument to restrict the application of customary human rights law to international organisations cannot be derived from the customary nature of the norm, but is based on the principle of speciality; international organisations operating in specific fields which do not come into contact with individuals may not be bound by human rights. If their constituent instruments do not contain competences to operate in such a field,[38] the international organisation will be prevented to act[39] and it is on the basis of these internal

---

des cours de l'Académie de La Haye, Volume 281 (1999), 9, 134–135. See also B. Kondoch, 'Human Rights Law and UN Peace Operations in Post-Conflict Situations', in N. D. White, D. Klaasen (eds.), *The UN, Human Rights and Post-Conflict Situations* (Manchester University Press, 2005), 19, 36–41; V. Gowlland-Debbas, The Security Council and Issues of Responsibility under International Law, Recueil des cours de l'Académie de La Haye, Volume 535 (2012), 185, 366; F. Naert, *International Law Aspects of the EU Security and Defence Policy, with a Particular Focus on the Law of Armed Conflict and Human Rights* (Antwerp, Intersentia, 2010), 394; a similar opinion is expressed by F. Morgenstern, *Legal Problems of International Organizations* (Cambridge University Press, 1986), 32.

[35] Cf. Interpretation of the Agreement of 25 March 1951 between the WHO and Egypt, Advisory Opinion (20 December 1980), para. 37.

[36] Cf. I. R. Gunning, 'Modernizing Customary International Law: The Challenges of Human Rights', *Virginia Journal of International Law*, 31 (1990–1991), 212–213, 221–227; J. E. Alvarez, 'International Organizations: Then and Now', *American Journal of International Law*, 100 (2006), 324, 332.

[37] Against such a view, J. Klabbers, 'International Institutions', in J. Crawford, M. Koskenniemi (eds.), *The Cambridge Companion to International Law* (Cambridge University Press, 2012), 228, 235.

[38] Cf. also G. Porretto, S. Vité, *The Application of International Humanitarian Law and Human Rights Law to International Organizations*, Research Paper Series No. 1, CUDIH, Geneva (2006), 45–46; N. Quénivet, 'Human Rights Law and Peacekeeping Operations', in M. Odello, R. Piotrowicz (eds.), *International Military Missions and International Law* (Leiden, Brill, 2011), 99, 125; F. Mégret, F. Hoffmann, 'The UN as a Human Rights Violator? Some Reflections on the United Nations Changing Human Rights Responsibilities', *Human Rights Quarterly*, 25 (2003), 314, 317; Peters, 'Article 25', supra note 11, 787, 824 mn. 119; A. Clapham, *Human Rights Obligations of Non-State Actors* (Oxford University Press, 2006), 69; Cameron, 'Human Rights Accountability', supra note 10, 267, in particular 275–277.

[39] Of course, there would always be the possibility of acts *ulta vires* by an agent or organ of the organisation.

rules of the organisation that human rights law would not be wholly or partially applicable.[40] In other words, it is argued that, human rights can only bind an organisation so far as it has relevant competences.[41] It also has to be strongly emphasised that in peacekeeping operations another limitation arises in the form of the mandate handed out by the Security Council. Another approach in doctrine relies on an argument similar to the transfer of power of states to international organisations, stating that customary law applies to all subjects of international law, and consequently to international organisations which possess international legal personality.[42]

Moving away from the application *in abstracto* of human rights law, it is noted that an international organisation is only bound in a specific situation to the extent that the organisation 'exercises functions in a way that can be equated with the exercise of jurisdiction by a State'.[43] This is less problematic for international organisations which administer a territory because they exercise functions and powers which are traditionally prerogatives of states and these comprehensive powers facilitate the establishment of jurisdiction.[44] In contrast, the establishment of jurisdiction for situations in which an international organisation is not administering a territory is complex.[45] It is also important to consider customary human rights norms as being part of the customary law of the international organisation itself, and particularly of the UN. This proposition is however problematic as the relevant practice by international organisations since

---

[40] Cf. O. Engdahl, 'Applicability/Application of Human Rights Law', in S. Kolanowski (ed.), *Proceedings of the Bruges Colloquium. International Organisations' Involvement in Peace Operations: Applicable Legal Framework and the Issue of Responsibility* (College of Europe, Bruges, 2011), 66, 69.

[41] De Brabandere, 'Human Rights Accountability of International Administrations', supra note 34, 331, 338.

[42] H. G. Schermers, 'The Legal Bases of International Organization Action', in R.-J. Dupuy (ed.), *Manuel sur les organisations internationals – A Handbook on International Organizations* (Leiden, Brill, 1998), 401–402; Tomuschat, *Human Rights*, supra note 34, 9, 134–135.

[43] J. F. Kleffner, 'Human Rights and International Humanitarian Law: General Issues', in T. D. Gill, D. Fleck (eds.), *The Handbook of the International Law of Military Operations* (Oxford University Press, 2010), 51, 67.

[44] Cf. also Forteau, 'Le droit applicable en matière de droits de l'homme', supra note 9, 7, 14–16.

[45] As the jurisprudence on extraterritorial application of human rights instruments to states shows, there is no consensus on the exact requirement, but it is a rather casuistic assembly. An additional layer of difficulty resides in the mere fact that this jurisprudence cannot be transferred and applied, mutatis mutandis to international organisations; see later on in this chapter.

the foundation of the UN is limited, and comprises only two cases of international administration.[46]

Further controversy has arisen from the identification of the specific norms which are part of customary human rights law. In some parts of legal scholarship it is opined that the whole corpus of human rights law as incorporated in the Universal Declaration on Human Rights is applicable,[47] while others are of the view that only a few specific fundamental norms are part of customary human rights law.[48] In any case, it is not disputed that the most fundamental norms are deemed to be of a customary nature, for example, violations of the rights of life through murder, torture and arbitrary detention.[49] Other authors suggest that even the right to an effective remedy is of a customary nature and applicable to international organisations, which would presuppose a previous violation of another right.[50]

[46] De Brabandere, 'Human Rights Accountability', supra note 34, 331, 337.
[47] B. Simma, P. Alston, 'The Sources of Human Rights Law: Custom, Jus Cogens, and General Principles', *Australian Yearbook of International Law*, 12 (1988-1989), 82, 84–85; M. G. Kaladharan Nayar, 'Introduction: Human Rights: The United Nations and United States Foreign Policy', *Harvard International Law Journal* (1978), 813, 816–817; T. Buergenthal, 'The Evolving International Human Rights System', *American Journal of International Law*, 100 (2006), 783, 787.
[48] Schachter, *International Law in Theory and Practice*, supra note 30, 12, 333–342; O. Schachter, 'New Custom: Power, Opinio Juris and Contrary Practice', in J. Makarczyk (ed.), *Theory of International Law at the Threshold of the 21st Century: Essays in Honour of Krzystof Skubiszewski* (Leiden, Brill, 1996), 531, 538–540; also R. K. M. Smith, *Textbook on International Human Rights* (Oxford University Press, 2012), 38–39; T. Meron, *Human Rights and Humanitarian Norms as Customary Law* (Oxford University Press, 1989), 82–89; Rehman considers the majority of the dispositions in the UDHR to be representing customary human rights law, J. Rehman, *International Human Rights Law. A Practical Approach* (London, Longman, 2010), 80–81.
[49] A. Cunningham, 'The European Convention on Human Rights, Customary International Law and the Constitution', *International and Comparative Law Quarterly*, 43 (1994), 537, 544; C. Bongiorno, 'A Culture of Impunity: Applying International Human Rights Law to the United Nations in East Timor', *Columbia Human Rights Law Review*, 33 (2002), 623, 644–645; O. De Schutter, 'Human Rights and the Rise of International Organisations: The Logic of Sliding Scales in the Law of International Responsibility' in J. Wouters, E. Brems, S. Smis (eds.), *Accountability for Human Rights Violations by International Organisations* (Antwerp, Intersentia, 2010), 51, 72–73; E. De Brabandere, 'Human Rights Accountability of International Administrations: Theory and Practice in East Timor' in J. Wouters, E. Brems, S. Smis (eds.), ibid., 331, 336; J. Wouters, E. Brems, S. Smis (eds.), 'Introductory Remarks', in J. Wouters, E. Brems, S. Smis (eds.), ibid., 1, 6; Tomuschat, *Human Rights*, supra note 30, 4.
[50] K. Wellens, 'Fragmentation of International Law and Establishing an Accountability Regime for International Organizations: The Role of the Judiciary in Closing the Gap', *Michigan Journal of International Law*, 25 (2004), 1159, 1162; D. Shelton, *Remedies under International Human Rights Law* (Oxford University Press, 2006), 123–130, 181–182.

Human Rights Obligations of International Organisations on the Basis of General Principles of Law

Human rights obligations also stem from general principles of law. Although they are not a subsidiary source of international law, they are less relevant in practice due to their often rather vague nature. Indeed, legal certainty is lacking in these 'elementary considerations of humanity'.[51] Furthermore, many norms considered as falling in this category will simultaneously constitute customary norms, so that the consideration of general principles of law in the present study will rather be limited.[52] The acceptance that general principles are one of the foundations of international law also leads to the conclusion that certain equally fundamental human rights norms must play an equal part.[53] Other arguments present general principles of international law as a tool to fill gaps in the law, so-called *non liquet* situations, equating them therefore with something akin to a *technique juridique* than with primary rules of international law.[54]

It is suggested that general principles are used to promote 'values that international law seeks to promote and protect',[55] focusing on human dignity and its position under international law.[56]

Other approaches suggest that certain procedural rights, for example the presumption of innocence and the right to a fair trial, are included, but it remains unclear what this entails.[57] Oswald suggests that there are certain criteria to comply with in relation to the treatment of detainees,

---

[51] ICJ, *The Corfu Channel Case (United Kingdom of Great Britain and Northern Ireland v. Albania)*, Merits, Judgment of 9 April 1949, 22. See also Quénivet, 'Human Rights Law and Peacekeeping Operations', supra note 38, 99, 130; De Schutter, 'Human Rights and the Rise of International Organisations', supra note 6, 51, 72.

[52] International Law Association, New Delhi Conference (2002), Committee on Accountability of International Organisations, Third Report consolidated and enlarged version of recommended rules and practices ('RRP-S'), 11; International Law Association, Berlin Conference (2004), Accountability of International Organisations, 22.

[53] M. Zwanenburg, 'Compromise or Commitment: Human Rights and International Humanitarian Law Obligations for UN Peace Forces', *Leiden Journal of International Law*, 11 (1998), 229, 236.

[54] A. Boyle, C. Chinkin, *The Making of International Law* (Oxford University Press, 2007), 285–286; H. Thirlway, 'The Sources of International Law', in M. Evans (ed.), *International Law* (Oxford University Press, 2010), 99, 108–109.

[55] Legality of the Threat or Use of Nuclear Weapons, Advisory Opinion (8 July 1996) (Judge Higgins, Dissenting Opinion), para. 41; *South West Africa Case (Ethiopia v. South Africa)*, Judgment of 18 July 1966, Second Phase (Dissenting Opinion, Judge Tanaka), 296.

[56] Boyle, Chinkin, *The Making of International Law*, supra note 54, 289; Quénivet, 'Human Rights Law and Peacekeeping Operations', supra note 38, 99, 130.

[57] Rehman, *International Human Rights Law*, supra note 48, 24.

including dignity and humanity.[58] However, as has been pointed out, these principles are derived from various human rights and IHL treaties.[59]

Arguments of legal theory are equally important while trying to connect general principles and the UN Charter as the constitution of the international order.[60] Brownlie submits that the Security Council is limited in its actions under Chapter VI and Chapter VII as human rights 'form part of the concept of international public order'.[61]

Facing all these difficulties and taking into account that these principles are inferred from human rights and humanitarian law, it is therefore preferable to discard any further attempt to apply human rights norms as being solely based on general principles. As it was pointed out, general principles are often intertwined with customary law, so that an implicit application to the conduct of international organisations, particularly in the field of human rights and humanitarian law cannot be excluded, but legal certainty, which itself could possibly be considered as a general principle, supports a restrictive approach. Therefore, the analysis of the applicable law to international organisations will be limited to customary international law. The analysis also showed that customary international law contains some problematic features such as the identification of state practice and *opinio iuris*, but there is general agreement concerning the most fundamental human rights norms which are also accepted in practice by international organisations.

The 'Territorial Problem' of Human Rights Application and Their Extraterritorial Application

The application of human rights to international organisations is problematic for another reason which is the application *ratione loci* or the territoriality of human rights. Human rights were traditionally granted by states to their citizens to give those rights against the state and also protection

---

[58] B. Oswald, 'The Treatment of Detainees by Peacekeepers: Applying Principles and Standards at the Point of Detention' in R. Arnold (ed.), *Law Enforcement Within The Framework of Peace Support Operations* (Leiden, Brill, 2008), 197, 206–208.

[59] Quénivet, 'Human Rights Law and Peacekeeping Operations', supra note 38, 99, 130; T. Meron, 'The Martens Clause, Principles of Humanity, and Dictates of Public Conscience', *American Journal of International Law*, 94 (2000), 78, 80.

[60] Cf. Fassbender, 'Sources of Human Rights Obligations', supra note 32, 71–92; H. G. Schermers, N. M. Blokker, *International Institutional Law* (Leiden, Martinus Nijhoff, 2011), 998, para. 1575; 1001, para. 1577.

[61] I. Brownlie, 'The Decisions of Political Organs of the United Nations and the Rule of Law', in R. St. J. MacDonald (ed.), *Essays in Honour of Wang Tieya* (Heidelberg, Springer, 1993), 91, 102.

by the State, and thus they are based on a vertical relationship between the bound human rights granting entity and the individual on the basis of the territory over which states exercise jurisdiction. A state may also have to respect its human rights obligations outside its own territory if it

> through the effective control of the relevant territory and its inhabitants abroad as a consequence of military occupation or through the consent, invitation or acquiescence of the government of that territory, exercises all or some of the public powers normally to be exercised by [the government of that territory].[62]

With regard to the application of human rights law to international organisations,

> large areas of international law are patently inapplicable to international organizations, which have no territory, confer no nationality and do not exercise jurisdiction in the same sense as States. Other rules ... either lack relevance ... or meet practical difficulties of implementation.[63]

Consequently, the traditional application of human rights *ratione loci* is impossible in the context of international organisations, which per se are aterritorial, and rather operate on the territories of states, except in circumstances where there is territorial administration by an international organisation in which they exercise competences and rights similar to a state.[64]

Nevertheless, 'the territorial–extraterritorial divide [of states] ... [is] useful, since it concerns a situation where states do not exercise the same powers that relate to their own territories – a situation similar to that of international organizations leading peace operations'.[65]

It is thus that the exercise of jurisdiction by international organisations under human rights law can be compared to the extraterritorial exercise of jurisdiction under human rights law by states. Excluding the scenarios of complete occupation of another territory by a state or international administration of a territory, both a state and an international organisation consequently exercise jurisdiction in very specific circumstances if they operate extraterritorially; the extent of their power over the population is limited.

---

[62] *Bankovic and others v. Belgium and others*, Admissibility, Decision of 12 December 2001, para. 80.
[63] Morgenstern, *Legal Problems*, supra note 34, 4.
[64] G. Verdirame, *The UN and Human Rights. Who Guards the Guardian?* (Cambridge University Press, 2011), 235.
[65] Engdahl, 'Applicability/Application of Human Rights Law', supra note 40, 66, 69.

Thus, it appears possible to apply the jurisprudence of international courts and tribunals for the extraterritorial exercise of jurisdiction by states in analogy to international organisations. However, it has to be emphasised that it is unclear whether this nexus in the form of 'jurisdiction' applies first of all under customary law and secondly to international organisations. Engdahl suggests that the practice of the European Court of Human Rights perhaps reflects – at least – regional customary law and that '[t]he applicability of human rights for international organizations would most certainly require some form of nexus towards individuals, and possibly also a requirement established with regard to some sort of effective control in customary law'.[66]

The question is how to apply 'jurisdiction' as it has developed in a territorial context to international organisations. One possibility is to interpret 'jurisdiction' in a functional sense. As argued by Besson, jurisdiction is both a normative threshold, triggering the application of human rights, and it also provides the conditions for the corresponding obligation to be feasible for the duty-bearer (functional element), although it has territorial, temporal and personal dimensions which are derived from the exercise of jurisdiction.[67] Peacekeeping operations normally operate in certain defined areas of a state and although they do not normally assume all governmental powers in these areas, they will exercise these functions under their mandate to guarantee peace and security for the local population. Therefore, as is also suggested by Naert, it has been proposed to equate the territory of an international organisation with that of its member states. In addition to this interpretation, Naert, however, argues that the notion of jurisdiction in its traditional conception is inapplicable and must be replaced by a criterion of functional jurisdiction.[68]

The analysis will therefore proceed on the basis of the case law of international courts and tribunals as developed in the *contexte étatique*.

Extraterritorial Jurisdiction under Human Rights Law Generally speaking, the application of IHL as well as international human rights is

---

[66] Engdahl, ibid., 66, 70.
[67] S. Besson, 'The Extraterritoriality of the European Convention on Human Rights: Why Human Rights Depend on Jurisdiction and What Jurisdiction Amount To', *Leiden Journal of International Law*, 25 (2012), 857, 863.
[68] Naert, *International Law Aspects*, supra note 34, 525–526, 545; J. Lett, 'The Age of Interventionism: The Extraterritorial Reach of the European Convention on Human Rights', in R. Arnold, G.-J. A. Knoops (eds.), *Practice and Policies of Modern Peace Support Operations under International Law* (Leiden, Brill, 2006), 111, 120.

triggered through factual considerations on the basis of human interaction, 'whenever the State through its agents exercises control and authority over an individual, and thus jurisdiction'.[69]

Whereas the threshold for the application of IHL is comparatively simple, consisting in the existence of an armed conflict of either an international or an internal character,[70] to define the threshold for the application of human rights law is more complicated. On the one hand, this is due to conceptual misunderstandings; on the other hand, it is by reason of divergent judgments between international human rights bodies or even within the very same: the European Court of Human Rights offers a prime example of the diversity in the jurisprudence on this issue.[71]

Regarding extraterritorial jurisdiction, one can distinguish between two principal models of the exercise of jurisdiction. Under the first model, extraterritorial jurisdiction is based on the factual connection between the state and the territory in which the relevant act took place – a spatial connection.[72] According to the second model, there is a factual connection between the state and the individual – a personal connection due to the exercise of state agent authority.[73] Both models rely on the specific circumstances in question.[74]

In this context, the exercise of jurisdiction in a form of authority or control over the person or a given territory has to be distinguished from the

---

[69] *Case of Al-Skeini and Others v. The United Kingdom*, Grand Chamber, Judgment, 7 July 2011, para. 137.

[70] Cf. M. Gondek, *The Reach of Human Rights in a Globalising World: Extraterritorial Application of Human Rights Treaties* (Antwerp, Intersentia, 2011), 66–69.

[71] Quénivet, 'Human Rights Law and Peacekeeping Operations', supra note 38, 99, 116. Cf. also Maastricht Principles on Extraterritorial Obligations of States in the area of Economic, Social and Cultural Rights (2012); Commentary to the Maastricht Principles on Extraterritorial Obligations of States in the Area of Economic, Social and Cultural Rights (2012).

[72] See, e.g., *Legal Consequences*, supra note 95, paras. 107–113; UN Doc. CCPR/C/21/Rev.1/Add.13 (2004), para. 10; *Case of Loizidou v. Turkey* (Preliminary Objections), Grand Chamber, Judgment, 23 March 1995, para. 62; *Case of Loizidou v. Turkey*, Judgment, Grand Chamber, Merits, 18 December 1996, para. 52; *Case of Issa and Others v. Turkey*, Second Section, Judgment, 16 November 2004, paras. 69–70.

[73] *Issa*, ibid., para. 71. It was confirmed in several other cases, i.e., *Case of Pad and Others v. Turkey*, Third Section, Decision as to the Admissibility, 28 June 2007, paras. 53–54; *Isaak and Others v. Turkey*, Third Section, Decision as to the Admissibility, 28 September 2006, under the heading 2(b)(ii); *Case of Solomou and Others v. Turkey*, Fourth Section, Judgment, 24 June 2008, paras. 44–45, 51; M. Milanovic, 'Al-Skeini and Al-Jedda in Strasbourg', *European Journal of International Law*, 23 (2012), 121–122.

[74] Cf. Naert, *International Law Aspects*, supra note 34, 645–646.

attribution of conduct, two different overlapping concepts which are often conflated in practice.[75] Jurisdiction for the purposes of human rights must also be distinguished from state jurisdiction to prescribe and enforce its domestic law.[76]

Territorial jurisdiction in the form of the first model amounts, according to the ECtHR in *Al-Skeini*, to 'the exercise of extra-territorial jurisdiction by a Contracting State when, through the consent, invitation or acquiescence of the Government of that territory, it exercises all or some of the public powers normally to be exercised by that Government'.[77]

In contrast, 'personal jurisdiction' is tantamount to 'the use of force by a State's agents operating outside its territory [which] may bring the individual thereby under the control of the State's authorities'.[78]

The European Court of Human Right's jurisprudence has stretched the spatial model to ever diminishing areas including mere places[79] and thereby has often even relied on a simultaneous application of both models of jurisdiction. In the case of *Medvedyev and Others*, involving a captured Cambodian ship on the high seas by a French navy vessel, the Court considered that France had 'full and exclusive control over the *Winner* [the ship] and its crew, at least *de facto*'.[80] In similar fashion, the Court also relied in the previously mentioned *Al-Skeini* case of a mixed model of jurisdiction, adding that 'the UK exercised authority and control over individuals killed in the course of such security operations'.[81]

As regards the detention of Iraqis by British soldiers being part of the Multi-National Force (MNF), the Court held likewise that 'given the total and exclusive *de facto*, and subsequently also *de jure*, control exercised by the United Kingdom authorities over the premises in question, the individuals detained there, including the applicants, were within the United Kingdom's jurisdiction'.[82]

---

[75] K. M. Larsen, *The Human Rights Treaty Obligations of Peacekeepers* (2012), 186.
[76] Milanovic, '*Al-Skeini* and *Al-Jedda* in Strasbourg', supra note 73, 121, 123. For an overview of the different definitions/concepts of jurisdiction, see Gondek, *The Reach of Human Rights*, supra note 70, 47–54, 56–57.
[77] *Al-Skeini*, supra note 69, 135.
[78] Ibid., para. 136.
[79] The test thereby becomes very artificial, Cf. M. Milanovic, *Extraterritorial Application of Human Rights Treaties* (Oxford University Press, 2011), 128–130, 151–160, 171; UN Doc. CAT/C/CG/2 (2008), 5, para. 16
[80] *Case of Medvedyev and Others v. France*, Judgment, Grand Chamber, 29 March 2010, para. 67.
[81] *Al-Skeini*, supra note 69, 60, para. 149.
[82] *Case of Al-Saadoon and Mufdhi v. The United Kingdom*, Fourth Section, Decision as to the Admissibility, 30 June 2009.

The Court therefore limited the exercise of jurisdiction to cases based on a mixed model of jurisdiction;[83] on the basis of public powers and in the exercise of specific security operations which is not only at odd with previous jurisprudence of the Court but equally illogical[84] if 'simply shooting suspects is apparently immune from scrutiny, so long as you are careful not to arrest them first'.[85] However, in the case of *Andreou v. Turkey*, the ECtHR was seized by the case of Mrs. Andreou who was hit by a bullet in the abdomen during a manifestation outside the UN buffer zone near Dherynia, close to the Greek–Cypriot National Guard checkpoint emanating from Turkish Armed Forces. She was injured severely.[86] The Court held that 'even though the applicant sustained her injuries in territory over which Turkey exercised no control, the opening of fire on the crowd from close range, which was the direct and immediate cause of those injuries, was such that the applicant must be regarded as "within [the jurisdiction]" of Turkey'.[87]

The threshold for the spatial test also covers a spectrum, 'ranging from the more entrenched and visible exercise of de facto government, administration, or public powers, to the more borderline cases of less permanent or overt state control as in *Issa* and *Ilascu*'.[88] The jurisprudence of the ECtHR regarding the exercise of personal jurisdiction is equally wide and varied which led Milanovic to conclude that it 'simply boils down to the proposition that a state has obligations under human rights treaties towards all individuals whose human rights it is able to violate'.[89]

---

[83] *Al-Skeini*, supra note 69, 58–59, paras. 141–142; 60, para. 149; A. Conte, 'Human Rights Beyond Borders: A New Era in Human Rights Accountability for Transnational Counter-Terrorism Operations?', *Journal of Conflict & Security Law*, 18 (2013), 233, 249.

[84] Larsen, *Human Rights Treaty Obligations*, supra note 75, 211.

[85] H. Hannum, 'Bombing for Peace: Collateral Damage and Human Rights. Remarks', *American Society of International Law Proceedings*, 96 (2002), 96, 98. See also A. Orakhelashvili, 'Human Rights Protection during Extra-territorial Military Operations: Perspectives at International and English Law', in N. White, C. Henderson (eds.), *Research Handbook on International Conflict and Security Law* (Cheltenham, Edward Elgar Publishing, 2013), 598, 608.

[86] *Georgia Andreou against Turkey*, Fourth Section, Decision as to the Admissibility, 3 June 2008, 2–3.

[87] Ibid., 11, second paragraph.

[88] Milanovic, *Extraterritorial Application*, supra note 79, 141.

[89] Ibid., 79, 207; also M. Scheinin, 'Extraterritorial Effect of the International Covenant on Civil and Political Rights', in F. Coomans, M. T. Kamminga (eds.), *Extraterritorial Application of Human Rights Treaties* (Antwerp, Intersentia, 2004), 73, 75; U. Karpenstein, F. C. Mayer, *EMRK. Konvention zum Schutz der Menschenrechte und Grundfreiheiten. Kommentar* (München, Beck, 2012), 48–49, mn. 24.

The jurisprudence of the Court further shows that its notion of 'jurisdiction' depends on the specific circumstances of a case; so the Court decided in *Al-Skeini* that 'in determining whether effective control exists, the Court will primarily have reference to the strength of the State's military presence in the area'.[90] In *Issa*, the Court considered that 'as a consequence of this military action, the respondent State could be considered to have exercised, temporarily, effective overall control of a particular portion of the territory of northern Iraq'.[91]

According to the jurisprudence of the Human Rights Committee under the ICCPR, the Covenant can be applicable extraterritorially as 'it does not imply that the State party concerned cannot be held accountable for violations of rights under the Covenant which its agents commit upon the territory of another State'.[92] In its General Comment No. 31 the Committee further elaborated the notion of jurisdiction and held that '[t]his principle [of jurisdiction] also applies to those within the power or effective control of the forces of a State Party acting outside its territory, regardless of the circumstances in which such power or effective control was obtained, such as forces constituting a national contingent of a State Party assigned to an international peace-keeping or peace-enforcement operation'.[93]

The distinction between 'power or effective control' suggests that the Human Rights Committee subscribes to both the spatial and the personal model of jurisdiction, but the Committee has never properly elaborated further upon its interpretation of 'jurisdiction'.[94] The ICJ endorsed the view of the Human Rights Committee regarding the extraterritorial

---

[90] *Al-Skeini*, supra note 69, para. 139.
[91] *Case of Issa*, supra note 72, para. 74.
[92] UN Doc. A/36/40 (1981), 182–183, para. 12.3; Views of the Human Rights Committee under Article 5(4) of the Optional Protocol to the International Covenant on Civil and Political Rights concerning Communication No. R.13/56, *Celiberti de Casariego v. Uruguay*, Annex XX, ibid., 188, para. 3; Appendix, Individual opinion submitted by a member of the Human Rights Committee under rule 94(3) of the Committee's provisional rules of procedure, Communication No. R.13/56, Christian Tomuschat, ibid., 189, second paragraph; D. McGoldrick, 'Extraterritorial Application of the International Covenant on Civil and Political Rights', in F. Coomans, M. T. Kamminga (eds.), *Extraterritorial Application of Human Rights Treaties* (Antwerp, Intersentia, 2004), 41, 55. The validity of such an interpretation can be already inferred from the travaux préparatoires, UN Doc. A/2929 (1955), chapter V, 48, para. 4.
[93] Human Rights Committee, General Comment No. 31 (80), supra note 72, para. 10; UN Doc. CCPR/CO/81/BEL (2004), 2, para. 6.
[94] Larsen, *Human Rights Treaty Obligations*, supra note 75, 181.

application of the ICCPR in its *Wall Case* advisory opinion.[95] The Human Rights Committee pronounced itself briefly and indirectly on the question of jurisdiction of international organisations in the case of *H.v.d.P. v. the Netherlands*, an employee of the European Patent Office who had claimed to be a victim of discrimination. The Committee said that 'the author's grievance... cannot, in any way, be construed as coming within the jurisdiction of the Netherlands or any other State party'.[96]

The Inter-American Commission on Human Rights likewise held that jurisdiction 'may, under given circumstances, refer to conduct with an extraterritorial locus where the person is concerned is present in the territory of one state, but subject to the control of another state – usually through the acts of the latter's agents abroad'.[97] Also in other cases, the Commission has adopted a wide approach to jurisdiction. It held in *Alejandre* that the shooting down of two civilian light aeroplanes in international airspace by a Cuban military aircraft 'agents of the Cuban State, although outside their territory, placed the civilian pilots... under their authority'.[98] In a case concerning the US military action in Panama, the Commission had decided likewise in a very short and unequivocal comment '[w]here it is asserted that a use of military force has resulted in noncombatants deaths, personal injury, and property loss, the human rights of noncombatants are implicated'.[99]

The border between the exercise of jurisdiction and the attribution of conduct can be rather fluid as 'often in order to assess jurisdiction, the link between the acts or omissions at stake and state agents needs to be assessed at once and at the same time, hence the difficulty in keeping them apart'.[100]

---

[95] UN Doc. CCPR/C/79/ADD.93 (1998), 3, para. 10; Legal Consequences of the Construction of a Wall in the Occupied Palestinian Territory, Advisory Opinion (9 July 2004), 47–48, paras. 110–111.
[96] UN Doc. A/42/40 (1987), 107, para. 403. Cf. also *Ilse Hess v. United Kingdom*, Commission, Decision on the Admissibility of the Application, 28 May 1975, 73–74.
[97] Case 10.951, *Coard et al. v. United States of America*, 29 September 1999, para. 39.
[98] Case 11.589, *Alejandre Jr., Costa, De la Peña, Morales v. Cuba*, 29 September 1999, para. 25.
[99] Case No. 10.573, *Salas and others v. United States [US Military Action in Panama]*, 14 October 1993, Analysis, para. 6.
[100] Besson, 'The Extraterritoriality of the European Convention on Human Rights', supra note 67, 857, 877. One can distinguish between the two in the following way: '[S]tate jurisdiction and attribution are distinct concepts. Ultimately, the latter is an issue of state control over the perpetrators of human rights violations, while the former is a question of a state's control over the victims of such violations through its agents, or, more generally, control over the territory in which they are located.' Milanovic, *Extraterritorial Application*, supra note 79, 51–52. Cf. also L. Boisson de Chazournes, V. Pergantis, 'À propos de l'arrêt Behrami et Saramati: Un jeu d'ombre et de lumière dans les relations entre l'ONU et les organisations régionales', in M. Kohen, R. Kolb, D. L. Tehindrazanarivelo (eds.),

For the purposes of applying the law of responsibility, a distinction is rather simple. Whereas any human rights body starts its analysis with establishing whether jurisdiction is given in the respective case, the law of responsibility starts with the attribution of conduct and, thus, jurisdiction will be dealt with in the analysis of the following requirement which is the breach of an international obligation.[101]

Jurisdiction under human rights law has also to be distinguished from jurisdiction under general international law[102]: 'It is this notion of jurisdiction – not the jurisdiction to prescribe rules of domestic law and to enforce them, but control over a territory and persons within it – that pervades international human rights treaties.'[103] Hence, in a certain way, one can apply 'jurisdiction' *mutatis mutandis* to international organisations.[104] The Draft Accession Agreement of the EU to the ECHR likewise foresaw the application of the same standard of jurisdiction to the EU for acts outside the territories of member states of the EU as for extraterritorial acts of a member state to the Convention.[105]

Perspectives of International Law in the 21st century/Perspectives du droit international au 21e siècle (Leiden, Brill, 2011), 191, 196.

[101] Milanovic, ibid., 51–52; cf. O. De Schutter, 'Globalization and Jurisdiction: Lessons from the European Convention on Human Rights', *Baltic Journal of International Law*, 6 (2006), 185, 188–192.

[102] Larsen, *Human Rights Treaty Obligations*, supra note 84, 173; Milanovic, ibid., 27. In other words, jurisdiction under general international law has the function to determine whether a claim made by a state to regulate some specific conduct is lawful or unlawful, B. H. Oxman, 'Jurisdiction of States' in R Wolfrum (ed.), *The Max Planck Encyclopedia of Public International Law* (Oxford University Press, 2008–), online edition (www.mpepil.com), paras. 1, 9; De Schutter, ibid., 185, 195–197.

[103] Milanovic, *Extraterritorial Application*, supra note 79, 32; L. G. Loucaides, 'Determining the Extra-territorial Effect of the European Convention: Facts, Jurisprudence and the Bankovic Case', *European Human Rights Law Review*, 4 (2006), 73, 91. See also H. Lauterpacht, *International Law and Human Rights* (London, Steven & Sons Ltd., 1968), 317, 364. For a codification in treaties, cf. Article 5(2) of the Convention on the Prohibition of the Use, Stockpiling, Production and Transfer of Anti-Personnel Mines and on their Destruction (1997); Principle 2 of the Rio Declaration on Environment and Development (1992).

[104] Cf. O. De Schutter, A. Eide, A. Khalfan et al., Commentary to the Maastricht Principles on Extraterritorial Obligations of States in the Area of Economic, Social and Cultural Rights (2012), *Human Rights Quarterly*, 34 (2012), 1084, 1122. Specifically for the context of a peacekeeping operation, cf. A. Tzanakopoulos, *Disobeying the Security Council. Countermeasure against Wrongful Sanctions* (Oxford University Press, 2011), 28.

[105] EU/Council of Europe, Fifth Negotiation Meeting between the CDDH Ad Hoc Negotiation Group and the European Commission on the Accession of the European Union to the European Convention on Human Rights, Final Report to the CDDH, Strasbourg, 5 April 2013, 5–6, para. 6. See generally M. den Heijer, A. Nollkaemper (eds.), 'SHARES Briefing Paper – A New Framework for Allocating International Responsibility: The EU Accession to the European Convention on Human Rights (2014)', available at www.sharesproject.nl.

In summary, the practice of international courts and tribunals in defining 'extraterritorial jurisdiction' is very varied and arguably also based on pragmatic reasons. If one bears in mind that at least in part of the jurisprudence, 'territorial jurisdiction' has been shrunk to include small geographical areas or even conflated with the personal notion of jurisdiction, it so appears that 'jurisdiction' is, indeed, used rather functionally. Consequently, there are no arguments against an application of both models of jurisdiction to international organisations whereby the exact threshold for the exercise of jurisdiction will depend on the specific circumstances of the case. The limitation of extraterritorial jurisdiction to certain specific circumstances is based on the idea that there has to be a sufficient nexus between the state, or in the case of the present study the international organisation, and the local population. Therefore, the question arose as to whether the human rights to be protected extraterritorially are also limited to these rights which would be relevant in the exercise of extraterritorial jurisdiction.

The Tailored Application of Human Rights Law to Peacekeeping Forces – From Bankovic to Al-Skeini   The applicants in the Bankovic case before the European Court of Human Rights argued that the extraterritorial application of human rights obligations of states can be 'divided and tailored'. Although the Court in *Bankovic* denied any such application of the European Convention,[106] this topic has since then been discussed rather extensively in academic writing and the discussion was rekindled following the judgment of the European Court of Human Rights in *Al-Skeini*.[107] Referring to *Bankovic*, the Court held that

> whenever the State through its agents exercises control and authority over an individual, and thus jurisdiction, the State is under an obligation under Article 1 to secure to that individual the rights and freedoms under Section 1 of the Convention that are relevant to the situation of that individual. In this sense, therefore, the Convention rights can be 'divided and tailored.'[108] [Emphasis added]

Interestingly, the ECtHR had already cited extensively in its *Beric* judgment[109] from a report of the Venice Commission in which it was stated '[i]t

---

[106] *Bankovic*, supra note 62, para. 75.
[107] *Al-Skeini*, supra note 69.
[108] Ibid., para. 137.
[109] *Berić and others v. Bosnia*, Fourth Section, Decision as to the Admissibility, 16 October 2007, para. 17.

would have been unrealistic to have insisted on immediate full compliance with all international standards governing a stable and full-fledged democracy in a post-conflict situation such as existed in BiH following the adoption of the [Peace] Agreement'[110] so that one might be inclined to think that the Court was slightly testing the water in *Beric*.[111] Nevertheless, the cryptic formulation of the ECtHR had instigated a debate about the interpretation; whether the judgment of the Court allows the 'cherry-picking' of rights or not.[112] The concurrent opinion by Judge Bonello and the follow-up judgment in *Hirsi Jamaa* confirm that the Court did have 'cherry-picking' in mind.[113] However, if one distinguishes between the obligations of a state on a general level and in a specific given case of alleged violations, *Al-Skeini* fits very well within the general practice of the Court as in any given case of alleged violations of human rights, the only human rights which actually matter are those which have allegedly been infringed. The Court also limited its view to the cases of people being under the authority of a state agent, so that, as it is also suggested by Miltner, for cases of control over a territory (territorial jurisdiction), a state party still has to guarantee all substantive rights of the Convention.[114]

[110] European Commission for Democracy Through Law (Venice Commission), Opinion on the Constitutional Situation in Bosnia and Herzegovina and the Powers of the High Representative, Venice, 11 March 2005, 23, para. 97. See also A. Gillman, W. Johnson (eds.), Operational Law Handbook, The Judge Advocate General's Legal Center & School (2012), 47–48, paras. III.A.–B; 51 D. 1; J. Cerone, 'Legal Responsibility Framework for Human Rights Violations Post-Conflict', in N. D. White, D. Klaasen (eds.), *The UN, Human Rights and Post-Conflict Situations* (Manchester University Press, 2005), 42, 48.

[111] O. Engdahl, 'The Future of Human Rights Law in Peace Operations', in O. Engdahl, P. Wrange (eds.), *Law at War: The Law as It Was and the Law as It Should Be. Liber Amicorum Ove Bring* (Leiden, Brill, 2008), 105, 109.

[112] Against: A. Cowan, 'A New Watershed? Re-evaluating *Banković* in Light of *Al-Skeini*', *Cambridge Journal of International and Comparative Law*, 1 (2012), 213, 222. In contrast, Miltner asserts that the judgment amounts to cherry-picking of Convention rights, B. Miltner, 'Revisiting Extraterritoriality after *Al-Skeini*: The ECHR and Its Lessons', *Michigan Journal of International Law*, 33 (2012), 693, 697. Cf. also F. Naert, 'The European Court of Human Rights' *Al-Jedda* and *Al-Skeini* Judgments: an Introduction and Some Reflections', *Military Law and the Law of War Review*, 50 (2011), 315, 317; Larsen, *Human Rights Treaty Obligations*, supra note 75, 81; R. Wilde, 'Triggering State Obligations Extraterritorially: The Spatial Test in Certain Human Rights Treaties', *Israel Law Review*, 40 (2007), 503, 519–520; M. Szydlo, 'Extra-territorial Application of the European Convention on Human Rights after *Al-Skeini* and *Al-Jedda*', *International Criminal Law Review*, 12 (2012), 271, 290.

[113] *Case of Hirsi Jamaa and Others v. Italy*, Grand Chamber, Judgment, 23 February 2012, para. 74; *Case of Al-Skeini and Others v. The United Kingdom*, Grand Chamber, Judgment, 7 July 2011 (Judge Bonello, Concurring Opinion), paras. 32–33.

[114] As confirmed in *Case of Hirsi Jamaa*, ibid., para. 74. Miltner, 'Revisiting Extraterritoriality', supra note 112, 693, 697–698.

Perhaps the Court also had the then pending accession of the EU to the Convention in mind, while elaborating its judgment. As the competences of international organisations are limited due to their own respective constitutive framework a tailored application of human rights is the only feasible option to apply human rights obligations to international organisations without exposing them to the risk of acting *ultra vires*. It is therefore submitted that, notwithstanding the cryptic judgment of the ECtHR in *Al-Skeini*, human rights can only be applied in a tailored and divided fashion to international organisations.

Peacekeeping operations also generally elude, in a certain way, the regulation of human rights. They are established to promote peace and security, but they are not 'human rights protecting operations' despite the recent emphasis on the protection of civilians in the mandates of operations. Hence, there may be a certain dichotomy between the human rights obligations of the peacekeepers and their mandate on the basis of a Security Council resolution.[115] Germany observed in the *Behrami/Saramati* case that 'account must be taken of the special difficulties under which such operations are normally deployed'.[116] Furthermore,

> [m]ore often than not, peace operations start after an armed conflict has brought death and destruction. Governmental institutions may not function properly, the infrastructure has suffered heavy damage, law and order have broken down, and the economic situation is disastrous... Accordingly, everyone knows that when a peace operation is launched the situation in the country concerned normally does not correspond to the standards of the International Covenant on Civil and Political Rights or those of the European Convention ... In conclusion, it must be acknowledged quite frankly that at least during a first stage of a peace operation, the standards of the Convention can hardly ever be maintained to a full extent.[117]

Other arguments raised are that a limited application of human rights law would prevent peacekeeping forces from being exposed to 'unworkable burdens with undue risk', thereby compromising any 'effective protective action' and consequently the whole mandate of the operation.[118] The very

---

[115] It is suggested by Larsen that a potential conflict arising out of a mandate to 'protect civilians under immediate threat' with the human rights obligations of the peacekeepers has to be considered as two non-related issues as the mandate in the form of a resolution is nothing more than an authorisation to use force to protect civilians but not an obligation to do so, Larsen, supra note 75, 392.
[116] Observations of the Federal Republic of Germany concerning application no. 78166/01: *Saramati v. France, Germany and Norway*, 18, para. 38.
[117] Ibid., 18, paras. 38–39; 19, para. 42.
[118] R. O. Weiner, F. N. Aolain, 'Beyond the Laws of War: Peacekeeping in Search of a Legal Framework', Columbia Human Rights Law Review, 27 (1995–1996), 293, 320, 352–353.

same arguments are invoked for a similar limited application of IHL to peacekeeping forces.[119] A wider debate has arisen as regards the possibility of a 'sliding scale of obligations' for armed groups whom, in contrast to states, are unable to respect all rules.[120]

Regarding the precise obligations of international organisations, some authors submit that the Security Council, for example, would only have 'due diligence' obligations regarding the application of human rights law,[121] and as such could not be held responsible for a failure to prevent a massacre or genocide, but only for the failure to conduct itself adequately.[122] In academic writing it is also suggested that it is necessary to distinguish between positive and negative obligations depending on the degree of control exercised over a given territory; negative

---

See also D. Lorenz, *Der territoriale Anwendungsberich der Grund- und Menschenrechte – zugleich ein Beitrag zum Individualschutz in bewaffnete Konflikten* (Berliner Wissenschafts-Verlag, 2005), 105; U. Erberich, *Auslandseinsätze der Bundeswehr und Europäische Menschenrechtskonvention* (München, Beck, 2004), in particular 5–31; see also especially Naert, *International Law Aspects*, supra note 34, 556–557, 564–565; Clapham, *Human Rights Obligations*, supra note 38, 68.

[119] Excluding, e.g., the dispositions on mandatory jurisdiction, Weiner, Aolain, ibid., 293, 320, 352–353.

[120] M. Sassòli, 'Introducing a Sliding-Scale of Obligations to Address the Fundamental Inequality between Armed Groups and States?', *International Review of the Red Cross*, 93 (2011), 426, 430–431; Y. Shany, 'A Rebuttal to Marco Sassòli', *International Review of the Red Cross*, 93 (2011), 432, 432–434; R. Provost, 'The Move to Substantive Equality in International Humanitarian Law: A Rejoinder to Marco Sassòli and Yuval Shany', *Review of the Red Cross*, 93 (2001), 437, 438–441. See more generally, G. Blum, 'On a Differential Law of War', *Harvard International Law Journal*, 52 (2011), 163, esp. 185–216; H. Shue, 'Laws of War, Morality and International Politics: Compliance, Stringency, and Limits', *Leiden Journal of International Law*, 26 (2013), 271–292.

[121] K. Schmalenbach, *Die Haftung Internationaler Organisationen im Rahmen von Militäreinsätzen und Territorialverwaltungen* (Frankfurt am Main, Peter Lang, 2004), 381–382; C. Eagleton, *International Organization and the Law of Responsibility*, Collected Courses of the Hague Academy of International Law, Vol. 076 (1950), 320, 400. Cf. UN Doc. S/4745 (1961), 7.

[122] A. Peters, 'Functions and Powers. Article 24', in B. Simma, D.-E. Khan, G. Nolte et al. (eds.), *The Charter of the United Nations. A Commentary, Volume I* (Oxford University Press, 2012), 761, 774 mn. 38; see R. A. Opie, 'Human Rights Violations by Peacekeepers: Finding a Framework for Attribution of International Responsibility', *New Zealand Law Review* (2006), 1, 22; cf. also N. Elaraby, 'Some Reflections on the Role of the Security Council and the Prohibition of the Use of Force in International Relations: Article 2(4) Revisited in the Light of Recent Developments', in T. Eitel, J. A. Frowein, K. Scarioth et al. (eds.), *Verhandeln für den Frieden. Liber Amicorum Tono Eitel* (Heidelberg, Springer, 2003), 41, 56; UN Doc. A/CN.4/553 (2005), 4, para. 10; Peters, ibid., 761, 774–775 mn. 40; Peters, 'Article 25', supra note 11, 787, 850 mn. 199.

obligations can always be respected by the control exercised by a state over its agents.[123]

Derogations under Human Rights Law as Another Method to Divide and Tailor the Application of Human Rights Law Other arguments for a limited application of human rights law to international organisations rely on the possibility of derogations under human rights treaties. In *Al-Skeini*, the European Court of Human Rights implicitly opened the door for extraterritorial human rights law derogations, referring to the ICJ and its judgment in the *Wall Case*, 'stating the International Court of Justice appeared to assume, that even in respect of extra-territorial acts, it would be in principle possible for a State to derogate from its obligations under the International Covenant on Civil and Political Rights'.[124] As human rights law serves to protect the individual, it would be, indeed, illogical to allow states to further limit their obligations on their own territory than when they act extraterritorially.[125]

Of course, these arguments can be only transposed to a certain extent from the territorial context of states to the 'aterritorial context' of international organisations, but the draft accession agreement of the EU to the European Convention on Human Rights likewise provides that the changes foreseen to the Convention 'may be interpreted as allowing the EU to take measures in derogation from its obligations under the Convention in relations to measures taken by one of its member States in time of emergency in accordance with Article 15 of the Convention'.[126] Hence, also from the perspective of derogations under human rights law, there are good arguments for limiting the application of human rights law to international

---

[123] Milanovic, *Extraterritorial Application*, supra note 79, 141; De Schutter, 'Globalization and Jurisdiction', supra note 101, 185, 245. This reasoning can also be applied to international organisations. Excluded are, obviously, cases of acts contravening instructions by agents.

[124] *Al-Skeini*, supra note 69, para. 90. Larsen concludes after a lengthy analysis that such a derogation is not *lex lata*: Larsen, *The Human Rights Treaty Obligations*, supra note 75, 299–311. Furthermore, he asserts that the *travaux préparatoires* of the Convention do not mention the issue of extraterritorial derogations, ibid., 306.

[125] K. M. Larsen, ' "Neither Effective Control Nor Ultimate Authority and Control": Attribution of Conduct in Al-Jedda', *Military Law and the Law of War Review*, 50 (2011), 347, 362.

[126] Fifth Negotiation Meeting supra note 105, 19, para. 28; EU/Council of Europe, Forth Negotiation Meeting between the CDDH Ad Hoc Negotiation Group and the European Commission on the Accession of the European Union to the European Convention on Human Rights, Draft Explanatory report to the Agreement on the Accession of the European Union to the Convention for the Protection of Human Rights and Fundamental Freedoms, Strasbourg, 8 January 2013, 5–6, para. 23.

organisations to what is feasible under their mandate and thereby also in the context of peacekeeping operations.[127] A particular problem is posed by the fact that the UN could invoke the Charter and Security Council resolutions 'to the extent that they reflect an international law obligation – to justify what might otherwise be regarded as non-compliance'.[128] The general and particularly the recent practice of the UN and regional organisations shows a strict adherence to international human rights standards,[129] but nevertheless the Security Council could at least theoretically derogate from these human rights in a resolution which does not involve rules of *jus cogens*.

In conclusion, the application of human rights law to international organisations is, indeed, tailored and limited to these rights as they are not only relevant in the specific circumstances, but as they may also be protected by the powers of the respective international organisations. This division of human rights law in its extraterritorial application is intrinsically linked to the question of jurisdiction. The following part of this chapter analyses the application of IHL to peacekeeping operations of international organisations. It illustrates very clearly that further difficulties arise in determining the applicable law in peacekeeping operations in addition to those encountered in the human rights law context. A particular problem is posed by the relationship between human rights and humanitarian law.

Application of IHL

IHL regulates the conduct of hostilities in armed conflict. The aim of IHL is to limit the effects of war on people and property and to protect particularly vulnerable persons.

---

[127] F. Naert, 'Applicability/Application of Human Rights Law to IOs involved in Peace Operations', in S. Kolanowski (ed.), *Proceedings of the Bruges Colloquium. International Organisations' Involvement in Peace Operations: Applicable Legal Framework and the Issue of Responsibility* (2011), 45, 49–50; Naert, *International Law Aspects*, supra note 34, 584. Cf. *House of Lords, R (on the application of Al-Jedda) (FC) (Appellant) v. Secretary of State for Defence (Respondent)*, Decision of 12 December 2007, Opinion of Lord Bingham of Cornhill, para. 32; Lord Brown of Eaton-Under-Heywood, para. 150; *Bankovic*, supra note 62, para. 62; H. Duffy, *The 'War on Terror' and the Framework of International Law* (Cambridge University Press, 2005), 296.

[128] UN Doc. A/CN.4/637/Add.1 (2011), 36, para. 3.

[129] L. Hultman, 'UN Peace Operations and Protection of Civilians: Cheap Talk or Norm Implementation?', *Journal of Peace Research*, 50 (2012), 59, 66–71; M. Dembinski, B. Schott, 'Converging around Global Norms? Protection of Civilians in African Union and European Union Peacekeeping in Africa', *African Security*, 6 (2013), 276, 282–284, 286–287.

Application *Ratione Personae* of IHL to Activities of International Organisations

The UN and the regional organisations which are part of the present study possess international legal personality and they therefore can be addressees of norms of IHL.[130] Regarding the UN particularly, the purposes and principles of the UN Charter, its mandate for maintaining international peace and security, and its competence to deploy military forces, which can become involved in conflict situations amounting to an armed conflict, lead to the conclusion that IHL is applicable.[131]

The *Institut de droit international* started to address in earnest the issue of the application of IHL in the context of the UN in 1971. The issued resolution considered humanitarian rules of IHL, including the Geneva Conventions, to be applicable 'as of right' to the UN, entailing an obligation to comply with IHL in all circumstances when engaged in hostilities.[132]

Other international organisations are bound by IHL if they possess international legal personality, have the capacity under their respective constitutive instrument to deploy military forces[133] and if they do deploy

---

[130] T. Ferraro, 'IHL Applicability to International Organisations Involved in Peace Operations', in S. Kolanowski (ed.), *Proceedings of the Bruges Colloquium. International Organisations' Involvement in Peace Operations: Applicable Legal Framework and the Issue of Responsibility* (2011), 15, 17. See generally M. Zwanenburg, 'United Nations and International Humanitarian Law', in R. Wolfrum (ed.), *The Max Planck Encyclopedia of Public International Law* (Oxford University Press, 2008–), online edition (www.mpepil.com); J. Peck, 'The U.N. and the Laws of War: How Can the World's Peacekeepers Be Held Accountable?', *Syracuse Journal of International Law and Commerce*, 21 (1995), 283–310.

[131] Kolb, Porretto, Vité, *L'application du droit international humanitaire*, supra note 2, 124–125. See also Peters, 'Article 25', supra note 11, 787, 827 mn. 129–828 mn. 132.

[132] *Institut de Droit International*, Resolution (Session of Zagreb 1971), Conditions of Application of Humanitarian Rules of Armed Conflict to Hostilities in which United Nations Forces May Be Engaged, Article 2. See also *Institut de Droit International*, Resolution (Session of Wiesbaden 1975), Conditions of Application of Rules Other Than Humanitarian Rules, of Armed Conflict to Hostilities in Which United Nations Forces May Be Engaged and *Institut de Droit International*, Resolution (Session of Berlin 1999), The Application of International Humanitarian Law and Fundamental Human Rights in Armed Conflicts in which Non-State Entities Are Parties, notably paras. II, IX and XI.

[133] K. E. Sams, 'IHL Obligations of the UN and other International Organisations Involved in International Missions', in M. Odello, R. Piotrowicz (eds.), *International Military Missions and International Law* (Leiden, Brill, 2011), 45, 53; E. David, *Principes de droit des conflits armés* (Brussels, Bruylant, 2008), 225–226, paras. 1.192–1.193; 234, para. 1.202; J. P. Bialke, 'United Nations Peace Operations: Applicable Norms and the Application of the Law of Armed Conflict', *Air Force Law Review*, 50 (2001), 1, 37; UN Doc. A/56/326 (2001), 9, para. 19; Status of Mission Agreement (SOMA) on the Establishment and Management of the Ceasefire Commission in the Darfur Area of the Sudan (CFC) (2004), para. 8(a), M. H. Hoffman, 'Peace Enforcement Actions and Humanitarian Law: Emerging Rules for "Interventional Armed Conflict"', *International Review of the Red Cross*, 82 (2000), 193,

military forces; a corollary of the capacity to use military force is to be titular of rights and obligations of IHL.[134] Therefore, the objective capacities of the organisations determine their subjective capacities to be bound by IHL and the precise legal content incumbent upon them.[135] Nevertheless, the UN Charter has also an effect on regional organisations deploying military troops as part of a UN operation or on the basis of a Security Council authorisation. The Charter confers on the UN both the responsibility to maintain international peace and security, and to develop and encourage the respect of human rights and fundamental liberties. Therefore, in practice, the mandates provided by the Security Council will contain the requirement to respect the applicable human rights and IHL.

Application *Ratione Materiae* of IHL

In contrast to human rights law, IHL does not presuppose the exercise of jurisdiction over a given territory; it is based on a predominantly horizontal relationship protecting the subjects of the parties to the conflict on the grounds of the mutual interest of all parties.

Depending on the nature of the conflict, different regimes of IHL are applicable. International armed conflicts are – under the Geneva Conventions – conflicts between opposing states,[136] whereas non-international armed conflicts covers all other cases of armed violence.[137] The regime applying to international armed conflict is the most developed, establishing categories of protected persons which do not exist in internal armed conflict.

In doctrine it is debated whether the involvement of international organisations in an armed conflict leads to a qualification of this particular conflict as international or as non-international. There is generally agreement that the law of international armed conflict is applicable if international troops confront a state,[138] which would amount to an international

---

198–200; A Faite, J. L. Grenier (eds.), *Report of the Expert Meeting on Multinational Peace Operations: Applicability of International Humanitarian Law and Human Rights Law to UN Mandated Forces* (Geneva, 11–12 December 2003), 24–26.

[134] Kolb, Porretto, Vité, *L'application du droit international humanitaire*, supra note 2, 127–128. This was equally recognised by the latest resolution of the *Institut de droit international*, cf. *Institut de Droit International*, supra note 132, para. II.

[135] V. Falco, 'The Internal Legal Order of the European Union as a Complementary Framework for Its Obligations under IHL', *Israel Law Review*, 42 (2009), 168, 188.

[136] And certain specific exceptions under Article 1 of Additional Protocol 1 to the Geneva Conventions.

[137] Such as a state versus an armed group or armed groups against each other.

[138] Kolb, Porretto, Vité, *L'application du droit international humanitaire*, supra note 2, 183; Sams, 'IHL Obligations of the UN', supra note 133, 45, 63; Faite, Grenier, 'Report of the Expert Meeting', supra note 133, 63. Cf. H. P. Aust, 'Article 2 (5)', in B. Simma, D.-E.

conflict *sui generis*, because in the final analysis it is not very different from a group of states involved in an armed conflict against another state.[139]

The issue is unresolved if one takes the example of the use of force by an international organisation against an organised armed group. The predominant view extends the application of the law of international armed conflict in which an international organisation takes part, to the opponent, notwithstanding if it is a state or an armed group.[140] Some authors agree that the status of an international organisation is sufficient to elevate the conflict to an international armed conflict.[141] This view is popular from a human rights point of view as it increases the level of protection for all parties involved in the conflict.[142]

This approach might better be suited to accommodating the reality of a peacekeeping operation. Modern peacekeeping operations often operate in conditions between war and peace where there might be fighting in

---

Khan, G. Nolte et al. (eds.), *The Charter of the United Nations. A Commentary*, Volume I (Oxford University Press, 2012), 235, 247 mn. 26 with further references. Generally see C. Wickremasinghe, G. Verdirame, 'Responsibility and Liability for Violations of Human Rights in the Course of UN Field Operations', in C. Scott (ed.), *Torture as Tort. Comparative Perspectives on the Development of Transnational Human Rights Litigation* (Oxford, Hart Publishing, 2001), 465, 473; F. Naert, 'The Application of International Humanitarian Law and Human Rights Law in CSDP Operations', in E. Cannizzaro, P. Palchetti, R. A. Wessel (eds.), *International Law as Law of the European Union* (Leiden Brill, 2012), 189, 197.

[139] Ferraro, 'IHL Applicability to International Organisations Involved in Peace Operations', supra note 130, 15, 19. It is therefore also unproblematic if an International Organisation intervenes in a NIAC in favour of rebel armed forces against the government as the respective organisation would be opposed to the government of the state. See V. Koutroulis, 'International Organisations Involved in Armed Conflict: Material and Geographical Scope of Application of Humanitarian Law', in S. Kolanowski (ed.), *Proceedings of the Bruges Colloquium. International Organisations' Involvement in Peace Operations: Applicable Legal Framework and the Issue of Responsibility* (2011), 29, 32; *Prosecutor v. Vlastimir Đorđević*, Judgment, Case No. IT-05-87/1 'Kosovo', Tr. Ch. II, 23 February 2011, 629, para. 1580.

[140] Sams, 'IHL Obligations of the UN', supra note 133, 45, 63; C. Greenwood, 'International Humanitarian Law and United Nations Military Operations', *Yearbook of International Humanitarian Law*, 1 (1998), 3, 26. See also *Prosecutor v. Dusko Tadić a/k/a 'Dule'*, Decision on the Defence Motion on Jurisdiction, Case No. IT-94-1, Tr.Ch., 10 August 1995; T. Meron, 'International Criminalization of Internal Atrocities', *American Journal of International Law*, 89 (1995), 554, 564–565; A. Aust, *Handbook of International Law* (2010), 237–238.

[141] Kolb, Porretto, Vité, *L'application du droit international humanitaire*, supra note 2, 184; Schmalenbach, *Die Haftung*, supra note 121, 363. With regard to the two opposing opinions and with further arguments, see the debate between David and Engdahl, E. David, O. Engdahl, 'How Does the Involvement of a Multinational Peacekeeping Force Affect the Classification of a Situation?', *International Review of the Red Cross*, 95 (2013), 659–679.

[142] Critical of this opinion, C. Beerli, 'Keynote Address', S. Kolanowski (ed.), *Proceedings of the Bruges Colloquium. International Organisations' Involvement in Peace Operations: Applicable Legal Framework and the Issue of Responsibility* (2011), 9, 11.

one part of a country and relative peace in other parts of the country perhaps with only very few skirmishes.[143] Therefore, under the law of internal armed conflict, one would arrive at the paradoxical situation that IHL might be applicable in one part of the territory, but not in the rest of the country.[144]

The opposing opinion is that 'there is no reason to think that the involvement of a UN force in a situation of armed conflict will of itself render the conflict "international" for the purpose of the application of the *ius in bello*'.[145] They therefore argue for an application of the law of internal conflict if the conflict involves an international organisation on one side and an armed group on the other side.[146] Thus, one must analyse 'each belligerent relationship to determine [the] applicable law'.[147] Once again, it is however questionable whether such a view is compatible with modern armed conflicts. Such a distinction would lead to an obligation of any international organisation to provide different standards of treatment depending on the adversaries, which is impractical in modern armed conflicts. It would also emphasise the separation of the two legal regimes which is less relevant in customary humanitarian law.[148] On the other hand, if an

---

[143] M. Odello, R. Piotrowicz, 'Legal Regimes Governing International Military Missions', in M. Odello, R. Piotrowicz (eds.), *International Military Missions and International Law* (Leiden, Brill, 2011), 25, 41; Contrary Ferraro, 'IHL Applicability to International Organisations', supra note 130, 15, 19.

[144] But see Sams, 'IHL Obligations of the UN', supra note 133, 45, 65; *The Prosecutor v. Jean-Paul Akayesu*, Judgment, Case No. ICTR-96-4-T, T. Ch. I, 2 September 1998, paras. 635–636.

[145] H. McCoubrey, N. D. White, *The Blue Helmets: Legal Regulation of United Nations Military Operations* (Dartmouth Publishing, 1997), 172. Cf. also David, *Principes de droit des conflits armés*, supra note 133, 160–161, 179–180; Koutroulis, 'International Organisations Involved in Armed Conflict', supra note 139, 29, 34–35.

[146] David, *Principes de droit des conflits armés*, supra note 133, 177; J. Cerone, 'Legal Responsibility Framework for Human Rights Violations', supra note 110, 42, 69; Naert, *International Law Aspects*, supra note 34, 483–484. See in particular, Ferraro, 'IHL Applicability to International Organisations', supra note 130, 15, 21; also M. Zwanenburg, 'International Organisations vs. Troops Contributing Countries: Which Should Be Considered as the Party to an Armed Conflict During Peace Operations?', in S. Kolanowski (ed.), *Proceedings of the Bruges Colloquium. International Organisations' Involvement in Peace Operations: Applicable Legal Framework and the Issue of Responsibility* (2011), 23, 25.

[147] Sams, 'IHL Obligations of the UN', supra note 133, 45, 63; Faite, Grenier, 'Report of the Expert Meeting', supra note 133, 63–64; ICRC, International Humanitarian Law and the Challenges of Contemporary Armed Conflicts, Report for the 31st International Conference of the Red Cross and Red Crescent, Doc. 31IC/11/5.1.2. (2011), 31, last para; Ferraro, 'IHL Applicability to International Organisations', supra note 130, 15, 17–18; Naert, 'The Application of International Humanitarian Law', supra note 138, 189, 197–198.

[148] Cf. also Sams, ibid., 45, 63; also R. Kolb, *Droit humanitaire et opérations de paix internationale* (Basel, Helbing & Lichtenhahn, 2006), 57–58.

armed conflict involves a state and an international organisation as a coalition and an armed group as an opponent, members of the latter would be exposed to different treatment depending on whether they are in the hands of forces of the organisation or of the state and there would be an application of the traditional rules of intervention by a third state.[149]

The practice seems to favour the application of the law of international armed conflict, thus the bulletin of the Secretary-General, which foresees the application of IHL, refers to the law of international armed conflict in Article 1 of bulletin.[150] In the same regard, the Convention on Safety of United Nations Personnel (1994), speaks of the law of international armed conflict (Article 2, para. 2).[151] This disposition was specifically accepted during the negotiations as 'il a été généralement admis qu'il était impossible à l'Organisation d'être impliquée dans un conflit armé interne, car une fois qu'elle ou le personnel associé s'engage dans un conflit contre une force locale, le conflit prend, par définition, une envergue "internationale"'.[152] Other examples of practice are less clear. With regard to Somalia, the UN and the US argued that the law of non-international armed conflict was applicable, but one has to keep in mind that Somalia was a so-called failed state with no effective government so that the armed opposition resembled an armed group rather than a government.[153] Concerning the Democratic Republic of Congo, the UN considered itself bound by the whole body of IHL.[154] However this particular question of the nature of an armed conflict between an international organisation and an armed group might

---

[149] Sams, ibid., 45, 63–64; *Military and Paramilitary Activities in and against Nicaragua (Nicaragua v. United States of America)*, Merits, Judgment (27 June 1986), para. 219; *Prosecutor v. Dario Kordić and Mario Čerkez*, Judgment, Case No. IT-95-14/2-A, Appeals Chamber, 17 December 2004, para. 320.

[150] See also Article 2(2). Kolb, Porretto, Vité, *L'application du droit international humanitaire*, supra note 2, 186; statements by several states during the elaboration of the 1994 Convention also indicate that a conflict involving UN troops falls under the regime of the law of IAC, UN Doc. A/AC.242/2 (1994), 43, paras. 166–170.

[151] The application of both the bulletin as well as the Convention is not mutually exclusive. The legal determination whether an armed conflict exists is a factual consideration and taking into account the saving clause of the Convention in Article 20(a)), both regimes can apply.

[152] P. Kirsch, 'La Convention sur la sécurité du personnel des Nations Unies et du personnel associé', in C. Emanuelli (ed.), *Les casques bleus: policiers ou combatants?/Blue helmets: policemen or combattants?* (Montréal, Wilson & Lafleur, 1997), 47, 56.

[153] Kolb, Porretto, Vité, *L'application du droit international humanitaire*, supra note 2, 187–188.

[154] Greenwood, supra note 140, 3, 26; Kolb, Porretto, Vité, ibid.; D. W. Bowett, *United Nations Forces: A Legal Study* (Clark, The Lawbook Exchange, Ltd., 1964), 509–510. See also S. Sheeran, S. Case, *The Intervention Brigade: Legal Issues for the UN in the Democratic Republic of the Congo*, International Peace Institute (2014).

be left undecided, as many treaty rules applicable in international armed conflicts, especially concerning the conduct of hostilities, are equally applicable in non-international conflicts on the basis of customary humanitarian law.[155]

The Relationship between Human Rights and IHL

In peacekeeping operations, situations may arise in which peacekeepers find themselves confronted with attacks involving the use of potentially deadly force. Such a scenario is independent from the question as to whether a peacekeeping operation has a mandate to use military force for purposes other than self-defence,[156] and it may trigger the application of IHL which therefore raises the question of the ways in which the two bodies of law, human rights law and IHL, can be reconciled in such a situation. It is now generally understood that both IHL and human rights law are applicable during armed conflict; they are complementary and not alternative.[157] Whereas, mostly in Europe this view is not only accepted but also supported, in contrast the American and Israeli position is that human rights law does not or should not apply in times of armed conflict.[158] In cases of overlap, the American perspective is that IHL applies as *lex specialis*.[159] In the past decades, an approximation

---

[155] For instance, Article 3 is applicable in international as well as in non-international armed conflicts, *Military and Paramilitary Activities*, supra note 149, para. 218; *Prosecutor v. Dusko Tadić a/k/a 'Dule'*, Decision on the Defence Motion for Interlocutory Appeal on Jurisdiction, Case No. IT-94-1, App.Ch., 2 October 1995, para. 102. Sams, 'IHL Obligations of the UN', supra note 133, 45, 63; M. Bothe, 'Peacekeeping', in B. Simma, D.-E. Khan, G. Nolte et al. (eds.), *The Charter of the United Nations. A Commentary*, Volume I (Oxford University Press, 2012), 1171, 1190 mn. 28; Beerli, 'Keynote Address', supra note 142, 9, 11.

[156] One example of such a mandate is the mandate of the intervention brigade in MONUSCO.

[157] J. Crawford, *Brownlie's Principles of Public International Law* (Oxford University Press, 2012), 654; O. Ben-Naftali, 'Introduction: International Humanitarian Law and International Human Rights Law – Pas de Deux', in O. Ben-Naftali (ed.), *International Humanitarian Law and International Human Rights Law* (Oxford University Press, 2011), 3, 4–6.

[158] G. D. Solis, *The Law of Armed Conflict. International Humanitarian Law in War* (Cambridge University Press, 2010), 24; F. J. Hampton, 'The Relationship between IHL and Human Rights Law from the Perspective of a Human Rights Treaty Body', *International Review of the Red Cross*, 90 (2008), 549, 550; L. Doswald-Beck, S. Vité, 'Le droit international humanitaire et le droit des droits de l'homme', *International Review of the Red Cross*, 75 (1993), 99, 112. The Israeli position might be based on political considerations regarding the Occupied Territories.

[159] Solis, ibid., 24; M. J. Dennis, 'Application of Human Rights Treaties Extraterritorially in Times of Armed Conflict and Military Occupation', *American Journal of International Law*, 99 (2005), 119, 133. But see A. Gillman, W. Johnson (eds.), *Operational Law Handbook, The Judge Advocate General's Legal Center & School* (2012), 46–47, paras. B.1–3; Fourth Periodic Report of the United States of America to the United Nations Committee

and partial convergence of IHL and human rights law occurred;[160] both fields of law are concerned with the protection of the human person[161] which has become a major issue in international law, as well as in international relations.[162] This is despite the different origins of both fields. Human Rights have grown out of constitutional, and thereby domestic, law in contrast to IHL which has a firm foundation in international law.[163]

The International Court of Justice elaborated at length on the relationship between human rights law and IHL in the *Wall Case*:

> the Court considers that the protection offered by human rights conventions does not cease in case of armed conflict, save through the effect of provisions for derogation of the kind to be found in Article 4 of the International Covenant on Civil and Political Rights. As regards the relationship between international humanitarian law and human rights law, there are thus three possible situations: some rights may be exclusively matters of international humanitarian law; others may be exclusively matters of human rights law; yet others may be matters of both these branches of international law. In order to answer the question put to it, the Court will have to take into consideration both these branches of international law, namely human rights law and, as *lex specialis*, international humanitarian law.[164]

---

on Human Rights Concerning the International Covenant on Civil and Political Rights (2011), para. 507.

[160] C. Droege, 'Elective Affinities? Human Rights and Humanitarian Law', *International Review of the Red Cross*, 90 (2008), 501, 548.

[161] Solis, *The Law of Armed Conflict*, supra note 158, 26.

[162] UN Doc. A/RES/60/1 (2005), paras. 138, 143; S/RES/1296 (2000); S/RES/1738 (2006). See also N. Krisch, 'Article 39', in B. Simma, D.-E. Khan, G. Nolte et al. (eds.), *The Charter of the United Nations. A Commentary, Volume II* (Oxford University Press, 2012), 1272, 1284 mn. 22–1285 mn. 24. Cf. C. True-Frost, 'The Security Council and Norm Consumption', *New York University Journal of International Law & Politics*, 40 (2007), 115, 138–174.

[163] A. A. Cançado Trindade, 'Desarrollo de las relaciones entre el derecho internacional humanitario y la protección internacional de los derechos humanos en su amplia dimensión', *Revista Instituto Interamericano de Derechos Humanos*, 16 (1992), 39, especially 45–49; R. Murphy, 'United Nations Military Operations and International Humanitarian Law: What Rules Apply to Peacekeepers?', *Criminal Law Forum*, 14 (2003), 153, 156–157; J.-M. Henckaerts, 'Concurrent Application of International Human Rights Law and International Humanitarian Law: Victims in Search of a Forum', *Human Rights & International Legal Discourse*, 1 (2007), 95, 97–100, 106–109; UN Doc. E/CN.4/Sub.2/2005/14 (2005), 12–14, paras. 41–50.

[164] *Legal Consequences*, supra note 95, para. 106. The Court reconfirmed its finding in *Congo v. Uganda, Case Concerning Armed Activities on the Territory of the Congo (Democratic Republic of the Congo v. Uganda)*, Judgment of 19 December 2005, para. 216.

This slightly cryptic judgment did not elucidate the position of the ICJ, but instead created confusion.[165] It was interpreted as a statement on the relationship between the two regimes per se and not as a pronouncement on how to establish the applicable legal framework in a specific context. In that regard, the advisory opinion of the ICJ in the *Legality of the Threat or Use of Nuclear Weapons Case* was clearer. The Court explicitly examined the relationship between one specific norm, the right to life under the ICCPR, and its application in times of armed conflict under IHL.[166] This norm-by-norm approach is well justified, as one cannot automatically presume that a specific norm of IHL will be *lex specialis* as regards the corresponding human rights norm.[167] Given that there are different human rights instruments, one might also allow derogation in specific cases which would allow the application of IHL, whereas in another instrument the same right might be regulated more restrictively.[168] Furthermore, depending on the norms in question, an interpretation might also allow an alignment of

---

[165] A better analysis of the relationship is contained the *Abella Case* of the Inter-American Commission on Human Rights, Case 11.137, *Juan Carlos Abella v. Argentina*, 18 November 1997, paras. 157–170. See generally D. Bethlehem, 'The Relationship between International Humanitarian Law and International Human Rights Law in Situations of Armed Conflict', *Cambridge Journal of International and Comparative Law*, 2 (2013), 180–182.

[166] *Legality of the Threat or Use of Nuclear Weapons*, supra note 51, para. 25. The Court held: 'the protection of the International Covenant on Civil and Political Rights does not cease in times of war, except by operation of Article 4 of the Covenant whereby certain provisions may be derogated from in a time of national emergency. Respect for the right to life is not, however, such a provision. In principle, *the right not arbitrarily to be deprived of one's life applies also in hostilities*. The test of what is an arbitrary deprivation of life, however, then falls to be determined by the applicable *lex specialis*, namely, the law applicable in armed conflict which is designed to regulate the conduct of hostilities'.

[167] L. Doswald-Beck, 'The Right to Life in Armed Conflict: Does International Humanitarian Law Provide All the Answers?', *International Review of the Red Cross*, 88 (2006), 881, 883–887, 890; H. Krieger, 'A Conflict of Norms: The Relationship between Humanitarian Law and Human Rights Law in the ICRC Customary Law Study', *Journal of Conflict & Security Law*, 11 (2006), 265, 271, 280–281; Henckaerts, 'Concurrent Application', supra note 163, 95, 119; A. Reidy, 'La pratique de la Commission et de la Cour européennes des droits de l'homme en matière de droit international humanitaire', *Revue Internationale de la Croix-Rouge*, 80 (1998), 551, 556–558, 561, 564; Erberich, supra note 118, 44–48; J. Cerone, 'Human Dignity in the Line of Fire: The Application of International Human Rights Law during Armed Conflict, Occupation, and Peace Operations', *Vanderbilt Journal of Transnational Law*, 39 (2006), 1447, 1453–1454; R. Cryer, 'The Interplay of Human Rights and Humanitarian Law: The Approach of the ICTY', *Journal of Conflict & Security Law*, 15 (2010), 511, 514. Cf. also *Case of Varnava and Others v. Turkey*, Grand Chamber, Judgment, 18 September 2009, para. 185; *Case of Al-Jedda v. The United Kingdom*, Judgment, Grand Chamber, Judgment, 7 July 2011, para. 107.

[168] Cf. Article 7 ICCPR and Article 5 ECHR.

the two norms, preventing a norm conflict according to which one norm is superseded by another.[169] Therefore, the norm deemed to be *lex specialis* is the norm with the 'more precise or narrower material and/or personal scope of application that prevails', in other words the one which has the larger 'common contact surface area' with the given situation.[170]

The nature of the armed conflict is also determinative for the relationship between two specific norms. Human rights are more likely to fill the lacunae in respect to the protection of persons in non-international armed conflict than in international armed conflicts.[171] There are also other areas of law which can be identified as falling more squarely under IHL or human rights law.[172] In relation to peacekeeping, it is argued that human rights apply in non-coercive operations and both bodies of law apply in coercive operations; however the correct criterion is an assessment of whether an armed conflict exists.[173]

As the competences of all international organisations are determined by their constitutive instruments, is even more important to determine the normative relationship between IHL and human rights law on a case-by-case basis.

Finally, an issue which has been more or less neglected in academic writing is the distinction between jurisdiction under human rights and humanitarian law for international organisations. It appears from the very few publications on this topic that the application of the regime of human rights law may be simply dismissed due to a lack of jurisdiction under

---

[169] M. Milanovic, 'A Norm Conflict Perspective on the Relationship between International Humanitarian Law and Human Rights Law', *Journal of Conflict & Security Law*, 14 (2010), 459, 468; cf. Human Rights Committee, General Comment 29, States of Emergency (Article 4), UN Doc. CCPR/C/21/Rev.1/Add.11 (2001), para. 3; Human Rights Committee, General Comment No. 31 (80), supra note 72, para. 11.

[170] M. Sassòli, L. M. Olson, 'The Relationship between International Humanitarian and Human Rights Law Where It Matters: Admissible Killing and Internment of Fighters in Non-international Armed Conflicts', *International Review of the Red Cross*, 90 (2008), 599, 604.

[171] Solis, *The Law of Armed Conflict*, supra note 158, 25; T. Meron, 'The Humanization of Humanitarian Law', *American Journal of International Law*, 94 (2000), 239, 240; Naert, *International Law Aspects*, supra note 34, 622–624; Krieger, 'A Conflict of Norms', supra note 167, 265, 274–275.

[172] A. Roberts, 'Transformative Military Occupation: Applying the Laws of War and Human Rights', *American Journal of International Law*, 100 (2006), 580, 594–595, 599–601; K. Watkin, 'Controlling the Use of Force: A Role for Human Rights Norms in Contemporary Armed Conflict', *American Journal of International Law*, 98 (2004), 1, 24–34, especially 26, 28.

[173] N. Tsagourias, 'EU Peacekeeping Operations: Legal and Theoretical Issues', in M. Trybus, N. D. White (eds.), *European Security Law* (Oxford University Press, 2007), 102, 118.

human rights law, which would leave IHL as the only applicable body of law.[174]

Naerts also asserts – on the basis of an analysis of the situation in Iraq in 2003 – that the Security Council can, by passing a resolution, set aside some provisions of IHL on the basis of Article 103 of the UN Charter.[175]

In summary, the relationship between IHL and HR has to be analysed in the context of a specific norm and the application of both fields of law may also be dependent on external factors – in terms of the respective norms – such as jurisdiction or the superseding powers of the Security Council.

A special regime of IHL is the law of occupation. It is argued in this book, that the law of occupation is not applicable to peacekeeping operations. Accordingly, it is only addressed very briefly. First of all, international territorial administration by an international organisation, corresponds rather to a situation of *occupatio pacifica* in contrast to *occupatio bellica* under the law of occupation.[176]

Moreover, the mandate of an international organisation, for example, the mandate of UNMIK, expressly includes a mandate of transformative authority which goes beyond safeguarding the status quo.[177] A large part if not the majority of academic writing denies an application of the law of occupation to international organisations.[178] Many international organisations are legally not even able to occupy a territory in the absence of

---

[174] F. Lattanzi, 'La frontière entre droit international humanitaire et droits de l'homme', in E. Decaux, A. Dieng, M. Sow (eds.), *From Human Rights to International Criminal Law. Studies in Honour of an African Jurist, the Late Judge Laïty Kama/ Des droits de l'homme au droit international pénal. Etudes en l'honneur d'un juriste africain, feu le juge Laïty Kama* (Leiden, Brill, 2007), 519, 569–570; Similarly, see Milanovic, 'A Norm Conflict Perspective', supra note 169, 459, 461; *Case of Issa*, supra note 72, paras. 68–74; Doswald-Beck, 'The Right of Life', supra note 167, 881, 899.

[175] Naert, *International Law Aspects*, supra note 34, 500–502; F. Naert, 'Detention in Peace Operations: The Legal Framework and Main Categories of Detainees', *Military Law & Law of the War Review*, 45 (2006), 51, 54; M. Zwanenburg, 'Existentialism in Iraq: Security Council Resolution 1483 and the Law of Occupation', *International Review of the Red Cross*, 86 (2004), 745, 755–757, 763–768; ICRC, Expert Meeting, Occupation and Other Forms of Administration of Foreign Territory, Report (2012), 83.

[176] Schmalenbach, *Die Haftung*, supra note 121, 358–362.

[177] Sams, 'IHL Obligations of the UN', supra note 133, 45, 66, 68; S. Ratner, 'Foreign Occupation and International Territorial Administration: The Challenges of Convergence', *European Journal of International Law*, 16 (2005), 695, 700; C. Stahn, *The Law and Practice of International Territorial Administration. Versailles to Iraq and Beyond* (Cambridge University Press, 2008), 155.

[178] G. H. Fox, *Humanitarian Occupation* (Cambridge University Press, 2008), 219; S. Wills, 'Continuing Impunity of Peacekeepers: The Need For a Convention', *Journal of International Humanitarian Legal Studies*, (2013), 1, 8–9.

competences under their internal law;[179] any such act would correspond to the international organisation acting *ultra vires*.[180] In practice, the UN has also never recognised the application of the law of occupation.[181]

Breach of an International Obligation in the Form of a Mandate of a Peacekeeping Operation

Another important source for potential breaches of international obligations in peacekeeping operations is the mandate of the operation itself.

Article 10(2) ARIO stipulates that a breach of an international obligation by an international organisation 'includes the breach of any international obligation that may arise for an international organization towards its members under the rules of the organization'. The Commentary of the ILC to Article 10 explains that paragraph 2 of the disposition includes generally – contrary to that which its wording might suggest – all rules of the organisation which may form part of international law.[182] Consequently Article 10(2) has to be interpreted as covering also cases of breaches of an international obligation by an organisation under its own rules towards other legal entities than its members.

Resolutions of organs of an organisation are considered to be part of the rules of the organisation according to Article 2(b) ARIO.[183] Thus, it can be questioned whether the breach of a mandate in the form of a Security Council Resolution by a peacekeeping operation would amount to a breach of an international obligation. According to the Commentary of the ILC, it is disputed which or whether rules of international organisations are part of international law or can only be seen as part of the internal law of the organisation.[184]

The ICJ observed in the *Kosovo* advisory opinion that '[t]he Constitutional Framework derives its binding force from the binding

---

[179] Internal law means the Constituent treaty as well as other relevant documents pertaining to its functioning on an external level.
[180] From the perspective of the law of international responsibility, 'consent' is a circumstance precluding wrongfulness.
[181] Sams, 'IHL Obligations of the UN and other International Organisations', supra note 133, 45, 68–69.
[182] UN Doc. A/66/10) (2011), 98, para. 8.
[183] The UN itself in its comments to the ILC stated that decisions and resolutions of the principal organs of the UN may fall under the rules of the organisation as well as the establishment and conduct of peacekeeping operations which has developed almost entirely through practice, UN Doc. A/CN.4/637/Add.1 (2011), 7, para. 5.
[184] UN Doc. A/66/10 (2011), 97–98, para. 5.

character of resolution 1244 (1999) and thus from international law' and concluded that 'Security Council resolution 1244 (1999) and the Constitutional Framework form part of ... international law'.[185] Mandates of the Security Council, in the form of a resolution, are nowadays rather lengthy documents containing various, specific obligations. Therefore, it appears first of all that it would be necessary to determine not whether the resolution is part of international law, but rather whether one or several specific dispositions are part of international law.

One needs to distinguish between non-binding provisions and provisions which – by the language and the context of the resolution – are binding upon regional organisations. Mere recommendations do not create legal obligations and they could therefore also not hold the SC responsible if they are acted upon by a regional organisation.[186] However the question is, even if a regional organisation is not obliged to deploy a peacekeeping operation as it was established in the previous chapter, nonetheless specific dispositions in the mandate for this peacekeeping operations could legally bind this regional organisation.

It is now standard practice of the Security Council to include dispositions regarding the protection of civilians in mandates as well as dispositions such as 'during the deployment of operation X, organisation Y shall ensure the respect of the applicable human rights, international humanitarian and refugee law'.

The Security Council emphasised anew the importance of the protection of civilians in the context of peacekeeping operations, in a Presidential Statement accompanied by a seventy-eight-page *aide-memoire* in February 2014.[187]

Article 10(1) ARIO stipulates that the breach of an international obligation exists 'regardless of the origin or character of the obligation concerned'. Therefore, any breach of a rule of international law as enshrined in the mandate of a peacekeeping operation would be a breach of an international obligation, without prejudice to the question as to whether the potentially corresponding human rights obligation of the international

---

[185] Accordance with International Law of the Unilateral Declaration of Independence in Respect of Kosovo, Advisory Opinion of 22 July 2010, 42–43, paras. 88–89, 93.
[186] Authorisations addressed to member states or organisations by an international organisation to commit an act that would be internationally wrongful if committed by the latter lead to the authorising organisation being responsible under Article 17 ARIO.
[187] UN Doc. S/PRST/2014/3 (2014). See also Human Rights Due Diligence Policy on United Nations Support to Non-United Nations Security Forces, UN Doc. A/67/777–S/2013/110 (2013).

organisation was also breached. It is therefore not necessary to construe the violation of a Security Council Resolution as a violation of an international obligation through a piggybacking approach; considering the mandate of the Resolution to contain implicit or explicit obligations under human rights law, IHL or any other particular body of law.[188] In practice, it could be problematic to determine the exact nature of a disposition in a mandate and it is even more problematic as the potentially corresponding rule of human rights or IHL is not codified but stems from customary international law. The UN therefore emphasised that it would be necessary for the organisation to clarify in its definition of rules that not a violation of the rules as such – entails the responsibility of the organisation, but the violation of the international law obligations it might contain.[189]

Based on the presumption that regional organisations are bound on a customary law basis by the dispositions of the UN Charter with regard to maintaining international peace and security, another interesting question arises: What are the implications regarding the law of responsibility if a binding obligation by the Security Council as part of a mandate addressed to a regional organisation is either not executed or violated in practice?

First of all, one would have to distinguish between the different kinds of obligations; the conditions for a breach of a due diligence or an obligation of means by a regional organisation are different from the conditions for a breach of an obligation of result. This distinction is also relevant if one considers regional organisations as *not* directly bound by the UN Charter, but in the contrary case, this distinction of obligations could have a direct bearing upon the distribution of responsibility.

One could argue that all international organisations are responsible for supervising the implementation of binding decisions by their members. Failing to do so the UN would have violated its positive obligation of monitoring the conduct and the regional organisation would have violated its negative obligation to abstain from certain conduct.[190] The situation would be different for a third organisation cooperating with both the UN

---

[188] Cf. Verdirame, *The UN and Human Rights*, supra note 64, 98.
[189] Responsibility of international organizations, Comments and observations received from international organizations, supra note 183, 7, para. 6. The District Court in The Hague likewise considered UNPROFOR's mandate as having 'a powers-creating character' but not as 'calling to life' enforceable obligations under international law; see *District Court in The Hague, Stichting Mothers of Srebrenica and Others v. The Netherlands*, Judgment, Case No. C/09/295247/HA ZA 07-2973, 16 July 2014, para. 4149.
[190] In the context of human rights law, a regional organisation owes in any case obligations to the UN as at least some human rights norms are considered to be obligations *erga omnes* and vice versa.

and the regional organisation in the peacekeeping operation as it would not be bound by the mandate.

Returning to the distinction between an obligation under the mandate of a peacekeeping operation and an independently existing obligation under human rights law, a derogation from human rights law by the peacekeeping operation would per se not constitute a violation of human rights law as it contains a separate obligation under international law.

This particular issue became, however, relevant in the case of *Al-Jedda* before the ECtHR and in the form of Article 103 of the UN Charter. The Court concluded that there was no contradiction between human rights law and Security Council Resolution 1546 and did not, accordingly, pronounce itself on the potential effect of Article 103 of the Charter.[191]

However, in the present context of cooperation between the UN and regional organisations, Article 103 is generally not relevant.[192] First of all, it applies to the member states of the UN and to agreements concluded by them which are contradictory to their obligations under the UN Charter.[193] Moreover, at least the most fundamental human rights norms are considered to be part of *jus cogens* and they would prevail over Article 103 at least, arguably, on their customary law basis. Nevertheless, if one takes the view that Article 103 applies equally to the UN itself, it would allow the organisation to invoke that disposition to justify non-compliance with an international obligation, also with regard to Article 32 ARIO which stipulates that '[t]he responsible international organization may not rely on its rules as justifications for failure to comply with its obligations under this Part'.[194]

The most interesting aspect is that such an application of Article 103 could even have an impact upon the distribution of responsibility between the UN and regional organisations in the context of peacekeeping

---

[191] Case of Al-Jedda v. The United Kingdom, Grand Chamber, Judgment, 7 July 2011, 56–60, paras. 101–109; cf. A. Conte, 'Human Rights beyond Borders: A New Era in Human Rights Accountability for Transnational Counter-Terrorism Operations?', *Journal of Conflict & Security Law*, 18 (2013), 233, 253.

[192] Unless one were to take the view that on the basis of customary law obligations of regional organisations towards the UN, as it was just argued, regional organisations could also be entitled to invoke Article 103 regarding obligations under international law which would be contravening their obligations towards the UN.

[193] Only a few authors argue that Article 103 applies to non-members; R. Kolb, *L'article 103 de la Charte des Nations Unies*, Recueil des cours de l'Académie de La Haye, Volume 367 (2013), 9, 76.

[194] The UN commented upon this particular point in its submissions to the ILC, UN Doc. A/CN.4/637/Add.1 (2011), 36 para. 3.

operations. If conduct arising during the deployment of a UN mandated operation were to be attributed jointly to the UN and a regional organisation and the Security Council would have explicitly derogated in the resolution from a specific human right,[195] the subsequent analysis of the breach of an international obligation would lead to the paradoxical situation that the UN could rely on Article 103 as a derogation in breach of any violation, whereas the regional organisation would, potentially, be responsible on its own,[196] despite the fact that the conduct was attributed to both of them.

This is not likely to arise in practice as the mandates given out by the Security Council do not generally contain obligations which would derogate from human rights law – rather the opposite – nor be so concise and specific to correspond to a particular human rights.[197] Although the mandate of recent peacekeeping operations are more precise regarding the competences and powers granted to the peacekeeping forces, the Security Council continues to rely likewise on the formula of 'all necessary means'.[198]

But this theoretical argument nevertheless underlines not only the complexity of the whole issue, but also the importance of the internal law of international organisations in applying the law of responsibility. In summary, if regional organisations are considered to be bound by the system of collective security as established by the UN, specific obligations handed out to these organisations by the UN Security Council could also impair the distribution of responsibility between the organisations.

---

[195] Presupposing that IHL would not be applicable, as otherwise the UN might be nevertheless bound by the corresponding or even *lex specialis* rule of IHL.

[196] It is harder to assess whether the result would be the same in the case of a UN-authorised operation. If one considers the SC Resolution establishing the operation as a mere authorisation and not of a delegation of powers of the Council, it would be difficult to argue that Article 103 would be applicable which could leave room for an application of Article 17 ARIO.

[197] Conte, 'Human Rights beyond Borders', supra note 191, 233, 260.

[198] Member states are very aware of the problems associated with such vague mandates. As pointed out by Gowlland-Debbas: 'It is understandable, therefore, that member states have treated such a delegation of the Council's powers to individual actors with extreme caution and that they have made numerous efforts to circumscribe Council authorisations, consistently insisting that the Council retain a degree of authority and control over such operations and avoid providing 'a blank cheque for excessive and indiscriminate use of force.' V. Gowlland-Debbas, 'The Limits of Unilateral Enforcement of Community Objectives in the Framework of UN Peace Maintenance', *European Journal of International Law*, 11 (2000), 361, 369.

Breach of an International Obligation in the Form of the Obligations Arising under the Internal Law of the Organisations

Breaches of international obligations of international organisations in the context of peacekeeping operations may also arise in the form of violations of the internal law of these organisations if these rules are also part of international law. The following part contains a brief analysis of the internal law of the AU, the UN and the EU on the basis of their particular relevance and involvement in all examined case studies.

African Union Since 2009, the AU has prioritised the development of a protection of civilians approach for AU-mandate peacekeeping operations[199] leading in 2010 to the adoption of the Draft Guidelines for the Protection of Civilians in African Union Peace Support Operations. According to the guidelines, the protection of civilians includes 'to ensure the full respect for the rights of ... the individual recognised under regional instruments including the African Charter of Human and Peoples' Rights ..., international law, including humanitarian, human rights and refugee law'.[200] In the same year, the Commission decided to mainstream the draft Guidelines for the Protection of Civilians in Peace Support Missions.[201] For the further elaboration of the Guidelines, the AU has consulted on a regular basis with the UN 'to ensure that the development of the Guidelines ... is aligned to the UN approach as closely as possible'.[202]

Regarding specifically the application of IHL, the status of mission agreement of the AU for the Ceasefire Commission in the Darfur region states that the AU shall ensure that the operation is conducted with full respect of the principles and rules of the Geneva Conventions and Additional Protocols.[203] The same disposition is inserted in the SOMA

---

[199] Progress Report of the Chairperson of the Commission, AU Doc. PSC/PR/2(CCLXXIX) (2011), 1, para. 5.
[200] Proposed Guidelines for the Protection of Civilians in African Union Peace Support Operations for Considerations by African Union (2010), 2, para. 1.
[201] Report of the Chairperson of the Commission, AU Doc. PSC/MIN/1(CCLXLV) (2010), 8, para. 33; Report of the Chairperson of the Commission, AU Doc. PSC/MIN/1(CCLXV) (2010), 9, para. 33; 22, para. 83(iii).
[202] Progress Report of the Chairperson of the Commission, supra note 199, 3, para. 12.
[203] Status of Mission Agreement (SOMA) on the Establishment and Management of the Ceasefire Commission in the Darfur Area of the Sudan (CFC) (2004), para. 8(a), available at www.africa-union.org/Darfur/Agreements/soma.pdf.

for AMISOM[204] so that one can probably conclude that it is the current practice of the AU now to demand respect for the principles and rules of the Geneva Conventions. In short, the internal documents of the AU confirm the application of human rights law and IHL without containing further specific rules regarding the application of these two areas of international law.

United Nations It is suggested that the UN is bound by human rights on the basis of its internal law. The Charter of the UN contains several references to the promotion and promulgation of human rights. These references are however, very generic and do not contain specific substantive obligations for the UN.[205] On the contrary, the human rights provisions in the UN Charter are rather 'scattered, terse, even cryptic',[206] so that one cannot read in the Charter what is not there.[207] But it is uncontroversial that international organisations 'may be bound by obligations arising under its constituent instrument'.[208] So it is beyond doubt that without the activities of the UN, human rights would not have become a 'subject of international interest' and it seems difficult to imagine if not illogical or immoral to consider the UN not to be bound at least by the most fundamental human rights and obligations it is promoting.[209] The Capstone document defines international human rights as an integral part of the normative framework of peacekeeping operations, but emphasises simultaneously that peacekeeping operations

---

[204] Status of Mission Agreement (SOMA) between the Transnational Federal Government of the Somali Republic and the African Union on the African Union Mission in Somalia (AMISOM), 5, paras. 9–10.
[205] Cf. also Kolb, Porretto, Vité, *L'application du droit international humanitaire*, supra note 27, 258–259.
[206] H. Steiner, P. Alston, R. Goodman, *International Human Rights in Context: Law, Politics, Morals* (Oxford University Press, 2008), 135.
[207] A. Tzanakopoulos, 'Hierarchy in International Law: The Place of Human Rights', in E. De Wet, J. Widmar (eds.), *Hierarchy in International Law: The Place of Human Rights* (Oxford University Press, 2012), 42, 61; N. Quénivet, 'Human Rights Law and Peacekeeping Operations', in M. Odello, R. Piotrowicz (eds.), *International Military Missions and International Law* (Leiden, Brill, 2011), 99, 118–119.
[208] Verdirame, *The UN and Human Rights*, supra note 64, 73.
[209] Cf. Kolb, Porretto, Vité, *L'application du droit international humanitaire*, supra note 27, 259–260; see also F. Mégret, F. Hoffmann, 'The UN as a Human Rights Violator? Some Reflections on the United Nations Changing Human Rights Responsibilities', *Human Rights Quarterly*, 25 (2003), 314, 317–320. Verdirame, *The UN and Human Rights*, supra note 64, 74.

'should be conducted/should act in accordance with ... international human rights law'.[210]

As confirmed by the Secretary-General in his report of 2011, the Bulletin on Observance by United Nations forces of IHL is 'binding upon all members of United Nations peace operations ... [and] signal[s] formal recognition of the applicability of International Humanitarian Law to United Nations peace operations'.[211] The bulletin covers the quintessential dispositions of IHL, including some which might not yet be deemed of enjoying a customary law character.[212] But it is not applicable to UN-authorised operations, and the responsibility 'to protect and ensure the respect' for IHL in the latter case rests with the state or regional organizations conducting the operation.[213] The Bulletin is applicable in peacekeeping operations when the use of force is permitted in self-defence.[214] It has to be pointed out that the Bulletin codifies some of the fundamental principles of IHL, but that it is not always in accordance with the respective dispositions of IHL. In paragraph 1.1 it is stated that '[t]he fundamental principles and rules of international humanitarian law set out in the present bulletin are applicable to United Nations forces when in situations of armed conflict they are actively engaged therein as combatants, to the extent and for the duration of their engagement'. Combatants can normally be always attacked under IHL whereas civilians can only be attacked during the time of their direct participation in hostilities, thus the Bulletin considers peacekeeping forces to be falling in-between the two categories. But it also provides that the UN force shall 'make a clear distinction at all times between civilians and combatants ... [and that] Attacks on civilians ... are prohibited'.[215]

---

[210] United Nations Peacekeeping Operations, Principles and Guidelines (2008), the so-called 'Capstone Doctrine', 14, para. 1.2; Note of Guidance on Integrated Missions, supra note 29, para. 3, 16.
[211] UN Doc. A/56/326 (2001), 9, para. 19. But see also Verdirame, *The UN and Human Rights*, supra note 64, 205–206; Zwanenburg, 'Compromise or Commitment', supra note 53, 176. See generally K. Grenfall, 'Perspective on the Applicability and Application of International Humanitarian Law: The UN Context', *International Review of the Red Cross*, 95 (2013), 645–652.
[212] D. Shraga, 'UN Peacekeeping Operations: Applicability of International Humanitarian Law and Responsibility for Operations-Related Damage', *American Journal of International Law*, 94 (2005), 406, 408.
[213] Ibid., 406, 408; UN Doc. ST/SGB/1999/13 (1999), 1, para. 1.1. In this regard, in Resolution 2085, the Security Council decided that AFISMA 'shall take all necessary measures, in compliance with applicable international humanitarian law and human rights law', UN Doc. S/RES/2085 (2012), 4, para. 9. Thus, the SC obliged a peacekeeping operation deployed by a regional organisation to respect the applicable legal framework.
[214] UN Doc. ST/SGB/1999/13 (1999), 1, para. 1.1.
[215] Ibid., para. 5.1.

It is binding only on an internal level, but does not possess a binding effect on the external sphere.[216]

European Union Article 6(1) TEU states that EU is founded on the principle of liberty, democracy, respect for fundamental rights and fundamental freedoms. Thereby it lays the ground for the incorporation of IHL into the European legal order as it would be a misnomer if principles 'so fundamental to the respect of the human person' would not fall under this formula.[217] Regarding the particular field of the CFSP, Article 21 TEU stipulates that 'the Union's action on the international scene shall be guided by the principles which have inspired its own creation ... the universality and indivisibility of human rights and fundamental freedoms, respect for human dignity'.[218]

Further human rights obligations of the EU derive from the EU's Charter of Fundamental Rights[219] which has the same legal value as the

---

[216] B. Dold, *Vertragliche und ausservertragliche Verantwortlichkeit im Recht der internationalen Organisationen* (Zürich, Schulthess, 2006), 71–72.

[217] V. Falco, 'The Internal Legal Order of the European Union as a Complementary Framework for Its Obligations under IHL', *Israel Law Review* 42 (2009), 168, 191; O. De Schutter, 'Human Rights and the Rise of International Organisations: The Logic of Sliding Scales in the Law of International Responsibility', in J. Wouters, E. Brems, S. Smis (eds.), *Accountability for Human Rights Violations by International Organisations* (Antwerp, Intersentia, 2010), 51, 106–107.

[218] D. Chalmers, G. Davies, G. Monti, *European Union Law* (2010), 660; Council of the European Union, EU Strategic Framework and Action Plan on Human Rights on Democracy, Luxembourg, 25 June 2012, 1–2; EU Guidelines, Human Rights and International Humanitarian Law (2009), 3, 12–13; cf. also Council of the European Union, Guidelines to EU Policy towards Third Countries on Torture and Other Cruel, Inhuman or Degrading Treatment or Punishment – An Update of the Guidelines, Brussels, 15 March 2012, 2; EU Guidelines on Children and Armed Conflict, 2, para. 7; Mainstreaming Human Rights and Gender into European Security and Defence Policy (2008), 11–12.

[219] D. Chalmers, G. Davies, G. Monti, *European Union Law* (Cambridge University Press, 2010), 230, 237–238; A. Clapham, 'A Human Rights Policy for the European Community', *Yearbook of European Law*, 10 (1990), 309, 311. See, for instance, C-540/03, *European Parliament v. Council of the European Union*, Judgment of the Court (Grand Chamber of 27 June 2006, I-5822–I-5823, paras. 38–39; I-5841, para. 107; C-275/06, *Productores de Música de España (Promusicae) v. Telefónica de España SAU*, Judgment (Grand Chamber) of 29 January 2008, paras. 1, 61–70; Joined Cases C-322/07 P, C-327/07 P and C-338/07 P, *Papierfabrik August Koehler AG (C-322/07 P), Bolloré SA (C-327/07 P) and Distribuidora Vizcaína de Papeles SL (C-338/07 P) v. Commission of the European Communities*, Judgment (Third Chamber) of 3 September 2009, especially para. 80; C-109/01, *Secretary of State for the Home Department v. Hacene Akrich*, Judgment of the Court of 23 September 2003, paras. 58–60; C-540/03, *European Parliament v. Council of the European Union*, Judgment (Grand Chamber) of 27 June 2006, especially para. 38, but see also paras. 52–59.

EU Treaties. Naert argues that the EU is already bound by the ECHR in substance on the basis of an operation of Article 6 TEU.[220] In contrast, Gaja argues that the status of the ECHR under EU law is not completely clear. Article 6(3) speaks of fundamental rights as guaranteed by the ECHR which points towards a binding effect within EU law, and suggests a status of the ECHR under EU law equivalent to other provisions in the treaties.[221]

Regarding the application of IHL under the EU's internal law, it is submitted that the updated EU Guidelines on promoting compliance with IHL cannot be considered as binding the EU, by a unilateral act, to comply with IHL.[222] But it can be argued that, indirectly, although on a policy level, they induce a behavior of compliance of the EU per se with IHL. EU Heads of Mission as well as Commanders of EU civilian and military operations are obliged to include an assessment of the IHL situation in their reports about a given State or conflict. Furthermore, the importance of preventing and suppressing violations of IHL by third parties shall be considered, where appropriate in the drafting of mandates of EU crisis management operations.[223] Therefore, this strict policy, which may also include sharing information for the purposes of criminal

---

[220] F. Naert, 'Applicability/Application of Human Rights Law to IOs involved in Peace Operations', in S. Kolanowski (ed.), *Proceedings of the Bruges Colloquium. International Organisations' Involvement in Peace Operations: Applicable Legal Framework and the Issue of Responsibility* (2011), 45, 47–48. See also Chalmers, Davies, Monti, *European Union Law*, ibid., 230.

[221] G. Gaja, 'Accession to the ECHR', in A. Biondi, P. Eeckhout, S. Ripley (eds.), *EU Law after Lisbon* (Oxford University Press, 2012), 180, 194; see C-415/05 P, *Al Barakaat International Foundation v. Council of the European Union and Commission of the European Communities*, Opinion of Advocate General Poiares Maduro, 23 January 2008, para. 44; Joined Cases C-402/05 P and C-415/05 P, *Yassin Abdullah Kadi and Al Barakaat International Foundation v. Council of the European Union and Commission of the European Communities*, Judgment of the Court (Grand Chamber) of 3 September 2008, paras. 283–285; C-4/73, *J. Nold, Kohlen- und Baustoffgroßhandlung v. Commission of the European Communities*, Judgment of the Court of 14 May 1974, p. 507, para. 13; C-36/75, *Roland Rutili v. Ministre de L'intérieur*, Judgment of 28 October 1975, p. 1232, para. 32; C-299/95, *Friedrich Kremzow v. Republic Österreich*, Judgment (Fifth Chamber) of 29 May 1997, p. I-2646, para. 19. The ICCPR has been considered as a source in the case of Orkem, C-374/87 *Orkem v. Commission of the European Communities*, Judgment of 18 October 1989, p. 3351, para. 31.

[222] They rather correspond to the second obligation of states under the Geneva Conventions, not only to respect, but also *to ensure respect of* international humanitarian law. See generally F. Naert, 'Observance of International Humanitarian Law by Forces under the Command of the European Union', *International Review of the Red Cross*, 95 (2013), 637–643.

[223] Updated EU guidelines on promoting compliance with international humanitarian law (IHL), Doc. 2009/C 303/06 (2009), paras. 15(b), 16(f).

prosecution by the ICC,[224] also puts pressure on EU staff to comply with IHL. Furthermore, the EU should cooperate, where appropriate, with the UN and relevant regional organisations for the promotion of compliance with IHL.[225] As the UN and other international organisations have adopted a similar policy, monitoring and ensuring the compliance of IHL by third parties, there is an overlapping network of policy mechanisms to ensure compliance with IHL, also ensuring respect of IHL by the staff of international organisations.[226]

In summary, the protection of human rights and humanitarian law has been incorporated in the internal law of the majority of the examined international organisations. By this fact, it may give rise to international responsibility, potentially independent of other violations of human rights or humanitarian law, and purely on the basis of international law. Should a mandate by the UN Security Council contain a slightly divergent disposition from the internal law of the obligation, it would once again be required to reach a harmonious interpretation of the conflicting dispositions.

Conclusions

The inquiry into the applicable law in respect to peacekeeping operations has shown that the legal framework is rather complex. Both international human rights and IHL can be applicable whereby both fields of law raise certain issues. In addition to the debate over the applicable body of humanitarian law to peacekeeping operations, the exercise of jurisdiction by international organisations under human rights law is also problematic. It was argued that the two models of jurisdiction developed in the jurisprudence of international courts and tribunals are applicable to international organisations. The unclear customary status of many dispositions further complicates the picture.

These two models of jurisdiction under human rights law may have a connotation in the context of the question of joint responsibility of international organisations for peacekeeping operations. The fact that

---

[224] Ibid., para. 16(f).
[225] Ibid., para. 16(e).
[226] See, e.g., Security Council Resolution 1502, UN Doc. S/RES/1502 (2003), Preamble, Statement by the President of the Security Council with Annex, Protection of Civilians in Armed Conflict, Aide-Memoire, UN Doc. S/PRST/2009/1 (2009); Statement by Ms. Patricia O'Brien, Under-Secretary-General for Legal Affairs at Thirtieth Annual Seminar for Diplomats on International Humanitarian Law, 20 March 2013; Secretary-General's Bulletin, supra note 214; ICRC, Customary IHL, Rule 139. Respect for International Humanitarian Law, available at www.icrc.org/customary-ihl/eng/docs/v1_rul_rule139.

the criterion of normative control is applicable signifies that all involved organisations generally also exercise jurisdiction under human rights law jointly, whether it is under the personal, the spatial or a combined personal–spatial model of jurisdiction. In the case of at least one international organisation aiding and assisting one or more international organisation(s), their human rights obligations might also be different. The aiding and assisting organisation might only exercise jurisdiction under the personal model, whereas the other organisation(s) could be exercising jurisdiction under the spatial model; the aiding and assisting organisation could then only be bound by negative obligations under human rights law, whereas the other organisation(s) could be bound by positive human rights obligations. Simultaneously, it is possible that one organisation will be bound by a norm of IHL and another organisation will be bound by rule of human rights law.

But even if the conduct giving rise to the internationally wrongful act is attributed to several international organisations on the basis of the normative control criterion, they can exercise jurisdiction under human rights law on the basis of different models. One could imagine that forces of the organisation deploying the peacekeeping operation have arrested an individual. For the purposes of that organisation, the individual might be under the jurisdiction of that organisation on the basis of the personal model, whereas the other organisations might exercise jurisdiction on the basis of the spatial model.

The mandate of the peacekeeping operation and the internal law of the involved organisations constitute two additional layers of potential obligations which can give rise to breaches of international law during the deployment of a peacekeeping operation thereby further multiplying the likelihood that international organisations are jointly responsible. Also under the mandate of a peacekeeping operations different obligations may arise for both the UN and the regional organisation. The former may be obliged to monitor the conduct of the latter and the latter may be bound to abstain from a certain conduct.

6

Conclusions and Recommendations

To 'promote international co-operation and to achieve international peace and security' and 'to unite our strength to maintain international peace and security' – these were the wishes of the founders of the League of Nations and the UN – and universal peace remains a desirable ideal.[1] Peacekeeping operations deployed by the UN and regional organisations have become a major tool for conflict regulation in the twenty-first century.

Universalist and regionalist positions, with regard to maintaining international peace and security, have converged in the practice of international organisations. Cooperation between international organisations has emerged as the key driver in defining roles or niches in the system of collective security and in establishing a division of labour for the mutual benefit of the involved organisations. This development included the institutionalisation of relations among the actors, as well as an increase in cooperation in the operational context – during the deployment of peacekeeping operations. This process benefitted from the wide margin of discretion provided for the Security Council under the UN Charter. International law has played a double role with regard to cooperation between international organisations and the maintenance of international peace and security. On the one hand, peacekeeping operations as a tool for conflict resolution could not have been 'invented' without the recognition of the concept of 'implied powers' as applicable to international organisations. On the other hand, the non-existence of established international legal rules regulating the conduct of international organisations and questions of their responsibility under international law resulted in a decades-long purely practice-driven approach, which in turn created further legal uncertainties.

The *bon mot* that international humanitarian law is always one war behind concerning the regulation of armed conflict, as referred to in the introduction of this study, is most certainly also applicable to the context of

---

[1] Preamble of the Covenant of the League of Nations and of the Charter of the UN respectively.

the international responsibility of international organisations. For several centuries, following the Westphalian peace, the system of international law was based on the principle of the sovereign equality of states and characterised by a purely bilateral conception of the relations among states. The possibility that several actors could be jointly responsible was absolutely *systemfremd* (alien to the system). The Articles on State Responsibility as codified in 2001 therefore only admit the possibility of joint responsibility in the limited circumstances of aid or assistance, direction and control, or coercion. In addition, an article on plurality of responsible states was inserted in the project, without, however, defining the necessary criteria for a joint attribution of conduct. The 2011 Articles on the Responsibility of International Organisations did not contain any assimilation of the criteria for the attribution of conduct on recent practice, but they were transferred from the previous set of Articles on State Responsibility. They are therefore an expression of several centuries of practice within a state-centric system, at least to the extent that they define the rules on the attribution of conduct.

As it was rightly acknowledged by the ILC and its Special Rapporteur, the practice of international organisations is sparse in some areas due to the fact that they are new entities in the international arena, at least in comparison to states. Moreover, the feedback or enthusiasm of international organisations in commenting on the project was not overwhelming, which is not surprising per se. From an organisational point of view, the legal uncertainties associated with the non-existence or at least non-codification of applicable rules on responsibility were outmatched by the liberty of conduct it afforded them. One could even raise the question whether the cooperation among international organisations, and in particular the high intensity of cooperation in the area of the maintenance of international peace and security had taken place if legal rules with regard to the responsibility of international organisations would have existed when the UN and the first regional organisations were founded.

The central research question this book endeavoured to explore, whether international organisations cooperating in peacekeeping operations can be jointly responsibility for violations of international law occurring during the deployment of such operations, can be responded to affirmatively. In particular the case studies illustrated that there are instances in which internationally wrongful acts can be attributed not only to one, but to two or several international organisations. The case studies nonetheless also highlighted that due to the incredibly varied nature of peacekeeping operations and the continuing evolution of relations among the UN and regional organisations in some instances, the conduct might not be attributable to two or more organisations, but just to one.

An analysis of the applicable legal framework to peacekeeping operations illustrated that the complex interplay of cooperation mechanisms and arrangements is accompanied by a complicated network of applicable norms which multiplies the potential for joint responsibility of international organisations. The fact that internationally wrongful acts of peacekeepers could possibly be attributed jointly to international organisations – applying the normative control criterion – on the basis of violations of different primary norms increases the flexibility and the likelihood that international organisations can be hold responsible under international law.

In the end, the Articles on the Responsibility of International Organisations have proven to be unsuitable for regulating the responsibility of international organisations in the context of peacekeeping operations as they are based on the premise that cooperation among international organisations is the exception rather than the rule. Whereas, on the one hand, it could be seen as a lacuna, on the other hand, it was already highlighted in the discussions within the ILC that the context of peacekeeping operations might be too specific to fall under any general rule of attribution.[2] The decision of the commission to abstain from including any specific disposition on peacekeeping operations therefore allows for an elaboration of an applicable rule by other actors, as well as in practice. The present study proposed the creation of a new criterion of attribution, namely 'normative control' based on the intertwined cooperation arrangements between international organisations on various levels of command and control in a peacekeeping operation and in conformity with the *lex specialis* rule contained in Article 64 ARIO.

Nevertheless, the present study has illustrated that the evolution of relations among the UN and regional organisations was also induced by several external and internal factors, among which were scarcities of resources and competition for legitimacy, which also led the organisations to develop their competences in complementary areas and based on different doctrines to deploy peacekeeping operations. These non-legal, external factors also add to the difficulty in defining the applicable legal framework. In addition, the relations among international organisations, and particularly, in the area of maintaining international peace and security are continuously evolving and non-static. In the course of

---

[2] See Chapter 3.

their evolution, there may be other instances of confrontation or repositioning of certain organisations which would also affect some of the specific findings of this study, such as the emerging division of labour for maintaining international peace and security on the African continent and they could also necessitate an adaptation of the normative control criterion at some point in the future. Furthermore, another obstacle exists in the form of a casuistic approach taken by international organisations in cooperating in peacekeeping operations. A thorough study and analysis of other case studies of peacekeeping operations might allow shedding more light on the criterion for the attribution of conduct in peacekeeping operations.

However, two new obstacles are already on the horizon, which concern the further multiplication of actors involved in peacekeeping operations. On the one hand, inter-mission cooperation between peacekeeping operations is increasing; on the other, peacekeeping operations have now started to use private contractors for certain tasks such as guard duties around camps.[3] States have also resorted to deploying troops in peacekeeping operations which are part of bi- or multinational cooperation arrangements, following the concepts of smart defence or sharing and pooling. In mid-February 2014, for example, France and Germany announced the deployment of parts of the Franco–German brigade to Mali as part of EUTM Mali. The brigade itself is under joint French–German command, but it is incorporated into the command structure of Eurocorps. This new multiplication of involved actors will further increase the likelihood for joint responsibility and consequently will also increase the likelihood that the threshold for the application of the normative control criterion will be surpassed.

The development towards more cooperation between international legal entities and the multiplication of actors, however, is not confined to the particular field of peacekeeping operations, but appears in all areas of activities regulated by international law. Thus, even on a larger scale, it is necessary to reflect upon the current state of the development of the law and mechanisms of international responsibility in order to prevent a further disconnect between the legal framework and reality. The more power international organisations have, the more important the effective

---

[3] With regard to the implications in terms of international responsibility for the acts of these private contractors, see, e.g., P. Palchetti, 'The Allocation of Responsibility for Internationally Wrongful Acts Committed in the Course of Multinational Operations', *International Review of the Red Cross*, 95 (2013), 727, 731–732.

regulation of responsibility of international organisations is.[4] Arguments of legal certainty also warrant the formulation of such a recommendation. As it was pointed out by Thomas Franck:

> The fairness of international law, as of any other legal system, will be judged, first by the degree to which the rules satisfy the participants' expectations of justifiable distribution of costs and benefits and secondly by the extent to which the rules are made and applied in accordance with what the participants perceive as right process.[5]

Any alternative approach focusing solely on a specific field of international law could possibly also contribute to a further fragmentation of international law.

A start would be to adapt the framework for international dispute settlement which in its current state is based on a bilateral conception. As the analysis in Chapter 3 illustrated, the invocation of international responsibility also raises certain problems which are in similar fashion an expression of the bilateral conception of international dispute settlement. In doctrinal writings, it has been suggested that it could be possible to establish an international or World Court for Human Rights which would have the competence to review the conduct of peacekeeping operations.[6]

However, this is an idea which would possibly cause more problems than it would solve, including a further fragmentation of international law. In any case, it is unlikely that states would subscribe to such an idea, as the opposition of a considerable group of states towards a ratification of the Rome Statute of the ICC demonstrates. One could rather envisage the Security Council requesting an advisory opinion from the International Court of Justice regarding the application of human rights law to international organisations, as well as the criterion for the attribution of conduct to two or more international organisations. An advisory opinion of the ICJ would have the advantage over a World Court for Human Rights that it would be universally accepted, without being, legally binding, therefore safeguarding also a margin of discretion for states and international organisations.

---

[4] Cf. E. Paasivirta, P. J. Kuijper, 'Does One Size Fit All? The European Community and the Responsibility of International Organizations', *Netherlands Yearbook of International Law*, XXXVI (2005), 169, 173.
[5] T. M. Franck, *Fairness in International Law and Institutions* (Oxford University Press, 1998), 7.
[6] M. Nowak, 'The Need for a World Court of Human Rights', *Human Rights Law Review*, 7 (2007), 251–259.

The question is, however, whether such a proposal would correspond to the interests of the UN, other international organisations and states alike. Major changes to the international legal system are not possible without the involvement and the agreement of states. Although, in practice, the UN assumes that it is exclusively responsible for the conduct of UN Peacekeepers, it is unlikely that the UN would voluntarily subscribe to an acceptance of responsibility for the conduct of UN authorised forces or for any conduct of other international organisations under the concept of joint responsibility. It is also implausible that other international organisations would voluntarily accept joint responsibility.

Of course, a UN internal attempt of regulation would also be feasible, for instance, within the Sixth Committee of the GA which is the primary forum for the consideration of legal questions in the GA, or even within the SC – Article 64 ARIO refers expressly to the existence of *lex specialis* rules. With regard to the Security Council, however, the Latin expression of '*Quis custodiet ipsos custodies?*' (Who guards the Guardian?) comes to mind. Bearing in mind the mandate of the Security Council, it could be questioned as to whether the Security Council could possibly elaborate a just and fair rule of attribution or as to whether such an attempt at regulation would not correspond to putting the fox in charge of the henhouse. The wider participation in the GA might be better suited to accommodate any such concerns.

The law of international responsibility in its current state of development also enhances the probability of a further augmentation of cooperation among states and international organisations alike. As long as they do not enter into cooperation arrangements with the intent of committing violations of international law, the existing legal framework will not allow joint responsibility.

The dispositions under the ARIO, as well as under the Articles on State Responsibility, require an element in the form of intent to allow the attribution of conduct also to one or more other actors and as indicated above, they do not define the criterion under which states or international organisations could otherwise be held responsible. Therefore, the lack of effective regulation creates some leeway for international organisations and states to enhance their cooperation arrangements without a real or substantial risk of being held accordingly responsible.

Consequently, although international organisations might be unwilling to contribute to the regulation of cases of joint responsibility, their involvement in any attempt at regulation, be it in the form of cooperation agreements specifying the distribution of responsibility or via a request of an advisory opinion of the ICJ, would be, from their point of view, beneficial, as it would allow them to influence and even steer the outcome. In any case, they could contribute their expertise to the regulation attempts. The alternative is that courts and tribunals will attempt to regulate this question insofar as they have jurisdiction. Bearing in mind the forthcoming accession of the EU to the European Convention of Human Rights, further judgments, not only on the responsibility of international organisations but also on joint responsibility, can be expected.[7]

The role of states with regard to potential further regulations of joint responsibility appears to be unclear. On the one hand, the elaboration of rules on the joint responsibility of international organisations will possibly increase their protection from being held responsible for acts of organs which were seconded to these organisations. On the other hand, the development of rules on the joint responsibility of international organisations could trigger the development of similar rules for states; the ARIO were also based upon the Articles on State Responsibility. An important aspect in this discussion is the arrangement for financial restitution within the different international organisations. So far, there is no standard model for international organisations to process claims for financial restitution and to pay compensation, including for damages arising in the context of peacekeeping operations. Of course, reasons of legal certainty and transparency support a proposal of a standardised regulation of financial damages by international organisations. The problem is that states, despite being generally willing to cooperate with international organisations, could be opposed to any regulation at the organisational level as it could be perceived as a transfer of competences and a loss of sovereignty.[8]

According to Article 40 ARIO, a responsible international organisation 'shall take all appropriate measures (...) to ensure that its members provide it with the means for effectively fulfilling its obligations under this Chapter' and the 'members of a responsible international organization shall take all the appropriate measures that may be required (...) in order to enable the organization to fulfil its obligations'. Thus, depending on the nature of arrangements for financial restitution in an international organisation, the main contributors to the budget of the organisation might be

---

[7] The ECtHR in *Al-Skeini* and also the Dutch Court of Appeal in the Srebrenica cases did not exclude the possibility of joint responsibility.
[8] In contrast, from the perspective of international organisations, it is a rather appealing idea as it also creates jobs within the organisation. This ambivalent attitude of states was also confirmed during interviews with members of staff at the General Staff College of the German Armed Forces, as well as at the German Ministry of Defence.

opposed to any efforts or undertakings which would increase the likelihood of international organisations being responsible, if compensation would be paid by the general budget of the organisation and not primarily or entirely by those states whose agents or organs might have contributed to or caused the internationally wrongful act. Thus, it appears that within the wider framework of the international community, any attempt or undertaking to further regulate the responsibility of international organisations can only be carried out effectively if states agree.[9]

With the focus once more on the specific subject of the present study, several practical recommendations can be made.

First, with regard to the fields of human rights and humanitarian law, it would be commendable if the UN and regional organisations were to engage in activities regarding the clarification of rules applicable in peacekeeping operations. The UN could, for example, adopt a bulletin on human rights obligations to be observed while deploying peacekeeping operations.[10] Legal uncertainty, particularly in the form of diluted responsibility, can also negatively impair the efficiency and performance during the deployment of a peacekeeping operation 'as the various actors involved might not feel fully in charge'.[11]

Moreover, bearing in mind in particular the complex cooperation arrangements for AFISMA, it is recommended that the UN and regional organisations include dispositions regarding the distribution of responsibility in their respective agreements if they cooperate in peacekeeping operations.[12] It is even more relevant and necessary to prevent blame shifting between the various involved actors as in the Srebrenica cases where both the Netherlands denied responsibility and the UN claimed immunity, which in the end, also corresponds to a denial of responsibility.[13]

---

[9] Their participation is in any case necessary, as members of the organisations, who ultimate decide upon the actions undertaken by the organisations whose members they are.

[10] N. Quénivet, 'Human Rights Law and Peacekeeping Operations', in M. Odello, R. Piotrowicz (eds.), *International Military Missions and International Law* (Antwerp, Intersentia, 2011), 99, 102. The Human Rights due diligence policy on UN support to non-UN security forces as adopted in 2013 may be considered as a first step in the right direction, UN Doc. A/67/777–S/2013/110 (2013). See also H. P. Aust, 'The UN Human Rights Due Diligence Policy: An Effective Mechanism against Complicity of Peacekeeping Forces', *Journal of Conflict and Security Law*, 20 (2015), 61, in particular 71–73.

[11] T. Tardy, 'Hybrid Peace Operations: Rationale and Challenges', *Global Governance*, 20 (2014), 95, 112.

[12] Cf. also A. Orakhelashvili, *Collective Security* (2011), 328.

[13] A. Nollkaemper, D. Jacobs, 'Shared Responsibility in International Law: A Concept Paper', ACIL Research Paper No 2011-07 (SHARES Series), finalised 2 August 2011, available at www.sharesproject.nl, 20.

CONCLUSIONS AND RECOMMENDATIONS 329

Regarding the wider question of the relationship between the UN and regional organisations, it is recommended to elaborate upon a standard model agreement which may be used to expand and formalise consultation and cooperation between the UN and regional organisations for the specific context of the maintenance of international peace and security.[14] It could even include articles regarding the question of international responsibility. The AU had also recommended enhanced consultations between the AU PSC and the UN Security Council.[15]

As noted by the Security Council itself, there is a need 'for a comprehensive analysis of lessons learned from practical cooperation between the United Nations and the African Union'[16] and this statement is equally valid for the practical cooperation between the UN and other regional organisations. Hopefully, the envisaged reforms by the Secretary-General following the publication of the report by the High-Level Independent Panel in June 2015 will bear fruits.

Regarding the interaction and the relations with the AU, the Security Council needs to address in a systematic manner the issue of the funding of AU peace support operations undertaken with the consent of the UN, through the use of UN assessed contribution as it was highlighted once again also by the High-Level Panel.[17] Such an engagement is not only necessary to increase the effective maintenance of international peace and security on the African continent, but also in order to address the legal implications of the power wielded by the UN over the AU with regard to the payment of AU peacekeeping operations. Naturally, the EU is also advised to do so accordingly for the financial mechanisms on the basis of its African Peace Facility. The assessment currently carried out for that purpose by the UN Secretariat, the AU and other partners upon the request of the UN Secretary-General allows for some optimism.[18] Nevertheless, there remain sceptical voices among the members of the Security Council; the UK argues, for example, that it will pay in any case, be it based on UN assessed contributions or as part of the African Peace Facility of the EU.[19]

---

[14] Cf. UN Doc. A/59/565 (2004), 85, para. 272(b).
[15] Ibid.
[16] UN Doc. S/RES/2033 (2012), Preamble, 2.
[17] Report of the Chairperson of the Commission, AU Doc. PSC/AHG/3.(CCCXCVII) (2013), 3, para. 6.
[18] UN Doc. A/70/357 and S/2015/682 (2015), 11, para. 48.
[19] C. Hull Wiklund, G. Ingerstad, *The Regionalisation of Peace Operations in Africa. Advantages, Challenges and the Way Ahead* (2015), FOI, 56.

The example of Mali and the CAR showed that the UN and regional organisations have to adapt to new security challenges and that includes improving the rapid deployment capacities of all international organisations, as well as the joint operation planning.[20]

Finally, it is recommended that NATO institutionalises its relations with the UN and establishes a permanent mission to the UN in New York.[21] It would allow the Alliance to be more actively involved in debates at the UN and it would prevent that NATO is further sidelined regarding the deployment of peacekeeping operations.

The limited scope of this study only permitted an insight into the specific field of cooperation of the UN and four regional organisations in peacekeeping operations. The study confirmed the original premise it was set out to explore, the question as to whether the existing legal framework would be appropriate to regulate the conduct of international organisations cooperation in peacekeeping operations. But it also became evident that a major transformation of international law is currently taking place towards a less state-centric, multi-actor network of institutionalised and multifarious relations which poses questions with regard to the general regulation of international responsibility under international law, as well as the general direction and conception of international law as a system. This study might serve as a stepping stone for further studies and inquiries with regard to these complex questions with which the international community is confronted.

---

[20] ECOWAS criticised that the UN was unable to respond more effectively to the offensive by terrorist groups in the south of Mali and the deadly hostage-taking situation at the natural gas facility in Algeria and that there 'is a need to further explore the possibilities offered by the normative framework for peacekeeping operations, in particular in the timely articulations of the provisions of Chapters VI, VII and VIII of the Charter of the United Nations'. Statement by Côte d'Ivoire speaking on behalf of ECOWAS, UN Doc. S/PV.6903 (2013), 52.

[21] Such a proposition was already contained in the report NATO 2020: Assured Security; Dynamic Engagement. Analysis and Recommendations of the Group of Experts on a New Strategic Concept for NATO, 17 May 2010, 25. The AU decided to strengthen its Permanent Mission to the UN in New York in September 2013, 'including through the establishment of a dedicated standby team to support African members on the Security Council', Peace and Security Council, AU Doc. PSC/AHG/COMM/1.(CCCXCVII) (2013), 5, para. 9v.

SELECT BIBLIOGRAPHY

Books, Articles and Other Literature

Abass, A., *Regional Organizations and the Development of Collective Security: Beyond Chapter VIII of the UN Charter* (Oxford, Hart Publishing, 2004).

Akehurst, M., 'Enforcement Actions by Regional Agencies with Special References to the Organization of American States', *British Yearbook of International Law*, 42 (1967), 175–227.

Akuffo, E. A., 'Cooperating for Peace and Security or Competing for Legitimacy in Africa? The Case of the African Union in Darfur', *African Security Review*, 19 (2010), 74–89.

   'The Politics of Interregional Cooperation: The Impact of NATO's Intervention in Libya on its Relations with the African Union', *African Conflict & Peacebuilding Review*, 4 (2014), 108–128.

Allain, J., 'The True Challenges to the United Nations System of the Use of Force: The Failures of Kosovo and Iraq and the Emergence of the African Union', *Max Planck Yearbook of United Nations Law*, 8 (2004), 237–289.

Arnold, R., Knoops, G.-J. A. (eds.), *Practice and Policies of Modern Peace Support Operations under International Law* (Leiden, Brill, 2006).

Aust, H. P., *Complicity and the Law of State Responsibility* (Cambridge University Press, 2011).

   'The UN Human Rights Due Diligence Policy: An Effective Mechanism against Complicity of Peacekeeping Forces', *Journal of Conflict and Security Law*, 20 (2015), 61–73.

Bah, A. S., Jones, B. D., *Peace Operations Partnerships: Lessons and Issues from Coordination to Hybrid Arrangements* (Center on International Cooperation, New York University, 2008).

Ballas, A., 'It Takes Two (or More) to Keep the Peace: Multiple Simultaneous Peace Operations', *Journal of International Peacekeeping*, 15 (2011), 384–421.

Bashua, A., 'Challenges and Prospects of AU–UN Hybrid Operations', *Journal of International Peacekeeping*, 18 (2014), 92–101.

Bell, C. A., 'Reassessing Multiple Attribution: The International Law Commission and the *Behrami* and *Saramati* Decision', *New York University Journal of International Law and Politics*, 42 (2010), 501–548.

Besson, S., 'The Extraterritoriality of the European Convention on Human Rights: Why Human Rights Depend on Jurisdiction and What Jurisdiction Amount To', *Leiden Journal of International Law*, 25 (2012), 857–884.

Bethlehem, D., 'The Relationship between International Humanitarian Law and International Human Rights Law in Situations of Armed Conflict', *Cambridge Journal of International and Comparative Law*, 2 (2013), 180–195.

Bialke, J. P., 'United Nations Peace Operations: Applicable Norms and the Application of the Law of Armed Conflict', *Air Force Law Review*, 50 (2001), 1–64.

Biondi, A., Eeckhout, P., Ripley, S. (eds.), *EU Law after Lisbon* (Oxford University Press, 2012).

Biscop, S., 'The UK's Change of Course: A New Chance for the ESDI', *European Foreign Affairs Review*, 4 (1999), 253–268.

Biscop, S., Whitman, R. G. (eds.), *The Routledge Handbook of European Security* (London, Routledge, 2013).

Blokker, N., 'Is the Authorization Authorized? Powers and Practice of the UN Security Council to Authorize the Use of Force by "Coalitions of the Able and Willing"', *European Journal of International Law*, 11 (2000), 541–568.

Blokker, N., Schrijver, N. (eds.), *The Security Council and the Use of Force: Theory and Reality. A Need for Change?* (Leiden, Brill, 2005).

Boisson de Chazournes, L., *Les relations entre organisations régionales et organisations universelles*, Recueil des cours de l'Académie de La Haye, Volume 347 (2010), 79–406.

Boisson de Chazournes, L., Kohen, M. (eds.), *International Law and the Quest for Its Implementation/Le droit international et la quête de sa mise en oeuvre. Liber Amicorum Vera Gowlland-Debbas* (Leiden, Brill, 2010).

Boon, K. E., 'Are Control Tests Fit for the Future? The Slippage Problem in Attribution Doctrines', *Melbourne Journal of International Law*, 15 (2014), 1–48.

Boulden, J. (ed.), *Responding to Conflict in Africa. The United Nations and Regional Organizations* (London, Palgrave/Macmillan, 2013).

Boutin, B., 'Responsibility of the Netherlands for the Acts of Dutchbat in *Nuhanović* and *Mustafić*: The Continuous Quest for a Tangible Meaning for "Effective Control" in the Context of Peacekeeping', *Leiden Journal of International Law*, 25 (2012), 521–535.

Brosig, M., 'The Multi-Actor Game of Peacekeeping in Africa', *International Peacekeeping*, 17 (2010), 327–342.

'The Emerging Peace and Security Regime in Africa: The Role of the EU', *European Foreign Affairs Review*, 16 (2011), 107–122.

Cardwell, P. J. (ed.), *EU External Relations Law and Policy in the Post-Lisbon Era* (Heidelberg, Springer, 2012).

Cerone, J., 'Human Dignity in the Line of Fire: The Application of International Human Rights Law During Armed Conflict, Occupation, and Peace Operations', *Vanderbilt Journal of Transnational Law*, 39 (2006), 1447–1510.

Charbonneau, B., 'What Is So Special about the European Union? EU–UN Cooperation in Crisis Management in Africa', *International Peacekeeping*, 16 (2009), 546–561.

Chesterman, S., 'The Use of Force in UN Peace Operations', External Study, *UN Peacekeeping Best Practices* (2004).

Clapham, A., *Human Rights Obligations of Non-State Actors* (Oxford University Press, 2006).

Coomans, F., Kamminga, M. T. (eds.), *Extraterritorial Application of Human Rights Treaties* (Antwerp, Intersentia, 2004).

Cowan, A., 'A New Watershed? Re-evaluating *Banković* in Light of *Al-Skeini*', *Cambridge Journal of International and Comparative Law*, 1 (2012), 213–227.

Cox, K. E., 'Beyond Self-Defense: United Nations Peacekeeping & the Use of Force', *Denver Journal of International Law and Policy*, 27 (1998–1999), 239–273.

Crawford, J., Koskenniemi, M. (eds.), *The Cambridge Companion to International Law* (Cambridge University Press, 2012).

Crawford, J., Pellet, A., Olleson, S. (eds.), *The Law of International Responsibility* (Oxford University Press, 2010).

Crawford, J., *Brownlie's Principles of Public International Law* (Oxford University Press, 2012).

State Responsibility. The General Part (Cambridge University Press, 2013).

Dannenbaum, T., 'Translating the Standard of Effective Control into a System of Effective Accountability: How Liability Should Be Apportioned for Violations of Human Rights by Member State Troop Contingents Serving as United Nations Peacekeepers', *Harvard International Law Journal*, 51 (2010), 113–192.

'Killings at Srebrenica, Effective Control, and the Power to Prevent Unlawful Conduct', *International and Comparative Law Quarterly*, 61 (2012), 713–728.

D'Aspremont, J., 'The Limits to the Exclusive Responsibility of International Organizations', *Human Rights & International Legal Discourse*, 1 (2007), 217–229.

'The Articles on the Responsibility of International Organizations: Magnifying the Fissures in the Law of International Responsibility', *International Organizations Law Review*, 9 (2012), 15–28.

David, E., *Principes de droit des conflits armés* (Brussels, Bruylant, 2008).

David, E., Engdahl, O., 'How Does the Involvement of a Multinational Peacekeeping Force Affect the Classification of a Situation?', *International Review of the Red Cross*, 95 (2013), 659–679.

Dennis, M. J., 'Application of Human Rights Treaties Extraterritorially in Times of Armed Conflict and Military Occupation', *American Journal of International Law*, 99 (2005), 119–141.

Derblom, M., Hagström Frisell, E., Schmidt, J., 'UN–EU–AU Cooperation in Peace Operations in Africa', FOI, Swedish Defence Research Agency (2008).

Dersso, S. A., 'The Role and Place of Human Rights in the Mandate and Works of the Peace and Security Council of the AU: An Appraisal', *Netherlands International Law Review*, 58 (2011), 77–103.

De Schutter, O., 'Globalization and Jurisdiction: Lessons from the European Convention on Human Rights', *Baltic Journal of International Law*, 6 (2000), 185–247.

de Wet, E., *The Chapter VII Powers of the United Nations Security Council* (Oxford, Hart Publishing, 2004).

'The Evolving Role of ECOWAS and the SADC in Peace Operations: A Challenge to the Primacy of the United Nations Security Council in Matters of Peace and Security?', *Leiden Journal of International Law*, 27 (2014), 353–369.

Direk, Ö. F., 'Responsibility in Peace Support Operations: Revisiting the Proper Test for Attribution Conduct and the Meaning of the "Effective Control" Standard', *Netherlands International Law Review*, 61 (2014), 1–22.

Dold, B., *Vertragliche und ausservertragliche Verantwortlichkeit im Recht der internationalen Organisationen* (Zürich, Schulthess, 2006).

Doswald-Beck, L., Vité, S., 'Le droit international humanitaire et le droit des droits de l'homme', *International Review of the Red Cross*, 75 (1993), 99–128.

Doswald-Beck, L., 'The Right to Life in Armed Conflict: Does International Humanitarian Law Provide All the Answers?', *International Review of the Red Cross*, 88 (2006), 881–904.

Duffy, H., *The 'War on Terror' and the Framework of International Law* (Cambridge University Press, 2005).

Eagleton, C., *International Organization and the Law of Responsibility*, Collected Courses of the Hague Academy of International Law, Volume 076 (1950), 320–425.

Evans, M., Koutrakos, P. (eds.), *The International Responsibility of the European Union* (Oxford, Hart Publishing, 2013).

Faite, A., Grenier, J. L. (eds.), Report of the Expert Meeting on Multinational Peace Operations: Applicability of International Humanitarian Law and Human Rights Law to UN Mandated Forces, Geneva, 11–12 December 2003.

Franck, T. M., *Fairness in International Law and Institutions* (Oxford University Press, 1995).

'Collective Security and UN Reform: Between the Necessary and the Possible', *Chicago Journal of International Law*, 6 (2005–2006), 597–616.

Gal-Or, N., Ryngaert, C., 'From Theory to Practice: Exploring the Relevance of the Draft Articles on the Responsibility of International Organizations (DARIO) – The Responsibility of the WTO and the UN', *German Law Journal*, 13 (2012), 511–541.

Gill, T. D., Fleck, D. (eds.), *The Handbook of the International Law of Military Operations* (Oxford University Press, 2010).

Ginsberg, R. H., Penska, S., *The European Union in Global Security* (London, Palgrave Macmillan, 2012).

Glick, R. D., 'Lip Service to the Laws of War: Humanitarian Law and United Nations Armed Forces', *Michigan Journal of International Law*, 17 (1995), 53–107.

Gondek, M., *The Reach of Human Rights in a Globalising World: Extraterritorial Application of Human Rights Treaties* (Antwerp, Intersentia, 2011).

Gowlland-Debbas, V., 'The Limits of Unilateral Enforcement of Community Objectives in the Framework of UN Peace Maintenance', *European Journal of International Law*, 11 (2000), 361–383.

The Security Council and Issues of Responsibility under International Law, Recueil des cours de l'Académie de La Haye, Volume 535 (2012), 185–444.

Gray, C., *International Law and the Use of Force* (Oxford University Press, 2008).

Greenwood, C., 'International Humanitarian Law and United Nations Military Operations', *Yearbook of International Humanitarian Law*, 1 (1998), 3–34.

Grenfall, K., 'Perspective on the Applicability and Application of International Humanitarian Law: The UN Context', *International Review of the Red Cross*, 95 (2013), 645–652.

Griep, E., *Regionale Organisationen und die Weiterentwicklung der VN-Friedenssicherung seit dem Ende des Kalten Krieges* (Baden-Baden, Nomos, 2012).

Haugevik, K. M., 'New Partners, New Possibilities. The Evolution of Inter-organizational Security Cooperation in International Peace Operations', NUPI Report, Security in Practice No. 6 (2007).

Henckaerts, J.-M., 'Concurrent Application of International Human Rights Law and International Humanitarian Law: Victims in Search of a Forum', *Human Rights & International Legal Discourse*, 1 (2007), 95–124.

Hestermeyer, H., König, D., Matz-Lück, N., et al. (eds.), *Coexistence, Cooperation and Solidarity. Liber Amicorum Rüdiger Wolfrum* (Leiden, Brill, 2012).

Instituto Hispano-Luso-Americano de Derecho Internacional, 'Las organizaciones internacionales y el Derecho de la responsabilidad', El XIV Congreso del Instituto Hispano-Luso-Americano de Derecho Internacional, San José, 1985.

Iyi, J.-M., 'The AU/ECOWAS Unilateral Humanitarian Intervention Legal Regimes and the UN Charter', *African Journal of International and Comparative Law*, 21 (2013), 489–519.

Kelsen, H., *The Law of the United Nations. A Critical Analysis of Its Fundamental Problems* (London Institute of World Affairs, 1950).

'Is the North Atlantic Treaty a Regional Arrangement?', *The American Journal of International Law*, 45 (1951), 162–166.

Kioko, B., 'The Right of Intervention under the African Union's Constitutive Act: From Non-Interference to Non-Intervention', *International Review of the Red Cross*, 85 (2003), 807–825.

Klabbers, J., *An Introduction to International Institutional Law* (Cambridge University Press, 2009).

Klein, P., *La responsabilité des organisations internationales dans les ordres juridiques internes et en droit des gens* (Brussels, Bruylant, 1998).

Kohen, M., Kolb, R., Tehindrazanarivelo, D. L. (eds.), *Perspectives of International Law in the 21st Century/Perspectives du droit international au 21e siècle* (Leiden, Brill, 2011).

Kolanowski, S. (ed.), *Proceedings of the Bruges Colloquium. International Organisations' Involvement in Peace Operations: Applicable Legal Framework and the Issue of Responsibility* (2011).

Kolb, R., *L'article 103 de la Charte des Nations Unies*, Recueil des cours de l'Académie de La Haye, Volume 367 (2013), 9–252.

Kolb, R., Porretto, G., Vité, S., *L'application du droit international humanitaire et des droits de l'homme aux organisations internationales. Forces de paix et administrations civiles transitoires* (Brussels, Bruylant 2005).

Koops, J. A., Macqueen, N., Tardy, T., et al., *The Oxford Handbook of United Nations Peacekeeping Operations* (Oxford University Press, 2015).

Koutrakos, P., *The EU Common Security and Defence Policy* (Oxford University Press, 2013).

Krause, J., Ronzitti, N. (eds.), *The EU, the UN and Collective Security. Making Multilateralism Effective* (London, Routledge, 2012).

Krieger, H., 'A Conflict of Norms: The Relationship between Humanitarian Law and Human Rights Law in the ICRC Customary Law Study', *Journal of Conflict & Security Law*, 11 (2006), 265–291.

Hartwig, M., *Die Haftung der Mitgliedstaaten für Internationale Organisationen* (Heidelberg, Springer, 1993).

Labbé, J., Boutellis, A., 'Peace Operations by Proxy: Implications for Humanitarian Action of UN Peacekeeping Partnerships with Non-UN Security Forces', *International Review of the Red Cross*, 95 (2013), 539–559.

Larsen, K. M., 'Attribution of Conduct in Peace Operations: The "Ultimate Authority and Control" Test', *European Journal of International Law*, 19 (2008), 509–531.

'"Neither Effective Control Nor Ultimate Authority and Control": Attribution of Conduct in *Al-Jedda*', *Military Law and the Law of War Review*, 50 (2011), 347–368.

The Human Rights Treaty Obligations of Peacekeepers (Cambridge University Press, 2012).

Leck, C., 'International Responsibility in United Nations Peacekeeping Operations: Command and Control Arrangements and the Attribution of Conduct', *Melbourne Journal of International Law*, 10 (2009), 346–364.

Lilly, D., 'The Changing Nature of the Protection of Civilians in International Peace Operations', *International Peacekeeping*, 19 (2012), 628–639.

Lowe, V., Roberts, A., Welsh, J., et al. (eds.), *The United Nations Security Council and War* (Oxford University Press, 2008).

Lüder, S. R., *Völkerrechtliche Verantwortlichkeit bei Teilnahme an 'Peace-keeping'-Missionen der Vereinten Nationen* (Heidelberg, Springer, 2004).

Major, C., 'EU–UN Cooperation in Military Crisis Management: The Experience of EUFOR RD Congo in 2006', Occasional Paper, n°72, September 2008, EUISS.

Maluwa, T., 'Reimaging African Unity: Some Preliminary Reflections on the Constitutive Act of the African Union', *African Yearbook of International Law*, 9 (2001), 3–38.

McCoubrey, H., White, N. D., *The Blue Helmets: Legal Regulation of United Nations Military Operations* (Dartmouth Publishing Company, 1997).

Mégret, F., Hoffmann, F., 'The UN as a Human Rights Violator? Some Reflections on the United Nations Changing Human Rights Responsibilities', *Human Rights Quarterly*, 25 (2003), 314–342.

Meron, T., *International Law in the Age of Human Rights. General Course on Public International Law*, Collected Courses of the Hague Academy of International Law, Volume 301 (2003), 9–489.

Milanović, M., Papić, T., 'As Bad as It Gets: The European Court of Human Rights's *Behrami* and *Seramati* Decision and General International Law', *International and Comparative Law Quarterly*, 58 (2009), 267–296.

Milanovic, M., *Extraterritorial Application of Human Rights Treaties* (Oxford University Press, 2011).

 '*Al-Skeini* and *Al-Jedda* in Strasbourg', *European Journal of International Law*, 23 (2012), 121–139.

Miltner, B., 'Revisiting Extraterritoriallity after *Al-Skeini*: The ECHR and Its Lessons', *Michigan Journal of International Law*, 33 (2012), 693–747.

Muhire, Y. G., *The African Union's Right of Intervention and the UN System of Collective Security* (2013), PhD thesis, Utrecht University.

Müller, L., 'The Force Intervention Brigade – United Nations Forces Beyond the Fine Line between Peacekeeping and Peace Enforcement', *Journal of Conflict & Security Law*, 20 (2015), 359–380.

Murithi, T., 'The African Union's Foray into Peacekeeping: Lessons from the Hybrid Mission in Darfur', *Journal of Peace, Conflict and Development*, 14 (2009), 1–19.

Murithi, T. (ed.), *Handbook of Africa's International Relations* (London, Routledge, 2014).

Murphy, R., 'United Nations Military Operations and International Humanitarian Law: What Rules Apply to Peacekeepers?', *Criminal Law Forum*, 14 (2003), 153–194.

 UN Peacekeeping in Lebanon, Somalia and Kosovo. Operational and Legal Issues in Practice (Cambridge University Press, 2007).

Naert, F., 'Detention in Peace Operations: The Legal Framework and Main Categories of Detainees', *Military Law & Law of the War Review*, 45 (2006), 51–78.

 International Law Aspects of the EU' Security and Defence Policy, with a Particular Focus on the Law of Armed Conflict and Human Rights (Antwerp, Intersentia, 2010).

 'The European Court of Human Rights' *Al-Jedda* and *Al-Skeini* Judgments: An Introduction and Some Reflections', *Military Law and the Law of War Review*, 50 (2011), 315–320.

'Observance of International Humanitarian Law by Forces under the Command of the European Union', *International Review of the Red Cross*, 95 (2013), 637–643.

Nedeski, N., Nollkaemper, A., 'Responsibility of International Organizations 'in Connection with Acts of States", *International Organizations Law Review*, 9 (2012), 33–52.

Nollkaemper, A., 'Dual Attribution: Liability of the Netherlands for Conduct of Dutchbat in Srebrenica', *Journal of International Criminal Justice*, 9 (2011), 1143–1157.

'Concerted Adjudication in Cases of Shared Responsibility', SHARES Research Paper 40 (2014), ACIL 2014-17, available at www.sharesproject.nl

Nollkaemper, A., Jacobs, D., 'Shared Responsibility in International Law: A Concept Paper', ACIL Research Paper No 2011-07 (SHARES Series), 2 August 2011, available at www.sharesproject.nl

Nollkaemper, A., van der Wilt, H. (eds.), *System Criminality in International Law* (Cambridge University Press, 2009).

Nollkaemper, A., Plakokefalos, I., Schechinger, J. N. M. (eds.), *Principles of Shared Responsibility in International Law. An Appraisal of the State of Art* (Cambridge University Press, 2014).

Nolte, G., 'From Dionisio Anzilotti to Roberto Ago: The Classical International Law of Responsibility and the Traditional Primacy of a Bilateral Conception of Inter-state Relations', *European Journal of International Law*, 13 (2002), 1083–1098.

Nowak, M., 'The Need for a World Court of Human Rights', *Human Rights Law Review*, 7 (2007), 251–259.

Odello, M., Piotrowicz, R. (eds.), *International Military Missions and International Law* (Leiden, Brill, 2011).

Oke, Y., 'Substitute for the United Nations? Extending the Frontiers of the North Atlantic Treaty Organisation and Implications for African Unity', *African Journal of International and Comparative Law*, 21 (2013), 120–141.

Olsen, G. R., 'The EU and Military Conflict Management in Africa: For the Good of Africa or Europe?', *International Peacekeeping*, 16 (2009), 245–260.

Omorogbe, E. Y., 'Can the African Union Deliver Peace and Security?', *Journal of Conflict & Security Law*, 16 (2011), 35–62.

Opie, R. A., 'Human Rights Violations by Peacekeepers: Finding a Framework for Attribution of International Responsibility', *New Zealand Law Review*, (2006), 1–34.

Orakhelashvili, A., *Collective Security* (Oxford University Press, 2011).

Paasivirta, E., Kuijper, P. J., 'Does One Size Fit All? The European Community and the Responsibility of International Organizations', *Netherlands Yearbook of International Law*, XXXVI (2005), 169–226.

Palchetti, P., 'The Allocation of Responsibility for Internationally Wrongful Acts Committed in the Course of Multinational Operations', *International Review of the Red Cross*, 95 (2013), 727–742.

Palchetti, P., Wessel, R. A. (eds.), *International Law as Law of the European Union* (Leiden, Brill, 2012).

Paliwal, S., 'The Primacy of Regional Organizations in International Peacekeeping: The African Example', *Virginia Journal of International Law*, 51 (2010), 185–230.

Papastavridis, E., 'Interpretation of Security Council Resolutions under Chapter VII in the Aftermath of the Iraqi Crisis', *International & Comparative Law Quarterly*, 56 (2007), 83–118.

Peck, J., 'The U.N. and the Laws of War: How Can the World's Peacekeepers Be Held Accountable?', *Syracuse Journal of International Law and Commerce*, 21 (1995), 283–310.

Poulton, R., Trillo, E., Kukkuk, L., *Part 1 of the African Peace Facility Evaluation: Reviewing the Procedures of the APF and Possibilities of Alternative Future Sources of Funding. Final Report* (2010).

Quigley, J., 'The "Privatization" of Security Council Enforcement Action: A Threat to Multilateralism', *Michigan Journal of International Law*, 17 (1995–1996), 249–283.

Ragazzi, M. (ed.), *International Responsibility Today. Essays in Memory of Oscar Schachter* (Leiden, Brill, 2005).

(ed.), *Responsibility of International Organizations. Essays in Memory of Sir Ian Brownlie* (Leiden, Brill, 2013).

Ratner, S., 'Foreign Occupation and International Territorial Administration: The Challenges of Convergence', *European Journal of International Law*, 16 (2005), 695–719.

Reichard, M., 'Some Legal Issues Concerning the EU–NATO Berlin Plus Agreement', *Nordic Journal of International Law*, 73 (2004), 37–64.

The EU–NATO Relationship: A Legal and Political Perspective (Farnham, Ashgate, 2006).

Reidy, A., 'La pratique de la Commission et de la Cour européennes des droits de l'homme en matière de droit international humanitaire', *Revue Internationale de la Croix-Rouge*, 80 (1998), 551–568.

Reinisch, A., 'Aid or Assistance and Direction and Control between States and International Organizations in the Commission of Internationally Wrongful Acts', *International Organizations Law Review*, 7 (2010), 63–77.

Ringsmose, J., Rynning, S. (eds.), *NATO's New Strategic Concept: A Comprehensive Assessment*, DIIS Report (2011).

Rodt, A. P., Okeke, J. M., 'AU–EU Partnership: Strengthening Policy Convergence and Regime Efficacy in the African Peace and Security Complex?', *African Security*, 6 (2013), 211–233.

Roxin, C., 'Organisationsherrschaft und Tatentschlossenheit', *Zeitschrift für internationale Strafrechtsdogmatik*, 1 (2006), 293–300.

Ryniker, A., 'Quelques commentaires à propos de la Circulaire du Secrétaire général des Nations Unies du 6 août 1999', *Revue internationale de la Croix-Rouge*, 836 (1999), 795–805.

Ryngaert, C., 'Apportioning Responsibility between the UN and Member States in UN Peace-Support Operations: An Inquiry into the Application of the "Effective Control" Standard after *Behrami*', *Israel Law Review*, 45 (2012), 151–178.

Sands, P., Klein, P., *Bowett's Law of International Institutions* (London, Sweet & Maxwell, 2009).

Sari, A., 'Jurisdiction and International Responsibility in Peace Support Operations: The *Behrami* and *Saramati* Cases', *Human Rights Law Review*, 8 (2008), 151–170.

'UN Peacekeeping Operations and Article 7 ARIO: The Missing Link', *International Organizations Law Review*, 8 (2012), 77–85.

Sarooshi, D., *The United Nations and the Development of Collective Security. The Delegation by the Security Council of Its Chapter VII Powers* (Oxford University Press, 2000).

Sassòli, M., Olson, L. M., 'The Relationship between International Humanitarian and Human Rights Law where It Matters: Admissible Killing and Internment of Fighters in Non-International Armed Conflicts', *International Review of the Red Cross*, 90 (2008), 599–627.

Sassòli, M., 'Introducing a Sliding-Scale of Obligations to Address the Fundamental Inequality between Armed Groups and States?', *International Review of the Red Cross*, 93 (2011), 426–431.

Saura, J., 'Lawful Peacekeeping: Applicability of International Humanitarian Law to United Nations Peacekeeping Operations', *Hastings Law Journal*, 58 (2007), 479–531.

Schachter, O., *International Law in Theory and Practice. General Course on Public International Law*, Recueils des cours de l'Académie de La Haye, Volume 178 (1982), 12–395.

Schermers, H. G., Blokker, N. M., *International Institutional Law* (Leiden, Martinus Nijhoff, 2011).

Schmalenbach, K., *Die Haftung Internationaler Organisationen im Rahmen von Militäreinsätzen und Territorialverwaltungen* (Frankfurt am Main, Peter Lang, 2004).

Schreuer, C., 'Regionalism v. Universalism', *European Journal of International Law*, 6 (1995), 477–499.

Seyersted, F., 'United Nations Forces Some Legal Problems', *British Yearbook of International Law*, 37 (1961), 351–475.

Shaw, M. N., *International Law* (Cambridge University Press, 2008).

Sheeran, S. P., 'A Constitutional Moment? United Nations Peacekeeping in the Democratic Republic of Congo', *International Organizations Law Review*, 8 (2011), 55–135.

Sheeran, S., Case, S., *The Intervention Brigade: Legal Issues for the UN in the Democratic Republic of the Congo* (International Peace Institute, 2014).

Shraga, D., 'UN Peacekeeping Operations: Applicability of International Humanitarian Law and Responsibility for Operations-Related Damage', *American Journal of International Law*, 94 (2005), 406–412.

Sicilianos, L.-A., 'L'autorisation par le Conseil de sécurité de récourir à la force: une tentative d'évaluation', *Revue générale de droit international public*, 106 (2002), 5–48.

Simma, B., Alston, P., 'The Sources of Human Rights Law: Custom, Jus Cogens, and General Principles', *Australian Yearbook of International Law*, 12 (1988–1989), 82–108.

Simma, B., Khan, D.-E., Nolte, G., et al. (eds.), *The Charter of the United Nations. A Commentary. Volumes I & II* (Oxford University Press, 2012).

Sloan, J., *The Militarisation of Peacekeeping in the Twenty-First Century* (Oxford, Hart Publishing, 2011).

Société française pour le droit international/Institut International des droits de l'homme, *Journée d'études de Strasbourg. La soumission des organisations internationales aux normes internationales relatives aux droits de l'homme* (Paris, A. Pedone, 2009).

Soma, A. T., 'Les relations entre l'Union Africaine et la Communauté Economique des Etats de l'Afrique de l'Ouest en matière den maintien de la paix', *African Yearbook of International Law*, 18 (2012), 345–388.

Stephens, D., 'The Lawful Use of Force by Peacekeeping Forces: The Tactical Imperative', *International Peacekeeping*, 12 (2005), 157–172.

Szydlo, M., 'Extra-Territorial Application of the European Convention on Human Rights after *Al-Skeini* and *Al-Jedda*', *International Criminal Law Review*, 12 (2012), 271–291.

Tardy, T., 'Limits and Opportunities of UN–EU Relations in Peace Operations: Implications for DPKO' (2003).

United Nations – European Union Relations in Crisis Management (International Forum for the Challenges of Peace Operations, 2008).

'Hybrid Peace Operations: Rationale and Challenges', *Global Governance*, 20 (2014), 95–118.

Tharoor, S., 'The Changing Face of Peace-keeping and Peace-Enforcement', *Fordham International Law Journal*, 19 (1995), 408–426.

Tomuschat, C., *International Law: Ensuring the Survival of Mankind on the Eve of a New Century. General Course on Public International Law*, Recueil des cours de l'Académie de La Haye, Volume 281 (1999), 9–438.

Törő, C., 'The Practice and Patterns of EU Military Operations in Concert with the United Nations', *Journal of Conflict & Security Law*, (2015), 1–27.

Trybus, M., White, N. D. (eds.), *European Security Law* (Oxford University Press, 2007).

Tsagourias, N., White, N. D., *Collective Security. Theory, Law and Practice* (Cambridge University Press, 2013).

Tzanakopoulos, A., *Disobeying the Security Council. Countermeasure against Wrongful Sanctions* (Oxford University Press, 2011).

van Nieuwkerk, A., 'The Regional Roots of the African Peace and Security Architecture: Exploring Centre-Periphery Relations', *South African Journal of International Affairs*, 18 (2011), 169–189.

Van Vooren, B., Blockmans, S., Wouters, J. (eds.), *The EU's Role in Global Governance: The Legal Dimension* (Oxford University Press, 2013).

Verdirame, G., *The UN and Human Rights. Who Guards the Guardian?* (Cambridge University Press, 2011).

Villani, U., *Les Rapports entre l'ONU et les organisations régionales dans le domaine du maintien de la paix*, Recueil des cours de l'Académie de La Haye, Volume 290 (2001), 225–436.

Vines, A., 'A Decade of African Peace and Security Architecture', *International Affairs*, 89 (2013), 89–109.

Virally, M., *L'Organisation Mondiale* (Paris, A. Colin, 1972).

von Bogdandy, A., 'The European Union as a Human Rights Organization? Human Rights and the Core of the European Union', *Common Market Law Review*, 37 (2000), 1307–1338.

Wallensteen, P., Bjurner, A. (eds.), *Regional Organizations and Peacemaking. Challengers to the UN?* (London, Routledge, 2015).

Walter, C., *Vereinte Nationen und Regionalorganisationen* (Heidelberg, Springer, 1996).

'Security Council Control over Regional Action', *Max Planck Yearbook of United Nations Law*, 1 (1997), 129–193.

Watkin, K., 'Controlling the Use of Force: A Role for Human Rights Norms in Contemporary Armed Conflict', *American Journal of International Law*, 98 (2004), 1–34.

Weiner, R. O., Aolain, F. N., 'Beyond the Laws of War: Peacekeeping in Search of a Legal Framework', *Columbia Human Rights Law Review*, 27 (1995–1996), 293–354.

Weiss, T., Daws, S. (eds.), *The Oxford Handbook on the United Nations* (Oxford University Press, 2007).

Wellens, K., 'Fragmentation of International Law and Establishing an Accountability Regime for International Organizations: The Role of the Judiciary in Closing the Gap', *Michigan Journal of International Law*, 25 (2004), 1159–1181.

Weller, M. (ed.), *The Oxford Handbook on the Use of Force in International Law* (Oxford University Press, 2014).

White, N. D., *The Law of International Organisations* (Manchester University Press, 2005).

White, N. D., Ülgen, Ö., 'The Security Council and the Decentralised Military Option: Constitutionality and Function', *Netherlands International Law Review*, 44 (1997), 378–413.

Wilde, R., 'Triggering State Obligations Extraterritorially: The Spatial Test in Certain Human Rights Treaties', *Israel Law Review*, 40 (2007), 503–526.

Williams, P. D., Boutellis, A., 'Partnership Peacekeeping: Challenges and Opportunities in the United Nations–African Union Relationship', *African Affairs*, 113 (2014), 254–278.

Wolfrum, R., 'Der Beitrag regionaler Abmachungen zur Friedenssicherung: Möglichkeiten und Grenzen', *Heidelberg Journal of International Law*, 53 (1993), 576–602.

Wouters, J., Brems, E., Smis, S. (eds.), *Accountability for Human Rights Violations by International Organisations* (Antwerp, Intersentia, 2010).

Wyss, M., Tardy, T. (eds.), *Peacekeeping in Africa: The Evolving Security Architecture* (London, Routledge, 2014).

Yamashita, H., 'Peacekeeping Cooperation between the United Nations and Regional Organisations', *Review of International Studies*, 38 (2012), 165–186.

Yusuf, A. A., 'The Right of Intervention by the African Union: A New Paradigm in Regional Enforcement Action?', *African Yearbook of International Law*, 11 (2003), 3–21.

Yusuf, A. A., Ouguergouz, F. (eds.), *The African Union: Legal and Institutional Framework* (Leiden, Brill, 2012).

Zwanenburg, M., 'Existentialism in Iraq: Security Council Resolution 1483 and the Law of Occupation', *International Review of the Red Cross*, 86 (2004), 745–769.

Accountability of Peace Support Operations (Leiden, Brill, 2005).

Cases

International Court of Justice

Certain Expenses of the United Nations (Article 17, Paragraph 2 of the Charter), Advisory Opinion (20 July 1962).

Competence of the General Assembly for the Admission of a State to the United Nations, Advisory Opinion (3 March 1950).

Difference Relating to Immunity from Legal Process of a Special Rapporteur of the Commission on Human Rights, Advisory Opinion (29 April 1999).

Effect of Awards of Compensation Made by the United Nations Administrative Tribunal, Advisory Opinion (13 July 1954).

Interpretation of the Agreement of 25 March 1951 between the WHO and Egypt, Advisory Opinion (20 December 1980).

Legal Consequences for States of the Continued Presence of South Africa in Namibia (South West Africa) Notwithstanding Security Council Resolution 276 (1970), Advisory Opinion (21 June 1971).

Legal Consequences for States of the Continued Presence of South Africa in Namibia (South West Africa) Notwithstanding Security Council Resolution 276 (1970), Advisory Opinion (21 June 1971) (Judge Fitzmaurice, Dissenting Opinion).

Legal Consequences of the Construction of a Wall in the Occupied Palestinian Territory, Advisory Opinion (9 July 2004).

Legality of the Threat or Use of Nuclear Weapons, Advisory Opinion (8 July 1996).

Legality of the Threat or Use of Nuclear Weapons, Advisory Opinion (8 July 1996) (Judge Higgins, Dissenting Opinion).

Legality of the Use by a State of Nuclear Weapons in Armed Conflict, Advisory Opinion (8 July 1996).

Military and Paramilitary Activities in and against Nicaragua (*Nicaragua v. United States of America*), Merits, Judgment (27 June 1986).

North Sea Continental Shelf Cases (*Federal Republic of Germany v. Denmark and Federal Republic of Germany v. the Netherlands*), Judgment (20 February 1969).

Reparation for Injuries Suffered in the Service of the United Nations, Advisory Opinion (11 April 1949).

European Court of Human Rights

Georgia Andreou against Turkey, Fourth Section, Decision as to the Admissibility, 3 June 2008.

Agim Behrami and Bekir Behrami against France, Ruzdhi Saramati against France, Germany and Norway, Decision on Admissibility, 2 May 2007.

Bankovic and others v. Belgium and others, Admissibility, Decision of 12 December 2001.

Berić and others v. Bosnia, Fourth Section, Decision as to the Admissibility, 16 October 2007.

Case of A. and Others v. The United Kingdom, Grand Chamber, Judgment, 19 February 2009.

Case of Al-Jedda v. The United Kingdom, Grand Chamber, Judgment, 7 July 2011.

Case of Al-Saadoon and Mufdhi v. The United Kingdom, Fourth Section, Decision as to the Admissibility, 30 June 2009.

Case of Al-Skeini and Others v. The United Kingdom, Grand Chamber, Judgment, 7 July 2011.

Case of Al-Skeini and Others v. The United Kingdom, Grand Chamber, Judgment, 7 July 2011 (Judge Bonello, Concurring Opinion).

Case of Hirsi Jamaa and Others v. Italy, Grand Chamber, Judgment, 23 February 2012.

Case of Ilaşcu and Others v. Moldova and Russia, Judgment of the Grand Chamber, 8 July 2004.

Case of Ilaşcu and Others v. Moldova and Russia, Judgment of the Grand Chamber, 8 July 2004 (Judge Sir Nicholas Bratza joined by Judges Rozakis, Hedigan, Thomassen and Pantiru, Partly Dissenting Opinion).

Case of Issa and Others v. Turkey, Second Section, Judgment, 16 November 2004.
Case of Loizidou v. Turkey (Preliminary Objections), Grand Chamber, Judgment, 23 March 1995.
Case of Loizidou v. Turkey, Judgment, Grand Chamber, Merits, 18 December 1996.
Case of Medvedyev and Others v. France, Judgment, Grand Chamber, 29 March 2010.
Case of Pad and Others v. Turkey, Third Section, Decision as to the Admissibility, 28 June 2007.
Case of Perks and Others v. The United Kingdom, Third Section, Judgment, 12 October 2009.
Case of Rantsev v. Cyprus and Russia, Judgment, 7 January 2010.
Case of Solomou and Others v. Turkey, Fourth Section, Judgment, 24 June 2008.
Case of Varnava and Others v. Turkey, Grand Chamber, Judgment, 18 September 2009.
Case of Velinov v. The Former Yugoslav Republic of Macedonia, First Section, Judgment, 19 September 2013.
Isaak and Others v. Turkey, Third Section, Decision as to the Admissibility, 28 September 2006.
Gajic v. Germany, First Section, Decision as to the Admissibility, 28 August 2007.
Kasumaj v. Greece, First Section, Decision as to the Admissibility, 5 July 2007.
Kyriakoula Stephens against Cyprus, Turkey and the United Nations, First Section, Decision as to the Admissibility, 11 December 2008.
Observations of the Federal Republic of Germany Concerning Application No. 78166/01: *Saramati v. France, Germany and Norway*.

European Court of Justice

C-286/90, *Anklagemyndigheden v. Peter Michael Poulsen and Diva Navigation Corp.* [1992] ECR 1-6019.
C-162/96, *Racke v. Hauptzollamt Mainz* [1998] ECR 1-3665.
C-316/91, *European Parliament v. Council of the European Union*, Judgment, 2 March 1994.
C-299/95, *Friedrich Kremzow v. Republic Österreich*, Judgment (Fifth Chamber), 29 May 1997.
C-109/01, *Secretary of State for the Home Department v. Hacene Akrich*, Judgment, 23 September 2003.
C-540/03, *European Parliament v. Council of the European Union*, Judgment (Grand Chamber), 27 June 2006.
C-91/05, *Commission of the European Communities v. Council of the European Union* [2005], Judgment (Grand Chamber), 20 May 2008.
C-415/05 P, *Al Barakaat International Foundation v. Council of the European Union and Commission of the European Communities*, Opinion of Advocate General Poiares Maduro, 23 January 2008.

Joined Cases C-402/05 P and C-415/05 P, *Yassin Abdullah Kadi and Al Barakaat International Foundation v. Council of the European Union and Commission of the European Communities*, Judgment (Grand Chamber), 3 September 2008.

Joined Cases C-322/07 P, C-327/07 P and C-338/07 P, *Papierfabrik August Koehler AG (C-322/07 P), Bolloré SA (C-327/07 P) and Distribuidora Vizcaína de Papeles SL (C-338/07 P) v. Commission of the European Communities*, Judgment (Third Chamber), 3 September 2009.

T-135/01, *Yassin Abdullah Kadi v. Council of the European Union and Commission of the European Communities* [2005].

T-306/01, *Ahmed Ali Yussuf and Al Barakaat International Foundation v. Council of the European Union and Commission of the European Communities* [2005].

Inter-American Commission on Human Rights/Inter-American Court of Human Rights.

Velásquez Rodríguez v. Honduras, Judgment, 29 July 1988, Inter-Am Ct. H.R.

Case No. 10.573, *Salas and others v. United States [US Military Action in Panama]*, 14 October 1993.

Case 10.951, *Coard et al. v. United States of America*, 29 September 1999.

Case 11.589, *Alejandre Jr., Costa, De la Peña, Morales v. Cuba*, 29 September 1999.

International Criminal Court

Decision on the Confirmation of Charges, *Prosecutor v. Thomas Lubanga Dyilo* (ICC-01/04-01/06), Pre-Trial Chamber I, 29 January 2007.

Decision on the Prosecutor's Application for a Warrant of Arrest against Jean-Pierre Bemba Combo (ICC-01/05-01/08), Pre-Trail Chamber III, 10 June 2008.

Decision on the Confirmation of Charges, *Prosecutor v. Germain Katanga and Mathieu Ngudjolo Chui* (ICC-01/04-01/07), Pre-Trial Chamber I, 30 September 2008.

Judgment pursuant to Article 74 of the Statute, *Prosecutor v. Thomas Lubanga Dyilo* (ICC-01/04-01/06), Trial Chamber I, 14 March 2012.

International Criminal Tribunal for the Former Yugoslavia

Prosecutor v. Dusko Tadić a/k/a 'Dule', Decision on the Defence Motion on Jurisdiction, Case No. IT-94-1, Tr. Ch., 10 August 1995.

Prosecutor v. Dusko Tadić a/k/a 'Dule', Decision on the Defence Motion for Interlocutory Appeal on Jurisdiction, Case No. IT-94-1, App.Ch., 2 October 1995.

Prosecutor v. Duško Tadić a/k/a 'Dule', Judgment, Case No. IT-94-1, Ap. Chamber, 15 July 1999.

Prosecutor v. Milomir Stakić, Judgment, Case No. IT-97-24-T, T. Ch. II, 31 July 2003.

Prosecutor v. Dario Kordić and Mario Čerkez, Judgment, Case No. IT-95-14/2-A, Appeals Chamber, 17 December 2004.
Prosecutor v. Vlastimir Đorđević, Judgment, Case No. IT-05-87/1 'Kosovo', Tr. Ch. II, 23 February 2011.
Prosecutor v. Momčilo Perišić, Judgment, Case No. IT-04-81-A, Appeals Chamber, 28 February 2013.

International Criminal Tribunal for Rwanda

The Prosecutor v. Jean-Paul Akayesu, Judgment, Case No. ICTR-96-4-T, T. Ch. I, 2 September 1998.
The Prosecutor v. André Rwamakuba, Decision on Appropriate Remedy, Case No. ICTR 98-44C-T, T. Ch. III, 31 January 2007.

Human Rights Committee

Appendix, Individual opinion submitted by a member of the Human Rights Committee under Rule 94(3) of the Committee's provisional rules of procedure, Communication No. R.13/56, Report of the Human Rights Committee, Supplement No. 40, UN Doc. A/36/40 (1981).
Consideration of Reports Submitted by States Parties under Article 40 of the Covenant, Concluding Observations of the Human Rights Committee, Israel, UN Doc. CCPR/C/79/ADD.93 (1998).
Consideration of Reports Submitted by States Parties under Article 40 of the Covenant, Concluding Observations of the Human Rights Committee, Belgium, UN Doc. CCPR/CO/81/BEL (2004).
General Comment 29, States of Emergency (Article 4), UN Doc. CCPR/C/21/Rev.1/Add.11 (2001).
General Comment No. 31(80), The Nature of the General Legal Obligations Imposed on States Parties to the Covenant, UN Doc. CCPR/C/21/Rev.1/Add.13 (2004).
Human Rights Committee, Summary Record of the 2384th Meeting, UN Doc. CCPR/C/SR.2384 (2006).
Report Submitted by the United Nations Interim Administration Mission in Kosovo to the Human Rights Committee on the Human Rights Situation in Kosovo since June 1999, Kosovo (Serbia and Montenegro), UN Doc. CCPR/C/UNK/1 (2006).
Danyal Shafiq v. Australia, Communication No. 1324/2004, UN Doc. CCPR/C/88/D/1324/2004 (2006).
Views of the Human Rights Committee under Article 5(4) of the Optional Protocol to the International Covenant on Civil and Political Rights Concerning Communication No. R.12/52, *López Burgos v. Uruguay*, Annex XIX to Report of the Human Rights Committee, Supplement No. 40, UN Doc. A/36/40 (1981).

Domestic Courts

Belgium

Tribunal civil de Bruxelles (71e chambre), M. et autres/Etat belge, ministre de la Défense nationale et A. et autres, 8 décembre 2010.

United Kingdom

House of Lords, R (on the application of Al-Jedda) (FC) (Appellant) v Secretary of State for Defence (Respondent), Decision, 12 December 2007.

The Netherlands

District Court in The Hague, Nuhanović v. The Netherlands, Judgment, LJN BF0181, Case No. 265615/HA ZA 06-1671(English translation), 10 September 2008.
District Court in The Hague, Mustafić v. The Netherlands, Judgment, LJN BF0182, Case No. 265618/HA ZA 06-1672 (English translation), 10 September 2008.
District Court in The Hague, Stichting Mothers of Srebrenica and Others v. The Netherlands, Judgment, Case No. C/09/295247/HA ZA 07-2973, 16 July 2014.
Court of Appeal in The Hague, Nuhanović v. The State of the Netherlands, Judgment, LJN BR5388, Case No. 200.20.174/01, 5 July 2011.
Court of Appeal in The Hague, Mustafić v. The State of the Netherlands, Judgment, LJN BR5386, Case No. 200.020.173/01, 5 July 2011.
Supreme Court of the Netherlands, The State of the Netherlands (Ministry of Defence and Ministry of Foreign Affairs) v. Hasan Nuhanović, Judgment, First Chamber, 12/03324, LZ/TT, 6 September 2013.
Supreme Court of the Netherlands, The State of the Netherlands (Ministry of Defence and Ministry of Foreign Affairs) v. Mehida Mustafić, Damir Mustafić, Alma Mustafić, Judgment, First Chamber, 12/03329, LZ/TT, 6 September 2013.

Documents of International Organisations

United Nations

Annex to the letter dated 1 August 2013 from the Permanent Representative of Argentina to the United Nations addressed to the Secretary-General, Cooperation between the United Nations and regional and subregional organizations in maintaining international peace and security, Concept note, UN Doc. S/2013/446 (2013).
Annex to the letter dated 14 October 2013 from the Permanent Representative of Rwanda to the United Nations addressed to the President of the Security Council, Joint communiqué of the seventh annual consultative meeting between members of the Security Council of the United Nations and the Peace and Security Council of the African Union, UN Doc. S/2013/611 (2013).

Budget for the United Nations Multidimensional Integrated Stabilization Mission in Mali for the period from 1 July 2013 to 30 June 2014, Report of the Advisory Committee on Administrative and Budgetary Questions, UN Doc. A/68/653 (2013).
Communiqué of the consultative meeting of members of the Security Council of the United Nations and the Peace and Security Council of the African Union (2008), Annex to UN Doc. S/2010/392/Add.1 (2010).
Communiqué of the consultative meeting of members of the Security Council of the United Nations and the Peace and Security Council of the African Union, Annex to UN Doc. S/2010/392 (2010).
Comprehensive review of the whole question of peace-keeping operation in all their aspects, Report of the Special Committee on Peacekeeping Operations, UN Doc. A/50/230 (1995).
Comprehensive review of the whole question of peacekeeping operations in all their aspects, Report of the Special Committee on Peacekeeping Operations, UN Doc. A/54/87 (1999).
Comprehensive review of the whole question of peacekeeping operations in all their aspects, Report of the Special Committee on Peacekeeping Operations, UN Doc. A/54/839 (2000).
Comprehensive review of the whole question of peacekeeping operations in all their aspects, Report of the Special Committee on Peacekeeping Operations, UN Doc. A/55/1024 (2001).
Comprehensive review of the whole question of peacekeeping operations in all their aspects, Report of the Special Committee on Peacekeeping Operations, UN Doc. A/57/767 (2003).
Declaration, Enhancing UN–AU Cooperation: Framework for the Ten-Year Capacity Buildling Programme for the African Union, Annex to UN Doc. A/61/630 (2006).
Department of Peacekeeping Operations and Department of Field Support, Policy, February 2008, Authority, Command and Control in United Nations Peacekeeping Operations.
Department of Peacekeeping Operations and Department of Field Support, A New Partnership Agenda. Charting a New Horizon for UN Peacekeeping (2009).
Department of Peacekeeping Operations and Department of Field Support, The New Horizon Initiative: Progress Report No. 1 (October 2010).
Evaluation of the implementation and results of protection of civilians mandates in United Nations peacekeeping operations, Report of the Office of Internal Oversight Services, UN Doc. A/68/787 (2014).
Financing of the United Nations Interim Administration Mission in Kosovo, Report of the Advisory Committee on Administrative and Budgetary Questions, UN Doc. A/55/624 (2000).

Responsibility of International Organizations, Interoffice Memorandum to the Director of the Codification Division, Office of Legal Affairs and Secretary of the International Law Commission regarding the topic Responsibility of International Organizations (2004), *United Nations Juridicial Yearbook*, 352–356.

Lesson Learned Unit, Department of Peacekeeping Operations, Cooperation between the United Nations and Regional Organizations/Arrangements in a Peacekeeping Environment, Suggested Principles and Mechanisms (1999).

Liability of the United Nations for Claims Involving Off-duty Acts of Members of Peace-keeping Forces – Determination of 'Off-Duty' versus 'On-Duty' Status, Memorandum to the Director, Office for Field Operation and External Support Activities, *United Nations Juridical Yearbook* (1986), 300–301.

Panel on United Nations Peace Operations, Report of the Panel on United Nations Peace Operations, UN Doc. A/55/305 and S/2000/809 (2000).

Peacekeeping, The Right of Self-Defence of United Nations Peacekeeping Forces and the Exercise of that Right – Article 51 of the Charter of the United Nations, Memorandum to the Senior Political Adviser to the Secretary-General (1993), *United Nations Juridical Yearbook*, 371–372.

Peacekeeping Best Practices Unit, Department of Peacekeeping Operations, *Handbook on United Nations Multidimensional Peacekeeping Operations* (2003).

Report of the African Union–United Nations Panel on Modalities for Support to African Union Peacekeeping Operations, UN Doc. A/63/666-S/2008/813 (2008).

Report of the High-Level Panel on Threats, Challenges and Change, A More Secure World: Our Shared Responsibility, UN Doc. A/59/565 (2004).

Report of the High-Level Independent Panel on Peace Operations on Uniting Our Strengths for Peace: Politics, Partnership and People, UN Doc. A/70/95 and S/2015/446 (2015).

Report of the Special Committee on Peacekeeping Operations and Its Working Group, 2004 substantive session (New York, 29 March–16 April 2004), UN Doc. A/58/19 (2004).

Report of the Special Committee on Peacekeeping Operations and Its Working Group, 2005 substantive session (New York 31 January–25 February 2005), 2005 resumed session (New York, 4–8 April 2005), UN Doc. A/59/19/Rev.1.

Report of the Special Committee on Peacekeeping Operations and Its Working Group, 2006 second resumed session (18 December 2006), 2007 substantive session (28 February–16 March and 23 May 2007), 2007 resumed session (11 June 2007), UN Doc. A/61/19/Rev.1 (2008).

Report of the Special Committee on Peacekeeping Operations and Its Working Group, 2008 substantive session (10 March–4 April and 3 July 2008), UN Doc. A/62/19 (2008).

Report of the Special Committee on Peacekeeping Operations, 2010 substantive session (22 February–19 March), UN Doc. A/64/19 (2010).

Report of the Special Committee on Peacekeeping Operations, 2011 substantive session (New York, 22 February–18 March and 9 May 2011), UN Doc. A/65/19 (2011).

Report of the Special Committee on Peacekeeping Operations, 2012 substantive session (New York, 21 February–16 March and 11 September 2012), UN Doc. A/66/19 (2012).

Report submitted by the United Nations Interim Administration Mission in Kosovo to the Human Rights Committee on the Human Rights Situation in Kosovo since June 1999, UN Doc. CCPR/C/UNK/1 (2006).

United Nations, Documents de la Conférence des Nations Unies sur l'Organisation Internationale, San Francisco, 1945, Tome IX, Commission II, Assemblée Générale (1945).

United Nations, Documents de la Conférence des Nations Unies sur l'Organisation Internationale, San Francisco, 1945, Tome XII, Commission III, Conseil de Sécurité (1945).

International Law Commission

Gaja, G., Second report on responsibility of international organizations, UN Doc. A/CN.4/541 (2004).

Gaja, G., Third report on responsibility of international organisations, UN Doc. A/CN.4/553 (2005).

Gaja, G., Fourth report on responsibility of international organisations, UN Doc. A/CN.4/564 (2006).

Gaja, G., Seventh report on responsibility of international organizations, UN Doc. A/CN.4/610 (2009).

Gaja, G., Eighth report on responsibility of international organizations, UN Doc. A/CN.4/640 (2011).

International Law Commission, Responsibility of international organizations, Comments and observations received by international organizations, UN Doc. A/CN.4/545 (2004).

International Law Commission, Responsibility of international organizations, Comments and observations received from governments and international organizations, UN Doc. A/CN.4/556 (2005).

International Law Commission, Responsibility of international organizations, Comments and observations received from international organizations, UN Doc. A/CN.4/582 (2007).

International Law Commission, Responsibility of international organizations, Comments and observations received from international organizations, UN Doc. A/CN.4/637 (2011).

International Law Commission, Responsibility of international organizations, Comments and observations received from international organizations, UN Doc. A/CN.4/637/Add.1 (2011).
International Law Commission, Responsibility of International Organizations, Text and titles of draft articles 1 to 67 adopted by the drafting committee on second reading in 2011, UN Doc. A/CN.4/L.778 (2011).
International Law Commission, Report of the International Law Commission on the Work of Its Fiftieth Session, 20 April–12 June 1998, 27 July–14 August 1998, General Assembly Official Records, Fifty-third Session, Supplement No. 10, UN Doc. A/53/10 (1998).
International Law Commission, Report on the Work of Its Fifty-Fifth Session (5 May–6 June and 7 July–8 August 2003), General Assembly Official Records, Fifty-Eighth Session, Supplement No. 10 (A/58/10) (2003).
International Law Commission, Report on the Work of Its Fifty-Seventh Session (2 May–3 June and 11 July–5 August 2005), General Assembly Official Records, Sixtieth Session, Supplement No. 10 (A/60/10) (2005).
International Law Commission, Report on the Work of Its Fifty-Eighth Session (1 May–9 June and 3 July–11 August 2006), General Assembly Official Records, Sixty-First Session, Supplement No. 10 (A/61/10) (2006).
International Law Commission, Report on the Work of Its Fifty-Sixth Session (3 May–4 June and 5 July–6 August (2004), General Assembly Official Records, Fifty-Ninth Session, Supplement No. 10 (A/59/10) (2004).
International Law Commission, Report on the Work of Its Sixty-First Session (4 May–5 June and 6 July–7 August 2009), General Assembly, Official Records, Sixty-Fourth Session, Supplement No. 10, UN Doc. A/64/10 (2009).
International Law Commission, Report of the International Law Commission, Sixty-Third session (26 April–3 June and 4 July–12 August 2011), General Assembly, Official Records, Sixty-Sixth Session, Supplement No. 10 (A/66/10) (2011).
International Law Commission, Responsibility of International Organizations, Comments and observations received from Governments, UN Doc. A/CN.4/547 (2004).
International Law Commission, Responsibility of International Organizations, Comments and observations received from governments and international organizations, UN Doc. A/CN.4/556 (2005).

Security Council

An Agenda for Peace: Preventive Diplomacy, Peacemaking and Peace-keeping, UN Doc. S/25996 (1993).
Annex to the letter dated 29 August 2002 from the Permanent Representative of Mauritius to the United Nations addressed to the President of the Security

Council, Recommendations of the Ad Hoc Working Group on Conflict Prevention and Resolution in Africa to the Security Council, UN Doc. S/2002/979 (2002).

Annex to the letter dated 12 June 2012 from the Permanent Representative of South Africa to the United Nations addressed to the President of the Security Council, Communiqué of the consultative meeting between members of the Security Council of the United Nations and the Peace and Security Council of the African Union, UN Doc. S/2012/444 (2012).

Secretary-General

Administrative and budgetary aspects of the financing of the United Nations peace-keeping operations: financing of the United Nations peace-keeping operations, Reform of the procedures for determining reimbursement to member states for contingent-owned equipment, Note by the Secretary-General, UN Doc. A/50/995 (1996).

Administrative and budgetary aspects of the financing of the United Nations peace-keeping operations: financing of the United Nations peacekeeping operations, UN Doc. A/51/903 (1997).

Administrative and budgetary aspects of the financing of the United Nations peace-keeping operations: financing of the United Nations peace-keeping operations, Reform of the procedures for determining reimbursement to member states for contingent-owned equipment, Note by the Secretary-General, UN Doc. A/51/967 (1997).

Comprehensive review of the whole question of peace-keeping operations in all their aspects: command and control of United Nations peace-keeping operations, Report of the Secretary-General, UN Doc. A/49/681 (1994).

Cooperation between the United Nations and the Organization of African Unity, Report of the Secretary-General, Addendum, UN Doc. A/48/475/Add.1 (1993).

Cooperation between the United Nations and regional and other organizations, Report of the Secretary-General, UN Doc. A/67/280-S/2012/614 (2012).

Enhancement of African peacekeeping capacity, Report of the Secretary-General, UN Doc. A/54/63–S/1999/171 (1999).

Enhancement of African peacekeeping capacity, Report of the Secretary-General, UN Doc. A/59/591 (2004).

Implementation of the recommendations of the Special Committee on Peacekeeping Operations, Report of the Secretary-General, UN Doc. A/58/694 (2004).

Implementation of the recommendations of the Special Committee on Peacekeeping Operations, Report of the Secretary-General, UN Doc. A/59/608 (2004).

Implementation of the recommendations of the Special Committee on Peacekeeping Operations, Report of the Secretary-General, UN Doc. A/60/640 (2005).

Implementation of the recommendations of the Special Committee on Peacekeeping Operations, Report of the Secretary-General, Addendum, UN Doc. A/60/640/Add.1 (2005).
Implementation of the recommendations of the Special Committee on Peacekeeping Operations, Report of the Secretary-General, Addendum, UN Doc. 61/668/Add.1 (2006).
Implementation of the recommendations of the Special Committee on Peacekeeping Operations, Report of the Secretary-General, UN Doc. A/61/668 (2007).
Implementation of the recommendations of the Special Committee on Peacekeeping Operations, Report of the Secretary-General, UN Doc. A/62/627 (2007).
Implementation of the recommendations of the Special Committee on Peacekeeping Operations, Report of the Secretary-General, UN Doc. A/64/573 (2009).
Implementation of the recommendations of the Special Committee on Peacekeeping Operations, Report of the Secretary-General, UN Doc. A/65/680 (2011).
Implementation of the recommendations of the Special Committee on Peacekeeping Operations, Report of the Secretary-General, UN Doc. A/65/680/Add.1 (2011).
Implementation of the recommendations of the Special Committee on Peacekeeping Operations, Report of the Secretary-General, UN Doc. A/67/632 (2012).
Letter dated 2 January 2015 from the Secretary-General addressed to the President of the Security Council, UN Doc. S/2015/3 (2015).
Partnering for peace: moving towards partnership peacekeeping, UN Doc. S/2015/229 (2015).
Report of the Secretary-General, Administrative and budgetary aspects of the financing of the United Nations peacekeeping operations: financing the United Nations peacekeeping operations, UN Doc. A/51/389 (1996).
Report of the Secretary-General, The causes of conflict and the promotion of durable peace and sustainable development in Africa, UN Doc. A/52/871– S/1998/318 (1998).
Report of the Secretary-General on inter-mission cooperation and possible cross-border operations between the United Nations Mission in Sierra Leone, the United Nations Mission in Liberia and the United Nations Operation in Côte d'ivoire, UN Doc. S/2005/135 (2005).
Report of the Secretary-General on the relationship between the United Nations and regional organizations, in particular the African Union, in the maintenance of international peace and security, UN Doc. S/2008/186 (2008).
Report of the Secretary-General, A regional-global security partnership: challenges and opportunities, UN Doc. A/ 61/204&S/2006/590 (2006).
Secretary-General, An agenda for peace, UN Doc. S/25996 (1993).
Secretary-General's Bulletin, Observance by United Nations forces of international humanitarian law, UN Doc. ST/SGB/1999/13 (1999).

Secretary-General, In larger freedom: towards development, security and human rights for all, UN Doc. A/59/2005 (2005).
Secretary-General, Note by the Secretary-General, UN Doc. A/59/565 (2004).
Supplement to an agenda for peace: Position paper of the Secretary-General on the occasion of the fiftieth anniversary of the United Nations, UN Doc. A/50/60–S/1995/1 (1995).
Support to African Union peacekeeping operations authorized by the United Nations, Report of the Secretary-General, UN Doc. A/64/359–S/2009/470 (2009).
Support to African Union peacekeeping operations authorized by the United Nations, Report of the Secretary-General, UN Doc. A/65/510 and S/2010/514 (2010).
Text of the exchange of letters dated 20 February 1965 between the Secretary-General of the United Nations and the Minister for Foreign Affairs of Belgium concerning the settlement of claims lodged against ONUC by Belgian Nationals (1965), UN Doc. S/6597, Annex 1.
The future of United Nations peace operations: implementation of the recommendations of the High-level Independent Panel on Peace Operations, UN Doc. A/70/357 and S/2015/682 (2015).

General Assembly

General Assembly, Declaration on the Enhancement of Cooperation between the United Nations and Regional Arrangements or Agencies in the Maintenance of International Peace and Security, UN Doc. A/RES/49/57 (1994) Annex.
General Assembly, Fifty-Eight Session, Official Records, Sixth Committee, Summary Record of the 14th Meeting, UN Doc. A/C.6/58/SR.14 (2003).
General Assembly, Fifty-Eight Session, Official Records, Sixth Committee, Summary Record of the 15th Meeting, UN Doc. A/C.6/58/SR.15 (2003).
General Assembly, Fifty-Ninth Session, Official Records, Sixth Committee, Summary Record of the 21st Meeting, UN Doc. A/C.6/59/SR.21 (2004).
General Assembly, Sixtieth Session, Official Records, Sixth Committee, Summary Record of the 12th Meeting, UN Doc. A/C.6/60/SR.12 (2005).
General Assembly, Sixtieth Session, Official Records, Sixth Committee, Summary Record of the 13th Meeting, UN Doc. A/C.6/60/SR.13 (2005).
General Assembly, Sixty-First Session, Official Records, Sixth Committee, Summary Record of the 15th Meeting, UN Doc. A/C.6/61/SR.15 (2006).
General Assembly, Sixty-Fourth Session, Official Records, Sixth Committee, Summary Record of the 15th Meeting, UN Doc. A/C.6/64/SR.15 (2009).
General Assembly, Sixty-Sixth Session, Official Records, Sixth Committee, Summary Record of the 18th Meeting, UN Doc. A/C.6/66/SR.18 (2011).

General Assembly, International Law Commission, Sixty-Fourth Session, Report of the International Law Commission on the Work of Its Sixty-Third Session (2011), Topical summary of the discussion held in the Sixth Committee of the General Assembly during its sixty-sixth session, prepared by the Secretariat, Addendum, UN Doc. UN Doc. A/CN.4/650/Add.1 (2012),

Resolution adopted by the General Assembly, Comprehensive review of the whole question of peace-keeping operations in all their aspects, UN Doc. A/RES/48/42 (1994).

Thematic evaluation of cooperation between the Department of Peacekeeping Operations/Department of Field Support and regional organizations, Report of the Office of Internal Oversight Services, UN Doc. A/65/762 (2011).

European Union

A secure Europe in a better world, European Security Strategy (2003).

Council of the European Union, the EU and Africa: Towards a strategic partnership, Brussels, 19 December 2005.

Council of the European Union, the Africa–EU Strategic Partnership. A joint Africa–EU strategy, 16344/07 (Presse 291) (2007).

Council of the European Union. EU concept for military command and control, Brussels, 24 September 2012.

EU Guidelines, Human Rights and International Humanitarian Law (2009).

EU Guidelines on Children and Armed Conflict.

EU–NATO Declaration on ESDP, 16 December 2002.

EU–UN Co-operation in Military Crisis Management Operations, Elements of Implementation of the EU–UN Joint Declaration (2004).

First Action Plan (2008–2010) for the Implementation of the Africa–EU Strategic Partnership.

Fourth EU–Africa Summit, 2–3 April 2014, Brussels, Declaration.

Fourth EU–Africa Summit, 2–3 April 2014, Brussels, Roadmap 2014–2017.

Joint Africa EU Strategy Action Plan 2011–2013.

Joint Declaration on UN–EU Co-operation in Crisis Management (2003).

Joint Statement on UN–EU Cooperation in Crisis Management (2007).

Key Deliverables of the Joint Africa–EU Strategy Second Action Plan 2011–2013 (living document, as of July 2012).

Plan of Action to Enhance EU CSDP Support to UN Peacekeeping, EEAS 01024/12, Brussels, 13 June 2012.

Preparing the December 2013 European Council on Security and Defence, Final report by the High Representative/Head of the EDA on the common security and defence policy, Brussels, 15 October 2013.

Securing Peace and Stabilitiy for Africa. The EU-funded African peace facility (2004).

Speech of High Representative Catherine Aston on main aspects and basic choices of the Common Foreign and Security Policy and the Common Security and Defence Policy, Brussels, 11 May 2011, A 179/11.
The European Union and the United Nations: The choice of multilateralism.
Updated European Union guidelines on promoting compliance with international humanitarian law (IHL) (2009/C 303/06).

African Union

50th Anniversary Solemn Declaration by Heads of State and Government of the African Union assembled to celebrate the golden jubliee of the OAU/AU.
Africa, our common destiny, Guideline document (2004).
Common African position on the UN review of peace operations, PSC/PR/2(DII), 29 April 2015.
Consultative meeting between the African Union (AU) – Regional economic communities (RECs)/regional mechanisms for conflict prevention, management and resolution (RMs) and the European Union (EU) on the EU support to the operationalization of the African Peace and Security Architecture (APSA), Akosombo, Ghana, 10–11 December 2009.
Experts' meeting on the relationship between the AU and the regional mechanisms for conflict prevention, management and resolution, Addis Ababa, 22–23 March 2005, Roadmap for the Operationalization of the African Standby Force (2005).
Joint Africa EU Strategy. Action Plan 2011–2013, Introductory Part.
Mali/African Union/Peace and Security Council, 323rd Meeting, New York, June 12, 2012, AU Doc. PSC/PR/COMM.(CCCXXIII) (2012).
Memorandum of understanding on cooperation in the area of peace and security between the African Union, the regional economic communities and the coordinating mechanisms of the regional standby brigades of Eastern Africa and Northern Africa (2008).
Policy framework for the establishment of the African Standby Force and the Military Staff Committee (Part I), Document adopted by the third meeting of African Chiefs of Defense Staff, 15–16 May 2003, Addis Ababa.
Policy framework on the establishment of the African Standby Force and the Military Staff Committee, AU Doc. Assembly/AU/Dec.35 (III) (2004).
Progress report of the chairperson of the Commission on the Development of Guidelines for the Protection of Civilians in African Union Peace Support Operations, PSC/PR/2(CCLXXIX) (2011).
Progress report of the chairperson of the Commission on the African-led International Support Mission in Mali, Peace and Security Council, 358th Meeting, 7 March 2013, PSC/PR/2(CCCLVIII).
Proposed guidelines for the protection of civilians in African Union peace support operations for considerations by the African Union (2010).

Protocol on amendments to the Constitutive Act of the African Union (2003).
Protocol relating to the establishment of the Peace and Security Council of the African Union (2002).
Report of the African Union High-Level Implementation Panel for Sudan and South Sudan, PSC/PR/COMM.1(CCCLIII) (2013).
Report of the chairperson of the Commission on Follow-up Steps on the Common African Position on the review of United Nations Peace Operations, PSC/AHG/3.(DXLVII).
Report of the chairperson of the Commission on the African Union–United Nations Partnership: The need for greater coherence, PSC/AHG/3.(CCCXCVII) (2013).
Report of the chairperson of the Commission on the Operationalisation of the Rapid Deployment Capacity of the African Standby Force and the Establishment of an 'African Capacity for Immediate Reponse to Crises', PSC/Exp/VI/STCDSS/(i-a)2013 (2013).
Report of the chairperson of the Commission on the Partnership between the African Union and the United Nations on Peace and Security. Towards greater strategic and political coherence, PSC/PR/2.(CCCVII) (2012).
Solemn declaration on a Common African Defence and Security Policy (2004).
Solemn declaration of the Assembly of the Union on the Situation in Mali, Addis Ababa, 27 and 28 January 2013.

North Atlantic Treaty Organization

Active engagement in cooperative security: A more efficient and flexible partnership policy (2011).
'An alliance for the 21st century', Washington Summit Communiqué issued by the Heads of State and Government participating in the meeting of the North Atlantic Council in Washington, DC, 24 April 1999.
Bucharest Summit Declaration, Issued by the Heads of State and Government participating in the meeting of the North Atlantic Council in Bucharest, 3 April 2008.
Chicago Summit Declaration, Issued by the Heads of State and Government participating in the meeting of the North Atlantic Council in Chicago, 20 May 2012.
EU–NATO Declaration on ESDP, 16 December 2002.
Lisbon Summit Declaration, Issued by the Heads of State and Government participating in the meeting of the North Atlantic Council in Lisbon, 20 November 2010.
Strategic concept for the defence and security of the members of the North Atlantic Treaty Organisation, Active Engagement, Modern Defence, 2010.

The Alliance's strategic concept, Approved by the Heads of State and Government participating in the meeting of the North Atlantic Council in Washington, DC, 24 April 1999.
Wales Summit Declaration, Issued by the Heads of State and Government participating in the meeting of the North Atlantic Council in Wales from 4 to 5 September 2014.

Economic Community of West African States

A proactive mechanism for change, Strategic Plan 2011–2015.
Extraordinary session of the authority of ECOWAS Heads of State and Government, Abuja, Federal Republic of Nigeria, 11 November 2012.
The ECOWAS conflict prevention framework, Regulation MSC/REG.1/01/08.

Documents of Other International Bodies

Institut de droit international

Resolution (Session of Berlin 1999), The application of International Humanitarian Law and fundamental human rights in armed conflicts in which non-state entities are parties.
Resolution (Session of Lisbonne 1995), The legal consequences for member states of the non-fulfilment by international organizations of their obligations toward third parties.

International Law Association

New Delhi Conference (2002), Committee on Accountability of International Organisations, Third report consolidated and enlarged version of recommended rules and practices ('RRP-S').
Berlin Conference (2004), Accountability of international organisations.
Sofia Conference (2012), Study group on the responsibililty of international organizations.

International Committee of the Red Cross

International humanitarian law and the challenges of contemporary armed conflicts, Report for the 31st International Conference of the Red Cross and Red Crescent, Doc. 31IC/11/5.1.2. (2011).

INDEX

Abyei Joint Oversight Committee (AJOC), 228
accountability, 3–4, 35, 68, 238
Act on Reciprocal Assistance and American Solidarity, 19
Action Plan for ESDP, 109–110
ad hoc agreements, 22
ad hoc authorised operation, 38, 70
Additional Protocols, 314
Afghanistan, 82
Africa, 155
   armed conflict, 14n46
   regional organisation, peacekeeping operations by, vii
African Charter on Human and Peoples' Rights, 273
African Immediate Crisis Reponse Capacity (AICRC), 146
African ownership, 99n177, 99–100, 109, 114–115, 115n275, 145, 246, 260
African Peace and Security Architecture (APSA), 100, 109–111, 126–128, 148, 151, 159, 202, 239, 243
   African Union and the sub-regional organisations relations, regulation of, 149–150
African Peace Facility (APF), 112–114, 119, 142, 144, 329
African Peace Facility Fund, 185
African Standby Force (ASF), 116, 141, 149, 151
African Union (AU), 9, 13–14, 36n86, 62n204, 129–130, 155, 157, 159, 161, 199, 201, 217, 251, 329

APF. *See* African Peace Facility
authority, 128, 152
ECOWAS and, 155
   ECOWAS as the stronger actor, 150–153
   normative framework, 149–150
establishment of, 130
European Union and, 117
financial burden of, 136, 142
High-Level Implementation Panel on Sudan (AUHIP), 226, 230
Mission for Mali and the Sahel (MISAHEL), 246
NATO and, 79–81
Normative Framework, 130–131
Peace and Security Architecture, 130, 137, 148
Peace Support Operations Divisions, 111, 149
Peace Support Operations Doctrine, 28n48
Political and Security Committee (PSC), 131, 134–135, 149, 152, 219, 221, 235–236, 241, 244–245, 250, 259, 329
Special Task Force, 39
United Nations and, 131–137
   aid for self-help, 140–142
   division of labour, 147
   early steps, 137–139
   institutionalisation, 145–149
   support packages for AU peace operations, 142–144
   World Summit, 139–140
African Union Mission in Somalia (AMISOM), 39n94, 113, 315

African Union Mission in Sudan
   (AMIS), 80, 217
African Union Non-Aggression and
   Common Defence Pact, 133, 135
African Union/United Nations Hybrid
   operation in Darfur (UNAMID),
   9, 116, 203
   assessment of control arrangements,
      223–225
   budget performance report for, 9n37
   chain of command and operational
      control, 222–223
   establishment, 219
   mandate, 219–220
   political oversight, 220–221
   strategic control, 221–222
African-led International Support
   Mission in the Central
   African Republic (MISCA), 203,
   250–252
   assessment, 255–256
   EU support missions and financial
      support, 254–255
   mandate, 252
   political process and control,
      252–253
   UN assessed contributions, 253–254
African-led International Support
   Mission to Mali (AFISMA), 1,
   39n94, 60, 128, 145, 183–184,
   203, 227, 233, 328
   assessment, 242–243
   chain of command of, 239
   mandate, 237
      establishment and elaboration,
         234–237
   operational control, 238–239
   operational/financial support,
      239–240
   political and strategic control, 238
   political process, 239–240
Agenda for Peace, An, 21, 42, 124
aggression, act of, 26
Agreement for the Adoption of the
   Doha Document for Peace in
   Darfur, 220
Agreement of the Framework on
   Cooperation, 103

aid and assistance, 83, 114, 172–175,
   177, 194–195
air strikes, 9, 33
Alejandre case, 291
Al-Jedda case, 167–168, 208, 312
Allied Harmony, 106
Al-Skeini case, 288, 290, 293–295, 297
Amani Africa, 111
Amani Africa II, 111
Amicus Curiae Brief, 187
Andreou v. Turkey, 289
Annan, Kofi, 22, 29, 37n89, 65n213, 77
anti-sniping patrols, 33
Applicable International Law to
   Peacekeeping Operations of
   International Organisations,
   272–273
applicable legal framework, 12, 24,
   284, 323
Arab League, 55
Arab Spring, 98
arbitrary detention or murder, 163
Argentine Presidency of the Security
   Council, 156
argumentum e contrario, 47
armed conflicts, 7, 14n46, 65, 130, 287
   non-international, 303
Articles of the International Law
   Commission, 4, 165, 177–178, 180,
   184, 191, 201, 216
   Article 7, 180
Articles on Responsibility of
   International Organizations, 165
Articles on State Responsibility, 322,
   326–327
Articles on State Responsibility of
   International Organisations, 11
Articles on the Responsibility of
   International Organisations
   (ARIO), 2, 11, 114, 163–164,
   192, 195, 208, 263, 269, 322–323,
   326–327
   Article 2 (b), 309
   Article 4, 208
   Article 7, 165–172, 179, 192
   Article 10 (1), 310
   Article 10 (2), 309
   Article 14, 173–175, 194, 215

INDEX 363

Article 15, 175
Article 17, 52n147, 192
Article 32, 312
Article 40, 327
Article 48, 177, 195
Article 48 (3), 200
Article 49, 196
Article 62, 196
Article 64, 178–179, 323, 326
Article 65, 179
assessment of, 177–178
Articles on the Responsibility of International Organizations (ARIO), 165–178
Ashton, C., 99
aterritorial context, of international organisations, 285, 297
attribution of conduct, 10, 66, 270–271, 324. *See also* new criterion of attribution
  AFISMA, of, 233–234
  attribution of responsibility and, distinguish between, 164
  exercise of jurisdiction and, 291
  joint, 170
  KFOR, of, 204–216
  MINUSCA, for, 249–250
  MINUSMA, of, 233–234
  MISCA, for, 249–250
  UNAMID, of, 217–225
  UNISFA, of, 226–227
  UNMISS, of, 226–227
attribution, criterion of, 164
Aust, H.P., 195
Australian–New Zealand Agreement 1944, 18
auxiliary responsibility, 92, 174, 177, 193

Ban Ki-moon, vii, 23, 157
Bankovic case, 293
Behrami/Saramati case, 11n41, 44n109, 166n24, 166–168, 192n159, 199, 204–205, 207–208, 295
Belgium, 41
Berdal, M., 7n29, 24n34
Berić and others v. Bosnia, 167, 293

Berlin Plus agreements, 102–103, 103n203, 106, 106n219, 118
Besson, S., 286
Bodeau-Livinec, F., 183
Boisson de Chazournes, L., 60
Bonello, G., 294
Bosnia, 33–38. *See also Berić and others v. Bosnia*
Boutros-Ghali, B., 7n26, 21, 23, 32, 32n68, 58, 124
Brahimi Report, 24, 58
breach of an international obligation
  in the form of a mandate of a peacekeeping operation, 309–313
  in the form of the obligations arising under the internal law of the organisations, 314
    African Union, 314–315
    European Union, 317–319
    United Nations, 315–317
Brownlie, I., 284
Brussels European Council 2008 Presidency Conclusions, 90
Bulletin on Observance, 316–317

Cameroon, 46n121
capacity-building through training of groups, 111
Capstone document, 315
Case concerning the Land and Maritime Boundary between Cameroon and Nigeria (Cameroon v. Nigeria), 46n121
casuistic approach, to international peacekeeping, 66, 129, 159, 324
causality, 193
Central African Republic (CAR), 64n212, 161, 203, 249, 330. *See also* MINUSCA; MISCA, MISCA; United Nations Multidimensional Integrated Stabilization Mission in the Central African Republic
Certain Expenses case, 57
(C)ESDP, 85
Cessation of Hostilities Agreement, 231
chasse gardée, 68, 262
Chicago Summit Declaration, 82

364   INDEX

children, protection of, 30n56
civil law, 191
civil war, 58
civilians
    killing of, 163
    protection of, 30n56
coalition of the willing, 21, 48
codification projects, 3–6, 131, 179
Cold War, 20
    Security Council after the end
        of, 21–25
collective security, 44, 47, 64, 161
collective self-defence, 29, 47
Commander in Chief Allied
    Forces, Southern Europe
    (CINCSOUTH), 210
Common African Position on the UN
    Review of Peace Operations, 143
Common Foreign and Security Policy
    (CFSP), 84–88, 87n106, 98–99
    implementation of, 88–89
Common Security and Defence Policy
    (CSDP), 86–88, 99, 104, 112,
    116, 119
Commonwealth, 46
comparative advantages, 147, 152–153
compensations, 164, 169, 191, 327–328
competition, 68
competitive attitudes, 154
complicity, 194–195
Conakry Peace Agreement, 125
conflicts, prevention and mediation
    of, 158
consent, 58
    lack of, and peace enforcement, 32
consent of the host-state, 27–28, 32, 57
Constituent Treaty of 1975, 120
constitutionalisation of international
    law, 186
Constitutive Act, 130, 149–150
    Article 4, African Union and,
        131–137
contexte étatique, 162, 286
control, notion of, 183–184
Convention on Safety of United
    Nations Personnel, 303
cooperation between international
    organisations, 1–2, 68–69,

153–154, 321. *See also specific
    organisations*
cooperation in the operational
    context, 321
cooperation with the UN, 269
cooperative effort, 189
co-perpetration, 188–189, 193
Corten, O., 136
Côte d'Ivoire, 126
Council of Elders, 121
Court of First Instance, 169, 274–275
Cox, K.E., 30n55
Craig, P., 86n101
criminal law, international, 186–189
    liability in, 187–189
cross-judging in situations of shared
    responsibility, 200
customary international law, 12, 268,
    271, 278, 311
    human rights and, 278–282
Cyprus, 106

damage of property
    unintentional, 191
    willful, 191
Darfur, 9, 39, 115, 136.
    See also UNAMID
D'Aspremont, J, 52
Dayton Peace Agreements, 76
de Hoop Scheffer, Jaap, ix, 83
de lege ferenda, 13
*Declaration on a Common African
    Defence and Security Policy*, 138
Declaration on the Enhancement of
    Cooperation (1994), 51, 58
delegation of powers
    and authorisation, distinction
        between, 55n164
    on the law of responsibility, 193
Democratic Republic of the Congo
    (DRC), 34, 39, 49, 96, 105, 303
Department for Peacekeeping
    Operations (DPKO), 126
directed and controled organisations,
    175–176
District Court in The Hague, 168
diversification, in peacekeeping
    operations, 35

division of labour, 37–40, 153, 269–271
domestic law, 164
Draft Accession Agreement of the EU to the ECHR, 199, 292, 297
Draft Guidelines for the Protection of Civilians in African Union Peace Support Operations, 314
Duch Case, 187
due diligence obligations, 296
Dumbarton Oaks proposals, 16–19, 64

Eagleton, C., 184
East African Intergovernmental Authority on Development (IGAD), 231
Economic Community of Central African States (ECCAS), 39n94, 251
Economic Community of West African States (ECOWAS), 10n39, 13–14, 54, 111, 119–120, 128–129, 159, 185–186, 199, 201
   African Union and, 126–128
   European Union and, 128
   Normative Framework, 120–123
   operation in Liberia, 38
   United Nations and, 123–128
Economic Community of West African States (ECOWAS) Cease-fire Monitoring Group (ECOMOG), 121–125
Economic Community of West African States (ECOWAS) Standby Force (ESF), 121
effective control, 167–168
effective overall control, 167
Eichmann case, 189
enforcement action, 50–57. *See also* peace enforcement
   limitations of, 51
Engdahl, O., 286
erga omnes, 178, 196
Eritrea, 49n134
Ethiopia, 49n134
Euro Recamp, 111
Euro(-atlantic) regional organisations, peacekeeping by, vii

European Commission (EC), 112, 169–170
European Community, 93
European Convention on Human Rights (ECHR), 11, 199, 273, 318, 327
   Article 15, 297
European Court of Human Rights (ECtHR), 166–167, 184, 198–199, 204–205, 207, 287–290, 293–294, 297, 312
European Defence Community Treaty of 1952, 102
European Development Fund (EDF), 113
European External Action Service (EEAS), 112
European Security and Defence Policy (ESDP), 85, 102
European Security Strategy, 89, 91, 104
European Union (EU), 1, 11, 13, 36n86, 36–38, 55, 83–84, 117–119, 155, 157, 159, 161, 190, 199, 201, 327
   Action Plan (2011–2013), 110, 114
   African Union and, 109–114, 117, 155
   equal standing, 114–117
   attribution of conduct, 119
   Charter of Fundamental Rights, 317
   division of labour, 98–101, 117
   effective multilateralism, 92–93
   embargo on weapons, 54
   foundation, 84–85
   framework, 84–85
   implementation of the CFSP, 88–89
   legal framework, 86–88
   limited military engagement on the African continent, 98–101
   NATO and, 101–109, 117
   peacekeeping and, 96–98
   Political and Security Committee (PSC), 88, 104, 110, 112–113, 257
   Pooling and Sharing initiatives, 107
   security policy, 89–91
   train and equip initiative, 112
   United Nations and, 91–96, 118, 155
European Union Force (EUFOR) Chad/CAR, 116

European Union Force (EUFOR) RCA, 254
European Union Force (EUFOR) RD Congo, 39
European Union permanent Planning Team (EUPT), 111
European Union Training Mission (EUTM) Mali, 98, 240, 243, 324
  MINUSMA and, 248
European Union Training Mission (EUTM) Somalia, 98
Europiean Commission (EC), 190
extraterritorial jurisdiction
  personal connection, 287–288, 293
  spatial connection, 287–288, 293
  by states, 285–286
  under human rights law, 286–293

factual control, 189, 193
Federal Republic of Yugoslavia (FRY), 216
financial activities, 35, 68, 96, 98, 107, 109, 112–114, 116–117, 124–126, 130, 136, 138, 140–144, 151, 155, 159, 175, 225, 235, 242, 253–254, 256, 327, 329
force, use of, 7, 25, 33, 37, 133
  authorisation of, 56–57
  decentralisation, 60
  objective and subjective capacities, 300
  for peace enforcement, 23
  as self-defence, 28–29, 57, 206
France, 36n86, 64n212, 176, 254, 324
Franck, T., 62n202, 325
Frowein, J., 62n201
fund activities, 35, 99, 112–114, 125, 144, 154, 175, 240, 253–255, 329
fundamental rights, 12, 317–318

G8-Forum, 258
Gaja, G., 181, 318
Gajic v. Germany, 167
General Assembly, 20, 42, 46, 326
general law, 267
general principles of law, 278, 283–284
Geneva Conventions, 300, 314

genocide, 130
Genocide case, 180, 190
Germany, 91, 98, 107, 295, 324
globalisation, 2, 2n6, 5
Gowlland-Debbas, V., 7n26
Griep, E., 78, 93
Grotius, H., 184
Guinea-Bissau, 154

H.v.d.P. v. the Netherlands, 291
Haiti, 54
Hammarskjöld, D., 30n57
Helsinki European Council, 105
Helsinki Headline Goal, 90
Higgins, R., 33, 33n69
High-Level Independent Panel, 142, 148, 158, 260, 329
Hirsch, M., 2n6
Hirsi Jamaa, 294
human rights, 328
  international humanitarian law and, relationship between, 304–309
  obligations on the basis of customary international law, 278–282
  obligations on the basis of general principles of law, 283–284
  obligations of members, 273–276
  obligations, as part of general international law, 278
  territorial problem of, 284–286
  treaties, specific case of accession to, 276–278
Human Rights Committee, 290–291
human rights law, 30
  application to peacekeeping forces, 293–297
  derogations under, 297–298
  extraterritorial jurisdiction under, 286–293
  violations of, 163
humanisation of international law, 161
hybrid peace operations, 8–9, 39, 116, 155, 217–218, 225

immunity of international organisations, 4n16, 201
Implementation Force (IFOR), 76
  operation in Yugoslavia, 59

implied powers, 321
individual criminal responsibility, 26n42
Indonesia, 54
Institut de droit international, 3, 299
institutional partnership, 70
institutionalisation of relations among international organisations, 158, 321
Instituto Hispano-Luso-America, 3
Instituto Hispano-Luso-Americano de Derecho Internacional, 3
Integrated Mission Task Force (IMTF), 35n80
Integrated Missions Planning Process (IMPP), 35n80
integrated operations, 38–39
Inter-American Commission on Human Rights, 291
Inter-American Convention on Human Rights, 273
interconnectivity, 5
interdependence, 5
inter-mission cooperation, 9, 324
internal crisis, 58
International Civilian Mission in Haiti (MICIVIH), 39
International Court of Justice (ICJ), 25n39, 46n121, 57, 171, 180, 185, 190, 197, 267, 276, 290, 297, 305–306, 309, 325, 327
International Courts and Tribunals, 162
International Covenant on Civil and Political Rights (ICCPR), 273, 290–291, 297, 306
International Criminal Court (ICC), 26n42, 188
international criminal law, 186–189
International Criminal Tribunal for the former Yugoslavia (ICTY), 187
international dispute settlement, 325
International Financial Institutions, 175
international humanitarian law (IHL), 12, 31, 34, 181, 273, 286, 298, 311, 314, 316, 318–319, 321, 328
  application *ratione materiae* of, 300–304
  application *ratione personae* of, 299–300
  armed conflicts and, 4
  generally, 298
  human rights and, relationship between, 304–309
  violations of, 163, 246
International Humanitatian Law (IHL) application under the EU's internal law, 318–319
international law, 321, 324
  constitutionalisation of, 186
  fragmentation of, 325
  humanisation of, 161
  violations of, 31
International Law Association (ILA), 3, 172, 181
International Law Commission (ILC), ix, 3, 20n18, 27n45, 176–177, 181, 192, 195, 309, 322. *See also* Articles on the Responsibility of International Organisations (ARIO)
  ICJ and, 171
  notion of control, 183
international military operation, 16
international responsibility, 31, 163, 197
international responsibility, law of, 6, 13, 32, 43, 59, 119, 128, 158–159, 178, 186, 198, 207–208, 326
  delegation of powers, 193
  practice of the United Nations, 162–165
International Security Assistance Force (ISAF), 82
internationally wrongful acts, 10, 13, 129, 320
inter-organisational cooperation, 4
intra-mission cooperation, 261–264
investor state arbitration, 180
Iraq war, 6
Issa case, 290

Joint Africa–European Union Strategy, 109, 111
joint attribution of conduct, 170–171
Joint Border Verification and Monitoring Mechanism, 228

joint coordination mechanism (JCM), 238
joint criminal enterprise, 187, 193
Joint Declaration on EU–UN Cooperation in Crisis Management, 92
Joint Guardian operation, 209
Joint Implementation Commission (JIC), 213
joint responsibility, 177–178, 195, 319, 322, 326–327
Joint Support and Coordination Mechanism (JSCM), 223
Joint UN–AU Framework for an Enhanced Partnership in Peace and Security, 148
Jordan, 36n86
jurisdiction, application of, 286
jurisprudence, and policy, 6
jus cogens, 298, 312

Kadi case, 274
Kasumaj v. Greece, 167
Kelsen, H., 47n126, 49n135
Kosovo, 38, 78. *See also* Kosovo Force
Kosovo case, 267, 309
Kosovo Force (KFOR), 77, 82, 176, 203
  application of the law of international responsibility, 208–209
  cooperation arrangements assessment, 215–216
  institutional and normative framework, 209–215
  mandate, 209–210
  UNMIK and, 205, 210–215
  operational/mission level, 213–215
  political level, 211–213
  strategic level, 213

Latin-America, 19
League of Nations, 321
legal framework of peacekeeping and peace enforcement operations, 25–27
legality issue, 25n39
Legality of the Threat or Use of Nuclear Weapons Case, 306

lex specialis rule, 11, 178–179, 304, 306, 323
liability in criminal law, 187–189
Liberia, 38, 123, 125
Libya, 78, 98, 108, 136
Lisbon Strategic Concept, NATO, 75
Lisbon Treaty, 87n106, 93
Lockerbie case, 198
logistical support, viii, 107, 125, 138, 140, 151, 173, 185, 193, 228, 235, 239–240, 242–243, 245, 251, 253, 256–257

Maastricht Treaty, 84
Mali, 35, 39n94, 55, 60, 64n212, 115–116, 127, 129, 145, 151–152, 161, 203, 324, 330. *See also* African-led International Support Mission to Mali; United Nations Multidimensional Integrated Stabilization Mission in Mali
  Resolution 2085, 1
Mali Integrated Task Force (MITF), 238, 248
Malian Defence Forces, 237
Mediation and Security Council, 121–122
Medvedyev and Others case, 288
Member States, 25
Memorandum of Understanding, 149–150
mens rea, 191–192
Mexico, 2
MICOPAX, 250–251
militarised peacekeeping operations, 30
military capacity of organisations, 37n89
Military Staff Committee, 141
military-technical agreement (MTA), 210, 215–216
Miltner, B., 294
MINUSCA. *See* United Nations Multidimensional Integrated Stabilization Mission in the Central African Republic
MINUSMA. *See* United Nations Multidimensional Integrated Stabilization Mission in Mali

Monetary Gold principle, 198–199
multiple simultaneous peace operations, in the same conflict, 160
multiplication of tasks, in peacekeeping operations, 7–8, 29, 37, 162

Naert, F., 61n197, 286, 308, 318
Namibia case, 267
National Movement for the Liberation of Azawad (NMLA), 233
National Patriotic Front of Liberia (NPFL), 54
nemo plus juris transferre potest quam ipse habet, 275
Netherlands, 19, 168–169, 207
network of cooperation, 8–10
new criterion of attribution, 178–180. *See also* attribution of conduct
  application of, 195–201
  defining, 182–186
  distinguishing from cases of other forms of responsibility, 193–195
  inspiration from other international legal rules, 186–189
  need for a special rule, 180–182
  normative control, 189–192
New Horizon Agenda, 97
Nicaragua case, 185, 193
Nigeria, 46n121
no-fly zones, 33
Nollkaemper, A., 198
non liquet situations, 283
non-international armed conflict, law of, 303
non-members of United Nations obligations for, 52, 264–266, 268
non-military sanctions, unauthorised, 54–55
normative control, 189–193, 263, 270, 320, 323
  application of, 195–201
North Atlantic Charter (NAC), 75n40
North Atlantic Council, 209–210
North Atlantic Treaty, 71–76
North Atlantic Treaty Organisation (NATO), 9, 13–14, 20, 38, 45, 47, 62n201, 70n15, 81–83, 156, 159, 201, 204–205, 209–210, 330
  African Union and, 79–81
  Assuming New Tasks of Security Proliferation and Projection, 75–76
  European Union and, 101–109, 117–118
  exclusion zones, acquiescence in, 33
  formal submission under Chapter VIII of the UN Charter, 72–73
  foundation of, 71–72
  history, 76–77
  military-technical agreement (MTA), 210, 215–216
  More Efficient and Flexible Partnership Policy, 81
  observer status in the General Assembly, 77
  Smart Defence, 107
  Strategic Concept, 83
  transformation and strategic redirection after, 73–74
  United Nations and, 77–79

objective responsibility, 192
occupatio bellica, 308
occupatio pacifica, 308
Oil Platforms case, 186
OPCON, 209
Operation Artemis, 39, 96–97, 105–106
Operation Concordia, 106
Operation EUFOR Tchad/RCA, 97
operational collaboration, 70
operational power transfer, 38–39
opinio iuris, 278, 284
  state practice and, distinguish between, 278–279
Organisation for Security and Co-operation in Europe (OSCE), 39, 46
Organisation international de la francophonie, 46
Organisation of African Unity (OAU), 49
Organisation of American States (OAS), 39, 47, 54
Organisation of Islamic Cooperation (OIC), 1, 46

Organisation of Southeast Asian Nations (ASEAN), 13
Oswald, B., 283

pacta tertiis nec nocent nec prosunt, 51
Panel on United Nations Peace Operations, 36n84
parallel operations, 38–39
partnership peacekeeping, vii
payment
   for damages, 163, 327
   for maintenance of peace and security, 99
Peace Agreements, 59
peace enforcement operations, 269
peacekeeping and peace enforcement, distinction between, 31n61
peacekeeping operations
   peace enforcement and, distinction between, 30n59
peacekeeping operations. *See also specific organisations*
   Article 53 of the UN Charter and, 57–59
   coercive character, 58
   definitions, 27
   generally, 1
   peace enforcement and, distinction between, 27–29, 32
   post-Cold War, 29–32
personal jurisdiction, 287, 293
Petersberg Tasks, 85, 85n95
Plan of Action to Enhance EU CSDP Support to UN Peacekeeping (2012), 100–101
Political Violence Task Force, 214
positive and negative obligations, 296, 311
private military and security companies (PMSCs), 10n39
private military and security contractors, 9, 324
Prodi report, 142
professionalisation, of peacekeeping, 35
profileration of international organisations, 6–8
Protocol establishing the Peace and Security Council, 130
Protocol Relating to Mutual Assistance on Defence, 122
Protocol Relating to the Establishment of the Peace and Security Council, 135
Protocol Relating to the Mechanism for Conflict Prevention, Management, Resolution, Peace-Keeping and Security of 1999 (MCPMRPS), 121–123
Provisions on the Common Security and Defence Policy (CSDP), 86

ratione loci, 284–285
reciprocal dependence, 155
Regional Arrangements and Agencies, 9, 41–43, 58
regional criterion, 47
regional economic communities (RECs), 111, 117, 150, 158
   within the APSA, 152–153
regional organisations, vii, 8, 10
   in Article 52 of UN Charter, 45–48
   UN Charter and, 271
regional organisations, relations among, 67–71
regionalism, 7–8, 18
Reichard, M., 118
Reparations case, 171, 267, 276
reporting mechanisms, 68, 72, 113, 144, 252
Rome Statute of the ICC, 26n42, 325
Rwanda, 157, 169
Rwandan presidency of the Council, 157

safe areas, 33
Sahel, 161, 238. *See also* African-led International Support Mission to Mali
San Francisco conference, 19
Sarooshi, D., 205
Schwebel, S.M., 198
Secretary-General, 20, 24, 33
Security Council, 6, 9, 20, 46, 49–50, 125, 150
   after the end of Cold War, 21–25
   authorisation for, 17
   authorisation of, 16, 24, 28, 53, 56–58

INDEX 371

authority, 32, 52–53, 55–58, 61, 64, 88, 114, 122–123, 166, 206, 265
Chapters VII and Chapters VIII, distinction between, 31
control mechanism, 52
control over support package allocation, 143
insisting on joint planning and joint mission assessment processes, 157
mandate from, 65
peacekeeping and peace enforcement and, distinction between. *See* peacekeeping operations
practice of, 59–63
pragmatic approach by, 61
Resolution 101, 265
Resolution 418, 266
Resolution 757, 51
Resolution 781, 73
Resolution 787, 14n47, 73
Resolution 788, 54, 122
Resolution 816, 56
Resolution 836, 33n69
Resolution 841, 54
Resolution 940, 59
Resolution 1001, 124
Resolution 1080, 59
Resolution 1132, 125
Resolution 1234, 49
Resolution 1244, 77, 206, 209–210, 212, 215, 310
Resolution 1484, 96
Resolution 1509, 125
Resolution 1546, 312
Resolution 1575, 106
Resolution 1625, 37n90
Resolution 1633, 126
Resolution 1769, 218–219
Resolution 1809, 116
Resolution 1990, 227
Resolution 2056, 60
Resolution 2057, 230
Resolution 2071, 60
Resolution 2085, 1, 50n137, 238, 240
Resolution 2086, 60
Resolution 2093, 146
Resolution 2098, 34, 35n78

Resolution 2100, 238
Resolution 2121, 250–251, 253
Resolution 2127, 250–253
Resolution 2149, 256
Resolution 2164, 37n86
Resolution 2167, 157
self-defence, use of force as, 29, 47, 57, 206
sequential operations, 38–39
sexual exploitation, 163
shared responsibility, 200
Sierra Leone, 36, 52n150, 125
Simma, B., 186
sliding scale of obligations, 296
Society of Nations, 17
socio-political-legal approach, 4
Somalia, 30, 33–37, 115, 146, 148, 303
South Sudan, 203, 226. *See also* UNMISS; UNISFA
Southern African Development Community, 49
Special Political Mission, 146
special rule for peacekeeping operations, recommendations for, 180–182
speciality, principle of, 197, 276–277, 280
Srebrenica, 168, 328
Stahn, C., 213
state practice, 284
  opinio iuris and, distinguish between, 278–279
Status of Mission Agreement (SOMA), 200, 314
Stephens v. Cyprus, Turkey and the United Nations, 167
Strategic Concept, 74–75
structures of international organisations, 8
sub-contracting, 96
subregional organisations, 22, 62, 112, 131, 139–141, 149–150, 153, 157–158, 252, 255, 259, 348. *See also specific organisations*
subsidiary responsibility, 196
Sudan, 106. *See also* UNMISS; UNISFA
sui generis, 11, 162, 180, 202, 301
Support Operation AMIS II, 115
Supreme Allied Commander Europe (SACEUR), 210

Supreme Court of the Netherlands, 169
Syria, 6, 55, 99

Tadić decision, 187, 193
Talmon, S., 266–267
Temporary Arrangements Agreement for the Administration and Security of the Abyei Area, 228
terra incognita, 161
territorial jurisdiction, 287–288, 293
terrorism, 180
Tharoor, S., 33
third party intervention, 199–200
third-generation peacekeeping operations, 29, 57
threat to the peace, 26
Tomuschat, C., 185, 205
treaties, 53
 ratifications, 218, 273, 275
treaty law, 12
Treaty of Amsterdam, 85
Treaty of Lisbon, 87n106, 94, 99, 266
Treaty of Maastricht, 84n90
Treaty on European Union (TEU), 87, 89n115
 Article 21, 317
 Article 6, 318
 Article 6(1), 317
Treaty on the Functioning of the European Union (TFEU), 86, 87n106
Tripartite Coordination Mechanism on UNAMID, 221
troop-contributing countries (TCC), 185
Turkey, 106

ultra vires, 51, 295
UN Charter, 6–7, 10, 24, 43n107, 94, 130, 132–137, 150, 315, 321
 Article 2(6), 265
 Article 103, 134, 308, 312–313
 Article 39, 62n202
 Article 43, 33, 85, 122, 269
 Article 48 (2), 264–265
 Article 51, 19
 Article 52, 45–50, 64, 153
 Article 53, 44, 48–52, 57–59, 64, 206
 Article 53 (1), 53–57
 Chapter VI, 9, 25

Chapter VII, 1, 7n26, 9, 25, 59–63
Chapter VIII, 1, 9, 40–41, 59–63, 265–270
 influence of Chapter VII over, 43–45
 relevance of practice for interpretation of, 41–43
 cooperation under, 17–20
UN Office in West Africa (UNOWA), 126
UN Support Office for AMISOM (UNSOA), 146
UNFICYP, 167
Unified Protector, 78
United Kingdom, 91, 167
United Nations
 and regional organisations, 43n107
United Nations (UN), vii, 6, 13, 27, 58, 69, 99, 153, 157, 159, 200–201, 321
 African Union and, 155
 authorised operations, 167
 authorised operations and, 208
 on 'effective control', 170
 European Union and, 101
 financial measures, 35
 funding by, 35
 Integrated Peacebuilding Office in the Central African Republic (BINUCA), 253
 internal law of, 269–270
 NATO and, 210–215
 new ways of planning and conducting peacekeeping operations, 158
 practice of, 164, 167, 267
 regional organisations and, 8, 10, 48–50, 67–71, 158, 323, 329
 standing forces, 23, 33
 universalism and regionalism, 17–20
United Nations Assistance Mission for Rwanda (UNAMIR), 169
United Nations Interim Administration in Kosovo (UNMIK), 39, 77
 mandate, 308
United Nations Interim Security Force for Abyei (UNISFA), 203
 assessment, 232–233
 inter-mission cooperation, 228–229
 mandate, 227–228
 Political Control/Chain of Command, 228

United Nations Mission in Liberia
(UNMIL), 125
United Nations Mission in Sierra Leone
(UNAMSIL), 36
United Nations Mission in Sudan
(UNMIS), 9n37
United Nations Mission in the
Democratic Republic of Congo
(MONUC), 96
United Nations Mission in the Republic
of South Sudan (UNMISS), 203
assessment, 232–233
inter-mission cooperation, 232
mandate, 229–230
political level and political process,
228–229
United Nations Multidimensional
Integrated Stabilization Mission
in Mali (MINUSMA), 39n94,
65n212, 203
assessment, 248–249
cooperation with the EU/EUTM
Mali, 248
Force Commander appointment, 246
mandate, 243
elaboration of, 244–246
political control, 246–247
strategic and operational level,
247–248
United Nations Multidimensional
Integrated Stabilization Mission
in the Central African Republic
(MINUSCA), 203, 256–257
assessment, 259–261
mandate, 257
political process and control,
257–258
strategic control, 259
United Nations Observer Mission in
Liberia (UNOMIL), 124
United Nations Observer Mission in
Sierra Leone (UNOMSIL), 36

United Nations Operation in Liberia
(UNMIL), 38
United Nations Organization
Stabilization Mission in the
Democratic Republic of Congo
(MONUSCO), 36n86
United Nations Protection Force
(UNPROFOR), 33, 56, 168
United Nations–African Union Joint
Task Force on Peace and Security,
145
United States, 36n86, 71, 104, 108
Uniting for Peace Resolution, 18
universal and regional organisations,
factors influencing the relations
between, 68
Universal Declaration on Human
Rights, 282
universalism versus regionalism, 41, 44,
154, 321
Ushakov, N., 195
USSR, 71

Vienna Convention on the Law of
Treaties
Article 31, 53
Article 34, 51, 273
Villani, U., 55
Virally, M., 68, 264

Wall Case, 291, 297, 305
Walter, C., 60
Western European Union (WEU),
62n201, 85, 94, 102, 104
women, protection of, 30n56
World Court for Human Rights, 325
World Summit (2005), 139
World Trade Organization (WTO)
Geographical Indications Dispute, 190

Yugoslavia, 9, 30, 33, 55, 76, 84
Yusuf case, 274

Lightning Source UK Ltd.
Milton Keynes UK
UKHW02f0835280618
324916UK00007B/89/P